COOKING
for
◇ TODAY ◇

COOKING
for
TODAY

◇ ◇

Translated by Frederick Gelhar
Edited by Audrey Ellis

BLACK CAT

Metrication

In this book quantities are given in Metric, Imperial and American measures. Exact conversion from one measure to another does not usually give very convenient working quantities and so the metric measures have been rounded off into units of 25 grams.

When making any of the recipes in this book, only follow one set of measures as they are not interchangeable.

Spoon measures: All spoon measures given in this book are level unless otherwise stated.

Flour: All flour is plain (all purpose) unless otherwise stated.

The material in this book has previously appeared in Dr Oetker KÜCHEN-BIBLIOTHEK

© Ceres-Verlag Rudolf-August Oetker KG
© English translation, Macdonald & Co (Publishers) Ltd, 1987

This edition published in 1987 by Black Cat, an imprint of Macdonald & Co (Publishers) Ltd, Greater London House, Hampstead Road, London NW1

A BPCC company

Reprinted 1988

ISBN 0-7481-0003-2

Printed and bound in Yugoslavia by Mladinska Knjiga, Ljubljana

CONTENTS

INTRODUCTION

Cooking for Today has been specially written for the cook of today. Whether catering on a day-to-day basis for the family, or entertaining friends, every busy cook needs a constantly renewed fund of recipe ideas, and *Cooking for Today* provides over 700 of these. Clear, workable section divisions make the recipe material readily accessible for easy reference and are specially designed to help plan every kind of menu, from healthy breakfasts and simple midweek suppers to weekend meals and elaborate special occasion buffets.

The recipes themselves are a pleasure to use, featuring easy-to-follow ingredients lists and clear, concise methods. Many of the recipes are supplemented with serving ideas, useful variations and cook's tips. giving handy hints and information on a wide variety of basic and more sophisticated cooking techniques.

Most of the recipes are fully illustrated, not only for easy identification but also to provide ideas for garnishing and presentation, which are such important aspects of cooking.

Throughout, *Cooking for Today* makes emphatic use of the fresh fruit and vegetables which are now universally recognized as vital in the modern diet. Although there are substantial sections on meat, poultry, game and fish, vegetarians will find a wealth of ideas for main and accompanying vegetable dishes, salads and snacks. The Soups section contains some interesting and unusual fruit soups, while Desserts features a selection of fruit-based sweets, from simple fruit salads and compotes to more elaborate mousses and rich ice creams. Editing this unique book, so lavishly illustrated in glorious colour, has been a great pleasure, which I hope readers will share in using it.

Audrey Ellis

THE MAGIC OF MICROWAVE

The microwave oven is now a feature of many modern kitchens, making all the difference to the life of the busy cook. Food cooked in a fraction of the conventional time, frozen dishes defrosted in seconds, minimal cleaning and big savings on fuel are just some of the reasons that make the microwave oven invaluable, once a few basic rules, as laid down in manufacturer's handbooks, have been mastered.

A very special feature of *Cooking for Today* is its unique combination of microwave and conventional cooking, making it invaluable for *every* kitchen. Where appropriate, a microwave version of the cooking method is given alongside that for a standard oven. In addition, specially for the benefit of microwave cooks, a wealth of microwave tips are presented throughout the text, giving all kinds of handy hints on how to make the most of this revolutionary cooking process.

SPECIAL OCCASION MENUS

SUMMER DINNER PARTY FOR 4

Eggs in tarragon aspic
(PAGE 59)

Baked sole with asparagus
(PAGE 146)

Broccoli with herbed wine sauce
(PAGE 349)

Pistachio parfait
(PAGE 470)

Cold cucumber soup
(PAGE 23)

Veal Cordon Bleu
(PAGE 190)

Simply cooked garden peas
(PAGE 350)

Berry salad with sabayon
(PAGE 456)

WINTER DINNER PARTY FOR 4

Whitebait London style
(PAGE 150)

Venison and pineapple with Béarnaise sauce
(PAGE 285)

French bean bundles in bacon
(PAGE 344)

Praline ring
(PAGE 431)

Tortellini with mushroom and wine sauce
(PAGE 86)

Halibut steaks with herbed cream cheese topping
(PAGE 121)

Mangetout peas in almond butter
(PAGE 351)

Bavarois with orange liqueur
(PAGE 442)

BUFFET SUPPER FOR 8

Lobster cocktails
(PAGE 113)

Avocado with Roquefort cream
(PAGE 417)

Fruit garnished chicken legs
(PAGE 250)

Fish pâté en croûte
(PAGE 106))

Mixed salad with cream dressing
(PAGE 396)

Elegant rice salad
(PAGE 327)

Peach crown
(PAGE 429)

Wine cream with pistachio nuts
(PAGE 438)

FESTIVE PICNIC FOR 8

Chicken pie with puff pastry top
(PAGE 281)

Smoked salmon and apple sandwiches
(PAGE 55)

Cucumber salad
(PAGE 380)

Mushroom salad
(PAGE 419)

Cinnamon pudding
(PAGE 424)

Fresh fruit

FAMILY MENUS

SUNDAY LUNCH

Boiled beef with apple horseradish sauce
(PAGE 155)

Simply cooked leeks
(PAGE 341)

Saucy potatoes
(PAGE 332)

Strawberry and marsala mousse
(PAGE 438)

★

Roast leg of lamb with mint crust
(PAGE 17)

French beans Parma style
(PAGE 342)

Potato croquettes
(PAGE 336)

Peaches in white wine with soufflé topping
(PAGE 423)

MIDWEEK SUPPER

Wholemeal lasagne with pine kernels
(PAGE 305)

Sweet pepper and tomato salad
(PAGE 379)

★

Chicken, grape and cheese salad
(PAGE 395)

Potatoes baked in foil
(PAGE 336)

CHILDREN'S HIGH TEA

Cauliflower bake with cheese topping
(PAGE 88)

Chocolate pudding
(PAGE 422)

★

Macaroni with peas and ham
(PAGE 307)

Lemon cheese cream
(PAGE 46)

★

Potato pizza
(PAGE 339)

Yogurt jelly
(PAGE 432)

BREAKFAST

Apple with yogurt and oats
(PAGE 49)

Peasant's breakfast
(PAGE 334)

★

Muesli with fresh and dried fruit
(PAGE 45)

Ham, cheese and egg ramekins
(PAGE 74)

★

Pancakes with syrup
(PAGE 82)

Scrambled eggs with bacon
(PAGE 75)

VEGETARIAN
MENUS

WINTER

Carrot soup
(PAGE 19)

Savoury potato pudding
(PAGE 330)

Apple compote
(PAGE 454)

SPRING

Springtime egg salad starter
(PAGE 53)

Home-made noodles with pesto sauce
(PAGE 302)

Apricot dessert with cinnamon cream
(PAGE 436)

SUMMER

Cold courgette soup with tomatoes
(PAGE 36)

Spanish salad platter
(PAGE 392)

Black Forest cherry cream
(PAGE 432)

AUTUMN

Greek tomato salad starter
(PAGE 53)

Baked fettucine
(PAGE 58)

Individual caramel custards
(PAGE 431)

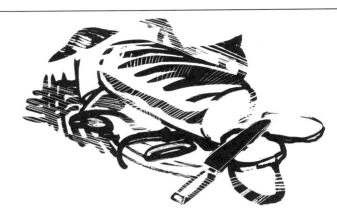

QUICK MENUS

Layered salad cocktails
(PAGE 388)

Ribbon noodles with seafood
(PAGE 300)

Bananas with almond snow
(PAGE 460)

★

Cream cheese with cucumber and black olives
(PAGE 407)

Iceberg lettuce with tongue and mixed fruit
(PAGE 370)

Vanilla milk fondue
(PAGE 440)

★

Artichoke bottoms piped with pâté
(PAGE 412)

Gourmet smoked salmon
(PAGE 401)

Quick peach delight
(PAGE 450)

★

Avocado coupes
(PAGE 405)

Veal miniature escalopes
(PAGE 409)

Orange slices with almonds
(PAGE 457)

Sweet pepper cream soup
Serves 4

Ingredients	Metric-Imperial	American
Sweet peppers, about	450 g/1 lb	1 lb
Onions	225 g/8 oz	8 oz
Canned, drained sauerkraut	225 g/8 oz	1¼ cups
Oil	2–3 tbs	3–4 tbs
Beef stock (bouillon)	1 L/1¾ pints	4⅓ cups
Dry white wine	3–4 tbs	4–5 tbs
Double cream (heavy)	150 ml/¼ pint	⅔ cup

Halve and deseed the peppers and cut into strips. Peel and finely chop the onions. Loosen the sauerkraut with 2 forks and chop it finely.

Heat the oil in a pan and use to fry the onion until limp. Add the pepper strips, sauerkraut and stock and bring to the boil. Simmer for 20 minutes. Stir in the wine and cream and season to taste with salt and pepper. Reheat just to boiling point before serving.

Cream of vegetable soup
Serves 4

Ingredients	Metric-Imperial	American
2 medium-sized onions		
Prepared vegetables such as leeks, carrots, kohlrabi, celery	750 g/1¾ lb	1¾ lb
Margarine	40 g/1½ oz	3 tbs
Beef stock (bouillon)	1 L/1¾ pints	4⅓ cups
Milk	300 ml/½ pint	1¼ cups
Salt and pepper		
Ground nutmeg		
2 egg yolks		
Medium-dry sherry	4 tbs	5 tbs
Whipping cream	150 ml/¼ pint	⅔ cup

Peel and chop the onions. Cut the other vegetables into large pieces. Fry the onion in the margarine in a large pan until golden brown. Add the stock and milk and bring to the boil. Put in the vegetables, season with a little salt, pepper and nutmeg and simmer, covered, for 15–20 minutes.

If desired, remove and reserve the pieces of leek and celery then liquidize or sieve the soup and return to the pan. Reheat. Beat the egg yolks with the sherry, stir into the soup with the cream. Reheat just to boiling point. Adjust the seasoning. Chop the reserved leek and celery and mix into the soup. Serve with French bread or hot cheese straws.

Variation: Add any favourite vegetable to this versatile soup.

Chervil and parsley soup
(Photo p. 12–13)

Serves 4

Ingredients	Metric-Imperial	American
Selection of pot vegetables		
Butter or margarine	40 g/1½ oz	3 tbs
Beef stock (bouillon)	1 L/1¾ pints	4⅓ cups
Cornflour (cornstarch)	2 tbs	3 tbs
Chopped chervil	50 g/2 oz	1 cup
Chopped parsley	25 g/1 oz	½ cup
Whipping cream	150 ml/¼ pint	⅔ cup
Salt and pepper		

Clean the vegetables, peel if necessary and cut into strips. Melt the butter or margarine in a pan and fry the vegetables gently. Add the stock, bring to the boil and simmer for 15 minutes.

Moisten the cornflour with a little cold water and stir into the soup. Bring to the boil, stirring, and simmer for a further 5 minutes. Mix the herbs and cream into the soup and season to taste with salt and pepper. Reheat but do not allow to boil. If liked, serve with bread croûtons.

Note: Pot vegetables usually include 1 leek or onion, 1 carrot, 1 piece of swede (rutabaga) or a small turnip.

Pumpkin soup

Serves 4

Ingredients	Metric-Imperial	American
Beef bones, about	1 kg/2¼ lb	2¼ lb
Water	1½ L/2½ pints	3¼ pints
Salt and pepper		
Selection of pot vegetables		
2 bay leaves		
White peppercorns	1 tsp	1 tsp
1 medium-sized onion		
Butter or margarine	50 g/2 oz	¼ cup
Cubed pumpkin flesh	1 kg/2 lb	6 cups
Pine kernels (nuts)	50 g/2 oz	½ cup
Chopped dill weed	2 tbs	3 tbs
Whipping cream	125 ml/4 fl oz	½ cup
Sugar		

Wash the beef bones under running cold water. Place in a large pan, add the water and a little salt and bring to the boil. Skim the surface. Clean the pot vegetables, peel if necessary then roughly chop. Add to the pan with the bay leaves and peppercorns. Allow to simmer for about 1½ hours, skimming occasionally.

When the liquid has reduced to about 1 L/1¾ pints (4⅓ cups), strain the stock and reserve.

Peel and chop the onion. Melt 40 g/1½ oz (3 tbs) of the butter or margarine in a clean pan and fry the onion until golden. Add the pumpkin cubes and hot stock, bring to the boil then simmer for about 15 minutes, until the pumpkin is soft. Lift out and reserve a few pumpkin cubes for the garnish then liquidize or sieve the soup and return to the pan.

Melt the remaining butter in a pan and fry the pine kernels until golden. Add the chopped dill, cream and reserved pumpkin pieces to the soup and season to taste with salt, pepper and a little sugar. Reheat but do not allow to boil. Sprinkle with the pine kernels at serving time.

Variation: Use slivered almonds instead of pine kernels.

Microwave method

Boil the water, place in a large bowl and add the bones, bay leaves and peppercorns. Cover and cook on full power for 5 minutes. Meanwhile, clean the pot vegetables, peel if necessary then roughly chop. Add to the bowl, cover and cook on medium power for 45 minutes. Strain and measure 1 L/1¾ pints (4⅓ cups) of the stock.

Put three quarters of the butter and the onion in a large bowl. Cover and cook on full power for 4 minutes. Stir in the pumpkin cubes and cook on full power for 2 minutes. Add the stock and season lightly with salt and pepper. Cook on full power for 10 minutes. Reduce power to medium and cook for 10 minutes. Remove a few pumpkin cubes for the garnish and liquidize the soup. Return to the bowl.

Heat the remaining butter in a small bowl on full power for 1 minute. Add the pine kernels, cover and cook on full power for 2 minutes.

Stir the dill, cream and reserved pumpkin pieces into the soup and adjust the seasoning. Cover and reheat on medium power for 1 minute. Serve, sprinkled with the pine kernels.

Opposite: Cream of vegetable soup
Above: Pumpkin soup

Cheese soup with spring onions
Serves 4

Ingredients	Metric-Imperial	American
Butter	50 g/2 oz	¼ cup
Flour (all-purpose)	40 g/1½ oz	⅓ cup
Beef stock (bouillon)	1 L/1¾ pints	4⅓ cups
Gouda cheese	225 g/8 oz	8 oz
Whipping cream	2 tbs	3 tbs
Salt and pepper		
Ground nutmeg		
4 large spring onions (scallions)		

Melt 40 g/1½ oz (3 tbs) of the butter in a pan, mix in the flour and cook, stirring, until golden. Whisk in the stock, bring to the boil and simmer for 5 minutes.

Dice the cheese and add to the pan with the cream. Simmer, stirring, until the cheese has melted. Season to taste with salt, pepper and nutmeg.

Trim and chop the onions. Melt the remaining butter in a pan, add the onion and fry for about 3 minutes. Sprinkle over the soup shortly before serving.

Variation: Substitute Cheddar cheese for Gouda.

Tomato soup crowned with cream
Serves 4

Ingredients	Metric-Imperial	American
Tomatoes	450 g/1 lb	1 lb
Streaky bacon (strips)	50 g/2 oz	4 strips
Butter or margarine	15 g/½ oz	1 tbs
1 onion		
2 cloves of garlic		
Flour (all-purpose)	40 g/1½ oz	⅓ cup
Beef stock (bouillon)	750 ml/1¼ pints	3 cups
Tomato purée (paste)	2 tbs	3 tbs
Dried oregano	½ tsp	½ tsp
Whipped cream	4 tbs	4 tbs
Chopped dill weed or parsley	1 tsp	1 tsp

Chop the tomatoes. Dice the bacon and heat in a pan until the fat runs. Add the butter or margarine. Peel and finely chop the onion and garlic and fry lightly in the fat. Sprinkle on the flour and stir well. Add the tomatoes, stock, tomato purée and oregano. Bring to the boil, stirring. Cover and simmer for 10 minutes.

Liquidize or sieve the soup and divide among 4 soup plates. Float a spoonful of cream on each portion and sprinkle with dill or parsley.

Queen's soup with chicken and almonds
Serves 4

Ingredients	Metric-Imperial	American
Butter or margarine	40 g/1½ oz	3 tbs
Flour (all-purpose)	40 g/1½ oz	⅓ cup
Chicken stock (bouillon)	1 L/1¾ pints	4⅓ cups
Diced cooked chicken	225 g/8 oz	1⅓ cups
Ground almonds	2 tbs	3 tbs
Cooked cauliflower florets or asparagus tips	100 g/4 oz	⅔ cup
1 egg yolk		
Milk	125 ml/4 fl oz	½ cup
Meat extract, optional		

Melt the butter or margarine in a pan, mix in the flour and cook until golden brown, stirring all the time. Gradually whisk in the stock, bring to the boil and simmer for about 10 minutes.

Add the chicken to the pan with the almonds and cooked vegetables. Reheat. Beat the egg yolk with the milk and stir into the soup. Season to taste with a little meat extract, if liked.

Variations: Use veal stock instead of chicken stock. If desired, garnish the soup with chopped dill.

Above: Tomato soup crowned with cream
Opposite: Israeli avocado soup

Israeli avocado soup
Serves 4

Ingredients	Metric-Imperial	American
Butter	40 g/1½ oz	3 tbs
Flour (all-purpose)	40 g/1½ oz	⅓ cup
Beef stock (bouillon)	750 ml/1¼ pints	3 cups
1 large ripe avocado		
Salt and pepper		
Dry white wine	125 ml/4 fl oz	½ cup
Lightly whipped cream	4 tbs	4 tbs
Chopped dill weed or parsley	1 tsp	1 tsp

Melt the butter in a pan, mix in the flour and cook, stirring, until golden. Gradually add the stock and bring to the boil, stirring constantly. Cook for 3 minutes.

Halve the avocado, remove the stone (pit) and scoop out the flesh. Liquidize or sieve and add to the soup. Season with salt and pepper to taste and stir in the wine. Reheat without allowing to boil. Divide among 4 soup plates, top each portion with cream and sprinkle with dill or parsley.

Cream of Brussels sprouts
Serves 4

Ingredients	Metric-Imperial	American
Brussels sprouts	450 g/1 lb	1 lb
Boiling water	300 ml/½ pint	1¼ cups
Salt and cayenne pepper		
Hot water	450 ml/¾ pint	2 cups
Meat extract	1 tsp	1 tsp
Cornflour (cornstarch)	1 tsp	1 tsp
1 egg yolk		
Whipping cream	2 tsp	2 tsp
Softened butter	1 tsp	1 tsp
Sugar		
Chopped parsley	1 tsp	1 tsp

Trim the Brussels sprouts. Have the boiling water ready in a pan, add the sprouts and a little salt. Bring back to the boil and simmer for 10 minutes or until just tender.

Remove 10 sprouts and cut into quarters. Liquidize the remainder of the sprouts in the cooking liquid or sieve and return to the pan. Add the hot water and meat extract and bring to the boil. Simmer for a further 5 minutes.

Moisten the cornflour with a little cold water and mix into the soup. Stir until boiling. Combine the egg yolk and cream and beat into the soup. Put in the butter, reserved sprout quarters, salt, cayenne and sugar to taste. Reheat but do not allow to boil. Serve sprinkled with parsley.

Egg flower soup
Serves 4

Ingredients	Metric-Imperial	American
Flour (all-purpose)	2 tbs	3 tbs
Milk	1 tbs	1 tbs
1 egg		
Salt	½ tsp	½ tsp
Ground nutmeg	¼ tsp	¼ tsp
Beef stock (bouillon)	1 L/1¾ pints	4⅓ cups
Chopped parsley	1 tsp	1 tsp

Beat together the flour, milk, egg, salt and nutmeg. Put the stock in a pan and bring to boiling point.

Pour the egg mixture into the stock in a thin stream over the back of a spoon. Bring the soup just to the boil again then serve sprinkled with parsley.

Variations: Use chicken stock (bouillon) instead of beef for a lighter soup. Garnish the soup with chopped spring onion (scallion). A crushed clove of garlic could be added to the stock.

Note: The 'egg flower' name of this famous Chinese soup comes from the technique of adding the egg to the soup making attractive flowerlike ribbons.

Sweet-sour banana soup
Serves 4

Ingredients	Metric-Imperial	American
5 ripe bananas		
Whipping cream	150 ml/¼ pint	⅔ cup
Wine vinegar	4 tbs	5 tbs
Sugar	1–2 tsp	1–2 tsp
Onion powder	½ tsp	½ tsp
Chicken stock (bouillon)	750 ml/1¼ pints	3 cups
Salt		
Few sprigs of mint		

Peel and mash 4 of the bananas. Mix in the cream and stir in the vinegar, sugar and onion powder.

Heat the stock in a pan and gradually whisk in the banana mixture. Bring to the boil and simmer for about 5 minutes. Season to taste with salt and serve garnished with slices of the remaining banana and sprigs of mint.

Microwave hint
For a comforting hot toddy, fill a micro-proof mug with milk, add 2 tsp clear honey (or to taste) and heat on full power for 4 minutes. Stir in whisky or brandy as preferred.

Italian fish soup
Serves 6–8

Ingredients	Metric-Imperial	American
Mussels	1 kg/2¼ lb	2¼ lb
Olive oil	8 tbs	⅔ cup
Cleaned whole fish such as cod, haddock, plaice (flounder)	2 kg/4½ lb	4½ lb
Squid	350 g/12 oz	12 oz
Lemon juice	2 tbs	3 tbs
Water	2 L/3½ pints	4½ pints
4 tomatoes		
1 carrot		
1 onion		
Celery	1 head	1 bunch
1 clove of garlic		
1 red sweet pepper		
Dried thyme	1 tsp	1 tsp
Dry white wine	300 ml/½ pint	1¼ cups
12 shelled cooked prawns (shrimp)		
Salt and pepper		
6–8 slices French bread		

Put the mussels in cold water and leave for several hours. Scrub well and remove the beards. Wash again thoroughly and discard any that are open.

Heat 3 tbs (4 tbs) of the oil in a large pan, add the mussels, cover and cook for 5 minutes. Discard any that have not opened. Reserve a few mussels in the shell for the garnish and remove the remainder from the shell. Reserve these and the cooking liquid.

Wash the fish and squid under running cold water, drain and pat dry. Remove heads, tails, fins and bones from the fish and cut the flesh into 5 cm/2 inch long strips. Sprinkle with the lemon juice and allow to stand for about 15 minutes. Put the fish trimmings into the water and boil for 15 minutes. Strain and discard the trimmings, reserving the stock. Cut the squid into rings. Peel and quarter the tomatoes and peel and slice the carrot and onion. Trim the celery, remove any strings and chop finely. Peel and chop the garlic. Deseed and dice the pepper.

Heat a further 3 tbs (4 tbs) of the oil in a large pan and use to sauté the thyme, tomato, red pepper and vegetables for a few minutes. Add the wine and cook to reduce by one third. Pour in the fish stock and liquid from the mussels, bring to the boil and simmer, covered, for 10 minutes. Put in the squid and simmer for a further 10 minutes. Now put in the fish and 15 minutes later finally add the shelled mussels and prawns. Reheat and season to taste with salt and pepper.

Fry the bread slices in the remaining oil, put a slice into the bottom of each soup plate and fill with soup. Garnish with the mussels in the shell.

Microwave hint
To check whether a chosen dish or container is suitable for use in the microwave cooker, place a heatproof jug inside it and add about 150 ml/¼ pint (⅔ cup) water to the jug. Place the dish in the cooker and process on full power for 1½ minutes. The dish is suitable if the water is heated, if the water remains cold it should not be used.

Carrot soup
Serves 4

Ingredients	Metric-Imperial	American
Carrots	450 g/1 lb	1 lb
2 large potatoes		
Celery	3 sticks	3 stalks
2 onions		
Butter	25 g/1 oz	2 tbs
Water	1 L/1¾ pints	4⅓ cups
Salt and pepper		
Whipping cream	75 ml/3 fl oz	⅓ cup
Chopped parsley	1 tbs	1 tbs
Little extra butter		

Peel and dice the carrots and potatoes and trim and chop the celery. Peel and chop the onions. Melt the butter in a large pan, put in the onion and fry until golden brown. Add the prepared vegetables, stir and cook for a further 3 minutes. Pour in the water, season lightly with salt and pepper, bring to the boil and simmer for 15 minutes.

Liquidize or sieve and return to the pan. Blend in the cream, adjust the seasoning and reheat. At serving time, sprinkle with the parsley and top with a few small pieces of butter.

Opposite: Sweet-sour banana soup
Below: Italian fish soup

Basic light soup
Serves 4

Ingredients	Metric-Imperial	American
Butter or margarine	40 g/1½ oz	3 tbs
Flour (all-purpose)	40 g/1½ oz	⅓ cup
Any vegetable, poultry or meat stock (bouillon)	1 L/1¾ pints	4⅓ cups
Salt and pepper		

Melt the butter or margarine in a pan, mix in the flour and cook, stirring, until golden. Whisk in the liquid, bring to the boil and simmer for about 10 minutes. Season to taste.

Fresh green pea soup
Serves 4

Ingredients	Metric-Imperial	American
1 small carrot		
1 small new potato		
Butter	50 g/2 oz	¼ cup
Shelled green peas	225 g/8 oz	1⅓ cups
Flour (all-purpose)	40 g/1½ oz	⅓ cup
Chicken stock (bouillon)	1 L/1¾ pints	4⅓ cups
Salt		
Chopped parsley	1 tbs	1 tbs

Scrape and finely dice the carrot and potato. Melt the butter in a pan, put in the vegetables and stir lightly. Cook for 3 minutes. Sprinkle on the flour and cook, stirring, for a further 2 minutes. Blend in the stock, stir until boiling and simmer for 10 minutes, or until the vegetables are tender. Season to taste with salt and serve sprinkled with parsley.

Serving suggestion: Float semolina dumplings in the soup.

Basic dark soup
Serves 4

Ingredients	Metric-Imperial	American
Butter or margarine	50 g/2 oz	¼ cup
Flour (all-purpose)	50 g/2 oz	½ cup
1 onion (optional)		
Any vegetable, poultry or meat stock (bouillon)	1 L/1¾ pints	4⅓ cups
Salt and pepper		

Melt the butter or margarine in a pan, mix in the flour and cook, stirring, until brown. If using the onion, peel and finely chop and add to the roux when it is light brown. Whisk in the liquid, bring to the boil and simmer for about 10 minutes. Season to taste with salt and pepper.

Serving suggestion: A small amount of diced cooked meat or root vegetables may be added to the soup.

Bean soup with tomatoes
Serves 4

Ingredients	Metric-Imperial	American
Dried cannellini beans	150 g/5 oz	⅔ cup
Water or beef stock (bouillon)	1¼ L/2¼ pints	2¾ pints
1 leek		
6 tomatoes		
Butter or margarine	15 g/½ oz	1 tbs
Tomato purée (paste)	1 tbs	1 tbs
Flour (all-purpose)	1 tbs	1 tbs
Salt		
Dried thyme	¼ tsp	¼ tsp
Garlic salt		
Meat extract		
Tabasco pepper sauce	5 drops	5 drops
4 frankfurter sausages		

Wash the beans and soak them for 12–24 hours in the water or stock. Bring the beans to the boil in the soaking liquid, cover and cook for 1½ hours.

Meanwhile, clean, trim and slice the leek. Add to the pan and cook for a further 15 minutes, or until the beans are tender.

Remove about a quarter of the beans from the soup with a slotted spoon and reserve. Liquidize or sieve the soup.

Pour boiling water over the tomatoes, drain, peel and chop. Melt the butter in a clean pan, add the tomato and tomato purée and stir in the flour. Whisk in the soup, put in the reserved beans and add a little salt and the thyme. Bring to the boil, stirring. Simmer for about 15 minutes then adjust the seasoning with garlic salt, a little meat extract and the Tabasco. Slice the sausages and reheat in the soup before serving.

Left: Fresh green pea soup
Opposite: Bean soup with tomatoes

Clear meat broth
Serves 4

Ingredients	Metric-Imperial	American
1 onion		
1 carrot		
1 turnip or piece of swede (rutabaga)		
Oil	1 tbs	1 tbs
Beef bones	225 g/8 oz	8 oz
Stewing steak (chuck)	350 g/12 oz	12 oz
Water	2 L/3½ pints	4¼ pints
Salt and pepper		
Meat extract		
Chopped parsley	1 tsp	1 tsp

Peel and slice the onion, carrot and turnip or swede. Heat the oil in a large pan, put in the onion and fry gently until brown. Have the bones divided into pieces. Wash them and add to the pan with the meat, water, remaining vegetables and a little salt and pepper. Bring to the boil, cover and simmer for about 2½ hours, or until the meat is tender.

Strain the broth and adjust the seasoning to taste with a little meat extract and extra salt and pepper. Serve sprinkled with parsley and if liked, accompanied by hot cheese straws. Serve the meat separately.

Meat broth with noodles
Serves 4

Ingredients	Metric-Imperial	American
Beef stock (bouillon)	1 L/1¾ pints	4⅓ cups
Small pasta shapes such as stars or letters	40 g/1½ oz	⅓ cup
Chopped parsley	1 tbs	1 tbs

Bring the meat stock to the boil in a pan, add the pasta and cook, stirring occasionally, for 10–15 minutes. Serve garnished with parsley.

Lentil soup
Serves 4

Ingredients	Metric-Imperial	American
Lentils	225 g/8 oz	1 cup
Beef stock (bouillon)	1¼ L/2¼ pints	2¾ pints
Selection of pot vegetables including 1 onion		
Dried thyme	¼ tsp	¼ tsp
Cornflour (cornstarch)	1 tsp	1 tsp
Water	1 tsp	1 tsp
Salt		
2–3 frankfurter sausages		
Finely snipped chives	1 tbs	1 tbs

Soak the lentils in the stock overnight. Bring them to the boil in the soaking liquid, cover and simmer for 45 minutes.

Clean the pot vegetables, peel if necessary and chop. Remove half or all the lentils, liquidize or sieve and return to the pan with the vegetables and thyme. Blend the cornflour with the water, mix into the soup and bring to the boil, stirring. Cover and simmer for a further 45 minutes, or until the lentils and vegetables are tender. Add salt to taste. Slice the frankfurters and reheat in the soup. Serve sprinkled with chives.

Microwave method
Wash the lentils and remove any black seeds. Put the lentils in a large pyrex bowl, cover with boiling stock and cook on full power for 15 minutes.

Meanwhile clean the pot vegetables, peel or scrape where necessary and cut into small even-sized pieces. Keep in a bowl of cold water.

Sieve or purée the lentils in a blender or food processor and return to the bowl with the vegetables, thyme and seasoning. Blend the cornflour with the water and add to the soup. Mix well and return to the microwave for 25 minutes on full power. Add a little boiling water if the mixture is too thick.

Taste for seasoning and make sure the vegetables are cooked. Slice the frankfurters and add to the soup. Return to full power for 10 minutes, leave to stand for 5 minutes. Serve sprinkled with chopped chives.

Left: Clear meat broth
Opposite: French onion soup

French onion soup
Serves 4

Ingredients	Metric-Imperial	American
2 large onions		
Margarine	75 g/3 oz	$\frac{1}{3}$ cup
Beef stock (bouillon)	1 L/1$\frac{3}{4}$ pints	4$\frac{1}{3}$ cups
Dry white wine	4 tbs	5 tbs
Salt and pepper		

Peel and slice the onions. Melt the margarine in a pan, put in the onion and cook until transparent. Add the stock, bring to the boil, cover and simmer for about 20 minutes. Pour in the wine and reheat without allowing to boil. Season to taste with salt and pepper.

Variation: For a slightly thickened soup, add 30 ml/2 tbs plain (all-purpose) flour to the onions before the stock is added.
Serving suggestion: Top portions of the soup with croûtons and grated cheese or accompany with cheese on toast, grilled until golden..

Cold cucumber soup
Serves 4

Ingredients	Metric-Imperial	American
1 clove of garlic		
1 small cucumber		
Salt and pepper		
Natural yogurt (plain)	300 ml/$\frac{1}{2}$ pint	1$\frac{1}{4}$ cups
Cold chicken stock (bouillon)	150 ml/$\frac{1}{4}$ pint	$\frac{2}{3}$ cup
Worcestershire sauce	1 tsp	1 tsp
Chopped parsley		

Peel and crush the garlic. Peel and grate or chop the cucumber then liquidize. Add the garlic and season to taste with salt and pepper. Leave to stand for about 30 minutes.
  Stir the yogurt, stock and Worcestershire sauce into the cucumber mixture. Sprinkle with the parsley and serve very cold with a few ice cubes in the tureen.

Remark: This uncooked soup is delicious and very easy to make.

Italian bean and vegetable soup
Serves 6–8

Ingredients	Metric-Imperial	American
Dried cannellini beans	150 g/5 oz	⅔ cup
Water	1 L/1¾ pints	4⅓ cups
Salt and pepper		
Streaky bacon (strips)	100 g/4 oz	8 strips
1 onion		
2 cloves of garlic		
Floury potatoes	225 g/8 oz	8 oz
Carrots	225 g/8 oz	8 oz
Courgettes (zucchini)	225 g/8 oz	8 oz
2 sticks of celery (stalks)		
2 leeks		
Tomatoes	225 g/8 oz	8 oz
Olive oil	4 tbs	5 tbs
Dried basil	½ tsp	½ tsp
Frozen peas	225 g/8 oz	1⅓ cups
Beef stock (bouillon)		
2 bay leaves		
Long grain rice	150 g/5 oz	⅔ cup
Grated Parmesan cheese	2 tbs	3 tbs

Soak the beans in the water for 12–24 hours. Bring to the boil in the soaking liquid, add a little salt, cover and simmer for about 1¼ hours, or until the beans are nearly soft. Drain the beans, reserving the cooking liquid.

Chop the bacon. Peel and chop the onion and garlic. Peel and chop the potatoes and carrots. Top and tail the courgettes and cut into slices. Trim and thinly slice the celery and leek. Pour boiling water over the tomatoes, drain, peel and cut into quarters.

Heat the oil in a large pan and cook the onion, garlic and bacon until transparent. Add the potato and basil and cook for 2 minutes. Put in the carrot, courgette, celery, leek and peas and cook gently for 10 minutes, stirring occasionally. Make the reserved bean cooking liquid up to 2 L/3½ pints (4½ pints) with beef stock. Add to the vegetables with the cooked beans and bay leaves. Bring to the boil, season to taste with salt and pepper, cover and simmer for 45 minutes. Stir in the rice and cook for a further 15 minutes. Put in the tomato pieces and cook on for another 5 minutes. Discard the bay leaves and serve the soup sprinkled with the cheese.

Vegetable bouillon
Serves 4

Ingredients	Metric-Imperial	American
1 medium-sized kohlrabi		
1 medium-sized carrot		
1 medium-sized onion		
1 stick of celery (stalk)		
Asparagus pieces	100 g/4 oz	⅔ cup
1 leek		
Butter or margarine	40 g/1½ oz	3 tbs
Water	1¼ L/2¼ pints	5¾ cups
1 bunch of parsley		
Salt and pepper		

Peel the kohlrabi, carrot and onion. Trim the celery, asparagus and leek. Chop all the vegetables. Melt the butter or margarine in a pan, add the vegetables and stir lightly. Cook for 2 minutes. Add the water, bring to the boil, cover and simmer for about 45 minutes. Add the washed parsley and cook for a further 15 minutes.

Strain and season to taste with salt and pepper. This bouillon can be used instead of meat or bone stock (bouillon).

Variations: Use parsnip, core of cauliflower or cabbage or the outer leaves of white or savoy cabbage instead of the vegetables suggested. Frozen vegetables can be substituted if fresh are not available.

Microwave hint
When using heatproof glass or ceramic containers in the microwave cooker, make sure they have no metal trim or screws in lids. Remember to remove any detachable handles too.

Above: Italian bean and vegetable soup
Opposite: Piquant oxtail soup

Piquant oxtail soup
Serves 4

Ingredients	Metric-Imperial	American
1 medium-sized onion		
Oil	1 tbs	1 tbs
1 small dill pickled cucumber		
Honey	1 tsp	1 tsp
Pinch of curry powder		
Pinch of sweet paprika pepper		
Oxtail soup	425 ml/15 oz can	15 oz can
Red wine or brandy, optional	1 tbs	1 tbs

Peel and chop the onion. Heat the oil in a pan, add the onion and cook until transparent. Dice the cucumber, put into the pan with the honey, curry powder and paprika. Cook for a further 1 minute, stirring. Blend in the soup and bring to the boil. If liked, stir the wine or brandy into the soup before serving.

Clear veal broth
Serves 4

Ingredients	Metric-Imperial	American
Selection of pot vegetables		
Veal bones	225 g/8 oz	8 oz
Breast of veal	225 g/ 8 oz	8 oz
Water	1½ L/2½ pints	3⅓ pints
Salt and pepper		
Meat extract		
Drained canned asparagus tips	100 g/4 oz	about 6
Cooked green peas	100 g/4 oz	⅔ cup

Clean the pot vegetables, peel if necessary and chop. Have the bones divided into pieces. Wash them and place in a pan with the meat, water, chopped vegetables and a little salt. Cover and simmer for about 1½ hours.

Strain the broth and return to the pan. Adjust the seasoning to taste with salt, pepper and a little meat extract. Stir in the asparagus and peas, reheat and serve.

Spring vegetable soup
Serves 4

Ingredients	Metric-Imperial	American
2 medium-sized carrots		
4 stalks of asparagus		
1 leek		
2 medium-sized tomatoes		
Diced celeriac	175 g/6 oz	1 cup
Cauliflower florets	100 g/4 oz	1 cup
Chicken stock (bouillon)	1 L/1¾ pints	4⅓ cups
Salt and pepper		
Meat extract		
Chopped parsley	2 tbs	3 tbs

Peel the carrots and cut into slices with a crinkle cutter. Trim the asparagus and cut into short lengths. Clean, trim and slice the leek. Pour boiling water over the tomatoes, drain, peel and roughly chop.

Put all the prepared vegetables into a pan with the stock and bring to the boil. Cover and simmer for about 20 minutes, or until the vegetables are tender. Season to taste with salt, pepper and a little meat extract and serve sprinkled with parsley.

Serving suggestion: Add sponge dumplings to the soup.

Dried green pea soup
Serves 4

Ingredients	Metric-Imperial	American
Dried green peas	225 g/8 oz	1 cup
Beef stock (bouillon)	1¼ L/2¼ pints	2¾ pints
Bacon or ham trimmings	up to 225 g/8 oz	up to 8 oz
1 bouquet garni		
Pinch of dried marjoram		
1 onion		
Bacon fat or butter	15 g/½ oz	1 tbs
Flour	1 tbs	1 tbs
Salt and pepper		
Meat extract		
Chopped parsley	1 tbs	1 tbs

Soak the peas in the stock for 12–24 hours. Bring to the boil in the soaking liquid, add the bacon or ham, cover and simmer for about 1 hour. Add the bouquet garni and marjoram and cook for a further 45 minutes, or until the peas are tender.

Discard the bouquet garni and bacon or ham. Liquidize or sieve the soup.

Peel and chop the onion. Cook in the bacon fat or butter in a large pan until transparent. Sprinkle on the flour and cook for 1 minute, stirring. Whisk in the soup and cook for a further 15 minutes. Season to taste with salt, pepper and a little meat extract. Serve sprinkled with parsley and accompanied by croûtons.

Right: Spring vegetable soup
Opposite: Beef, mushroom and rice soup

Beef, mushroom and rice soup
Serves 4

Ingredients	Metric-Imperial	American
1–2 small pieces of beef bone, optional		
Braising steak (chuck)	450 g/1 lb	1 lb
Water	1½ L/2½ pints	6¼ cups
Salt		
Mushrooms	225 g/8 oz	8 oz
Butter	15 g/½ oz	1 tbs
Dried tarragon	½ tsp	½ tsp
Long grain rice	50 g/2 oz	¼ cup
Drained canned asparagus pieces	100 g/4 oz	⅔ cup
Meat extract		
Chopped parsley	1 tbs	1 tbs

Wash the bones if used and place in a pan with the meat and water. Add a little salt and bring to the boil. Skim the surface, cover the pan and simmer for about 1¾ hours.

Slice the mushrooms. Melt the butter in a clean pan, put in the mushrooms and tarragon and cook gently for about 10 minutes, stirring occasionally.

Remove the meat and bones from the stock, dice the meat and discard the bones. Cook the rice in the stock for 15 minutes then add the mushrooms, asparagus pieces and meat. Season with a little meat extract, reheat to boiling point and serve sprinkled with parsley.

Microwave hint

Some suitable dishes you want to use in the microwave cooker may not have lids. (Microwave recipes often recommend cooking covered, as a layer of steam builds up under the cover, keeping the food moist and warming it up more quickly.) An inverted plate will take the place of a cover or lid.

Vegetable soup with cheese dumplings
Serves 4–6

Ingredients	Metric-Imperial	American
Veal bones	1 kg/2¼ lb	2¼ lb
Breast of veal	1 kg/2¼ lb	2¼ lb
Water	3½ L/6 pints	7½ pints
1 lime or small lemon		
1 small celeriac		
2 small parsnips		
2 beef stock cubes (bouillon)		
Salt and pepper		
Carrots	225 g/8 oz	8 oz
Cauliflower florets	225 g/8 oz	2 cups
1 bunch of spring onions (scallions)	225 g/8 oz	8 oz
Shelled green peas	225 g/8 oz	1⅓ cups
Mange tout peas (sugar peas)	225 g/8 oz	8 oz
For the dumplings:		
Water	125 ml/4 fl oz	½ cup
Butter or margarine	50 g/2 oz	¼ cup
Salt	1 tsp	1 tsp
Flour	75 g/3 oz	¾ cup
Grated Gouda cheese	100 g/4 oz	1 cup
3 eggs		
Freshly ground pepper		
Ground nutmeg		

Have the veal bones in small pieces. Put them in a large pan with the veal and water. Bring to the boil and skim the surface. Halve the lime, peel and roughly chop the celeriac and parsnips. Add these to the pan and simmer, uncovered, for about 1½ hours. Remove the lime or lemon.

Discard the bones. Lift out the meat, cut it into small pieces and reserve. Crumble the stock cubes into the stock and add extra salt and pepper if necessary. Peel the carrots and cut into strips. Add to the pan with the cauliflower. Cook for 15 minutes. Trim and chop the spring onions, put into the soup with the peas, mange tout and reserved meat. Cook for a further 30 minutes.

Meanwhile, make the dumplings. Put the water, margarine and salt into a pan and bring to the boil. Remove from the heat and put in all the flour. Beat over low heat for about 1 minute, until the mixture forms a ball. Beat in the cheese and eggs and season with pepper and nutmeg to taste.

Have ready a pan of boiling salted water. With 2 wet teaspoons, form small dumplings from the cheese mixture and drop into the boiling water. Allow to simmer for 6 minutes. Remove with a slotted spoon, drain well and serve in the soup.

Serving suggestion: As an alternative to the dumplings, accompany the soup with mouthwatering garlic bread to transform soup into a snack or light lunch.

Pea soup with pickled pork and frankfurters
Serves 4

Ingredients	Metric-Imperial	American
Dried green peas	350 g/12 oz	1½ cups
Beef stock (bouillon)	2 L/3½ pints	4¼ pints
Pickled belly of pork (pork sides)	450 g/1 lb	1 lb
Potatoes	450 g/1 lb	1 lb
Selection of pot vegetables (see pge 15)		
Dried marjoram	½ tsp	½ tsp
Salt and pepper		
4 frankfurters		

White wine soup with kiwi fruit
Serves 4

Ingredients	Metric-Imperial	American
Apple juice	400 ml/14 fl oz	1¾ cups
Sweet white wine	350 ml/12 fl oz	1½ cups
Sugar	40 g/1½ oz	3 tbs
Cornflour (cornstarch)	2 tbs	3 tbs
2 egg yolks		
Double cream (heavy)	125 ml/4 fl oz	½ cup
Vanilla essence (extract)	1 tsp	1 tsp
Lemon juice		
Extra sugar		
2 kiwi fruit		

Put the apple juice, wine and sugar into a pan and bring to the boil. Blend the cornflour with a little cold water, add to the soup and stir until boiling. Simmer for 1 minute. Beat the egg yolks with the cream and whisk into the soup. Reheat, stirring, but do not allow to boil. Stir in the vanilla and add lemon juice and extra sugar to taste.

Peel and slice the kiwi fruit, add the slices to the soup and serve hot or cold.

Snow dumplings
Serves 4

Ingredients	Metric-Imperial	American
2 egg whites		
Caster sugar (granulated)	2 tsp	2 tsp
Finely grated chocolate or a mixture of ground cinnamon and sugar for sprinkling		

Have ready a pan of boiling fruit soup or water. Whisk the egg whites until stiff, add the sugar and whisk again until glossy.

Remove the pan from the heat. Take small quantities of the dumpling mixture using a teaspoon and drop them into the soup or water. Put the lid on the pan and leave for 5 minutes, until the dumplings become firm. Remove with a slotted spoon, drain and serve sprinkled with chocolate or cinnamon sugar as desired.

Wash the peas, place in a large pan, pour on the stock and leave to soak for 12–24 hours.

Rinse the pork and remove the skin. Peel and dice the potatoes. Trim the pot vegetables, peel if necessary and chop. Add to the pan with the pork, potato, herbs and a little seasoning. Bring to the boil. Cover and simmer for about 2 hours, or until the peas are tender.

Remove the pork, cut into small dice and return to the soup. Adjust the seasoning to taste. Put in the frankfurters and reheat them in the soup. Serve with crisply fried bread croûtons.

Variation: Instead of the pickled pork use a piece of bacon
Other continental sausages could be used, sliced if necessary.

Try making croûtons using wholemeal (wholewheat) bread instead of white.

Left: Pea soup with pickled pork and frankfurters

Cold apricot soup
Serves 4

Ingredients	Metric-Imperial	American
Ripe apricots	450 g/1 lb	1 lb
Water	1 L/1¾ pints	4⅓ cups
Sugar	100 g/4 oz	½ cup
½ stick of cinnamon		
2 slices of lemon		
Cornflour (cornstarch)	4 tbs	5 tbs
Few drops of vanilla essence (extract)		
Lemon juice		

Cover the apricots with boiling water, drain and peel. Cut in half and remove the stones (pits). Reserve a few apricot halves for the garnish and cut the remainder into 1 cm/½ inch wide strips.

Put the water, sugar, cinnamon stick and lemon slices into a pan and bring to the boil. Add the apricot strips and cook for about 15 minutes. Discard the cinnamon and lemon slices. Liquidize or sieve the soup, return to the pan and reheat. Blend the cornflour with a little cold water, mix into the soup and stir until boiling. Simmer for 3 minutes. Add the vanilla essence and lemon juice to taste and leave to cool. Stir the reserved apricot halves into the soup and, if wished, serve with Snow dumplings (see page 31).

Microwave method
Cover the apricots with boiling water, drain and peel. Cut the apricots in half and remove the stones, reserving a few halves for garnish. Cut the remaining halves into 1 cm/½ inch strips.

Mix the boiling water, sugar, cinnamon stick and lemon slice in a large pyrex bowl and cook on full power for 6 minutes. Add the apricot strips and cook on full power again for 10 minutes. Leave to cool slightly.

Purée the soup in a blender or food processor or pass through a coarse sieve. Mix the cornflour with a little cold water and then add some of the hot soup. Mix well until no lumps are present then add to the soup. Whisk the cornflour mixture and soup until smooth, add vanilla essence and lemon juice to taste.

Return to the microwave at full power for 10 minutes. Whisk when the soup is removed, leave to cool and chill. Stir in the apricot garnish before serving.

Cold cherry soup with snow dumplings
Serves 4

Ingredients	Metric-Imperial	American
Morello cherries	675 g/1½ lb	1½ lb
Red or white wine	300 ml/½ pint	1¼ cups
Water	750 ml/1¼ pints	3 cups
Pared strip of lemon rind		
Lemon juice	1 tbs	1 tbs
1 stick of cinnamon		
1 whole clove		
Sugar	75 g/3 oz	⅓ cup
Cornflour (cornstarch)	2 tbs	3 tbs
For the dumplings:		
Milk	500 ml/18 fl oz	2¼ cups
Grated lemon rind	½ tsp	½ tsp
Sugar	25 g/1 oz	2 tbs
Pinch of salt		
Semolina	150 g/5 oz	scant 1 cup
1 egg		

Remove stalks and stones (pits) from the cherries. Put the wine, water, lemon rind, lemon juice, cinnamon stick, clove and sugar into a pan and bring to the boil. Add the cherries and poach for 8 minutes. Moisten the cornflour with a little

cold water, add to the pan and stir until boiling. Simmer for 1 minute. Discard the rind, cinnamon and clove and cool.

To make the dumplings, bring the milk, lemon rind, sugar and salt to the boil. Off the heat, add the semolina and stir vigorously until the mixture forms a ball. Heat for 1 minute, stirring. Transfer to a bowl and beat in the egg.

Fill a large pan two thirds full with salted water and bring to boiling point. Using 2 wet teaspoons, form small dumplings from the semolina mixture and drop into the simmering salted water. Cook gently for 5–7 minutes, remove with a slotted spoon, drain and serve with the soup.

Above: Cold apricot soup

Cold gooseberry soup
Serves 4

Ingredients	Metric-Imperial	American
Water	300 ml/½ pint	1¼ cups
Pared rind of ½ lemon		
½ stick of cinnamon		
Dessert gooseberries	1 kg/2¼ lb	2¼ lb
Red wine	350 ml/12 fl oz	1½ cups
Sugar	150 g/5 oz	⅔ cup

Bring the water, lemon rind and cinnamon stick to the boil. Add the gooseberries and cook for 8 minutes until soft. Discard the cinnamon and rind. Liquidize the soup. Add the wine and sugar and stir until boiling. Cool for 4 hours.

Chocolate soup
Serves 4

Ingredients	Metric-Imperial	American
Cornflour (cornstarch)	3 tbs	4 tbs
Milk	1 L/1¾ pints	4⅓ cups
Grated plain chocolate	75 g/3 oz	¾ cup
Vanilla essence (extract)	1 tsp	1 tsp
Pinch of salt		
Sugar		

Moisten the cornflour with a little of the milk. Put the remaining milk and the chocolate in a pan and bring to the boil. Add the cornflour mixture and cook gently for 3 minutes, stirring all the time. Add the vanilla essence and salt then sugar to taste. Stir well until dissolved.

Tip: To intensify the chocolate flavour, add 2 tbs (3 tbs) very strong coffee to the milk. For special occasions, also add the same amount of coffee liqueur after the soup is removed from the heat.

Cold strawberry soup
Serves 4

Ingredients	Metric-Imperial	American
Strawberries	675 g/1½ lb	1½ lb
Caster sugar (granulated)	2–3 tbs	3–4 tbs

Orange juice	225 ml/8 fl oz	1 cup

Reserve a few strawberries for the garnish and hull the remainder. Liquidize these or sieve. Stir in the sugar and orange juice, mix well and chill. Stir the soup and garnish.

Cold apple soup with borage
Serves 4

Ingredients	Metric-Imperial	American
Tart dessert apples	450 g/1 lb	1 lb
Medium white wine	225 ml/8 fl oz	1 cup
Lemon juice	125 ml/4 fl oz	½ cup
Water	300 ml/½ pint	1¼ cups
Sugar	150 g/5 oz	⅔ cup
Cornflour (cornstarch)	2 tbs	3 tbs
Few borage leaves and flowers		

Peel, quarter and core the apples and cut into slices. Put the wine, lemon juice and water in a pan and bring to the boil. Add the apple slices and simmer until they are tender but not soft. Remove the apple slices and reserve.

Add the sugar to the cooking liquid and bring to the boil. Moisten the cornflour with a little cold water, stir into the pan and simmer for 2 minutes. Return the apple to the soup, chill. Garnish with borage leaves and flowers.

Above: Cold apple soup with borage
Opposite: Cold strawberry soup

Rhubarb soup with berries
Serves 4

Ingredients	Metric-Imperial	American
Rhubarb	450 g/1 lb	1 lb
Sugar	100 g/4 oz	½ cup
Medium white wine	300 ml/½ pint	1¼ cups
Raspberries	225 g/8 oz	8 oz
Strawberries	450 g/1 lb	1 lb
For the dumplings:		
1 egg white		
Caster sugar (granulated)	2 tbs	3 tbs
Ground cinnamon	1 sp	1 tsp

Wash the rhubarb and cut into small pieces. Put the sugar into a pan and heat, stirring, until it becomes golden brown. Pour in the wine and heat, stirring, until the caramel has dissolved. Add the rhubarb and raspberries, bring to the boil, cover and simmer for 10 minutes. Press through a sieve and return to the pan. Hull the strawberries and cut them in half. Stir into the soup and leave to cool.

Whisk the egg white until stiff, add 1 tsp of the sugar and whisk again until glossy. Bring a pan of water to the boil and remove it from the heat. Take small portions of the egg white mixture using a teaspoon and drop these into the water. Cover the pan and leave for 5 minutes, until the dumplings become firm. Remove with a slotted spoon, drain and float on the soup. Combine the remaining sugar and the cinnamon and sprinkle over the dumplings.

Refreshing savoury banana soup
Serves 4

Ingredients	Metric-Imperial	American
Beef or chicken stock (bouillon)	600 ml/1 pint	2½ cups
Pinch of curry powder		
2 ripe bananas		
Lemon juice	1 tsp	1 tsp
Salt		
Double cream (heavy)	2 tbs	3 tbs
Few toasted slivered almonds		

Put the stock and curry powder into a pan and bring to the boil. Peel the bananas and mash them in a large bowl. Sprinkle with lemon juice and whisk in the boiling stock. Season to taste with salt and blend in the cream. Cool and then chill. Serve the soup garnished with the toasted slivered almonds.

Blackcurrant soup with apples
Serves 4

Ingredients	Metric-Imperial	American
Blackcurrants	350 g/12 oz	12 oz
Sugar	75 g/3 oz	1/3 cup
Pared strip of lemon rind		
1 stick of cinnamon		
Water	500 ml/18 fl oz	2 1/4 cups
2 medium-sized cooking apples		
Juice of 1 lemon		
Cornflour (cornstarch)	2 tbs	3 tbs
Little extra sugar		

Wash the blackcurrants and place in a pan with the sugar, lemon rind, cinnamon stick and water. Bring to the boil then simmer for about 15 minutes, or until the fruit is soft. Press the soup through a sieve, discarding the lemon rind and cinnamon. Make up to 750 ml/1 1/4 pints (3 cups) with more water if necessary.

Peel, quarter and core the apples. Cut into slices and place in a pan with the fruit soup and lemon juice. Bring to the boil and cook for 5 minutes. Moisten the cornflour with a little cold water, add to the soup and stir until thickened. Simmer for a further 5 minutes and add extra sugar to taste. Serve hot or cold.

Cold kiwi fruit soup with white wine
Serves 4

Ingredients	Metric-Imperial	American
Sweet white wine	600 ml/1 pint	2 1/2 cups
Caster sugar (granulated)	4 tbs	5 tbs
4 whole cloves		
1 stick of cinnamon		
Maple syrup	4 tbs	5 tbs
5 kiwi fruit		
Whipping cream	125 ml/4 fl oz	1/2 cup
Few sprigs of mint		

Put the wine, sugar, cloves and cinnamon in a pan and bring to the boil. Remove from the heat and stir in the maple syrup. Leave to cool then strain.

Peel the kiwi fruit, cut a few slices and reserve for the garnish. Sieve the remaining fruit to remove the seeds. Beat the purée into the spiced wine with the cream. Chill. Serve portions of the soup decorated with slices of kiwi fruit and mint sprigs.

Opposite: Rhubarb soup with berries
Below: Cold kiwi fruit soup with white wine

Russian cold beetroot soup

Serves 4

Ingredients	Metric-Imperial	American
Cucumber juice freshly pressed from unpeeled cucumber	350 ml/12 fl oz	1½ cups
Sour cream	450 ml/¾ pint	2 cups
½ red sweet pepper		
½ green sweet pepper		
½ cucumber		
2 hard-boiled eggs		
Diced pickled beetroot	175 g/6 oz	1 cup
Vodka	3 tbs	4 tbs
Salt and freshly ground pepper		
Snipped chives	2 tbs	3 tbs

Combine the cucumber juice and sour cream. Deseed and dice the peppers and dice the cucumber. Shell and chop the eggs. Stir the beetroot, pepper dice, cucumber, egg and vodka into the sour cream mixture. Season to taste with salt and pepper and chill. Serve sprinkled with chives.

Tip: If you do not have a juice extractor, liquidize the cucumber and press out the juice firmly through a fine sieve.

Cold courgette soup with tomatoes

Serves 4

Ingredients	Metric-Imperial	American
Tomatoes	350 g/12 oz	12 oz
3 small courgettes (zucchini)		
Natural yogurt (plain)	450 ml/¾ pint	2 cups
Whipping cream	150 ml/¼ pint	⅔ cup
Milk	125 ml/4 fl oz	½ cup
1–2 cloves of garlic		
Chopped mint	1 tbs	1 tbs
Chopped tarragon	1 tbs	1 tbs
Chopped dill weed	1 tsp	1 tsp
Chopped parsley	1 tsp	1 tsp
Salt and pepper		
Few lettuce leaves, optional		
1 hard-boiled egg		
Few sprigs of mint		

Pour boiling water over the tomatoes, drain, peel and roughly chop. Peel the courgettes and cut into thin slices. Whisk together the yogurt, cream and milk. Add the courgette slices and tomato. Peel and finely chop the garlic and stir into the soup with the herbs. Season with salt and pepper and chill for several hours to allow the flavour to develop.

If using the lettuce leaves, arrange them to line a glass serving dish. Pour in the soup. Shell and chop the egg, sprinkle over the soup and garnish with sprigs of mint.

Serving suggestion: Buttered wholemeal bread or slices of white bread fried in butter make a good accompaniment.

White wine soup with dumplings
Serves 4

Ingredients	Metric-Imperial	American
Water	300 ml/½ pint	1¼ cups
1 stick of cinnamon		
Pared rind of ½ lemon		
Cornflour (cornstarch)	3 tbs	4 tbs
Medium white wine	750 ml/1¼ pints	3 cups
1 egg yolk		
Sugar	100 g/4 oz	½ cup
Snow dumplings (see page 31)		

Put the water, cinnamon stick and lemon rind in a large pan and bring slowly to the boil. Discard the cinnamon stick. Moisten the cornflour with a little cold water, add to the pan and stir until boiling. Cook for 3 minutes.

Remove from the heat, take out the lemon rind and stir in the wine. Beat the egg yolk with a little cold water, blend into the soup and reheat, stirring, but do not allow to bcil. Stir in the sugar and remove from the heat. Leave to ccol and serve the soup cold with a few Snow dumplings floating on each portion.

Opposite: Russian cold beetroot soup
Above: White wine soup with snow dumplings

Avocado soup with almonds
Serves 4

Ingredients	Metric-Imperial	American
2 ripe avocados		
Lemon juice	2 tbs	3 tbs
Chicken stock (bouillon)	300 ml/½ pint	1¼ cups
Double cream (heavy)	100 ml/4 fl oz	½ cup
Medium white wine	3 tbs	4 tbs
Salt and freshly ground pepper		
Toasted slivered almonds	1 tbs	1 tbs

Halve the avocados, discard the stones (pits) and scoop out the flesh. Liquidize with the lemon juice.

Put the stock in a pan and bring to the boil. Stir in the cream and wine. Remove from the heat and beat in the avocado purée. Season to taste with salt and pepper. Cool and then chill the soup. Divide between 4 soup plates and serve sprinkled with almonds.

Cold melon soup with grapes
Serves 4

Ingredients	Metric-Imperial	American
Green grapes	100 g/4 oz	4 oz
Apricots	150 g/5 oz	5 oz
1 eating apple		
1 cantaloup melon		
Lemon juice	3 tbs	4 tbs
Sweet white wine	500 ml/18 fl oz	2¼ cups
Cornflour (cornstarch)	1 tsp	1 tsp
Clear honey	1 tbs	1 tbs
Pine kernels (nuts)	50 g/2 oz	½ cup

Wash the grapes, apricots and apple and cut in half. Remove the pips or stones (pits) from the grapes and apricots. Core and thinly slice the apple. Cut the melon in half, remove the seeds and dice the flesh from one half, discarding the rind. Put the diced melon in a pan with the remaining fruit and pour over the lemon juice and wine. Bring to the boil, cover and simmer for 20 minutes.

Liquidize or sieve, return to the pan and reheat. Moisten the cornflour with a little cold water, add to the pan and stir until boiling. Simmer for 3 minutes and stir in the honey.

Using a melon baller, cut balls from the remaining half of the melon and put into the soup. Allow to cool. Toast the pine kernels, tossing then in a pan without fat over moderate heat until golden brown. Just before serving, sprinkle them over the soup.

Microwave hint
When a soup or sauce contains a high proportion of milk, use a large container because the food will foam up and rise much more than if water or stock is the main liquid ingredient.

Fruit soup compote
Serves 4

Ingredients	Metric-Imperial	American
Dried fruit such as apples, apricots or prunes	100 g/4 oz	⅔ cup
Water	1¼ L/2¼ pints	2¾ pints
Lemon juice	1 tsp	1 tsp
Ground cinnamon	½ tsp	½ tsp
Cornflour (cornstarch)	2 tbs	3 tbs
Vanilla essence (extract)		
Caster sugar (granulated)		

Wash the dried fruit and leave to soak in the water for 12 hours. Bring to the boil in the soaking water and add the lemon juice and cinnamon. Cover and simmer for about 25 minutes.

Liquidize or sieve and return to the pan. Reheat. Moisten the cornflour with a little cold water, add to the soup and stir until boiling. Simmer for 3 minutes and add a little vanilla essence and sugar to taste. Leave until cold and serve with ratafia biscuits (miniature almond macaroons).

Above: Cold melon soup with grapes
Opposite: Avocado soup with almonds

Cold morello soup
Serves 4

Ingredients	Metric-Imperial	American
Morello cherries	450 g/1 lb	1 lb
Water	1¼ L/2¼ pints	5¾ cups
Pared strip of orange rind		
Sugar	225 g/8 oz	1 cup
1 packet raspberry flavoured blancmange powder (pudding)	33 g/scant 1¼ oz	3 tbs
Medium white wine	3 tbs	4 tbs

Remove the stalks and stones (pits) from the cherries. Place the water in a large pan and bring to the boil. Add the cherries and orange rind and put in approximately three quarters of the sugar. Stir well and simmer for 10 minutes.

Moisten the blancmange powder with a little cold water, add to the pan and stir until boiling. Simmer for a further 5 minutes. Remove from the heat, stir in the wine and add as much of the remaining sugar as wished. Allow the soup to cool and remove the orange rind before serving.

Below: Cold morello soup
Opposite: Cold wine soup with figs

Cold wine soup with figs
Serves 4

Ingredients	Metric-Imperial	American
Canned figs	425 g/15 oz can	15 oz can
2 slices of lemon		
1 stick of cinnamon		
Ground cardamom	¼ tsp	¼ tsp
Sugar	1–2 tbs	2–3 tbs
Arrowroot	4 tsp	4 tsp
Medium white wine	450 ml/¾ pint	scant 2 cups

Drain the figs and make up the syrup to 600 ml/1 pint (2½ cups) with water. Put the liquid into a large pan with the lemon slices, cinnamon stick, cardamom and sugar and bring to the boil. Blend the arrowroot with a little cold water, add to the pan and stir until boiling. Simmer for 1 minute.

Remove from the heat, discard the lemon slices and cinnamon stick and blend in the wine. Cut 4 of the figs into strips and stir into the soup. Allow to cool and then chill before serving. Any extra figs can be added to a fruit salad.

Savoury almond cream soup
Serves 4

Ingredients	Metric-Imperial	American
2 onions		
Butter or margarine	25 g/1 oz	2 tbs
Ground almonds	100 g/4 oz	1 cup
Beef stock (bouillon)	600 ml/1 pint	2½ cups
Whipping cream	125 ml/4 fl oz	½ cup
White wine	125 ml/4 fl oz	½ cup
Salt and pepper		
Ground nutmeg		
2 egg yolks		
Water	2 tbs	3 tbs
Toasted slivered almonds	1 tbs	1 tbs

Peel and finely chop the onions. Melt the butter or margarine in a pan, put in the onion and cook until transparent. Sprinkle in the almonds and allow to cook for 1 minute, stirring. Pour in the stock, bring to the boil and blend in half the cream. Simmer for 10 minutes.

Strain, return to the pan and stir in the wine. Season to taste with salt, pepper and nutmeg and reheat just to boiling point. Beat the egg yolks with the water and whisk into the soup. Allow to cool. Whip the remaining cream until thick and serve the soup cold, topped with cream and almonds.

Orange, honey and oat breakfast dish
Serves 1

Ingredients	Metric-Imperial	American
2 small oranges		
Clear honey	1 tbs	1 tbs
Rolled oats	4 tbs	5 tbs
Sprig of mint		

Peel the oranges. Cut one slice and reserve for the decoration then divide the remaining orange flesh into small pieces, discarding the pith. Fold in the honey and leave to stand for 5 minutes. Stir in the oats and serve in a small bowl decorated with the reserved orange slice and a sprig of mint.

Variation: Add 1 tbs chopped almonds or mixed nuts to the above ingredients then pour over a little cream.

Pear, melon and raspberry salad
Serves 6

Ingredients	Metric-Imperial	American
1 honeydew melon		
Raspberry cordial	4 tbs	5 tbs
Lemon juice	1 tbs	1 tbs
Caster sugar (granulated)	3 tbs	4 tbs
2 pears		
Raspberries	225 g/8 oz	8 oz
Sweet white wine	4 tbs	5 tbs

Cut the melon in half, if desired in a zig-zag pattern. Discard the seeds, scoop out the flesh and dice. Place in a bowl, add the raspberry cordial, lemon juice and sugar. Increase the amount of sugar to taste. Peel, quarter and core the pears. Dice the flesh. Add to the melon mixture with the raspberries. Pour the wine over, spoon into the melon halves and chill before serving.

Note: The fruit may be divided among 6 small dessert dishes instead of being served in the melon halves.

Above: Orange, honey and oat breakfast dish
Opposite: Muesli with fresh and dried fruit

Creamy peach purée

Serves 4–6

Ingredients	Metric-Imperial	American
4 peaches		
Milk	3 tbs	4 tbs
tCream cheese	250 g/9 oz	generous 1 cup
Sugar	75 g/3 oz	⅓ cup
Vanilla essence (extract)	2 tsp	2 tsp
Lemon juice	2 tbs	3 tbs
Whipping cream	125 ml/4 fl oz	½ cup

Pour boiling water over the peaches, drain and peel. Halve and remove the stones (pits). Cut the flesh into pieces and purée with the milk in a blender or food processor. When smooth, add the cream cheese, sugar, vanilla and lemon juice, and blend again. Whip the cream and fold into the peach mixture. Serve in small glass dessert dishes topped with grated chocolate if liked.

Traditional muesli

Serves 4

Ingredients	Metric-Imperial	American
Rolled oats	200 g/7 oz	2 cups
Milk	300 ml/½ pint	1¼ cups
Whipping cream	125 ml/4 fl oz	½ cup
4 dessert apples		
Lemon juice	2 tbs	3 tbs
2 bananas		
4 oranges		
Chopped hazelnuts (filberts) or almonds	50 g/2 oz	½ cup
Clear honey	2 tbs	3 tbs

Put the oats in a bowl and pour the milk and cream over them. Allow to stand for a few minutes.

Peel, quarter and core the apples, and cut the flesh into small pieces. Sprinkle with the lemon juice. Peel and slice the bananas. Peel the oranges, and cut into small pieces removing all the pith. Combine the fruit and nuts with the honey, and fold into the oat mixture.

Muesli with fresh and dried fruit

Serves 4

Ingredients	Metric-Imperial	American
Milk	125 ml/4 fl oz	½ cup
Grated rind of 1 lemon		
Lemon juice	1 tbs	1 tbs
Rolled oats	3 tbs	4 tbs
Clear honey	3 tbs	4 tbs
Seedless raisins	2 tbs	3 tbs
2 dessert apples		
4 dried dates or figs		
1 banana		
Strawberries	100 g/4 oz	4 oz
Chopped walnuts	2 tbs	3 tbs
Chopped almonds	2 tbs	3 tbs

Place the milk in a pan and bring to the boil. Remove from the heat and stir in the lemon rind and juice, the oats, honey and raisins. Leave to stand for 30 minutes.

Peel and grate the apples, discarding the cores. Stone (pit) the dates if using. Coarsely chop the dates or figs. Peel and slice the banana. Hull and halve the strawberries. Fold the fruit and nuts into the oat mixture. Divide among 4 breakfast bowls and serve with yogurt.

Yogurt with honey and hazelnuts

Serves 1

Ingredients	Metric-Imperial	American
Hazelnuts (filberts)	25 g/1 oz	¼ cup
Natural yogurt (plain)	150 ml/¼ pint	⅔ cup
Clear honey	2 tbs	3 tbs
Pinch of ground cinnamon		

Coarsely chop the hazelnuts and toss in a frying pan over moderate heat without any fat until golden brown. Allow to cool. Stir together the yogurt and honey in a breakfast bowl. Fold in the hazelnuts and sprinkle with the cinnamon.

Simple cheese cream
Serves 4

Ingredients	Metric-Imperial	American
Water	3 tbs	4 tbs
Powdered gelatine	1 tbs	1 tbs
Curd cheese (sieved cottage)	225 g/8 oz	8 oz
3 eggs		
Caster sugar (granulated)	75 g/3 oz	⅓ cup
Lemon juice	2 tbs	3 tbs

Put the water into a small bowl and sprinkle on the gelatine. Leave to stand for 10 minutes. Place over hot water and stir until the gelatine has completely dissolved.

Beat the cheese until soft. Separate the eggs and put the yolks into a bowl with the sugar. Whisk until pale and creamy. Gradually whisk in the cheese and the lemon juice. Stir 3 tbs (4 tbs) into the dissolved gelatine then add this to the bowl and mix well. Whisk the egg whites in a clean bowl until stiff and fold into the cheese mixture. Pour at once into a glass serving dish and leave to set.

Fruit salad
Serves 4

Ingredients	Metric-Imperial	American
4 oranges		
4 dried figs		
Seedless raisins	2 tbs	3 tbs
Sultanas (seedless white raisins)	2 tbs	3 tbs
Caster sugar (granulated)	4 tbs	5 tbs
Lemon juice	1 tbs	1 tbs
Sweet wine or fruit syrup	4 tbs	5 tbs
Almonds or hazelnuts (filberts)	25 g/1 oz	¼ cup

This salad is particularly delicious as both dried and fresh fruit are combined. Peel the oranges and divide into segments, discarding the pith. Place the figs, raisins and sultanas in a bowl and pour over hot water to cover. Leave to stand for 10 minutes, until the fruit is plump. Drain well and chop coarsely. Put the orange segments and fig mixture in layers in a glass serving dish, sprinkling the layers with sugar. Spoon over the lemon juice and wine or fruit syrup. Serve decorated with nuts.

Variations: The following combinations make delightfully refreshing salads.
1 Apples, oranges, sugar, lemon juice and nuts.
2 Apples, oranges, bananas, sugar, lemon juice and nuts.
3 Apples, figs, sugar and lemon juice.
4 Apples, oranges, bananas, pineapple, sugar and wine.
5 Apples, oranges, pears, pineapple, sugar and fruit syrup.
6 Oranges, bananas, sugar and lemon juice.
7 Plums, pears, peaches, sugar and lemon juice.

Lemon cheese cream
Serves 4

Ingredients	Metric-Imperial	American
Water	4 tbs	5 tbs
Powdered gelatine	2 tsp	2 tsp
Curd cheese (sieved cottage)	225 g/8 oz	8 oz
Milk	125 ml/4 fl oz	½ cup
Caster sugar (granulated)	100 g/4 oz	4 oz
Grated rind and juice of ½ lemon		
Whipping cream	125 ml/4 fl oz	½ cup
Vanilla essence (extract)	2 tsp	2 tsp
Maraschino cherries (cocktail)		

Place the water in a small bowl and sprinkle on the gelatine. Leave to stand for 10 minutes. Place over hot water and stir until the gelatine has completely dissolved.

Beat the cheese in a bowl until soft. Gradually beat in the milk, sugar, lemon rind and juice. Stir 3 tbs (4 tbs) of the mixture into the dissolved gelatine than add this to the bowl and mix well. Whip the cream with the vanilla until stiff and fold into the cheese mixture. Transfer to a glass serving bowl and chill until set. Decorate with cherries before serving.

Raspberries with crunchy oats
Serves 4

Ingredients	Metric-Imperial	American
Butter	25 g/1 oz	2 tbs
Rolled oats	100 g/4 oz	generous 1 cup
Caster sugar (granulated)		
Grated lemon rind	1 tsp	1 tsp
Raspberries	450 g/1 lb	1 lb
Whipping cream	125 ml/4 fl oz	½ cup
Vanilla essence (extract)	1 tsp	1 tsp

Melt the butter in a frying pan, add the oats and stir until they are golden. Sprinkle in 2 tbs (3 tbs) sugar and fry for a further 1 minute, stirring once during this time. Leave to cool.

Fold the lemon rind into the raspberries and sweeten with sugar to taste, if necessary. Whip the cream with a further 1 tsp of sugar and the vanilla essence until stiff.

Divide the raspberry mixture among individual dessert dishes and top with the vanilla cream. Sprinkle with the fried oat topping before serving.

Opposite: Fruit salad
Above: Raspberries with crunchy oats

Curd cheese with raspberries
Serves 4

Ingredients	Metric-Imperial	American
Water	5 tbs	6 tbs
Powdered gelatine	1 tbs	1 tbs
Curd cheese (sieved cottage)	225 g/8 oz	8 oz
Caster sugar (granulated)	75 g/3 oz	⅓ cup
Lemon juice	2 tbs	3 tbs
Chopped almonds	40 g/1½ oz	⅓ cup
Rolled oats	4 tbs	5 tbs
Raspberries	275 g/10 oz	10 oz

Put the water in a small bowl and sprinkle on the gelatine. Leave to stand for 10 minutes then place over hot water and stir until the gelatine has completely dissolved.

Beat the cheese until soft then gradually beat in the sugar, lemon juice, almonds, oats and dissolved gelatine. Fold in the raspberries.

Rinse 4 moulds with cold water then fill with the cheese mixture and chill until set. Dip the containers quickly into hot water and turn out on to dessert plates. If liked, decorate with whipped cream and a few more raspberries.

Variation: Other soft summer fruits could be used instead of the raspberries.

Peach and oat snack
Serves 1

Ingredients	Metric-Imperial	American
Rolled oats	4 tbs	5 tbs
Milk	125 ml/4 fl oz	½ cup
2 peaches		
Caster sugar (granulated)	1 tbs	1 tbs
Little whipped cream		

Stir the oats into the milk. Leave to stand for 10 minutes. Halve and stone (pit) the peaches and cut the flesh into pieces. Fold into the oat mixture with the sugar. Serve in a bowl and decorate with cream before serving.

Strawberries with corn flakes
Serves 1

Ingredients	Metric-Imperial	American
Strawberries	100 g/4 oz	4 oz
Orange juice	2 tbs	3 tbs
Caster sugar (granulated)	1 tbs	1 tbs
Corn flakes	3 tbs	4 tbs
Whipping cream	2 tbs	3 tbs

Hull and halve the strawberries. Mix with the orange juice and sugar and allow to stand for 10 minutes. Serve in a bowl or deep plate topped with the corn flakes and cream.

Radish and bean sprout sandwich
Serves 1

Ingredients	Metric-Imperial	American
Butter for spreading		
1 slice of wholemeal bread (wholewheat)		
5 radishes		
1 rasher lean back bacon (Canadian)		
Bean sprouts	1–2 tbs	2–3 tbs

Butter the bread. Trim and thinly slice the radishes and arrange on the bread. Fry the bacon in a greased frying pan until crisp. Drain on absorbent kitchen paper and place on the radishes. Sprinkle with the bean sprouts and serve.

Variations: Instead of beans, the seeds of lentils, peas, mustard and cress, watercress, mustard or fennel may be grown instead, and make excellent alternatives. The sprouts can easily be produced on a wet cloth placed on a tray, on a windowsill. They may be stored in a refrigerator for 2 days afterwards before cutting, without further growth.

Avocado fruit salad with yogurt dressing
Serves 4

Ingredients	Metric-Imperial	American
1 ripe avocado		
1 large banana		
Lemon juice	3 tbs	4 tbs
2 oranges		
Fresh dates	150 g/5 oz	5 oz
Strawberries	100 g/4 oz	4 oz
1 kiwi fruit		
Seedless raisins	50 g/2 oz	1/3 cup
Natural yogurt (plain)	150 ml/1/4 pint	2/3 cup
Sour cream	2 tbs	3 tbs
Vanilla essence	1 tsp	1 tsp
Sugar	2 tbs	3 tbs

Halve, peel and stone (pit) the avocado then slice the flesh. Peel and slice the banana. Sprinkle the avocado and banana slices with two thirds of the lemon juice. Peel the oranges and divide into segments, discarding the pith. Halve the dates, discard the stones (pits) and hard skin and cut into strips. Hull and halve or quarter the strawberries. Peel the kiwi fruit, cut in half lengthways and then slice. Combine all the fruit and the raisins and divide among dessert bowls.

To make the sauce, mix together the yogurt, cream, vanilla essence, sugar and the remaining lemon juice and pour over the fruit in the bowls. Serve immediately.

Opposite: Peach and oat snack
Below: Apple with yogurt and oats

Apple with yogurt and oats
Serves 2

Ingredients	Metric-Imperial	American
2 medium-sized dessert apples		
Natural yogurt (plain)	150 ml/1/4 pint	2/3 cup
Caster sugar (granulated)	1 tbs	1 tbs
Rolled oats	40 g/1 1/2 oz	scant 1/2 cup

Quarter and core the apples and then dice finely. Mix into the yogurt with the sugar and oats. Divide between 2 breakfast bowls for serving.

Tomato and yogurt drink
Serves 1

Ingredients	Metric-Imperial	American
1 large tomato		
1 gherkin (small dill pickle)		
Natural yogurt (plain)	150 ml/1/4 pint	2/3 cup
Salt and pepper		

Cut 1 slice from the tomato and reserve. Chop the rest of the tomato and the gherkin. Stir these into the yogurt and season to taste with salt and pepper. Serve in a glass, garnished with the tomato slice.

Cucumber juice drink
Serves 1

Ingredients	Metric-Imperial	American
20 cm/8 inch length cucumber		
Whipping cream	1 tbs	1 tbs
Salt and pepper		
Few ice cubes		
Sprig dill		

Halve the cucumber lengthways and scoop out the seeds. Cut into pieces and process in a juice extractor or blender.

Stir the cream into the cucumber liquid, stir in salt and pepper to taste. Pour the cucumber drink over ice cubes in a tall glass and garnish with a sprig of fresh dill and a thin slice of cucumber if liked.

Tomato melon drink
Serves 1

Ingredients	Metric-Imperial	American
Tomatoes	225 g/8 oz	8 oz
2 slices of honeydew melon		
Lemon juice	1 tsp	1 tsp
Small pinch of cayenne pepper		
Few drops of Worcestershire sauce		
Salt		
Whipped cream	1 tbs	1 tbs
Sweet paprika pepper		

Pour boiling water over the tomatoes, drain and peel. Cut in half, scoop out the seeds and roughly chop the flesh. Remove the rind from the melon slices and dice the flesh. Liquidize with the tomato in the lemon juice, adding the cayenne and Worcestershire sauce. Add salt to taste and transfer to a tall glass. Float the cream on top and sprinkle this with a little paprika.

Exotic fruit cocktail
Serves 4

Ingredients	Metric-Imperial	American
4 Ogen melons		
Canned lichees	225 g/8 oz can	8 oz can
Canned mango	225 g/8 oz can	8 oz can
For the sauce:		
Lemon juice	2 tbs	3 tbs
Cherry liqueur	2 tbs	3 tbs
Brandy	4 tbs	5 tbs
Vanilla essence (extract)	1 tsp	1 tsp
Icing sugar (confectioners')	2 tbs	3 tbs
Ice cubes		
Maraschino cherries (cocktail)		

Cut the top third off each melon and vandyke the edge. Remove and dice the flesh, discard the melon seeds and place in a bowl. Drain and stone (pit) the lichees and drain the mango. Cut the fruit into pieces, add to the melon flesh.

To make the sauce, stir together the lemon juice, cherry liqueur, brandy and vanilla. Sift the sugar over the top and stir in. Fold into the fruit, cover and chill for at least 1 hour.

Crush some ice cubes then spoon it into 4 glass dishes.

Divide the fruit mixture among the melon 'shells' and bed these firmly into the ice. Decorate with cherries and serve with boudoir biscuits (ladyfingers) and whipped cream.

Grapefruit and peach cocktails with oats
Serves 2

Ingredients	Metric-Imperial	American
1 grapefruit		
1 peach		
Natural yogurt (plain)	150 ml/¼ pint	⅔ cup
Caster sugar (granulated)		
Rolled oats	4 tbs	5 tbs
Maraschino cherries (cocktail)		

Cut the grapefruit in half and carefully remove the flesh with a grapefruit knife. Cut into small pieces, discarding the pith. Halve and stone (pit) the peach and cut the flesh into small pieces. Fold the fruit into the yogurt with 2 tbs (3 tbs) sugar and the oats. Add a little more sugar to taste if preferred. Divide between the grapefruit 'cups' and serve decorated with cherries.

Opposite left: Cucumber juice drink
Opposite right: Tomato melon drink
Above: Grapefruit and peach cocktails with oats
Right: Exotic fruit cocktail

51

Avocado and radish salad
Serves 4

Ingredients	Metric-Imperial	American
1 round lettuce		
1 head of fennel (Florence)		
1 bunch of radishes		
1 small red and 1 small green sweet pepper		
1 avocado		
For the dressing:		
Oil	5 tbs	6 tbs
Vinegar	2 tbs	3 tbs
Salt and pepper		
Sugar	½ tsp	½ tsp
Snipped chives	1 tbs	1 tbs

Discard the outer leaves of the lettuce. Remove the remaining leaves from the stem and tear into small pieces. Wash, if necessary, and drain well. Trim and clean the fennel then quarter and cut into thin strips. Trim and slice the radishes. Halve and deseed the peppers, and cut the flesh into thin strips. Halve the avocado lengthways, discard the stone (pit) then peel and cut the flesh into slices. Mix all the salad ingredients lightly together in a glass bowl.

To make the dressing, beat together the oil and vinegar, season with salt, pepper and sugar to taste, and stir in the chives. Toss lightly with the salad and allow to stand for a few minutes before serving.

Note: This salad makes a good meal starter, served in individual glass dishes, or a light meal with the addition of a little cooked pasta or rice.

Asparagus and prawn cocktails in orange cups
Serves 4

Ingredients	Metric-Imperial	American
Canned asparagus tips	425 g/15 oz can	15 oz can
Shelled cooked prawns (shrimp)	225 g/8 oz	8 oz
For the dressing:		
Salad cream from a bottle	5 tbs	6 tbs
Whipping cream	2 tbs	3 tbs
Dry sherry	1 tbs	1 tbs
Lemon juice	2 tsp	2 tsp
2 oranges		

Drain the asparagus, and combine with the prawns in a salad bowl. To make the dressing, mix together the salad cream, whipping cream, sherry and lemon juice. Fold into the salad ingredients. Halve the oranges and scoop out the flesh, discarding the pith. Add to the salad. Divide the mixture among the orange 'cups'. Serve each person with an orange cup, surrounded by toast triangles.

Note: To make the 'cups' stand steady on the plates, slice a tiny sliver of rind from the bottom of each before filling and check that it will stand evenly.

Greek tomato salad starter
Serves 4

Ingredients	Metric-Imperial	American
Tomatoes	450 g/1 lb	1 lb
Black olives	50 g/2 oz	1/3 cup
Feta cheese	150 g/5 oz	5 oz
For the dressing:		
Oil	3 tbs	4 tbs
Lemon juice	3 tbs	4 tbs
Salt and pepper		
1 medium-sized onion		
Chopped mint	1 tbs	1 tbs

Thinly slice the tomatoes and place in a bowl with the olives. Crumble the feta cheese and combine with the ingredients in the bowl.

To make the dressing, beat together the oil and lemon juice with salt and pepper to taste. Peel and finely chop the onion and add to the dressing with the mint. Pour over the tomato salad and chill for at least 30 minutes to allow the flavours to combine. Serve in individual dishes.

Variations: Substitute chopped oregano or basil for the mint.

Optional ingredients to add to this versatile salad are a 50 g/2 oz can drained anchovy fillets, 1 small shredded head endive (chicory), 1/2 sliced cucumber and some shredded cos (romaine) lettuce.

Note: Greek feta cheese has a salty sour flavour as it is preserved in brine. A semi-soft white cheese with a flaky, crumbly texture, feta is excellent cooked or uncooked in Greek dishes.

Springtime egg salad starter
Serves 2

Ingredients	Metric-Imperial	American
1 large white radish	225 g/8 oz	8 oz
15 cm/6 in length cucumber		
2 tomatoes		
Few lettuce leaves		
1 soft-boiled egg		
For the dressing:		
Sour cream	4 tbs	5 tbs
French mustard	1 tsp	1 tsp
Medium-dry sherry	1 tsp	1 tsp
Salt and pepper		
Snipped chives	1 tbs	1 tbs

Peel and thinly slice the radish. Slice the cucumber and tomatoes. Line 2 cocktail glasses with lettuce leaves and arrange the salad ingredients in them. Shell and halve the egg.

To make the dressing, mix together the cream, mustard and sherry and season to taste with salt and pepper. Spoon over the salad ingredients. Top each starter with an egg half, sprinkle with the chives and serve immediately.

Opposite: Avocado and radish salad
Below: Springtime egg salad starter

Carrot and apple sandwich
Serves 1

Ingredients	Metric-Imperial	American
2 carrots		
1 small dessert apple		
Lemon juice	1 tsp	1 tsp
Apple juice	1 tbs	1 tbs
1 slice of wholemeal bread (wholewheat)		
Butter for spreading		
Cottage cheese	100 g/4 oz	½ cup
1 slice of lemon		
Few sprigs of mustard and cress		

Peel the carrots and apple and grate coarsely. Combine with the lemon and apple juices.

Spread the bread with butter and then with the cheese. Top with the carrot mixture and garnish with the lemon slice and watercress.

Note: The topping can be placed on 2 slices of bread.

Ham and salad sandwich
Serves 1

Ingredients	Metric-Imperial	American
Butter for spreading		
1 slice of rye bread		

	Metric-Imperial	American
Few lettuce leaves		
1 slice of cooked ham		
1 hard-boiled egg		
1 tomato		
3 radishes		
4 cucumber slices		
Snipped chives	1 tsp	1 tsp

Butter the bread, cover with lettuce leaves and place the ham on top. Shell and slice the egg, and slice the tomato and radishes. Arrange on the ham with the cucumber slices. Sprinkle with the chives before serving.

Cream cheese and radish sandwich
Serves 1

Ingredients	Metric-Imperial	American
Small bunch of radishes		
Curd cheese (sieved cottage)	100 g/4 oz	4 oz
Evaporated milk (canned unsweetened)	1 tbs	1 tbs
Snipped chives	1 tbs	1 tbs
Salt and pepper		
1 slice of wholemeal (wholewheat) bread		
Butter for spreading		

Trim the radishes, finely chop half of them, and thinly slice the remainder. Beat together the cheese and milk. Stir in

Smoked salmon and apple sandwiches
Serves 4

Ingredients	Metric-Imperial	American
Butter for spreading		
4 slices of dark rye bread		
4 slices of white bread		
4 lettuce leaves		
4 slices of smoked salmon		
Creamed horseradish	3 tbs	4 tbs
4 apple slices		
Lemon juice	1 tsp	1 tsp
4 sprigs of dill weed		

Butter all the bread slices. Place a lettuce leaf on each slice of rye bread and cover with a slice of salmon. Spread this lightly with horseradish cream. Peel and core the apple slices if necessary, put one on each sandwich, sprinkle with lemon juice and top with a sprig of dill. Cover with the white bread slices, trim the sandwiches and cut in half diagonally.

most of the chives and season to taste with salt and pepper. Fold in the chopped radish and half the slices. Spread the bread with butter and then with the cheese mixture. Garnish with the remainder of the radish slices and the rest of the chives.

Opposite left: Carrot and apple sandwich
Opposite centre: Ham and salad sandwich
Opposite right: Cream cheese and radish sandwich
Below: Smoked salmon and apple sandwiches

Shrimp sandwiches
Serves 4

Ingredients	Metric-Imperial	American
Butter for spreading		
4 slices of wholemeal bread (wholewheat)		
4 lettuce leaves		
1 small cucumber		
4 radishes		
Shelled cooked shrimps	225 g/8 oz	8 oz
Chopped dill weed		

Butter the bread slices and top each with a lettuce leaf. Slice the cucumber, discarding the ends, and trim and slice the radishes. Divide the shrimps among the bread slices and arrange a line of overlapping cucumber and radish slices on either side of the shrimps. Sprinkle with the dill before serving.

Variation: Use prawns instead of shrimps.

Stuffed red peppers
Serves 4

Ingredients	Metric-Imperial	American
4 medium-sized red sweet peppers		
1 onion		
Streaky bacon (strips)	150 g/5 oz	10 strips
Minced beef and pork combined (ground)	225 g/8 oz	8 oz
1 egg		
Rolled oats	4 tbs	5 tbs
Salt and pepper		
Water	125 ml/4 fl oz	½ cup

Cut the tops off the peppers to form lids. Scoop out and discard the seeds. Peel and chop the onion, and chop the bacon. Combine the onion, one third of the bacon, the minced meat, egg and oats, and season to taste with salt and pepper. Use to stuff the peppers, and cover with the lids.

Heat the remainder of the bacon in a pan until the fat runs, pour in the water and stand the stuffed peppers upright in the pan. Bring to the boil, cover and simmer for 50 minutes, or until the peppers are tender.

Serve with boiled brown rice or mashed potatoes and a fresh tomato sauce, if liked.

Above: Stuffed red peppers
Opposite: Bacon-wrapped pineapple on toast

Microwave method

Cut the tops off the peppers to form lids. Scoop out the inside and discard the seeds. Put the peppers on a plate with 3 tablespoons cold water, cook on full power for 5 minutes and drain.

Peel and chop the onion and derinded bacon. Mix the onion, one-third of the bacon, the minced beef, egg, oats and seasoning together. Stuff the peppers with the mixture.

Put the peppers upright in a suitable deep dish with 125 ml/4 fl oz (½ cup) of water and cook on full power for 5 minutes, allow to stand for 3 minutes. Place the remaining bacon evenly on top of the peppers and cook for 3 minutes on full power, put the lids on top and cook for a further 3 minutes. Serve with brown rice and tomato sauce.

Stuffed ham rolls in aspic
Serves 4

Ingredients	Metric-Imperial	American
2 beef stock cubes (bouillon)		
Boiling water	600 ml/1 pint	2½ cups
Powdered gelatine	2 tbs	2 tbs
White wine vinegar	2 tbs	3 tbs
Worcestershire sauce	1 tsp	1 tsp
Salt and pepper		
Sliced cooked tongue	100 g/4 oz	4 oz
Salami	50 g/2 oz	2 oz
Mayonnaise	3 tbs	4 tbs
Chopped parsley	1 tbs	1 tbs
4 slices of cooked ham		
2 hard-boiled eggs		
1 medium-sized pickled cucumber (dill pickle)		
Tomato wedges		

Make up the stock cubes with the water. Put a few tablespoons of the stock into a small bowl and sprinkle on the gelatine. Allow to stand for 10 minutes. Combine with the rest of the stock and stir until the gelatine has completely dissolved. Add the vinegar, Worcestershire sauce and season with salt and pepper to taste, to make aspic.

Wash and dry 4 empty 227 g/8 oz margarine cartons, or use containers of a similar size. Pour a little of the aspic into each chosen mould to form a base and chill until set.

Meanwhile, cut the tongue and salami into thin strips and combine with the mayonnaise and parsley. Spread this mixture on the ham slices and roll them up, trimming the ends of the rolls straight. Cut the rolls in half crossways, if necessary, so that they will fit into the containers. Shell and slice the eggs and slice the pickled cucumber. Arrange egg slices on the set aspic, top with the ham rolls and surround with slices of pickled cucumber and any remaining egg slices. Pour over a little more aspic and chill again. When set, divide the rest of the aspic among the 4 containers and chill until firm.

Loosen the edges of the aspic with the tip of a knife if necessary then dip the bases of the containers quickly into very hot water and turn out on plates. Serve each aspic mould garnished with tomato wedges.

Bacon-wrapped pineapple on toast
Serves 4

Ingredients	Metric-Imperial	American
4 slices of white bread		
Brandy	4 tbs	5 tbs
Garlic powder	1 tsp	1 tsp
8 lettuce leaves		
4 small tomatoes		
Salt		
2 canned pineapple slices		
4 rashers streaky bacon (strips)		
Butter	15 g/½ oz	1 tbs
4 stuffed green olives		

Toast the bread slices, and sprinkle one side of each with a little of the brandy and the garlic powder. Cover each slice with 2 lettuce leaves. Slice the tomatoes thinly, and arrange over the lettuce. Sprinkle lightly with salt.

Drain the pineapple slices, cut in half, and wrap each half slice in bacon, securing this with a wooden cocktail stick (toothpick).

Melt the butter in a frying pan and use to brown the bacon wrapped pineapple slices on both sides. Arrange them on the sandwiches and sprinkle with the remaining brandy. Cover the ends of the sticks with stuffed olives before serving.

Savoury avocado sandwiches
Serves 4

Ingredients	Metric-Imperial	American
1 large ripe avocado		
Danish Blue cheese	75 g/3 oz	3 oz
Butter	75 g/3 oz	⅓ cup
Lemon juice	1 tsp	1 tsp
Pepper		
4 slices of wholemeal bread (wholewheat)		
1 bunch of watercress		
4 tomatoes		
Lemon slices		

Halve, peel and stone (pit) the avocado. Cut into pieces and purée with the cheese, butter and lemon juice. Season with pepper to taste.

Spread the bread slices with some of the avocado mixture. Trim, wash and carefully dry the watercress, and divide into sprigs. Arrange a border of cress round each slice of bread. Slice the tomatoes and arrange, overlapping, in a ring round the centre of each sandwich. Put the remaining avocado cream into a large piping bag fitted with a star tube (pipe). Top the tomato slices with rosettes of the avocado mixture. Serve garnished with lemon slices.

Tip: Prepare the sandwiches just before they are required, as the avocado mixture tends to become oily if kept waiting.

Microwave hint
Earthenware dishes and plates can safely be used in the microwave cooker on medium and low power if they are indicated as suitable for the conventional oven up to 200°C/400°F/Gas Mark 6. However, avoid using them to cook mixtures containing a high proportion of sugar as these get very hot.

Baked fettucine
Serves 5–6

Ingredients	Metric-Imperial	American
Ribbon noodles	350 g/12 oz	12 oz
2 onions		
1 clove of garlic		
Tomatoes	450 g/1 lb	1 lb
Butter	50 g/2 oz	¼ cup
Minced beef and pork combined	450 g/1 lb	1 lb
Salt and pepper		
Sweet paprika pepper		
Dried thyme	½ tsp	½ tsp
Grated Parmesan cheese	2 tbs	3 tbs

Cook the noodles in plenty of boiling salted water for 8 minutes, stirring occasionally. Drain, refresh with cold water and drain again. Peel and chop the onions and garlic. Pour boiling water over the tomatoes, then drain, peel and chop.

Melt half the butter in a pan, and cook the onion and garlic until transparent. Add the meat to the pan and cook, stirring, until it looks brown and crumbly. Season with salt, pepper, paprika and thyme. Add the tomatoes to the pan and cook for another 5 minutes. Put two thirds of the noodles in a greased casserole, cover with the mixture, a little of the remaining butter, and then with the rest of the noodles. Sprinkle with the cheese and dot with the rest of the butter. Bake, uncovered, in a preheated hot oven, 220°C, 425°F, Gas Mark 7, for 35 minutes.

Variation: For a vegetarian fettucine dish, omit the meat and use 100g/4 oz courgettes (zucchini) and 1 medium-sized aubergine (eggplant). Slice the courgettes and aubergines without peeling, sprinkle with salt and allow to stand. While the onion is cooking, rinse and drain the courgettes and aubergine. Add them to the onion and cook for 5 minutes. Season and finish as recipe.

Apple halves with bacon and cheese
Serves 4

Ingredients	Metric-Imperial	American
4 medium-sized dessert apples		
Medium-dry sherry	8 tbs	8 tbs
4 rashers of streaky bacon (8 strips)		
8 slices of Gouda cheese		
Sweet paprika pepper		
Lettuce leaves		
8 sprigs of parsley		

Peel and halve the apples and remove the cores without cutting completely through the flesh. Place the apple halves, cut sides downwards, in an oiled grill (broiler) pan. Cook under high heat for about 4 minutes then turn and put 1 tbs sherry into the hollow of each apple half.

Halve the bacon slices crossways and use to top the apple halves. Cover each with a slice of cheese and return to the grill for about 5 minutes, or until the cheese has melted and the bacon is cooked. Sprinkle with paprika, serve on a bed of lettuce and garnish with parsley sprigs before serving.

Eggs in tarragon aspic
Serves 6

Ingredients	Metric-Imperial	American
1 onion		
1 carrot		
3 sprigs of tarragon		
Strong beef stock (bouillon)	750 ml/1¼ pints	3 cups
Powdered gelatine	2 tbs	3 tbs
Water	6 tbs	½ cup
Dry sherry	125 ml/4 fl oz	½ cup
Yeast extract	½ tsp	½ tsp
Salt and pepper		
Stuffed green olives		
Chervil leaves		
6 soft-boiled eggs		
3 slices of cooked ham		
Few lettuce leaves		
Tomato wedges		

Peel and quarter the onion. Peel and slice the carrot. Place both in a pan with the tarragon and one third of the stock, bring to the boil then simmer for 10 minutes. Strain the stock, reserving the carrot slices. Meanwhile, sprinkle the gelatine over the water and allow to stand for 10 minutes.

Return the stock to the pan, reheat, add the softened gelatine and stir until it has completely dissolved. Add the remainder of the stock, the sherry and yeast extract and season with salt and pepper to taste.

Rinse 6 small glass dessert dishes with cold water. Pour a little of the aspic mixture into each dish and allow to set. Cover with the reserved carrot slices, sliced olives and chervil leaves. Pour in more aspic and allow to set. Carefully shell the eggs then halve the ham slices and wrap each egg in a piece of ham. Place a wrapped egg in the centre of each

dish and pour in the remaining aspic round them. Chill again to set.

Before serving, loosen the edges of the aspic moulds with the tip of a knife, dip the bases of the dishes quickly into very hot water, and turn out on to small plates lined with lettuce leaves. Garnish with tomato wedges and serve with buttered toast.

Opposite: Baked fettucine
Above: Eggs in tarragon aspic

59

Potato and cheese bake
Serves 4

Ingredients	Metric-Imperial	American
Medium-sized potatoes	1 kg/2¼ lb	2¼ lb
Salt and pepper		
Fresh breadcrumbs	25 g/1 oz	½ cup
Butter	50 g/2 oz	¼ cup
Grated Cheddar cheese	75 g/3 oz	¾ cup

Peel the potatoes and place in a pan. Cover with salted water, bring to the boil, cover and simmer for 10 minutes. Drain and slice while still warm.

Arrange the potato slices, overlapping, in a greased shallow ovenproof dish and sprinkle with salt, pepper and the breadcrumbs. Dot with the butter and sprinkle with the cheese. Bake, uncovered, in a preheated moderately hot oven, 200°C, 400°F, Gas Mark 6, for 20 minutes, or until the cheese topping is golden brown.

Microwave method

Peel the potatoes and slice into even-sized pieces. Place in a suitable dish and add 475 ml/16 fl oz (2 cups) of cold water. Place in the microwave and cook on full power for 6 minutes. Allow to stand for 5 minutes and drain.

Butter a shallow dish which can be used in the microwave and sprinkle with half the breadcrumbs, salt and pepper. Arrange the potato slices overlapping in layers, sprinkling each layer with half the cheese and a little seasoning. Mix the remaining breadcrumbs and cheese together and spoon evenly over the top of the potatoes. Dot the top of the dish with butter.

Cook on full power for 10 minutes and allow to stand for 5 minutes. Test with a skewer and if potatoes seem too firm cook for a further 5 minutes (the type of potato will affect the cooking time).

Place under a hot grill or broiler for a few minutes until the top turns golden. Serve hot.

Escalopes of veal hollandaise
Serves 4

Ingredients	Metric-Imperial	American
4 slices of white bread		
Butter for frying		
4 escalopes of veal		
Salt and pepper		
Chopped mixed herbs	2 tbs	3 tbs
For the sauce:		
Butter	100 g/4 oz	½ cup
2 egg yolks		
Tarragon vinegar	1 tsp	1 tsp
Water	2 tbs	3 tbs
Salt and pepper		
Sugar		
Lemon juice		

Cut 4 rounds from the bread slices. Melt about 25 g/1 oz (2 tbs) butter in a frying pan and use to fry the bread rounds until brown on both sides, adding more butter if necessary. Remove from the pan. Beat the escalopes lightly. Add a little more butter to the pan and use to fry the escalopes for about 5 minutes on each side, or until golden brown on both sides. Remove, trim to the same shape and size as the bread rounds and place one on each. Season with salt and pepper and sprinkle with the herbs. If the dish is to be served hot, keep the bread and veal warm in the oven.

To make the sauce, place the butter in the top of a double boiler or in a bowl over a pan of simmering water and allow to melt. Add the egg yolks, vinegar and water and whisk gently until the mixture thickens. Season with salt, pepper and sugar to taste and sharpen the flavour with a little lemon juice. If the sauce is not required immediately, keep it warm over the hot water to prevent it from curdling. Serve the escalopes hot or cold with the hollandaise and a green salad.

Snails in garlic butter
Serves 4

Ingredients	Metric-Imperial	American
24 canned snails together with the shells		
1 small onion		
1 clove of garlic		
Softened butter	75 g/3 oz	⅓ cup
Chopped parsley	1 tbs	1 tbs
Pinch of cayenne pepper		
Salt and freshly ground black pepper		

Wash the snail shells in hot water and drain well. Put about ½ tsp of the snail liquid and 1 snail into each shell. Set aside.

Peel and finely chop the onion and garlic and beat into the butter with the parsley. Season with the cayenne, and salt and pepper to taste. Use the garlic butter to top the snails in the shells.

Put a layer of coarse salt in a shallow ovenproof dish and stand the stuffed snail shells in this. Place, uncovered, in a preheated hot oven, 220°C, 425°F, Gas Mark 7, for about 10 minutes. Serve with French bread.

Opposite: Potato and cheese bake
Right: Snails in garlic butter

61

Stuffed cucumber
Serves 4

Ingredients	Metric-Imperial	American
2 small cucumbers		
Salt and pepper		
For the filling:		
Canned tuna	200 g/7 oz can	7 oz can
2 hard-boiled eggs		
2 egg yolks		
Made mustard	2 tsp	2 tsp
Lemon juice or vinegar	1 tbs	1 tbs
Pinch of sugar		
Salt and pepper		
Oil	125 ml/4 fl oz	½ cup

Peel the cucumbers and cut into 5 cm/2 inch lengths. Scoop out almost all the seeds, leaving a 'base' in each cucumber shell. Sprinkle inside and out with salt and leave upside-down to drain for 10 minutes.

To make the filling, drain and flake the tuna. Shell and chop the eggs and combine with the tuna. Beat the egg yolks in a small bowl with the mustard, lemon juice or vinegar, sugar and seasoning to taste, until slightly thickened. Gradually beat in the oil. Fold into the fish mixture and use to fill the cucumber shells. If liked, garnish the cucumber with lemon slices, tomato wedges and parsley sprigs before serving.

Gourmet sandwiches
Serves 4

Ingredients	Metric-Imperial	American
4 slices of white bread		
4 lettuce leaves		
Whipping cream	125 ml/4 fl oz	½ cup
Creamed horseradish from a jar	2-3 tbs	3-4 tbs
Lemon juice		
Salt		
8 slices of smoked salmon		
Canned hearts of palm	100 g/4 oz	4 oz
4 canned artichoke bottoms		
Red lumpfish roe	4 tsp	4 tsp
4 lemon slices		
Few stuffed green olives		

Toast the bread slices and trim off the crusts. Top each slice of toast with a lettuce leaf.

Whip the cream until stiff and stir in horseradish to taste. Add lemon juice and salt to taste. Spread on the slices of smoked salmon and roll up. Cut the hearts of palm into 8 slices. Divide the salmon rolls, hearts of palm slices and artichoke bottoms among the toast slices. Top with lumpfish roe and serve at once garnished with lemon slices and olives.

Fruit cocktail with shrimps
Serves 4

Ingredients	Metric-Imperial	American
1 orange		
1 banana		
1 dessert apple		
Canned drained morello cherries	175 g/6 oz	1 cup
Shelled cooked shrimps	150 g/5 oz	scant 1 cup
Lettuce leaves		
For the dressing:		
Natural yogurt (plain)	150 ml/¼ pint	⅔ cup
Lemon juice	1 tbs	1 tbs
Slivered almonds	25 g/1 oz	¼ cup
Salt		
Sugar		

Peel the orange, discard the white pith and chop the flesh. Peel and dice the banana. Peel, quarter and core the apple then dice the flesh. Stone (pit) the cherries if necessary and mix with the other prepared fruit. Add the shrimps. Line 4 cocktail glasses with lettuce leaves and fill with the shrimp mixture.

To make the dressing, mix together the yogurt and lemon juice. Fold in the almonds and season with salt and sugar to taste. Spoon over the cocktails and serve garnished with tomato waterlilies if wished.

Left: Stuffed cucumber
Opposite: Ham and horseradish rolls

Ham and horseradish rolls
Serves 4

Ingredients	Metric-Imperial	American
Water	2 tbs	3 tbs
Powdered gelatine	1 tsp	1 tsp
Curd cheese (sieved cottage)	225 g/8 oz	8 oz
Creamed horseradish	3 tbs	4 tbs
Lemon juice	1 tbs	1 tbs
Salt		
Sugar		
Whipping cream	225 ml/8 fl oz	1 cup
8 large slices of cooked ham		
Tomato slices		
Sprigs of parsley		

Put the water in a small bowl and sprinkle on the gelatine. Leave to stand for 10 minutes then place over hot water and stir until the gelatine has completely dissolved.

Beat together the cheese, horseradish and lemon juice and season to taste with salt and sugar. Whip the cream until thick then whisk in the dissolved gelatine and continue beating until the cream is stiff. Fold into the cheese mixture. Spread over the ham slices. Roll these up and secure with wooden cocktail sticks (toothpicks). Serve on a dish garnished with tomato slices and parsley sprigs.

Cheese sandwiches with cucumber salad
Serves 4

Ingredients	Metric-Imperial	American
1 small cucumber		
Oil	2 tbs	3 tbs
Lemon juice	3 tbs	4 tbs
Salt and pepper		
Chopped dill	1 tbs	1 tbs
4 radishes		
Blue Brie or Danish Saga	225 g/8 oz	8 oz
Butter for spreading		
4 slices of wholemeal bread (wholewheat)		
4 lettuce leaves		

Thinly slice the cucumber. Stir together the oil and lemon juice and season to taste with salt and pepper. Fold in the cucumber slices and dill. Trim the radishes and cut a deep cross in the top of each. Slice the cheese.

Butter the bread slices and place a lettuce leaf on each. Divide the cucumber salad among the sandwiches. Top with the cheese slices and garnish each portion with a radish.

Ham with red wine and mushroom sauce
Serves 4

Ingredients	Metric-Imperial	American
1 large mild onion		
Mushrooms	100 g/4 oz	4 oz
Canned ham	450 g/1 lb can	1 lb can
8 juniper berries		
Red wine	300 ml/½ pint	1¼ cups
Butter	75 g/3 oz	⅓ cup
Flour (all-purpose)	2 tbs	3 tbs
Pepper		
Ground nutmeg		

Peel and chop the onion. Slice the mushrooms. Take the jelly from the ham and place it in a pan with the juniper berries. Heat, stirring, until the jelly has melted. Pour in the wine and boil until reduced by about one third.

Melt the butter in a separate pan and use to fry the onion until soft. Put in the mushrooms and cook until limp. Sprinkle on the flour and cook, stirring, for 2 minutes. Strain in the wine liquid and bring to the boil, stirring constantly. Add pepper and nutmeg to taste. Thinly slice the ham and serve with the hot sauce.

Turkey breast sandwiches
Serves 4

Ingredients	Metric-Imperial	American
2 turkey breast fillets	150 g/5 oz each	5 oz each
Salt and pepper		
Sweet paprika pepper		
Oil	3 tbs	4 tbs
4 canned drained pineapple slices		
8 slices of white bread		
Butter for spreading		
4 lettuce leaves		

Cut each turkey fillet in half horizontally to give 2 thin layers, and sprinkle all over with salt, pepper and paprika. Heat the oil in a frying pan and use to cook the turkey slices for 2–3 minutes on each side, or until done to taste. Remove from the heat and keep warm. Add the pineapple slices to the oil remaining in the pan and cook until golden on each side.

Spread the bread slices with butter and top 4 of them with lettuce leaves.

Top each of the lettuce leaves with a turkey fillet and pineapple slice and cover with the remaining bread slices. Serve at once.

Bacon-wrapped potato and tomato platter

(Photo p. 42–43)

Serves 4

Ingredients	Metric-Imperial	American
New potatoes	675 g/1½ lb	1½ lb
Salt		
12 tomatoes		
Butter	3 tbs	4 tbs
Chopped sage	1 tsp	1 tsp
Freshly ground black pepper		
8 rashers streaky bacon (strips)		
Sage leaves (optional)		

Clean the potatoes in boiling salted water for about 20 minutes, or until tender.

Meanwhile, cut a cross in each tomato and place in a greased shallow ovenproof dish. Dot with butter, sprinkle with sage and season with salt and pepper. Place in a preheated moderately hot oven, 200°C, 400°F, Gas Mark 6, for 15–20 minutes.

Cut the bacon in half crossways and grill until crisp. Drain the potatoes, toss in the remaining butter and divide among 4 individual warmed serving dishes. Add 3 tomatoes to each dish and top with the bacon. Garnish with sage leaves if using and serve hot.

Below: Lamb cutlets with mint
Opposite: Potato pancakes with mushrooms

Calves' kidneys flambés

Serves 4

Ingredients	Metric-Imperial	American
Calves' kidneys (beef)	450 g/1 lb	1 lb
Milk	150 ml/¼ pint	⅔ cup
1 onion		
1 red and 1 green sweet pepper		
Button mushrooms	100 g/4 oz	4 oz
Butter	40 g/1½ oz	3 tbs
Salt and pepper		
Sweet paprika pepper		
Dry white wine	125 ml/4 fl oz	½ cup
Oil	4 tbs	5 tbs
Brandy	4 tbs	5 tbs
Chopped parsley	1 tbs	1 tbs

Halve the kidneys and snip out the cores. Place in a bowl and pour the milk over. Leave to stand for 1 hour. Drain well and cut the kidneys into thin slices.

Peel and chop the onion. Halve and deseed the peppers and cut the flesh into strips. Slice the mushrooms. Melt the butter in a pan, add the onion and pepper strips and cook for 3 minutes, stirring frequently. Put in the mushrooms and season with salt, pepper and paprika. Cook, stirring now and then, for 5 minutes. Pour in the wine, bring to the boil, cover and simmer for a further 5 minutes.

Heat the oil in a separate pan, add the kidney slices and cook for about 5 minutes on each side. Remove with a slotted spoon, sprinkle with salt and pepper and keep hot. Add the vegetable mixture to the oil remaining in the pan and put the kidney slices in the centre. Heat the brandy in a ladle, pour over the kidney then ignite. As soon as the flames die down, stir the ingredients together carefully and serve on a bed of freshly boiled rice, sprinkled with parsley.

Lamb cutlets with mint

Serves 4

Ingredients	Metric-Imperial	American
8–12 lamb cutlets		
Salt and freshly ground white pepper		
Chopped mint	3 tbs	4 tbs
3 cloves of garlic		
Butter	3 tbs	4 tbs
Lemon juice	2 tbs	3 tbs
Whipping cream	150 ml/¼ pint	⅔ cup
Sprigs of mint		

Trim excess fat from the cutlets then sprinkle them all over with salt and pepper. Rub with some of the chopped mint. Peel and finely chop the garlic.

Melt the butter in a pan, add half the garlic and remaining chopped mint and cook for 2 minutes. Put in the cutlets and fry for 3 minutes on each side, in batches if necessary, or until done to taste. Transfer to a warm serving dish and spoon over the pan juices.

Mix together the remaining garlic, the lemon juice and cream. Garnish with mint and hand the sauce separately.

Potato pancakes with mushrooms
Serves 4–6

Ingredients	Metric-Imperial	American
Potatoes	1½ kg/3 lb 5 oz	3 lb 5 oz
Milk	125 ml/4 fl oz	½ cup
4 eggs		
Salt and pepper		
2 onions		
Chopped dill weed	1 tbs	1 tbs
Snipped chives	2 tbs	3 tbs
Chopped mint	1 tbs	1 tbs
Chopped parsley	4 tbs	5 tbs
Butter or margarine	100 g/4 oz	½ cup
Mushrooms	450 g/1 lb	1 lb
Whipping cream	150 ml/¼ pint	⅔ cup
Dry white wine	2 tbs	3 tbs

Peel and coarsely grate the potatoes and place in a clean kitchen cloth on a colander over a bowl. Leave the potato to drain into the bowl for 10 minutes. Pour off the clear liquid from the bowl and add the potato to the starch sediment. Mix in the milk and eggs and season with salt and pepper to taste. Peel and grate the onions and fold half into the potato with the dill, chives, mint and half the parsley.

Reserve half the butter or margarine and melt a little of the remainder in a frying pan.

Using a small ladleful of the potato mixture each time, spread to make thin round pancakes and cook them until golden brown on both sides. Keep hot and make the remaining pancakes in the same way, adding more of the butter to the pan during cooking as necessary. Stack up the pancakes on a plate and keep hot.

Halve or quarter large mushrooms. Melt the reserved butter or margarine in a pan and use to cook the rest of the onion until transparent. Add the mushrooms, season with salt and pepper and stir well. Cover and cook for about 10 minutes, shaking the pan frequently. Pour in the cream, stir until boiling and simmer until slightly reduced. Stir in the wine and remaining parsley and adjust the seasoning if necessary. Serve with the potato pancakes.

Red cabbage slaw
Serves 4

Ingredients	Metric-Imperial	American
Red cabbage	450 g/1 lb	1 lb
1 medium-sized onion		
Golden syrup (corn)	2 tbs	3 tbs
Vinegar	3 tbs	4 tbs
French mustard	1 tsp	1 tsp
Salt and pepper		

Trim and quarter the cabbage, cut out the core and shred the leaves. Wash and drain well. Peel the onion and cut into thin rings. Combine the cabbage and onion in a salad bowl. For the dressing, beat together the syrup, vinegar, and mustard. Season. Fold into the salad.

Onion soup with cheese croûtons
Serves 6

Ingredients	Metric-Imperial	American
Large mild onions	1 kg/2¼ lb	2¼ lb
Butter or margarine	75 g/3 oz	⅓ cup
Beef stock (bouillon)	750 ml/1¼ pints	3 cups
Dry white wine	300 ml/½ pint	1¼ cups
Salt and pepper		
For the croûtons:		
6 slices of bread		
Very finely grated Gouda cheese	100 g/4 oz	1 cup

Peel and quarter the onions, then cut into slices. Melt the butter or margarine in a pan and use to cook the onion until transparent. Add the stock and wine and season to taste with salt and pepper. Bring to the boil, cover and simmer for 10 minutes.

Meanwhile, make the cheese croûtons. Toast the bread slices on one side only then sprinkle the untoasted side with the cheese. Grill (broil) until the cheese has melted then cut each slice into pieces.

Spoon the soup into 6 plates and top each portion with cheese croûtons before serving.

Variation: Other cheese with good melting properties could be substituted such as Swiss Gruyère. The croûtons can be made from white or wholemeal (wholewheat) bread; alternatively use 1 cm (½ in) slices from a French loaf

Gammon steaks with curry sauce
Serves 4

Ingredients	Metric-Imperial	American
2 oranges		
Butter	40 g/1½ oz	3 tbs
4 small round gammon (raw ham) or bacon steaks	100 g/4 oz each	4 oz each
2 tart dessert apples		
1 onion		
Curry paste	½-1 tbs	½-1 tbs
Dry white wine	5 tbs	6 tbs
Whipping cream	300 ml/½ pint	1¼ cups
Salt and pepper		
Canned drained apricot halves		
Slivered almonds or sweet paprika pepper		

Peel the oranges and divide into segments, discarding all the pith. Reserve any juice. Melt two thirds of the butter in a frying pan and use to cook the gammon steaks for about 4 minutes on each side, or until done to taste. Transfer to a warm serving dish and keep hot. Add the orange segments to the fat remaining in the pan and heat through. Arrange on the dish with the steaks.

Meanwhile, peel, core and slice the apples. Peel and chop the onion. Melt the remaining butter in a pan and use to cook the onion and apple slices for 3 minutes, stirring frequently. Sprinkle in the curry powder and cook, stirring, for a further 1 minute. Add the orange juice, wine and cream and stir until boiling. Simmer for 3 minutes, or until the apples are just tender. Season with salt and pepper. Liquidize or sieve and return to the pan. Reheat.

Pour a little of the curry sauce over the steaks and garnish with apricot halves. Sprinkle with almonds or with paprika and hand the remaining sauce separately.

Savoury roast beef sandwiches
Serves 4

Ingredients	Metric-Imperial	American
Butter for spreading		
4 slices of wholemeal bread (wholewheat)		
4 lettuce leaves		
Sliced roast beef	225 g/8 oz	8 oz
French mustard	1 tbs	1 tbs
16 cucumber slices		
8 radishes		
2 spring onions (scallions)		

Butter the bread slices, cover each with a lettuce leaf, then with roast beef, spread this with mustard and arrange 4 cucumber slices on top. Trim and chop the radishes and spring onions and sprinkle over the sandwiches before serving.

Californian salad

Serves 4

Ingredients	Metric-Imperial	American
1 small or half a large iceberg lettuce		
1 small honeydew melon		
3 oranges		
3 carrots		
Shelled peas	100 g/4 oz	⅔ cup
For the dressing:		
Natural yogurt (plain)	150 ml/¼ pint	⅔ cup
Whipping cream	2 tbs	3 tbs
Lemon juice	1 tbs	1 tbs
Salt and pepper		
Sugar		
Chopped hazelnuts (filberts)		

Discard any rough outer leaves from the lettuce and tear the remaining leaves into pieces, discarding the core. Halve the honeydew, discard the seeds and scoop out the flesh using a melon baller. Peel the oranges and divide into segments, discarding any pith but reserving any juice. Peel and slice the carrots. Place the carrot slices and peas in a pan of boiling salted water, bring back to the boil and simmer for 3 minutes. Drain and allow to cool. Put all these salad ingredients into a glass bowl or into individual dishes.

To make the dressing, stir together the yogurt, cream, lemon juice and reserved orange juice and season to taste with salt, pepper and sugar. Spoon over the salad and sprinkle with nuts. If liked, garnish the salad with tarragon leaves.

Tomato salad with feta cheese

Serves 4–6

Ingredients	Metric-Imperial	American
Tomatoes	1 kg/2¼ lb	2¼ lb
Feta cheese	225 g/8 oz	8 oz
For the dressing:		
Olive oil	175 ml/6 fl oz	¾ cup
Lemon juice	4 tbs	5 tbs
Chopped dill weed	6 tbs	½ cup
Salt and pepper		

Cut each tomato into 8 wedges. Crumble the cheese. Combine the tomato and cheese in a bowl.

To make the dressing, beat together the oil, lemon juice and dill with salt and pepper to taste. Spoon over the tomato salad and leave to stand for 30 minutes before serving.

Note: Feta cheese orginates from Greece and is made from goats' or sheep's milk or a mixture of the two. The pressed and salted curds are matured in their own whey.

Courgette salad with cream cheese

Serves 4

Ingredients	Metric-Imperial	American
Courgettes (zucchini)	550 g/1¼ lb	1¼ lb
Caster sugar (granulated)	1 tbs	1 tbs
Lemon juice	3 tbs	4 tbs
Lettuce leaves		
Cream cheese	75 g/3 oz	⅓ cup
Whipping cream	6 tbs	½ cup
Sweet paprika pepper		

Top, tail and slice the courgettes. Dissolve the sugar in the lemon juice and stir into the courgette slices in a bowl. Cover and chill well.

Line a platter with lettuce leaves and arrange the courgette salad on top. Beat the cheese until soft then gradually beat in the cream. Spoon over the courgette salad and sprinkle with paprika before serving.

Opposite: Onion soup with cheese croûtons
Above: Californian salad

French turkey breast rolls
Serves 4–8

Ingredients	Metric-Imperial	American
Turkey breast roll	750 g/1¾ lb	1¾ lb
8 rashers of streaky bacon (16 strips)		
Dried oregano	1 tsp	1 tsp
Chopped thyme	1 tbs	1 tbs
Salt and white pepper		
Olive oil	3 tbs	4 tbs
Aubergines (eggplant)	225 g/8 oz	8 oz
3 medium-sized onions		
2 red sweet peppers		
Tomatoes	225 g/8 oz	8 oz
1 clove of garlic		
Chopped basil	1 tbs	1 tbs
Lemon wedges		
Lemon juice		

Cut the turkey breast roll into 16 thin slices. Halve the bacon slices. Sprinkle the turkey slices with the oregano, thyme and a little salt and pepper. Top with the bacon then roll up each turkey slice and secure with wooden cocktail sticks (toothpicks) or tie with fine string.

Heat the oil in a frying pan and use to fry the turkey rolls for about 5 minutes, or until golden brown on all sides. Remove from the pan and leave to cool. Discard the sticks or strings.

Meanwhile, dice the aubergines, sprinkle with salt and leave to stand for 10 minutes. Drain and dry on absorbent kitchen paper. Peel and chop the onions. Halve and deseed the peppers and cut the flesh into small pieces. Pour boiling water over the tomatoes, drain, peel and chop. Add the onion to the fat remaining in the pan with the pepper and cook until the onion begins to soften. Put in the aubergine and tomato and add a little water if the mixture is too dry. Cover and cook gently for 15 minutes. Peel and crush the garlic and add to the pan with the basil. Stir well, cover and simmer for a further 10 minutes. Add salt and pepper to taste and leave to cool.

Spread the vegetable mixture in a shallow dish and top with the turkey rolls. Garnish the dish with lemon wedges and sprinkle the rolls with a little lemon juice before serving.

Opposite: French turkey breast rolls
Right: Beefsteak tartare

Beefsteak tartare
Serves 8

Ingredients	Metric-Imperial	American
2 onions		
Very lean rump or fillet steak	750 g/1¾ lb	1¾ lb
Oil	1 tbs	1 tbs
French mustard	2 tbs	3 tbs
Green peppercorns	1 tsp	1 tsp
Salt		
Sweet paprika pepper		
8 egg yolks		
Sprigs of marjoram (optional)		

Peel and chop the onions. Mince the steak very finely and mix with the onion, oil and mustard. Crush the peppercorns lightly and add to the steak mixture then season to taste with salt and paprika.

Arrange the meat mixture in 8 portions on a serving dish. Make a hollow in the top of each portion with the back of a spoon and place an egg yolk in each hollow. Garnish with sprigs of marjoram. Hand small dishes of onion rings, coarsely ground black pepper, gherkins (small dill pickles), snipped chives, sweet paprika pepper, canned anchovy fillets, drained capers and chopped parsley with the steak tartare and serve with brown bread and butter.

Chicken breasts with lime sauce
Serves 4

Ingredients	Metric-Imperial	American
4 boneless chicken breasts, total weight	550 g/1¼ lb	1¼ lb
Salt and pepper		
Flour		
1 egg		
Chopped almonds	100 g/4 oz	1 cup
Butter or margarine	40 g/1½ oz	3 tbs
2 limes		
Whipping cream	300 ml/½ pint	1¼ cups
Chopped lemon balm	2 tbs	3 tbs
Dry vermouth	2 tbs	3 tbs
Lettuce leaves		
½ small green sweet pepper		
Lime slices		

Skin the chicken breasts, season with salt and pepper and dust with flour. Beat the egg and place in a shallow dish. Dip the breasts into the egg then coat with almonds. Melt the butter or margarine in a frying pan and use to cook the chicken fillets for about 4 minutes on each side, or until brown. Leave to cool.

Grate the rind from 1 lime and squeeze the juice from both. Mix together the lime rind and juice with the cream, lemon balm and vermouth. Season with salt to taste.

Shred the lettuce leaves and arrange on a serving dish. Top with the chicken breasts and spoon over half the sauce. Deseed the pepper and cut the flesh into thin strips. Scatter over the chicken breasts and garnish the dish with lime slices. Hand the remaining sauce separately.

Pea soufflé
Serves 4

Ingredients	Metric-Imperial	American
Butter	40 g/1½ oz	3 tbs
Flour	40 g/1½ oz	⅓ cup
Milk	450 ml/¾ pint	scant 2 cups
Salt and pepper		
Ground nutmeg		
2 eggs		
Frozen peas	350 g/12 oz	2 cups
Little extra flour (all-purpose)		

Melt the butter in a pan, sprinkle in the flour and stir until the roux is golden. Gradually add the milk and bring to the boil, stirring constantly. Simmer for 5 minutes. Season to taste with salt, pepper and nutmeg.

Separate the eggs. Whisk the yolks into the sauce then stir in the defrosted peas. Whisk the eggs whites in a clean bowl until stiff and fold into the pea mixture.

Grease an ovenproof dish and sprinkle the inside with a little flour. Turn in the pea mixture and place, uncovered, in a preheated moderately hot oven, 200°C, 400°F, Gas Mark 6, for about 20 minutes, until golden. Serve immediately.

Potato nests with pea and ham filling
Serves 4

Ingredients	Metric-Imperial	American
Potatoes	750 g/1¾ lb	1¾ lb
2 eggs		
Butter	25 g/1 oz	2 tbs
Salt and pepper		
Ground nutmeg		
1 egg yolk		
Water	1 tbs	1 tbs
For the filling:		
Cooked ham	75 g/3 oz	3 oz
Butter	25 g/1 oz	2 tbs
Frozen peas	175 g/6 oz	1 cup
Water	125 ml/4 fl oz	½ cup
Cornflour (cornstarch)	1 tsp	1 tsp
Dry white wine	1 tbs	1 tbs
Salt and pepper		

Cook the potatoes in plenty of boiling salted water until tender. Drain and peel while still hot. Mash until smooth and beat in the 2 eggs and the butter. Season to taste with salt, pepper and nutmeg. Transfer to a piping bag fitted with a large star tube (pipe).

Grease a baking sheet (cookie sheet) and pipe out 4 nests from the potato. Beat the egg yolk with the water and brush this mixture over the nests. Bake, uncovered, in a preheated moderately hot oven, 200°C, 400°F, Gas Mark 6 for about 15 minutes, or until golden brown.

Meanwhile, make the filling. Dice the ham. Melt the butter in a pan and add the defrosted peas and ham and cook, stirring, for 3 minutes. Add the water and bring to the boil. Cover and simmer for 10 minutes. Moisten the cornflour with the wine and add to the pan. Stir until thickened. Season to taste with salt and pepper and simmer for 2 minutes. Spoon into the hot potato nests and serve at once.

Sardines on toast
Serves 4

Ingredients	Metric-Imperial	American
4 slices of toasting bread		
Butter for spreading		
Canned sardines in oil	100 g/4 oz can	4 oz can
Little lemon juice		
Pinch of black pepper		
2 hard-boiled eggs		
Few onion rings		
Tomato ketchup (catsup)		
Sprigs of parsley		

Toast the bread and when cool spread with butter. Drain the sardines and divide among the toast slices. Sprinkle with lemon juice and season with pepper. Shell and slice the eggs and arrange the slices on the sardines. Garnish with onion rings, ketchup and parsley sprigs and serve at once.

Opposite: Chicken breasts with lime sauce
Above right: Pea soufflé
Centre right: Potato nests with pea and ham filling
Below right: Pea and prawn toasts

Pea and prawn toasts
Serves 4–8

Ingredients	Metric-Imperial	American
Frozen peas	225 g/8 oz	1⅓ cups
Butter	75 g/3 oz	⅓ cup
Salt and pepper		
Garlic salt		
Cream cheese	225 g/8 oz	8 oz
Whipping cream	2 tbs	3 tbs
8 slices of toasting bread		
Shelled cooked shrimps	225 g/8 oz	1⅓ cups
Chopped dill weed	2 tbs	3 tbs

Defrost the peas. Melt half the butter in a pan, stir in the peas, cover and cook gently for 8 minutes, stirring occasionally. Season with salt and pepper and leave to cool. Cream the remaining butter until soft. Season with garlic salt to taste and mix into the cheese with the whipping cream and more salt and pepper to taste.

Toast the bread and spread with the cheese mixture. Mix together the cooked peas and shrimps. Divide among the toast slices and serve, sprinkled with the dill weed.

Ham, cheese and egg ramekins
Serves 4

Ingredients	Metric-Imperial	American
Cooked ham	50 g/2 oz	2 oz
Grated Cheddar cheese	40 g/1½ oz	⅓ cup
4 eggs		

Chop the ham and mix with the cheese. Crack one egg into each of 4 well buttered ramekin dishes or heatproof cups and top with the ham and cheese mixture. Cover the dishes with foil and stand them in a large pan. Pour in hot but not boiling water to come half-way up the sides of the dishes. Bring the water to simmering point, cover the pan and cook for about 10 minutes, or until the eggs are lightly set.

Turn each ramekin out on to a heated individual serving plate. Serve at once, with fingers of hot buttered toast.

Microwave method

Chop the ham into fine dice and mix with the cheese. Butter four ramekin dishes well and break one egg into each dish. Sterilise a skewer or a large needle with boiling water and pierce the egg yolks.

Divide the ham and cheese mixture between the four ramekin dishes, topping each egg with the mixture. Place the ramekins in the microwave and cover all four dishes with a piece of kitchen paper and cook on full power for 4 minutes. Allow to stand for 2 minutes.

Line a serving dish with lettuce leaves and turn the eggs in the ramekin dishes out on to the lettuce. Serve at once.

Below: Fried egg
Opposite: Egg ramekins with mustard sauce

Boiled eggs

Ingredients	Metric-Imperial	American
Water		
Eggs		

Eggs for boiling must be fresh to ensure superb flavour. To cook evenly, they must be completely covered in water. If the eggs are very cold, they should be brought to room temperature so that the shells do not crack when placed in the boiling water. After cooking they can be dipped into cold water so that they do not continue to cook and become hard, and they can be peeled more easily later if necessary.

Bring a pan of water to the boil then carefully lower the eggs into the water and start timing from this moment. Keep the water boiling gently.

Soft-boiled eggs – cook for 4 minutes
Hard-boiled eggs – cook for 10 minutes

Fried eggs

Ingredients	Metric-Imperial	American
Butter	25 g/1 oz	2 tbs
6 eggs		
Salt		

Melt the butter in a frying pan. Carefully crack the eggs then slide them into the pan side-by-side. Sprinkle with salt and cook for about 5 minutes, or until lightly set.

Variation: Crack the eggs on to a greased heatproof plate, put this over a pan of boiling water and cook until set.

Egg ramekins with mustard sauce
Serves 4

Ingredients	Metric-Imperial	American
8 eggs		
Lean bacon (Canadian)	75 g/3 oz	1–2 slices
Salt and pepper		
Snipped chives	2 tbs	3 tbs
For the sauce:		
Whipping cream	225 ml/8 fl oz	1 cup
French mustard	2 tsp	2 tsp
Salt		
Sprigs of parsley		

Grease 4 large ramekin dishes, break the eggs and slide 2 into each dish. Chop the bacon and sprinkle over the eggs with the chives. Season to taste with salt and pepper. Set the ramekin dishes on a baking sheet (cookie sheet). Place, uncovered, in a preheated moderate oven, 180°C, 350°F, Gas Mark 4, for about 8 minutes, or until the eggs are firm.

Meanwhile, place the cream in a pan and cook gently, stirring frequently, until reduced by half. Beat in the mustard and season to taste with salt. Loosen the cooked eggs, turn out on warm plates, and garnish with sprigs of parsley. Serve with the mustard sauce.

Scrambled eggs with chives
Serves 4

Ingredients	Metric-Imperial	American
6 eggs		
Milk	4 tbs	5 tbs
Salt		
Snipped chives	1 tbs	1 tbs
Butter	25 g/1 oz	2 tbs

Beat the eggs with the milk and season to taste with salt. Stir in the chives. Melt the butter in a pan, add the egg mixture and stir over moderate heat until lightly set but still creamy. Do not allow to become dry. Serve at once.

Scrambled eggs with bacon
Serves 4

Ingredients	Metric-Imperial	American
6 eggs		
Milk	6 tbs	½ cup
Salt		
Streaky bacon (strips)	75 g/3 oz	6 strips

Beat the eggs with the milk and season to taste with salt. Chop the bacon, place in a frying pan and cook until golden brown. Pour the egg mixture into the pan and stir over moderate heat until the eggs are lightly set but still creamy. Serve at once, on hot buttered toast, or garnished with triangles of fried bread.

Variations: Replace the bacon with 8 anchovy fillets, finely chopped, or 100 g/4 oz lightly fried sliced button mushrooms.

Poached eggs

Ingredients	Metric-Imperial	American
Water	1 L/1¾ pints	4⅓ cups
Vinegar	2 tbs	3 tbs
4 eggs		

Put the water and vinegar into a pan and bring to the boil. Reduce the heat so that the water barely simmers. Crack each egg into a cup and carefully slide into the simmering water. Allow to cook for about 4 minutes, until lightly set. Remove with a slotted spoon, dip into cold water for just a moment to halt the cooking, and trim around the eggs.

Stuffed eggs
Serves 2

Ingredients	Metric-Imperial	American
4 hard-boiled eggs		
Cream cheese	175 g/6 oz	¾ cup
Drained capers	2 tbs	3 tbs
Single cream	1 tbs	1 tbs
Salt and pepper		
2 tomatoes		

Shell and halve the eggs. Remove the yolks and mash then mix in the cream cheese. Chop the capers and add to the cheese mixture with the cream. Season to taste.

Cut a cross in the top of each tomato and squeeze lightly to open the cut. Scoop out the seeds. Pipe cheese filling into the egg white halves and into the tomatoes.

Fried eggs with bacon
Serves 2

Ingredients	Metric-Imperial	American
Streaky bacon (strips)	75 g/3 oz	6 strips
2 eggs		
Salt		

Place the bacon in a frying pan and cook until golden brown and crisp. Remove and keep hot. Carefully crack the eggs and slide them into the bacon fat in the pan. Sprinkle with salt and cook over low heat until the eggs are firm. Serve with the bacon on a hot dish, garnished with fresh herbs if liked.

Above: Fried egg with bacon
Opposite: Scrambled eggs with tomatoes

Pancakes with bacon
Serves 4

Ingredients	Metric-Imperial	American
Flour (all-purpose)	225 g/8 oz	2 cups
Baking powder	1 tsp	1 tsp
3 eggs		
Salt		
Milk	450 ml/¾ pint	scant 2 cups
Streaky bacon (strips)	175 g/6 oz	12 strips
Oil for frying		

Sift the flour and baking powder into a bowl and make a well in the centre. Put in the eggs, salt and milk and beat, gradually drawing in the dry ingredients, until the batter is smooth. Cut the bacon into small pieces.

Heat a little oil in a frying pan and add a few bacon pieces. Cook until golden. Pour in a small ladleful of the batter and tilt the pan until it covers the base. Cook the pancake until golden brown on both sides. Make more pancakes in the same way, stacking up cooked ones on a warm plate. Keep hot. When all the pancakes are cooked, serve with a green salad.

Scrambled eggs with tomatoes
Serves 4

Ingredients	Metric-Imperial	American
6 eggs		
Milk	6 tbs	½ cup
Salt		
3 tomatoes		
Margarine	40 g/1½ oz	3 tbs

Beat together the eggs and milk and season to taste with salt. Slice the tomatoes.

Melt the margarine in a pan, pour in the egg mixture and stir over moderate heat for 2 minutes. Put in the tomato slices and cook for a further 3 minutes, stirring frequently, until the eggs are creamy but not dry and the tomato slices heated through.

Microwave hint
To cook scrambled eggs by microwave, whisk the eggs in a suitable bowl and season with salt and pepper. Stir in 1 tbsp cream for every 2 eggs. Cook, uncovered, on full power for 1 minute. Stir the cooked egg at the edges into the centre. Cook for a further minute, but do not allow to set fully. Stir again and leave to stand for 1 minute, by which time the eggs should be set.

Scrambled eggs with rolled oats
Serves 4

Ingredients	Metric-Imperial	American
4 eggs		
Milk	4 tbs	5 tbs
Rolled oats	4 tbs	5 tbs
Salt		
Parma ham (prosciutto)	100 g/4 oz	4 oz
Butter	15 g/½ oz	1 tbs
4 slices of wholemeal (wholewheat) bread		
Snipped chives	1 tbs	1 tbs

Beat together the eggs, milk and oats and season to taste with salt. Roughly chop the ham. Melt the butter in a pan, pour in the egg mixture and stir over moderate heat until the eggs are lightly set but still creamy. Spoon over the bread slices and serve at once, sprinkled with the ham and chives.

Omelettes with mushrooms
Serves 2

Ingredients	Metric-Imperial	American
Mushrooms	350 g/12 oz	12 oz
Streaky bacon (strips)	100 g/4 oz	8 strips
Butter	40 g/1½ oz	3 tbs
Cornflour (cornstarch)	1 tsp	1 tsp
Salt and pepper		
Chopped parsley	2 tbs	3 tbs
For the omelettes:		
4 eggs		
Milk	2 tbs	3 tbs

Slice the mushrooms and chop the bacon. Melt one third of the butter in a pan, add the bacon and cook, stirring frequently, until golden. Remove the bacon bits from the pan. Add the mushrooms to the bacon fat and cook, stirring occasionally, until soft. Return the bacon bits. Moisten the cornflour with a little cold water, add to the pan and cook, stirring, until thickened. Season to taste with salt and pepper and stir in the parsley. Keep hot.

To make the omelettes, beat together the eggs and milk. Melt half the remaining butter in a pan, add half the egg mixture and cover the pan. Cook gently until the top is lightly set and the underside golden. Slide the omelette on to a warm plate and fill with half the mushroom mixture. Keep hot while making another omelette in the same way.

Chicken-stuffed crêpes
Serves 4

Ingredients	Metric-Imperial	American
Flour (all-purpose)	150 g/5 oz	1¼ cups
2 eggs		
Milk	125 ml/4 fl oz	½ cup
Whipping cream	125 ml/4 fl oz	½ cup
Pinch of salt		
For the filling:		
Boneless chicken breasts	350 g/12 oz	12 oz
Flour (all-purpose)	1 tbs	1 tbs
Sweet paprika pepper	½ tsp	½ tsp
Curry powder	½ tsp	½ tsp
Butter	50 g/2 oz	¼ cup
Whipping cream	150 ml/¼ pint	⅔ cup
Dry white wine	5 tbs	6 tbs
Salt		
2 bananas		

Sift the flour into a bowl and make a well in the centre. Put in the eggs, milk and cream and add the salt. Beat, gradually drawing in the dry ingredients, until the batter is smooth.

To make the filling, slice the chicken breasts. Combine the flour, paprika and curry powder and use to coat the chicken slices. Melt a quarter of the butter in a pan, add the chicken slices and cook for about 3 minutes, stirring occasionally. Mix in the cream and wine and bring to the boil, stirring.

Simmer for 2 minutes and add salt to taste. Peel and slice the bananas, add to the meat and heat through. Keep hot.

Melt a little of the remaining butter in a frying pan, add a small ladleful of the batter and tilt the pan until it covers the base. Cook until golden on both sides. Remove from the pan and keep hot while making more crêpes in the same way. When all are cooked, place a little filling on each one and roll up. Serve at once, on a hot dish.

Opposite: Omelette with mushrooms
Above: Baked soufflé omelette

Baked soufflé omelette
Serves 4

Ingredients	Metric-Imperial	American
4 eggs		
Caster sugar (granulated)	100 g/4 oz	½ cup
Cornflour (cornstarch)	2 tbs	3 tbs
Icing sugar (confectioners') for sprinkling		

Separate the eggs and beat the yolks with the sugar until foamy. Whisk the egg whites in a clean bowl until stiff and place on the egg yolk mixture. Sift the cornflour evenly over the top of the egg whites and fold the ingredients together lightly but thoroughly.

Transfer the mixture to a well buttered flat ovenproof dish and bake, uncovered, in a preheated moderately hot oven, 190°C, 375°F, Gas Mark 5, for about 25 minutes, or until golden brown. Dust generously with icing sugar and serve at once.

Variations: For a fruity Baked Soufflé Omelette, place a layer of raspberries or blackberries in the dish before adding the egg mixture. For a special occasion, flavour the mixture with 2 tbs of a fruit-flavoured liqueur, such as Grand Marnier, Cointreau or framboise.

Pancakes with horseradish cheese cream
Serves 4

Ingredients	Metric-Imperial	American
Flour (all-purpose)	150 g/5 oz	1¼ cups
Rolled oats	2 tbs	3 tbs
3 eggs		
Mineral or soda water	250 ml/9 fl oz	generous 1 cup
1 onion		
Grated Cheddar cheese	50 g/2 oz	½ cup
Chopped mixed herbs	2 tbs	3 tbs
Salt		
Oil for frying		
Sprigs of watercress		
For the cream:		
Curd cheese (sieved creamed cottage)	225 g/8 oz	1 cup
Whipping cream	4 tbs	5 tbs
Grated horseradish from a jar	1 tsp	1 tsp
Rolled oats	3 tbs	4 tbs
Snipped chives	2 tbs	3 tbs
Salt		

Sift the flour into a bowl, stir in the oats and make a well in the centre. Beat the eggs with the water and pour into the well. Beat, gradually drawing in the dry ingredients, until the batter is well combined. Leave the batter to stand for at least 1 hour.

Meanwhile, make the horseradish cheese cream. Beat together the curd cheese and cream and stir in the horseradish, oats and chives and season to taste with salt.

Peel and chop the onion and stir into the batter with the grated cheese and herbs. Season to taste with salt.

Heat a little oil in a frying pan, add a small ladleful of the batter and spread to make a round pancake. Cook until golden brown on both sides. Make more pancakes in the same way and stack cooked ones on a plate. Keep hot. Garnish with watercress and serve with the cheese cream.

Buckwheat pancakes
Serves 4

Ingredients	Metric-Imperial	American
Buckwheat flour	250 g/9 oz	2¼ cups
Lukewarm water	500 ml/18 fl oz	2¼ cups
3 egg yolks		
Caster sugar (granulated)	1 tsp	1 tsp
2 egg whites		
Butter	50 g/2 oz	¼ cup

Put the flour into a bowl and gradually whisk in the water. Leave to stand for 1 hour. Beat in the egg yolks and sugar. Whisk the egg whites until stiff and fold into the batter.

Melt some of the butter in a frying pan, add a small ladleful of the batter and spread to make a round thin pancake. Fry until golden brown on both sides. Make more pancakes in the same way and stack cooked ones on a warm plate. Keep hot. Serve with fried bacon.

Jam and cream pancakes
Serves 4

Ingredients	Metric-Imperial	American
Flour (all-purpose)	250 g/9 oz	2¼ cups
Baking powder	2 tsp	2 tsp
3 eggs		
Milk	500 ml/18 fl oz	2¼ cups
Sugar	1 tbs	1 tbs
Pinch of salt		
Oil for frying		
Strawberry jam		
Lightly whipped cream		

Sift the flour and baking powder into a bowl and make a well in the centre. Beat together the eggs, milk, sugar and salt and pour half into the bowl. Beat, gradually drawing in the dry ingredients and adding the remaining egg mixture, until the batter is smooth. Leave to stand for 30 minutes.

Heat a little oil in a frying pan, pour in a small ladleful of the batter and tilt the pan until it coats the base thinly. Cook until golden brown on both sides. Make more pancakes in the same way, stacking cooked ones on a warm plate. Keep hot. When all the pancakes are cooked, spread with jam and spoon over a little cream. Serve while the pancakes are still warm.

Stuffed cornflour pancakes
Serves 4

Ingredients	Metric-Imperial	American
Cornflour (cornstarch)	150 g/5 oz	generous 1 cup
3 eggs		
Sugar	1 tsp	1 tsp
Milk	500 ml/18 fl oz	2¼ cups
Pinch of salt		
For the filling:		
Salami	225 g/8 oz	8 oz
Grated Gouda or Cheddar cheese	225 g/8 oz	2 cups
Hot cooked peas	275 g/10 oz	1⅔ cups
Oil for frying		

Sift the cornflour into a bowl and make a well in the centre. Beat together the eggs, sugar, milk and salt and gradually add this to the cornflour, beating vigorously, until the batter is smooth. Leave to stand for 2 hours.

To make the filling, dice the salami and mix with the cheese and peas.

Heat a little of the oil in a small frying pan, add a ladleful of the batter and tilt the pan until it makes a thin layer. Cook until golden brown on both sides. Make more pancakes in the same way and stack cooked ones on a warm plate. Keep hot. When all the pancakes are cooked, place a little of the filling on one half of each pancake and fold the other half over. Transfer to a hot dish and serve while still warm.

Opposite: Pancakes with horseradish cheese cream
Above: Apple pancake

Apple pancakes
Serves 4

Ingredients	Metric-Imperial	American
Dessert apples	1 kg/2¼ lb	2¼ lb
Oil for frying		
For the batter:		
Flour (all-purpose)	250 g/9 oz	2¼ cups
Baking powder	2 tsp	2 tsp
3 eggs		
Milk	500 ml/18 fl oz	2¼ cups
Caster sugar (granulated)	2 tbs	3 tbs
Pinch of salt		

Peel, quarter, core and thinly slice the apples.

To make the batter, sift the flour and baking powder into a bowl and make a well in the centre. Beat together the eggs, milk, 1 tbs sugar and the salt and add half to the bowl. Beat, gradually drawing in the dry ingredients and adding the remaining egg mixture, until the batter is smooth.

Heat a little oil in a frying pan, add a small ladleful of the batter and tilt the pan until it coats the base thinly. Add a few of the apple slices and cook until the pancake is golden brown on both sides. Make more pancakes in the same way, stacking cooked ones on a plate. Keep hot. Serve the pancakes while still warm, sprinkled with the sugar.

Variations: Use halved and stoned (pitted) plums or sliced bananas in place of the apples.

Soufflé omelettes with cream cheese and strawberry filling
Serves 2

Ingredients	Metric-Imperial	American
Strawberries	225 g/8 oz	8 oz
Cream cheese	75 g/3 oz	⅓ cup
Caster sugar (granulated)	25 g/1 oz	2 tbs
Vanilla essence (extract)	½ tsp	½ tsp
Whipping cream	125 ml/4 fl oz	½ cup
For the omelettes:		
3 eggs		
Grated rind of ½ lemon		
Caster sugar (granulated)	25 g/1 oz	2 tbs
Cornflour (cornstarch)	1 tsp	1 tsp
Butter or margarine	25 g/1 oz	2 tbs

Hull and halve the strawberries. Beat together the cream cheese, sugar and vanilla essence. Whisk the cream until stiff and fold into the cheese mixture with two thirds of the strawberries.

To make the omelettes, separate the eggs and beat the yolks with the lemon rind and sugar. Whisk the egg whites in a clean bowl until stiff, place on the egg yolk mixture and sift the cornflour over the top. Fold the ingredients together lightly.

Melt half the butter in a pan and add about half the egg mixture. Cover the pan and cook over low heat for about 10 minutes, or until golden underneath and lightly set on top. Spoon half the filling on to the omelette, fold over and slide carefully on to a warm plate. Keep hot while making another omelette in the same way. Decorate the omelettes with the remaining strawberries and serve at once.

Soufflé omelettes
Serves 2

Ingredients	Metric-Imperial	American
3 eggs		
Grated rind of ½ lemon		
Lemon juice	4 tsp	4 tsp
Caster sugar (granulated)	25 g/1 oz	2 tbs
Cornflour (cornstarch)	2 tsp	2 tsp
Butter	25 g/1 oz	2 tbs
Cranberry sauce		
Icing sugar (confectioners') for sprinkling		

Separate the eggs and beat the yolks with the lemon rind and juice and the sugar until foamy. Whisk the egg whites in a clean bowl until stiff. Place on the egg yolk mixture and sift the cornflour over the top. Fold the ingredients together lightly.

Melt about half the butter in a frying pan, put in half the egg mixture, cover the pan and cook gently for about 10 minutes, or until the omelette is golden brown underneath and lightly set on top. Spoon a little cranberry sauce over half the omelette, fold over and slide carefully on to a warm plate. Keep hot while you make another omelette in the same way. Serve the Soufflé Omelettes at once, lightly sifted with icing sugar.

Pancakes with syrup
Serves 4

Ingredients	Metric-Imperial	American
Flour (all-purpose)	200 g/7 oz	1¾ cups
Baking powder	1 tsp	1 tsp
4 eggs		
Milk	500 ml/18 fl oz	2¼ cups
Caster sugar (granulated)	2 tsp	2 tsp
Pinch of salt		
Ground cinnamon	2 tsp	2 tsp
Butter	75 g/3 oz	⅓ cup
Maple syrup		

Sift the flour and baking powder into a bowl and make a well in the centre. Beat the eggs with the milk, sugar, salt and cinnamon. Gradually beat into the dry ingredients until the batter is smooth. Melt one third of the butter and beat into the batter then leave to stand for at least 30 minutes.

Melt a little of the remaining butter in a frying pan, pour in a small ladleful of the batter and tilt the pan until it makes a thin layer. Cook until golden brown on both sides. Make more pancakes in the same way, stacking cooked ones on a warm plate. Keep hot. Roll the pancakes and serve warm with maple syrup.

Buttermilk pancakes
Serves 4

Ingredients	Metric-Imperial	American
Flour (all-purpose)	250 g/9 oz	2¼ cups
5 eggs		
Caster sugar (granulated)	1 tsp	1 tsp
Salt		
Grated rind of 1 lemon		
Buttermilk	500 ml/18 fl oz	2¼ cups
Water	125 ml/4 fl oz	½ cup
Butter	50 g/2 oz	¼ cup
Redcurrant jelly		
Icing sugar (confectioners') for sprinkling		

Sift the flour into a bowl and make a well in the centre. Beat together the eggs, sugar, salt, grated lemon rind, buttermilk and water. Pour into the bowl and beat, drawing in the dry ingredients, until the batter is smooth. Leave to stand for 30 minutes.

Melt a little of the butter in a frying pan, add a small ladleful of the batter and tilt the pan until it makes a thin layer. Cook until golden brown on both sides. Make more pancakes in the same way, stacking cooked ones on a warm plate. Keep hot. When all the pancakes are cooked, spread them with redcurrant jelly and roll up. Serve generously sifted with icing sugar.

Sweet plum puff
Serves 4

Ingredients	Metric-Imperial	American
Ripe plums	550 g/1¼ lb	1¼ lb
Sugar	125 g/4½ oz	scant ⅔ cup
Ground cinnamon	1 tsp	1 tsp
3 eggs		
Curd cheese (sieved creamed cottage)	450 g/1 lb	2 cups
Softened butter	75 g/3 oz	⅓ cup
Cornflour (cornstarch)	1 tbs	1 tbs
Vanilla essence (extract)	2 tsp	2 tsp
Rum	2 tbs	3 tbs
Grated rind and juice of 1 lemon		

Stone (pit) the plums and place in a greased ovenproof dish. Mix together 2 tbs (3 tbs) of the sugar and the cinnamon and sprinkle over the plums.

Separate the eggs and beat the yolks with the cheese, butter, cornflour, vanilla essence, rum, lemon rind and juice and the remaining sugar. Stiffly whisk the egg whites in a clean bowl and fold into the cheese mixture. Spoon over the plums. Bake, uncovered, in a preheated moderate oven, 180°C, 350°F, Gas Mark 4, for 1 hour, until golden brown on top. Serve sprinkled with more cinnamon if wished.

Variation: To give a more interesting surface, reserve about 5 of the plums and drop them into the cheese topping just before baking.

Microwave hints

● A soufflé omelette is particularly successful when cooked by microwave. Separate the eggs, beat the whites until stiff but not dry. Blend the egg yolks with 2 tbs (3 tbs) milk for each yolk, seasoning to taste, and then gradually fold in the whisked whites. Microwave a knob of butter in a medium-sized shallow pie dish at full power for 30 seconds. Pour in the egg mixture and cook on medium power for 5 minutes, lifting the edges of the omelette with a spatula half-way through cooking time. Fold carefully in half with the spatula and slide on to a serving dish.

● To cook scrambled eggs by microwave, whisk the eggs in a suitable bowl and season with salt and pepper. Stir in 1 tbs cream for every 2 eggs and cook, uncovered, on full power for 1 minute. Stir the cooked egg at the edges into the centre. Cook for 1 further minute, but do not allow to set fully. Stir again and leave to stand for 1 minute, by which time the eggs should be fully set.

● When preparing baked eggs in individual ramekins, first make a bed of chopped spinach or cooked chopped potato in the dishes, break the eggs on top, sprinkle with salt, pepper and grated cheese. Cook the ramekins, 2 at a time, for 1½ minutes on full power. Remove and leave to stand for 1 minute to allow the eggs to finish cooking.

● To make an omelette to cut in strips and use as a garnish, put 15 g/½ oz (1 tbs) butter in a suitable small round dish and cook on full power for 30 seconds. Swirl the butter over the base and sides of the dish. Beat 2 eggs with 1 tsp soy sauce and add salt and pepper to taste. Pour into the dish, cover with pierced cling film and cook on full power for 1 minute. Remove and rotate the dish to distribute the uncooked egg mixture. Cook, covered, on full power for a further 1 minute. If not fully set, cook, uncovered, for a further 30 seconds. Cool, then cut into narrow strips.

● Never cook eggs in the shell by microwave as they tend to explode. Even eggs broken into a dish for poaching may explode unless the membrane is pricked with a fine pointed skewer in one or two places.

● To make a baked custard, whisk together 2 eggs in a medium-sized suitable dish. Warm 300 ml/½ pint (1¼ cups) milk with 2 tbs (3 tbs) caster sugar (granulated) on full power for 1 minute. Whisk into the eggs and flavour with vanilla to taste. Bake at full power for 3 minutes then allow to stand for 2 minutes.

Garlic sausage and potato medley
Serves 4

Ingredients	Metric-Imperial	American
Small potatoes	750 g/1¾ lb	1¾ lb
Streaky bacon (strips)	225 g/8 oz	16 strips
Onions	350 g/12 oz	12 oz
Garlic sausage	225 g/8 oz	8 oz
Curd cheese (sieved creamed cottage)	450 g/1 lb	2 cups
Whipping cream	225 ml/8 fl oz	1 cup
6 eggs		
Snipped chives	2 tbs	3 tbs
Caraway seeds	2 tsp	2 tsp
Salt and pepper		

Cook the potatoes in plenty of boiling salted water for 15 minutes. Drain, refresh with cold water and peel. Reserve 4 slices (8 strips) of the bacon and chop the rest. Place in a frying pan and cook until the bacon is crisp. Remove the bacon bits and reserve. Peel and thinly slice the onion and fry in the bacon fat until golden brown. Slice the sausage.

Beat together the cheese, cream, eggs, chives and caraway seeds and season to taste with salt and pepper. Place half the bacon bits, onion, potatoes and sausage slices in a greased ovenproof dish and spoon over half the cheese mixture. Level the surface. Repeat these layers once. Top with the reserved bacon and place, uncovered, in a preheated moderately hot oven, 200°C, 400°F, Gas Mark 6, for 50 minutes. Leave to stand for 10 minutes before serving.

Variations: Replace the garlic sausage with frankfurters or spicy chorizo sausage.

Kohlrabi and potatoes au gratin
Serves 4

Ingredients	Metric-Imperial	American
4 small kohlrabi		
Potatoes	450 g/1 lb	1 lb
4 onions		
Salami	100 g/4 oz	4 oz
Grated cheese such as Emmental or Cheddar	200 g/7 oz	1¾ cups
Salt and pepper		
2 eggs		
Whipping cream	125 ml/4 fl oz	½ cup
Milk	225 ml/8 fl oz	1 cup
Sweet paprika pepper		
Fresh breadcrumbs	3 tbs	4 tbs
Butter	25 g/1 oz	2 tbs

Remove the leaves from the kohlrabi. Peel and thinly slice the kohlrabi, potatoes and onions. Slice the salami then cut into strips. Arrange these ingredients in layers in a greased ovenproof dish, sprinkling the kohlrabi and potato layers with some of the cheese and a little seasoning, and ending with a layer of potato slices.

Beat together the eggs, cream and milk and season to taste with salt and paprika. Pour evenly over the ingredients in the dish. Mix the rest of the cheese with the breadcrumbs, sprinkle over the top then dot with the butter. Bake, uncovered, in a preheated moderately hot oven, 200°C, 400°F, Gas Mark 6, for 45 minutes, or until the top is golden brown and the potato is tender.

Variations: Fennel, leeks or thinly sliced swedes (rutabaga) or carrots would all make suitable substitutes for kohlrabi.

Microwave hint
Small packs of frozen vegetables can be cooked by microwave from frozen in the freezer bag. Pierce the bag in two places and place it on absorbent kitchen paper in the cooker so that the liquid running from the bag will be absorbed.

Microwave hint
To cook vegetables in a cook bag by microwave, secure the end of the bag loosely with an elastic band so that steam does not build up and cause the bag to burst.

Left: Garlic sausage and potato medley
Opposite: Kohlrabi and potatoes au gratin

Colourful vegetable bake
Serves 4

Ingredients	Metric-Imperial	American
Macaroni	225 g/8 oz	8 oz
2 onions		
1 clove of garlic		
1 green sweet pepper		
1 carrot		
Butter	15 g/½ oz	1 tbs
Cooked ham	225 g/8 oz	8 oz
Whipping cream	150 ml/¼ pint	⅔ cup
Grated cheese	100 g/4 oz	1 cup

Break the macaroni into short lengths and cook in plenty of boiling salted water for 8 minutes. Drain, refresh with cold water and drain again. Peel and chop the onions and garlic. Halve and deseed the pepper and cut the flesh into strips. Peel and slice the carrot.

Melt the butter in a frying pan and cook the onion, garlic, pepper and carrot for 6 minutes, stirring frequently. Cut the ham into strips. Mix the onion mixture with the macaroni, ham and cream and transfer to a greased ovenproof dish. Sprinkle with the cheese and place, uncovered, in a preheated hot oven, 220°C, 425°F, Gas Mark 7, for 30 minutes, or until golden brown on top.

Microwave hint
Green vegetables with a high water content, such as cucumber, cook more quickly by microwave than denser, drier vegetables such as cabbage.

Below: Colourful vegetable bake
Opposite: Special potato bake

Mixed vegetables au gratin *(Photo p. 72–73)*
Serves 4

Ingredients	Metric-Imperial	American
Parsnips	675 g/1½ lb	1½ lb
2 medium-sized onions, red-skinned if possible		
Savoy cabbage	1 lb	1 lb
4 sticks of celery		
Streaky bacon (strips)	200 g/7 oz	14 strips
Whipping cream	225 ml/8 fl oz	1 cup
Salt and pepper		
Ground nutmeg		
Grated Cheddar cheese	75 g/3 oz	¾ cup

Peel and thinly slice the parsnips. Place the slices in a pan, cover with salted water and bring to the boil. Cover and simmer for 8 minutes. Drain well. Peel and slice the onions and divide the slices into rings. Remove the rough outer leaves from the cabbage, cut it in half and remove the stalk. Shred the leaves. Trim the celery, removing any strings, and cut into thin slices. Add the onion rings, cabbage and celery to a pan of boiling salted water, bring back to the boil, cover and simmer for 8 minutes. Drain and refresh with cold water. Chop the bacon.

Layer the vegetables and bacon in a greased ovenproof dish, spooning a little cream over each layer and sprinkling it with salt, pepper, nutmeg and cheese. Finish with a layer of parsnip slices. Spoon the rest of the cream evenly over the top and sprinkle with the remaining cheese. Bake, uncovered, in a preheated hot oven, 220°C, 425°F, Gas Mark 7, for 45 minutes, or until golden brown on top.

Variations: Cauliflower or broccoli florets could replace the cabbage, and runner (green) beans used instead of celery.

Special potato bake
Serves 4

Ingredients	Metric-Imperial	American
Potatoes	1 kg/2¼ lb	2¼ lb
Cooked ham	225 g/8 oz	8 oz
Hot chicken stock		
(bouillon)	225 ml/8 fl oz	1 cup
Whipping cream	150 ml/¼ pint	⅔ cup
2 eggs		
Salt and white pepper		
Ground nutmeg		
Cornflour (cornstarch)	1 tbs	1 tbs
Grated Parmesan cheese	25 g/1 oz	¼ cup
Butter	15 g/½ oz	1 tbs

Cook the potatoes in plenty of boiling salted water for 20 minutes, or until tender. Peel, allow to cool then slice. Dice the ham and layer with the potato in a shallow greased ovenproof dish, finishing with a layer of potato.

To make the sauce, beat together the stock, cream and eggs and season to taste with salt, pepper and nutmeg. Moisten the cornflour with a little cold water and stir well into the stock mixture. Pour over the potatoes, sprinkle with the cheese and dot with the butter. Bake, uncovered, in a preheated moderately hot oven, 200°C, 400°F, Gas Mark 6, for 35 minutes, or until golden brown on top.

Variation: For Herbed potato bake, add 2-3 tbs (3-4 tbs) chopped fresh thyme, or 1 tbs dried thyme, to the cream and egg mixture.

Microwave hint

To cook three large peeled potatoes by microwave, stir together 4 tbs (5 tbs) water and a pinch of salt in a suitable dish. Cut each potato in 4 pieces, place in the dish, cover and cook on full power for 8 minutes. Test for tenderness. If too firm, cook for another 2 minutes. Allow to stand for 3 minutes before serving.

Cauliflower bake with cheese topping
Serves 5–6

Ingredients	Metric-Imperial	American
1 large cauliflower		
Cooked ham	225 g/8 oz	8 oz
Whipping cream	225 ml/8 fl oz	1 cup
1 egg		
Green peppercorns	1 tsp	1 tsp
Lean bacon (Canadian)	100 g/4 oz	2 slices
Butter	50 g/2 oz	¼ cup
Flour (all-purpose)	2 tbs	3 tbs
Milk	125 ml/4 fl oz	½ cup
3 eggs		
Grated Parmesan cheese	50 g/2 oz	¼ cup

Trim off any leaves from the cauliflower and remove as much of the stalk as possible. Place in a pan with salted water to cover and bring to the boil. Simmer for 12 minutes then drain well and divide into florets.

Mince the ham or purée in a food processor. Mix with the cream, egg and peppercorns. Roughly chop the bacon and fold in. Place half the ham and cream mixture in a greased ovenproof dish, top with half the cauliflower florets then repeat these layers once.

Melt the butter in a pan, sprinkle in the flour and stir until the roux is golden. Whisk in the milk and bring to the boil, stirring. Simmer for 5 minutes. Separate the eggs, mix the yolks with the cheese and stir into the sauce, removing the pan from the heat. Whisk the egg whites in a clean bowl until stiff and fold into the sauce. Spoon over the ingredients in the dish. Place, uncovered, in a preheated moderately hot oven, 200°C, 400°F, Gas Mark 6, for about 35 minutes, or until golden brown on top. Serve with a tomato sauce.

Celery and turkey surprise
Serves 4

Ingredients	Metric-Imperial	American
Turkey breast	750 g/1¾ lb	1¾ lb
Toasting bread	100 g/4 oz	4 slices
Chicken stock (bouillon)	125 ml/4 fl oz	½ cup
1 egg		
Dry white wine, sherry or cider	3 tbs	4 tbs
Whipping cream	3 tbs	4 tbs
Lemon juice	1 tsp	1 tsp
Finely grated rind of ½ lemon		
Dijon mustard		
1 carton mustard and cress		
Butter	75 g/3 oz	⅓ cup
Salt and freshly ground pepper		
2 small heads of celery		
Flour (all-purpose)	40 g/1½ oz	⅓ cup
Hot milk	500 ml/18 fl oz	2¼ cups
Gorgonzola or Stilton cheese	100 g/4 oz	4 oz
Ground nutmeg		

Dice the turkey. Trim off the crusts from the bread, soak it in the stock then squeeze out most of the moisture. Finely mince the turkey and bread or purée in a food processor. Mix with the remaining stock, the egg, wine, cream, lemon juice and rind, mustard and snipped mustard and cress. Melt half the butter and add to the turkey mixture. Season to taste with salt and pepper.

Trim the celery, removing any strings, and cut each stick in half crossways. Put half the celery pieces into a greased ovenproof dish with the hollow side upwards. Spoon the turkey mixture over and cover with the rest of the celery pieces, hollow side downwards.

Melt the remaining butter in a pan, sprinkle in the flour and stir until the roux is pale and golden. Whisk in the milk and bring to the boil, stirring. Simmer for 5 minutes. Crumble in the cheese and stir until it has melted. Season to taste with salt, pepper and nutmeg and pour over the ingredients in the dish. Place, uncovered, in a preheated moderately hot oven, 200°C, 400°F, Gas Mark 6, for about 1 hour and 5 minutes. To prevent overbrowning, protect the surface with a sheet of foil during the last 20 minutes of cooking time if necessary. Serve with a green salad.

Opposite: Celery and turkey surprise
Above: Cauliflower bake with cheese topping

Tomato and pasta bake
Serves 4

Ingredients	Metric-Imperial	American
Pasta twists	225 g/8 oz	2⅔ cups
Tomatoes	750 g/1¾ lb	1¾ lb
Parma ham (prosciutto)	100 g/4 oz	4 oz
3 eggs		
Milk	125 ml/4 fl oz	½ cup
Chopped parsley	2 tbs	3 tbs
Snipped chives	2 tbs	3 tbs
Salt and pepper		
Grated Parmesan cheese	2 tbs	3 tbs
Fresh breadcrumbs	2 tbs	3 tbs

Cook the pasta in plenty of boiling salted water for about 8 minutes. Drain, refresh briefly with cold water and drain again. Pour boiling water over the tomatoes, drain, peel and slice. Chop the ham.

Place the tomato slices in a greased ovenproof dish and cover with the ham and pasta. Beat the eggs with the milk, parsley and chives and season to taste with salt and pepper. Pour over the pasta. Mix the cheese with the breadcrumbs and sprinkle over the top. Place, uncovered, in a preheated moderately hot oven, 200°C, 400°F, Gas Mark 6, for 35 minutes, protecting the surface with a sheet of foil if necessary during the last 15 minutes of baking to prevent overbrowning.

Below: Tomato and pasta bake

Savoury cheese pudding, Caernarvon style
Serves 4

Ingredients	Metric-Imperial	American
6 thick slices bread		
Butter	50 g/2 oz	¼ cup
Grated strong Cheddar cheese (sharp)	275 g/10 oz	2½ cups
Salt and pepper		
Dry wholegrain mustard (powder)	1 tsp	1 tsp
4 eggs		
Milk	750 ml/1¼ pints	3 cups

Toast the slices of bread on one side only then butter the untoasted side generously. Place two slices, toasted side downwards, in a buttered ovenproof dish and sprinkle with one third of the cheese and a little salt, pepper and mustard. Repeat the layers twice.

Beat the eggs in a bowl. Put the milk into a pan and bring to the boil. Add the milk to the eggs and whisk well. Pour evenly over the ingredients in the dish and leave to stand for 30 minutes. Place, uncovered, in a preheated moderate oven, 180°C, 350°F, Gas Mark 4, for 30 minutes, or until well risen and golden brown.

Welsh rarebit
Serves 2

Ingredients	Metric-Imperial	American
Grated strong Cheddar cheese (sharp)	100 g/4 oz	1 cup

	Metric-Imperial	American
Butter	25 g/1 oz	2 tbs
Milk	3 tbs	4 tbs
Pinch of dry mustard (powder)		
Salt and pepper		
2 slices bread		
Butter for spreading		

Put the cheese, butter and milk into a pan and heat gently, stirring, until smooth. Add the mustard and season to taste with salt and pepper.

Meanwhile, toast the bread slices on both sides and spread with butter. Cover the toast with cheese mixture and place under a hot grill (broiler) until the topping is golden brown.

Variation: Substitute beer for the milk in the cheese mixture.

Spinach and potato grill
Serves 4

Ingredients	Metric-Imperial	American
Potatoes	750 g/1¾ lb	1¾ lb
Milk	300 ml/½ pint	1¼ cups
Streaky bacon (strips)	150 g/5 oz	10 strips
Grated Cheddar cheese	150 g/5 oz	1¼ cups
Salt and pepper		
Spinach	750 g/1¾ lb	1¾ lb
1 onion		
1 clove of garlic		
Butter	15 g/½ oz	1 tbs

Peel and slice the potatoes. Place the milk in a pan and bring to the boil. Put in the potato slices, bring back to the boil, cover and simmer for about 10 minutes, or until the potatoes are tender. Chop the bacon and stir into the potato mixture with one third of the cheese. Season with salt and pepper and place in the centre of a heatproof dish.

Wash the spinach, drain and place in a pan with just the water clinging to the leaves. Cover and cook for about 5 minutes, shaking the pan occasionally, or until the spinach is limp. Peel and chop the onion and garlic. Melt the butter in a pan and use to cook the onion and garlic until soft. Stir in the spinach and mix well over the heat for 2 minutes. Spoon around the potato mixture in the dish and sprinkle with the remaining cheese. Place under a hot grill (broiler) for about 7 minutes, or until the potatoes are golden brown.

Microwave method
Peel and slice the potatoes; arrange one layer overlapping in a round dish suitable for the microwave. Leave an empty ring round the edge. Chop the bacon and arrange some of the bacon with a sprinkling of cheese and seasoning on the first layer of potatoes. Continue until all the ingredients are used. Heat the milk in a bowl at full power in the microwave for 5 minutes. Pour on top of the potatoes and cover. Cook on full power for 15 minutes.

Wash the spinach, drain and cook in the microwave for 5 minutes. Drain again.

Peel and chop the onion and crush the garlic and mix with the spinach. Arrange in the empty space round the edge of the potatoes and dot with butter. Cook on full power for 5 minutes.

If a brown top is required place the dish under a hot grill (broiler) until the top of the potatoes are golden.

Layered meat and corn bake
Serves 4

Ingredients	Metric-Imperial	American
1 onion		
1 clove of garlic		
Oil	1 tbs	1 tbs
Minced beef and pork combined (ground)	450 g/1 lb	1 lb
Mild chilli powder	1 tsp	1 tsp
Salt and pepper		
Ground cinnamon		
Canned sweetcorn kernels	350 g/12 oz can	12 oz can
Salami	150 g/5 oz	5 oz
Tomatoes	450 g/1 lb	1 lb
Chopped oregano		
Grated Gouda cheese	175 g/6 oz	1½ cups
Fresh breadcrumbs	2 tbs	3 tbs
Butter	15 g/½ oz	1 tbs

Peel and chop the onion and garlic. Heat the oil in a pan and use to cook the onion and garlic until transparent. Add the meat and cook, stirring, until it is brown and crumbly. Sprinkle in the chilli powder and salt, pepper and cinnamon to taste. Transfer to a greased ovenproof dish and level the surface.

Drain the corn and cut the salami into strips. Pour boiling water over the tomatoes, drain, peel and roughly chop.

Spoon the corn over the meat mixture, top with the salami strips, then with the tomato. Sprinkle with pepper and oregano to taste. Mix together the cheese and breadcrumbs, sprinkle over the ingredients in the dish and dot with the butter. Place, uncovered, in a preheated moderately hot oven, 200°C, 400°F, Gas Mark 6, for 35 minutes, or until golden brown on top.

Mixed noodles with ham
Serves 4

Ingredients	Metric-Imperial	American
Plain ribbon noodles	100 g/4 oz	4 oz
Spinach ribbon noodles	100 g/4 oz	4 oz
Tomatoes	450 g/1 lb	1 lb
Cooked ham	225 g/8 oz	8 oz
3 eggs		
Whipping cream	150 ml/¼ pint	⅔ cup
Salt and pepper		
Snipped chives	2 tbs	3 tbs
Chopped parsley	2 tbs	3 tbs
Cream cheese	225 g/8 oz	1 cup
Sour cream	2 tbs	3 tbs

Cook the noodles, keeping plain and spinach separate, in pans of boiling salted water for 8 minutes. Drain and refresh briefly with cold water. Drain again. Pour boiling water over the tomatoes, drain, peel and slice. Dice the ham. Beat together the eggs and whipping cream and season to taste with salt and pepper.

Place the plain and spinach noodles on opposite sides of a greased shallow ovenproof dish. Fill the centre with layers of tomato and ham. Pour the egg mixture over the ingredients in the dish and sprinkle most of the herbs over the top. Cook, uncovered, in a preheated moderately hot oven, 200°C, 400°F, Gas Mark 6, for 40 minutes. Meanwhile, beat together the cream cheese, sour cream and remaining herbs. Take the dish from the oven and spoon the cream cheese mixture over the top just before serving.

Left: Layered meat and corn bake
Opposite: Yellow and green noodles with ham

Pasta and cottage cheese bake
Serves 4

Ingredients	Metric-Imperial	American
Short cut macaroni	200 g/7 oz	2⅓ cups
Oil	1 tbs	1 tbs
Cottage cheese	225 g/8 oz	1 cup
Whipping cream	150 ml/¼ pint	⅔ cup
3 eggs		
Caraway seeds	1 tsp	1 tsp
Snipped chives	2 tbs	3 tbs
Salt and pepper		
2 frankfurters		
Streaky bacon (strips)	50 g/2 oz	4 strips

Cook the pasta in plenty of boiling salted water, adding the oil, for 10 minutes. Drain, refresh briefly with cold water and drain again.

Beat together the cottage cheese, cream, eggs, caraway seeds and chives and season to taste with salt and pepper. Slice the frankfurters.

Combine the pasta, cheese mixture and sausage slices and transfer to a greased ovenproof dish. Lay the bacon on top. Place, uncovered, in a preheated moderately hot oven, 200°C, 400°F, Gas Mark 6, for 1 hour and 5 minutes. Protect the top with a sheet of foil for the last 20 minutes of cooking time to prevent overbrowning. Serve with a tomato and onion salad.

Smoked cod soufflé
Serves 4

Ingredients	Metric-Imperial	American
Smoked cod fillets	350 g/12 oz	12 oz
Milk	300 ml/½ pint	1¼ cups
Butter	50 g/2 oz	¼ cup
Flour (all-purpose)	40 g/1½ oz	⅓ cup
4 eggs		
Lemon juice	2 tsp	2 tsp
Anchovy essence (extract)	1 tsp	1 tsp
Grated Cheddar cheese	50 g/2 oz	½ cup
Cayenne pepper		
Salt		
Grated Parmesan cheese	1 tbs	1 tbs

Courgettes au gratin
Serves 4

Ingredients	Metric-Imperial	American
Courgettes (zucchini)	450 g/1 lb	1 lb
Salt and pepper		
2 onions		
Cooked ham	100 g/4 oz	4 oz
Flour (all-purpose)	2 tbs	3 tbs
2 eggs		
Ground nutmeg		
Oil	2 tbs	3 tbs
Grated Gruyère cheese	100 g/4 oz	1 cup

Top and tail the courgettes and grate coarsely. Sprinkle with salt, place in a clean kitchen cloth and squeeze out the moisture. Peel and chop the onions and chop the ham. Mix together the courgettes, onion, ham, flour and eggs and season to taste with salt, pepper and nutmeg.

Put the oil into an ovenproof dish and place this in a preheated hot oven, 220°C, 425°F, Gas Mark 7, for 3 minutes. Turn the courgette mixture into the dish and level the surface. Return the dish to the oven and cook, uncovered, for 30 minutes. Sprinkle with the cheese and return to the oven for a further 5 minutes, or until the cheese has melted.

Poach the fish fillets in the milk for about 5 minutes, or until just cooked through. Drain off the milk and reserve. Remove skin and bones from the fish and flake the flesh.

Melt the butter in a small pan, sprinkle in the flour and cook, stirring, for 1 minute. Gradually add the reserved milk and bring to the boil, stirring constantly. Simmer for 3 minutes and remove from the heat. Separate the eggs and beat the yolks into the sauce, one at a time. Then beat in the lemon juice, anchovy essence and Cheddar cheese. Lastly, stir in the flaked fish and season with a pinch of cayenne and salt to taste. Whisk the egg whites in a clean bowl until stiff and fold into the fish mixture. Transfer to a large greased soufflé dish standing on a baking sheet (cookie sheet) or to a deep ovenproof dish. Sprinkle the Parmesan over the top and place, uncovered, in a preheated moderately hot oven, 200°C, 400°F, Gas Mark 6, for 2 minutes, then reduce the heat to 190°C, 375°F, Gas Mark 5, and continue baking for a further 30 minutes, or until the soufflé is well risen and golden brown. Serve immediately.

Above: Pasta and cottage cheese bake
Right: Courgettes au gratin

Potato, leek and minced beef bake
Serves 4

Ingredients	Metric-Imperial	American
Potatoes	750 g/1¾ lb	1¾ lb
4 leeks		
2 onions		
2 cloves of garlic		
Oil	2 tbs	3 tbs
Minced beef and pork combined (ground)	450 g/1 lb	1 lb
Salt and pepper		
Cayenne pepper		
Sour cream	225 ml/8 fl oz	1 cup
Chopped parsley	2 tbs	3 tbs
Grated Cheddar cheese	100 g/4 oz	1 cup
Butter	15 g/½ oz	1 tbs

Cook the potatoes in plenty of boiling salted water for about 20 minutes, or until tender. Drain, peel while still hot, leave to cool then slice. Trim and clean the leeks and cut into slices. Blanch the slices in boiling salted water for 3 minutes then drain well. Peel and chop the onions and garlic.

Heat the oil in a large frying pan and use to cook the onion and garlic until transparent. Add the meat and cook, stirring, until it looks brown and crumbly. Season with salt, pepper and a pinch of cayenne. Stir together the sour cream and parsley and season with salt and pepper.

Place half the potato and leek slices in a greased ovenproof dish and sprinkle with salt. Spoon over half the cream mixture and place the meat on top. Cover with the remaining potato and leek, sprinkle with more salt and pepper and spoon over the rest of the cream mixture. Sprinkle with the cheese and dot with the butter. Bake, uncovered, in a preheated moderately hot oven, 200°C, 400°F, Gas Mark 6, for about 30 minutes, or until the top is brown.

Moussaka
Serves 4

Ingredients	Metric-Imperial	American
4 large aubergines (eggplant)		
Salt		
Oil	125 ml/4 fl oz	½ cup
8 tomatoes		
Minced lamb	550 g/1¼ lb	1¼ lb
2 cloves of garlic		
Chopped parsley	2 tbs	3 tbs

Chopped thyme	1 tsp	1 tsp
1 egg		
Natural yogurt (plain)	150 ml/¼ pint	⅔ cup
Grated Cheddar cheese	50 g/2 oz	½ cup

Cut the aubergines into 1.25 cm/½ inch thick slices, sprinkle with salt and leave to stand for 30 minutes then rinse and dry on absorbent kitchen paper. Heat the oil in a pan and use to fry the aubergine slices until golden brown on both sides. Drain well and keep hot. Slice the tomatoes.

Remove excess oil from the pan, leaving about 2 tbs (3 tbs). Add the lamb and cook, stirring, until it looks brown and crumbly. Peel and chop the onions and garlic, add to the pan with the parsley and oregano and half the basil and thyme. Cook for a further 10 minutes, stirring frequently.

Put half the aubergine slices into a well oiled ovenproof dish, sprinkle with some of the remaining herbs, lay half the tomato slices on top and sprinkle with the rest of the herbs. Spoon the meat over, level the surface and cover with the last of the aubergine and tomato slices. Press down lightly. Beat together the egg and yogurt, spoon over the ingredients in the dish and sprinkle with the cheese. Cook, uncovered, in a preheated moderately hot oven, 200°C, 400°F, Gas Mark 6, for 40 minutes, or until golden brown.

Opposite: Potato, leek and minced beef bake
Above: Moussaka

Microwave method

Cut the aubergines into 1.25 cm/½ inch slices, sprinkle with salt and leave to stand on a tray to allow excess bitter juices to drain. Dry on absorbent kitchen paper. Heat the oil in a browning dish on full power for 1 minute. Cover the dish with aubergine slices and cook for 2 minutes. This stage will have to be done in batches. Remove the aubergines on to a baking tray and put each batch under a hot grill for 1½ minutes. Although this sounds complicated it is much less messy than frying the aubergines. Drain the aubergines on absorbent kitchen paper.

Heat remaining oil from the aubergines in the browning dish and stir the lamb into the hot oil. Cook on full power for 3 minutes, remove and break the mixture up with a fork until crumbly again.

Peel and chop the onions and garlic, add to the lamb with half the parsley, oregano, basil and thyme. Mix well and cook on full power for 2 minutes.

Place half the aubergines on the bottom of a microwave casserole dish, sprinkle with some of the remaining herbs and top with tomato slices. Add the rest of the herbs and spoon the meat on top. Level the mixture and press down with the back of a spoon. Cover with the remaining aubergine and tomato slices. Put in the microwave at full power for 8 minutes.

Meanwhile beat the egg and yogurt together with a little seasoning. Remove the moussaka from the microwave and spread the yogurt mixture on top. Sprinkle with cheese and cook on full power for 5 minutes. Flash under a hot grill to make the top golden brown. Serve with a Greek salad of lettuce, tomato, cucumber and Feta cheese.

Fluffy vanilla pudding
Serves 4

Ingredients	Metric-Imperial	American
4 eggs		
Hot water	3 tbs	4 tbs
Vanilla essence (extract)	1 tsp	1 tsp
Caster sugar (granulated)	100 g/4 oz	½ cup
Cornflour (cornstarch)	2 tbs	3 tbs

Separate the eggs and place the yolks in a bowl with the water and vanilla essence. Whisk until foamy then gradually add two thirds of the sugar and beat until the mixture is smooth and creamy. Whisk egg whites until stiff. Gradually whisk in the remaining sugar until firm.

Sift the cornflour over the surface of the egg yolk mixture, top with the meringue and fold the ingredients lightly together. Transfer to a greased soufflé dish and bake, uncovered, in a preheated moderately hot oven, 190°C, 375°F, Gas Mark 5, for about 20 minutes, or until well risen and golden brown.

Individual apricot soufflés
Serves 4

Ingredients	Metric-Imperial	American
Ripe apricots	450 g/1 lb	1 lb
4 eggs		
Hot water	3 tbs	4 tbs
Caster sugar (granulated)	100 g/4 oz	½ cup
Cornflour (cornstarch)	2 tbs	3 tbs
Butter	15 g/½ oz	1 tbs
Icing sugar (confectioners')		

Halve and stone (pit) the apricots and purée the flesh in a blender or food processor. Separate the eggs and place the yolks in a bowl with the water. Whisk until foamy then gradually beat in two thirds of the sugar, until the mixture is creamy. Blend the cornflour with the apricot purée and beat

into the egg yolk mixture. Whisk the egg whites until stiff then gradually whisk in remaining sugar until firm. Fold into apricot mixture.

Transfer to 4 well buttered ramekin dishes standing on a baking sheet (cookie sheet). Dot with butter and place, uncovered, in a preheated moderately hot oven, 190°C, 375°F, Gas Mark 5, for 20 minutes, or until golden brown. Sift a little icing sugar over the tops and serve at once.

Cream cheese soufflé
Serves 4

Ingredients	Metric-Imperial	American
Butter	65 g/2½ oz	⅓ cup
Caster sugar (granulated)	150 g/5 oz	⅔ cup
2 eggs, beaten		

Pinch of salt		
Cream cheese	450 g/1 lb	2 cups
Semolina	125 g/4½ oz	¾ cup
Custard powder (vanilla pudding)	40 g/1½ oz	⅓ cup
Baking powder	1 tbs	1 tbs
Dessert apples	450 g/1 lb	1 lb
Seedless raisins	40 g/1½ oz	¼ cup
Milk	3 tbs	4 tbs

Beat 50 g/2 oz (¼ cup) of the butter with the sugar until light and fluffy. Gradually beat in the eggs, lemon essence, salt and cream cheese, then the semolina, custard powder and baking powder.

Peel, core and chop the apples and add to the mixture with the raisins and milk. Transfer to a greased ovenproof soufflé dish and dot with the remaining butter. Bake, in a preheated moderately hot oven, 190°C, 375°F, Gas Mark 5, for about 1 hour, or until well risen and golden brown.

Cider cooked apples with bread topping
Serves 4

Ingredients	Metric-Imperial	American
4 day-old soft bread rolls		
2 tart dessert apples		
Cider or apple juice	4 tbs	5 tbs
Sugar	75 g/3 oz	1/3 cup
Seedless raisins	50 g/2 oz	1/3 cup
Slivered almonds	40 g/1 1/2 oz	1/3 cup
3 eggs		
Milk	300 ml/1/2 pint	1 1/4 cups
Grated rind of 1 lemon		
Melted butter	25 g/1 oz	2 tbs

Slice the bread rolls and arrange half the slices, overlapping, in the base of a greased ovenproof dish. Peel, quarter and core the apples and cut the flesh into thick slices. Put the cider into a pan with half the sugar and heat gently until the sugar dissolves then add the apple slices and cook until just tender. Spoon over the bread in the dish and scatter the raisins and almonds on top. Cover with the rest of the bread slices.

Beat together the eggs, milk, remaining sugar and lemon rind. Pour evenly over the pudding and sprinkle with the butter. Bake, uncovered, in a preheated moderately hot oven, 190°C, 375°F, Gas Mark 5, for 45 minutes, or until golden brown on top. Serve hot.

Plum and pear soufflé
Serves 4–6

Ingredients	Metric-Imperial	American
Firm ripe pears	450 g/1 lb	1 lb
Lemon juice	2 tbs	3 tbs
Chopped hazelnuts (filberts)	100 g/4 oz	1 cup
Fresh breadcrumbs	50 g/2 oz	1 cup
Soft brown sugar (light)	50 g/2 oz	1/4 cup
Plums	1 kg/2 1/4 lb	2 1/4 lb
Water	125 ml/4 fl oz	1/2 cup
4 eggs		
Butter	65 g/2 1/2 oz	5 tbs
Caster sugar (granulated)	50 g/2 oz	1/4 cup
Whipping cream	225 ml/8 fl oz	1 cup
Flour (all-purpose)	100 g/4 oz	1 cup
Salt	1/4 tsp	1/4 tsp

Peel the pears, halve lengthways and remove the cores. Sprinkle with the lemon juice and place, cut surface downwards, in a greased ovenproof dish. Mix half the nuts with the breadcrumbs and brown sugar and sprinkle one third of this mixture over the pears. Halve and stone the plums and place in a pan with the water. Bring to the boil, cover the pan and cook gently for 5 minutes. Drain the plums and spoon them over the pears. Sprinkle with the remaining nut mixture.

Separate the eggs. Beat about two thirds of the butter until soft and gradually add the egg yolks. Place the sugar in a pan and heat gently, stirring, until it melts and turns golden. Add the remaining butter and when it has melted, stir in the cream. Heat gently, stirring, until the caramel has dissolved. Do not boil. Gradually beat the caramel cream into the egg yolk mixture. Fold in the remaining nuts and the flour. Leave to cool.

Whisk the egg whites in a clean bowl with the salt until stiff then fold into the nut mixture. Spoon over the fruit and level the surface. Bake, uncovered, in a preheated moderate oven, 180°C, 350°F, Gas Mark 4, for 35 minutes, covering the top lightly with a sheet of foil for the last 10 minutes of cooking time to prevent overbrowning.

Strawberry soufflé pudding
Serves 6

Ingredients	Metric-Imperial	American
Strawberries	750 g/1 3/4 lb	1 3/4 lb
Caster sugar (granulated)	200 g/7 oz scant	1 cup
Flour (all-purpose)	65 g/2 1/2 oz	scant 2/3 cup
2 eggs		
Pinch of salt		
Milk	125 ml/4 fl oz	1/2 cup
Grated rind of 1 lemon		
Pinch of ground nutmeg or mixed spice		

Hull and halve the strawberries. Place about two thirds of them in a dish and sprinkle with 2 tbs (3 tbs) of the sugar. Set aside. Reserve a further 2 tbs (3 tbs) of the sugar. Purée the rest of the strawberries with the remaining sugar in a

blender or food processor. Chill the strawberry purée. Separate the eggs. Mix together the flour, salt, egg yolks, milk, lemon rind, nutmeg or mixed spice and the reserved sugar, to make a soft dough.

Place half the dough in a greased ovenproof soufflé dish. Top with the sugared strawberries, reserving the juice. Cover with the rest of the dough. Bake, uncovered, in a preheated moderately hot oven, 190°C, 375°F, Gas Mark 5, for 45 minutes. Meanwhile, whisk the egg whites in a clean bowl until stiff. Add one third to the strawberry purée with the reserved juice and mix lightly. Fold in the remaining egg white. Spoon into the soufflé dish, swirl the top slightly. Reduce oven heat to 180°C, 350°F, Gas Mark 4, and cook for a further 25 minutes, until golden brown on top.

Above: Strawberry soufflé
Opposite: Cider-cooked apples with bread topping

For the sauce:

	Metric-Imperial	American
Hot mustard	4 tbs	5 tbs
Dry mustard (powder)	1 tsp	1 tsp
Sugar	3 tbs	4 tbs
Wine vinegar	2 tbs	3 tbs
Oil	5 tbs	6 tbs
Chopped dill	3 tbs	4 tbs

Wash the trout in running cold water and dry well. Cut in half lengthways and remove the bones. Put one half in a dish with the skin side downwards. Lay the dill over the fish. Mix together the salt, sugar and pepper, scatter over the dill then sprinkle with the brandy. Put the other half of the fish on top. Cover with foil and then weight down with a board and several full cans of food to flatten the fish. Chill for 2–3 days, occasionally basting with the liquid.

Remove the trout, dry on absorbent kitchen paper, then skin. Slice flesh and arrange on serving platter.

To make the sauce mix the mustards with the sugar and wine vinegar. Mix in oil and dill. Serve with the trout.

Left: Marinated salmon trout
Below: Trout in aspic with horseradish sauce

FISH DISHES

Fish offers as much variety as meat when you consider how many different categories there are – the rich, strongly flavoured oily fish like herring, mackerel, trout and salmon; the more subtle and delicate white fish, which may be as finely textured as sole or as robust as cod. Fish has great nutritional value combined with easy digestibility and, in the case of white fish, a low fat content. This makes it the perfect choice for a healthy diet, especially for invalids and slimmers. Then there is the luxury of shellfish, in all its exotic forms and flavours.

Marinated salmon trout
Serves 4

Ingredients	Metric-Imperial	American
1 cleaned salmon trout	1 kg/2¼ lb	2¼ lb
Roughly chopped dill weed	25 g/1 oz	½ cup
Coarse salt	2 tbs	3 tbs
Sugar	1 tbs	1 tbs
Freshly ground white pepper	1 tbs	1 tbs
Brandy	1 tbs	1 tbs

Trout in aspic with horseradish sauce
Serves 6

Ingredients	Metric-Imperial	American
Cold water	4 tbs	5 tbs
Powdered gelatine	4 tsp	4 tsp
1 small onion		
Strong chicken stock (bouillon)	400 ml/14 fl oz	1¾ cups
4 juniper berries		
6 peppercorns		
Pinch of saffron strands		
White wine	250 ml/9 fl oz	generous 1 cup
Wine vinegar	1 tbs	1 tbs
Salt and pepper		
Few drops of Tabasco pepper sauce		
2 hard-boiled eggs		
2 tomatoes		
6 smoked trout fillets		
Cooked or canned asparagus tips	150 g/5 oz	scant 1 cup
Few sprigs of dill weed		
For the sauce:		
Whipping cream	150 ml/¼ pint	⅔ cup
Grated horseradish from a jar	2 tbs	3 tbs
Salt		
Lemon juice		

Put the water into a small bowl and sprinkle on the gelatine. Leave to stand for 10 minutes. Peel and chop the onion. Skim off any fat from the stock, place in a pan and add the onion, juniper berries, peppercorns and saffron. Bring to the boil and simmer for 5 minutes. Strain through a cloth into another pan, bring back to the boil, remove from the heat and stir in the gelatine mixture until it has completely dissolved. Mix in the wine and vinegar, add salt and pepper to taste and the Tabasco.

Shell and slice the eggs and slice the tomatoes. Skin the fish. Arrange the trout, egg, tomato and asparagus tips on six plates and garnish with dill. Pour the aspic over the ingredients and chill until set.

To make the sauce, stir together the cream and horseradish and add salt and lemon juice to taste. Serve with the trout in aspic and hot toast.

Smoked trout as hors d'oeuvre
Serves 1

Ingredients	Metric-Imperial	American
1 endive leaf		
1 chicory leaf (Belgian endive)		
1 orange slice		
1 smoked trout fillet		
Lemon juice	1 tsp	1 tsp
Grated horseradish from a jar	1 tsp	1 tsp
Whipping cream	1 tbs	1 tbs
Chopped dill weed	1 tsp	1 tsp
Lemon juice		
Salt and pepper		

Arrange the salad leaves on a plate with the orange slice. Skin the trout and place on the salad. Sprinkle the fish with lemon juice and add the horseradish to the plate. Mix together the cream and dill with lemon juice, salt and pepper to taste. Spoon over the fish and serve with hot toast.

Delicate fish pâté en croûte
Serves 4

Ingredients	Metric-Imperial	American
2 cleaned trout	225 g/8 oz each	8 oz each
1 onion		
Snipped chives	1 tbs	1 tbs
White wine	125 ml/4 fl oz	½ cup
Oil	5 tbs	6 tbs
Flour (all-purpose)	300 g/11 oz	2¾ cups
4 eggs		
Cold water	1 tbs	1 tbs
Salt	½ tsp	½ tsp
Pork dripping or white vegetable fat	100 g/4 oz	½ cup
Plaice fillets (flounder)	450 g/1 lb	1 lb
Chopped dill	2 tbs	3 tbs
Fresh breadcrumbs	2 tbs	3 tbs
Finely grated rind of 1 lemon		
Whipping cream	150 ml/¼ pint	⅔ cup
Melted butter	50 g/2 oz	¼ cup
Salt and pepper		
Milk	1 tsp	1 tsp

Skin and bone the trout. Wash and dry well. Place the fillets in a dish. Peel and slice the onion and separate the slices into rings. Mix together the chives, wine and oil and pour over the trout flesh. Add the onion, cover and chill overnight.

Above: Smoked trout as hors d'oeuvre
Opposite: Delicate fish pâté en croûte

Bake the pie in a preheated moderately hot oven, 190°C, 375°F, Gas Mark 5, for 30 minutes. Beat together the reserved egg yolk and milk and use to brush the surface of the pie. Return to the oven for a further 45 minutes, or until golden brown. Loosen the pie with a round-bladed knife but leave it in the tin to cool. When cold, remove and wrap in foil. Store in the refrigerator for 1–2 days before cutting. Serve with green salad and remoulade sauce.

Microwave hint

To save time, when using frozen fish fillets, cook them straight from the freezer by microwave. Defrost 450 g/1 lb fillets on low power for 3–4 minutes. The excess liquid created can be drained off and used to prepare a sauce mixture made from, for instance, milk, cornflour (cornstarch) and anchovy essence. Meanwhile, cook the defrosted fish on full power for a further 2 minutes and test that the flesh flakes with a fork. Add any excess liquid to the sauce and cook on medium power for 3 minutes. Stir well and pour over the fish.

Microwave hint

Whole fish, such as trout, can be cooked from frozen. Defrost a trout weighing 450 g/1 lb on low power for 6 minutes, then cook on full power for 4 minutes, turning halfway through cooking time.

Sift the flour into a bowl and make a well in the centre. Separate one egg and add half the yolk and half the white to the bowl with 1 more egg. Reserve the rest of the egg yolk and egg white separately. Put in the water and salt and mix in a little of the flour to make a very wet sticky dough. Dice the fat, add to the bowl and mix all the ingredients together. Knead until smooth. Cover and chill for at least 4 hours.

Skin the plaice fillets and mince finely or purée in a food processor. Stir in the remaining 2 eggs, the dill, breadcrumbs, lemon rind, cream and butter. Season to taste with salt and pepper.

Knead the dough until smooth, take two thirds and roll this out on a lightly floured surface. Grease a large loaf-shaped tin measuring approximately 30 cm/12 inches by 12.5 cm/5 inches. Cut rectangles from the rolled dough to line the base, short sides and long sides of the chosen tin. Put the base into the tin and brush the edges with some of the reserved egg white. Position the sides in the tin, brushing the edges again with egg white and press all the joins together to seal.

Spoon half the plaice mixture into the base of the pastry case. Remove the trout fillets from the marinade, dry on absorbent kitchen paper and arrange on the plaice mixture. Top with the remaining plaice mixture. Trim the pastry case to about 1.25 cm/½ inch above the level of the filling. Roll out the remaining dough to make a lid and cut 2–3 2.5 cm/1 inch steam vents in it. Cut fancy shapes from the pastry trimmings using cocktail cutters. Brush the lid with egg white, position the pastry decorations then brush the edges of the pastry case with egg white and put on the lid. Seal the edges together well.

Vegetable and fish casserole with saffron rice
Serves 6

Ingredients	Metric-Imperial	American
Onions	225 g/8 oz	8 oz
6 sticks of celery (stalks)		
Grated rind and juice of 1 lime or small lemon		
4 cloves of garlic		
Margarine	65 g/2½ oz	5 tbs
Leeks	1 kg/2¼ lb	2¼ lb
Chicken stock (bouillon)	1 L/1¾ pints	4⅓ cups
White fish fillets such as cod or haddock	1½ kg/3 lb 5 oz	3 lb 5 oz
6 shelled cooked jumbo prawns (shrimp)		
Frozen peas	175 g/6 oz	1 cup
1 sprig of tarragon		
Chopped basil	2 tbs	3 tbs
Chopped parsley	2 tbs	3 tbs
Salt		
For the saffron rice:		
2 sweet peppers		
Saffron strands	¼ tsp	¼ tsp
Salted water	500 ml/18 fl oz	2¼ cups
Long grain rice	200 g/7 oz	scant 1 cup

Peel and slice the onions. Trim the celery, removing any strings. Slice thinly and sprinkle with the lemon juice. Peel and chop the garlic. Melt the margarine in a large pan and use to cook the onion, celery and garlic for 5 minutes. Trim and clean the leeks and cut into slices. Add to the pan with the stock and bring to the boil. Simmer for 5 minutes.

Meanwhile, wash and dry the fish. Discard the skin and cut the flesh into bite-sized pieces. Add the fish, prawns and peas to the soup with the tarragon. Bring to the boil, cover and simmer for 10 minutes. Put in the chopped herbs and lemon rind and season to taste with salt.

To cook the rice, deseed and chop the pepper. Put the salted water into a pan, add the pepper and saffron and bring to the boil. Sprinkle in the rice, bring back to the boil, cover and simmer for 12 minutes, or until the rice is tender and the water absorbed. Serve with the fish casserole.

Microwave method

Peel the onion and cut into strips. Trim the celery, remove the strings and slice thinly. Sprinkle the celery with lemon juice. Peel and chop the garlic.

Melt the margarine in a browning dish on full power for 1 minute, tip in the onion, celery and garlic and cook on full power for 2 minutes.

Trim and clean the leeks and cut into slices. Put into a large pyrex bowl. Add the cooked vegetables and the hot stock. Cook on full power for 10 minutes.

Meanwhile prepare the fish by skinning and cutting into bite-sized pieces. Add the fish with the prawns, peas and tarragon to the bowl of stock. Cover and cook for 10 minutes. Stir in the chopped herbs and lemon rind and allow to stand for 3 minutes.

Mix the saffron in a little liquid from the soup and allow to stand. Put 475 ml/16 fl oz (2 cups) of boiling water into a suitable dish with a pinch of salt. Sprinkle in the rice with the chopped deseeded pepper and the saffron. Cover and cook for 8 minutes or until water is absorbed. Remove and fork the rice and allow to stand for 2 minutes.

Return the fish to the microwave and allow to cook for a further 8 minutes. Check that the fish is cooked before serving with the rice.

Plaice fillets with mayonnaise on toast
Serves 4

Ingredients	Metric-Imperial	American
Plaice fillets (flounder)	350 g/12 oz	12 oz
Flour (all-purpose)		
Fat or oil for shallow frying		
4 slices of white bread		
For the mayonnaise:		
1 egg yolk		
Tarragon vinegar	2 tbs	3 tbs
French mustard	1 tsp	1 tsp
Salt		
Sugar		
Oil	125 ml/4 fl oz	½ cup
Snipped chives	1 tbs	1 tbs
Tomato ketchup	1 tbs	1 tbs

First make the mayonnaise. Beat the egg yolk with the vinegar, mustard and a little salt and sugar. Gradually beat in the oil until the dressing is thick. Adjust the seasoning if necessary and fold in the chives and ketchup.

Wash and dry the plaice fillets. Cut into 2.5 cm/1 inch strips and coat the strips in flour. Melt a little fat, or heat oil, in a pan and use to fry the plaice strips for 2–3 minutes, turning them occasionally, until evenly golden brown. Keep hot.

Toast the bread and arrange the hot fish on it. Spoon the mayonnaise over the top and serve at once.

Below: Vegetable and fish casserole with saffron rice
Opposite: Plaice fillets with mayonnaise on toast

109

Matjes herring in cream cheese sauce
Serves 4

Ingredients	Metric-Imperial	American
6 matjes herring fillets		
2 medium-sized onions,		
red-skinned if possible		
2 dessert apples		
Double cream (heavy)	125 ml/4 fl oz	½ cup
Cream cheese	225 g/8 oz	8 oz
Salt and pepper		

Lemon juice
Few sprigs of dill

Cut the herring fillets into bite-sized pieces. Peel and slice the onions and divide the slices into rings. Peel, core and dice the apples.

Whip the cream until thick. Beat the cream cheese until soft and combine with the cream. Fold in the herring pieces, onion rings and diced apple. Add salt, pepper and lemon juice to taste and chill for 1 hour. Serve with potatoes or wholemeal bread and butter, garnished with dill.

Above: Matjes herring in cream
Opposite: Matjes herring in cream cheese sauce

Matjes herring in cream
Serves 6

Ingredients	Metric-Imperial	American
6 matjes herring fillets		
For the sauce:		
Onions	225 g/8 oz	8 oz
2 gherkins (small dill pickles)		
Whipping cream	350 ml/12 fl oz	1½ cups
Vinegar	4 tbs	5 tbs
Mustard seeds	1 tbs	1 tbs
8 peppercorns		

Soak the herring fillets in water for 2 hours if very salty. Drain and dry on absorbent kitchen paper. Cut into 2.5 cm/1 inch wide strips.

To make the sauce, peel and slice the onions and slice the gherkins. Beat together the cream, vinegar, mustard seeds and peppercorns. Add the onion and gherkin and the herring fillets. Chill for 24 hours before serving.

Fried sardines in sherry sauce
Serves 6

Ingredients	Metric-Imperial	American
Cleaned sardines	675 g/1½ lb	1½ lb
Lemon juice	2 tbs	3 tbs
Salt and pepper		
Flour (all-purpose)	2 tbs	3 tbs
Butter	50 g/2 oz	¼ cup
Oil	2 tbs	3 tbs

For the marinade:		
Water	300 ml/½ pint	1¼ cups
Wine vinegar	2 tbs	3 tbs
2 onions		
1 carrot		
1 leek		
Mustard seeds	1 tsp	1 tsp
6 peppercorns		
Ground ginger		
Sugar		
Sherry	500 ml/18 fl oz	2¼ cups

Wash and dry sardines. Sprinkle with lemon juice, leave for 15 minutes. Dry again, and coat in flour.

Melt the butter in a large frying pan, add the oil and fry the sardines, in batches, for 3–4 minutes, turning once, until crisp and brown. Remove, drain, leave to cool.

To make the marinade, put the water and vinegar in a pan. Peel and slice the onion, then divide the slices into rings. Peel and chop the carrot. Trim, clean and chop the leek. Add the onion, carrot and leek to the pan with the mustard seeds, peppercorns and a little ginger and sugar. Simmer for 15 minutes, add sherry and reheat.

Put the sardines in a bowl and pour the marinade over. Cool and then chill for 2 days.

Prawn cocktail
Serves 4

Ingredients	Metric-Imperial	American
Cooked shelled prawns (shrimp)	350 g/12 oz	2 cups
Lettuce leaves		
Lemon slices		
Cocktail cherries		
Sprigs of fresh herbs		
For the mayonnaise:		
1 egg yolk		
Lemon juice	1 tbs	1 tbs
Tomato ketchup	1 tbs	1 tbs
Sugar	1 tsp	1 tsp
Salt		
Oil	125 ml/4 fl oz	½ cup

First make the mayonnaise. Beat together the egg yolk, lemon juice, ketchup, sugar and a little salt. When the mixture has the consistency of thin cream gradually add the oil, beating until the dressing is thick. Add more salt to taste.

Defrost the prawns if frozen. Drain well. Line 4 dishes with lettuce leaves and divide the prawns among them. Spoon the mayonnaise over the top and garnish with lemon slices, cocktail cherries and herbs. Serve with toast or thinly sliced brown bread and butter.

Mackerel in dill marinade
Serves 4

Ingredients	Metric-Imperial	American
4 mackerel		
2 onions		
For the marinade:		
Wine vinegar	125 ml/4 fl oz	½ cup
Water	225 ml/8 fl oz	1 cup
10 peppercorns		
2 bay leaves		
5 juniper berries		
Sugar	1 tbs	1 tbs
Salt		
Chopped dill weed	2 tbs	3 tbs

Halve, bone and skin mackerel. Wash and dry. Peel and slice onions and divide into rings. Arrange mackerel fillets in a glass or earthenware jar. Top with onion rings.

Put vinegar, water, peppercorns, baby leaves, juniper berries, sugar and a little salt into a pan. Bring to the boil. Simmer for 5 minutes, then pour over fish. Cool then chill for 2 days. Drain, then serve on a dish sprinkled with dill.

Below: Prawn cocktails
Opposite: Rolled fillet of sole with herbed mayonnaise

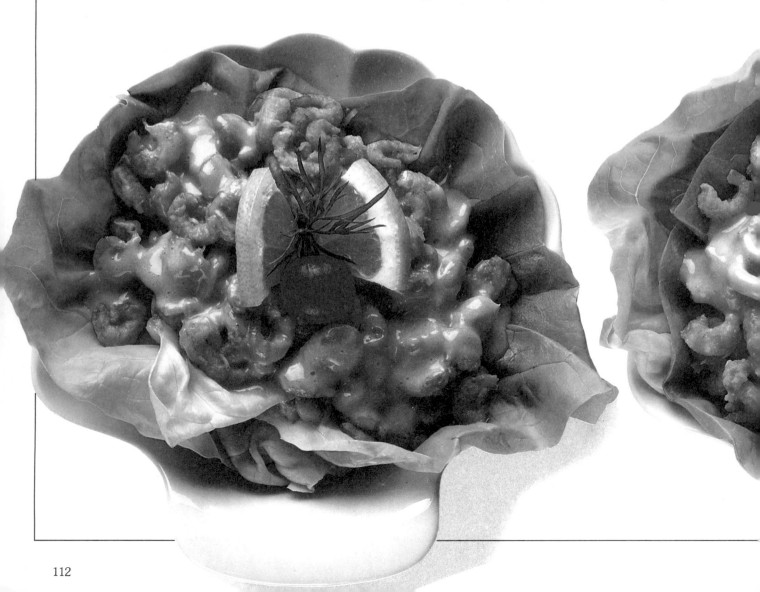

Lobster cocktail
Serves 4

Ingredients	Metric-Imperial	American
Butter	25 g/1 oz	2 tbs
1 clove of garlic		
Chopped dill weed	2 tbs	3 tbs
4 cooked shelled lobster tails		
Salt		
4 lettuce leaves		
For the sauce:		
Whipping cream	150 ml/¼ pint	⅔ cup
Dry sherry	1 tbs	1 tbs
Worcestershire sauce	1 tsp	1 tsp
Lemon juice	1 tsp	1 tsp
Salt and pepper		
Sugar		

Melt butter in a pan. Peel and crush garlic, add to butter with half the dill, cook for 3 minutes. Put in lobster tails, season with salt and heat through thoroughly. Leave to cool.

To make the sauce, stir together the cream, sherry, Worcestershire sauce and lemon juice and season with salt, pepper and sugar to haste.

Line 4 glasses with lettuce leaves, arrange lobster tails on top and spoon sauce over. Sprinkle with remaining dill.

Rolled fillets of sole with herbed mayonnaise
Serves 4

Ingredients	Metric-Imperial	American
12 sole fillets	750 g/1¾ lb	1¾ lb
White wine	125 ml/4 fl oz	½ cup
Water	125 ml/4 fl oz	½ cup
6 peppercorns		
Few mustard seeds		
Wine vinegar	2 tbs	3 tbs
Salt	1 tsp	1 tsp
Pepper	¼ tsp	¼ tsp
12 canned artichoke bottoms		
3 large tomatoes		
For the mayonnaise		
1 egg yolk		
Vinegar	2 tbs	3 tbs
French mustard	1 tsp	1 tsp
Sugar	1 tsp	1 tsp
Salt and pepper		
Oil	125 ml/4 fl oz	½ cup
Sour cream	4 tbs	5 tbs
Snipped chives	1 tbs	1 tbs
Chopped parsley	1 tbs	1 tbs

Roll up the sole fillets and secure with wooden cocktail sticks (toothpicks). Put the wine, water, peppercorns, mustard seeds, vinegar, salt and pepper into a pan and bring to the boil. Put in the fish rolls, bring back to the boil and simmer for about 5 minutes. Remove the fish rolls from the liquid, discard the sticks and chill.

To make the mayonnaise, beat together the egg yolk, vinegar, mustard, sugar and a little salt and pepper. When the mixture is the consistency of thin cream gradually add the oil and beat until the dressing is thick. Sir in the cream, chives and parsley and adjust the seasoning to taste with more salt and pepper.

Slice the artichoke bottoms and tomatoes. Place a slice of tomato on a slice of artichoke, top with a fish roll and secure with a cocktail stick. Make up the rest of the ingredients in the same way. Serve with the mayonnaise.

Trout Florentine
Serves 4

Ingredients	Metric-Imperial	American
Frozen leaf spinach	550 g/1¼ lb	1¼ lb
Streaky bacon (strips)	75 g/3 oz	6 strips
1 medium-sized onion		
Salt and pepper		
4 cleaned trout	225 g/8 oz each	8 oz each
Lemon juice	2 tbs	3 tbs
Flour (all-purpose)	4 tbs	5 tbs
Margarine	65 g/2½ oz	5 tbs
Dry white wine	3 tbs	4 tbs
Whipping cream	150 ml/¼ pint	⅔ cup

Defrost the spinach at room temperature and drain thoroughly. Chop the bacon, place in a large frying pan and heat gently until the fat runs. Peel and chop the onion, add to the bacon and cook until translucent. Put in the spinach and cook for about 5 minutes, stirring frequently. Season to taste with salt and pepper. Transfer to a greased shallow ovenproof dish.

Wash the trout and dry well. Sprinkle the fish inside and out with lemon juice and allow to stand for 15 minutes. Dry the fish on absorbent kitchen paper, sprinkle with salt and coat with the flour.

Wipe out the frying pan and use to melt the margarine. Add the trout and fry for 5 minutes on each side, or until golden brown. Place the fish side-by-side on top of the spinach and cook in a preheated moderately hot oven, 200°C, 400°F, Gas Mark 6, for 20 minutes.

Meanwhile, loosen the sediment in the frying pan with the wine, blend in the cream, season lightly with salt and pepper and bring to just below boiling point, stirring. Pour over the trout and return the dish to the oven for a further 5 minutes, until the fish are cooked through.

Cook's tip: 'Florentine' describes any dish cooked with spinach. White fish lends itself particularly well to the Florentine treatment, as do eggs and veal.
Variation: Omit the bacon, and use 100 g/4 oz thinly sliced button mushrooms instead.

Cod in tomato sauce
Serves 4

Ingredients	Metric-Imperial	American
1 small onion		
Water	1 L/1¾ pints	4⅓ cups
6 peppercorns		
1 bay leaf		
Few mustard seeds		
Salt	2 tsp	2 tsp
Freshly ground black pepper		
Tailpiece of cod, weight	750 g/1¾ lb	1¾ lb
For the sauce:		
1 small onion		
Butter or margarine	40 g/1½ oz	3 tbs
Flour (all-purpose)	40 g/1½ oz	⅓ cup
Tomato purée (paste)	3 tbs	4 tbs
Sugar		
Salt and pepper		
Sweet paprika pepper	½ tsp	½ tsp
Lemon juice	1 tsp	1 tsp

Peel and quarter the onion. Place in a pan with the water, peppercorns, bay leaf, mustard seeds, salt and a grinding of pepper. Bring to the boil, put in the cod, bring back to the boil then simmer for 10 minutes. Remove the fish from the pan, discard the skin and bones and cut the flesh into bite-sized pieces. Keep hot.

To make the sauce, strain the fish stock, measure and reserve 500 ml/18 fl oz (2¼ cups). Peel and chop the onion. Melt the butter or margarine in a pan and use to cook the onion until pale golden. Sprinkle in the flour and stir until the roux is pale brown. Gradually add the fish stock and stir until boiling. Simmer for 2 minutes. Mix in the tomato purée, add a pinch of sugar, salt and pepper to taste, the paprika and lemon juice. Cook for a further 5 minutes, taste and adjust the seasoning if necessary. Carefully add the fish pieces and heat through. If liked, serve sprinkled with chopped parsley.

Variation: Add fried onion rings, or strips of red sweet pepper to the sauce if desired.

Left: Trout Florentine
Opposite: Halibut in herbed butter

Halibut in herbed butter
Serves 4

Ingredients	Metric-Imperial	American
4 halibut steaks	225 g/8 oz each	8 oz each
Lemon juice	2 tbs	3 tbs
1 onion		
2 tomatoes		
Salt and pepper		
Butter	100 g/4 oz	½ cup
Chopped dill weed	2 tbs	3 tbs
Chopped tarragon	2 tbs	3 tbs
Chopped basil	2 tbs	3 tbs
Few drops of Worcestershire sauce		

Sprinkle the halibut steaks with the lemon juice and leave to stand for 15 minutes. Drain well. Peel and chop the onion, chop the tomatoes and put both these into a greased oval ovenproof dish. Sprinkle the fish with salt and pepper and place on top of the onion and tomato.

Beat the butter until soft and add the herbs. Season with the Worcestershire sauce and salt and pepper to taste. Dot the fish with the herbed butter, cover and cook in a preheated moderate oven, 180°C, 350°F, Gas Mark 4, for 35 minutes, or until cooked through. Serve with potatoes and a mixed salad.

Cook's tip: Dill, tarragon and basil have particular affinities with fish. Herb butter shaped into a roll, chilled, then cut into pats, also makes an attractive garnish for fish.

Carp in beer sauce
Serves 5

Ingredients	Metric-Imperial	American
1 cleaned carp	1.5 kg/3¼ lb	3¼ lb
1 large onion		
1 carrot		
Butter	25 g/1 oz	2 tbs
Flour (all-purpose)	1 tbs	1 tbs
Light ale (light beer)	500 ml/18 fl oz	2¼ cups
1 bay leaf		
2 whole cloves		
2 peppercorns		
Salt		
5 lemon slices		
Honey cake	100 g/4 oz	4 oz
Seedless raisins	1 tbs	
Shredded almonds	1 tbs	
Lemon juice	1 tsp	1 tsp
Sugar		
Little extra ale or red wine		

Wash the carp thoroughly, pat dry and cut into thick steaks. Peel and chop the onion. Peel the carrot and cut into julienne strips. Melt half the butter in a pan, add the onion and carrot and cook, stirring frequently, until limp. Remove and keep hot. Add the remaining butter to the pan, blend in the flour and stir until the roux is brown. Gradually whisk in the ale and bring to the boil, stirring. Add the bay leaf, cloves, peppercorns, ½ tsp salt and lemon slices. Simmer, covered, for 30 minutes. Strain into a large shallow pan.

Crumble the honey cake into the sauce and stir in the raisins and almonds. Bring to the boil, add the lemon juice and season to taste with more salt and a little sugar. Arrange the fish steaks side-by-side in the sauce and cook over low heat for about 20 minutes, adding more ale or red wine if necessary, until the fish is cooked through. Arrange fish on a warm serving dish and garnish with reserved vegetables and fresh lemon slices. Hand sauce separately.

Larded trout with vegetables
Serves 4

Ingredients	Metric-Imperial	American
2 cleaned trout	450 g/1 lb each	1 lb each
Lemon juice	2 tbs	3 tbs
Salt		
Streaky bacon (strips)	150 g/5 oz	10 strips
6 tomatoes		
2 medium-sized aubergines (eggplant)		
1 leek		
2 onions		
Butter or margarine	50 g/2 oz	¼ cup
For the sauce:		
Flour (all-purpose)	1 tbs	1 tbs
Sour cream	225 ml/8 fl oz	1 cup
Sweet paprika pepper		
Salt		

Trim the trout. Wash and dry on absorbent kitchen paper. Sprinkle with the lemon juice and leave to stand for 15 minutes. Dry again and sprinkle with salt. Cut the bacon into strips and use to lard the fish. Lay remaining bacon strips in a greased ovenproof dish.

Pour boiling water over the tomatoes, drain, peel and slice. Slice the aubergines. Trim and clean the leek and then slice. Peel and slice the onions. Arrange the vegetables on the bacon. Put the fish on top and dot with the butter or margarine. Cook, uncovered, in a preheated moderately hot oven, 200°C, 400°F, Gas Mark 6, for 35–40 minutes, or until the fish is cooked through. Transfer the fish, bacon and vegetables to a warm serving dish and keep hot.

Pour the juices from the cooking dish into a pan. Blend the flour with the sour cream, add to the pan and stir until boiling. Season to taste with paprika and salt and simmer for 5 minutes. Serve the sauce with the fish dish.

Variations: Diced sweet pepper, fennel, celery and carrots would also make good additions to the vegetable mixture.
Serving ideas: Serve the trout and vegetables with a gratin dauphinois or potato purée. No other vegetable accompaniment would be needed.

Left: Carp in beer sauce
Opposite: Larded trout with vegetables

Fish casserole, Provençal style
Serves 4

Ingredients	Metric-Imperial	American
2 onions		
1 leek		
Red, green and yellow sweet peppers	450 g/1 lb	1 lb
3 'beefsteak' tomatoes		
2 cloves of garlic		
Oil	3 tbs	4 tbs
Dried thyme	½ tsp	½ tsp
Pinch of dried sage		
1 bay leaf		
Dry white wine	125 ml/4 fl oz	½ cup
White fish fillets such as cod or haddock	750 g/1¾ lb	1¾ lb
Whipping cream	150 ml/¼ pint	⅔ cup
½ chicken or fish stock cube (bouillon)		
Cayenne pepper		
Salt		
Lemon juice		

Peel and chop the onions. Halve the leek lengthways, clean and then slice. Deseed the peppers and cut the flesh into strips. Pour boiling water over the tomatoes, drain, peel and cut into pieces. Peel and crush the garlic. Heat the oil in a pan, add the onion, leek, pepper, tomato and garlic and cook, stirring frequently, until limp. Sprinkle in the herbs, add the bay leaf and wine and bring to the boil. Simmer for 8 minutes.

Cut the fish into bite-sized pieces. Add the cream to the vegetable mixture and crumble in the stock cube. Stir well, add the fish pieces, season carefully with cayenne and salt and add a little lemon juice to taste. Cook gently for about 15 minutes, until the fish is cooked through. Serve with rice or boiled potatoes.

Baked halibut platter
Serves 4

Ingredients	Metric-Imperial	American
4 halibut steaks	225 g/8 oz each	8 oz each
Lemon juice	2 tbs	3 tbs
Salt and pepper		
Sweet paprika pepper		
Canned asparagus tips	225 g/8 oz can	8 oz can
Canned drained diced carrots	100 g/4 oz	⅔ cup
Canned drained peas	100 g/4 oz	⅔ cup
Melted butter	15 g/½ oz	1 tbs
For the sauce:		
1 small onion		
Canned mushrooms	225 g/8 oz can	8 oz can
Butter	25 g/1 oz	2 tbs
Flour (all-purpose)	1 tbs	1 tbs
Salt and pepper		

Sprinkle the halibut steaks with the lemon juice and leave to stand for 15 minutes. Pat dry and sprinkle with salt, pepper

and paprika. Place the steaks in the centre of a greased ovenproof platter.

Drain the asparagus and arrange round the fish with the carrots and peas. Sprinkle the fish and vegetables with salt and then with the butter. Cover with foil and place in a preheated moderately hot oven, 200°C, 400°F, Gas Mark 6, for 25 minutes, or until the fish is cooked through.

To make the sauce, peel and chop the onion. Drain the mushrooms and make the liquid up to 125 ml/4 fl oz (½ cup) with water if necessary. Heat the butter in a pan and use to fry the onion until golden. Add the mushrooms and heat through. Stir in the flour then gradually add the mushroom liquid and stir until boiling. Season to taste with salt and pepper and simmer for 5 minutes. Serve with the fish platter, garnished with a slice of lemon and sprig of dill weed if wished.

Microwave method
Sprinkle the steaks with lemon juice and leave to stand for 15 minutes. Place the steaks in a suitable deep dish with 125 ml/4 fl oz (½ cup of water), cover and cook on full power for 10 minutes.

Drain the liquid from the fish into a bowl. Drain the asparagus, carrots and peas. Arrange the vegetables around the fish. Sprinkle the fish with paprika and season the vegetables lightly.

To make the sauce, peel and chop the onion. Drain the mushrooms and make up the liquid to 125 ml/4 fl oz (½ cup) with the fish liquid. Put the browning dish in the microwave for 1 minute. Remove, add the butter and leave on full power for 40 seconds then add the onion and cook on full power for 2 minutes. Sprinkle in the flour and mix well with some of the reserved liquid. Make sure the sauce is smooth and free from lumps then add the mushrooms and seasoning. Return to the microwave at full power for 4 minutes. Remove and mix well, taste and adjust seasoning.

Pour the sauce over the fish. Dot the vegetables with butter and return to the microwave, covered, for 7 minutes. Serve straight from the dish.

Opposite: Fish casserole Provençale style
Above: Baked halibut platter

119

White fish steaks in beer sauce
Serves 4

Ingredients	Metric-Imperial	American
4 white fish steaks such as cod or haddock	225 g/8 oz each	8 oz each
Lemon juice	1 tbs	1 tbs
Salt		
Leeks	225 g/8 oz	8 oz
Carrots	225 g/8 oz	8 oz
Piece of celeriac	225 g/8 oz	8 oz
1 parsnip		
Butter or margarine	25 g/1 oz	2 tbs
Stout (dark beer)	225 ml/8 fl oz	1 cup
Light ale (light beer)	300 ml/½ pint	1¼ cups
½ chicken or fish stock cube (bouillon)		
4 peppercorns		
Freshly ground black pepper		
Grated lemon rind	½ tsp	½ tsp
Flour (all-purpose)	2 tbs	3 tbs
Sugar		

Sprinkle the fish steaks with the lemon juice and leave to stand for 15 minutes. Drain well and sprinkle with salt.

Clean the leeks, peel the carrots, celeriac and parsnip then cut all the vegetables into strips. Melt the butter or margarine in a pan, stir in the vegetables and cook until they are limp. Mix in the stout and ale, add the stock cube, peppercorns, 1 grinding of pepper and the lemon rind. Bring to the boil, cover and simmer for 10 minutes. Add the fish steaks to the sauce and simmer for a further 15 minutes, or until cooked through. Transfer the fish to a warm serving dish and keep hot.

Moisten the flour with a little cold water, add to the pan and stir until boiling. Adjust the seasoning with salt, pepper and sugar to taste and simmer for a further 10 minutes. Serve poured over the fish.

Microwave hint
To cook thin fillets of fish evenly by microwave, arrange them in a dish, tucking the thinnest part underneath the remainder of the fillet.

Above: White fish steaks in beer sauce
Opposite: Halibut steaks with herbed cream topping

Halibut steaks with herbed cream cheese topping

Serves 4

Ingredients	Metric-Imperial	American
4 halibut steaks	225 g/8 oz each	8 oz each
Lemon juice	2 tbs	3 tbs
1 carrot		
3 spring onions (scallions)		
2 courgettes (zucchini)		
Dry white wine	75 ml/3 fl oz	⅓ cup
Butter	15 g/½ oz	1 tbs
Fish stock (bouillon)	75 ml/3 fl oz	⅓ cup
Salt and pepper		
Cream cheese with herbs	225 g/8 oz	1 cup

Sprinkle the halibut steaks with the lemon juice and leave to stand for 15 minutes. Drain well.

Peel the carrot and cut into strips. Trim off the darker green ends of the spring onions then cut into slices obliquely. Top and tail the courgettes and slice thinly. Put the vegetables into a wide shallow pan with the wine, butter and stock. Bring to the boil, cover and simmer for 15 minutes. Put the fish steaks into the pan on the vegetables, season with salt and pepper then cover the pan again and simmer for a further 10 minutes, or until the fish is cooked.

Meanwhile, put the cream cheese into a bowl over a pan of simmering water and stir until creamy. Transfer fish and vegetables to a warm serving dish, top with cream cheese.

121

Fish with onions and green peppercorns
Serves 4

Ingredients	Metric-Imperial	American
4 hake fillets	225 g/8 oz each	8 oz each
Juice of 1 lemon		
Onions	225 g/8 oz	8 oz
Butter	25 g/1 oz	2 tbs
Salt and pepper		
Chopped tarragon	1 tsp	1 tsp
Light ale (light beer)	125 ml/4 fl oz	½ cup
Whipping cream	125 ml/4 fl oz	½ cup
Drained green peppercorns	1 tbs	1 tbs

Sprinkle the hake fillets with the lemon juice and leave to stand for 15 minutes. Drain well.

Peel and slice the onions. Melt the butter in a pan and use to fry the onion slices until limp. Sprinkle the fish with salt, pepper and the tarragon and place on the onion in the pan. Cover and cook for 10–15 minutes, or until the fillets are cooked through. Transfer them to a warm serving dish and keep hot.

Blend the ale and cream into the pan juices with the peppercorns. Stir until just below boiling and season to taste with salt and pepper. Pour over the fish and serve with boiled potatoes sprinkled with chopped dill weed.

Below: Fish with onions and green peppercorns
Opposite: Fried prawns with sherry and dill

Fillet of cod, Creole style
Serves 4

Ingredients	Metric-Imperial	American
Cod fillets	750 g/1¾ lb	1¾ lb
Lemon juice	2 tbs	3 tbs
Salt		
Canned sweetcorn kernels	200 g/7 oz can	7 oz can
Streaky bacon (strips)	75 g/3 oz	6 strips
Butter or margarine	25 g/1 oz	2 tbs
Chopped parsley or chervil	1 tbs	1 tbs

Cut the cod into 2.5 cm/1 inch cubes. Sprinkle with the lemon juice and leave for 15 minutes. Drain well and sprinkle with salt.

Drain the corn. Chop the bacon and place in a pan with the corn and half the butter. Cook, stirring frequently, until the bacon just begins to turn golden. Put the fish cubes into the centre of a greased shallow ovenproof dish and spoon the corn mixture around the fish. Dot the fish cubes with the remaining butter, cover the dish with lid or foil and cook in a preheated oven, 220°C, 425°F, Gas Mark 7, for 25–30 minutes, or until the fish is cooked through. Sprinkle with parsley or chervil and serve with fried or boiled potatoes.

Fish in white wine sauce
Serves 2–3

Ingredients	Metric-Imperial	American
White fish fillets such as sole or plaice (flounder)	450 g/1 lb	1 lb
Lemon juice	1 tbs	1 tbs
Salt		
1 onion		
Butter	25 g/1 oz	2 tbs
Dry white wine	125 ml/4 fl oz	½ cup
For the sauce:		
Whipping cream	150 ml/¼ pint	⅔ cup
Tomato ketchup	4 tbs	5 tbs
Salt and pepper		
Sugar		
Chopped parsley or chervil	1 tbs	1 tbs

Sprinkle the fish fillets with the lemon juice and leave them to stand for 15 minutes. Drain the fillets and sprinkle with salt. Set aside.

Peel and chop the onion. Melt the butter in a pan and use to fry the onion until transparent. Add the fish fillets and wine and bring to the boil. Cover and simmer for about 10 minutes, or until the fish is cooked through. Transfer the fish fillets to a warm serving dish and keep hot while you make the sauce.

To make the sauce, stir the cream and tomato ketchup into the cooking liquid and season to taste with salt, pepper and sugar. Stir until the sauce comes to boiling point, pour over the fish and serve sprinkled with parsley or chervil, accompanied by buttered new potatoes.

Fried prawns with sherry and dill
Serves 4

Ingredients	Metric-Imperial	American
Frozen shelled cooked jumbo prawns (shrimp)	450 g/1 lb	1 lb
3 cloves of garlic		
Butter	25 g/1 oz	2 tbs
Salt and pepper		
Dry sherry	3 tbs	4 tbs
Chopped dill weed	2 tbs	3 tbs
Lemon wedges		
Sprig of dill		

Defrost the prawns and drain well on absorbent paper.

Peel and very finely chop the garlic. Melt the bu... use to cook the garlic until transparent. Add the prawns, season with salt and pepper, pour on the sherry and add the chopped dill. Bring to the boil, cover and simmer for 5 minutes. Transfer the shellfish to a warm serving dish and garnish with lemon wedges and a sprig of dill. Spoon the pan juices over the prawns and serve with French bread and butter.

Simple poached cod
Serves 4

Ingredients	Metric-Imperial	American
Tail piece of cod	1.5 kg/3¼ lb	3¼ lb
Lemon juice	2 tbs	3 tbs
1 onion		
2 carrots		
1 leek		
Small piece of celeriac		
Mixed herbs	75 g/3 oz	3 oz
1 bay leaf		
10 black peppercorns		
5 white peppercorns		
3 whole cloves		
Mustard seeds	¼ tsp	¼ tsp
1 lemon, sliced		
Water	250 ml/9 fl oz	generous 1 cup
Vinegar	1 tbs	1 tbs
Salt	1 tsp	1 tsp

Sprinkle the cod with the lemon juice and leave to stand for 15 minutes. Drain well.

Peel and slice the onion and divide the slices into rings. Peel and slice the carrots, trim, clean and slice the leek. Peel the celeriac and cut into small pieces. Add the fish and all remaining ingredients to a large baking tin or fish kettle and cover with foil. Place in a preheated moderately hot oven, 190°C, 375°F, Gas Mark 5, for 40 minutes, or until the fish is cooked through. Transfer it to a warm dish and serve with melted butter if wished.

Microwave method
Sprinkle the fish with lemon juice and leave to stand for 15 minutes.

Peel and slice the onion and divide the slices into rings. Peel and slice the carrots; trim, clean and slice the leek. Peel the celeriac and cut into small pieces.

Put the fish into a suitable dish, arrange the vegetables around the fish with the remaining ingredients and the water. Cover and cook on full power for 10 minutes. Turn the fish carefully and baste with the liquid. Cook for a further 10 minutes on full power and allow to stand for 5 minutes.

Divide the fish and serve with a spoonful of vegetables and a little melted butter poured over each portion.

Steamed halibut
Serves 4

Ingredients	Metric-Imperial	American
4 halibut steaks	225 g/8 oz each	8 oz each
Lemon juice	2 tbs	3 tbs
Salt and pepper		
1 small onion		
Butter	25 g/1 oz	2 tbs
Water	2 tbs	3 tbs
10 black peppercorns		
1 bay leaf		
1 whole clove		
Sprigs of parsley		

Sprinkle the halibut steaks with lemon juice and le[ ] stand for 15 minutes. Drain well and sprinkle with sa[ ] pepper.

Peel and chop the onion. Melt the butter in a pan and use to cook the onion until transparent. Add the fish steaks with the water, peppercorns, bay leaf and clove. Cover and cook gently for 10 minutes, or until the fish is cooked through. Transfer to a warm serving dish and garnish with parsley.

Tunafish steaks Alhambra
Serves 4

Ingredients	Metric-Imperial	American
4 tuna steaks	200 g/7 oz each	7 oz each
Lemon juice	2 tbs	3 tbs
Salt and pepper		
Flour (all-purpose)	50 g/2 oz	½ cup
1 clove of garlic		
Butter	40 g/1½ oz	3 tbs
1 large onion		
4 tomatoes		
Oil	3 tbs	4 tbs
Dried oregano	1 tsp	1 tsp
White wine	125 ml/4 fl oz	½ cup

Sprinkle the tuna steaks with the lemon juice and leave to stand for 15 minutes. Drain and season with salt. Coat in flour. Peel and crush the garlic. Melt the butter in a frying pan, add the garlic and fry for 3 minutes. Remove garlic and fry fish steaks for about 2 minutes on each side.

Meanwhile, peel and chop the onion and tomatoes. Heat the oil in a pan, add the onion and cook gently until soft. Put in the tomato and cook for 3 minutes. Season with salt and pepper and spoon over steaks. Sprinkle with oregano and add the wine. Cover and cook gently for 10 minutes, or until steaks are cooked through. Transfer to a warm dish and spoon pan juices over.

Rolled fish fillets with tomato sauce
Serves 4

Ingredients	Metric-Imperial	American
White fish fillets such as sole or plaice (flounder)	750 g/1¾ lb	1¾ lb
Lemon juice	2 tbs	3 tbs
Salt		
Celery salt		
Sweet paprika pepper		
4 gherkins (dill pickles)		
Dry white wine	125 ml/4 fl oz	½ cup
For the sauce:		
1 small onion		
Tomatoes	350 g/12 oz	12 oz
Butter	25 g/1 oz	2 tbs
Flour (all-purpose)	25 g/1 oz	¼ cup
Water	175 ml/6 fl oz	¾ cup
Tomato purée	3 tbs	4 tbs
Lemon juice		
Few drops of Tabasco		

Sprinkle the fish fillets with the lemon juice and leave to stand for 30 minutes. Drain well and sprinkle with salt, celery salt and paprika. Cut the fillets into long strips about 5 cm/2 inches wide. Place a gherkin on each fillet strip, roll up and secure with a wooden cocktail stick (toothpick). Arrange the rolls in a greased ovenproof dish and pour over the wine. Cover with a lid or foil and cook in a preheated moderately hot oven, 190°C, 375°F, Gas Mark 5, for 10 minutes.

Meanwhile, make the tomato sauce. Peel and chop the onion and finely chop the tomatoes. Melt the butter in a pan, add the onion and tomato and cook, stirring frequently, until the onion is soft. Blend in the flour, gradually add the water and stir until boiling. Cook for 5 minutes then sieve and return to the rinsed pan. Mix in the tomato purée and add lemon juice, Tabasco, salt and paprika to taste. Cook for a further 5 minutes.

Transfer the fish rolls to a warm dish. Stir cooking juices into sauce and spoon over fish.

Microwave method

Sprinkle the fish fillets with lemon juice and leave to stand for 30 minutes. Drain and sprinkle with celery salt and paprika. Cut the fillets into long strips 5 cm/2 inches wide. Spread one side of each strip with mustard, roll up and secure with wooden cocktail sticks (toothpicks).

Arrange in a buttered dish which is suitable for the microwave, pour over the wine. Cover with a lid, or cling wrap with slits, and cook on full power for 5 minutes and allow to stand for 3 minutes.

Prepare the tomato sauce; peel and chop the onion and finely chop the tomatoes. Melt the butter in a pyrex bowl in the microwave for 1 minute on full power, add the onion and tomatoes and cook on full power for 2 minutes. Remove and stir in the flour, mix well and gradually add the water with the tomato purée, lemon juice, Tabasco, salt and paprika. Cook on full power for 5 minutes, stir and cook for a further 3 minutes.

Meanwhile remove sticks from fish. Pour wine juices into tomato sauce and sieve sauce over fish. Return dish to microwave. Reheat on full power for 5 minutes.

Below: Rolled fish fillet with tomato sauce
Opposite: Poached eel in green sauce

Rolled fish fillets in wine sauce
Serves 4

Ingredients	Metric-Imperial	American
White fish fillets such as plaice (flounder)	750 g/1 ¾ lb	1¾ lb
Lemon juice	2 tbs	3 tbs
Salt		
For the sauce:		
Butter	25 g/1 oz	2 tbs
Flour (all-purpose)	25 g/1 oz	¼ cup
Dry white wine	225 ml/8 fl oz	1 cup
Whipping cream	5 tbs	6 tbs
Salt		
Sugar		
Lemon juice		

Sprinkle the fillets with the lemon juice and allow to stand for 30 minutes. Drain, sprinkle with salt and cut into 5 cm/2 inch strips. Roll up each strip and secure with a cocktail stick. Place the rolls in a greased ovenproof dish.

To make the sauce, melt the butter in a pan, add the flour and stir until golden. Gradually add the wine and bring to the boil, stirring constantly. Blend in the cream, season with salt and sugar and add a little lemon juice to taste. Pour over the fish fillets, cover and cook in a preheated moderately hot oven, 190°C, 375°F, Gas Mark 5, for about 30 minutes, or until fish is cooked. Remove sticks before serving.

Poached mackerel with cheese sauce
Serves 4

Ingredients	Metric-Imperial	American
4 cleaned mackerel	225 g/8 oz each	8 oz each
Water	750 ml/1¼ pints	3 cups
1 bay leaf		
6 juniper berries		
Mustard seeds	¼ tsp	¼ tsp
Salt	1 tsp	1 tsp
Pinch of pepper		
Vinegar	4 tbs	5 tbs
For the sauce:		
Butter or margarine	25 g/1 oz	¼ cup
Flour (all-purpose)	25 g/1 oz	¼ cup
Grated Cheddar cheese	50 g/2 oz	½ cup
Whipping cream	4 tbs	5 tbs
Salt and pepper		
Sugar		

Trim the mackerel, wash and dry well. Put the water into a large pan with the bay leaf, juniper berries, mustard seeds, salt, pepper and vinegar and bring to the boil. Put in the fish, bring back to the boil, cover and simmer for about 10 minutes, or until the fish are cooked through. Carefully lift out and arrange on a warm serving dish. Keep hot.

To make the sauce, strain the cooking liquid, measure 350 ml/12 fl oz (1½ cups) and reserve. Melt the butter or margarine in a pan, blend in the flour and stir until golden. Whisk in the fish stock, bring to the boil and simmer for 5 minutes. Stir in the cheese and cream and season with salt, pepper and sugar to taste. Serve poured over the mackerel.

Poached eel in green sauce
Serves 4

Ingredients	Metric-Imperial	American
Cleaned eel	1 kg/2¼ lb	2¼ lb
Chopped parsley	50 g/2 oz	1 cup
Chopped tarragon	1 tsp	1 tsp
Salt and pepper		
Dry white wine	300 ml/½ pint	1¼ cups
Butter	25 g/1 oz	2 tbs
Flour (all-purpose)	1 tbs	1 tbs
1 egg yolk		
Whipping cream	4 tbs	5 tbs
Sugar		
Lemon juice		
Chopped dill weed	4 tbs	5 tbs

Wash the eel, dry well and cut into pieces about 5 cm/2 inches long. Place about three quarters of the parsley, tarragon, 1 tsp salt and the wine in a pan and bring to the boil. Put in the eel pieces, bring back to boiling point, cover and simmer for about 15 minutes, or until the eel is cooked through. Remove the fish with a slotted spoon and transfer to a warm serving dish. Keep hot.

Melt the butter in a pan, blend in the flour and stir until golden. Whisk in the stock from cooking the fish and bring to the boil. Cover and simmer for about 10 minutes. Remove from the heat, beat in the egg yolk and cream, add 1 tsp sugar, 1 tbs lemon juice, ¼ tsp pepper, the remaining parsley and half the dill. Stir well, reheat and adjust the seasoning with salt, pepper, sugar or lemon juice if required. Pour sauce over eel, garnish with remaining dill.

Pike fricassee
Serves 4

Ingredients	Metric-Imperial	American
1 cleaned pike	1–1.5 kg/ 2¼–3¼ lb	2¼– 3¼ lb
Vinegar		
Salt and pepper		
Butter	25 g/1 oz	2 tbs
For the sauce:		
Butter	25 g/1 oz	2 tbs
Flour (all-purpose)	25 g/1 oz	¼ cup
Beef stock (bouillon)	450 ml/¾ pint	scant 2 cups
Dry white wine	4 tbs	5 tbs
2 canned anchovy fillets		
Canned drained sliced mushrooms	150 g/5 oz	scant 1 cup
Drained chopped capers	1 tsp	1 tsp
1 egg yolk		
Whipping cream	2 tbs	3 tbs

Remove head from pike, wash fish well, dry and divide into portions. Sprinkle with vinegar, leave for 30 minutes. Dry well and sprinkle with salt.

Melt the butter in a pan, add the fish, cover and cook over low heat for 20 minutes, or until cooked.

To make the sauce, melt the butter in a pan, mix in the flour and stir until golden. Whisk in the stock and wine, bring to the boil and simmer for 5 minutes. Chop the anchovies, add to the sauce with the mushrooms and capers and simmer for a further 5 minutes. Remove from the heat, beat in the egg yolk and cream and season to taste with pepper.

Below: Pike fricassee
Opposite: Fish in lemon and caper sauce

French-style mussels
Serves 4

Ingredients	Metric-Imperial	American
Mussels	1.5 kg/3¼ lb	3¼ lb
2 small onions		
Butter	50 g/2 oz	¼ cup
1 leek		
1 small swede (rutabaga)		
1 large carrot		
Chopped parsley	1 tbs	1 tbs
Dry white wine	350 ml/12 fl oz	1½ cups
Garlic powder	½ tsp	½ tsp
Salt and pepper		

Leave the mussels in cold water for several hours, changing the water from time to time. Scrub the mussels, remove the beards and discard any that are open.

Peel and chop the onions. Melt the butter in a large pan and use to cook the onion until limp. Trim, clean and chop the leek, peel and chop the swede and the carrot. Add to the pan with the parsley and cook, stirring, for 3 minutes. Blend in the wine, garlic powder and a little salt and pepper and bring to the boil. Put in the mussels, bring back to the boil, cover and cook for about 10 minutes, shaking the pan occasionally. Discard any mussels that have not opened and transfer the remainder to a warm serving dish with the vegetables.

Fish in lemon and caper sauce
Serves 2

Ingredients	Metric-Imperial	American
White fish fillets such as cod or haddock	450 g/1 lb	1 lb
Lemon juice		
1 large onion		
Drained capers	1 tsp	1 tsp
Hot chicken stock (bouillon)	300 ml/½ pint	1¼ cups
Cornflour (cornstarch)	1 tbs	1 tbs
Tomato purée (paste)	½ tsp	½ tsp
French mustard	½ tsp	½ tsp
Salt and pepper		
Sweet paprika pepper		
2 gherkins (small dill pickles)		
Chopped parsley	1 tbs	1 tbs

Sprinkle fish with lemon juice, leave for 15 minutes.

Peel and chop the onion and place in a pan with the capers and stock. Bring to the boil, cover and simmer for 5 minutes. Moisten the cornflour with a little cold water, add to the pan and stir until boiling. Mix in the tomato purée and mustard and season to taste with salt, pepper and paprika. Cover again and simmer for a further 10 minutes.

Cut the gherkins into strips and the fish into bite-sized pieces, add both to the sauce, bring to the boil, cover and simmer for 10 minutes, or until the fish is cooked through. Transfer to a warm dish and serve sprinkled with the parsley.

Fish in a rice ring
Serves 4

Ingredients	Metric-Imperial	American
White fish fillets	750 g/1¾ lb	1¾ lb
Lemon juice	2 tbs	3 tbs
Salt	1 tsp	1 tsp
For the sauce:		
Butter	25 g/1 oz	2 tbs
Flour (all-purpose)	25 g/1 oz	¼ cup
Chicken stock (bouillon)	450 ml/¾ pint	scant 2 cups
Dry white wine	50 ml/2 fl oz	¼ cup
Drained capers	1 tsp	1 tsp
Lemon juice	1 tbs	1 tbs
Celery salt	½ tsp	½ tsp
Sweet paprika pepper	½ tsp	½ tsp
2 egg yolks		
Cold water	2 tbs	3 tbs
1 rice ring (see page 325)		
Lemon wedges		
Tomato wedges		
Chopped parsley	1 tbs	1 tbs

Sprinkle the fish with the lemon juice and leave to stand for 30 minutes. Dry on absorbent kitchen paper, sprinkle with the salt and cut into bite-sized pieces.

To make sauce, melt butter in a pan, mix in flour and stir until golden. Gradually add stock and wine and bring to boil, stirring constantly. Add fish, capers, lemon juice, celery salt and paprika. Return to boil, simmer for 15 minutes, until cooked through.

Beat the egg yolks with the water, add a little of the hot sauce and mix well. Pour this into the pan and stir carefully. Add salt to taste and serve in the rice ring garnished with lemon and tomato wedges and the parsley, with extra herbs in the rice if liked..

Microwave method
Sprinkle the fish fillets with lemon juice and leave for 30 minutes to absorb the flavour. Dry on absorbent kitchen paper and cut into bite-sized pieces.

To make sauce, put margarine in a pyrex bowl in microwave on full power for 45 seconds. Remove, stir in flour and return on full power for 40 seconds. Mix well.

Measure the stock and wine together, add a little to the flour mixture and beat well. Put the stock in a suitable container into the microwave at full power for 2 minutes.

Add some warmed stock to the sauce and stir well. Continue until half the stock is used then place in the microwave at full power for 2 minutes. Stir well when it is removed and add the remaining stock gradually, stirring vigorously. Tip in the fish pieces, capers, lemon juice, celery salt and paprika and mix gently until the ingredients are distributed evenly. Return to the microwave at full power, covered, for 5 minutes, remove and mix well. Return for a further 5 minutes at full power and allow to stand for 3 minutes. Mix again and check that the fish is cooked.

Beat the egg yolks with the water and pour in a little of the hot sauce. Gradually stir this egg mixture into the fish sauce gently to avoid breaking up the fish. Cook at full power for 2 minutes, remove and taste for seasoning.

Serve in the rice ring garnished with lemon and tomato wedges and a sprinkling of parsley.

Ham-wrapped fish rolls with leek
(Using a pressure cooker)
Serves 4

Ingredients	Metric-Imperial	American
4 large slices of Parma ham (prosciutto)		
4 plaice (flounder) or sole fillets	220 g/7 oz each	7 oz each
Lemon juice	2 tbs	3 tbs

Ingredients	Metric-Imperial	American
Pepper and salt		
French mustard	1 tbs	1 tbs
Leeks	750 g/1¾ lb	1¾ lb
Butter	25 g/1 oz	2 tbs
Water	125 ml/4 fl oz	½ cup
Flour (all-purpose)	2 tbs	3 tbs
Whipping cream	125 ml/4 fl oz	½ cup

Cut each slice of ham in half lengthways. Sprinkle the fish fillets with the lemon juice and leave to stand for 15 minutes. Drain well. Place each fish fillet between 2 slices of ham, spread one side with mustard, season to taste with pepper and roll up. Secure the rolls with wooden cocktail sticks (toothpicks).

Cut the leeks in half lengthways, clean and then cut into 2.5 cm/1 inch pieces. Melt the butter in the open pressure cooker, add the leek and cook, stirring, until limp. Pour in the water then arrange the fish rolls on top of the leek and put on the lid. Bring to full pressure and cook for 8 minutes. Remove the fish rolls and keep hot.

Blend the flour with the cream, add to the leek mixture and stir until boiling. Simmer for 2 minutes and season to taste with salt and pepper. Transfer to a warm dish and arrange the fish rolls on top, removing the sticks. Parslied potatoes and a tomato salad go well with this dish.

Opposite: Fish in a rice ring
Above: Ham-wrapped fish rolls with leek

Mushroom and fish casserole
Serves 4

Ingredients	Metric-Imperial	American
Cod fillets	550 g/1¼ lb	1¼ lb
Lemon juice	2 tbs	3 tbs
Salt and pepper		
Mushrooms	225 g/8 oz	8 oz
French beans (green)	225 g/8 oz	8 oz
Potatoes	350 g/12 oz	12 oz
2 large onions		
Margarine	50 g/2 oz	¼ cup
Water	250 ml/9 fl oz	generous 1 cup
Dry white wine	125 ml/4 fl oz	½ cup
Mushroom ketchup	1 tsp	1 tsp
Fish seasoning	¼ tsp	¼ tsp
Chopped parsley	2 tbs	3 tbs

Sprinkle the cod fillets with lemon juice and leave to stand for 15 minutes. Drain well, sprinkle with salt and pepper and cut into bite-sized pieces.

Slice the mushrooms. Top and tail the beans and cut into short lengths. Peel and dice the potatoes. Peel and slice the onions. Melt the margarine in a pan and use to cook the onion until golden. Add the mushrooms, beans and potato and cook, stirring, for 5 minutes. Season with salt and pepper, add the water and bring to the boil. Cover and simmer for 25 minutes. Add the fish and wine, bring back to the boil, cover and simmer for a further 15 minutes. Stir in the mushroom ketchup and fish seasoning then add more salt and pepper to taste if necessary. Transfer to a warm serving dish and sprinkle with the parsley.

Below: Mushroom and fish casserole
Right: Simple fried fillets of fish

Simple fried fillets of fish
Serves 4

Ingredients	Metric-Imperial	American
4 cod fillets	225 g/8 oz each	8 oz each
Lemon juice	2 tbs	3 tbs
Salt and pepper		
1 egg		
Water	2 tbs	3 tbs
Fresh breadcrumbs	75 g/3 oz	1½ cups
Flour (all-purpose)	50 g/2 oz	½ cup
Margarine	75 g/3 oz	⅓ cup

Sprinkle the cod fillets with the lemon juice and leave to stand for 30 minutes. Dry on absorbent kitchen paper and sprinkle with salt and pepper.

Beat the egg with the water and place in a shallow dish. Put the breadcrumbs on a sheet of greaseproof paper (waxed). Coat the fish first with flour, then dip into the egg mixture and cover all over with breadcrumbs.

Melt the margarine in a large frying pan, put in the fish fillets and fry for 5–6 minutes on each side, or until golden brown and cooked through. Drain on more kitchen paper and serve immediately on a warm dish.

Oven-baked cod
Serves 4

Ingredients	Metric-Imperial	American
1 cleaned cod, weight	1.5 kg/3¼ lb	3 lb 5 oz
Lemon juice	2 tbs	3 tbs
Salt		
Butter	40 g/1½ oz	3 tbs
Lemon slices		
Parsley sprigs		

Wash the cod and dry on absorbent kitchen paper. Sprinkle inside and out with the lemon juice and salt to taste.

Put an upturned cup in a well buttered ovenproof dish and place the fish over it, with the open side downwards, so that it stands up in the dish. Melt the butter and spoon over the fish to coat it. Place, uncovered, in a preheated moderate oven, 180°C, 350°F, Gas Mark 4, for 40 minutes, or until the fish is cooked through and the flesh flakes easily when tested. Transfer to a warm dish, garnish with lemon slices and parsley sprigs and serve with boiled potatoes and sauce tartare.

Microwave method
Wash the fish and dry thoroughly on absorbent kitchen paper. Sprinkle inside and out with lemon juice and a little salt on the inside.

Place a browning dish in the microwave with the butter, switch on to full power for 1 minute. Arrange the fish in the dish and coat all over with the butter. Cover the dish with a lid or cling wrap with slits and cook at full power for 10 minutes. Allow to stand for 5 minutes.

Turn the fish over carefully and cook on full power for 5 minutes.

Prepare the garnish of lemon slices and parsley. Serve in the cooking dish if suitable or transfer to a warm plate. Arrange the garnish and serve with boiled potatoes and sauce tartare.

Fried fish fillets with cream cheese and almonds

Serves 2

Ingredients	Metric-Imperial	American
2 plaice fillets (flounder)	225 g/8 oz each	8 oz each
Lemon juice	1 tbs	1 tbs
Salt and pepper		
1 egg		
Flour (all-purpose)	2 tbs	3 tbs
Fresh breadcrumbs	4 tbs	5 tbs
Oil	2 tbs	3 tbs
Cream cheese	75 g/3 oz	⅓ cup
Butter	25 g/1 oz	2 tbs
Slivered almonds	4 tbs	5 tbs

Lemon slices
Sprigs of parsley

Sprinkle the plaice fillets with the lemon juice, leave to stand for 15 minutes then drain and dry on absorbent kitchen paper. Sprinkle with salt and pepper.

Beat the egg and place in a flat dish. Coat the fish fillets first in the flour, then in beaten egg and finally cover them with breadcrumbs.

Heat the oil in a frying pan and cook the fish fillets for 5–6 minutes on each side, or until cooked through and golden brown. Transfer to a warm serving dish and keep hot.

Beat the cheese until smooth and use to top the fish fillets. Melt the butter in a pan, sprinkle in the almonds and fry, stirring, until golden. Spoon the nuts over the cheese topping and garnish the dish with lemon slices and parsley.

Fried herrings
Serves 4

Ingredients	Metric-Imperial	American
4 cleaned herrings	200 g/7 oz each	7 oz each
Flour (all-purpose)	2 tbs	3 tbs
Salt and pepper		
Oil	5 tbs	6 tbs
Lemon wedges		
Sprigs of herbs		

Wash the herrings and dry on absorbent kitchen paper. Season flour and use to coat the fish.

Fry fish in oil in frying pan for 8 minutes on each side, until cooked. Serve garnished with lemon and herbs.

Opposite: Fried fish fillets with cream cheese and almonds
Above: Fried herrings

Trout meunière
Serves 4

Ingredients	Metric-Imperial	American
4 cleaned trout	225 g/8 oz each	8 oz each
Salt		
Flour (all-purpose)	4 tbs	5 tbs
Oil	4 tbs	5 tbs
Butter	50 g/2 oz	¼ cup
Lemon juice	2 tbs	3 tbs
Worcestershire sauce	1 tbs	1 tbs

Chopped parsley
Lemon slices

Wash and dry trout, season and coat with flour.

Heat the oil in a frying pan, put in the fish and cook for about 10 minutes on each side, or until golden brown and cooked through. Pour out the oil in the pan and put in the butter. When it has melted, spoon it over the fish until they are coated. Transfer the fish to a warm dish and keep hot.

Stir lemon juice and Worcestershire sauce into pan and cook for 2 minutes. Spoon over fish. Serve garnished with parsley and lemon slices.

French mustard	1 tbs	1 tbs
Salt and pepper		
Fresh breadcrumbs		
Margarine	65 g/2½ oz	5 tbs

Soak the roll in cold water then squeeze out the moisture. Sprinkle the fish fillets with 2 tbs (3 tbs) lemon juice and leave to stand for 30 minutes.

Drain the fish and mince with the bread roll, or purée in a food processor. Peel and chop the onion. Heat the oil in a pan and use to cook the onion until softened. Combine the fish mixture, onion, egg, parsley and mustard with salt, pepper and lemon juice to taste. Form into round flat cakes with wet hands and coat in the breadcrumbs, patting them on well. Fry the fish cakes in the margarine for about 5 minutes on each side, or until golden brown, and cooked through.

Fried herrings with bacon
Serves 4

Ingredients	Metric-Imperial	American
8 cleaned herrings	150 g/5 oz each	5 oz each
Salt	2 tsp	2 tsp
Pepper	1 tsp	1 tsp
Streaky bacon (strips)	150 g/5 oz	10 strips
2 small onions		
Lemon wedges		
Chopped mixed herbs		

Wash and dry the herrings, then season.

Cut the bacon into strips and place in a large dry frying pan. Fry until crisp, then remove and reserve. Fry herrings in the bacon fat for about 5 minutes.

Meanwhile, peel and chop onions. Add to pan and cook for a further 5–6 minutes, or until fish are cooked through. Transfer to a warm serving dish. Return bacon bits to pan and reheat. Spoon bacon mixture over herrings and garnish with lemon wedges.

Opposite: Trout meunière
Below: Fried herrings with bacon

Fried fish cakes
Serves 4

Ingredients	Metric-Imperial	American
1 bread roll		
White fish fillets	450 g/1 lb	1 lb
Lemon juice		
1 medium-sized onion		
Oil	1 tbs	1 tbs
1 egg		
Chopped parsley	1 tbs	1 tbs

Fried plaice
Serves 4

Ingredients	Metric-Imperial	American
4 cleaned plaice (flounder)	300 g/11 oz each	11 oz each
Lemon juice	2 tbs	3 tbs
Salt and pepper		
Flour	3 tbs	4 tbs
Margarine	75 g/3 oz	⅓ cup

Wash and dry the plaice. Sprinkle with lemon juice and leave to stand for 30 minutes. Dry on absorbent kitchen paper, sprinkle inside and out with salt and pepper and coat in the flour.

Melt the margarine in a large frying pan, or in two pans if necessary, and use to cook the fish for about 5 minutes on each side, or until golden brown and cooked through. Serve hot with potato salad or herbed rice.

Variations: Instead of plaice use trout of the same weight, allowing cooking time of about 10 minutes on each side, or sole weighing about 250 g/9 oz each, allowing 6 minutes on each side, or until the fish are cooked through.

Fried plaice with streaky bacon
Serves 4

Ingredients	Metric-Imperial	American
4 cleaned plaice (flounder)	300 g/11 oz each	11 oz each
Lemon juice	2 tbs	3 tbs
Salt and pepper		
Flour	3 tbs	4 tbs
Oil	2 tbs	3 tbs
Streaky bacon (strips)	175 g/6 oz	12 strips
Lemon wedges		

Wash and dry the plaice. Sprinkle with the lemon juice and leave to stand for 30 minutes. Dry on absorbent kitchen paper, sprinkle inside and out with salt and pepper and coat in the flour.

Heat the oil in a large pan and fry the bacon lightly. Put in the fish and cook for about 15 minutes, turning the fish once during this time, or until they are cooked through and the bacon is crisp. If necessary, cook the fish and bacon in two separate pans. Transfer the plaice to a warm serving dish, lay the bacon on top and garnish with lemon wedges.

Fillets of fish with curry sauce
Serves 2

Ingredients	Metric-Imperial	American
White fish fillets	450 g/1 lb	1 lb
Lemon juice	2 tbs	3 tbs
Salt and pepper		
1 dessert apple		
Whipping cream	150 ml/¼ pint	⅔ cup
White wine	1 tbs	1 tbs
Salt	¼ tsp	¼ tsp
Sugar	1 tsp	1 tsp
Curry powder	1 tsp	1 tsp
Chopped mango chutney	1 tbs	1 tbs

Sprinkle fish fillets with lemon juice, leave for 15 minutes. Drain and season. Place in buttered ovenproof dish.

Peel, quarter and core apple, then dice flesh. Stir together cream, wine, salt, sugar, curry powder and chutney. Mix in apple and spoon over fish.

Cover and place in a preheated moderately hot oven, 190°C, 375°F, Gas Mark 5, for about 30 minutes, or until the fish is cooked through. Serve with rice.

Onion-stuffed cod
Serves 4

Ingredients	Metric-Imperial	American
1 cleaned cod	1.5 kg/3¼ lb	3¼ lb
Lemon juice	2 tbs	3 tbs
Salt and pepper		
For the stuffing:		
1 bunch of spring onions (scallions)		
Butter	50 g/2 oz	¼ cup
Chopped parsley	5 tbs	6 tbs
Worcestershire sauce		

Wash and dry cod. Sprinkle with lemon juice, leave for 30 minutes. Dry well, then season.

Trim and slice the spring onions. Cook gently in butter until soft. Stir in parsley, salt, pepper and Worcestershire sauce to taste.

Line a roasting tin with a sheet of foil. Put fish in centre, cavity upwards, and fill with onion stuffing. Season, cover with foil and place in a moderately hot oven, 200°C, 400°F, Gas Mark 6, for about 55 minutes, or until the fish is cooked through.

Opposite: Fried plaice
Above: Fillets of fish with curry sauce

Turbans of fish in Madeira sauce
Serves 4

Ingredients	Metric-Imperial	American
4 haddock fillets	200 g/7 oz each	7 oz each
Lemon juice	2 tbs	3 tbs
Salt and pepper		
Streaky bacon (strips)	50 g/2 oz	4 strips
1 onion		
2 gherkins (small dill pickles)		
Finely chopped red sweet pepper	1 tbs	1 tbs
French mustard	1 tbs	1 tbs
Double (heavy) cream	75 ml/3 fl oz	⅓ cup
Sour cream	50 ml/2 fl oz	¼ cup
Madeira	2 tbs	3 tbs
Sugar		
Grated cheese, such as Cheddar	25 g/1 oz	¼ cup
Butter	40 g/1½ oz	3 tbs

Sprinkle the haddock fillets with lemon juice and allow to stand for 30 minutes. Pat dry and season with salt and pepper. Cut the fillets into strips about 5 cm/2 inches wide, roll them up and secure with wooden cocktail sticks (toothpicks). Arrange in a well buttered ovenproof dish.

Chop the bacon, place in a frying pan and heat until the

fat runs. Peel and chop the onion and fry in the bacon fat until golden. Leave to cool. Dice the gherkins and stir into the onion mixture with the chopped pepper, mustard, creams and Madeira and add a little sugar to taste. Pour over the fish turbans, sprinkle with the cheese and dot with the butter. Cook, uncovered, in a preheated moderately hot oven, 200°C, 400°F, Gas Mark 6, for about 30 minutes, or until the fish is cooked through. Remove the sticks before serving.

Trout in bacon shirts
Serves 4

Ingredients	Metric-Imperial	American
4 cleaned trout	225 g/8 oz each	8 oz each
Salt		
Streaky bacon (strips)	350 g/12 oz	24 strips
Sour cream	300 ml/½ pint	1¼ cups

Pinch of cayenne pepper		
Sweet paprika pepper	1 tsp	1 tsp
Sugar	½ tsp	½ tsp

Wash and dry the trout and sprinkle inside and out with salt. Wrap the fish in **bacon** and place side-by-side in a well-buttered ovenproof dish. Place, uncovered, in a preheated moderately hot oven, 200°C, 400°F, Gas Mark 6, for 15 minutes. Meanwhile, mix the sour cream with the cayenne, paprika and sugar and add salt to taste. Spoon over the trout and cook for a further 5 minutes, or until the fish are cooked through. Transfer to a hot dish and serve with parslied potatoes and a leek salad.

Opposite: Turbans of fish in Madeira sauce
Above: Trout in bacon shirts

Baked fish fillets with curried rice
Serves 4

Ingredients	Metric-Imperial	American
White fish fillets such as		
cod or haddock	450 g/1 lb	1 lb
Lemon juice	2 tbs	3 tbs
Salt and pepper		
2 onions		
Cooked ham	100 g/4 oz	4 oz
Oil	1 tbs	1 tbs
Natural yogurt (plain)	300 ml/½ pint	1¼ cups
Snipped chives	2 tbs	3 tbs
Chopped dill weed	2 tbs	3 tbs
Chopped parsley	2 tbs	3 tbs
Sweet paprika pepper		
5 tomatoes		
Canned mushrooms	225 g/8 oz can	8 oz can
Fresh breadcrumbs	2 tbs	3 tbs
Butter	15 g/½ oz	1 tbs
Grated Cheddar cheese	150 g/5 oz	1¼ cups
For the curried rice:		
Curry powder	1 tsp	1 tsp
Salted water	600 ml/1 pint	2½ cups
Long grain rice	275 g/10 oz	1¼ cups
Butter	15 g/½ oz	1 tbs

Sprinkle the fish fillets with the lemon juice and leave to stand for 15 minutes. Season with salt and pepper.

Peel and chop the onions and chop the ham. Place in a pan with the oil and cook gently until the onion is soft. Mix together the yogurt and herbs and season to taste with salt, pepper and paprika. Slice tomatoes and drain mushrooms.

Spoon half the onion and ham into a well greased oval ovenproof dish, put the fish fillets on this, top with the remaining onion and ham and then with the tomato slices and mushrooms. Spoon the herbed yogurt evenly over the top, sprinkle with the breadcrumbs and dot with the butter.

Put the curry powder into an ovenproof dish and gradually stir in the salted water. Sprinkle in rice, stir, then flake butter over surface. Cover tightly with lid or foil.

Leaving the fish dish uncovered, place both dishes in a preheated moderately hot oven, 200°C, 400°F, Gas Mark 6, for 40 minutes. Sprinkle the fish mixture with the cheese, return to the oven and cook with the dish of rice for a further 10 minutes, until the fish is golden on top and the rice tender and the liquid absorbed.

Tuna in tomato sauce
Serves 4

Ingredients	Metric-Imperial	American
2 red sweet peppers		
1 canned red pimiento		
Large tomatoes	750 g/1¾ lb	1¾ lb
Chopped parsley	4 tbs	5 tbs
Onions	350 g/12 oz	12 oz
3 cloves of garlic		
Oil	6 tbs	½ cup
1 beef stock cube		
(bouillon)		
Sweet paprika pepper	1 tbs	1 tbs
Salt and freshly ground		
black pepper		
4 tuna steaks	200 g/7 oz each	7 oz each
Mushrooms	225 g/8 oz	8 oz

Deseed the peppers and pimiento. Pour boiling water over the tomatoes, drain, peel and scoop out the seeds. Chop the tomatoes, pepper and pimiento flesh and combine with the parsley. Peel and finely chop the onions and garlic.

Heat two thirds of the oil in a flameproof dish and use to fry the onion and garlic until softened. Add the tomato mixture and cook, stirring frequently, for 10 minutes. Crumble in the stock cube, stir well and season with the paprika and salt and pepper to taste. Put the tuna steaks into the tomato mixture, cover with lid or foil and place in a preheated hot oven, 220°C, 425°F, Gas Mark 7, for 30 minutes.

Slice the mushrooms, add to the dish and sprinkle with the remaining oil. Cover again and return to the oven for a further 15 minutes. Serve with rice or French bread, accompanied by a green salad.

preheated hot oven, 220°C, 425°F, Gas Mark 7, for 8 minutes. If liked, serve garnished with lemon twists and parsley sprigs, accompanied by French bread.

Microwave method

Open the oyster shells, remove the beards. Wash the oysters thoroughly and then gently remove the fish and keep in the refrigerator. Reserve the deep oyster shells and rinse well under cold running water.

Place the butter in a small bowl in the microwave for 30 seconds on full power, remove and beat in the parsley, dill, mustard, a little garlic powder, salt and pepper.

Divide two-thirds of this mixture amongst the deep oyster shells and place the oysters on top of the flavoured butter.

Mix the breadcrumbs and cheese together and sprinkle over the oysters; dot the remaining butter on top.

Place 6 shells at a time in the microwave and cook on full power for 4 minutes. Remove and flash under a hot grill (broiler) until golden.

Serve with lemon twists and parsley sprigs, accompanied by French bread.

Left: Baked fish fillets with curried rice
Below: Oysters baked in the shell

Oysters baked in the shell
Serves 4

Ingredients	Metric-Imperial	American
24 oysters		
Butter	75 g/3 oz	⅓ cup
Chopped parsley	1 tbs	1 tbs
Dried dill weed	½ tsp	½ tsp
French mustard	½ tsp	½ tsp
Garlic powder		
Salt and pepper		
Fresh breadcrumbs	1 tbs	1 tbs
Grated Gouda cheese	25 g/1 oz	¼ cup

If possible have the oysters opened for you. If you have to do this yourself, hold the deep shell in your hand and prise off the other shell with an oyster knife. Remove the beards, wash the oysters thoroughly then gently remove the fish and keep cool. Reserve the deep oyster shells.

Soften the butter and beat in the parsley, dill, mustard and season with garlic powder and salt and pepper to taste.

Divide two thirds of this mixture between the deep oyster shells and put the oysters on top. Mix the breadcrumbs with the cheese and sprinkle over the oysters. Dot the remaining butter mixture over the top. Place the filled shells on a baking sheet (cookie sheet) and place, uncovered, in a

Simple grilled plaice
Serves 4

Ingredients	Metric-Imperial	American
4 cleaned plaice (flounder)	300 g/11 oz each	11 oz each
Lemon juice	2 tbs	3 tbs
Salt		
Lemon wedges		
Sprigs of herbs		

Wash and dry the plaice, sprinkle with the lemon juice and leave for 15 minutes. Dry on absorbent kitchen paper.

Arrange the fish on the greased grid of a grill pan (broiler) and cook under high heat for about 5 minutes on each side, or until cooked through. Transfer to a warm dish, sprinkle with salt and serve garnished with lemon wedges and sprigs of herbs.

Variations: Other delicate white fish such as lemon sole or whiting may be cooked in the same way. Serve garnished with pots of herbs or citrus butter if liked.
Serving ideas: Serve with duchesse or Lyonnaise potatoes, grilled (broiled) tomatoes and French beans.

Grilled mackerel with sweet and sour cabbage
Serves 4

Ingredients	Metric-Imperial	American
2 cleaned mackerel	550 g/1¼ lb each	1¼ lb each
Lemon juice	1 tbs	1 tbs
For the cabbage:		
1 white cabbage	750 g/1¾ lb	1¾ lb
8 small onions		
Dripping or butter	50 g/2 oz	¼ cup
Salt and pepper		
8 juniper berries		
1 bay leaf		
Water	125 ml/4 fl oz	½ cup
2 tart dessert apples		
Vinegar		

Wash and dry the mackerel, sprinkle inside and out with the lemon juice and leave to stand for 15 minutes.

Discard the rough outer leaves of the cabbage, quarter and cut out the stalk. Slice the leaves thinly. Peel and quarter the onions. Melt the dripping or butter in a large pan and use to fry the onion until golden. Add the cabbage and cook for 5 minutes, stirring frequently. Season with salt and pepper, add the juniper berries, bay leaf and water and bring to the boil. Simmer for 5 minutes. Peel, quarter and core the apples then slice thinly. Stir into the cabbage mixture and cook for another 10 minutes. Adjust the seasoning, add a little vinegar to taste and keep the cabbage mixture hot.

While the cabbage is cooking, dry the fish on absorbent kitchen paper and sprinkle with salt and pepper. Slash the flesh and place the fish on the greased grid of a grill pan (broiler). Cook under high heat for about 7 minutes on each side, or until the fish is cooked through. Place the sweet and sour cabbage mixture on a hot dish and serve the grilled mackerel on top.

Fried mackerel in egg and breadcrumbs
Serves 4

Ingredients	Metric-Imperial	American
4 cleaned mackerel	275 g/10 oz each	10 oz each
For the marinade:		
Lemon juice	2 tbs	3 tbs
Chopped mixed herbs	3 tbs	4 tbs
Salt	1 tsp	1 tsp
Coarsely ground black pepper	1 tsp	1 tsp
For the coating:		
Butter	75 g/3 oz	⅓ cup
2 egg yolks		
Fresh breadcrumbs	75 g/3 oz	1½ cups

Trim the mackerel and remove the heads. Wash and dry.

To make the marinade, combine the lemon juice, herbs, salt and pepper. Use to brush the fish inside and out. Place in a dish and leave to stand for 3 hours. Dry the fish on absorbent kitchen paper, pour the juices in the dish through a sieve, retaining the herbs.

Soften one third of the butter and beat in the egg yolks and reserved herbs. Coat the fish with this mixture then cover them all over in breadcrumbs.

Melt the remaining butter in a large frying pan and use to cook the fish for about 20 minutes, turning them once during this time, or until cooked through.

Microwave hint
When microwave cooking a whole fish enclosed in a skin, i.e. trout or salmon, make a few small slits in the skin to allow the steam to escape during cooking.

Opposite: Simple grilled plaice
Grilled mackerel with sweet and sour cabbage

Grilled halibut with herbed butter pats
Serves 4

Ingredients	Metric-Imperial	American
4 halibut steaks	225 g/8 oz each	8 oz each
Lemon juice	2 tbs	3 tbs
Softened butter	50 g/2 oz	¼ cup
Chopped mixed herbs	2 tbs	3 tbs
Melted butter	25 g/1 oz	2 tbs
Salt and pepper		

Sprinkle the halibut with the lemon juice and leave to stand for 15 minutes. Cream the butter with the herbs. Shape the herbed butter into a roll about 4 cm/1½ inches in diameter and chill.

Pat the fish dry, brush with the melted butter and sprinkle with salt and pepper. Arrange on a greased grid and cook under a preheated grill (broiler) for about 6 minutes on each side, or until cooked through.

Cut the roll of herbed butter into 4 slices and place one on each fish steak. Serve with grilled tomatoes and garnish the dish with snipped mustard and cress if liked.

Baked sole with asparagus
Serves 4

Ingredients	Metric-Imperial	American
8 sole fillets	675 g/1½ lb	1½ lb
Lemon juice	2 tbs	3 tbs
Salt		
Melted butter	40 g/1½ oz	3 tbs
16 cooked or canned asparagus spears		
Sweet paprika pepper	1 tsp	1 tsp

Sprinkle the sole fillets with the lemon juice and leave to stand for 30 minutes. Dry on absorbent kitchen paper. Mix a little salt into the butter and use half of this to brush the skin side of the fillets. Take one fillet, wrap it, skin side inside, around 2 asparagus spears and tie into a knot. Repeat with the remaining fillets and asparagus.

Arrange the sole and asparagus knots on an oiled baking sheet (cookie sheet). Stir the paprika into the remaining butter and brush this over the fish. Bake, uncovered, in a preheated moderately hot oven, 190°C, 375°F, Gas Mark 5,

Prawns, Singapore-style
Serves 4

Ingredients	Metric-Imperial	American
Shelled cooked prawns (shrimp)	450 g/1 lb	1 lb
For the batter:		
Flour (all-purpose)	225 g/8 oz	2 cups
Baking powder	1 tsp	1 tsp
Curry powder	1 tsp	1 tsp
1 egg		
Light ale (light beer)	250 ml/9 fl oz	generous 1 cup

Salt
Oil for deep frying

Defrost the prawns if frozen. Drain well.

To make the batter, sift the flour, baking powder and curry powder into a bowl and make a well in the centre. Beat together the egg and ale with a little salt. Pour into the well in the dry ingredients, draw them in with a wooden spoon and beat well until the batter is smooth.

Heat oil in a deep fryer until it will brown a cube of day-old bread in 1 minute. Dip the prawns in the batter, allow any excess to drain off then fry, in batches, for 1 minute, or until golden brown. Drain well on absorbent kitchen paper and serve hot with a savoury dipping sauce of your choice.

for about 12 minutes, or until the fish is cooked through. Serve with hot toast.

Baked eel with sage
Serves 4

Ingredients	Metric-Imperial	American
Cleaned eel	750 g/1¾ lb	1¾ lb
Salt and pepper		
5 sage leaves		
Butter	25 g/1 oz	2 tbs

Wash and dry the eel and sprinkle with salt and pepper. Place in a greased ovenproof casserole and arrange the sage leaves on the fish. Dot with the butter and place, uncovered, in a preheated moderately hot oven, 200°C, 400°F, Gas Mark 6, for about 20 minutes, or until cooked through. Serve with buttered potatoes and a green salad.

Above: Grilled halibut with herbed butter pats
Right: Prawns, Singapore-style

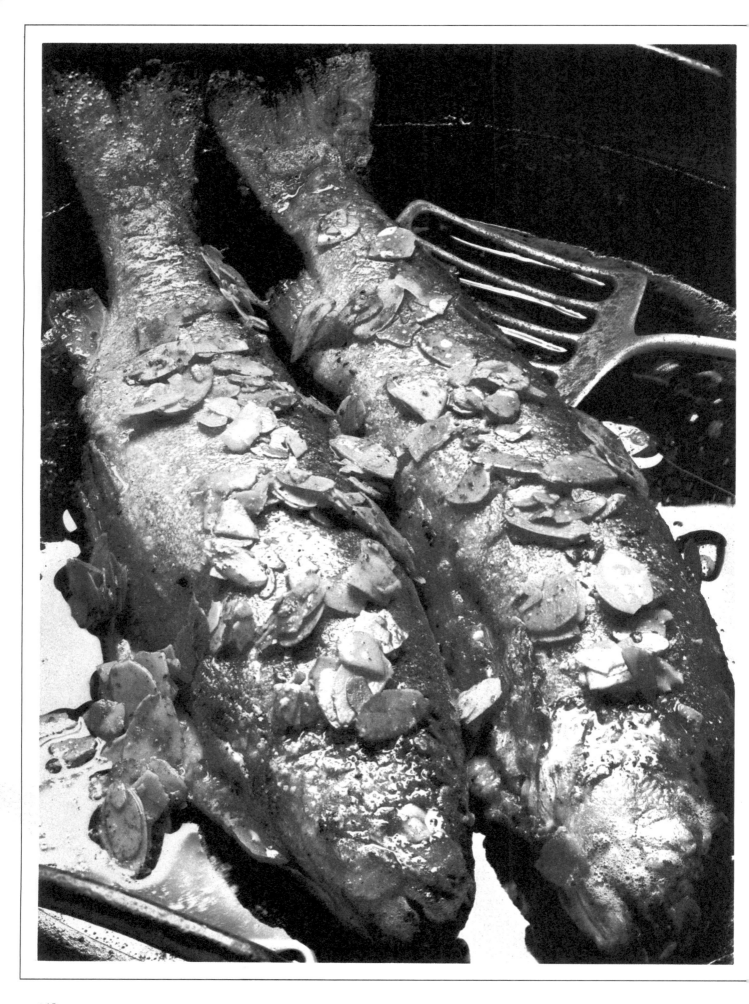

Fried trout with almonds
Serves 4

Ingredients	Metric-Imperial	American
4 cleaned trout		
Lemon juice	2 tbs	3 tbs
Salt and pepper		
1 egg		
Slivered almonds	40 g/1½ oz	⅓ cup
Flour	2 tbs	3 tbs
Oil for shallow frying		
Lemon slices		
Sprigs of dill weed		

Sprinkle the trout inside and out with lemon juice and leave to stand for 15 minutes. Dry on absorbent kitchen paper and sprinkle with salt and pepper.

Beat the egg and place in a dish. Sprinkle the almonds on a sheet of greaseproof paper (waxed). Coat the fish with the flour, dip in the egg and roll in the almonds, patting them on well.

Heat a little oil in a frying pan and use to cook the trout, two at a time, for about 7 minutes, turning them once, or until cooked through. Place the trout on a hot dish, garnish with lemon slices and sprigs of dill and serve with potatoes and peas.

Deep fried fillet of fish in batter
Serves 4

Ingredients	Metric-Imperial	American
White fish fillets such as cod or haddock	750 g/1¾ lb	1¾ lb
Lemon juice	2 tbs	3 tbs
Salt		
For the batter:		
Flour (all-purpose)	100 g/4 oz	1 cup
1 egg		
Milk	125 ml/4 fl oz	½ cup
Oil	1 tbs	1 tbs
Fat or oil for deep frying		

Sprinkle the fish with the lemon juice and leave to stand for 30 minutes. Dry on absorbent kitchen paper and sprinkle with salt. Cut into even-sized pieces.

To make the batter, sift the flour into a bowl and make a well in the centre. Drop in the egg, add the milk and oil and beat until the batter is smooth.

Heat fat or oil in a deep pan until it will brown a cube of day-old bread in 1 minute. Dip the pieces of fish into the batter, using a fork, allow excess batter to drain off and fry the fish pieces for about 5 minutes, or until golden brown and crisp. Cooking time will depend on the size of the fish pieces. Drain well and serve with a potato salad.

Vegetables and prawns in batter
Serves 4

Ingredients	Metric-Imperial	American
8 baby carrots		
8 very small parsnips		
2 heads of fennel (Florence)		
4 jumbo prawns in the shell (shrimp)		
Cleaned squid	225 g/8 oz	8 oz
Lemon juice	1 tbs	1 tbs
For the batter:		
Flour (all-purpose)	225 g/8 oz	2 cups
1 egg		
Light ale (light beer)	225 ml/8 fl oz	1 cup
Salt and pepper		
Fat or oil for deep frying		
8 sprigs of parsley		

Peel the carrots and parsnips and trim the green tops to about 1.25 cm/½ inch. Clean and quarter the fennel. Shell the prawns, leaving on just the end of the tail. Cut the squid into thin rings, sprinkle with the lemon juice and leave to stand for 15 minutes. Dry on absorbent kitchen paper.

To make the batter, sift the flour into a bowl and make a well in the centre. Beat the egg with the ale, pour into the dry ingredients, add a little salt and pepper and beat until the batter is smooth.

Heat fat or oil in a deep fryer until it will brown a cube of day-old bread in 1 minute.

Coat the vegetables in batter, allow excess to drain off, and cook, in batches, for about 10 minutes, or until golden brown and cooked through. Drain well on absorbent kitchen paper, sprinkle with salt and keep hot. Dip the prawns and squid rings in batter and fry these in the same way for about 5 minutes, or until golden brown. Drain as above. Finally, dip the parsley sprigs in batter and fry for about 2 minutes. As soon as all the ingredients are cooked and drained, serve on a hot plate.

Opposite: Fried trout with almonds
Right: Vegetables and prawns in batter

American mussel chowder
Serves 4

Ingredients	Metric-Imperial	American
20 mussels		
Water	1 L/1¾ pints	4⅓ cups
Lemon juice	2–3 tbs	3–4 tbs
1 piece of celeriac	100 g/4 oz	4 oz
2 tomatoes		
1 green sweet pepper		
Potatoes	225 g/8 oz	8 oz
1 onion		
Streaky bacon (strips)	75 g/3 oz	6 strips
Oil	3 tbs	4 tbs
1 chicken stock cube (bouillon)		
1 bay leaf		
Chopped thyme	1 tbs	1 tbs
Chopped marjoram	1 tbs	1 tbs
Pinch of cayenne pepper		
Dry white wine	4 tbs	5 tbs
Salt and pepper		

Soak the mussels in cold water for 4 hours, changing the water twice during this time. Drain, scrub and remove the beards. Discard any mussels which are open.

Put the water and lemon juice into a pan and bring to the boil. Add the mussels, bring back to the boil then simmer for 5 minutes. Drain, reserving the liquid. Discard any mussels which do not open. Make the reserved liquid up to 1 L/1¾ pints (4 ⅓ cups) with more water. Take the mussels from the shells.

Peel and dice the celeriac. Pour boiling water over the tomatoes, drain, peel and chop. Deseed the pepper and cut the flesh into strips. Peel and dice the potatoes. Peel and chop the onion and chop the bacon. Place the onion and bacon in a pan, add the oil and cook for 3 minutes. Pour in the reserved liquid, crumble in the stock cube and add the bay leaf, thyme, marjoram, cayenne, celeriac, tomato and cayenne. Bring to the boil, cover and cook for about 40 minutes, or until all the vegetables are tender. Stir in the mussels and wine and season to taste with salt and pepper.

Whitebait, London-style
Serves 4

Ingredients	Metric-Imperial	American
Flour (all-purpose)	50 g/2 oz	½ cup
Salt and pepper		
Oil for deep frying		
Whitebait	450 g/1 lb	1 lb
Lemon wedges		

Season flour and use to coat the fish lightly.

Heat the oil in a deep fryer until it will brown a cube of day-old bread in 1 minute. Using a frying basket, cook the whitebait, in batches, for 3 minutes. Drain on kitchen paper.

When all the fish have been fried, reheat the oil until it will brown a cube of bread in 40 seconds. Return the whitebait to the basket and fry briefly to brown and crisp. Drain well, season, garnish with lemon wedges and serve with brown bread and butter.

Creamy fish casserole
Serves 4

Ingredients	Metric-Imperial	American
1 small cleaned cod	900 g/2 lb	2 lb
Lemon juice	2 tbs	3 tbs
Selection of pot vegetables		
Water	1 L/1¾ pints	4⅓ cups
1 chicken or fish stock cube (bouillon)		
3 peppercorns		
1 bay leaf		
3 whole cloves		
Pared strips of lemon rind		
Oil	4 tbs	5 tbs
Salt and pepper		
1 egg yolk		
Whipping cream	4 tbs	5 tbs
Chopped parsley	2 tbs	3 tbs

Skin and bone the cod, reserving the trimmings. Cut the flesh into bite-sized pieces and sprinkle with the lemon juice.

Clean pot vegetables, peel if necessary, then chop. Put water into a pan and bring to boil. Crumble in stock cube and add peppercorns, bay leaf, cloves, lemon rind, pot vegetables and fish trimmings. Bring to boil, cover and simmer for 45 minutes. Strain stock and reserve.

Heat the oil in a large pan, add fish pieces and fry until golden brown. Add fish stock, bring to boil then simmer for 5 minutes. Season. Beat egg yolk with cream, spoon in a little hot cooking liquid and mix well. Pour into pan, remove from heat and stir carefully. Sprinkle with parsley.

Microwave hint
When cooking a whole fish in the microwave cooker, wrap a piece of thin foil around the tail and only remove this half way through cooking time. This prevents the tail from becoming very dry, fragile and breaking off when the fish is moved.

Opposite: American mussel chowder
Below: Creamy fish casserole

Silverside with mixed vegetables and chive sauce
Serves 4

Ingredients	Metric-Imperial	American
Beef stock (bouillon)	1 L/1¾ pints	4⅓ cups
Silverside of beef	550 g/1¼ lb	1¼ lb
Salt and pepper		
2 onions		
Turnip or swede (rutabaga)	225 g/8 oz	8 oz
Carrots	225 g/8 oz	8 oz
Chopped parsley	2 tbs	3 tbs
1 bay leaf		
3 black peppercorns		
For the mixed vegetables:		
Potatoes	450 g/1 lb	1 lb
Carrots	225 g/8 oz	8 oz
Leeks	225 g/8 oz	8oz
For the sauce:		
4 egg yolks		
White wine	4 tbs	5 tbs
Whipping cream	125 ml/4 fl oz	½ cup
Salt and pepper		
Sugar		
Snipped chives	4 tbs	5 tbs

Place the stock in a pan and bring to the boil. Put in the beef, bring back to simmering point, season with salt and pepper, cover and simmer for 1 hour. Peel and slice the onions and divide into rings. Peel and chop the turnips or swede, and the carrots. Add these three vegetables to the pan with the chopped parsley, the bay leaf and peppercorns. Cook for a further 1 hour. Lift out the meat, wrap it in foil and keep hot.

To make the vegetable accompaniment, peel and dice the potatoes and carrots. Strain the stock from cooking the meat, season to taste and measure 300 ml/½ pint (1¼ cups). Place in a pan and bring to the boil. Put in the potato

and carrot and cook for 5 minutes. Meanwhile, trim and clean the leeks then slice thinly. Add to the pan, bring to the boil, season with salt and pepper, cover and simmer for a further 15 minutes, or until the vegetables are tender.

To make the sauce, beat together the egg yolks, wine and cream. Season to taste with salt, pepper and sugar and place in a double boiler or in a bowl over a pan of simmering water. Whisk constantly for about 10 minutes until the sauce begins to thicken. Stir in the chives.

Slice the meat and arrange on a warm serving dish with the mixed vegetables. Spoon the sauce over.

Roast beef with Yorkshire pudding
Serves 6

Ingredients	Metric-Imperial	American
Rib of beef	2 kg/4½ lb	4½ lb
Beef dripping	25 g/1 oz	2 tbs
Salt and pepper		
For the puddings:		
Flour (all-purpose)	175 g/6 oz	1½ cups
Pinch of salt		
2 eggs		
Milk	300 ml/½ pint	1¼ cups
Water	50 ml/2 fl oz	¼ cup

Have the beef jointed with the chine bone removed. Place in a roasting tin with the dripping, sprinkle with salt and pepper, and cook, uncovered, in a preheated moderately hot oven, 200°C, 400°F, Gas Mark 6, for 2 hours, or, if the meat is preferred rare, 1 hour and 50 minutes. Transfer the beef to a warm serving dish and allow to stand for at least 10 minutes before carving.

Meanwhile, make the Yorkshire puddings. Sift the flour and salt together into a bowl and make a well in the centre. Drop in the eggs and half the milk and whisk until smooth. Gradually beat in the remaining milk and the water.

Twenty minutes before the beef is cooked, spoon off 4 tbs (5 tbs) of the dripping from the roasting tin and divide this among 12 deep bun tins (patty pans). Heat in the oven for 5 minutes then divide the batter among the tins. Place on a shelf above the meat for about 15 minutes, or until well risen and golden brown. Arrange on the dish with the beef and serve with horseradish sauce and gravy made with the meat juices.

Left: Silverside with mixed vegetables and chive sauce
Opposite: Boiled beef with apple-horseradish sauce

Boiled beef with apple-horseradish sauce

Serves 4

Ingredients	Metric-Imperial	American
Selection of pot vegetables		
Salted water	500 ml/18 fl oz	2¼ cups
Silverside of beef	750 g/1¾ lb	1¾ lb
Black peppercorns	1 tsp	1 tsp
2 whole cloves		
1 bay leaf		
For the sauce:		
4 dessert apples		
Lemon juice	1 tbs	1 tbs
Grated horseradish from a jar	4 tbs	5 tbs
Salt		

Clean the pot vegetables and peel if necessary. Put the salted water into a pan and bring to the boil. Add the meat, vegetables, peppercorns, cloves and bay leaf, bring to the boil, cover and simmer for 30 minutes. Remove the vegetables, and reserve. Cover the pan again and simmer the meat for a further 1 hour, or until tender. Lift out the beef, slice and place on a warm serving dish. Keep hot. Strain the stock into another pan, add the vegetables and reheat. Drain, arrange on the dish with the meat.

To make the sauce, peel, quarter and core the apples then grate finely. Mix with the lemon juice, and horseradish and add salt to taste. Serve the meat and vegetables with boiled potatoes and carrots and hand the sauce separately.

Pickled beef with horseradish cream
Serves 4

Ingredients	Metric-Imperial	American
Pickled silverside of beef	1 kg/2¼ lb	2¼ lb
Salted water	1.75 L/3 pints	7½ cups
1 medium-sized onion		
1 parsnip		
1 carrot		
1 small head of celeriac		
1 leek		
1 bay leaf		
2 juniper berries		
Few black peppercorns		
For the sauce:		
Whipping cream	125 ml/4 fl oz	½ cup
Grated horseradish from jar	5 tbs	6 tbs
Salt and pepper		
Lemon juice		

Put the beef and salted water into a pan, bring to the boil and skim. Cover and simmer for 1 hour. Peel the onion, parsnip, carrot and celeriac and trim and clean the leek. Cut all the vegetables into bite-sized pieces, add to the meat with the bay leaf, juniper berries and peppercorns and cook, covered, for a 1 further hour.

Lift out the meat, allow to stand for 10 minutes then cut into 1.25 cm/½ inch thick slices. Arrange on a warm serving dish and spoon over a little of the stock.

To make the sauce, whip the cream until thick, stir in the horseradish and add salt, pepper and a little lemon juice to taste. Serve the meat with boiled potatoes, stewed apples, the horseradish cream and cranberry sauce.

Tip: Season the stock to taste and serve with the vegetables as a first course, removing the bay leaf, juniper berries and peppercorns beforehand if possible.

Cold ox tongue with vegetables
Serves 8

Ingredients	Metric-Imperial	American
1 pickled ox tongue	1.25 kg/2¾ lb	2¾ lb
Selection of pot vegetables		
Canned asparagus	300 g/11 oz can	11 oz can
Canned peas	225 g/8 oz can	8 oz can
Canned French beans (green)	225 g/8 oz can	8 oz can
Cherry tomatoes	450 g/1 lb	1 lb
2 small onions		
Snipped chives	2 tbs	3 tbs
Chopped parsley	2 tbs	3 tbs
Oil	125 ml/4 fl oz	½ cup
Vinegar	125 ml/4 fl oz	½ cup
Salt and pepper		
Sugar		
Canned drained mushrooms	50 g/2 oz	⅓ cup
For the sauce:		
Whipping cream	125 ml/4 fl oz	½ cup
Mayonnaise	3 tbs	4 tbs
Chopped parsley	1 tbs	1 tbs
Lemon juice		

Soak the tongue in cold water overnight. Drain and place in a large pan. Clean the pot vegetables, peel if necessary and cut into pieces. Add to the pan and pour over water to cover. Bring to the boil, skim the surface then cover and simmer for about 3½ hours, or until the small bones at the base of the tongue can easily be removed. Drain the tongue, remove the skin, bones and gristle and leave to cool.

Drain the asparagus, peas and beans, reserving the liquid from the asparagus and beans. Pour boiling water over the tomatoes, drain and peel. Place each kind of vegetable in a bowl. Peel and chop the onions. Add half the onion and half the chives to the tomatoes, the remainder of the onion to the beans and half the parsley to the peas.

Beat together the oil, vinegar, and reserved vegetable liquid and season to taste with salt, pepper and sugar. Spoon a quarter of the dressing over each type of vegetable.

Leave to stand for about 30 minutes.

Cut the tongue into thick oblique slices and arrange in a curve on a serving platter. Surround with the marinated vegetables and mushrooms.

To make the sauce, whip the cream until thick and fold in the mayonnaise and herbs. Sharpen the flavour with a little lemon juice to taste. Serve with the tongue and vegetable platter.

Opposite: Pickled beef with horseradish cream
Above: Cold ox tongue with vegetables

Simple braised beef
Serves 4

Ingredients	Metric-Imperial	American
Top rump or topside of beef	1 kg/2¼ lb	2¼ lb
Salt and pepper		
Lard (shortening)	50 g/2 oz	¼ cup
Selection of pot vegetables		
1 tomato		
Hot water		
Flour (all-purpose)	2 tbs	3 tbs

Sprinkle the beef with salt. Melt the lard in a pan and use to brown the meat on all sides. Meanwhile, clean the pot vegetables and peel if necessary. Roughly chop the vegetables and tomato, add to the pan and cook for 3 minutes. Pour in hot water to come half-way up the meat and bring to the boil. Cover and simmer for 2½ hours, adding more hot water as the liquid evaporates. Lift out the meat, slice and arrange on a warm serving dish. Keep hot.

Strain the stock and make up to 450 ml/¾ pint (2 cups), with more water if necessary. Bring to the boil in a pan. Moisten the flour with a little cold water, add to the stock and stir constantly until thickened. Simmer for 4 minutes and adjust the seasoning to taste with salt and pepper. Serve the meat with potato croquettes and buttered beans and hand the sauce separately.

Braised beef, Chinese style
Serves 4

Ingredients	Metric-Imperial	American
Dried sliced mushrooms	3 tbs	4 tbs
Hot water	450 ml/¾ pint	2 cups
Top rump of beef	750 g/1¾ lb	1¾ lb
Salt and pepper		
Streaky bacon (strips)	50 g/2 oz	4 strips
1 onion		
Flour (all-purpose)	1 tbs	1 tbs
Whipping cream	3 tbs	4 tbs
Dry white wine	2 tbs	3 tbs
Beansprouts	175 g/6 oz	6 oz
Soy sauce		
Sugar		

Cover the mushrooms with a little hot water and set aside. Sprinkle the beef with salt and pepper. Chop the bacon, place in a pan and heat until the fat runs. Use the bacon fat to brown the piece of meat on all sides. Peel and chop the onion, add to the pan and fry until soft. Add some of the remaining hot water to the meat, bring to the boil, cover and simmer for 1¾ hours, adding more water as the liquid evaporates.

Drain the mushrooms, chop and add to the pan. Cover again and cook for a further 15 minutes. Transfer the meat to a warm dish and keep hot.

Blend the flour with the cream and add to the pan with the wine. Stir until boiling then put in the beansprouts and season to taste with soy sauce and sugar. Cook for 3 minutes. Slice the meat and serve with rice and lightly cooked Chinese cabbage. Hand the sauce separately.

Rump steaks with horseradish cream
Serves 4

Ingredients	Metric-Imperial	American
Whipping cream	125 ml/4 fl oz	½ cup
Grated horseradish from a jar	1 tbs	1 tbs
Salt and pepper		
4 rump steaks about 2.5 cm/1 inch thick		
Oil		
Sweet paprika pepper		

Whip the cream until thick and mix in the horseradish. Season to taste with salt. Chill until serving time.

Lightly beat the steaks and place on a greased grid in a grill pan (broiler). Cook under high heat for 1 minute on each side. Brush the steaks all over with oil, sprinkle with salt, pepper and paprika and cook for a further 2 minutes on each side, or until done to taste. Serve topped with the horseradish sauce and accompanied by potatoes and a green salad.

Piquant braised beef
Serves 6

Ingredients	Metric-Imperial	American
Top rump of beef	1.5 kg/3¼ lb	3¼ lb
Red wine	1 L/1¾ pints	4⅓ cups
2 carrots		
1 parsnip		
Celeriac	225 g/8 oz	8 oz
3 onions		
4 tomatoes		
1 clove of garlic		
Salt and pepper		
Dried rosemary	¼ tsp	¼ tsp
Dried marjoram	½ tsp	½ tsp
Oil	4 tbs	5 tbs
Streaky bacon (strips)	100 g/4 oz	8 strips
Tomato purée (paste)	2 tbs	3 tbs
Whipping cream	2 tbs	3 tbs

Put the beef into a dish large enough to take it comfortably and pour over the wine. The meat must be completely covered. Leave to marinate for about 48 hours, turning the meat occasionally.

Peel and chop the carrots, parsnip, celeriac and onions. Pour boiling water over the tomatoes, drain, peel and chop. Peel and crush the garlic. Remove the meat from the marinade and dry on absorbent kitchen paper. Sprinkle with salt, pepper, the rosemary and marjoram and rub with the garlic.

Heat the oil in a pan and use to brown the meat on all sides. Add the vegetables and cook for a further 2 minutes. Transfer the ingredients to a roasting tin and lay the bacon over the meat. Mix 500 ml/18 fl oz (2¼ cups) of the marinade with the tomato purée and add to the roasting tin. Cover and cook in a preheated moderate oven, 160°C, 325°F, Gas Mark 3, for about 2½ hours, adding more marinade to the pan as the liquid evaporates, until the meat is tender. Slice the meat, arrange on a warm serving dish and keep hot.

Sieve or liquidize the cooking juices and vegetables and place in a pan. Adjust the seasoning with salt and pepper and bring to boiling point. Remove from the heat, blend in the cream and serve with the meat, boiled potatoes and green beans or broccoli.

Opposite: Simple braised beef
Above: Braised beef with celery

Braised beef with celery
Serves 4

Ingredients	Metric-Imperial	American
Top rump of beef	750 g/1¾ lb	1¾ lb
Salt and pepper		
Oil	4 tbs	5 tbs
Selection of pot vegetables		
Sweet paprika pepper		
Beef stock	125 ml/4 fl oz	½ cup
Light ale (light beer)	400 ml/14 fl oz	1¾ cups
6 small carrots		
1 head of celery		
Small onions	225 g/8 oz	8 oz
Whipping cream	150 ml/¼ pint	⅔ cup

Sprinkle the beef with salt and pepper. Heat the oil in a pan and use to brown the meat on all sides. Clean the pot vegetables, peel if necessary then roughly chop. Add to the pan with 1 tsp paprika. Mix together the stock and beer and pour about half into the pan. Bring to the boil, cover and simmer for about 45 minutes, turning occasionally and adding more of the stock mixture to the pan as the liquid evaporates.

Peel the carrots. Trim the celery, removing any strings. Cut into short lengths. Peel the onions. Add these three vegetables to the pan, cover and cook for a further 1¼ hours. Lift out the meat, slice and arrange on a warm serving dish with the carrots, celery and onions. Keep hot.

Blend the cream into the contents of the pan and cook for 3 minutes, stirring constantly to loosen the sediment. Do not boil Adjust the seasoning with salt, pepper and paprika to taste. Serve poured over the meat, or hand separately.

to the pan, stir well, cover again and allow to cook for a further 30 minutes. Add the mushrooms, cook for 5 minutes more then adjust the seasoning with salt, pepper and paprika to taste. Sprinkle with the parsley and serve with boiled potatoes.

Microwave method

Cut the beef into bite-sized pieces and trim off any fat. Place the browning dish on full power for 1 minute then add the oil and put in the beef. Cook on full power for 2 minutes then turn the beef and return for a further 2 minutes. Season with salt, pepper and paprika; add the water and wine. Return to the microwave for 10 minutes and allow to stand for 5 minutes.

Halve and seed the peppers; cut the flesh into strips. Peel and slice the onions thinly. Remove the dish from the microwave and add the peppers and onion to the beef, stir well. Return on full power for 15 minutes.

Add the mushrooms to the beef and add more paprika if necessary; return on full power for 7 minutes. Allow to stand for 5 minutes and sprinkle with parsley before serving with boiled potatoes.

Sliced braised beef with vegetables
Serves 4

Ingredients	Metric-Imperial	American
1 clove of garlic		
Beef stock (bouillon)	400 ml/14 fl oz	1¾ cups
Brandy	2 tbs	3 tbs
Lemon juice	2 tbs	3 tbs
Oil	2 tbs	3 tbs
Salt and pepper		
Flank of beef	675 g/1½ lb	1½ lb
2 leeks		
4 carrots		
Mushrooms	225 g/8 oz	8 oz
Margarine	25 g/1 oz	2 tbs
Chopped tarragon	1 tsp	1 tsp
Chopped mint	1 tsp	1 tsp
Soy sauce	2 tsp	2 tsp

Peel and crush the garlic. Stir together one third of the beef stock, the brandy, lemon juice, oil and garlic and season with salt and pepper. Thinly slice the beef and place in a dish, pour over the marinade. Cover and leave to stand for 2 hours, turning the meat slices occasionally if they are not completely covered by marinade.

Trim and clean the leeks then cut into slices. Peel and thinly slice the carrots. Slice the mushrooms. Lift out the meat slices and drain well, reserving the marinade.

Melt the margarine in a pan and use to brown the meat slices on both sides. Add the vegetables and cook for a further 2 minutes. Pour in the remaining stock and the marinade, add the tarragon and mint and bring to the boil. Cover and simmer for 30 minutes. Add the soy sauce and simmer for a further 10 minutes, or until the meat is tender. Adjust the seasoning and serve with rice.

Goulash with sweet peppers
Serves 2

Ingredients	Metric-Imperial	American
Chuck steak	350 g/12 oz	12 oz
Oil	3 tbs	4 tbs
Salt and pepper		
Sweet paprika pepper		
Hot water	125 ml/4 fl oz	½ cup
Red wine	125 ml/4 fl oz	½ cup
4 sweet peppers, red and green		
2 large onions		
Canned mushrooms	100 g/4 oz	⅔ cup
Chopped parsley	1 tbs	1 tbs

Cut the beef into bite-sized pieces. Heat the oil in a pan and use to brown the meat all over. Season generously with salt, pepper and paprika and add the water and wine. Bring to the boil then cover and simmer for 45 minutes, adding more water to replace evaporated liquid if necessary.

Halve and deseed the peppers and cut the flesh into strips. Peel and slice the onions. Add the pepper and onion

Left: Goulash with sweet peppers
Opposite: Sliced braised beef with vegetables

Beef stew with wine and apricots
Serves 4

Ingredients	Metric-Imperial	American
Chuck steak	750 g/1¾ lb	1¾ lb
1 large onion		
Oil	4 tbs	5 tbs
Salt and pepper		
Water	300 ml/½ pint	1¼ cups
Medium white wine	350 ml/12 fl oz	1½ cups
Green peppercorns	1 tbs	1 tbs
Canned, drained apricot halves	225 g/8 oz	8 oz
Whipping cream	150 ml/¼ pint	⅔ cup
Ground cinnamon	¼ tsp	¼ tsp

Cut the beef into 2.5 cm/1 inch cubes. Peel and chop the onion. Heat the oil in a pan, add the meat and onion and fry until the meat is brown. Season with salt and pepper, pour in the water and wine and add the peppercorns. Bring to the boil, cover and simmer for 1 hour.

Sieve or liquidize half the apricots and add to the pan with the apricot halves and cook for a further 15 minutes. Stir in the cream and cinnamon, adjust the seasoning with salt and pepper and reheat.

Below: Beef stew with wine and apricots
Below right: Chinese beef with bamboo shoots
Opposite: Beef rolls with gherkins

Chinese beef with bamboo shoots
Serves 4

Ingredients	Metric-Imperial	American
Dried sliced mushrooms	1 tbs	1 tbs
Rump steak	450 g/1 lb	1 lb
Soy sauce	4 tbs	5 tbs
Rice wine or dry sherry	2 tbs	3 tbs
Cornflour (cornstarch)	2 tbs	3 tbs
Oil	250 ml/9 fl oz	generous 1 cup
1 leek		
Canned bamboo shoots	225 g/8 oz can	8 oz can
Hot water	250 ml/9 fl oz	generous 1 cup
Ground ginger	½ tsp	½ tsp
Salt		

Soak the mushrooms overnight in cold water. Cut the beef first into slices and then into thin strips. Stir together the soy sauce and rice wine or sherry and use to marinate the meat strips for about 30 minutes. Drain the meat strips well and coat in the cornflour.

Heat the oil in a large pan or wok and use to fry the meat lightly, in batches, until sealed. Drain and keep hot. Remove all but 5 tbs (6 tbs) of the oil from the pan.

Trim and clean the leek and cut into slices. Drain the bamboo shoots and cut into strips. Add the leek and bamboo shoots to the oil and fry for 3 minutes. Drain the mushrooms and add to the pan with the marinade, hot water, ginger and meat strips. Bring to the boil, stirring, then simmer, uncovered, for 15 minutes. Season to taste with salt and serve with freshly boiled rice.

Beef rolls with gherkins
Serves 4

Ingredients	Metric-Imperial	American
4 sirloin steaks	200 g/7 oz each	7 oz each
French mustard	100 g/4 oz	8 strips
Salt and pepper		
Sweet paprika pepper		
1 gherkin (small dill pickle)		
2 onions		
Streaky bacon (strips)	100 g/4 oz	8 strips
Lard (shortening)	25 g/1 oz	2 tbs
Water	300 ml/½ pint	1¼ cups
Selection of pot vegetables		
Red wine or beef stock (bouillon)	125 ml/4 fl oz	½ cup
Whipping cream	2 tbs	3 tbs
Brandy	2 tbs	3 tbs

Beat the steaks until fairly thin, spread one side with mustard and season with salt, pepper and paprika. Cut the gherkin lengthways into 4 strips. Peel and slice the onions. Top each piece of meat with a slice of bacon (2 strips), then with onion slices and finally a strip of gherkin. Roll up each piece of meat from the narrowest end and secure with fine string or skewers.

Melt the lard in a pan and use to brown the meat rolls on all sides. Add the water, bring to the boil, cover and simmer for about 30 minutes.

Meanwhile, clean the pot vegetables, peel if necessary and cut into pieces. Add to the pan, cover again and cook for a further 1 hour, replacing evaporated liquid with wine or stock. Remove the beef rolls, discard the string or skewers, and place on a warm serving dish. Keep hot while preparing a sauce.

Press the cooking liquid and vegetables through a sieve into another pan, stir in the cream and brandy and season to taste with salt, pepper and paprika. Heat through without boiling then serve the creamy wine sauce with the beef rolls accompanied by boiled noodles and rice and a colourful mixed salad or cooked red cabbage.

Braised pepper beef
Serves 4

Ingredients	Metric-Imperial	American
Flank of beef	750 g/1¾ lb	1¾ lb
Onions	450 g/1 lb	1 lb
Dripping	25 g/1 oz	2 tbs
Salt and pepper		
Black peppercorns	1 tsp	1 tsp
Pinch of hot paprika pepper		
3 bay leaves		
Lemon juice	1 tbs	1 tbs
Beef stock (bouillon)	500 ml/18 fl oz	2¼ cups
Fresh breadcrumbs	2 tbs	3 tbs
Lemon slices		

Cut the beef into 2.5 cm/1 inch cubes. Peel and chop the onions. Heat the fat in a pan and use to brown the meat cubes on all sides. Remove the meat, add the onion to the fat remaining in the pan and fry until golden.

Return the meat cubes and add 1 tsp salt, the peppercorns, paprika, bay leaves, lemon juice and stock to the pan. Stir well, bring to the boil then cover and simmer for about 1 hour, or until the meat is tender. Stir in the breadcrumbs and adjust the seasoning with salt and pepper to taste. Cook for a further 5 minutes, transfer to a warm dish and garnish with lemon slices. Serve with boiled potatoes and gherkins (dill pickles).

Braised beef with white wine
Serves 4

Ingredients	Metric-Imperial	American
Braising beef	750 g/1¾ lb	1¾ lb
Olive oil	4 tbs	5 tbs
2 cloves of garlic		
Chopped oregano	1 tsp	1 tsp
Salt and pepper		
5 tomatoes		
1 bay leaf		
Medium white wine	125 ml/4 fl oz	½ cup
Beef stock (bouillon)	125 ml/4 fl oz	½ cup
Onions	450 g/1 lb	1 lb
Butter	25 g/1 oz	2 tbs
Chopped parsley	3 tbs	4 tbs

Cut the beef into 2.5 cm/1 inch cubes. Heat the oil in a flameproof pan, and use to brown the meat cubes on all sides. Peel and finely chop the garlic. Push the meat to the sides of the pan, put the garlic into the centre, add the oregano and a little salt and fry for 2 minutes. Stir the ingredients together and season with pepper.

Meanwhile, pour boiling water over the tomatoes, drain, peel and chop. Add to the pan with the bay leaf, wine and stock. Cover and place in a preheated moderately hot oven, 200°C, 400°F, Gas Mark 6, for about 1 hour, or until the meat is tender. Adjust the seasoning if necessary.

Peel and slice the onions. Melt the butter in a pan and use to cook the onions until golden. Spoon over the braised beef and serve sprinkled with parsley.

Below: Braised pepper beef
Opposite: Braised beef with white wine

165

Beef olives with chicory
Serves 4

Ingredients	Metric-Imperial	American
4 small heads of chicory (Belgian endive)		
4 slices of flank of beef	175 g/6 oz each	6 oz each
Salt and white pepper		
Sweet paprika pepper		
Cayenne pepper		
4 slices of lean cooked ham		
Oil	4 tbs	5 tbs
Medium white wine	225 ml/8 fl oz	1 cup
For the sauce:		
3 tomatoes		
Flour (all-purpose)	2 tbs	3 tbs
Whipping cream	2 tbs	3 tbs
Salt		
Pinch of sugar		
Worcestershire sauce		

Remove any rough outer leaves from the chicory and cut a cross in the base of each. Sprinkle each slice of beef with salt and pepper, paprika and a little cayenne. Top each piece of meat with a slice of ham and then a chicory head. Starting from the narrowest end of the meat slices roll each up and secure with wooden cocktail sticks (toothpicks) or fine string.

Heat the oil in a pan and use to brown the beef rolls on all sides. Add half the wine, bring to boiling point, cover and simmer for 1¼ hours, adding the rest of the wine as the liquid evaporates. Transfer the beef olives to a warm serving dish and remove the sticks or string. Keep hot.

Pour boiling water over the tomatoes, drain, peel, halve and remove the seeds. Sieve or liquidize the flesh and add to the juices in the pan. Blend the flour with the cream, add to the pan and stir until boiling. Simmer for 3 minutes, season with salt and add the sugar and a few drops of Worcestershire sauce to taste. Serve with the beef olives accompanied by noodles or potatoes.

Microwave hint
To test pot-roasted or braised meat for doneness, use a microwave thermometer, which can be left inside the meat in a roasting bag. If your microwave has a probe, make a slit in the bag and insert the probe through the slit. If you have neither, remove the meat from the cooker and test with a conventional meat thermometer.

Microwave hint
Do not salt food on the surface, especially meat and vegetables, as it causes dehydration, and toughness. Sprinkle salt on meat after removing it from the microwave cooker.

Hungarian goulash
Serves 4

Ingredients	Metric-Imperial	American
Chuck steak	750 g/1¾ lb	1¾ lb
Oil	2 tbs	3 tbs
Salt and pepper		
Large mild onions	550 g/1¼ lb	1¼ lb
Sweet paprika pepper	2 tsp	2 tsp
1 red sweet pepper		
1 red chilli pepper		
2 large tomatoes		
Water	125 ml/4 fl oz	½ cup

Cut the beef into 2.5 cm/1 inch cubes. Heat the oil in a pan and use to brown the meat all over. Season with salt and pepper. Peel and chop the onions, add to the meat, sprinkle with the paprika and cook for a further 5 minutes. Halve and deseed both the peppers and cut the flesh into strips. Add to the pan and cook for a further 5 minutes.

Pour boiling water over the tomatoes, drain, peel and chop. Mix with the water and pour into the pan. Bring to the boil, cover and simmer for 1½ hours. Adjust the seasoning if necessary and serve with macaroni or ribbon noodles and a green salad.

Variations: Halve and deseed 1 green sweet pepper, cut the flesh into strips and use instead of the tomatoes.

Brown the beef in the oil with 1-2 crushed cloves of garlic at the beginning of the recipe.

Left: Hungarian goulash
Opposite: Beef goulash with feta cheese

Beef goulash with feta cheese
Serves 4-6

Ingredients	Metric-Imperial	American
Top rump of beef	1 kg/2¼ lb	2¼ lb
Olive oil	6 tbs	½ cup
Beef stock (bouillon)	750 ml/1¼ pints	3 cups
Tomato purée (paste)	4 tbs	5 tbs
Wine vinegar	3 tbs	4 tbs
Caraway seeds	½ tsp	½ tsp
1 cinnamon stick		
Salt and pepper		
Small onions	750 g/1¾ lb	1¾ lb
Feta cheese	100 g/4 oz	4 oz

Cut the beef into 2.5 cm/1 inch cubes. Heat the oil in a pan and use to brown the meat cubes on all sides. Pour in the stock, stir in the tomato purée, vinegar, caraway seeds and cinnamon stick and season with salt and pepper. Bring to the boil, cover and simmer for 1 hour.

Meanwhile, peel the onions. Blanch in a pan of boiling water for 1 minute then drain. Add to the meat mixture, cover and cook for a further 30 minutes. Adjust the seasoning to taste, remove the cinnamon stick and transfer the goulash to a warm serving dish. Crumble the cheese over the top.

Oxtail with bacon and celery
Serves 4

Ingredients	Metric-Imperial	American
Streaky bacon (strips)	200 g/7 oz	14 strips
Oxtail	1 kg/2¼ lb	2¼ lb
4 sticks of celery		
1 onion		
1 clove of garlic		
Medium white wine	225 ml/8 fl oz	1 cup
Canned tomatoes	2 × 396 g/14 oz cans	2 × 14 oz cans
Salt and pepper		
Beef stock (bouillon)		

Chop the bacon, place in a pan and heat until the fat runs. Have the oxtail divided into pieces about 4 cm/1½ inches long. Add to the pan and fry until sealed on all sides. Remove the oxtail.

Cut the celery into 2.5 cm/1 inch lengths. Peel and chop the onion and garlic. Put the celery, onion and garlic into the fat remaining in the pan and fry, stirring, for 3 minutes. Pour in the wine, bring to the boil then simmer for 5 minutes. Drain the tomatoes, quarter them then add to the pan with the liquid from the cans and the oxtail. Season well with salt and pepper, bring to the boil, cover and simmer for about 2 hours, replacing evaporated liquid with stock. Adjust the seasoning if necessary and serve with boiled potatoes.

Below: Oxtail with bacon and celery
Opposite: Braised sirloin steaks with stuffed olives

Braised sirloin steaks with stuffed olives
Serves 2

Ingredients	Metric-Imperial	American
2 large sirloin steaks on the bone		
Salt and pepper		
1 onion		
2 tomatoes		
Oil	4 tbs	5 tbs
15 stuffed green olives		
Green peppercorns	2 tbs	3 tbs
Beef stock (bouillon)	150 ml/¼ pint	⅔ cup
Flour (all-purpose)	1 tbs	1 tbs
Sour cream	125 ml/4 fl oz	½ cup

Sprinkle the steaks with pepper. Peel and chop the onion. Pour boiling water over the tomatoes, drain, peel and cut into wedges. Heat the oil in a large pan and use to brown the meat on both sides. Add the onion, olives, peppercorns, tomato wedges and stock, cover and cook gently for 20 minutes. Transfer the steak and olive mixture to a warm serving dish, sprinkle with salt and keep hot. Strain the cooking juices into a rinsed pan. Blend the flour with the cream, add to the sauce and stir until boiling. Simmer for 4 minutes and adjust the seasoning if necessary. Serve the steaks and olive mixture with the sauce.

Beef and kohlrabi stew
Serves 4

Ingredients	Metric-Imperial	American
Stewing steak (chuck)	675 g/1½ lb	1½ lb
Oil	4 tbs	5 tbs
Salt and pepper		
2 onions		
Beef stock (bouillon)	750 ml/1¼ pints	3 cups
2 carrots		
2 kohlrabi		
Chopped marjoram	1 tbs	1 tbs
Grated horseradish from a jar	1 tsp	1 tsp
Chopped parsley	1 tbs	1 tbs

Cut the beef first into slices, then into small strips. Heat the oil in a pan and use to brown the meat strips on all sides. Season with salt and pepper. Peel and chop the onions, add to the pan and cook until golden. Pour in the stock, bring to the boil, cover and simmer for 30 minutes.

Meanwhile, peel and slice the carrots and peel and roughly chop the kohlrabi. Add these to the pan with the marjoram and horseradish and season to taste with salt and pepper. Cook for a further 30 minutes. Sprinkle with the parsley before serving.

Stuffed fillet of beef with Danish Blue cream
Serves 6

Ingredients	Metric-Imperial	American
Pine kernels (nuts)	50 g/2 oz	½ cup
Oil	4 tbs	5 tbs
1 onion		
2 cloves of garlic		
Whipped cream	2 tbs	3 tbs
Dried herbs of Provence	2 tbs	3 tbs
Chopped mixed fresh herbs	4 tbs	5 tbs
Salt and pepper		
Fillet of beef	1 kg/2¼ lb	2¼ lb
Cherry tomatoes (optional)		
Sprigs of herbs		

For the sauce:

Whipping cream	150 ml/¼ pint	⅔ cup
Danish blue cheese	100 g/4 oz	4 oz

Place the pine kernels and 1 tsp of the oil in a frying pan and toss the nuts over moderate heat until golden. Cool and then grind. Peel and finely chop the onion and 1 clove of garlic. Heat about a quarter of the remaining oil in a pan and use to fry the onion and chopped garlic until transparent. Remove with a slotted spoon and mix with the ground pine kernels, whipped cream, half the dried and fresh herbs and salt and pepper to taste.

Remove any membrane from the fillet then make a deep lengthways slit in it and fill with the herb mixture. Close the opening and tie the meat with fine string. Place in an ovenproof dish.

Peel and very finely chop the second clove of garlic, add to the rest of the oil and season with salt and pepper. Stir in

Mustard steaks
Serves 4

Ingredients	Metric-Imperial	American
4 fillet steaks	100 g/4 oz each	4 oz each
Salt and pepper		
2 onions		
Dry mustard (powder)	3 tbs	4 tbs
2 eggs		
Chopped parsley	1 tbs	1 tbs
Whipping cream	2 tbs	3 tbs
Flour (all-purpose)	3 tbs	4 tbs
Butter	25 g/1 oz	2 tbs

Flatten the steaks slightly and sprinkle with salt and pepper. Peel and finely chop the onions. Beat together the onion, mustard, eggs, parsley, cream and flour. Coat the steaks with the mustard mixture.

Melt the butter in a frying pan, put in the steaks and cook for about 3 minutes on each side, or until done to taste. Serve with fried potatoes and a green salad.

Microwave hint
To reduce the frying or roasting time of chips or roast potatoes, place the prepared potatoes in a bowl. Cover and cook on full power for 3–5 minutes, depending upon the quantity, until the potatoes are thoroughly warmed through.

Left: Stuffed fillet of beef with Danish blue cream
Below: Mustard steaks

the remaining dried and fresh herbs. Spread this mixture over the meat, cover and leave to stand for about 2 hours.

Uncover the meat and place in a preheated hot oven, 220°C, 425°F, Gas Mark 7, for about 40 minutes, turning during this time. Leave the fillet to cool, remove the trussing string and cut the meat into slices. Arrange on a serving dish and garnish with cherry tomatoes and sprigs of herbs.

To make the Danish blue cream, half whip the cream. Press the cheese through a sieve and beat in the cream. Serve the meat with toast, French bread, sauté or new potatoes and a fennel salad. Hand the cheese cream separately.

Cook's tip: Freeze fresh herbs unblanched. First remove their stalks, then place the herbs in small polythene bags or containers. No need to thaw, just crumble the frozen herbs into the dish.

Beef Wellington
Serves 6

Ingredients	Metric-Imperial	American
1 fillet of beef	750 g/1¾ lb	1¾ lb
Butter	100 g/4 oz	½ cup
2 onions		
Button mushrooms	50 g/2 oz	2 oz
Whipping cream	125 ml/4 fl oz	½ cup
Salt and pepper		
Frozen puff pastry	450 g/l lb	1 lb
1 egg		
Milk	1 tsp	1 tsp

Remove any membrane from the fillet. Melt half the butter in a pan, add the fillet and fry until sealed on all sides. Leave to cool.

Peel and chop the onions and slice the mushrooms. Add the remaining butter to the pan and use to cook the onion and mushroom until the onion is transparent. Stir in the cream and season to taste with salt and pepper. Cook for 2 minutes, stirring. Allow to cool.

Defrost the pastry and roll out to a rectangle measuring just over twice the size of the fillet. Put a little of the onion mixture into the centre of the pastry, lay the fillet on top and cover with the remaining onion mixture. Separate the egg and lightly beat the white. Fold up the pastry to enclose the fillet, brush the edges with egg white and seal well together. Transfer to a dampened baking sheet (cookie sheet) with the seal downwards. Cut shapes from the pastry trimmings to decorate the pastry surface. Beat the egg yolk with the milk and use to brush the pastry. Position the decorations and brush these also with egg yolk. Place, uncovered, in a preheated moderately hot oven, 200°C, 400°F, Gas Mark 6 for 40-45 minutes, or until the pastry is golden brown. Serve with peas.

Microwave hint

It is important to cook certain dishes uncovered by microwave for reheating purposes, such as those that have been pre-fried, like fried or croquette potatoes. If covered, the coating tends to lose crispness and become soft.

Below: Beef Wellington
Opposite: Roast fillet of beef

Roast fillet of beef
Serves 4

Ingredients	Metric-Imperial	American
1 fillet of beef	1 kg/2¼ lb	2¼ lb
Salt and pepper		
Oil	2 tsp	2 tsp

Remove any membrane from the fillet and rub it with salt and pepper and the oil. Place in a greased roasting tin and cook, uncovered, in a preheated hot oven, 220°C, 425°F, Gas Mark 7, for 30 minutes, turning the meat once during this time, or until cooked to taste. Transfer the fillet to a warm dish and leave to stand for 10 minutes before slicing. Serve with lightly steamed broccoli and duchesse or sauté potatoes.

Beef in cream sauce
Serves 2

Ingredients	Metric-Imperial	American
Rump steak	275 g/10 oz	10 oz
1 onion		
1 cucumber		
2 tomatoes		
1 clove of garlic		
Butter	15 g/½ oz	1 tbs
Salt and pepper		
Whipping cream	150 ml/¼ pint	⅔ cup
Tomato purée (paste)	1 tsp	1 tsp
French mustard	½ tsp	½ tsp
½ beef stock cube (bouillon)		

Slice the beef and then cut the slices into thin strips. Peel and chop the onion and cucumber. Pour boiling water over the tomatoes, drain, peel and chop. Peel and crush the garlic and rub the inside of a pan with it. Put in the butter and use to fry the meat for 8 minutes, stirring frequently. Sprinkle with salt and pepper, remove and keep hot.

Add the onion to the fat remaining in the pan and cook until transparent. Put in the cucumber and tomato and heat through, stirring. Blend in the cream, tomato purée and mustard and crumble in the stock cube. Stir really well and bring to the boil. Simmer for 2 minutes then return the meat to the pan and heat through. Serve with fried potatoes.

Beef and pork patties
Serves 4

Ingredients	Metric-Imperial	American
1 bread roll		
2 medium-sized onions		
Minced beef and pork combined (ground)	675 g/1½ lb	1½ lb
1 egg		
Salt and pepper		
Sweet paprika pepper		
White vegetable fat	50 g/2 oz	¼ cup

Soak the roll in cold water then squeeze out the moisture. Peel and chop the onions. Mix together the soaked bread, onion, meat and egg. Season to taste with salt, pepper and paprika. With wet hands, form the meat mixture into 8 round flat patties.

Melt the fat in a large frying pan, put in the patties and fry for about 5 minutes on each side, or until golden brown.

Rump steaks in beer sauce

Serves 4

Ingredients	Metric-Imperial	American
Onions	450 g/1 lb	1 lb
Oil	2 tbs	3 tbs
4 rump steaks	175 g/6 oz each	6 oz each
Salt and pepper		
Chopped thyme		
Beef stock (bouillon)	75 ml/3 fl oz	⅓ cup
Light ale (light beer)	125 ml/4 fl oz	½ cup

Peel and slice the onions. Heat the oil in a frying pan and use to cook the onion until golden. Remove and keep hot.

Snip the fat around the steaks. Reheat the oil in the pan, put in the steaks and cook for 3–4 minutes on each side, or until done to taste. Sprinkle with salt, pepper and thyme and transfer to a warm serving dish. Put the onions on the steaks, keep hot. Add the stock and ale to the pan and stir up the sediment. Bring to the boil and cook for 3 minutes. Spoon a little over the steaks and hand the rest separately.

Opposite: Beef in cream sauce
Below: Rump steaks in beer sauce

Steaks with green peppercorn sauce
Serves 2

Ingredients	Metric-Imperial	American
2 fillet steaks	150 g/5 oz each	5 oz each
Salt and pepper		
Butter	15 g/½ oz	1 tbs
Brandy	2 tbs	3 tbs
Whipping cream	150 ml/¼ pint	⅔ cup
Green peppercorns	1 tbs	1 tbs

Sprinkle the steaks with salt and pepper. Melt the butter in a frying pan, put in the steaks and cook for about 3 minutes on each side, or until done to taste. Transfer to a warm serving dish and keep hot.

Add the brandy to the juices remaining in the pan and stir well. Blend in the cream and adjust the seasoning with salt and pepper. Stir in the peppercorns, bring to the boil and pour over the steaks. Serve with potatoes baked in their jackets, topped with sour cream mixed with chopped herbs.

	Metric-Imperial	American
Cayenne pepper		
Butter or margarine	·50 g/2 oz	¼ cup
Spinach	1 kg/2¼ lb	2¼ lb
Ground nutmeg		
Natural yogurt (plain)	300 ml/½ pint	1¼ cups

Peel and chop the onions and place in a strainer. Dip the onion, in the strainer, into boiling water for 2 minutes. Drain well. Peel the garlic and chop very finely. Mix the garlic and onion with the meat and sausagemeat, and eggs. Season generously with salt and pepper and add a little cayenne.

With wet hands form the mixture into small balls, each about the size of a walnut. Melt half the butter, add the meatballs and cook for about 15 minutes, turning until brown.

Remove any tough stalks from the spinach and wash well. Melt the remaining butter in a large pan. Drain the spinach and add to the pan with just the water clinging to the leaves. Put on the lid and cook for about 5 minutes, shaking the pan occasionally, or until the spinach is limp. Season with salt, pepper and nutmeg to taste. Transfer the spinach to a warm serving dish and top with the meatballs. Season the yogurt with salt and pepper and spoon over the meatballs.

Microwave method

Peel and chop the onions and place in a suitable dish in the microwave with a little water for 2 minutes on full power. Drain and put into a bowl with the crushed garlic, meat and eggs. Season generously with salt, pepper and a little cayenne.

Wet the hands and form the mixture into small balls, each about the size of a walnut. Put a browning dish into the microwave for 2 minutes on full power then add half the butter or margarine and return on full power for 40 seconds. Add the meat balls and cook for 3 minutes on full power, remove and turn and cook for a further 3 minutes.

Meanwhile remove any stalks from the spinach and wash well. Put the spinach in a suitable dish with the remaining butter and 1 tbs water, cover and cook for 5 minutes on full power.

Season the spinach and sprinkle with nutmeg. Arrange the meatballs on top and cook on full power for 6 minutes. Spoon the yogurt over the meatballs and sprinkle with a little cayenne; serve straight from the dish.

If there are too many meatballs divide the spinach and meat balls into two dishes and cook for 5 minutes each.

Turkish meatballs with yogurt sauce
Serves 4

Ingredients	Metric-Imperial	American
2 onions		
1 clove of garlic		
Minced beef and pork combined (ground)	350 g/12 oz	12 oz
Pork sausagemeat (bulk pork sausage)	100 g/4 oz	4 oz
2 eggs		
Salt and pepper		

Liver with pineapple and onion
Serves 2

Ingredients	Metric-Imperial	American
2 slices of calves' liver (beef)	100 g/4 oz each	4 oz each
Flour (all-purpose)	1 tbs	1 tbs
Margarine	50 g/2 oz	¼ cup
Salt and pepper		
1 medium-sized onion		
2 slices canned pineapple		
Chopped parsley	1 tbs	1 tbs

Coat the liver slices with the flour. Melt the margarine in a frying pan, put in the liver slices and cook for about 5 minutes on each side, or until done to taste. Season with salt and pepper, transfer to a warm dish and keep hot.

Peel and slice the onion and cut the pineapple into pieces. Add the onion and pineapple to the fat remaining in the pan and cook, stirring frequently, until the onion is soft. Spoon over the liver slices and sprinkle with the parsley. Serve with fried potatoes.

Variation: Use pigs' liver instead of calves' liver, but soak the slices in milk for 1 hour before cooking.

Cook 1 medium-sized sliced green pepper until soft with the onion and pineapple.

Sirloin steaks with courgettes
Serves 4

Ingredients	Metric-Imperial	American
4 large courgettes (zucchini)		
Butter	100 g/4 oz	½ cup
Whipping cream	3 tbs	4 tbs
Salt and pepper		
4 sirloin steaks	175 g/6 oz each	6 oz each
Chopped parsley	1 tbs	1 tbs

Peel the courgettes, halve them lengthways and cut into 2.5 cm/1 inch pieces. Melt 40 g/1½ oz (3 tbs) of the butter in a pan, stir in the courgette pieces and cook for 1 minute. Add the cream and season to taste with salt and pepper. Cover and cook gently for 15 minutes, or until the courgette is tender.

Snip the fat around the steaks. Melt the remaining butter in a frying pan, put in the steaks and cook for 3 minutes on each side, or until done to taste. Baste with the pan juices during cooking. Transfer the steaks to a warm serving dish, spoon the courgette mixture over them and garnish with the parsley. Serve with potatoes baked in their jackets and a radish or tomato salad.

Variation: For added flavour, gently cook 1 peeled and finely chopped onion and add to the courgette pieces.

Skewered baby meatballs
Serves 4

Ingredients	Metric-Imperial	American
1 bread roll		
1 large onion		
Minced beef and pork combined (ground)	450 g/1 lb	1 lb
1 egg		
Chopped marjoram	½ tsp	½ tsp
Salt and pepper		
Sweet paprika pepper		
1 red sweet pepper		
1 bunch of spring onions (scallions)		
4 bay leaves		
White vegetable fat	50 g/2 oz	¼ cup
Sprigs of marjoram		

Soak the roll in water then squeeze out the moisture. Peel and chop the onion and mix with the meat, bread, egg and chopped marjoram. Season to taste with salt, pepper and paprika and mix well. Deseed the pepper and cut the flesh into strips. Trim the spring onions leaving on about 15 cm/ 6 inches of the green part.

With wet hands, form the meat mixture into 16 balls. Thread the meatballs, pepper strips, onions and bay leaves on to 4 skewers.

Melt the fat in a large frying pan, put in the skewers and cook for about 8 minutes, turning them frequently and basting with the fat in the pan. Serve garnished with sprigs of marjoram accompanied by a risotto and orange and fennel salad.

Simple fried fillet steaks
Serves 4

Ingredients	Metric-Imperial	American
Butter	50 g/2 oz	¼ cup
4 fillet steaks	150 g/5 oz each	5 oz each
Salt and pepper		

Heat the butter in a frying pan, put in the steaks and cook for 4 minutes. Turn, sprinkle with salt and pepper and cook the second side for 3 minutes, or until done to taste. Transfer the steaks to a warm serving dish and spoon the pan juices over them.

Variation: Spread the steaks with French mustard before cooking then serve sprinkled with chopped herbs.

Opposite: Liver with pineapple and onion
Right: Skewered baby meatballs

179

Fillet steaks Lucullus
Serves 2

Ingredients	Metric-Imperial	American
2 tomatoes		
Mushrooms	50 g/2 oz	2 oz
2 fillet steaks	175 g/6 oz each	6 oz each
Salt		
16 black peppercorns		
Tomato purée (paste)	1 tsp	1 tsp
Chopped marjoram	2 tbs	3 tbs

Peel and chop the tomatoes. Slice the mushrooms. Season the steaks with salt. Lightly crush the peppercorns. Spread both sides of the steaks with the tomato purée then place each on foil and scatter over the peppercorns. Divide the tomatoes and mushrooms between the steaks and sprinkle with marjoram.

Fold up the foil and crimp the edges together to make airtight parcels. Place these on a baking sheet and cook in a preheated hot oven, 230°C, 450°F, Gas Mark 8 for 8 minutes. Fold back the foil and cook on for about 6 minutes.

Poached fillet of beef
(Photo p. 152–153)
Serves 4

Ingredients	Metric-Imperial	American
Fillet of beef	750 g/1¾ lb	1¾ lb
Salt and pepper		
Beef stock (bouillon)	1.5 L/2½ pints	6¼ cups
Coarsely ground black pepper	1 tbs	1 tbs
Chopped parsley	1 tbs	1 tbs

Remove any membrane from the fillet, sprinkle with salt and pepper on all sides and tie into a neat shape with fine string, making three loops on one long side. Thread the handle of a wooden spoon through these loops, so the meat can be suspended and covered in stock, without touching the pan base.

Put the stock into the chosen pan and bring to the boil. Suspend the meat in it, reduce the heat so that the stock barely simmers and cook for 20 minutes. Lift out the fillet and remove the string. Slice the meat and arrange on a hot dish. Sprinkle with the pepper and parsley.

Meatball stroganoff
Serves 4–6

Ingredients	Metric-Imperial	American
2 bread rolls		
2 medium-sized onions		
Minced beef and pork combined (ground)	750 g/1¾ lb	1¾ lb
3 eggs		
Salt and freshly ground pepper		
Ground nutmeg		
Butter or margarine	50 g/2 oz	¼ cup
For the sauce:		
Mushrooms	350 g/12 oz	12 oz
Onion	225 g/8 oz	8 oz
Whipping cream	225 g/8 fl oz	1 cup
French mustard	2 tsp	2 tsp
Salt and pepper		
Sugar		
2 large gherkins (dill pickles)		

Soak the rolls in cold water then squeeze out the moisture. Peel and chop the onions. Mix together the meat, onion, eggs and crumbled bread and season to taste with salt, pepper and nutmeg. With wet hands, form the mixture into 12 balls.

Melt the butter or margarine in a frying pan, add the meatballs and fry for about 12 minutes, turning frequently, until brown and cooked through. Transfer to a warm serving dish and keep hot.

To make the sauce, slice the mushrooms, peel and slice the onions and divide the slices into rings. Add the mushrooms and onions to the fat remaining in the pan and cook, stirring, until the onion is softened. Stir in the cream and mustard and season to taste with salt, pepper and sugar. Cook for 5 minutes, to reduce slightly. Meanwhile, cut the gherkins into strips. Add to the sauce and heat through. Spoon the sauce over the meatballs and serve with parslied potatoes and a cucumber salad.

Opposite: Fillet steaks Lucullus
Above: Meatball stroganoff

Beef strips with mushrooms
Serves 4

Ingredients	Metric-Imperial	American
Fillet of beef	550 g/1¼ lb	1¼ lb
Flour (all-purpose)	2 tbs	3 tbs
2 onions		
Butter	100 g/4 oz	½ cup
Mushrooms	225 g/8 oz	8 oz
Dry white wine	125 ml/4 fl oz	½ cup
Whipping cream	225 ml/8 fl oz	1 cup
Salt and pepper		

Remove any membrane from the beef and cut it into thin strips. Dust with the flour. Peel and chop 1 onion. Melt about one quarter of the butter in a pan, add half the chopped onion and half the meat and cook, stirring frequently, for 2 minutes until browned. Remove from the pan and keep hot. Melt a further quarter of the butter and use to brown the remaining meat and chopped onion in the same way.

Peel and chop the second onion and cut any large mushrooms in half or into quarters. Melt the rest of the butter in a pan, add the onion and mushrooms and cook for about 10 minutes, stirring frequently. Mix in the wine and cream, season with salt and pepper, add the meat mixture and cook, stirring, for about 6 minutes. Serve with potatoes baked in their jackets and mixed vegetables.

Above: Beef strips with mushrooms
Opposite: Peppered fillet steaks

182

Liver with onions and mushrooms
Serves 4

Ingredients	Metric-Imperial	American
4 slices calves' liver (beef)	100 g/4 oz each	4 oz each
Flour (all-purpose)	1 tbs	1 tbs
Butter or margarine	50 g/2 oz	¼ cup
Salt and pepper		
Onions	225 g/8 oz	8 oz
Drained canned mushrooms	200 g/7 oz	1¼ cups

Coat the liver with the flour. Heat half the butter or margarine in a frying pan and use to fry the liver slices for about 5 minutes on each side, or until done to taste. Sprinkle with salt and pepper, transfer to a warm dish and keep hot.

Peel and slice the onions, separate the slices into rings. Melt the remaining butter and use to cook the onion rings until golden. Add the mushrooms, season to taste with salt and pepper and heat through. Spoon over the liver and serve with mashed potato and baked apples.

Variation: Use pigs' liver instead of calves' liver and soak the slices in milk for 1 hour before cooking.

Peppered fillet steaks
Serves 4

Ingredients	Metric-Imperial	American
Black peppercorns	2 tbs	3 tbs
4 fillet steaks	150 g/5 oz each	5 oz each
Butter	40 g/1½ oz	3 tbs
Oil	1 tbs	1 tbs
Brandy	2 tbs	3 tbs
Whipping cream	150 ml/¼ pint	⅔ cup

Put the peppercorns between two sheets of greaseproof paper (waxed) and crush with a rolling pin. Press the crushed peppercorns into both sides of the steaks.

Heat the butter and oil in a frying pan, put in the steaks and cook for about 4 minutes on the first side. Turn and cook for 3 minutes on the second side, or until done to taste. Transfer the steaks to a warm serving dish and keep hot.

Stir the brandy into the pan juices and ignite. When the flames die down, stir in the cream and heat through well. Season to taste with salt. Spoon over the steaks and serve at once.

Microwave hint
If you find minced (ground) beef rather fatty, place in a micro-proof non-metal colander inside a casserole. The excess fat will drip through into the casserole during cooking.

Simple fried rump steaks
Serves 4

Ingredients	Metric-Imperial	American
4 rump steaks	175 g/6 oz each	6 oz each
Butter	50 g/2 oz	¼ cup
Salt and pepper		

Snip the fat around the steaks. Melt the butter in a frying pan, add the steaks and cook for 4 minutes. Turn, sprinkle with salt and pepper and cook for a further 3 minutes, or until done to taste, basting the steaks during cooking. Transfer to a warm serving dish and spoon over the pan juices.

Variations: Top the cooked steaks with fried onions and serve with horseradish sauce.

Veal goulash with capers
Serves 4

Ingredients	Metric-Imperial	American
Breast of veal	1.25 kg/2¾ lb	2¾ lb
Selection of pot vegetables		
2 onions		
3 bay leaves		
White peppercorns	1 tsp	1 tsp
Dry white wine	125 ml/4 fl oz	½ cup
Boiling water	750 ml/1¼ pints	3 cups
Butter		
Flour (all-purpose)	2 tbs	3 tbs
Salt and pepper		
Mushrooms	450 g/1 lb	1 lb
1 bunch of spring onions (scallions)		
Whipping cream	125 ml/4 fl oz	½ cup
Drained capers	50 g/2 oz	⅓ cup
Liquid from the jar of capers	1 tbs	1 tbs
Lemon juice		

Bone the veal and remove excess fat. Render this out in a pan and reserve. Chop the bones and dice the meat. Clean the pot vegetables, peel if necessary then chop. Peel and quarter the onions. Fry the bones, pot vegetables and onion quarters in the rendered fat for a few minutes. Add the bay leaves, peppercorns, wine and water to the pan and bring to the boil. Skim and then boil until the liquid is reduced to about 500 ml/18 fl oz (2¼ cups). Strain, leave to cool and remove the surface fat.

Take about 2 tbs (3 tbs) of the removed fat, and heat in a pan. Add butter to make up the quantity if necessary. Put in the meat and fry until brown all over. Sprinkle over the flour, stir well and cook for a further 1 minute. Gradually add the bone stock, season to taste with salt and pepper and bring to the boil, stirring constantly. Cover and simmer for about 1 hour.

Meanwhile, halve or quarter any large mushrooms. Add all the mushrooms to the pan and cook for a further 10 minutes. At the same time, trim the spring onions, leaving on about 7.5 cm/3 inches of the green part. Cut the onions into 1.25 cm/½ inch lengths. Add to the goulash and simmer for a further 5 minutes. Stir in the cream, capers and liquid from the jar. Add a little lemon juice to taste and adjust the seasoning with salt and pepper if necessary. Bring to the boil and simmer for 5 minutes more. Serve with noodles or rice and a courgette (zucchini) and tomato salad.

Simmered calves' kidneys
Serves 4

Ingredients	Metric-Imperial	American
Calves' kidneys (beef)	550 g/1¼ lb	1¼ lb
Salt and pepper		
Flour (all-purpose)	2 tbs	3 tbs
White vegetable fat	50 g/2 oz	¼ cup
Beef stock (bouillon)	225 ml/8 fl oz	1 cup
Sweet paprika pepper		
Lemon juice		
Chopped parsley	1 tbs	1 tbs

Cut the kidneys in half, snip out the cores then wash and drain. Pour boiling water over the kidneys and leave to stand for 30 minutes. Dry on absorbent paper and cut into slices. Sprinkle with salt and pepper and coat in the flour.

Melt the fat in a pan and use to cook the kidney slices for 5 minutes, stirring frequently. Add the stock and stir well to loosen the sediment. Bring to the boil, cover and simmer for 20 minutes. If liked, thicken the sauce with a little more flour moistened with cold water. Season to taste with paprika and add a little lemon juice to sharpen the flavour. Serve in a rice ring (see page 325 and sprinkle with the parsley.

Microwave hint
For an almost instant snack on a plate, lay a thin slice of ham on buttered toast, then put a thin slice of cheese on top. Processed cheese is particularly suitable, but not essential. Cook on full power for 30 seconds. The cheese will have melted, the ham and toast will be hot. Remember, two snacks cooked at the same time will take twice as long.

Opposite: Veal goulash with capers
Below: Simmered calves' kidneys

Swallows' nests
Serves 4

Ingredients	Metric-Imperial	American
4 hard-boiled eggs		
8 thin slices of gammon (raw ham)		
4 escalopes of veal	150 g/5 oz each	5 oz each
Butter	65 g/2½ oz	5 tbs
Chicken stock (bouillon)	300 ml/½ pint	1¼ cups
Flour (all-purpose)	1 tbs	1 tbs
Sour cream	2 tbs	3 tbs
Salt		

Shell the eggs. Put 2 slices of gammon on each escalope then top with an egg. Roll up from the narrowest end and secure each with a skewer or tie with fine string.

Melt the butter in a pan and use to brown the rolls on all sides. Pour in half the stock, bring to the boil, cover and simmer for 1 hour, adding more stock as the liquid evaporates. Lift out the veal rolls, discarding the skewers or string, and place on a warm serving dish. Keep hot.

Pour any remaining stock into the pan and stir well to loosen the sediment. Moisten the flour with a little cold water, add to the pan and stir. Simmer for 4 minutes, blend in the cream and season. Hand the sauce separately.

Braised boned leg of veal
Serves 6

Ingredients	Metric-Imperial	American
1 onion		
Dry red wine	1 L/1¾ pints	4⅓ cups
1 bay leaf		
1 whole clove		
1 cinnamon stick		
Sweet paprika pepper	1 tsp	1 tsp
Boned leg of veal	1.5 kg/3¼ lb	3¼ lb
Salt and pepper		
Streaky bacon (strips)	50 g/2 oz	4 strips
Flour (all-purpose)	1 tbs	1 tbs
Whipping cream	4 tbs	5 tbs

Peel and quarter the onion and place in a pan with the wine, bay leaf, clove and cinnamon. Bring to the boil then simmer for 5 minutes. Rub the paprika into the veal, place it in a dish and pour over the wine marinade. Cool and then cover and chill for 48 hours, turning the meat in the marinade occasionally.

Remove the veal from the marinade, dry on absorbent kitchen paper and sprinkle all over with salt and pepper. Chop the bacon and place in a flameproof dish. Heat until the fat runs then add the meat and brown on all sides. Put in the onion and spices from the marinade and cook until the onion is golden. Pour in 300 ml/½ pint (1¼ cups) of the marinade. Cook, uncovered, in a preheated moderately hot oven, 200°C, 400°F, Gas Mark 6, for about 1¾ hours, adding more marinade to the dish as the liquid evaporates and turning the meat occasionally. Slice the veal and arrange on a warm serving dish. Keep hot.

Add any remaining marinade to the cooking dish and stir well to loosen the sediment. Strain the liquid into a pan and bring to the boil. Blend the flour with a little cold water, add to the pan and stir until thickened. Simmer for 3 minutes, season with salt and pepper to taste and stir in the cream. Reheat. Serve the veal with chicory (Belgian endive) and herbed potatoes and hand the sauce separately.

Boiled calves' tongues
Serves 4

Ingredients	Metric-Imperial	American
Selection of pot vegetables		
Calves' tongues	675 g/1½ lb	1½ lb
Salted water		

Clean the pot vegetables, peel if necessary and roughly chop. Add the tongues to a pan of salted water, bring to the boil and skim. Put in the vegetables, bring back to the boil, cover and simmer for about 1¾ hours. The tongues are cooked when the tip can easily be pierced with a fork.

Lift out the tongues, rinse in cold water and remove the skin while they are still hot. Trim off the roots of the tongues and remove any small bones. Return to the hot stock until required. At serving time, drain the tongues, cut into finger-thick slices and transfer to a warm dish. Serve with mushroom sauce and a risotto.

Ragout of calves' hearts
Serves 4

Ingredients	Metric-Imperial	American
Calves' hearts	675 g/1½ lb	1½ lb
Salted water	500 ml/18 fl oz	2¼ cups
1 bay leaf		
3 whole cloves		
5 black peppercorns		
For the sauce:		
Margarine	50 g/ 2 oz	¼ cup
Flour (all-purpose)	50 g/2 oz	½ cup
1 medium-sized onion		
Salt and pepper		
Sugar		
Lemon juice	1 tbs	1 tbs
1 gherkin (dill pickle)		

Cut the hearts in half, remove any tubes and membranes and wash well. Leave to stand in cold water for 1 hour. Drain well and cut into bite-sized pieces.

Place the salted water in a pan with the bay leaf, cloves, peppercorns and meat. Bring to the boil then cover and simmer for 1½ hours. Remove the meat with a slotted spoon and strain the stock. If necessary make the stock up to 500 ml/18 fl oz (2¼ cups) with more water.

To make the sauce, melt the margarine in a pan, sprinkle in the flour and stir until the roux is golden. Peel and chop the onion, add to the pan and cook until the onion is softened. Gradually add the stock and bring to the boil, stirring constantly. Simmer for 5 minutes. Add the meat to the sauce, bring back to the boil and simmer for a further 5 minutes. Season with salt, pepper and sugar and sharpen the flavour with a little lemon juice to taste. Chop the gherkin and add to the ragout before serving.

Opposite: Swallows' nests
Above: Ragout of calves' hearts

Above: Ragout of veal with mushrooms
Opposite: Fillet of veal with grapes and almonds

188

Ragout of veal with mushrooms
Serves 8

Ingredients	Metric-Imperial	American
Butter or margarine	50 g/2 oz	¼ cup
Flour (all-purpose)	40 g/1½ oz	⅓ cup
Chicken stock (bouillon)	500 ml/18 fl oz	2¼ cups
Canned mushrooms	225 g/8 oz can	8 oz can
Diced cooked calves' tongues (beef)	400 g/14 oz	2¼ cups
Diced cooked veal	350 g/12 oz	2 cups
2 egg yolks		
Milk	2 tbs	3 tbs
Lemon juice	2 tbs	3 tbs
Dry white wine	1 tbs	1 tbs
Salt and pepper		
Worcestershire sauce		
Fresh breadcrumbs	2 tbs	3 tbs
Grated cheese such as Gouda or Cheddar	3 tbs	4 tbs

Melt three quarters of the butter or margarine in a pan, sprinkle in the flour and stir until the roux is golden. Gradually add the stock and bring to the boil, stirring constantly. Simmer for 5 minutes. Drain the mushrooms, slice or dice and add to the sauce with the tongue and veal. Bring to the boil again. Beat the egg yolks with the milk, beat into the sauce and remove the pan from the heat. Stir in the lemon juice and wine and season to taste with salt, pepper and a few drops of Worcestershire sauce. (Use a few drops only as Worcestershire sauce is strongly flavoured and coloured.)

Divide the ragout among 8 individual ovenproof dishes or deep scallop shells. Place these on a baking sheet (cookie sheet). Mix together the breadcrumbs and cheese and sprinkle over the dishes. Dot with the remaining butter and place, uncovered, in a preheated hot oven, 220°C, 425°F, Gas Mark 7, for about 12 minutes, or until the topping is golden brown. If liked, garnish the dishes with halved lemon slices and parsley sprigs.

Fillet of veal with grapes and almonds
Serves 4

Ingredients	Metric-Imperial	American
1 fillet of veal	550 g/1¼ lb	1¼ lb
Salt and pepper		
Oil	2 tbs	3 tbs
Butter or margarine	15 g/½ oz	1 tbs
Hot chicken stock (bouillon)	300 ml/½ pint	1¼ cups
Lemon juice		
Green grapes	225 g/8 oz	8 oz
Blanched almonds	100 g/4 oz	1 cup
Chopped mint	1 tbs	1 tbs

Rub the veal all over with salt and pepper. Heat the oil in a pan and use to brown the meat on all sides, cooking for about 10 minutes. Add the butter or margarine and continue cooking for a further 5 minutes, turning the meat frequently. Cook a few minutes longer if you prefer the meat to be well done. Remove the fillet from the pan, wrap in foil and keep hot.

Pour the stock into the fat remaining in the pan, season with salt and pepper and boil until reduced by one third. Sharpen the flour with a little lemon juice to taste. Halve the grapes, remove the seeds (pits) and add to the pan with the almonds.

Unwrap the meat, slice and heat through in the sauce. Serve in a hot dish, garnished with the mint and accompanied by buttered rice or French bread.

Veal stuffed with apricots
Serves 4

Ingredients	Metric-Imperial	American
Dried apricots	225 g/8 oz	8 oz
Sweet sherry	225 ml/8 fl oz	1 cup
4 thick escalopes of veal		
Salt and pepper		
Flour (all-purpose)	4 tbs	5 tbs
Oil	4 tbs	5 tbs
Whipping cream	225 ml/8 fl oz	1 cup
Pinch of sugar		

Soak the apricots in the sherry for 3 hours. Drain, reserving the liquid.

Cut a deep pocket in each escalope and sprinkle inside the pocket with salt and pepper. Use most of the apricots to stuff the pockets then close the openings and secure with skewers or wooden cocktail sticks (toothpicks). Sprinkle the stuffed escalopes with salt and pepper and coat in the flour. Heat the oil in a frying pan and use to cook the escalopes for about 7 minutes on each side. Remove and keep hot.

Add the reserved sherry marinade to the pan and stir well until boiling to loosen the sediment. Blend in the cream and simmer for about 20 minutes, to reduce slightly. Adjust the seasoning with salt, pepper and the sugar, return the escalopes to the pan and simmer for a further 10 minutes. Transfer to a warm dish, remove the skewers or sticks and garnish with the reserved apricots.

Veal 'Cordon Bleu'
Serves 4

Ingredients	Metric-Imperial	American
4 slices of cheese	40 g/1½ oz each	1½ oz each
4 slices of cooked ham	50 g/2 oz each	2 oz each
8 escalopes of veal	75 g/3 oz each	3 oz each
Salt and pepper		
2 eggs		
Fresh breadcrumbs	65 g/2½ oz	1¼ cups
Butter	65 g/2½ oz	5 tbs

The slices of cheese and ham should be about the same size as the escalopes. Beat the escalopes lightly and season with salt and pepper. Top 4 escalopes with cheese slices, then with ham slices and finally with the remaining escalopes. Press the layers firmly together.

Beat the eggs and use to coat the veal 'sandwiches' then cover them in breadcrumbs. Melt the butter in a frying pan and use to cook the stuffed and coated escalopes for about 5 minutes on each side, or until golden brown. Serve with baked potatoes topped with a sour cream sauce and with peas.

Roast veal with peaches
Serves 4

Ingredients	Metric-Imperial	American
1 boned shoulder of veal	1 kg/2¼ lb	2¼ lb
Salt and pepper		
Melted butter	15 g/½ oz	1 tbs
Selection of pot vegetables		
Medium white wine	300 ml/½ pint	1¼ cups
Sour cream	2 tbs	3 tbs

	Metric-Imperial	American
2 ripe but firm peaches		
Green grapes	100 g/4 oz	4 oz
Black grapes	100 g/4 oz	4 oz

Sprinkle the veal with salt and pepper. Brush with the butter and place in a greased roasting tin. Clean the pot vegetables, peel if necessary, then cut into small pieces. Add to the meat. Cook, uncovered, in a preheated moderately hot oven, 200°C, 400°F, Gas Mark 6, for 15 minutes. Turn the meat, pour in half the wine and cook for a further 1 hour, adding the rest of the wine as the liquid evaporates. Remove the meat to a warm serving dish and keep hot.

Stir up the roasting pan contents to loosen the sediment, strain into a pan and blend in the cream.

Peel, stone (pit) and slice the peaches. Halve the grapes and remove the seeds (pits). Add the fruit to the sauce and heat through. Remove with a slotted spoon and arrange round the veal on the serving dish. Adjust the seasoning of the sauce with salt and pepper to taste. Serve with the veal and fruit.

Liver with sage
Serves 4-6

Ingredients	Metric-Imperial	American
Onions	450 g/1 lb	1 lb
Butter	100 g/4 oz	½ cup
Calves' or lambs' liver	675 g/1½ lb	1½ lb
Salt and pepper		
Lemon juice	4 tbs	5 tbs
Dry white wine	150 ml/¼ pint	⅔ cup
Chopped sage	2 tbs	3 tbs
Chopped parsley	4 tbs	5 tbs

Peel and chop the onions. Melt half the butter in a pan and use to cook the onion until golden. Set aside.

Remove any membrane from the liver and cut into thin strips. Season with salt and pepper. Heat the remaining butter in a frying pan, add the liver strips and cook for about 5 minutes, stirring frequently, until brown. Remove from the pan, sprinkle with the lemon juice and keep hot.

Pour two thirds of the wine into the frying pan and heat, stirring to loosen the sediment. Add the fried onions and reheat. Put in the liver strips and sage. Adjust the seasoning with salt and pepper. Reheat then sprinkle over the parsley and remaining wine, reheat again and serve immediately.

Tips: Pigs' liver can be substituted for the calves' or lambs' liver but it should be soaked in milk for 1 hour before cooking.

Microwave hint
Fresh frozen sausages (not smoked varieties) can be defrosted and then cooked without a pause between the two processes. For 225 g/8 oz sausages, allow 5 minutes on low power. Leave to stand for 10 minutes to ensure complete defrosting. Cook on full power for 5 minutes, turning the sausages over once during cooking.

Left: Veal 'Cordon Bleu'
Opposite: Liver with sage

Liver, Berlin style
Serves 4

Ingredients	Metric-Imperial	American
4 slices of calves' liver		
(beef)	150 g/5 oz each	5 oz each
Flour (all-purpose)	2 tbs	3 tbs
Butter or margarine	65 g/2½ oz	5 tbs

Salt		
4 onions		
Hot water	2 tbs	3 tbs

Remove any membrane from the liver slices and coat them with the flour. Heat the butter or margarine in a frying pan, put in the liver slices and cook for about 5 minutes on each side, or until done to taste. Sprinkle with salt and transfer to a warm serving dish. Keep hot.

Wiener schnitzel
Serves 4

Ingredients	Metric-Imperial	American
4 escalopes of veal	75 g/3 oz each	3 oz each
Salt		
Flour (all-purpose)	1 tbs	1 tbs
1 egg		
Fresh breadcrumbs	40 g/1½ oz	¾ cup
Pork dripping	100 g/4 oz	½ cup
Hot water	2 tbs	3 tbs

Beat the escalopes until evenly thin but do not tear the flesh. Season the meat with salt then dust with the flour. Beat the egg and place in a shallow dish. Coat the escalopes in egg then cover with breadcrumbs.

Melt the dripping in a frying pan and use to cook the escalopes for about 7 minutes on each side, until golden brown and crisp. Drain and arrange on a warm serving dish.

Add the water to the cooking juices and heat, stirring to loosen the sediment. Serve with the schnitzels.

Italian veal with mushrooms
Serves 4

Ingredients	Metric-Imperial	American
Dried mushrooms	50 g/2 oz	½ cup
Lukewarm water	300 ml/½ pint	1¼ cups
Whipping cream	225 ml/8 fl oz	1 cup
Dry white wine	3 tbs	4 tbs
Fillet of veal	550 g/1¼ lb	1¼ lb
Butter	25 g/1 oz	2 tbs
Salt and pepper		

Soak the mushrooms in the lukewarm water in a pan for 30 minutes. Add the cream and wine, bring to the boil and cook until thickened, stirring frequently.

Slice the veal very thinly and then cut into strips. Melt the butter in a pan, put in the veal strips and season with salt and pepper. Cook for about 15 minutes, stirring occasionally. Stir into sauce, heat through and adjust the seasoning.

Peel and slice the onions and separate the slices into rings. Cook in the fat remaining in the pan until golden. Spoon over the liver. Add the water to the pan and heat, stirring to loosen the sediment. Pour over the liver and onions. Serve with mashed potatoes and a tomato or cucumber salad.

Above: Liver, Berlin style
Right: Italian veal with mushrooms

Aspic brawn mould
Serves 4

Ingredients	Metric-Imperial	American
Salted water	1 L/1¾ pints	4⅓ cups
Boneless veal	225 g/8 oz	8 oz
Boneless veal pork	225 g/8 oz	8 oz
Selection of pot vegetables		
1 medium-sized onion		
1 bay leaf		
4 black peppercorns		
Vinegar	125 ml/4 fl oz	½ cup
Salt		
Sugar		
Water	5 tbs	6 tbs
Powdered gelatine	1 tbs	1 tbs
Sprigs of parsley		

Put the salted water into a pan and bring to the boil. Add the veal and pork and bring back to boiling point. Skim. Clean the pot vegetables and extra onion, peel if necessary then add to the pan with the bay leaf and peppercorns. Cover and simmer for about 30 minutes, or until the meat is tender.

Lift out the veal and pork, leave to cool and then dice. Strain the stock, measure 375 ml/13 fl oz (1⅔ cups) and place in a clean pan with the vinegar. Season to taste with salt and sugar.

Put the water in a small bowl and sprinkle on the gelatine. Leave to stand for 10 minutes. Bring the stock and vinegar to the boil and stir in the softened gelatine until it has completely dissolved. Add the diced meat. Divide among cups or moulds previously rinsed in cold water. Chill until firmly set. Loosen the brawn from the containers with a knife blade, or dip them into hot water then turn out on a serving dish or plates. Garnish with parsley sprigs.

Ham and egg brawn
Serves 4

Ingredients	Metric-Imperial	American
Water	6 tbs	½ cup
Powdered gelatine	2 tbs	7 tsp
Beef stock (bouillon)	1 L/1¾ pints	4⅓ cups
Vinegar	150 ml/¼ pint	⅔ cup
Salt		
Cooked ham	350 g/12 oz	12 oz
4 tomatoes		
4 gherkins (small dill pickles)		
5 hard-boiled eggs		
Chopped parsley	5 tbs	6 tbs

Put the water into a small bowl and sprinkle on the gelatine. Leave to stand for 10 minutes. Put the stock into a pan and bring to the boil. Remove from the heat, add the soaked gelatine and stir until it has completely dissolved. Stir in the vinegar and season to taste with salt. Rinse a rectangular mould measuring about 30 cm/12 inches long with water. Pour in a thin layer of aspic and allow to set.

Trim off any fat from the ham then cut into dice. Halve the tomatoes, scoop out the seeds and dice the flesh. Chop the gherkins. Shell the eggs, chop 3 of them and slice the remainder.

Add ingredients to the mould in the order given, covering each layer with about 125 ml/4 fl oz (½ cup) of liquid aspic. Chill until this sets before adding the next ingredient. Make layers as follows: the egg slices; half the ham dice; half the gherkin; half the diced tomato mixed with half the parsley; the chopped egg; the remaining tomato and parsley; the rest of the gherkin; the remaining ham.

Chill the completed brawn until firmly set. Loosen it by dipping the mould into hot water then turn out and serve with brown bread and butter.

Pork steaks with fennel
Serves 4

Ingredients	Metric-Imperial	American
Fennel (Florence fennel)	450 g/1 lb	1 lb
Butter or margarine	100 g/4 oz	½ cup
Whipping cream	125 ml/4 fl oz	½ cup
Water	125 ml/4 fl oz	½ cup
Salt		
Flour	1 tbs	1 tbs
4 pork steaks		
Grated cheese such as Gouda or Cheddar	3 tbs	4 tbs
For the sauce:		
Water	125 ml/4 fl oz	½ cup
Flour	1 tsp	1 tsp
Sour cream	4 tbs	5 tbs

Trim the fennel and cut into thin strips. Melt half the butter or margarine and use to fry the fennel strips, stirring, for 2 minutes. Add the cream and water, season with salt, bring to the boil, cover and simmer for 20 minutes. Moisten the flour with a little cold water, add to the fennel mixture and cook, stirring, for 2 minutes.

Beat the pork steaks slightly to flatten. Sprinkle with salt. Melt the remaining butter or margarine in a frying pan and use to fry the steaks until brown on both sides. Transfer to a greased ovenproof dish, spoon the fennel mixture over the top and sprinkle with the cheese. Bake, uncovered, in a preheated hot oven, 220°C, 425°F, Gas Mark 7, for 25 minutes. Transfer the chops and fennel to a warm serving dish and keep hot.

Add the hot water to the cooking dish. Stir to loosen the sediment and pour into a pan. Moisten the flour with the sour cream, add to the pan and stir until boiling. Simmer for 2 minutes and adjust the seasoning with more salt if necessary. Serve the pork and fennel with potatoes and hand the sauce separately.

Opposite: Aspic brawn mould

195

Pork strips in beer sauce

Serves 4

Ingredients	Metric-Imperial	American
Fillet of pork	550 g/1¼ lb	1¼ lb
2 onions		
Pork dripping	25 g/1 oz	2 tbs
Sweet paprika pepper		
Salt	½ tsp	½ tsp
Stout (dark beer)	300 ml/½ pint	1¼ cups
1 bay leaf		
Pinch of ground allspice		
1 red sweet pepper		
1 tomato		
2 gherkins (small dill pickles)		
Sour cream	4 tbs	5 tbs

Remove any membrane from the pork, cut into thin slices and then into strips. Peel and chop the onions. Melt half the dripping in a pan and use to cook the onion until golden. Remove with a slotted spoon. Add the remaining dripping to the fat left in the pan and use to fry the meat strips until golden. Return the onion to the pan, add 1 tsp paprika, the salt, stout, bay leaf and allspice and bring to the boil. Cover and simmer for 5 minutes.

Halve and deseed the pepper and cut the flesh into strips. Pour boiling water over the tomato, drain, peel, scoop out the seeds and cut the flesh into strips. Add the tomato and pepper strips to the pork. Cover the pan again and cook for a further 15 minutes.

Cut the gherkins into strips, add to the pan, cook for a further 5 minutes then remove the bay leaf, blend in the cream and season with extra paprika to taste. Serve with potatoes or rice.

Tip: For a less expensive meal, use any boneless lean pork in place of the fillet.

Below: Pork strips in beer sauce
Opposite: Pork with spring onions, Chinese style

Pork with spring onions, Chinese style
Serves 4

Ingredients	Metric-Imperial	American
2 cloves of garlic		
Boneless lean pork	350 g/12 oz	12 oz
Soy sauce	2 tbs	3 tbs
Dry sherry	3 tbs	4 tbs
Grated root ginger	1 tsp	1 tsp
Cornflour (cornstarch)	1 tbs	1 tbs
Tomato ketchup	175 ml/6 fl oz	¾ cup
Finely chopped canned pineapple	2 tbs	3 tbs
Pineapple juice	4 tbs	5 tbs
Mild chilli sauce	2 tbs	3 tbs
3 bunches of spring onions (scallions)		
Slivered almonds	25 g/1 oz	¼ cup
Oil	2 tbs	3 tbs
Salt		

Peel and very finely chop the garlic. Cut the pork into small dice and mix with the soy sauce, sherry, garlic, ginger, cornflour, ketchup, pineapple and pineapple juice and the chilli sauce. Trim the spring onions and cut into 1.25 cm/½ inch lengths. Put the almonds into a dry frying pan and toss

over moderate heat until golden. Leave to cool.

Heat the oil in 2 frying pans. Drain the meat from the marinade, add to one of the pans and cook, stirring frequently, for 2 minutes. Put the spring onions into the second pan and fry for 1 minute. Remove both pans from the heat and sprinkle a little salt over the onions. Add the ketchup marinade to the pan of meat and bring to the boil, stirring. Simmer for 3 minutes then remove from the heat again, stir in the onion and sprinkle with the almonds. Serve immediately, with rice.

Microwave hint

To make a quick relish to serve with ham or pork by microwave, first remove the base and stem end from 8 small, thin-skinned oranges and slice into thin rings. Place them in a large bowl and add 1 large cinnamon stick, broken into 5-cm/2-in lengths, and 5 or 6 whole cloves. Prepare a batch of light sugar syrup and pour over the orange slices. Cover and cook on full power for 12 minutes, stirring halfway through, then leave to stand for 5 minutes before serving.

Roast pork with crackling
Serves 4

Ingredients	Metric-Imperial	American
1 leg of pork with skin	1.5 kg/3¼ lb	3¼ lb
Salt and pepper		
Oil	1 tbs	1 tbs
Rosemary leaves	1 tbs	1 tbs
Hot water	300 ml/½ pint	1¼ cups
Light ale (light beer)	3 tbs	4 tbs
Flour (all-purpose)	1 tbs	1 tbs
Sugar		
Whipping cream	4 tbs	5 tbs

Score the skin of the pork in trellis pattern with a sharp knife. Sprinkle liberally with salt and pepper, brush with the oil and sprinkle with the rosemary. Place in a greased roasting tin and cook, uncovered, in a preheated moderately hot oven, 200°C, 400°F, Gas Mark 6, for about 30 minutes. Add half the water to the tin and return it to the oven for a further 1½ hours, replacing evaporated liquid with more of the water. Baste the meat occasionally with the pan juices.

Brush the skin of the pork with ale then return it to the oven for a further 30 minutes, brushing with ale twice more during this time. Remove the meat to a warm serving dish and keep hot.

Add any remaining water to the tin and stir well to loosen the sediment. Strain into a pan and bring to the boil. Moisten the flour with a little more ale, add to the pan and stir until thickened. Adjust the seasoning with salt, pepper and sugar to taste and, if wished, add a little extra ale. Simmer for 5 minutes then remove from the heat and stir in the cream. Serve with potatoes and red cabbage.

Simmered pork with sherry sauce
Serves 2

Ingredients	Metric-Imperial	American
Boneless pork	450 g/1 lb	1 lb
Salt and pepper		
Dried rosemary		
Oil	1 tbs	1 tbs
1 medium-sized onion		
5 tomatoes		
Dry sherry	4 tbs	5 tbs

switch on for a further 30 seconds. Flatten one side of the meat on the dish immediately and return for 3 minutes on full power. This should brown one side, turn the meat over and cook on full power for a further 3 minutes.

In the meantime peel and chop the onion, skin the tomatoes and remove the seeds. Add the tomatoes and onion to the meat and return on full power for 3 minutes.

Pour over the sherry and 225 ml/8 fl oz/1 cup of hot water, cover the dish and cook on full power for 15 minutes. Turn the meat round and cook for 5 minutes. Remove to a plate.

Mix the flour with the evaporated milk. Purée the gravy in a blender or food processor with the flour and milk. Return to the dish and cook on full power for 3 minutes. Stir well.

Carve the meat into slices and place in the gravy. Return to reheat on full power for 5 minutes.

Grilled pork fillet
Serves 4

Ingredients	Metric-Imperial	American
2 fillets of pork	450 g/1 lb	1 lb
French mustard	2 tbs	3 tbs
Oil	1 tbs	1 tbs
Sweet paprika pepper	½ tsp	½ tsp
Salt		

Spread the fillets with mustard on all sides. Place on the grid of a grill pan (broiler). Mix together the oil and paprika and use to brush the meat carefully. Cook under high heat for 10 minutes, brushing with more of the oil mixture twice during this time. Turn the fillets, brush again with the spiced oil and cook for about 7 minutes, brushing the meat twice more, until done to taste. Sprinkle with salt before serving.

Flour (all-purpose)	2 tsp	2 tsp
Evaporated milk		
(unsweetened)	3 tbs	4 tbs

Sprinkle the pork on all sides with salt, pepper and rosemary. Heat the oil in a pan and use to brown the meat on both sides. Peel and chop the onion. Pour boiling water over the tomatoes, drain, peel, halve and remove the seeds. Add the onion and tomato to the pan with the sherry. Pour in enough water to come half-way up the meat. Bring to the boil then cover and simmer for 40 minutes, adding more water to the pan as the liquid evaporates. Transfer the pork to a warm serving dish and keep hot.

Add a little more hot water to the pan if necessary and stir up the sediment. Sieve the pan contents and return to the rinsed pan. Blend the flour with the evaporated milk. Add to the pan and cook, stirring constantly, until thickened. Simmer for 4 minutes and adjust the seasoning if necessary. Pour over the pork and serve at once.

Microwave method
Brush the pork on all sides with oil and sprinkle with freshly ground pepper and rosemary. Put the browning dish in the microwave on full power for 2 minutes, add the oil and

Opposite: Roast pork with crackling
Below: Simmered pork with sherry sauce

Sugar-glazed ham
Serves 6-8

Ingredients	Metric-Imperial	American
Bacon collar (Canadian piece)	2 kg/4½ lb	4½ lb
2 cloves of garlic		
5 whole cloves		
1 bay leaf		
3 onions		
3 tomatoes		
Sugar		
Flour	1 tbs	1 tbs
Salt and pepper		

Have the butcher cut the rind of the bacon joint into diamond shapes. Peel the garlic and cut into slivers. Make several slits into the rind of the bacon and insert pieces of garlic and the cloves. Cut the bay leaf into 6 pieces and put between the diamond shapes on the bacon skin. Peel the onion and cut this and the tomatoes into quarters.

Put the bacon into a roasting tin with the onion and tomato quarters then pour in enough hot water to come half-way up the joint. Cook, uncovered, in a preheated hot oven, 190°C, 375°F, Gas Mark 5, for 2 hours.

Remove the roasting tin from the oven, sprinkle the joint with sugar and return to the oven for a further 30 minutes. If the skin is becoming too dark, protect with a sheet of foil. Transfer the ham to a warm serving dish and make a sauce.

Add a little more water to the pan and stir to loosen the sediment. Sieve and make up to 450 ml/¾ pint (scant 2 cups) with more water. Place in a pan. Moisten the flour with a little cold water, add to the pan and stir until boiling. Simmer for 4 minutes, season to taste with salt and pepper and serve with the ham.

Pork with cheese glaze
(Using a chicken brick)
Serves 4

Ingredients	Metric-Imperial	American
Roasting pork	1.5 kg/3¼ lb	3¼ lb
Salt and pepper		
Sweet paprika pepper		
1 egg		
Grated Gouda cheese	75 g/3 oz	¾ cup
Cornflour (cornstarch)	1 tsp	1 tsp

Soak the chicken brick in water in the usual way. Remove the skin from the pork if necessary and sprinkle the joint with salt, pepper and paprika on all sides. Place in the chicken brick, cover and place in a preheated moderately hot oven, 200°C, 400°F, Gas Mark 6, for 2¼ hours.

Beat together the egg and cheese. Remove the dish from the oven, take off the lid and spread the cheese mixture over the meat. Return to the oven and cook, uncovered, for a further 15 minutes. Transfer the pork to a warm serving dish.

Make the cooking juices up to 300 ml/½ pint (1¼ cups) with water and place in a pan. Moisten the cornflour with a little cold water, add to the pan and stir. Simmer for 5 minutes. Season with salt, pepper and paprika and serve.

Skewered frankfurters with pickled cucumber

Serves 4

Ingredients	Metric-Imperial	American
Onions	225 g/8 oz	8 oz
Sweet peppers	225 g/8 oz	8 oz
Tomatoes	450 g/1 lb	1 lb
Salt and pepper		
Sweet paprika pepper		
Oil	3 tbs	4 tbs
4 large frankfurters		
2 large gherkins (dill pickles)		
4 thick slices of streaky bacon (8 strips)		

Peel and slice the onions then separate the slices into rings. Halve the peppers, deseed and cut the flesh into strips. Pour boiling water over about two thirds of the tomatoes, drain, peel and slice. Mix together the onion, pepper strips and tomato slices, season with salt, pepper and paprika to taste and stir in about two thirds of the oil. Place in a large shallow ovenproof dish.

Dip the frankfurters into boiling water for 1 minute then drain and cut into 2.5 cm/1 inch lengths. Slice the gherkins, quarter the remaining tomatoes and cut the bacon into pieces. Thread the sausage pieces, gherkin, tomato and bacon on to 4 skewers. Mix a little paprika into the remaining oil and use to brush the loaded skewers. Lay these on the vegetable mixture in the dish and cover with foil, making this slightly domed in the centre. Place in a preheated moderately hot oven, 200°C, 400°F, Gas Mark 6, for about 1 hour. Serve with crusty bread.

Left: Sugar-glazed ham
Below: Skewered frankfurters with pickled cucumber

201

Pork chops stuffed with pineapple and ham
Serves 4

Ingredients	Metric-Imperial	American
4 thick pork chops 8 oz each	225 g/8 oz each	
4 small canned pineapple slices		
4 slices of lean cooked ham		
Butter	25 g/1 oz	2 tbs
Sprigs of parsley		

Cut a deep pocket into each pork chop. Wrap each pineapple ring in a slice of ham and insert in a pocket in a chop. Close the openings and secure with wooden cocktail sticks (toothpicks).

Melt the butter in a frying pan and use to cook the stuffed chops for about 9 minutes on each side. Remove the sticks and serve garnished with parsley. These stuffed pork chops are delicious hot or cold.

Pork with mushrooms
Serves 4

Ingredients	Metric-Imperial	American
4 pork chops	200 g/7 oz each	7 oz each
Salt and pepper		
Sweet paprika pepper		
Margarine	25 g/1 oz	2 tbs
Canned drained mushrooms	150 g/5 oz	scant 1 cup
Chopped parsley	2 tbs	3 tbs
Brandy	1 tbs	1 tbs
Whipping cream	3 tbs	4 tbs

Sprinkle the chops with salt, pepper and paprika. Melt the margarine in a frying pan and use to cook the pork chops for 8 minutes. Turn, add the mushrooms to the pan and cook for a further 7 minutes, or until done to taste. Transfer the pork and mushrooms to a warm serving dish and sprinkle with the parsley and brandy.

French mustard	1 tsp	1 tsp
Green peppercorns	1 tsp	1 tsp
Whipping cream	150 ml/¼ pint	⅔ cup
Few drops of		
Worcestershire sauce		

Sprinkle the chops with salt, pepper and paprika. Heat the oil and butter in a frying pan and use to cook the chops for 5 minutes on each side, or until cooked through and brown on both sides. Transfer to a warm serving dish and keep hot.

Peel and chop the onion and fry in the fat remaining in the pan until golden. Stir the wine, mustard, peppercorns, cream and Worcestershire sauce into the fried onion and season to taste with salt and pepper. Cook, stirring, for 3 minutes. Serve the sauce with the pork chops.

Curried pork chops
Serves 4

Ingredients	Metric-Imperial	American
4 thin pork chops	175 g/6 oz each	6 oz each
Oil		
Salt and pepper		
Curry powder		
Tomato wedges		

Beat the pork chops slightly to flatten, brush with oil and sprinkle both sides with salt, pepper and curry powder. Place side-by-side on a large sheet of foil and fold this up to make a neat parcel, crimping the edges well together. Set the parcel on a baking sheet (cookie sheet) and place in a preheated moderately hot oven, 200°C, 400°F, Gas Mark 6, for about 30 minutes.

Transfer the pork to a warm dish, garnish and hand the cooking juices separately as a thin sauce.

Stir the cream into the juices in the pan and season to taste with salt, pepper and paprika. Reheat carefully; do not boil. Serve the pork with potatoes and a cucumber salad and hand the sauce separately.

Pork chops with creamy peppercorn sauce
Serves 4

Ingredients	Metric-Imperial	American
4 pork loin chops		
Salt and pepper		
Sweet paprika pepper		
Oil	2 tbs	3 tbs
Butter	15 g/½ oz	1 tbs
1 onion		
Dry white wine	6 tbs	½ cup

Pork chops in egg and breadcrumbs
Serves 4

Ingredients	Metric-Imperial	American
4 pork chops	200 g/7 oz each	7 oz each
Salt and white pepper		
1 egg		
Flour	2 tbs	3 tbs
Fresh breadcrumbs	40 g/1½ oz	¾ cup
Lard or pork dripping	50 g/2 oz	¼ cup

Sprinkle the chops on both sides with salt and pepper. Beat the egg and place in a shallow dish. Dust the chops with the flour, dip in the egg and coat all over in breadcrumbs, patting them on well.

Melt the fat in a frying pan and use to cook the chops for about 8 minutes on each side, until golden brown and cooked through.

Variation: Veal cutlets may be used instead of pork, reducing the cooking time to 5 minutes each side.

Roast hand of pork
Serves 4

Ingredients	Metric-Imperial	American
1 hand of pork (shoulder)	1 kg/2¼ lb	2¼ lb
Salt and pepper		
Sweet paprika pepper		
Hot water	150 ml/¼ pint	⅔ cup
1 onion		
1 tomato		

Sprinkle the pork on all sides with salt, pepper and paprika and place in a greased roasting tin. Cook, uncovered, in a preheated moderately hot oven, 200°C, 400°F, Gas Mark 6, for 15 minutes.

Pour in half the water and return the pork to the oven for 1 further hour, adding more of the water as the liquid evaporates. Peel and quarter the onion and quarter the tomato. Add these to the roasting tin and cook for a further 30 minutes. Lift out the meat, slice and arrange on a warm serving dish. Add any remaining water to the roasting tin and heat, stirring to loosen the sediment. Sieve and pour over the meat.

Pork with garlic and small onions
Serves 4

Ingredients	Metric-Imperial	American
4 pork chops	200 g/7 oz each	7 oz each
4 cloves of garlic		
Salt and pepper		
Sweet paprika pepper		
Small onions	225 g/8 oz	8 oz
Butter or margarine	25 g/1 oz	2 tbs
Dry white wine	4 tbs	5 tbs
Whipping cream	2 tbs	3 tbs

Trim off surplus fat from the chops. Peel and crush the garlic and rub well into both sides of the chops. Sprinkle with salt, pepper and paprika. Peel the onions.

Melt the butter or margarine in a pan, put in the onions and chops and cook for about 15 minutes, turning the chops several times. Transfer the chops and onions to a warm serving dish and keep hot.

Add the wine to the pan and heat, stirring to loosen the sediment. Blend in the cream and cook to reduce slightly. Season to taste with salt, pepper and paprika and pour over the chops or hand separately if preferred. Serve with potatoes and butter beans.

Microwave hint
Lean pork chops can become rather dry when cooked in the microwave. To avoid this, coat them in fine breadcrumbs, pressed well into the surface. Coat the inside of a preheated browning dish with oil and add the chops. Cook on full power for 2 minutes. Turn and cook for a further 2 minutes. Cover and cook on medium power for a further 20 minutes, turning the chops once.

Left: Pork chops in egg and breadcrumbs
Opposite: Pork with garlic and small onions

Bacon chops with apple sauce
Serves 4

Ingredients	Metric-Imperial	American
4 bacon chops (thick slices Canadian)	150 g/5 oz each	5 oz each
Pepper		
Oil	4 tbs	5 tbs
Apple purée (applesauce)	6 tbs	½ cup
Beef stock (bouillon)	125 ml/4 fl oz	½ cup

Sprinkle the chops with pepper on both sides. Heat the oil in a frying pan and use to cook the chops for about 5 minutes on each side. Transfer to a warm serving dish and keep hot.

Add the apple purée and stock to the pan juices and stir well. Bring to the boil and adjust the seasoning with salt and pepper to taste. Serve the chops with mashed potatoes and a mixed salad and hand the sauce separately.

Pork strips with beansprouts
Serves 4

Ingredients	Metric-Imperial	American
Boneless lean pork	450 g/1 lb	1 lb
Oil	2 tbs	3 tbs
Beansprouts	225 g/8 oz	8 oz
Dry white wine	2 tbs	3 tbs
Whipping cream	2 tbs	3 tbs
Soy sauce	4 tbs	5 tbs
Butter	50 g/2 oz	¼ cup
4 slices of brown bread		

Slice the pork thinly and then cut into strips. Heat the oil in a pan and use to fry the meat for about 5 minutes, stirring frequently. Put in the beansprouts and stir-fry with the meat for a further 1 minute. Pour in the wine, cream and soy sauce, bring to the boil then remove from the heat.

Meanwhile, melt the butter in a frying pan and use to fry the bread slices until golden brown on both sides. Serve with the pork and beansprouts accompanied by a tomato salad.

Microwave hint
To make a garnish by microwave for joints of pork or ham, turn the contents of a large can of apricot halves or whole apricots into a suitable dish, with all the syrup. Add ½ tsp each ground nutmeg, cinnamon and cloves and stir well. Cover and cook on full power for 7 minutes. Leave covered until completely cold. Lift out the fruit with a draining spoon and garnish.

Microwave hint
To make a quick apple sauce by microwave, peel and core 2 large cooking apples. Finely slice them into a pudding bowl and add 2 tbsp (3 tbsp) water and 25 g/1 oz (2 tbsp) butter. Cook, uncovered, on full power for 2 minutes. Mash and stir well. Add a pinch of allspice or nutmeg if liked.

Below: Bacon chops with apple sauce
Opposite: Pork strips with beansprouts

207

Crusty grilled pork
Serves 4

Ingredients	Metric-Imperial	American
Oil	4 tbs	5 tbs
White pepper and salt		
Chopped basil	4 tsp	4 tsp
4 pork shoulder steaks	150 g/5 oz each	5 oz each
Butter	50 g/2 oz	¼ cup
Fresh breadcrumbs	2 tbs	3 tbs
Whipping cream	1 tbs	1 tbs

Mix the oil with a pinch of pepper and half the basil. Brush this mixture over the pork steaks and leave for 15 minutes.

Melt the butter in a frying pan, put in the pork steaks and cook for about 7 minutes on each side. Sprinkle with salt and transfer to a greased grill pan (broiler). Mix together the breadcrumbs, cream and remaining basil and spread over the steaks. Place under a hot grill for about 5 minutes, or until the top is golden brown.

Turkish shashlik
Serves 4

Ingredients	Metric-Imperial	American
1 large banana		
2 medium-sized onions		
Boneless lean pork	275 g/10 oz	10 oz
4 thin slices calves' liver (beef)	225 g/8 oz	8 oz
Streaky bacon (strips)	150 g/5 oz	10 strips
Tomatoes	225 g/8 oz	8 oz
Few gherkins (small dill pickles)		
Oil		
Barbecue seasoning		

Peel the banana and onions. Cut the pork, liver and bacon into pieces about 2.5 cm/1 inch wide then cut the onion, banana, tomatoes and gherkins into pieces about the same size. Thread the ingredients alternately on 4 skewers and brush with oil.

Line the grid of a grill pan (broiler) with foil and arrange the loaded skewers on top. Cook under high heat for 6 minutes then turn, brush with more oil and cook again for 6 minutes, or until the pork is cooked through. Sprinkle with barbecue seasoning before serving.

Opposite: Crusty grilled pork
Below: Turkish shashlik

Skewered marinated pork fillet
Serves 4

Ingredients	Metric-Imperial	American
Fillet of pork	675 g/1½ lb	1½ lb
For the marinade:		
Olive oil	4 tbs	5 tbs
Lemon juice	4 tbs	5 tbs
Crushed juniper berries	1 tbs	1 tbs
Chopped oregano	1 tbs	1 tbs
Salt and pepper		

Cut the pork into slices about 2.5 cm/1 inch thick and place in a bowl.

To make the marinade, stir together the oil, lemon juice, juniper berries and oregano with salt and pepper to taste. Pour over the pork, cover and chill for about 3 hours, turning the meat occasionally.

Lift out the slices of pork and drain well. Thread on 4 skewers. Line the grid of a grill pan (broiler) with foil, place the skewers on top and cook under high heat for 8 minutes. Turn the skewers, brush with some of the marinade and cook for a further 7 minutes, or until done to taste.

Grilled sweet-sour pork
Serves 4

Ingredients	Metric-Imperial	American
Clear honey	2 tbs	3 tbs
Soy sauce	3 tbs	4 tbs
White wine	3 tbs	4 tbs
Oil	4 tbs	5 tbs
Dried rosemary	¼ tsp	¼ tsp
Dried thyme	¼ tsp	¼ tsp
Pepper and salt		
4 thin pork chops	175 g/6 oz each	6 oz each

Mix together the honey, soy sauce, wine and oil with the rosemary and thyme. Season with pepper.

Arrange the chops on the grid of a grill pan (broiler) and cook under high heat for 4 minutes on each side. Brush with the honey baste and cook for a further 4 minutes on each side, brushing frequently during this time with more of the honey mixture. Sprinkle with salt before serving.

Serving suggestion: Use any remaining honey baste to brush canned pineapple slices, sweet pepper strips or peeled, halved and cored pears. Grill (broil) these for about 4 minutes, turning once and brushing with more baste during cooking. Serve with the pork.

Opposite: Skewered marinated pork fillet
Above: Grilled pork spare rib chops

Grilled pork spare rib chops
Serves 4

Ingredients	Metric-Imperial	American
2 cloves of garlic		
Oil	5 tbs	6 tbs
Lemon juice	2 tbs	3 tbs
Few drops of Worcestershire sauce		
Few drops of Tabasco pepper sauce		
Coarsely ground black pepper and salt		
4 large spare rib chops		
Light ale (light beer)	125 ml/4 fl oz	½ cup

Peel and chop the garlic and mix with the oil, lemon juice, Worcestershire sauce and Tabasco. Season with pepper and pour over the chops. Leave to stand for 1 hour.

Drain the chops well and arrange on the grid of a grill pan (broiler). Cook under high heat for 5 minutes. Turn, brush with ale, cook for another 5 minutes then turn again and brush with more ale. Grill for a further 5 minutes, or until cooked through. Sprinkle with salt before serving.

Poached shoulder of lamb in butter sauce
Serves 4

Ingredients	Metric-Imperial	American
1 boned shoulder of lamb	750 g/1¾ lb	1¾ lb
Chicken stock (bouillon)	1 L/1¾ pints	4⅓ cups
Dry white wine	225 ml/8 fl oz	1 cup
1 large onion		
Baby carrots	450 g/1 lb	1 lb
Chilled butter	100 g/4 oz	½ cup
Drained capers	50 g/2 oz	⅓ cup
Grated lemon rind	2 tsp	2 tsp
Chopped parsley	2 tbs	3 tbs
Snipped chives	1 tbs	1 tbs
Chopped tarragon	1 tsp	1 tsp
Salt and pepper		

Cut the lamb into 4 equal-sized pieces. Mix together the stock and wine in a pan and bring to the boil. Peel and roughly chop the onion and add to the pan with the lamb. Bring back to the boil, cover and simmer for 15 minutes. Peel the carrots, add to the pan, cover again and cook for a further 15 minutes. Remove from the heat.

Dice the cold butter. Measure 300 ml/½ pint (1¼ cups) of the stock and place in a separate pan. Boil until reduced by about one third. Remove from the heat and quickly stir in the diced butter, capers, lemon rind, parsley, chives and tarragon and season to taste with salt and pepper.

Drain the lamb and carrots and arrange on a warm serving dish. Serve with the butter sauce, boiled potatoes and broccoli.

Microwave hint
To cook 3 large peeled potatoes by microwave, stir together 4 tbsp (5 tbsp) water and a pinch of salt in a suitable dish. Cut each potato in 4 pieces, place in the dish, cover and cook on full power for 8 minutes. Test for tenderness; if too firm, cook for another 2 minutes. Allow to stand for 3 minutes before serving.

Below: Poached shoulder of lamb in butter sauce
Opposite: Leg of lamb with cannellini beans and tomatoes

Boiled leg of lamb, old English style
Serves 6

Ingredients	Metric-Imperial	American
1 leg of lamb	2 kg/4½ lb	4½ lb
1 large onion		
8 whole cloves		
6 black peppercorns		
Salt	1 tsp	1 tsp
1 bouquet garni		
For the sauce:		
Butter	40 g/1½ oz	3 tbs
Flour (all-purpose)	40 g/1½ oz	⅓ cup
White wine vinegar	1 tsp	1 tsp
Drained capers	2 tbs	3 tbs
Liquid from caper jar	1 tsp	1 tsp
Salt and pepper		
2 egg yolks		
Single cream (light)	150 ml/¼ pint	⅔ cup

Place the leg of lamb in a large pan and add boiling water just to cover. Peel the onion and stick with the cloves, add to the pan with the peppercorns, salt and bouquet garni. Bring to the boil, skim, cover and simmer for 2 hours. Lift out the meat, cut into neat slices and arrange on a warm serving dish. Cover and keep hot. Strain the stock, measure 900 ml/1½ pints (3¾ cups) and reserve.

To make the sauce, melt the butter in a pan, sprinkle in the flour and cook for 1 minute, stirring. Gradually add the reserved stock and bring to the boil, stirring constantly. Put in the vinegar, capers and liquid from the jar and season to taste with salt and pepper. Simmer for 3 minutes. Mix the egg yolks with the cream, beat into the sauce and remove the pan from the heat. Serve the sliced lamb masked with the sauce.

Saddle of lamb with courgettes
Serves 4

Ingredients	Metric-Imperial	American
1 saddle of lamb	1 kg/2¼ lb	2¼ lb
Dried herbs of Provence		
Salt and pepper		
Hot water	225 ml/8 fl oz	1 cup
1 onion		
1 tomato		
Courgettes (zucchini)	1 kg/2¼ lb	2¼ lb

Remove excess fat from the lamb and sprinkle with the herbs and salt. Place in a greased roasting tin and place, uncovered, in a preheated hot oven, 220°C, 425°F, Gas Mark 7, for 10 minutes. Add a little of the water to the pan and continue cooking for a further 30 minutes.

Meanwhile, peel and quarter the onion and quarter the tomato. Peel and slice the courgettes. Add the onion, tomato and courgette to the pan with the rest of the water, baste with the pan juices, season the vegetables with salt and pepper and cook for a further 35 minutes.

Leg of lamb with cannellini beans and tomatoes

Serves 4–6

Ingredients	Metric-Imperial	American
Dried cannellini beans	350 g/12 oz	1½ cups
Onions	225 g/8 oz	8 oz
French beans (green)	350 g/12 oz	12 oz
Leg of lamb	1.5 kg/3¼ lb	3¼ lb
Salt and pepper		
Dried rosemary	1 tsp	1 tsp
Dried thyme	1 tsp	1 tsp
Oil	4 tbs	5 tbs
Canned tomatoes	2 × 396 g/14 oz cans	2 × 14 oz cans

3 cloves of garlic

Add the cannellini beans to a pan of boiling water, bring back to the boil and cook for 5 minutes. Drain. Peel and quarter the onions. Top and tail the beans and cut into short lengths. Remove any surplus fat from the lamb and rub it with salt, pepper, rosemary and thyme.

Heat the oil in a flameproof pan and use to brown the meat on all sides. Add the cannellini beans and French beans, the onion and tomatoes with the liquid from the can. Peel and finely chop the garlic, add to the pan and bring to the boil. Cover and place in a preheated cool oven, 130°C, 250°F, Gas Mark ½, for about 5 hours. Adjust the seasoning with salt and pepper before serving.

Note: As a perfect seal is essential for this method of cooking, make up a small quantity of flour and water pastry, roll into a thin rope and place around the rim of the dish and press the lid down firmly.

Braised boned leg of lamb
Serves 4

Ingredients	Metric-Imperial	American
3 onions		
3 cloves of garlic		
Water	300 ml/½ pint	1¼ cups
1 bay leaf		
8 juniper berries		
5 allspice berries		
Dried thyme	1 tsp	1 tsp
Vinegar	2 tbs	3 tbs
Dry white wine	300 ml/½ pint	1¼ cups
1 boned leg of lamb	1 kg/2¼ lb	2¼ lb
Salt and pepper		
Oil	3 tbs	4 tbs
Tomatoes	225 g/8 oz	8 oz
Sour cream	1 tbs	1 tbs
Flour (all-purpose)	2 tbs	3 tbs
Sugar		

Peel and quarter the onions and peel and quarter the garlic. Place the water in a large pan and add the onion, garlic, bay leaf, juniper and allspice berries, thyme and vinegar. Bring to the boil, simmer for 5 minutes and leave to cool. Add the wine to the pan then put in the lamb and leave to marinate for 24 hours, turning the meat occasionally.

Lift out the meat. Strain the marinade, reserving both the liquid and the vegetables and spice mixture. Dry the meat on absorbent kitchen paper, sprinkle with salt and pepper and if necessary tie into a neat shape with fine string.

Heat the oil in a pan and use to brown the meat on all sides. Quarter the tomatoes and add to the pan with the reserved vegetables and spice mixture. Cook for a further 5 minutes. Pour in half the marinade, bring to the boil, cover and simmer for about 1½ hours, adding more marinade as the liquid evaporates. Lift out the meat and keep hot.

Strain the pan juices into another pan and stir in the cream. Moisten the flour with a little cold water, add to the pan and bring to the boil, stirring constantly. Simmer for 4 minutes and adjust the seasoning with salt, pepper and a little sugar. Serve with the meat and boiled potatoes and butter (lima) beans.

Simple braised lamb
Serves 4

Ingredients	Metric-Imperial	American
Boneless lamb	1 kg/2¼ lb	2¼ lb
Dripping	25 g/1 oz	2 tbs
1 onion		
Lamb or chicken stock (bouillon)	300 ml/½ pint	1¼ cups
Salt and pepper		
Sweet paprika pepper		
Flour (all-purpose)	2 tbs	3 tbs

Remove any excess fat and membrane from the lamb. Chop the fat and place in a pan with the dripping. Heat and use to brown the lamb on all sides. Peel and chop the onion, add to the pan and cook for 2 minutes. Pour in half the

stock, add salt, pepper and paprika to taste, bring to the boil, cover and simmer for 1½ hours, adding more of the stock as the liquid evaporates. Transfer the lamb to a warm serving dish and keep hot.

Strain the cooking liquid into another pan. Moisten the flour with a little cold water, add to the pan and stir until boiling. Simmer for 4 minutes and adjust the seasoning with salt, pepper and paprika if necessary. Serve the meat with Brussels sprouts and potatoes and the hot sauce handed separately.

Lamb curry
Serves 4-6

Ingredients	Metric-Imperial	American
Boneless lamb	1.5 kg/3¼ lb	3¼ lb
Butter or margarine	50 g/2 oz	¼ cup
Onions	350 g/12 oz	12 oz
1 clove of garlic		
Salt and pepper		
Caraway seeds	½ tsp	½ tsp
Curry powder	2 tbs	3 tbs
1 sprig of thyme		
Water	350 ml/12 fl oz	1½ cups
Flour	2 tbs	3 tbs
Whipping cream	300 ml/½ pint	1¼ cups
2 pieces preserved ginger		
Slivered almonds	100 g/4 oz	1 cup

Cut the lamb into bite-sized pieces. Melt two thirds of the butter or margarine in a pan and use to brown the meat on all sides. Peel and chop the onions and garlic, add to the meat and cook until the onion is golden. Season with salt and pepper and add the caraway seeds, curry powder and thyme. Pour in two thirds of the water and bring to the boil. Cover and simmer for 30 minutes.

Blend the flour with a little of the remaining water. Add to the pan with the rest of the water and the cream and bring back to boiling point, stirring all the time. Cover and simmer for a further 15 minutes.

Meanwhile, slice the ginger. Melt the remaining butter in a pan and use to brown the almonds. Add to the curry with the ginger and adjust the seasoning with more salt if necessary. Serve with rice and a green salad.

Opposite: Lamb curry

Braised lamb with red wine
Serves 4

Ingredients	Metric-Imperial	American
½ shoulder of lamb	750 g/1¾ lb	1¾ lb
1 clove of garlic		
Salt	1 tsp	1 tsp
Coarsely ground pepper	½ tsp	½ tsp
Oil	3 tbs	4 tbs
1 onion		
6 spring onions (scallions)		
5 baby carrots		
1 head of celery		
2 tomatoes		
Red wine	125 ml/4 fl oz	½ cup

Remove excess fat and any membrane from the lamb. Peel and finely chop the garlic, mix with the salt and crush to a paste. Rub the garlic mixture and pepper into the meat.

Heat the oil in a flameproof pan and use to brown the meat on both sides. Remove it from the pan. Peel and quarter the onion. Trim and slice the spring onions. Peel and slice the carrots. Trim the celery, removing any strings, and cut into short lengths. Add the onion, spring onions, carrot and celery to the fat remaining in the pan and fry for a few minutes. Pour boiling water over the tomatoes, drain, peel and quarter. Add the tomatoes to the pan, stir and lay the lamb shoulder on top. Place, uncovered, in a preheated moderately hot oven, 200°C, 400°F, Gas Mark 6, for 20 minutes. Pour the wine into the pan and continue cooking for a further 25 minutes, or until the lamb is cooked through. Serve with boiled potatoes.

Roast leg of lamb with mint crust

Serves 4–6

Ingredients	Metric-Imperial	American
1 leg of lamb	2 kg/4½ lb	4½ lb
Salt and pepper		
Garlic salt		
Water	300 ml/½ pint	1¼ cups
Shallots or small onions	450 g/1 lb	1 lb
Chopped parsley	4 tbs	5 tbs
Chopped dill	4 tbs	5 tbs
Dried rosemary	1 tsp	1 tsp
Fresh breadcrumbs	1 tbs	1 tbs
Concentrated mint sauce	1 tsp	1 tsp
Butter	15 g/½ oz	1 tbs
Cooked or canned small carrots	225 g/8 oz	1½ cups
Red wine	225 ml/8 fl oz	1 cup
Flour (all-purpose)	1 tbs	1 tbs
Sour cream	225 ml/8 fl oz	1 cup
Sprigs of rosemary		

Remove excess fat and any membrane from the lamb and sprinkle it with salt, pepper and garlic salt. Place in a roasting tin and cook, uncovered, in a preheated moderately hot oven, 200°C, 400°F, Gas Mark 6, for 15 minutes. Add half the water to the tin and continue cooking for a further 1¼ hours.

Peel the shallots or onions. Add these to the roasting tin, baste with the pan juices and cook for a further 15 minutes.

Meanwhile, mix together the parsley, dill, rosemary, breadcrumbs, mint sauce and 1 tbs of the remaining water to make a paste. Spread it over the meat and dot with the butter. Add the carrots to the roasting tin, pour the red wine

over and return the tin to the oven for a further 15 minutes. Remove the meat, onions and carrots to a warm serving dish and keep hot.

Add the remaining water to the roasting tin and stir well to loosen the sediment. Blend together the flour and cream, add to the tin and stir until boiling. Simmer for 4 minutes and adjust the seasoning. Serve with the meat and vegetables, garnished with sprigs of rosemary if liked.

Microwave hint

To cook chops or cutlets with a glaze by microwave, trim the fat neatly and arrange the chops in a shallow dish. Mix together 3 tbsp (4 tbsp) bottled barbecue sauce and 1 tbsp clear honey, then stir in 1 tbsp Dijon or other French mustard. Brush half of the glaze over the chops. Leave to marinate for about 30 minutes, then brush with more glaze and arrange on a micro-proof roasting rack. Cook on full power for 3 minutes. Turn, brush with any remaining glaze and cook for a further 3 minutes. Leave to stand for 5 minutes before serving.

Opposite: Braised lamb with red wine
Above: Roast leg of lamb with mint crust

Boned shoulder of lamb with cauliflower
Serves 6

Ingredients	Metric-Imperial	American
4 carrots		
1 parsnip		
1 boned shoulder of lamb	1 kg/2¼ lb	2¼ lb
1 onion		
3 whole cloves		
Salted water	1.5 L/2½ pints	6¼ cups
10 black peppercorns		
Potatoes	750 g/1¾ lb	1¾ lb
1 cauliflower		
Salt and pepper		
Frozen peas	175 g/6 oz	1 cup
Chopped parsley	2 tbs	3 tbs

Peel 2 of the carrots and the parsnip. Cut the parsnip in quarters lengthways. Halve the carrots lengthways if large. Place the lamb on a board with the skin side downwards, lay the vegetables on top, roll the meat up enclosing the vegetables, and tie with fine string. Peel the onion and press the cloves into it.

Put the salted water into a large pan and bring to the boil. Add the meat, onion and peppercorns. Bring back to the boil, cover and simmer for 1½ hours. Remove the meat to a warm serving dish and keep hot.

While the meat is cooking, peel the potatoes and cut into small pieces. Peel and slice the remaining carrots, using a fluted cutter if possible. Divide the cauliflower into florets. Strain and measure 500 ml/18 fl oz (2¼ cups) of the meat stock and place in a pan. Season to taste with salt and pepper, add the potatoes and carrots, bring to the boil, cover and cook for 5 minutes. Put in the cauliflower florets and peas, bring back to simmering point, cover again and cook for a further 15 minutes, or until all the vegetables are tender. Drain and arrange round the meat. Sprinkle with the parsley and serve with horseradish sauce.

Lamb with courgettes and cheese topping
Serves 4

Ingredients	Metric-Imperial	American
Boneless leg of lamb	750 g/1¾ lb	1¾ lb
Oil	6 tbs	½ cup
2 onions		
4 tomatoes		
2 cloves of garlic		
Salt and pepper		
Lamb stock (bouillon)	300 ml/½ pint	1¼ cups
Chopped parsley		
4 courgettes (zucchini)		
Grated cheese such as		
Cheddar or Gouda	50 g/2 oz	½ cup

Cut the lamb into cubes. Heat half the oil in a pan and use to brown the meat on all sides. Peel and chop the onions, add to the meat and cook until softened. Pour boiling water over the tomatoes, drain, peel and chop. Peel and finely chop the garlic and add to the pan with the tomato, ½ tsp salt and a little pepper. Transfer to an ovenproof dish and stir in the stock and parsley. Cover and place in a preheated hot oven, 220°C, 425°F, Gas Mark 7, for 1 hour.

Meanwhile, top, tail and slice the courgettes. Heat the remaining oil in a pan and use to cook the courgette slices until tender, stirring frequently. Sprinkle with a little salt. Spoon the courgettes over the meat, sprinkle with the cheese and return to the oven for a further 10 minutes, or until the cheese is turning golden.

Above: Boned shoulder of lamb with cauliflower
Opposite: Lamb with courgettes and cheese topping

Saddle of lamb with coconut pears
Serves 6

Ingredients	Metric-Imperial	American
1 saddle of lamb	1.5 kg/3¼ lb	3¼ lb
Curry powder	1 tbs	1 tbs
Clear honey	125 ml/4 fl oz	½ cup
Lemon juice	2 tbs	3 tbs
6 ripe but firm pears		
Butter	50 g/2 oz	¼ cup
Shredded coconut	6 tbs	7 tbs
Sugar		

Remove the skin and any excess fat from the saddle and score the remaining fat with a sharp knife. Place in a roasting tin and cook, uncovered, in a preheated moderately hot oven, 200°C, 400°F, Gas Mark 6, for 20 minutes.

Meanwhile, mix together the curry powder, honey and lemon juice, brush this over the saddle and return it to the oven for a further 40 minutes, basting frequently with more of the honey mixture.

Meanwhile, peel the pears, halve lengthways and remove the cores. Place in a greased ovenproof dish. Melt the butter in a pan, add the coconut and cook, stirring, until it is turning golden. Spoon over the pears and sprinkle with a little sugar. Add the dish to the oven with the lamb for the last 25 minutes of cooking time.

Microwave hint
To keep meat tasty and moist during cooking, cook in a browning dish on full power for 2 minutes on each side. Meanwhile, peel and slice across a mild onion. Place the onion rings on the meat, overlapping over the surface. Cover and reduce the power to medium. Cook for a further 10-20 minutes, according to thickness, turning once and replacing the onion slices on top.

Microwave hint
One-stage methods are easy when cooking vegetables by microwave. For instance, chop up a cucumber roughly, place in a suitable shallow dish and pour over enough cream to cover. Sprinkle with salt and pepper and cook uncovered, on full power, for 10 minutes. Sprinkle with chopped mixed herbs and serve at once.

Leg of lamb stuffed with spinach
Serves 6

Ingredients	Metric-Imperial	American
1 boned leg of lamb	1.5 kg/3¼ lb	3¼ lb
Salt and pepper		
2 onions		
Butter or margarine	50 g/2 oz	¼ cup
Spinach	350 g/12 oz	12 oz
Gorgonzola cheese	150 g/5 oz	5 oz
Medium-hot made mustard	2 tbs	3 tbs
1 clove of garlic		
Chopped basil	2 tbs	3 tbs
Chopped thyme	1 tbs	1 tbs
Small new potatoes	1 kg/2¼ lb	2¼ lb
Hot water	300 ml/½ pint	1¼ cups
Whipping cream	225 ml/8 fl oz	1 cup

Sprinkle the lamb all over with salt and pepper, including inside the cavity. Peel and chop the onions. Melt half the butter or margarine in a pan and use to cook the onion until golden.

Wash the spinach, drain and place in a pan with the water clinging to the leaves. Cover and cook for about 5 minutes, shaking the pan occasionally, or until the spinach is limp. Drain and chop roughly. Cut the cheese into pieces and add to the fried onion with the mustard and spinach. Cook, stirring, for 2 minutes.

Peel and finely chop the garlic and mix with the basil, thyme and spinach mixture. Season with salt and pepper and purée in a food processor or blender.

Fill the cavity in the leg of lamb with about one third of the spinach mixture. Close the opening and tie the meat into a neat shape with thin string. Place in a roasting tin and cover with half the remaining spinach mixture. Dot with the rest of the butter and cook, uncovered, in a preheated hot oven, 220°C, 425°F, Gas Mark 7, for 30 minutes.

Meanwhile, scrub the potatoes and sprinkle with a little salt. Add to the roasting tin and return this to the oven, basting occasionally with the juices in the tin, for a further 50 minutes. Remove the meat, wrap in foil and keep hot. Place the potatoes in a warm serving dish and keep hot.

Add the water to the roasting tin and stir to loosen the sediment. Strain into a pan, stir in the remaining spinach mixture and the cream and cook to reduce slightly, stirring all the time. Season to taste with salt and pepper. Remove the trussing strings, slice the lamb and arrange on a warm platter. Serve with braised tomatoes and the potatoes and hand the sauce separately.

Opposite: Saddle of lamb with coconut pears
Above: Leg of lamb stuffed with spinach

Saddle of lamb with rosemary
Serves 4

Ingredients	Metric-Imperial	American
1 saddle of lamb	2 kg/4½ lb	4½ lb
Salt and pepper		
3 cloves of garlic		
3 onions		
Oil	2 tbs	3 tbs
Rosemary leaves	4 tbs	5 tbs
Hot water	150 ml/¼ pint	⅔ cup
1 egg		
Chopped parsley	3 tbs	4 tbs
2 slices of toasting bread		

Sprinkle the lamb with salt and pepper. Peel and crush the garlic and rub over the meat. Peel and quarter the onions. Put the oil into a roasting tin and sprinkle in about three quarters of the rosemary. Lay the saddle of lamb on this and surround with the onion quarters. Place, uncovered, in a preheated moderately hot oven, 200°C, 400°F, Gas Mark 6, for 10 minutes. Pour half the water into the roasting tin and cook for a further 1 hour and 5 minutes, adding more water as the liquid evaporates.

Meanwhile, chop the remaining rosemary and mix with the egg and parsley. Cut the bread into cubes. Take the roasting tin from the oven, brush the meat with the egg mixture and press on the bread cubes. Return to the oven for a further 15 minutes. Remove the saddle and carefully separate the meat from the bones. Transfer to a warm serving dish and keep hot.

Leg of lamb with mushrooms
Serves 4

Ingredients	Metric-Imperial	American
1 leg of lamb	1 kg/2¼ lb	2¼ lb
3 cloves of garlic		
Salt and pepper		
Margarine	50 g/2 oz	¼ cup
Selection of pot vegetables		
Flour (all-purpose)	1 tbs	1 tbs
Red wine	225 ml/8 fl oz	1 cup
Beef stock	300 ml/½ pint	1¼ cups
1 bay leaf		
5 black peppercorns		
Tomato purée (paste)	1 tsp	1 tsp
Sugar	½ tsp	½ tsp
Mushrooms	450 g/1 lb	1 lb

Remove surplus fat and any membrane from the lamb. Peel the garlic and cut into slivers. Make slits in the meat and insert a piece of garlic into each. Sprinkle with salt and pepper. Melt the margarine in a flameproof pan and use to brown the meat on all sides. Remove it from the pan.

Clean the pot vegetables, peel if necessary and then chop. Add these to the fat remaining in the pan and cook until golden. Sprinkle in the flour and stir well. Gradually add the wine and stock and stir until boiling. Put in the bay leaf, peppercorns, tomato purée and sugar and return the meat to the pan. Cover and place in a preheated moderately hot oven, 200°C, 400°F, Gas Mark 6, for about 1½ hours.

Add the mushrooms to the dish, baste with the cooking juices, cover and return to the oven for a further 30 minutes. Serve with potato dumplings.

Shoulder of lamb with onions and honey
Serves 4

Ingredients	Metric-Imperial	American
1 boned shoulder of lamb	1 kg/2¼ lb	2¼ lb
Pinch of saffron strands		
Ground cinnamon	¾ tsp	¾ tsp
Ground ginger	¾ tsp	¾ tsp
Clear honey	4 tbs	5 tbs
Lamb or chicken stock (bouillon)	1 L/1¾ pints	4⅓ cups
Small onions	1 kg/2¼ lb	2¼ lb
Salt		

Remove surplus fat and skin from the lamb and cut into 2.5 cm/1 inch cubes. Place in a flameproof dish with the saffron, cinnamon, ginger, half the honey and the stock. The liquid should come half-way up the meat. Cover and cook in a preheated moderately hot oven, 200°C, 400°F, Gas Mark 6, for 35 minutes.

Drain the cooking juices from the dish into a pan and boil until reduced to just less than half. Peel the onions, add to the meat and pour over the reduced stock. Season to taste with salt and stir in the rest of the honey. Half-cover the dish and return it to the oven for a further 30 minutes, or until the onions and lamb are browned and the liquid almost evaporated. Serve with caramelized potatoes.

Press the meat juices and onions through a sieve into a pan and reheat. Season to taste with salt and pepper and serve with the saddle, accompanied by sauté potatoes, broccoli and grilled tomatoes.

Lamb cutlets with pineapple
Serves 4

Ingredients	Metric-Imperial	American
12 small lamb cutlets		
Olive oil	5 tbs	6 tbs
Herbed vinegar	2 tsp	2 tsp
Dried rosemary	½ tsp	½ tsp
Dried basil	1 tsp	1 tsp
Salt		
Butter	20 g/¾ oz	4 tsp
4 small canned pineapple slices		
Dry sherry	3 tbs	4 tbs

Trim off surplus fat from the cutlets. Mix together half the oil, the vinegar, rosemary and basil and brush the cutlets with the mixture. Leave to stand for at least 2 hours. Sprinkle the cutlets with salt.

Heat the remaining oil in a frying pan and use to cook the cutlets for about 10 minutes, turning them frequently, until brown on both sides and cooked through.

Add the butter to the fat remaining in the pan. Cut the pineapple slices in half, add to the pan and fry until lightly browned. Pour in the sherry and boil to reduce slightly. Arrange the pineapple and cutlets on warm plates and spoon over the pan juices. Garnish with sprigs of basil if liked and serve with potato croquettes or garlic bread.

Lamb chops with coriander sauce
Serves 4

Ingredients	Metric-Imperial	American
1 large onion		
Oil	2 tbs	3 tbs
Ground coriander	1 tbs	1 tbs
Ground ginger	1 tsp	1 tsp
Caraway seeds	1 tsp	1 tsp
Natural yogurt (plain)	150 ml/¼ pint	⅔ cup
Salt and pepper		
4 double loin of lamb chops (butterfly)		

Peel and chop the onion. Heat half the oil in a frying pan and use to cook the onion until golden. Sprinkle in most of the coriander, the ginger and caraway seeds. Blend in the yogurt, reheat carefully, stirring, then remove from the heat, season to taste with salt and pepper and keep warm.

Trim off excess fat from the chops then brush them all over with the remaining oil and sprinkle with the rest of the coriander. Place on a grid in a grill pan (broiler). Cook under high heat for 5 minutes on each side, or until cooked through. Serve the chops on hot plates topped with some of the coriander sauce. Garnish each portion with lemon slices and fresh herbs if wished. Hand the remaining sauce separately.

Tip: The sauce is also delicious with fried lambs' or calves' (beef) liver.

Lamb with onion purée
Serves 6–8

Ingredients	Metric-Imperial	American
1 boned leg of lamb	2 kg/4½ lb	4½ lb
3 cloves of garlic		
Salt and pepper		
Chopped thyme	2 tbs	3 tbs
Oil	2 tbs	3 tbs
3 onions		
3 carrots		
Water	300 ml/½ pint	1¼ cups
For the purée:		
Onions	1 kg/2¼ lb	2¼ lb
Streaky bacon (strips)	75 g/3 oz	6 strips
Butter	15 g/½ oz	1 tbs
Water	125 ml/4 fl oz	½ cup
Whipping cream	6 tbs	½ cup
Pinch of cayenne pepper		

Remove surplus fat and any skin from the lamb. Peel the garlic and cut into slivers. Make small slits in the meat and insert the garlic pieces. Sprinkle the lamb with salt, pepper and thyme.

Heat the oil in a roasting tin and use to brown the joint on all sides. Peel and quarter the onions and peel and slice the carrots. Add to the tin and place, uncovered, in a preheated hot oven, 220°C, 425°F, Gas Mark 7, for about 30 minutes. Add half the water to the tin and cook for a further 1½ hours, replacing evaporated liquid with the remaining water. Lift out the meat, slice and keep hot.

Press the meat juices and vegetables through a sieve into a pan and bring to the boil. Add a little hot water if the sauce is too thick. Season with salt and pepper to taste. Keep hot.

While the meat is cooking, make the onion purée. Peel and slice the onions. Chop the bacon and place in a pan until the fat runs and the bacon is golden. Remove the bacon bits with a slotted spoon and discard. Add the butter to the bacon fat and when it has melted, put in the water and onion slices. Bring to the boil, cover and cook until the onion is soft, stirring occasionally. Purée the pan contents and reheat. Stir in the cream and season with the cayenne.

Spread some of the onion purée on a warm serving dish and arrange the slices of lamb on top. Put the remaining onion purée into a warm serving dish. Serve with the lamb platter and sauce.

Romanian sweet pepper pot with minced lamb
Serves 4

Ingredients	Metric-Imperial	American
Minced lamb (ground)	450 g/1 lb	1 lb
6 small green sweet peppers		
2 large onions		
Potatoes	450 g/1 lb	1 lb
Meat stock (bouillon)	500 ml/18 fl oz	2¼ cups
Salt		
Celery salt		
Sweet paprika pepper		
Tomatoes	275 g/10 oz	10 oz
Sour cream	150 ml/¼ pint	⅔ cup

Put the lamb into a large pan and heat, stirring, until the fat runs and the meat looks brown and crumbly. Halve and deseed the peppers and cut the flesh into strips. Peel and chop the onions. Add the pepper strips and onion to the pan and cook, stirring frequently, until softened. Peel and dice the potatoes, add to the meat mixture, pour in the stock and season to taste with salt, celery salt and paprika. Bring to the boil, cover and simmer for 45 minutes.

Pour boiling water over the tomatoes, drain, peel and chop. Add to the pan, cover again and cook for a further 15 minutes. Stir in the cream, adjust the seasoning to taste and serve piping hot in a casserole dish.

Grilled lamb chops with red peppers
Serves 4

Ingredients	Metric-Imperial	American
4 small red sweet peppers		
Butter or margarine	15 g/½ oz	1 tbs
Cornflour (cornstarch)	1 tsp	1 tsp
Whipping cream	125 ml/4 fl oz	½ cup
Salt and pepper		
4 double loin of lamb chops (butterfly)		
Oil		
Sweet paprika pepper		

Halve and deseed the peppers and cut the flesh into thin strips. Melt the butter or margarine in a pan, stir in the pepper strips, cover and simmer for 25 minutes, or until soft. Blend the cornflour with the cream and season with salt and pepper. Pour into the pan and stir until boiling. Simmer for 3 minutes and adjust the seasoning if necessary.

Meanwhile, trim off excess fat and skin from the chops. Place them on the grid of a grill pan (broiler). Brush with oil, sprinkle with paprika and cook under high heat for about 5 minutes on each side, brushing the chops again with oil and sprinkling them with paprika when turning, or until cooked through. Serve with buttered rice and top with the pepper mixture.

Lamb cutlets with spring onions
Serves 1

Ingredients	Metric-Imperial	American
2 lamb cutlets		
Salt and pepper		
Ground coriander		
Small potatoes	200 g/7 oz	7 oz
Butter	40 g/1½ oz	3 tbs
1 bunch of spring onions		
Mushrooms	100 g/4 oz	4 oz
Whipping cream	3 tbs	4 tbs
Grated Cheddar or Gouda cheese	25 g/1 oz	¼ cup

Trim off most of the fat from the cutlets. Sprinkle them with salt, pepper and coriander. Peel the potatoes. Melt two thirds of the butter in a frying pan and use to cook the cutlets for about 5 minutes, or until brown on both sides. Remove from the pan, wrap in foil and keep hot. Add the potatoes to the fat remaining in the pan and stir well. Cover and cook for 15 minutes, turning occasionally. Trim the onions and halve them lengthways. Add to the potatoes, cover and cook for a further 5 minutes.

Slice the mushrooms. Melt the remaining butter in a pan and use to cook the mushrooms, stirring frequently, until soft. Purée with the cream and add coriander to taste.

Place the potatoes and onions on a flameproof plate and top with the cutlets. Spread these with the mushroom mixture and sprinkle with the cheese. Cook under a hot grill (broiler) for 5 minutes.

Microwave hint
To cook a meat loaf evenly without a ring mould, place a glass in the centre of a round dish and pack the mixture round it. When cooked, gently remove the glass before turning out the loaf. This prevents an uncooked centre when the edges are ready.

Below: Grilled lamb chops with red peppers
Opposite: Lamb cutlets with spring onions

Corn, beef and pork casserole
Serves 4

Ingredients	Metric-Imperial	American
Boneless beef	225 g/8 oz	8 oz
Boneless pork	225 g/8 oz	8 oz
Margarine	40 g/1½ oz	3 tbs
1 onion		
1 red and 1 green sweet pepper		
Salt and pepper		
Cayenne pepper		
Beef stock (bouillon)	300 ml/½ pint	1¼ cups
Frozen peas	350 g/12 oz	2 cups
Canned sweetcorn kernels	325 g/11½ oz can	11½ oz can
Chopped parsley	2 tbs	3 tbs

Dice the meat. Heat the margarine in a pan and use to fry the meat until browned on all sides. Peel and chop the onion. Halve and deseed the peppers and cut the flesh into strips. Add the onion and pepper strips to the pan and cook for 5 minutes, stirring occasionally. Season with salt, pepper and a little cayenne, pour in the stock and bring to the boil. Cover and simmer for 1¼ hours.

Add the peas to the pan with the corn and liquid from the can and continue cooking for a further 6 minutes. Adjust the seasoning with salt and pepper to taste and serve sprinkled with parsley. Serve with hot rolls.

Carrot and cannellini bean casserole
Serves 4

Ingredients	Metric-Imperial	American
Dried cannellini beans	100 g/4 oz	⅔ cup
Cold water	750 ml/1¼ pints	3 cups
Boneless belly of pork	400 g/14 oz	14 oz
Carrots	1 kg/2¼ lb	2¼ lb
Potatoes	450 g/1 lb	1 lb
Dessert apples	225 g/8 oz	8 oz
2 onions		
Butter or margarine	40 g/1½ oz	3 tbs
Salt and pepper		
Hot water	400 ml/14 fl oz	1¾ cups
Chopped parsley	2 tbs	3 tbs

Soak the beans in the cold water for 24 hours. Bring the beans to the boil in the soaking water then cover and cook for 1 hour, or until the beans are tender.

Meanwhile, remove any skin from the pork and dice the meat. Peel and dice the carrots and potatoes. Peel, quarter and core the apples then slice. Peel and chop the onions. Melt the butter or margarine in a pan, add the meat and fry until brown on all sides. Put in the onion and cook until golden. Season with salt and pepper, add the carrot, potato and apple and stir in the hot water. Bring to the boil, cover and simmer for about 50 minutes, or until the pork and vegetables are tender.

Drain the beans and add to the meat mixture. Adjust the seasoning to taste and serve the casserole sprinkled with the chopped parsley.

Beef casserole with turnips and apples
Serves 6–8

Ingredients	Metric-Imperial	American
Boneless brisket of beef	1.25 kg/2¾ lb	2¾ lb
Streaky bacon (strips)	65 g/2½ oz	5 strips
Sugar	50 g/2 oz	¼ cup
Onions	750 g/1¾ lb	1¾ lb
Turnips	750 g/1¾ lb	1¾ lb
Salt and pepper		
Dried marjoram	1½ tsp	1½ tsp
Whole grain dry mustard (powder)	2 tbs	3 tbs
Potatoes	750 g/1¾ lb	1¾ lb
Caraway seeds	1 tsp	1 tsp
Cooking apples	1 kg/2¼ lb	2¼ lb
Beef stock (bouillon)	400 ml/14 fl oz	1¾ cups

Trim off any excess fat from the beef then cut into 2.5-cm/1-inch pieces. Chop the bacon and heat in a large pan until the fat runs. Sprinkle in the sugar and cook until it turns golden.

Peel the onions and cut into wedges. Peel and dice the turnips. Add both vegetables to the pan and cook, stirring, for 4 minutes. Season with salt and sprinkle in the marjoram. Place the meat on the vegetables in the pan, season with pepper and sprinkle with the mustard powder. Peel the potatoes, cut into small pieces, place on the meat, season with salt and sprinkle with the caraway seeds. Peel, core and slice the apples, put into the pan on the potatoes and pour the stock over the top. Bring to the boil, cover and simmer for 1¾ hours.

Transfer the contents of the pan to a warm serving dish, stirring the ingredients lightly together. Adjust the seasoning with salt and pepper to taste before serving.

Opposite: Corn, beef and pork casserole
Below: Beef casserole with turnips and apples

Leek casserole with sausages
Serves 4

Ingredients	Metric-Imperial	American
Leeks	1 kg/2¼ lb	2¼ lb
3 carrots		
1 piece of celeriac	100 g/4 oz	4 oz
Potatoes	750 g/1¾ lb	1¾ lb
1 onion		
Streaky bacon (strips)	75 g/3 oz	6 strips
Oil	1 tbs	1 tbs
Beef stock (bouillon)	1 L/1¾ pints	4⅓ cups
4 smoked mettwurst sausages		
Salt and pepper		
Chopped parsley	2 tbs	3 tbs

Trim the leeks, cut in half lengthways and wash well. Cut into 1.25 cm/½ inch wide slices. Peel and slice the carrots. Peel and dice the celeriac and potatoes. Peel and chop the onion. Chop the bacon, place in a pan and heat until the fat runs. Add the oil, celeriac, onion and carrot and fry until the onion is golden. Put in the potatoes, most of the stock and the sausages. Bring to the boil and simmer for 10 minutes.

Add the leeks to the pan, season to taste with salt and pepper and add the remaining stock. Bring back to the boil and cook for a further 10 minutes. Remove the sausages, slice and return to the pan. Simmer for a further 10 minutes and serve sprinkled with the parsley.

Below: Leek casserole with sausages
Opposite: Ham and potato bake

Ham and potato bake
Serves 4

Ingredients	Metric-Imperial	American
Potatoes	1 kg/2¼ lb	2¼ lb
Cooked ham	225 g/8 oz	8 oz
For the sauce:		
Beef stock (bouillon)	225 ml/8 fl oz	1 cup
Whipping cream	150 ml/¼ pint	⅔ cup
2 eggs		
Cornflour (cornstarch)	1 tbs	1 tbs
Salt and pepper		
Ground nutmeg		
Grated Parmesan cheese	25 g/1 oz	¼ cup
Butter	15 g/½ oz	1 tbs

Cook the potatoes in a pan of boiling water (salted) for about 20 minutes, or until tender. Drain, peel, leave to cool and then slice. Roughly chop the ham. Arrange the potato slices and ham in layers in a greased ovenproof dish, finishing with a layer of potato slices.

To make the sauce, beat together the stock, cream and eggs. Moisten the cornflour with a little cold water and stir into the cream mixture. Season to taste with salt, pepper and nutmeg and pour over the ingredients in the dish. Sprinkle with the cheese, dot with the butter and place, uncovered, in a preheated moderately hot oven, 200°C, 400°F, Gas Mark 6, for about 35 minutes, or until browned on top.

Microwave hint
When cooking braised or pot-roasted meat by microwave, pierce the meat deeply on all surfaces with a fork to ensure even cooking.

Microwave hint
Melamine cooking utensils and plates are not suitable for microwave cooking as, in spite of the appearance, this substance actually contains metal.

231

Beef and ham casserole
Serves 4

Ingredients	Metric-Imperial	American
Potatoes	1 kg/2¼ lb	2¼ lb
Margarine	75 g/3 oz	⅓ cup
Minced beef (ground)	225 g/8 oz	8 oz
Cooked ham	175 g/6 oz	6 oz
Salt and pepper		
Flour (all-purpose)	40 g/1½ oz	⅓ cup
Beef stock (bouillon)	300 ml/½ pint	1¼ cups
Milk	225 ml/8 fl oz	1 cup
Fresh breadcrumbs	2 tbs	3 tbs
Butter	25 g/1 oz	2 tbs

Cook the potatoes in boiling salted water for about 20 minutes, or until tender. Drain, peel and leave to cool. Slice. Melt half the margarine in a pan and use to cook the beef, stirring frequently, until it looks brown and crumbly. Chop the ham and mix into the meat. Season with salt and pepper.

Use about one third of the potato slices to make a layer in a greased ovenproof dish. Cover with half the meat mixture, add another one third of the potato slices and the rest of the meat mixture. Top with the last of the potato slices, arranging them slightly overlapping.

Melt the remaining margarine in a pan, sprinkle in the flour and stir until the roux is golden. Gradually add the stock and milk and bring to the boil, stirring constantly. Simmer for 5 minutes, add salt and pepper to taste and pour evenly over the ingredients in the dish. Sprinkle with the breadcrumbs, dot with the butter and bake, uncovered, in a preheated moderately hot oven, 200°C, 400°F, Gas Mark 6, for 35 minutes, or until golden brown on top.

Variation: Instead of the sauce given above, heat 225 ml/8 fl oz (1 cup) sour cream with 300 ml/½ pint (1¼ cups) beef stock (bouillon) and thicken with 1 tbs cornflour (cornstarch) moistened with a little water. Beat in 2 eggs and season to taste. Pour over the potato mixture and sprinkle with grated cheese instead of the breadcrumbs.

Above: Beef and ham casserole
Opposite: Aubergine and minced lamb bake

Aubergine and minced lamb bake
Serves 4

Ingredients	Metric-Imperial	American
Tomatoes	450 g/1 lb	1 lb
Aubergines (eggplant)	450 g/1 lb	1 lb
Salt and pepper		
Oil	2 tbs	3 tbs
2 onions		
Minced lamb	450 g/1 lb	1 lb
Sweet paprika pepper		
Dried thyme	½ tsp	½ tsp
Pinch of dried rosemary		
3 eggs		
Flour (all-purpose)	1 tbs	1 tbs
Natural yogurt (plain)	150 ml/¼ pint	⅔ cup

Pour boiling water over the tomatoes, drain, peel and slice. Cut the aubergines into thin slices. Sprinkle these with salt and leave to stand for 30 minutes. Rinse, drain and dry on absorbent kitchen paper.

Heat the oil in a pan and use to fry the aubergine slices until just golden on both sides. Remove from the pan. Peel and chop the onions, add to the fat remaining in the pan and fry until soft. Put in the lamb and cook, stirring frequently, until it looks brown and crumbly. Season to taste with salt, pepper and paprika and add the thyme and rosemary. Cook for 5 minutes.

Arrange the meat mixture, aubergine and tomato slices in layers in a greased ovenproof dish, ending with a layer of aubergine slices and sprinkling each layer with salt, pepper and paprika. Place, uncovered, in a preheated moderately hot oven, 190°C, 375°F, Gas Mark 5, for 30 minutes.

Meanwhile, beat together the eggs, flour and yogurt, pour over the bake and return to the oven for a further 15 minutes, or until turning golden brown on top.

Microwave hint

Defrosting minced (ground) beef by microwave can be difficult because the outer layer begins to cook while the centre is still frozen. To avoid this, defrost the pack for 3 minutes on Low power, then scrape off the defrosted outer layer. Continue defrosting and scraping off the outer layer every few minutes.

Lentil casserole with smoked pork
Serves 4

Ingredients	Metric-Imperial	American
Green lentils	350 g/12 oz	1½ cups
Beef stock (bouillon)	1.5 L/2½ pints	6¼ cups
Mild cured pork	450 g/1 lb	1 lb
Potatoes	450 g/1 lb	1 lb
Selection of pot vegetables		
Salt and pepper		
Chopped thyme	1 tbs	1 tbs
Chopped parsley		

Place the lentils and the stock in a pan and leave to stand overnight. Bring to the boil, add the pork, cover and simmer for 1 hour.

Peel the potatoes and cut into pieces. Clean the pot vegetables, peel if necessary, then slice. Add to the pan with the potatoes and season with salt and pepper. Put in the thyme, bring back to the boil, cover and simmer for a further 30 minutes, or until the potatoes are tender. Lift out the meat. If liked, remove a few of the potato pieces, mash until smooth then stir back into the casserole. Cut the meat into strips and either return to the pan, or serve separately, sprinkled with parsley.

Potato casserole with sliced sausage
Serves 4

Ingredients	Metric-Imperial	American
Selection of pot vegetables		
Salted water	1.5 L/2½ pints	6¼ cups
Shin of beef	450 g/1 lb	1 lb
4 allspice berries		
2 bay leaves		
Floury potatoes	1 kg/2¼ lb	2¼ lb
Chopped marjoram	1 tbs	1 tbs
Frankfurters	225 g/8 oz	8 oz
Salt and pepper		
Chopped parsley	1 tbs	1 tbs

Clean the pot vegetables, peel if necessary, then chop. Put the salted water into a pan, add the beef, allspice, chopped vegetables and the bay leaves and bring to the boil. Skim then cover and simmer for 2 hours. Strain the stock into another pan, reserving the meat and chopped vegetables. Dice the meat.

Peel and dice the potatoes. Add to the stock with the marjoram, bring to the boil, cover and simmer for 15 minutes. Remove about one third of the potatoes with a slotted spoon. Sieve or liquidize the contents of the pan with the reserved chopped vegetables. Return to the pan and add the diced meat and potato. Slice the frankfurters, stir into the stew and reheat. Adjust the seasoning with salt and pepper to taste and serve the casserole sprinkled with the chopped parsley.

Microwave method
Clean the pot vegetables, peel or scrape then chop into even-sized pieces. Put the vegetables into a bowl with the water (unsalted), the beef, allspice and bay leaves. Cook on

Meanwhile peel and dice the potatoes and put in another large bowl. Strain the stock from the meat over the potatoes, add the marjoram and a little seasoning. Cook in the microwave for 25 minutes.

Retain the vegetables and cut the meat into small dice when it is cool enough to handle.

Remove one-third of the potatoes with a slotted spoon and retain on a plate. Sieve or purée in a blender or food processor the vegetables, potatoes and some of the stock.

Return the puréed vegetables to the bowl and stir in remaining stock, beef and diced potatoes. Slice the frankfurters, stir into the stew, taste for seasoning. Cook for a further 20 minutes at full power. Serve sprinkled with parsley.

Microwave hint

Pot-roasting joints, such as topside or silverside, is particularly successful if cooked slowly by microwave. Place the marinated meat in a roasting bag together with the marinade and a few sliced onions and carrots. Secure the bag loosely with an elastic band or a strip cut from the top of the bag, taking care that the liquid will not spill out. Cook on medium power for at least 1 hour. Allow to stand for 10 minutes before carving.

Left: Lentil casserole with smoked pork
Below: Pot au feu with cauliflower (recipe page 237)

full power for 15 minutes then skim. Cover with cling-film with slits and cook for a further 15 minutes, allow to stand for 5 minutes. Stir round and turn the meat; cook for a further 15 minutes on full power.

Carrot casserole with pork
Serves 4-6

Ingredients	Metric-Imperial	American
Dried cannellini beans	100 g/4 oz	⅔ cup
Water	750 ml/1¼ pints	3 cups
Boneless belly of pork	225 g/8 oz	8 oz
2 onions		
Butter or margarine	25 g/1 oz	2 tbs
Braising beef	450 g/1 lb	1 lb
Salt and pepper		
Carrots	1 kg/2¼ lb	2¼ lb
Potatoes	450 g/1 lb	1 lb
Piece of celeriac	100 g/4 oz	4 oz
Cooking apples	225 g/8 oz	8 oz
Chopped mixed herbs	2 tbs	3 tbs

Place the beans in a pan, pour the water over and leave to stand overnight. Dice the pork, removing any rind. Peel and chop the onions. Melt the butter or margarine in a large pan and use to brown the pork and the piece of beef. Put in the onion and fry until golden. Season with salt and pepper. Drain the beans and make the soaking liquid up to 750 ml/1¼ pints (3 cups) with more water. Add to the meat with the soaked beans. Bring to the boil, cover and simmer for 30 minutes. Peel and dice the carrots, potatoes and celeriac and cook for a further 15 minutes. Peel, core and slice the apples, add to the stew and cook for a further 10 minutes. Take out the beef, cut into dice and return to the stew. Adjust the seasoning with salt and pepper and serve sprinkled with the herbs.

Savoy cabbage with beef and bacon
Serves 4

Ingredients	Metric-Imperial	American
Savoy cabbage	1kg/2¼ lb	2¼ lb
1 large onion		
Streaky bacon (strips)	150g/5 oz	10 strips
Braising beef	450g/1 lb	1 lb
Salt and pepper		
Water	125ml/4 fl oz	½ cup

Discard any rough outer leaves from the cabbage, quarter it and cut out the core. Shred the leaves. Peel and slice the onion.

Line the base of a flameproof dish with the bacon. Put the onion slices on top and cook gently for 10 minutes. Divide the beef into 4 portions and add to the dish with the cabbage. Season with salt and pepper and pour the water over. Cover and place in a preheated moderately hot oven, 200°C, 400°F, Gas Mark 6, for 1½ hours, or until tender.

Pot au feu with cauliflower
Serves 4

Ingredients	Metric-Imperial	American
Shin of beef	350 g/12 oz	12 oz
Beef stock (bouillon)	1.5 L/2½ pints	6¼ cups
2 large chicken legs		
1 small cauliflower		
2 carrots		
1 stick of celery		
1 onion		
2 potatoes		
2 tomatoes		
Chopped basil	1 tbs	1 tbs
Dried marjoram	½ tsp	½ tsp
Salt and pepper		
Ground nutmeg		
Chopped parsley	1 tbs	1 tbs

Put the beef into a pan and pour the stock over. Bring to the boil, cover and simmer for 1 hour. Add the chicken legs and cook for a further 30 minutes.

Divide the cauliflower into florets. Peel and slice the carrots. Slice the celery, removing any strings. Peel and chop the onion. Peel and dice the potatoes. Pour boiling water over the tomatoes, drain, peel and chop. Add the vegetables, basil and marjoram to the pan, season with salt, pepper and nutmeg to taste and bring back to simmering point. Cover and cook for another 25 minutes.

Remove the meat and chicken from the pan, discard any bones and cut the flesh into pieces. Return to the pan, reheat and adjust the seasoning if necessary. Serve sprinkled with parsley. *Illustrated on p. 235.*

Bean casserole with lamb and tomatoes
Serves 4

Ingredients	Metric-Imperial	American
Dried cannellini beans	250 g/9 oz	1¼ cups
Water	1 L/1¾ pints	4⅓ cups
Shoulder of lamb	750 g/1¾ lb	1¾ lb
Onions	225 g/8 oz	8 oz
3 cloves of garlic		
Oil	4 tbs	5 tbs
Dried rosemary	1 tsp	1 tsp
Salt and pepper		
Canned tomatoes	396 g/14 oz can	14 oz can
Cayenne pepper	¼ tsp	¼ tsp

Put the beans into a pan and pour the water over. Leave to soak overnight. Bring the beans to the boil in the cooking liquid, skim then cover and simmer for 35 minutes.

Dice the lamb, discarding skin and bones. Peel and chop the onions and garlic. Heat the oil in a pan and use to brown the meat and onions. Sprinkle in the rosemary and season with salt and pepper. Drain the cooking liquid from the beans into the meat mixture and add two thirds of the garlic. Bring to the boil, cover and simmer for 15 minutes. Add the beans and tomatoes with the liquid from the can and the cayenne. Bring back to boiling point, cover and cook for 1 further hour. Stir in the remaining garlic and adjust the seasoning with salt to taste. Serve with french bread.

Variation: Try haricot beans instead of cannellini.

Opposite: Carrot casserole with pork
Right: Bean casserole with lamb and tomatoes

Salt beef with young turnips and spinach
Serves 6–8

Ingredients	Metric-Imperial	American
Salt beef	1.5 kg/3¼ lb	3¼ lb
Water	1.5 L/2½ pints	6¼ cups
Carrots	750 g/1¾ lb	1¾ lb
Turnips	750 g/1¾ lb	1¾ lb
Onions	350 g/12 oz	12 oz
Potatoes	1 kg/2¼ lb	2¼ lb
1 bunch of parsley		
Frozen spinach	225 g/8 oz	8 oz
Salt and pepper		
Sugar		
Dry mustard (powder)	2 tsp	2 tsp
Whipping cream	225 ml/8 fl oz	1 cup
Grated horseradish from a jar	3 tbs	4 tbs

Put the beef into a pan and pour the water over. Bring to the boil, skim and cook, uncovered, for 1 hour, turning once.

Peel the carrots and cut into thick oblique slices. Peel the turnips and cut into wedges. Peel and slice the onions. Add the carrot, turnip and onion to the pan and cook for a further 30 minutes.

Remove the meat and cut into large dice. Peel and coarsely grate the potatoes. Strip the parsley leaves from the stalks and add to the pan with the potato, spinach and meat dice. Season with salt, pepper and sugar to taste then stir in the mustard powder. Bring to the boil, cover and simmer for a further 30 minutes. Meanwhile, half-whip the cream and stir in the horseradish. Serve the casserole with the horseradish cream.

Green bean and lamb casserole
Serves 4-6

Ingredients	Metric-Imperial	American
Boneless lean lamb	1 kg/2¼ lb	2¼ lb
Dripping	40 g/1½ oz	3 tbs
Small onions	350 g/12 oz	12 oz
2 cloves of garlic		
Water	1 L/1¾ pints	4⅓ cups
Salt and pepper		
French beans (green)	750 g/1¾ lb	1¾ lb
Potatoes	450 g/1 lb	1 lb
2 green sweet peppers		
Dried savory	½ tsp	½ tsp
Chopped parsley	1 tbs	1 tbs

Cut the lamb into bite-sized cubes. Melt the dripping in a pan and use to brown the meat on all sides. Peel and halve the onions and peel and finely chop the garlic. Add to the pan and fry until golden. Pour in half the water, add salt and pepper and bring to the boil. Cover and simmer for 30 minutes.

Top and tail the beans and cut into short lengths. Peel the potatoes and cut into small pieces. Deseed the peppers and cut the flesh into strips. Add the beans, potato and pepper strips to the pan with the savory and remaining water and bring back to the boil. Cover and simmer for a further 45 minutes. Adjust the seasoning with salt and pepper if necessary and serve sprinkled with the parsley.

Microwave method
Dice the meat. Put the browning dish in the microwave for 2 minutes on full power then add the dripping and return for 45 seconds. Add the meat to the dish and cook for 2 minutes on full power. Turn the meat and brown on the other side for 3 minutes.

Peel and half the onions and crush the garlic. Remove the meat to a casserole dish and cook the onions and garlic for 2 minutes each side at full power in the browning dish. Add to the casserole with half the water and some seasoning. Cover and cook on full power for 15 minutes, allow to stand for 5 minutes.

Top and tail the beans and cut into short lengths. Peel the potatoes and cut into small pieces. Deseed the peppers and cut the flesh into strips. Put the potatoes in a bowl with half the remaining water and cook on full power for 10 minutes, drain and retain the water.

Add the potatoes, beans and peppers to the lamb casserole with the savory. Some of the potato water may be added if more liquid is needed. Cover and cook on full power for 20 minutes. Test the lamb and the potatoes to make sure they are tender. If not, cook for a further 10 minutes. Taste and adjust seasoning if necessary. Serve sprinkled with the parsley.

Opposite: Salt beef with young turnips and spinach
Below: Green bean and lamb casserole

Larded turkey thigh with vegetables
Serves 4

Ingredients	Metric-Imperial	American
Oil	4 tbs	5 tbs
Streaky bacon (strips)	200 g/7 oz	14 strips
1 turkey thigh, with bones	1 kg/2¼ lb	2¼ lb
Salt and pepper		
Hot water	1 L/1¾ pints	4⅓ cups
Small onions	450 g/1 lb	1 lb
1 small head of celeriac	about 225 g/8 oz	about 8 oz
Carrots	225 g/8 oz	8 oz
1 small parsnip		
1 leek		
Sour cream	125 ml/4 fl oz	½ cup
Flour (all-purpose)	2 tbs	3 tbs
Chopped parsley (optional)	1 tbs	1 tbs

Put the oil into a roasting tin and place in a preheated moderately hot oven, 200°C, 400°F, Gas Mark 6, for 5 minutes.

Meanwhile, cut the bacon into thin strips and use to lard the underside of the turkey joint. Rub the skin with salt and pepper. Add the turkey to the hot oil in the roasting tin and place, uncovered, in the oven for 10 minutes. Add a little of the hot water to the tin and baste the turkey well with the pan juices. Return to the oven and continue cooking for 1 further hour, basting occasionally and adding more water as necessary. Peel the onions, peel and slice the celeriac, carrot and parsnip. Trim and clean the leek and cut into slices. Add the vegetables to the tin, baste all the ingredients well with the pan juices and cook for 1 further hour, until the turkey is cooked through.

Transfer the turkey and vegetables to a warm serving dish and keep hot. Pour any remaining water into the tin and stir well to loosen the sediment. Strain into a pan. Blend the cream with the flour, add to the pan and stir until boiling. Simmer for 2 minutes and adjust the seasoning with salt and pepper. Sprinkle parsley, if using, over the turkey and vegetables and hand the sauce separately.

Cheese-stuffed turkey breasts with wine sauce
Serves 4

Ingredients	Metric-Imperial	American
4 slices of turkey breast	200 g/7 oz each	7 oz each
Pepper and salt		
3 portions Camembert cheese, total weight	150 g/5 oz	5 oz
Cranberry sauce	4 tsp	4 tsp
Sweet paprika pepper		
Flour (all-purpose)	4 tbs	5 tbs
Butter	50 g/2 oz	¼ cup
1 large lemon		
For the sauce:		
Dry white wine	200 ml/7 fl oz	scant 1 cup
Sugar	25 g/1 oz	2 tbs
Water	4 tbs	5 tbs
Brandy	3 tbs	4 tbs
Whipping cream	125 ml/4 fl oz	½ cup
4 sprigs of mint		

Cut a deep pocket in each turkey breast and sprinkle inside the pockets with pepper. Slice the Camembert and use the slices together with the cranberry sauce to fill the pockets. Close the openings with wooden cocktail sticks (toothpicks). Rub the turkey breasts with salt and paprika and coat in the flour, shaking off any excess.

Melt the butter in a frying pan and fry the stuffed turkey breasts in it for 5 minutes on each side. Meanwhile, grate the lemon rind then peel the fruit and remove the pith. Cut out the lemon segments with a sharp knife. Arrange the turkey breasts on a warm serving dish and top with the lemon segments. Keep hot.

To make the sauce, pour half the wine into the frying pan and stir to loosen the sediment. Heat the sugar and water in another pan, stirring continuously, then allow to become brown. Add the remainder of the wine and the brandy. Bring to the boil, pour in the turkey juices and wine from the frying pan and add the lemon rind. Reheat, remove from the heat and stir in the cream. Pour over the turkey breasts and serve garnished with mint.

Larded turkey thigh with vegetables
Right: Cheese-stuffed turkey breasts with wine

Turkey rolls with Feta cheese
Serves 4

Ingredients	Metric-Imperial	American
4 slices of turkey breast	150 g/5 oz each	5 oz each
Feta cheese	100 g/4 oz	4 oz
1 egg yolk		
Chopped tarragon	1 tsp	1 tsp
Chopped basil	1 tsp	1 tsp
Chopped parsley	1 tsp	1 tsp
Salt and pepper		
Garlic powder	½ tsp	½ tsp
Oil	2 tbs	3 tbs
Flour (all-purpose)	1 tbs	1 tbs
Hot chicken stock (bouillon)	300 ml/½ pint	1¼ cups
Medium sherry	1 tbs	1 tbs
Whipping cream	3 tbs	4 tbs
4 lemon slices		
4 sprigs of parsley		
For the pepper rice:		
Long-grain rice	275 g/10 oz	scant 1¼ cups
1 red sweet pepper		
1 medium-sized green sweet pepper		
Oil	2 tbs	3 tbs

Flatten the slices of turkey breast slightly. Crumble the cheese and mix with the egg yolk and herbs. Season to taste with salt and pepper. Spread over the slices, roll them up and secure with fine string. Sprinkle with salt and garlic powder. Heat the oil in a pan and use to brown the turkey rolls on all sides. Sprinkle in the flour and stir carefully. Blend in the hot stock and bring to the boil. Cover and simmer for 15 minutes. Transfer the turkey rolls to a warm serving dish, remove the strings and keep hot.

Stir the sherry and cream into the sauce, reheat and adjust the seasoning if necessary. Pour over the turkey rolls and garnish the dish with lemon slices and parsley sprigs.

For the pepper rice, cook the rice in plenty of boiling salted water for 12 minutes, or until tender. Drain, refresh with cold water and drain again. Place in a warm serving dish and keep hot. Halve the peppers, deseed and dice finely. Heat the oil in a pan, cook the diced pepper in it until softened and fold into the rice.

Microwave hint
Make up a thickened glaze for poultry with dry flesh, such as poussins and guinea fowl. Try mixing equal quantities of soy sauce and white wine with a little vegetable oil. For each 150 ml/¼ pint (2/3 cup) of sauce, stir in 1 tsp cornflour (cornstarch) until blended. Cook on full power for 1½ minutes. Stir again before brushing the poultry with the glaze before cooking.

Turkey strips with kiwi fruit
Serves 4

Ingredients	Metric-Imperial	American
Flour (all-purpose)	100 g/4 oz	1 cup
Baking powder	1 tsp	1 tsp
1 egg		
Water	150 ml/¼ pint	⅔ cup
Salt		
Turkey breast slices	550 g/1¼ lb	1¼ lb
Oil		
Grated fresh ginger	1 tbs	1 tbs
Button mushrooms	100 g/4 oz	4 oz
2 spring onions (scallions)		
2 large kiwi fruit		
Slivered almonds	40 g/1½ oz	⅓ cup
Chicken stock (bouillon)	125 ml/4 fl oz	½ cup
Dry sherry	2 tbs	3 tbs
Soy sauce	4 tbs	5 tbs
Sugar	2 tsp	2 tsp
White wine vinegar	2 tbs	3 tbs
Cornflour (cornstarch)	2 tsp	2 tsp

Sift the flour and baking powder into a bowl and make a well in the centre. Beat the egg with the water and a pinch of salt. Pour into the dry ingredients and beat well until the batter is smooth.

Cut the turkey breast slices into 1 cm/½ inch wide strips, turn them into the batter and stir well.

Heat sufficient oil in a deep pan until a cube of day-old bread will brown in 1 minute. Fry the coated turkey strips, in batches, for 2–3 minutes, or until golden brown and crisp. Drain well and keep hot in a warm serving dish.

Heat 2 tbs (3 tbs) oil in a separate pan and use to fry the ginger for 2 minutes. Toss the mushrooms in a clean pan without oil over moderate heat for 4 minutes. Trim and chop the spring onions and peel and thickly slice the kiwi fruit. Add the mushrooms, spring onions and kiwi fruit to the ginger with the almonds and cook for 2 minutes.

Combine the stock, sherry, soy sauce, sugar, vinegar and cornflour. Blend well together and pour over the mushroom mixture. Cook, stirring, for a further 3 minutes. Pour over the turkey strips and serve immediately with freshly boiled rice.

Microwave hint
All poultry benefits from being glazed before cooking by microwave. The simplest glaze is 1 tsp Worcestershire sauce mixed with 25 g/1 oz (2 tbsp) melted butter. Brush all over the bird before cooking.

Left: Turkey rolls with feta cheese
Below: Turkey strips with kiwi fruit

Turkey schnitzels
Serves 4

Ingredients	Metric-Imperial	American
4 turkey escalopes	150 g/5 oz each	5 oz each
Salt		
1 egg		
Flour	50 g/2 oz	½ cup
Dried breadcrumbs	50 g/2 oz	½ cup
Margarine	75 g/3 oz	⅓ cup

Sprinkle the escalopes with salt. Beat the egg lightly. Turn the escalopes in flour then dip them in the egg and lastly coat with breadcrumbs, pressing them on well.

Melt the margarine in a large frying pan and fry all the escalopes for about 12 minutes, or until golden brown on both sides. Serve with creamed potatoes and a green salad.

Chicken in sherry sauce
Serves 4

Ingredients	Metric-Imperial	American
4 chicken legs		
Salt and pepper		
Butter	25 g/1 oz	2 tbs
1 onion		
Flour (all-purpose)	15 g/½ oz	2 tbs
Ground turmeric	2 tsp	2 tsp
Hot chicken stock (bouillon)	225 ml/8 fl oz	1 cup
Whipping cream	125 ml/4 fl oz	½ cup
Medium dry sherry	125 ml/4 fl oz	½ cup

Sprinkle the chicken legs well with salt and pepper. Heat the butter in a frying pan and use to brown the chicken portions on both sides. Continue cooking, covered, for 15–20 minutes, or until cooked through. Arrange on a warm serving dish and keep hot.

Peel and chop the onion, add to the fat left in the pan and cook for 2 minutes. Sprinkle in the flour and stir until brown. Add the ground turmeric, mix well and blend in the stock. Stir until boiling and simmer for 5 minutes. Remove from the heat and stir in the cream. Reheat but do not allow to boil. Pour in the sherry and reheat again. Spoon some of the sauce over the chicken and hand the remainder separately. If liked, garnish the dish with fresh herbs and serve with buttered rice.

Opposite: Turkey schnitzel
Left: Chicken in sherry sauce

Curried chicken legs
Serves 4

Ingredients	Metric-Imperial	American
4 large chicken legs		
Salt and pepper		
Vegetable fat	25 g/1 oz	2 tbs
2 onions		
4 canned peach halves plus syrup from the can		
Hot water		
Curry powder		
Toasted slivered almonds	25 g/1 oz	¼ cup
Ground cinnamon	½ tsp	½ tsp

Sprinkle the chicken legs with salt and pepper. Heat the fat in a frying pan and use to brown the chicken on all sides, then remove and keep hot. Peel and chop the onions, add to the fat remaining in the pan and fry for a few minutes. Make up the peach syrup to 300 ml/½ pint (1¼ cups) with hot water and blend in 1 tbs curry powder and ½ tsp salt. Add to the pan together with the chicken legs. Bring to the boil and simmer for 25 minutes. If liked, remove the chicken legs and put under the grill (broiler) for a few minutes.

Below: Curried chicken legs
Right: Deep-fried chicken

Meanwhile, adjust the seasoning of the sauce adding extra curry powder and salt if necessary. Put the chicken legs on a warm dish with the peach halves stuffed with half the almonds. Pour the sauce over the chicken and sprinkle with the remaining almonds and then with the cinnamon.

Deep-fried chicken
Serves 4

Ingredients	Metric-Imperial	American
2 eggs		
Pepper		
Sweet paprika pepper		
Salt	1 tsp	1 tsp
8 small chicken pieces, total weight	1.25 kg/2¾ lb	2¾ lb
Dried breadcrumbs	about 8 tbs	about ⅔ cup

Oil for deep frying

Beat together the eggs, a little pepper and paprika and the salt. Dip the chicken pieces into the egg mixture and coat with breadcrumbs, pressing them on well.

Heat oil in a deep fryer until it will brown a cube of day-old bread in 1 minute. Fry the chicken pieces, in two batches if necessary, for 8–10 minutes, or until golden brown. Drain well on absorbent kitchen paper. Serve hot and garnish with tomato wedges, lemon slices and parsley if wished.

Casserole of turkey, Burgundy style
Serves 4
(Photo p. 240–241)

Ingredients	Metric-Imperial	American
1 turkey leg with bones	1 kg/2¼ lb	2¼ lb
Salt and pepper		
Garlic powder	½ tsp	½ tsp
Sweet paprika pepper	½ tsp	½ tsp
Oil	4 tbs	5 tbs
1 large onion		
Chicken stock (bouillon)	300 ml/½ pint	1¼ cups
Cooked ham	225 g/8 oz	8 oz
Canned mushrooms	225 g/8 oz can	8 oz can
Red wine	225 ml/8 fl oz	1 cup
Flour (all-purpose)	2 tbs	3 tbs
Sour cream	2 tbs	3 tbs
Chopped mixed herbs	1 tbs	1 tbs

Sprinkle the turkey with salt, pepper, the garlic powder and paprika. Heat the oil in a large pan and use to fry the turkey joint on all sides, until sealed. Peel and chop the onion, add to the pan and cook for 2 minutes. Pour over the stock. Cut the ham into strips, drain and quarter the mushrooms. Add both ingredients to the turkey together with half the wine. Bring to boil, cover and simmer for 1½ hours, or until turkey is tender. Remove to a warm serving dish, keep hot.

Combine the flour and remaining wine, add to the pan and stir until boiling. Simmer for 2 minutes, blend in the cream. Pour over the turkey. Serve sprinkled with herbs.

Chicken braised in wine
(Using a pressure cooker)
Serves 4

Ingredients	Metric-Imperial	American
8 small chicken pieces, total weight	1.25 kg/2¾ lb	2¾ lb
Salt and pepper		
Streaky bacon (strips)	75 g/3 oz	6 strips
Butter or margarine	50 g/2 oz	¼ cup
1 onion		
Leeks	225 g/8 oz	8 oz
Red wine	300 ml/½ pint	1¼ cups
Chicken stock (bouillon)	225 ml/8 fl oz	1 cup
4 whole cloves		
1 bay leaf		
1 sprig of rosemary		
Flour (all-purpose)	2 tbs	3 tbs

Sprinkle the chicken portions with salt and pepper. Chop the bacon and heat in the open pressure cooker until the fat runs. Add the butter or margarine and use to brown the chicken pieces on all sides. Peel and chop the onion and slice the leeks thinly. Add to the pan and fry, stirring, for 2 minutes. Reserve 3 tbs (4 tbs) of the wine, and add the rest to the pan with the stock, cloves and herbs. Close the cooker and bring to full pressure. Cook for 10 minutes.

Remove the chicken to a warm serving dish and keep hot. Mix the flour with the remaining wine, add to the ingredients still in the pan and stir until boiling. Simmer for 5 minutes then pour over the chicken. Serve with mashed potatoes and a chicory (Belgian endive) salad.

Below: Chicken braised in wine
Right: Fruit-garnished chicken legs

Fruit-garnished chicken legs
Serves 4

Ingredients	Metric-Imperial	American
Oil	2 tbs	3 tbs
Sweet paprika pepper	½ tsp	½ tsp
Curry powder	½ tsp	½ tsp
Salt and pepper		
4 chicken legs		
Hot water	125 ml/4 fl oz	½ cup
Canned mandarin segments, peach slices and pineapple slices		
Drained cocktail cherries		
Powdered gelatine	1 tbs	1 tbs
Medium white wine	3 tbs	4 tbs

Mix together first 4 ingredients. Spread over the chicken. Arrange in a greased roasting tin and cook, uncovered at 200°C, 400°F, Gas Mark 6 for 10 minutes. Add a little water and cook for a further 30–35 minutes, adding more water as it evaporates and basting until cooked. Transfer to a rack over a baking sheet (cookie sheet) and cool.

Drain the fruit, reserving the syrups. Make the syrups up to 250 ml/9 fl oz (generous 1 cup) with water. Dissolve the gelatine in the wine in a small bowl over a pan of hot water. Stir into the fruit juice and leave to thicken. Spoon over each chicken leg repeat until well covered. Leave to set. Pour left-over aspic into a tin and leave this to set. Cut into cubes. Serve on a dish, garnished with aspic cubes.

Chicken breasts with Marsala sauce
Serves 3

Ingredients	Metric-Imperial	American
3 boneless chicken breasts		
Salt and pepper		
Chopped sage		
3 thin slices Parma ham		
Butter	40 g/1½ oz	3 tbs
Marsala	4 tbs	5 tbs
Whipping cream	150 ml/¼ pint	⅔ cup

Sprinkle the chicken breasts with salt, pepper and sage and wrap each one in a slice of ham. Secure with wooden cocktail sticks (toothpicks).

Melt the butter in a frying pan and cook the wrapped chicken breasts for 10–15 minutes, turning them occasionally, until cooked through. Remove from the pan and keep hot.

Add the Marsala to the juices left in the pan and stir well. Blend in the cream and bring to the boil, stirring constantly. Remove from the heat and season to taste with salt. Discard the sticks from the chicken breasts and serve them in the sauce, accompanied by a risotto and green salad.

Chicken fillets with herbed mayonnaise and avocado
Serves 6

Ingredients	Metric-Imperial	American
Boneless chicken breasts, total weight	675 g/1½ lb	1½ lb
Salt and pepper		
Grated rind of 1 lime or small lemon		
Butter	40 g/1½ oz	3 tbs

For the mayonnaise:

	Metric-Imperial	American
2 egg yolks		
Juice of 1 lemon or lime		
Salt and pepper		
Sugar		
Oil	250 ml/9 fl oz	generous 1 cup
Chopped tarragon	1 tbs	1 tbs
Chopped parsley	1 tbs	1 tbs
3 ripe avocados		
Snipped cress		
Lime or lemon slices		

Place the chicken breasts in a dish and sprinkle with salt, pepper and citrus rind. Cover and leave for 1 hour, turning

the chicken once during this time. Melt the butter in a frying pan and cook the chicken breasts for about 5 minutes on each side, or until cooked through. Leave to cool.

To make the mayonnaise, beat together the egg yolks, 1 tbs lime or lemon juice and salt, pepper and sugar to taste. Gradually beat in the oil until the mayonnaise thickens. Adjust the seasoning with a little more citrus juice, salt, pepper and sugar if wished. Fold in the tarragon and parsley.

Peel the avocados, remove the stones (pits) and cut the flesh into 1 cm/½ inch thick slices. Arrange these, fan-like, on a serving dish. Sprinkle with herbs and citrus juice. Slice the chicken breasts obliquely and arrange on the avocado slices. Spoon the mayonnaise over the top and garnish with more herbs and lime or lemon slices.

Left: Chicken breasts with Marsala wine
Above: Chicken fillets with herbed mayonnaise and avocado

253

Stewed chicken with basil
Serves 4

Ingredients	Metric-Imperial	American
Boneless chicken breasts, total weight	750 g/1¾ lb	1¾ lb
Oil	4 tbs	5 tbs
Salt and pepper		
2 onions		
Dry white wine	125 ml/4 fl oz	½ cup
Lime or lemon juice	2 tsp	2 tsp
1 chicken stock cube (bouillon)		
Cornflour (cornstarch)	2 tsp	2 tsp
2 egg yolks		
Whipping cream	225 ml/8 fl oz	1 cup
Chopped basil	3 tbs	4 tbs
Worcestershire sauce	1 tsp	1 tsp

If wished, first discard the skin from the chicken fillets then cut the flesh into 2.5 cm/1 inch cubes. Heat the oil in a pan and use to brown the chicken cubes. Add a little salt and pepper. Peel and chop the onions, add to the pan and cook until transparent. Stir in the wine and citrus juice and crumble in the stock cube. Bring to the boil and simmer for 15 minutes, until cooked through.

Moisten the cornflour with a little cold water, add to the pan and stir until boiling. Simmer for 5 minutes and remove from the heat. Mix together the egg yolks and cream, stir into the chicken mixture and reheat but do not allow to boil. Fold in the basil, add the Worcestershire sauce and adjust the seasoning with salt and pepper to taste. Serve immediately with rice or French bread.

Variation: Instead of chicken use turkey breasts in this recipe. Most large supermarkets now stock a wide selection of turkey pieces. It is a low-fat meat.

Microwave method

Remove the skin from the chicken fillets and cut the flesh into 2.5 cm/1 inch cubes.

Put the browning dish in the microwave for 1 minute on full power. Pour in the oil and switch on for a further 40 seconds. Add the chicken and return on full power for 2 minutes. Turn the chicken cubes and cook another 2 minutes.

Peel and chop the onions, add to the microwave dish and cook for 3 minutes on top of the chicken.

Heat the wine and the fruit juice for 1 minute on full power and crumble in the stock cube. Mix well with a spoon to make sure it has dissolved. Pour over the chicken, cover the dish and cook for 6 minutes. Leave to stand for 3 minutes.

Mix the cornflour with a little cold water, spoon a little juice from the chicken into the cornflour and mix well. Gradually add the egg yolks, cream, basil, Worcestershire sauce, salt and pepper to the cornflour and mix well.

Stir this mixture into the chicken and mix until evenly distributed. Return to the microwave on half power for 10 minutes. Serve hot with French bread or rice.

Paella supreme
Serves 4

Ingredients	Metric-Imperial	American
Fresh mussels	450 g/1 lb	1 lb
Dry white wine	125 ml/4 fl oz	½ cup
Spanish chorizo sausage	50 g/2 oz	2 oz
2–3 cloves of garlic		
Olive oil	6–7 tbs	about ½ cup
8 small chicken pieces		
Salt and pepper		
4 small onions		
Lean boneless pork	225 g/8 oz	8 oz
5 tomatoes		
1 green sweet pepper		
Cooked jumbo prawns (shrimp)	225 g/8 oz	8 oz
Long-grain rice	250 g/9 oz	generous 1 cup
Frozen peas	100 g/4 oz	⅔ cup
4 canned drained artichoke hearts		
Powdered saffron	½ tsp	½ tsp
Chicken stock (bouillon)	750 ml/1¼ pints	3 cups
Few stuffed green olives		

Soak the mussels in plenty of clean water for several hours. Scrub and remove the beards. Discard any mussels which do not open. Bring the wine to the boil in a pan, add the mussels and cook for about 5 minutes, stirring occasionally. Discard any mussels which remain closed. Reserve a few mussels in the shell and shell the remainder. Slice the sausage and peel and chop the garlic. Heat the oil and use to fry the sausage and garlic for 2–3 minutes. Remove the sausage bits from the pan and keep hot. Sprinkle the chicken pieces with salt and pepper and brown in the oil remaining in the pan. Peel and chop the onions, add to the chicken and fry until transparent. Dice the pork, add to the pan and cook for 3 minutes. Pour boiling water over the tomatoes, drain, peel, halve and remove the seeds. Roughly chop the flesh. Deseed and chop the pepper. Add the tomato and pepper to the meat and cook gently, covered, for about 30 minutes. Meanwhile, shell most of the prawns.

Remove the chicken pieces and stir the rice into the remaining pan contents. Transfer to a large ovenproof dish, return the chicken and add the sausage, shelled mussels and prawns and those in the shell, the peas and artichoke hearts. Mix the saffron with the stock and pour over the ingredients. Cover and cook in a preheated moderately hot oven, 200°C, 400 oF, Gas Mark 6, for about 20 minutes, or until the rice is tender. Adjust the seasoning with salt and pepper if necessary and serve hot, garnished with olives.

Left: Stewed chicken with basil
Right: Paella suprème

Indonesian chicken
Serves 4

Ingredients	Metric-Imperial	American
Selection of pot vegetables		
1 chicken	1 kg/2¼ lb	2¼ lb
1 onion		
2 carrots		
1 piece of celeriac	100 g/4 oz	4 oz
1 stick of celery (stalk)		
Margarine	40 g/1½ oz	3 tbs
Curry powder	4 tsp	4 tsp
1 banana		
1 apple		
3 drained canned pineapple slices		
Salt		
Sugar		

Clean the pot vegetables, peel if necessary and cut into small pieces. Cook the chicken with these vegetables in boiling salted water for about 1 hour. Remove the chicken, take the flesh from the bones and cut into strips, discarding skin and bones. Strain the stock and measure 500 ml/18 fl oz (2¼ cups).

Peel and chop the onion, carrots and celeriac and trim and slice the celery. Heat the margarine in a pan and cook the vegetables for about 10 minutes, stirring occasionally. Stir in the curry powder and cook for a further few minutes.

Add the chicken strips and measured stock and bring to the boil. Peel the banana and peel and core the apple. Dice the pineapple, banana and apple and stir into the curry mixture. Heat for 3–5 minutes and season to taste with salt and pepper. Serve with buttered cooked long grain rice and a mixed green salad.

Chicken fricassee
Serves 4

Ingredients	Metric-Imperial	American
1 chicken	1.25 kg/2¾ lb	2¾ lb
2 medium-sized onions		
2 carrots		
1 small turnip or swede (rutabaga)		
1 bay leaf		
6 peppercorns		
For the sauce:		
1 onion		
Butter	25 g/1 oz	2 tbs
Mushrooms	225 g/8 oz	8 oz
Curry powder	½ tsp	½ tsp
Flour (all-purpose)	40 g/1½ oz	⅓ cup
Canned asparagus tips	175 g/6 oz	1 cup
Frozen peas	175 g/6 oz	1 cup
Whipping cream	2 tbs	3 tbs
Salt and pepper		
1 egg yolk		
Cold milk	2 tsp	2 tsp
Chopped parsley	1 tbs	1 tbs

Bring the chicken to the boil in plenty of salted water in a large pan. Peel the onions, carrot and turnip or swede and add to the chicken with the bay leaf and peppercorns. Bring back to the boil and simmer for about 1¼ hours, or until the chicken is tender. Remove from the pan, take the flesh from the bones and dice it, discarding skin and bones. Strain the stock and if necessary make up to 750 ml/1¼ pints (3 cups) with hot water. Chop the carrots and reserve. Discard the other vegetables.

To make the sauce, peel and chop the onion. Melt the butter in a pan and use to cook the onion until transparent. Slice the mushrooms and add to the pan. Cook for 3 minutes, stirring occasionally. Sprinkle with the curry powder and flour and cook for 2 minutes, stirring. Blend in the measured stock and stir until boiling. Simmer for 5 minutes. Add the asparagus and peas to the sauce and simmer for 5 minutes more. Mix in the cream, chicken and reserved carrot. Adjust the seasoning with salt and pepper then bring to the boil. Beat the egg yolk with the milk, remove the pan from the heat and beat in the egg yolk mixture. Sprinkle with parsley and serve with rice.

Left: Indonesian chicken
Right: Chicken fricassee

Chicken casserole, Spanish style
(Using a pressure cooker)
Serves 4

Ingredients	Metric-Imperial	American
Olive oil	4 tbs	5 tbs
8 small chicken pieces, total weight	1 kg/2¼ lb	2¼ lb
2 red sweet peppers		
Canned mushrooms	225 g/8 oz can	8 oz can
Long grain rice	150 g/5 oz	⅔ cup
Frozen peas	275 g/10 oz	1⅔ cups
Tomato purée (paste)	4 tbs	5 tbs
Chicken stock (bouillon)	600 ml/1 pint	2½ cups
Dried basil	¼ tsp	¼ tsp
Pinch of dried rosemary		
Salt and pepper		

Heat the oil in the open pressure cooker and use to brown the chicken pieces on all sides.

Halve and deseed the peppers and cut the flesh into wide strips. Add to the chicken and cook, stirring occasionally, for a few minutes.

Halve the mushrooms and add to the cooker with the liquid from the can, the rice, peas, tomato purée, stock, basil and rosemary. Season to taste with salt and pepper. Close the cooker, bring to full pressure and cook for about 10 minutes. Transfer to a warm serving dish.

Chicken on fruity risotto
Serves 4

Ingredients	Metric-Imperial	American
Butter	15 g/½ oz	1 tbs
Long-grain rice	250 g/9 oz	generous 1 cup
Hot chicken stock (bouillon)	500 ml/18 fl oz	2¼ cups
2 apples		
2 bananas		
Juice of 2 oranges		
Salt and white pepper		
Sweet paprika pepper		
Curry powder		
Oil	1 tbs	1 tbs
4 chicken legs		
Parsley sprigs (optional)		
Orange wedges (optional)		

Melt the butter in a large saucepan, add the rice and fry until translucent. Add the hot chicken stock, bring to the boil, stir once, cover and slightly simmer for 12 minutes, or until the rice is tender and the liquid absorbed.

Peel and roughly grate the apples. Peel and slice the bananas. Mix the apple and banana with the orange juice and stir into the cooked rice. Reheat and season to taste with salt, pepper, paprika and curry powder. Set aside but keep hot.

Meanwhile, combine the oil with ½ tsp paprika pepper and brush this over the chicken. Cook under a hot grill (broiler) for 10–12 minutes on each side, basting occasionally, or until cooked through.

Put the fruity risotto onto a warm serving dish and arrange the chicken legs on top. If liked, garnish the dish with parsley sprigs and orange wedges.

Cheesy chicken rice
(Using a pressure cooker)
Serves 4

Ingredients	Metric-Imperial	American
1 onion		
Oil	5 tbs	6 tbs
Long-grain rice	250 g/9 oz	generous 1 cup
Cooked, boneless chicken	350 g/12 oz	12 oz
Chicken stock (bouillon)	500 ml/18 fl oz	2¼ cups
Salt and pepper		
Grated Cheddar cheese	65 g/2½ oz	⅔ cup

Peel and chop the onion. Heat the oil in the open pressure cooker and use to fry the onion until soft. Add the rice and cook for a few minutes. Cut the chicken into small pieces and add with the stock. Season to taste with salt and pepper. Close the cooker and bring to full pressure. Cook for about 8 minutes. Stir in the cheese before serving.

Left: Chicken casserole, Spanish style
Right: Chicken on fruity risotto

Chicken with braised carrots
Serves 4

Ingredients	Metric-Imperial	American
Carrots	750 g/1¾ lb	1¾ lb
4 chicken legs	200 g/7 oz each	7 oz each
Salt and pepper		
Ground nutmeg	½ tsp	½ tsp
Margarine	40 g/1½ oz	3 tbs
3 onions		
Hot chicken stock	225 ml/8 fl oz	1 cup
Cornflour (Cornstarch)	2 tsp	2 tsp
Chopped parsley	1 tbs	1 tbs

Peel the carrots and cut into small strips. Rub the chicken legs with salt, pepper and nutmeg. Melt the margarine in a pan and use to brown the chicken legs on all sides. Peel and slice the onions. Add to the chicken with the carrots. Season with salt and pepper and pour in half the stock. Bring to the boil, cover and simmer for 25–30 minutes, or until the chicken is cooked through.

Remove the chicken pieces to a warm serving dish and keep hot. Add the remaining stock to the vegetables in the pan and bring to the boil. Moisten the cornflour with a little cold water, mix into the vegetables and cook, stirring constantly, for 1 minute. Spoon the vegetables round the chicken and serve sprinkled with parsley.

Chicken breasts in cream sauce
Serves 4

Ingredients	Metric-Imperial	American
Boneless chicken breasts, total weight	450 g/1 lb	1 lb
Salt and pepper		
Sweet paprika pepper		
Butter	25 g/1 oz	2 tbs
Flour (all-purpose)	25 g/1 oz	¼ cup
Canned sliced mushrooms with liquid	150 g/5 oz	⅔ cup
Whipping cream	125 ml/4 fl oz	½ cup

Thinly slice the chicken breasts and sprinkle with salt, pepper and paprika. Melt the butter in a pan and use to fry the chicken slices for 7 minutes, stirring occasionally, until golden brown.

Sprinkle the flour into the pan and stir and cook for a further 1 minute. Drain the liquid from the mushrooms and make up to 250 ml/9 fl oz (generous 1 cup) with water. Gradually add to the pan, stirring constantly until boiling. Put in the mushrooms and cream and cook for 5 minutes, stirring occasionally. Season well with salt, pepper and paprika to taste.

Boned and stuffed chicken legs with pineapple
Serves 4

Ingredients	Metric-Imperial	American
4 chicken legs		
Gouda cheese	100 g/4 oz	4 oz
4 slices of Parma ham (prosciutto)		
4 slices of drained canned pineapple		
Little oil		
Sweet paprika pepper		
Chopped parsley	1 tbs	1 tbs

Bone the chicken legs. Cut the cheese into 4 equal strips, wrap each in a slice of ham and place inside the chicken portions. Sew up with fine string using a larding needle.

Arrange the stuffed chicken portions on the grid of the grill pan (broiler) and cook under high heat for about 12 minutes on each side, or until cooked through. Meanwhile, add the pineapple slices to the grid, brush with oil and sprinkle with paprika. Cook for 5 minutes then turn, brush with oil and sprinkle again with paprika and cook for a further 5 minutes. Remove the trussing threads from the chicken.

Arrange the pineapple slices on a hot serving dish, put a chicken portion on each and sprinkle with parsley.

Left: Chicken with braised carrots
Right: Chicken breasts with cream sauce

Fried chicken livers with mixed vegetables
Serves 4

Ingredients	Metric-Imperial	American
Small potatoes	750 g/1¾ lb	1¾ lb
Butter or margarine	65 g/2½ oz	5 tbs
Oil	2 tbs	3 tbs
Salt and pepper		
Button onions	225 g/8 oz	8 oz
Carrots	450 g/1 lb	1 lb
2 bay leaves		
Leeks	225 g/8 oz	8 oz
Chopped thyme	1 tsp	1 tsp
Chicken livers	450 g/1 lb	1 lb
Few sprigs of parsley		

Peel the potatoes. Heat half the butter or margarine and the oil in a pan, add the potatoes and fry gently for about 20 minutes, turning them occasionally. Season with salt to taste.

Peel the onions, peel and thickly slice the carrots. Add the onions and carrot to the potatoes with the bay leaves and cook for a further 20 minutes, stirring now and then. Trim and clean the leek and cut into thick slices. Add to the pan and cook, stirring frequently, for 10 minutes more. Season with pepper and add the thyme.

In a separate pan, melt the remaining butter or margarine. Add the livers and cook for 8–10 minutes, turning often, until brown and cooked through. Fold into the vegetable mixture and garnish with small sprigs of parsley.

Chicken livers with apples
Serves 4

Ingredients	Metric-Imperial	American
Cooking apples	450 g/1 lb	1 lb
Onions	450 g/1 lb	1 lb
Butter	150 g/5 oz	⅔ cup
Salt and pepper		
Flour (all-purpose)	4 tbs	5 tbs
Chicken livers	450 g/1 lb	1 lb
4 slices of rye bread		
Sprigs of marjoram or parsley		

Peel, quarter and core the apples and cut into fairly thick wedges. Peel the onions, slice and divide into rings. Melt about one third of the butter in a pan, add the onion rings and fry until golden brown. Remove from the pan, sprinkle with salt and keep hot.

Add another third of the butter to the pan and use to fry the apple wedges, turning them occasionally, until golden. Keep these hot with the onions.

Coat the livers with the flour. Add the remaining butter to the pan, put in the livers and cook for 8–10 minutes, turning now and then, until brown and cooked through. Toast the bread, place each slice on a warm plate and top with livers, apple and onion. Sprinkle with salt and pepper if wished and serve at once, garnished with sprigs of marjoram or parsley.

Left: Fried chicken livers with mixed vegetables
Right: Chicken livers with apples

Braised chicken with peppers and paprika
Serves 4

Ingredients	Metric-Imperial	American
Salt and pepper		
4 chicken pieces		
Oil	3 tbs	4 tbs
Streaky bacon (strips)	100 g/4 oz	8 strips
1 onion		
2 cloves of garlic		
2 red sweet peppers		
Canned tomatoes	225 g/8 oz can	8 oz can
Chicken stock (bouillon)		
Whipping cream	3 tbs	4 tbs
Chilli sauce	3–4 tbs	4–5 tbs
Sweet paprika pepper		

Rub a little pepper into the chicken pieces. Heat the oil in a

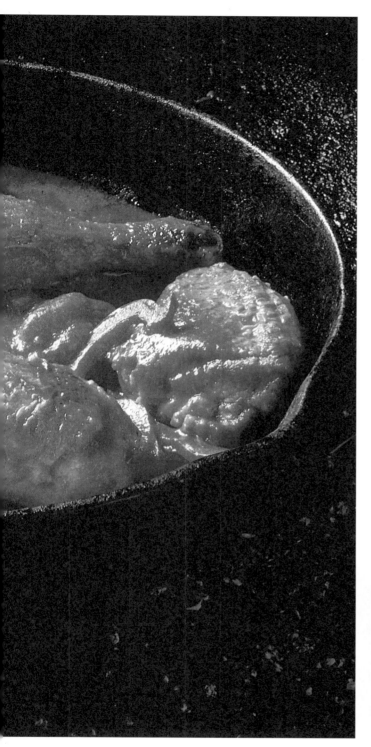

chicken portions into the sauce, bring back to the boil then simmer for 25 minutes. Adjust the seasoning with salt, pepper and paprika to taste and put in the tomatoes. Cook for a further 5 minutes and serve hot.

Roast chicken, Normandy style
Serves 4

Ingredients	Metric-Imperial	American
1 roasting chicken	1.25 kg/2¾ lb	2¾ lb
Salt and pepper		
1 large sprig of tarragon		
2 medium-sized cooking apples		
Cider	125 ml/4 fl oz	½ cup
Butter	50 g/2 oz	¼ cup

Rub the outside and sprinkle the inside of the chicken with salt and pepper. Put the tarragon inside. Peel, quarter and core the apples. Pour the cider into an ovenproof dish and put in the chicken, breast downwards. Surround with the apple quarters. Melt the butter and brush half of it over the chicken and apples. Cook, uncovered, in a preheated moderately hot oven, 200°C, 400°F, Gas Mark 6, for 30 minutes.

Turn the chicken over so that the breast is upwards. Use the remaining butter to brush over the chicken and apples and return the dish to the oven for a further 45 minutes, or until the chicken is cooked through. Serve the chicken and apples on a bed of boiled rice if liked.

Left: Braised chicken with peppers and paprika
Below: Roast chicken, Norman style

pan and fry the chicken for about 15 minutes, until brown on both sides. Remove the chicken.

Chop the bacon, add to the fat remaining in the pan and fry until just turning golden. Peel and chop the onion and garlic and fry lightly in the bacon fat. Halve the peppers, remove the seeds and cut the flesh into strips. Add to the pan. Drain the tomatoes and make the liquid up to 500 ml/18 fl oz (2 cups) with stock.

Pour the tomato stock, cream and chilli sauce into the pan and stir until boiling. Cook until slightly reduced. Put the

	Metric-Imperial	American
Water	350 ml/12 fl oz	1½ cups
Tomato purée (paste)	3 tbs	4 tbs
Hot paprika pepper	1 tsp	1 tsp
Dried marjoram	½ tsp	½ tsp
Sour cream	3 tbs	4 tbs
Cornflour (cornstarch)	1 tbs	1 tbs

Rub the chicken pieces with salt and sweet paprika. Heat the oil in a pan and use to brown the chicken portions on both sides. Peel and chop the onion and garlic, add to the pan and fry gently for 1 minute. Pour in half the water and bring to the boil. Simmer for 40 minutes, adding more of the water as the liquid evaporates. Remove the chicken.

Measure the cooking liquid and make up to 350 ml/12 fl oz (1½ cups) with more water. Return to the pan, stir in the tomato purée and add the hot paprika and 1 tbs sweet paprika plus the marjoram. Bring back to the boil. Combine the sour cream and cornflour, add to the pan and stir until the sauce boils. Adjust the seasoning with salt, return the chicken portions to the pan and bring to the boil again. Simmer for 10 minutes and serve with noodles or rice.

Left: Paprika braised chicken
Below: Chicken on a bed of onions

Paprika braised chicken
Serves 4

Ingredients	Metric-Imperial	American
4 chicken pieces, total weight	1 kg/2¼ lb	2¼ lb
Salt		
Sweet paprika pepper		
Oil	2–3 tbs	3–4 tbs
1 onion		
1 clove of garlic		

Chicken on a bed of onions
Serves 4

Ingredients	Metric-Imperial	American
Oil	2 tbs	3 tbs
8 small chicken pieces, total weight	1.25 kg/2¾ lb	2¾ lb
Salt and pepper		
Button onions	450 g/1 lb	1 lb
Carrots	225 g/8 oz	8 oz
Butter	40 g/1½ oz	3 tbs
Roughly chopped thyme	1 tbs	1 tbs
2 bay leaves		
Whipping cream	125 ml/4 fl oz	½ cup

Heat the oil in a pan and add the chicken pieces. Fry, turning them occasionally, for 20 minutes. Remove the chicken from the pan, sprinkle with salt and pepper and keep hot.

Peel and quarter the onions and peel and slice the carrots. Add the butter to any fat remaining in the pan, put in the carrot and onion and fry, stirring occasionally, until golden. Sprinkle on the thyme, put in the bay leaves and return the chicken. Season to taste and cook, covered, for a further 20 minutes, stirring carefully now and then. Mix in the cream and reheat. Serve with buttered noodles.

Curry-glazed chicken with fried bananas
Serves 4

Ingredients	Metric-Imperial	American
1 dessert apple		
3 bananas		
Curry powder		
Sugar	¼ tsp	¼ tsp
Salt		
Clear honey	1½ tsp	1½ tsp
1 roasting chicken	1.25 kg/2¾ lb	2¾ lb
Butter	15 g/½ oz	1 tbs

Peel and core the apple and cut into thin rings. Peel and thinly slice one banana. Mix the fruit with ½ tsp curry powder and the sugar and add a little salt. Sprinkle the chicken inside and out with salt and fill with the curried fruit. Truss the bird into a neat shape. Oil a sheet of heavy duty foil and enclose the chicken loosely. Place on a baking sheet (cookie sheet). Bake in a preheated hot oven, 220°C, 425°F, Gas Mark 7, for 1 hour.

Open up the foil. Mix ½ tsp curry powder with the honey and brush this over the chicken. Return to the oven, with the foil open, for a further 15 minutes, brushing twice with the glaze and turning the chicken over once during this time.

Remove the stuffing and place on a warm serving dish with the chicken. Keep hot.

Peel the remaining bananas and cut in half lengthways. Melt the butter in a shallow pan, put in the bananas and fry gently, turning them occasionally, until well heated through. Drain in the juices from the cooking foil and spoon these over the bananas. Serve with the chicken and stuffing.

Roast lemon and garlic chicken
Serves 4

Ingredients	Metric-Imperial	American
4 cloves of garlic		
Juice of ½ lemon		
Salt		
Oil	2 tbs	3 tbs
1 roasting chicken	1.25 kg/2¾ lb	2¾ lb
1 medium-sized cooking apple		
Pared rind of ½ lemon		
Small bunch of parsley		
Sour cream	4 tbs	5 tbs
Chopped rosemary	1 tsp	1 tsp

Peel and crush the garlic. Mix together the lemon juice, garlic, ½ tsp salt and the oil. Coat the chicken inside and out with the garlic mixture, wrap loosely in foil and leave for 30 minutes for flavours to blend.

Peel, quarter and core the apple. Stuff the chicken with the apple quarters, lemon rind and stalks from the parsley. Truss the bird into a neat shape.

Thread on a spit or place in a roasting tin. Spit-roast for 40 minutes, or roast, uncovered, in a preheated moderately hot oven, 200°C, 400°F, Gas Mark 6, for 1 hour and 10 minutes, or until the juice runs clear when the thickest part is pierced with a skewer.

Mix together the cream and rosemary with a little salt. Brush the chicken with this mixture and spit-roast for a further 5 minutes, or cook 10 minutes in the oven, until the skin is well browned and the chicken cooked through. Discard the stuffing, divide the chicken into 4 portions and place on a warm dish garnished with parsley. Serve with French bread or fried potatoes and a mixed salad.

Simple chicken spaghetti
Serves 4

Ingredients	Metric-Imperial	American
Spaghetti	275 g/10 oz	10 oz
Butter	25 g/1 oz	2 tbs
Cooked, boneless chicken	350 g/12 oz	12 oz
Sweet paprika or freshly ground black pepper		
Grated Cheddar or Gouda cheese	50 g/2 oz	½ cup

Cook the spaghetti in plenty of boiling salted water for 10 minutes, or until tender but still firm to the bite. (If liked, break the pasta into finger lengths.) Drain, refresh briefly with cold water and drain again. Cut the chicken into small pieces. Rinse and dry the pan, melt the butter in it, add the spaghetti and chicken. Cook for about 2 minutes, stirring constantly until the chicken is warmed through. Turn into a warm serving dish. Mix together paprika or black pepper to taste with the cheese and sprinkle over the pasta.

Left: Curry-glazed chicken with fried bananas
Below: Roast lemon and garlic chicken

Chicken in wine with marjoram
Serves 4

Ingredients	Metric-Imperial	American
2 cloves of garlic		
Butter	50 g/2 oz	¼ cup
Salt and pepper		
4 chicken pieces		
Chopped marjoram	3 tbs	4 tbs
Dry white wine	225 ml/8 fl oz	1 cup
Sweet peppers, green, red and yellow	450 g/1 lb	1 lb
Tomatoes	450 g/1 lb	1 lb

Peel and finely chop the garlic. Mix together the butter, garlic and seasoning to taste. Spread this mixture over the chicken pieces. Place in a greased ovenproof dish or roasting tin and sprinkle with half the marjoram. Cook, uncovered, in a preheated hot oven, 220°C, 425°F, Gas Mark 7, for 20 minutes. Pour in half the wine and continue cooking for a further 20 minutes.

Halve and deseed the peppers and cut the flesh into small strips. Add to the chicken with the rest of the wine and cook for 5 minutes. Meanwhile, pour boiling water over the tomatoes, drain, peel and cut into quarters. Add these to the chicken, baste all the ingredients with the liquid in the dish and cook on for 15 minutes more. Serve sprinkled with the remaining marjoram.

Left: Chicken with wine and marjoram
Right: Apple-stuffed roast duck

Apple-stuffed roast duck
(Using a chicken brick)
Serves 4

Ingredients	Metric-Imperial	American
1 ovenready duck	1.25 kg/3¼ lb	3¼ lb
Salt and pepper		
2 large tart dessert apples		
Seedless raisins	50 g/2 oz	⅓ cup
Sugar		
Cornflour (cornstarch)	1 tsp	1 tsp

Prepare the chicken brick by soaking it in water in the usual way.

Sprinkle the cavity of the duck with salt. Peel, quarter and core the apples. Combine the apple and raisins and add a little sugar if desired. Use to stuff the duck. Close the opening and secure with a skewer or wooden cocktail sticks (toothpicks).

Rub the outside of the duck with salt and pepper. Place in the prepared chicken brick, put on the lid and cook in a preheated moderately hot oven, 200°C, 400°F, Gas Mark 6, for about 2 hours, until the duck is cooked through. Cut the duck into 4 portions with poultry shears if wished and place with the stuffing on a hot dish.

Skim excess fat from the pan juices. Stir up the sediment and strain into a pan. Moisten the cornflour with a little cold water, add to the juices and stir until boiling. Simmer for 1 minute and adjust the seasoning with salt and pepper. Serve with the duck and stuffing.

Simple roast duck
Serves 4

Ingredients	Metric-Imperial	American
1 ovenready duck	2 kg/4½ lb	4½ lb
Salt and pepper		
Hot water		
Cold salted water		
Flour (all-purpose)	2 tbs	3 tbs

Sprinkle the inside of the duck with salt. Place, breast upwards, on a trivet in a roasting tin with 2 tbs (3 tbs) water. Roast, uncovered, in a preheated moderately hot oven, 200°C, 400°F, Gas Mark 6, for a total of 1¾ hours. During roasting time prick the duck occasionally under the wings and legs to allow the fat to run freely. After 30 minutes drain off the accumulated fat. As soon as the juices in the pan begin to brown, add a little hot water and baste the duck. Replace the evaporated juices with more hot water as often as is necessary. After 1½ hours brush the duck with cold salted water and increase the heat to 220°C, 425°F, Gas Mark 7 for the last 15 minutes of cooking to make the skin crisp and golden brown.

When the duck is cooked, place it on a warm serving dish and keep hot, or serve cut into portions.

Skim excess fat from the juices in the roasting tin then loosen the sediment by stirring in a little more hot water. Strain the juices into a pan and make up to about 300 ml/½ pint (1¼ cups) with more water. Moisten the flour with a little cold water, add to the pan and stir until boiling. Simmer for a few minutes and adjust the seasoning with salt and pepper. Serve the duck and sauce with red cabbage and apple slices with cranberries.

Below: Simple roast duck
Right: Boiled duck with Chinese vegetables

Boiled duck with Chinese vegetables

Serves 4

Ingredients	Metric-Imperial	American
Soy sauce	225 ml/8 fl oz	1 cup
Water	2 L/3½ pints	4½ pints
1 ovenready duck	2 kg/4½ lb	4½ lb
Carrots	225 g/8 oz	8 oz
2 red sweet peppers		
2 green sweet peppers		
Mushrooms	150 g/5 oz	5 oz
Fat or oil for deep frying		
Beansprouts	225 g/8 oz	8 oz
Cornflour (cornstarch)	1 tbs	1 tbs
Salt		

Reserve 2 tbs (3 tbs) soy sauce and place the rest in a large pan with the water. Add the duck and bring to the boil. Cover and simmer for 40 minutes, turning the bird once during this time. Remove the duck from the liquid, take the flesh from the bones and cut into large pieces. Measure 350 ml/12 fl oz (1½ cups) of the stock and reserve

Peel the carrots and cut into strips. Halve the peppers, deseed and cut the flesh into strips. Slice the mushrooms. Heat fat or oil in a deep pan until it will brown a cube of day-old bread in 1 minute. Cook the duck meat, in batches, for 3–4 minutes, or until golden brown. Drain well on absorbent kitchen paper. Cut into strips and keep hot.

Cook the vegetables separately in the oil, the carrot strips for about 2 minutes, the pepper strips for about 1 minute, the mushrooms and beansprouts for about 30 seconds each. Drain all the vegetables well and place in a pan with the reserved stock and soy sauce. Moisten the cornflour with a little cold water or more of the stock. Add to the pan and stir until boiling. Simmer for 1 minute. Put the vegetables and sauce on a warm serving dish and top with the duck.

Spit-roasted duck with oranges
Serves 4

Ingredients	Metric-Imperial	American
1 ovenready duck	2 kg/4½ lb	4½ lb
Sweet paprika pepper	2 tsp	2 tsp
Salt and pepper		
3 oranges		
Orange liqueur	6 tbs	½ cup
Flour (all-purpose)	2 tbs	3 tbs
4 sprigs of parsley		

Trim surplus skin from the duck, truss the legs and wings closely with fine string, and close the openings at either end with wooden cocktail sticks (toothpicks). Rub the skin with the sweet paprika and thread the duck on a spit. Cook for about 20 minutes under a preheated grill, collecting the fat that runs out in a grill pan. Season the fat with 1 tsp salt and a little pepper and baste the duck with the seasoned fat.

Grate the rind from 1 orange and mix with the liqueur. Squeeze the juice from this orange and reserve. Peel and slice the other 2 oranges. Put the slices into the grill pan under the duck. Continue cooking for a further 40 minutes, basting from time to time with the juices in the grill pan, or until the duck is cooked through. Baste with the liqueur mixture and cook for another 10 minutes.

Serve the duck on a hot platter on a bed of the well-drained orange slices. Keep hot.

Mix the flour with a little cold water. Carefully skim off surplus fat from the grill pan and stir up the juices. Make these up to 300 ml/½ pint (1¼ cups) with hot water and strain into a pan. Add the orange juice and the flour mixture and cook, stirring, until the sauce thickens. Simmer for 3 minutes then adjust the seasoning with salt and pepper and transfer to a warm sauceboat. Garnish the duck with the parsley and serve with the sauce.

Note: If preferred, cook the duck on a trivet in a roasting tin, putting the oranges in the bottom of the tin, allowing 1¾ hours in a preheated moderately hot oven, 200°C, 400°F, Gas Mark 6, or until the bird is cooked through.

Roast duck with spring onions
Serves 4

Ingredients	Metric-Imperial	American
3 bunches of spring onions (scallions)		
Butter	40 g/1½ oz	3 tbs
Sugar	25 g/1 oz	2 tbs
Soy sauce	5 tbs	6 tbs
1 ovenready duck with giblets	2.5 kg/5½ lb	5½ lb
Salt		
Boiling water	225 ml/8 fl oz	1 cup
Dry sherry	4 tbs	5 tbs
Ground ginger	½ tsp	½ tsp
Whipping cream	125 ml/4 fl oz	½ cup
Little extra soy sauce and sherry		
1 slice peeled root ginger		

Trim the spring onions, leaving 15 cm/6 inches of the green part. Heat the butter in a frying pan and fry the onions in it for 2 minutes. Sprinkle on the sugar and stir carefully until it melts. Spoon over half the soy sauce and set aside for the onions to cool. Do not discard the pan juices.

Remove the giblets from the duck and rub the skin with salt. Tuck under the skin of the neck to close the opening. Stuff the duck with the spring onions so that some of the green part protrudes from the other opening. Tie the legs close to the body with fine string.

Place the duck, breast upwards, in a roasting pan together with the giblets. Brush the skin with the juices from the pan in which the onions were cooked. Roast, uncovered, in a preheated moderately hot oven, 200°C, 400°F, Gas Mark 6, for 15 minutes.

Pour half the boiling water into the tin and return it to the oven for a further 30 minutes. Mix together the remaining soy sauce, the sherry and ground ginger and spoon into the tin. Cook for another 1 hour, or until the duck is crisp, brown and cooked through. Transfer the duck to a warm serving dish and remove the trussing strings. Keep the duck hot until ready to serve.

Discard the giblets. Add the remaining water to the roasting tin and stir well to loosen the sediment. Cook over moderate heat for a few minutes, stirring, until slightly reduced.

Strain the pan juices and skim off surplus fat. Stir in the cream and adjust the seasoning with a little more soy sauce and sherry if desired. Cut the ginger into fine strips and sprinkle over the duck. Hand the sauce separately. Serve with stir-fried rice and button mushrooms.

Below: Spit-roasted duck with oranges
Right: Roast duck with spring onions

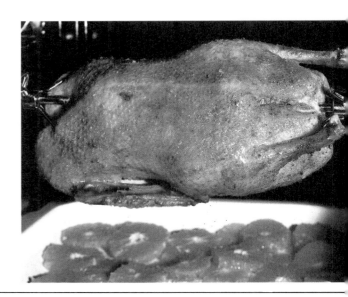

Herbed roast ducklings
Serves 4

Ingredients	Metric-Imperial	American
2 young ovenready young ducklings	1–1.25 kg/2¼–2¾ lb each	2¼–2¾ lb each
Salt and freshly ground black pepper		
Chopped marjoram	1 tbs	1 tbs
Chopped thyme	1 tbs	1 tbs
Chopped basil	1 tbs	1 tbs
Red wine	2 tbs	3 tbs
Flour (all-purpose)	2 tbs	3 tbs
Extra chopped herbs (optional)		

Rub the skin of the ducklings with salt, pepper and the herbs. Set the ducks on a trivet in a roasting tin and cook, uncovered, in a preheated hot oven, 220°C, 425°F, Gas Mark 7, for 55 minutes.

Take the tin from the oven and cut off the breast fillets from the sides of both ducklings. Wrap these in foil and keep hot. Replace the birds in the roasting tin, return to the oven and cook for a further 10 minutes, or until the legs are cooked. Remove the ducks and divide into serving pieces. Cut each breast fillet obliquely into thick slices. Arrange all the duck meat on a warm serving dish and keep hot, until ready to serve.

Skim surplus fat from the roasting tin, pour in the red wine and cook, stirring, over moderate heat to loosen the sediment. Strain into a pan. Moisten the flour with a little cold water, add to the pan and stir until boiling. Simmer for 2 minutes and adjust the seasoning with salt and pepper if necessary. Stir in extra herbs if wished. Serve with the duck accompanied by leeks, potato pancakes and stuffed onions, or new potatoes and garden peas.

Below: Herbed roast duckling
Right: Duck with grape sauce

Duck with grape sauce
Serves 4

Ingredients	Metric-Imperial	American
1 ovenready duck with giblets	2½ kg/5½ lb	5½ lb
Salt and freshly ground black pepper		
Chopped marjoram	2 tbs	3 tbs
Hot water		
Green grapes	225 g/8 oz	8 oz
Redcurrant jelly	2 tbs	3 tbs
Port	4 tbs	5 tbs
Hot mustard	½ tsp	½ tsp
Lemon juice	2 tsp	2 tsp
Flour (all-purpose)	2 tbs	3 tbs
Extra port (optional)		

Rub the skin and sprinkle the cavity with salt, pepper and marjoram. Truss the bird into a neat shape with fine string. Place in a roasting tin, putting the giblets next to it. Roast, uncovered, in a preheated hot oven, 220°C, 425°F, Gas Mark 7, for 45 minutes. Prick the duck under the wings and the legs twice. Pour off the fat from the roasting tin and add a little hot water. Continue cooking for a further 15 minutes, adding more water to the tin as it evaporates.

Halve the grapes and remove the pips (pits). Beat together the redcurrant jelly, port, mustard and lemon juice. Brush the duck with half the mixture, add the grapes to the roasting tin and cook for a further 20 minutes. Brush the duck with the remaining port mixture and cook for 10 minutes more, or until cooked through.

Transfer the duck to a warm serving dish and remove the trussing strings. Keep hot. Discard the giblets. Add 125 ml/4 fl oz (½ cup) hot water to the juices in the roasting tin and stir over moderate heat to loosen the sediment. Skim off excess fat. Moisten the flour with a little cold water, add to the juices and stir until boiling. Simmer for 2 minutes and adjust the seasoning with salt and pepper. Add a little extra port if wished. Serve with the duck.

Breast of goose with orange sauce
Serves 4

Ingredients	Metric-Imperial	American
1 breast of goose	1 kg/2¼ lb	2¼ lb
Salt and pepper		
2 carrots		
1 piece of celeriac		
Hot water	500 ml/18 fl oz	2¼ cups
Juice of 2 oranges		
Orange slices		
Flour (all-purpose)	2 tbs	3 tbs
Sprigs of parsley		

Rub the skin of the goose with salt and pepper and place it in a roasting tin. Cook, uncovered, in a preheated moderately hot oven, 200°C, 400°F, Gas Mark 6, for 30 minutes. Drain off the accumulated fat.

Peel the carrots and celeriac, add to the roasting tin and cook for a further 10 minutes. Add some of the water and continue cooking for a further 45 minutes, turning the goose over twice and adding more water to the tin as it evaporates. Pour the orange juice over the goose and cook on for 15 minutes more.

Lift out the goose, remove the meat from the bones and arrange the slices on the goose carcase, interleaving them with orange slices. Keep hot.

Strain the pan juices into a small pan, moisten the flour with a little cold water, add to the pan and stir until boiling. Simmer for 3 minutes and adjust the seasoning. Garnish the goose with parsley and hand the sauce separately.

Note: If necessary, ask the poulterer to remove the breast section for you. Cook the rest of the goose for another meal.

Spit-roasted turkey roll
Serves 4

Ingredients	Metric-Imperial	American
Rolled turkey joint	1 kg/2¼ lb	2¼ lb
Oil	1 tbs	1 tbs
Salt and freshly ground white pepper		
Sweet paprika pepper		
Prepared mustard	½ tsp	½ tsp

Thread the turkey joint on a spit, or place in a roasting tin. Mix together the oil and salt, pepper and paprika to taste and the mustard. Brush this mixture over the meat, making sure it is well coated.

Spit-roast over a pan for 45–60 minutes, basting occasionally with the pan drippings, until cooked through. Alternatively, roast in a preheated moderately hot oven, 200°C, 400°F, Gas Mark 6, for 1 hour and 10 minutes, basting now and then, or until cooked through.

Leave the joint to cool then slice and serve with French bread and a celery salad.

Roast turkey roll with mushrooms
(Using a chicken brick)
Serves 4

Ingredients	Metric-Imperial	American
Rolled turkey joint, weight	1 kg/2¼ lb	2¼ lb
Salt and freshly ground pepper		
Chopped thyme	1 tsp	1 tsp
Canned mushrooms with liquid	500 g/18 oz	2¼ cups
Cornflour (cornstarch)	1 tsp	1 tsp

Prepare the chicken brick by soaking it in water in the usual way.

Rub the turkey roll with salt, pepper and the thyme and place in the prepared chicken brick. Drain the mushrooms, reserving the liquid, and add to the turkey. Put on the lid and place in a preheated moderately hot oven, 200°C, 400°F, Gas Mark 6, for 1 hour. Remove from the oven and add the liquid from the mushrooms. Cover again and cook for a further 30 minutes. Slice the turkey and transfer to a warm serving dish with the mushrooms. Keep hot until ready to serve.

Pour the juices from the chicken brick into a pan. Moisten the cornflour with a little cold water, add to the pan and stir until boiling. Simmer for 1 minute, adjust the seasoning if necessary and serve with the turkey and mushrooms.

Left: Breast of goose with orange sauce
Right: Turkey with cauliflower in chive sauce

Turkey with cauliflower in chive sauce
Serves 4

Ingredients	Metric-Imperial	American
Salted water	1.25 L/2¼ pints	2¾ pints
1 turkey thigh, with bones	1 kg/2¼ lb	2¼ lb
1 bunch of parsley		
6 peppercorns		
Carrots	350 g/12 oz	12 oz
2 sticks of celery (stalks)		
2 leeks		
1 cauliflower	450 g/1 lb	1 lb
For the sauce:		
2 hard-boiled eggs		
Hot prepared mustard	2 tsp	2 tsp
Oil	125 ml/4 fl oz	4 fl oz
Vinegar		
Salt and pepper		
Snipped chives	2 tbs	3 tbs

Put the water into a pan and bring to the boil. Add the turkey, parsley and peppercorns and bring to the boil. Cover and simmer for 50 minutes.

Peel the carrots and cut into 3 cm/1¼ inch strips with a fluted cutter. Clean the celery and cut into 4 cm/1½ inch lengths. Add the carrot and celery to the pan, bring back to the boil, cover and simmer for 10 minutes. Trim and clean the leeks, cut into 4 cm/1½ inch lengths. Divide the cauliflower into florets. Add the leek and cauliflower to the turkey and cook for a further 15 minutes. Leave the ingredients to cool in the stock.

To make the sauce, shell the eggs and press through a sieve. Mix with the mustard and oil and add vinegar, salt and pepper to taste. Fold in the snipped chives.

Drain the turkey and vegetables well. Arrange the vegetables on a serving dish and spoon the sauce over them. Slice the turkey and set the slices, overlapping slightly, on the vegetables. Serve with French bread and garnish the dish with a bunch of chives if wished.

Rabbit casserole with lentils and mushrooms

Serves 4–6

Ingredients	Metric-Imperial	American
1 saddle of rabbit	550 g/1¼ lb	1¼ lb
4 rabbit legs, total weight	1 kg/2¼ lb	2¼ lb
Salt and pepper		
Butter or margarine	50 g/2 oz	¼ cup
Streaky bacon (strips)	225 g/8 oz	16 strips
Chopped thyme	2 tsp	2 tsp
Calvados or brandy	3 tbs	4 tbs
Brown lentils	250 g/9 oz	generous 1 cup
Beef stock (bouillon)	1 L/1¾ pints	4⅓ cups
Mushrooms	225 g/8 oz	8 oz
2 cloves of garlic		
Wine vinegar	1 tbs	1 tbs
Red wine	125 ml/4 fl oz	½ cup

Cut the rabbit saddle into 4 portions. Rub all the rabbit pieces with salt and pepper. Melt two thirds of the butter or margarine in a large pan and fry the bacon slices for 5 minutes. Remove from the pan and reserve. Fry the rabbit pieces in the same fat until golden on all sides. Put in half the thyme, the Calvados or brandy and the lentils. Cook for 5 minutes, stirring occasionally. Add the stock and bring to the boil. Cover the pan and simmer for 45 minutes, stirring now and then.

Meanwhile, melt the remaining butter or margarine in a frying pan. Halve or quarter the mushrooms according to size, add to the pan and fry for 2 minutes. Peel and finely chop the garlic, add to the mushrooms and season with salt and pepper. Put in the vinegar and wine. Stir well and cook for a further 10 minutes. Add the contents of the pan to the rabbit and lentil mixture with the reserved bacon, bring back to simmering point and cook for 15 minutes. Remove the lid and cook on for 5 minutes more to reduce slightly. Adjust the seasoning if necessary, garnish with the remaining thyme and serve with French bread.

Microwave hint

To cook lentils by microwave, wash well, then place in a suitable container and cover with boiling water. Put a plate over the container and cook on full power for 10 minutes. Leave to stand for 5 minutes, then cook for a further 10 minutes, or until the pulses are tender but not breaking up.

Left: Rabbit casserole with lentils and mushrooms
Right: Chicken pie with puff pastry top

Chicken pie with puff pastry top

Serves 4

Ingredients	Metric-Imperial	American
Frozen puff pastry	350 g/12 oz pack	12 oz pack
Boneless chicken breasts, total weight	450 g/1 lb	1 lb
Oil	2 tbs	3 tbs
Salt and pepper		
Mushrooms	450 g/1 lb	1 lb
Dry white wine	125 ml/4 fl oz	½ cup
Whipping cream	3 tbs	4 tbs
Snipped chives	2 tbs	3 tbs
1 egg yolk		

Defrost the pastry at room temperature. Dice the chicken breasts. Heat the oil in a pan and brown the chicken pieces on all sides. Season with salt and pepper and add the mushrooms, wine and cream. Stir well and heat through. Put the mixture into a greased ovenproof pie dish and sprinkle with the chives.

Roll out the pastry to make a lid. Moisten the edge of the dish with water, put on the pastry lid and press well around the rim of the dish to seal. Trim off any surplus pastry and roll out again to make shapes to decorate the pie. Beat the egg yolk and use to brush the surface of the pastry. Position the decorations and brush these with egg yolk. Cut a small steam vent. Bake, uncovered, in a preheated moderately hot oven, 200°C, 400°F, Gas Mark 6, for about 40 minutes, or until golden brown.

Venison steaks with slivered almonds
Serves 4

Ingredients	Metric-Imperial	American
4 venison leg steaks	125 g/4 oz each	4 oz each
Salt and pepper		
Ground nutmeg		
White vegetable fat	40 g/1½ oz	3 tbs
Toasted slivered almonds	75 g/3 oz	¾ cup
Whipping cream	150 ml/¼ pint	⅔ cup

Sprinkle the steaks with salt and nutmeg. Melt the fat in a frying pan and use to cook the steaks for 2–4 minutes on each side, or until brown and cooked to taste. Arrange on a warm serving dish, sprinkle with the almonds and keep hot.

Venison skewers and Cumberland sauce
Serves 4

Ingredients	Metric-Imperial	American
Boned saddle of venison	450 g/1 lb	1 lb
Streaky bacon (strips)	100 g/4 oz	8 strips
1 mild pickled cucumber (dill pickle)		
Oil	4 tbs	5 tbs
Salt and pepper		
For the sauce:		
Pared rind of 1 orange		
Red wine	3 tbs	4 tbs
Redcurrant jelly	225 g/8 oz	2/3 cup
Made mustard	2 tsp	2 tsp
Salt		
Lemon juice		
Little extra red wine		

First make the sauce. Cut the orange rind into shreds. Put the wine into a small pan with the orange shreds and cook until reduced by about half. Leave to cool. Put the redcurrant jelly in a small pan and heat gently, stirring, until melted. Mix in the mustard and cooled wine and orange shreds. Season to taste with salt, lemon juice and more red wine to taste. Transfer to a small dish.

Remove any membrane from the meat and cut into small pieces. Cut the bacon into pieces about the same size and thinly slice the cucumber. Thread the ingredients on 4 skewers. Heat the oil in a large frying pan, put in the skewers and cook gently for about 12 minutes, turning. Sprinkle with salt and pepper and serve with the Cumberland sauce.

Stir the cream into the juices remaining in the pan and cook over low heat for a few minutes, stirring frequently, until slightly thickened and reduced. Adjust the seasoning with salt and pepper and serve the sauce with the steaks.

Above: Venison steaks with slivered almonds
Right: Venison skewers with Cumberland sauce

Venison steaks with morello cherries
Serves 2

Ingredients	Metric-Imperial	American
Streaky bacon (strips)	25 g/1 oz	4 strips
1 onion		
Flour (all-purpose)	1½ tsp	1½ tsp
Sour cream	125 ml/4 fl oz	½ cup
Salt		
2 venison leg steaks	150 g/5 oz each	5 oz each
Butter	15 g/½ oz	1 tbs
2 slices white bread		
Butter for frying (optional)		
Juniper berries		
Canned drained stoned (pitted) morello cherries	75 g/3 oz	½ cup
Redcurrant jelly	2 tbs	3 tbs
2 orange slices		

Chop the bacon and heat in a pan until the fat runs. Peel and chop the onion and fry in the bacon fat for 3 minutes. Sprinkle on the flour and stir until golden. Blend in the cream and bring to the boil, stirring constantly. Simmer for 10 minutes and season to taste with salt.

Slightly flatten the steaks. Heat the butter and fry the steaks for 2–4 minutes on each side, until cooked to taste. Remove from the pan with the juices and keep hot. Toast the bread slices or fry them in a little extra butter. Pour 2 tbs (3 tbs) water into the pan in which the steaks were cooked and stir to loosen the sediment. Pour this into the sauce.

Arrange the bread slices, one on top of the other, on a warm dish and top with the steaks. Crush the juniper berries and sprinkle over the top. Warm the cherries with the redcurrant jelly in a pan, stirring until the jelly has melted. Cut out the centre of the orange slices and place the rings on the plate. Spoon in the cherry mixture. Hand the sauce separately.

Venison and pineapple with Béarnaise sauce
Serves 4

Ingredients	Metric-Imperial	American
Boned saddle of venison	550 g/1¼ lb	1¼ lb
French wholegrain mustard	1 tbs	1 tbs
Oil	3 tbs	4 tbs
Salt and pepper		
Butter	15 g/½ oz	1 tbs
4 canned well drained pineapple slices		
Chopped basil		
For the sauce:		
Butter	100 g/4 oz	½ cup
1 small onion		
Wine vinegar	1 tsp	1 tsp
Medium white wine	2 tbs	3 tbs
Chopped tarragon	1 tsp	1 tsp
Chopped basil	1 tsp	1 tsp
Coarsely ground black pepper		
2 egg yolks		
Salt		
Sugar		

First make the sauce. Warm the butter until just melted then leave to cool slightly. Peel and chop the onion. Place in a small pan with the vinegar, wine, tarragon and basil and season with a little pepper. Cook until reduced by half. Transfer to a double boiler or a bowl over a pan of simmering water and beat in the egg yolks. Stir until the sauce begins to thicken then gradually whisk in the butter. Season to taste with salt, pepper and sugar and keep warm over hot water.

Remove any membrane from the meat and cut into slices about 2.5 cm/1 inch thick. Flatten the slices slightly then spread both sides with mustard. Heat the oil in a pan and use to fry the steaks for about 5 minutes on each side, or until cooked to taste. Sprinkle with salt and pepper and keep warm until ready to serve.

Melt the butter in another pan and use to fry the pineapple slices until golden brown on both sides. Arrange the pineapple slices on a warm serving dish, top with the steaks and spoon Béarnaise sauce over the top. Sprinkle with basil and serve at once.

Left: Venison steaks with morello cherries
Right: Strips of venison, Hungarian style

Strips of venison, Hungarian style
Serves 4

Ingredients	Metric-Imperial	American
1 red sweet pepper		
1 green sweet pepper		
4 onions		
Boned venison	450 g/1 lb	1 lb
Butter or margarine	50 g/2 oz	¼ cup
Salt and pepper		
Sweet paprika pepper		
Beef stock (bouillon)	300 ml/½ pint	1¼ cups
Drained pickled beetroot	175 g/6 oz	6 oz
1 pickled cucumber		
Cornflour (cornstarch)	2 tsp	2 tsp
Sour cream	4 tbs	5 tbs
Chopped parsley	1 tbs	1 tbs

Deseed the peppers and cut the flesh into strips. Peel, halve and slice the onions. Discard any membrane from the meat and cut into strips. Melt the butter or margarine in a pan and fry the venison for 6 minutes, stirring. Remove from pan.

Add the onion to the fat remaining in the pan and cook until golden. Put in the pepper strips and cook for a further 2 minutes, stirring. Season to taste with salt, pepper and paprika and pour in the stock. Bring to the boil and simmer for 30 minutes. Cut the beetroot and pickled cucumber into strips and stir into the pepper mixture with the venison. Bring to the boil and simmer for 10 minutes.

Moisten the cornflour with the sour cream, add to the pan and stir until boiling. Simmer for 2 minutes and adjust the seasoning if necessary. Garnish with the parsley.

Casseroled rabbit legs
Serves 4

Ingredients	Metric-Imperial	American
4 rabbit legs		
Salt		
Dried marjoram		
Very fat bacon (strips)	100 g/4 oz	8 strips
1 large onion		
1 carrot		
1 piece of turnip or swede (rutabaga)		
Flour (all-purpose)	1 tsp	1 tsp
Tomato purée (paste)	1 tsp	1 tsp
Orange liqueur	1–2 tbs	1–2 tbs
For the marinade:		
2 cloves of garlic		
Red wine	450 ml/¾ pint	scant 2 cups
2 bay leaves		
Dried thyme	¼ tsp	¼ tsp
Dried marjoram	¼ tsp	¼ tsp
1 whole clove		
Juice of 1 orange		
Salt and black pepper		
Chopped parsley		
Selection of pot vegetables		

First make the marinade. Peel and crush the garlic and add to the wine with the bay leaves, thyme, marjoram, clove, orange juice and a little seasoning. Clean the pot vegetables, peel if necessary and chop. Add to the wine mixture. Remove any membrane from the rabbit legs, place in a dish and pour over the marinade. Cover and leave for at least 6 hours, turning occasionally.

Lift out the rabbit portions and dry with absorbent kitchen paper. Rub with salt and marjoram. Chop the bacon, place in a pan and heat until the fat runs. Put in the rabbit and brown the portions on both sides. Peel and chop the onion, carrot and turnip, add to the pan and cook gently until the onion is soft. Sprinkle on the flour and stir well. Strain the marinade and add half of it to the pan. Stir until boiling and simmer for about 1 hour, adding more marinade as the sauce reduces. Arrange the rabbit on a warm serving dish and keep hot. Strain the sauce, add the tomato purée and boil until slightly reduced. Blend in orange liqueur to taste and pour the sauce over the rabbit. Sprinkle over the parsley. Serve with potato croquettes.

Braised hare
Serves 4

Ingredients	Metric-Imperial	American
4 legs of hare		
10 juniper berries		
Salt and pepper		
White vegetable fat	50 g/2 oz	¼ cup
3 medium-sized onions		
1 bay leaf		
6 black peppercorns		
Hot water	500 ml/18 fl oz	2¼ cups
Flour (all-purpose)	2 tbs	3 tbs

Remove any membrane from the hare. Crush the juniper berries and rub these into the hare with salt and pepper. Melt the fat in a pan and use to brown the hare portions on both sides. Peel and chop the onions, add to the hare with the bay leaf and peppercorns and cook until the onion is soft. Pour in half the water and bring to the boil. Simmer, uncovered, for 1½ hours, adding more water to the pan as the liquid evaporates and turning the hare now and then, until tender. Remove the hare to a warm serving dish and keep hot.

Strain the cooking liquid and return to the rinsed pan. Moisten the flour with a little cold water, add to the pan and stir until boiling. Simmer for 2 minutes and adjust the seasoning with salt and pepper to taste. Pour over the hare and serve with boiled potatoes and red cabbage.

Ragout of hare with mushrooms
Serves 4

Ingredients	Metric-Imperial	American
4 legs of hare		
White vegetable fat	50 g/2 oz	¼ cup
1 onion		
2 cloves of garlic		
8 black peppercorns		
Dried thyme	1 tsp	1 tsp
1 bay leaf		
Flour (all-purpose)	1 tbs	1 tbs
Red wine	225 ml/8 fl oz	1 cup
Beef stock		
(bouillon)	300 ml/½ pint	1¼ cups
Mushrooms	350 g/12 oz	12 oz
Salt and pepper		

Divide each leg of hare into two pieces and remove any membrane. Melt the fat in a pan, put in the hare pieces and brown on all sides. Peel and chop the onion, add to the hare and fry until golden. Peel the garlic, put in a mortar and pound until smooth with the peppercorns and thyme. Add this mixture to the pan with the bay leaf. Sprinkle on the flour and stir well. Gradually add the wine and stock and stir until boiling. Cover and simmer for 1¼ hours. Remove the bay leaf.

Slice the mushrooms, add to the pan and cook for a further 15 minutes, or until the hare is tender. Adjust the seasoning with salt and pepper and serve with boiled new potatoes and a selection of vegetables.

Minced game in pastry puffs
Serves 4

Ingredients	Metric-Imperial	American
Game meat such as		
venison or hare	225 g/8 oz	8 oz
Streaky bacon (strips)	65 g/2½ oz	5 strips
1 onion		
Chopped parsley	2 tbs	3 tbs
Chopped thyme	2 tsp	2 tsp
Whipping cream	2 tbs	3 tbs
Port	1 tbs	1 tbs
Salt		
Frozen puff pastry	350 g/12 oz pack	12 oz pack
1 egg, separated		

Remove any membrane from the meat. Finely mince the game and bacon together. Peel and chop the onion and mix into the meat with the parsley, thyme, cream and port. Season to taste with salt.

Defrost the pastry and roll out to a rectangle measuring about 40 cm × 30 cm/16 × 12 inches and cut this into twelve 10 cm/4 inch squares. Divide the meat mixture among the pastry squares.

Whip the egg white and use to brush the edges of the pastry squares. Gather the four corners together over the filling on one square then seal along the cut edges. Secure the pastry corners with a wooden cocktail stick (toothpick). Make up the remaining puffs in the same way. Beat the egg yolk, brush over the puffs and place them on a dampened baking sheet (cookie sheet).

Bake in a preheated hot oven, 220°C, 425°F, Gas Mark 7, for about 15 minutes, or until golden brown. Remove the sticks and serve the puffs with Cumberland or cranberry sauce, and steamed carrots.

Left: Casseroled rabbit legs
Above: Braised hare

287

Saddle of venison with brandied prunes
Serves 6

Ingredients	Metric-Imperial	American
Stoned prunes (pitted)	450 g/1 lb	1 lb
Armagnac or brandy	125 ml/4 fl oz	½ cup
1 saddle of venison, with bones	2 kg/4½ lb	4½ lb
Salt and pepper		
4 sprigs of thyme		
Streaky bacon (strips)	175 g/6 oz	12 strips
2 spring onions (scallions)		
Chopped venison bones	225 g/8 oz	8 oz
Red wine	350 ml/12 fl oz	1½ cups
Water	300 ml/½ pint	1¼ cups
Button onions	350 g/12 oz	12 oz
Toasted split almonds (halved almonds)	50 g/2 oz	½ cup

Put the prunes in a pan, pour over water to cover and bring to the boil. Drain and place the prunes in a bowl. Pour over the Armagnac or brandy and leave to stand.

Remove the fillets from the underside of the saddle of venison and set aside. Rub the saddle with salt and pepper. Strip the leaves from the sprigs of thyme, sprinkle these over the saddle and pat them in. Take two thirds of the bacon and lay the strips over the saddle. Place the joint in a greased roasting tin. Trim and chop the spring onions and place round the saddle with the venison bones. Roast, uncovered, in a preheated moderately hot oven, 200°C, 400°F, Gas Mark 6, for 10 minutes. Combine the wine and water and add half to the pan. Cook for a further 35 minutes, basting the meat occasionally with the pan juices and adding more wine liquid as they evaporate. Remove the venison, wrap in foil and keep hot. Discard the bones.

Peel and quarter the onions. Chop half the remaining bacon, place in a pan and heat until the fat runs. Add the onions and cook until soft. Keep hot.

Bring the ingredients in the roasting tin to the boil. Strain into a pan and boil again to reduce slightly. Add the brandied prunes and season with salt and pepper to taste.

Chop the last of the bacon, place in a frying pan and heat until the fat runs. Sprinkle the reserved venison fillets with salt and pepper, add to the bacon fat and fry for 5 minutes, turning occasionally. Remove the cooked meat from the saddle, slice and arrange the slices again on the carcase. Place on a warm serving dish with the fillets. Lift out the prunes from the sauce and arrange on the serving dish with the almonds and onions. Hand the sauce separately and serve with rice.

Leg of venison, hunter style
Serves 2

Ingredients	Metric-Imperial	American
Leg of venison joint, with bones	550 g/1¼ lb	1¼ lb
3 juniper berries		
Salt and pepper		
Chopped mixed herbs such as thyme, marjoram, rosemary, sage		
1 large onion		
Butter	25 g/1 oz	2 tbs
Red wine	125 ml/4 fl oz	½ cup
Cranberry sauce	2 tbs	3 tbs
Whipping cream	150 ml/¼ pint	⅔ cup

Remove any membrane from the meat. Crush the juniper berries and rub into the meat with salt and the herbs. Peel and chop the onion. Melt the butter in a flameproof dish, add the meat and brown on all sides. Put in the onion, cover the pan and place in a preheated moderate oven, 180°C, 350°F, Gas Mark 4, for about 30 minutes. Remove the joint to a warm serving dish and keep hot.

Add the wine to the dish and stir well to loosen the sediment. Strain into a pan and mix in the cranberry sauce and cream. Stir until boiling and adjust the seasoning with salt and pepper. Spoon a little sauce over the meat and hand the rest separately. Serve with braised fennel (Florence) and potato croquettes.

Left: Saddle of venison with brandied prunes
Right: Leg of venison, hunter style

Casseroled saddle of hare with morello cherries
(Using a chicken brick)
Serves 4

Ingredients	Metric-Imperial	American
Canned stoned morello cherries (pitted)	425 g/15 oz can	15 oz can
Red wine	125 ml/4 fl oz	½ cup
Salt and pepper		
1 saddle of hare, with bones	675 g/1½ lb	1½ lb
Few sprigs of parsley		
Cornflour (cornstarch)	2 tbs	3 tbs

Prepare the chicken brick by soaking in water in the usual way.

Drain the cherries and measure 125 ml/4 fl oz (½ cup) of the syrup. Reserve a few of the cherries and put the remainder into the prepared chicken brick. Combine the measured cherry syrup and wine and season with a little salt. Add to the cherries. Rub salt and pepper into the hare and set it on the cherries in the pot. Put on the lid and place in a preheated moderately hot oven, 200°C, 400°F, Gas Mark 6, for about 1 hour, or until the hare is cooked through. Transfer the joint to a warm serving dish and garnish with the reserved cherries and parsley sprigs. Keep hot.

Measure the cherries and liquid from the chicken brick, make up to 300 ml/½ pint (1¼ cups) with water if necessary and pour into a pan. Moisten the cornflour with a little cold water, add to the pan and stir until boiling. Simmer for 1 minute, adjust the seasoning to taste and pour the sauce round the saddle of hare in the dish.

Partridges in creamed lentils
Serves 4

Ingredients	Metric-Imperial	American
Lentils	275 g/10 oz	scant 1¼ cups
2 carrots		
3 onions		
¼ head of celeriac		
2 leeks		
Butter or margarine	50 g/2 oz	¼ cup
Beef stock (bouillon)	2 L/3½ pints	4¼ pints
Salt and pepper		
4 partridges	250 g/9 oz each	9 oz each
2 whole cloves		
Lean bacon (Canadian)	100 g/4 oz	2 slices
Sour cream	225 ml/8 fl oz	1 cup
Port	1 tbs	1 tbs

Put the lentils in a pan, pour over cold water to cover and leave to soak overnight. Drain.

Peel the carrots, 2 of the onions and the celeriac. Trim and clean the leeks. Cut the vegetables into thin strips. Melt the butter or margarine in a large flameproof pan, add the vegetable strips and cook for a few minutes, stirring occasionally. Put in the lentils and stock and bring to the boil.

Meanwhile, rub salt into the skin of the partridges and sprinkle more into the cavities. Peel the remaining onion and press in the cloves. Add to the pan with the partridges. Cover and cook in a preheated moderately hot oven, 200°C, 400°F, Gas Mark 6, for about 1 hour, or until the partridges and lentils are tender.

Take out the partridges, remove the flesh from the bones and dice it. Chop the bacon, place in a pan and heat gently until just turning golden. Stir into the lentil mixture with the partridge meat and sour cream. Reheat, stirring, add the port and adjust the seasoning to taste with salt and pepper.

Rabbit in tarragon sauce
Serves 4

Ingredients	Metric-Imperial	American
1 rabbit	2 kg/4½ lb	4½ lb
Chopped tarragon	3 tbs	4 tbs
Mild French mustard	75 g/3 oz	⅓ cup
Butter	50 g/2 oz	¼ cup
Salt and pepper		
Dry white wine	175 ml/6 fl oz	¾ cup
Chicken stock (bouillon)	225 ml/8 fl oz	1 cup
French beans (green)	450 g/1 lb	1 lb
Dried savory	½ tsp	½ tsp
8–10 thin rashers of streaky bacon (strips)		

Sugar	1 tsp	1 tsp
Whipping cream	150 ml/¼ pint	⅔ cup
Few drops of		
Worcestershire sauce		

Discard any membrane from the rabbit, divide into portions, removing the legs and cutting the saddle into 3 or 4 pieces. Stir the tarragon into the mustard. Melt the butter in a roasting tin. Sprinkle the rabbit portions with salt and pepper and spread with half the tarragon mustard. Arrange in the tin and cook, uncovered, in a preheated moderately hot oven, 200°C, 400°F, Gas Mark 6, for 30 minutes. Pour in the wine and stock, return to the oven and cook for a further 15 minutes.

Meanwhile, top and tail the beans, place in a pan with the savory and salted water to cover. Bring to the boil and simmer for 3 minutes. Drain, divide into portions and wrap each bundle in bacon. Place these in the roasting tin with the rabbit, return to the oven and cook for a further 30 minutes. Arrange the bean bundles and rabbit pieces on a warm serving dish and keep hot.

Strain the cooking juices into a pan and boil until reduced by half. Stir together the remaining mustard, sugar and cream and blend into the liquid. Bring to the boil, stirring. Add the Worcestershire sauce and more salt and pepper to taste. Spoon some of the sauce over the rabbit and hand the remainder separately.

Left: Casseroled saddle of hare with morello cherries
Below: Rabbit in tarragon sauce

Roast guinea fowl in sour cream sauce
Serves 2

Ingredients	Metric-Imperial	American
1 guinea fowl with giblets		
Salt		
Butter	15 g/½ oz	1 tbs
Soy sauce	1 tbs	1 tbs
Hot chicken stock (bouillon)	125 ml/4 fl oz	½ cup
Flour (all-purpose)	1 tbs	1 tbs
Sour cream	3 tbs	4 tbs
Green grapes	100 g/4 oz	4 oz

Sprinkle the cavity of the fowl with salt then rub more into the skin. Put the giblets inside with the butter. Truss the bird into a neat shape and place in a greased roasting tin. Sprinkle over the soy sauce and cook, uncovered, in a moderately hot oven, 200°C, 400°F, Gas Mark 6, for 10 minutes.

Add half the stock and baste the fowl. Return to the oven and cook for a further 35 minutes, basting twice during this time with the pan juices and adding more stock as the liquid evaporates, or until the fowl is cooked through. Transfer the guinea fowl to a warm serving dish and keep hot.

Halve the grapes and remove the pips (pits). Add 2 tbs (3 tbs) water to the roasting tin and stir to loosen the sediment. Strain into a pan. Blend the flour with the sour cream, add to the pan and stir until boiling. Add the grapes, bring to the boil again and simmer for 2 minutes. Adjust the seasoning if necessary. Serve the sauce with the guinea fowl.

Guinea fowl in tuna fish sauce
Serves 4

Ingredients	Metric-Imperial	American
1 large guinea fowl		
Salted water		
Selection of pot vegetables		
1 bunch of parsley		
8 sprigs of basil		
For the sauce:		
1 egg yolk		
French mustard	1 tsp	1 tsp
Wine vinegar	2 tsp	2 tsp
Salt and pepper		
Canned tuna	200 g/7 oz can	7 oz can
Olive oil	75 ml/3 fl oz	⅓ cup
2 hard-boiled eggs		
Drained capers	1 tbs	1 tbs
Lemon juice		
Dry white wine		
Tomato wedges		
Lemon slices		

Put the guinea fowl in a pan large enough to accommodate it easily. Pour over salted water to cover, bring to the boil and skim. Clean the pot vegetables, peel if necessary and cut into large pieces. Add to the pan with the parsley and half the basil. Bring back to the boil, cover and simmer for

45–60 minutes, or until the fowl is tender. Remove it from the pan and leave to cool. Divide the fowl into portions and discard the skin. Arrange on a serving dish. Strip the leaves from the remaining sprigs of basil and sprinkle over the guinea fowl portions.

To make the sauce, beat together the egg yolk, mustard, vinegar and a little seasoning until well blended. Drain the tuna and gradually beat the oil into the egg yolk mixture with the olive oil to make a thick dressing. Shell and finely chop the eggs. Flake the tuna then mash or chop finely with the capers. Mix the egg, tuna and capers into the dressing. Add a little lemon juice and wine to taste. Spoon the dressing over the guinea fowl and garnish with tomato wedges and lemon slices. Serve with French bread.

Braised partridges with vine leaf stuffing
Serves 4

Ingredients	Metric-Imperial	American
4 partridges		
Salt and freshly ground pepper		
Chopped oregano		
Canned stuffed vine leaves		
4 preserved vine leaves		
8 rashers smoked streaky bacon (16 strips)		
Butter	40 g/1½ oz	3 tbs

Partridges in red wine sauce
Serves 4

Ingredients	Metric-Imperial	American
4 partridges	200 g/7 oz each	7 oz each
Salt and pepper		
Streaky bacon (strips)	100 g/4 oz	8 strips
Butter or margarine	40 g/1½ oz	3 tbs
1 onion		
5 juniper berries		
Chopped sage	1 tsp	1 tsp
Red wine	125 ml/4 fl oz	½ cup
Hot water		
Flour (all-purpose)	2 tsp	2 tsp
Sour cream	4 tbs	5 tbs

Sprinkle the cavities of the partridges with salt and pepper then rub more seasoning into the skin. Cover the breast of each bird with bacon and secure with fine string. Melt the butter in a frying pan and use to brown the birds all over, one at a time.

Transfer the partridges to a roasting tin and spoon over any fat left in the pan. Peel and quarter the onion and add to the roasting tin with the juniper berries, sage and wine. Cook, uncovered, in a moderately hot oven, 200°C, 400°F, Gas Mark 6, for 45–60 minutes, basting the birds with the pan juices occasionally and adding a little water to the pan as the liquid evaporates, until the birds are cooked through. Lift out the partridges, remove the trussing strings, cut each bird in half and arrange on a warm serving dish.

Add a further 2 tbs (3 tbs) water to the roasting tin and stir well to loosen the sediment. Strain into a small pan. Blend the flour with the sour cream, add to the pan and stir until boiling. Adjust the seasoning with salt and pepper and simmer for 2 minutes. Transfer to a warm sauce boat. Serve the partridges and sauce with potato croquettes and Brussels sprouts.

Red wine	125 ml/4 fl oz	½ cup
Sour cream	225 ml/8 fl oz	1 cup
Grated rind of ½ lemon		
Blackberry or		
blackcurrant liqueur	2–3 tbs	3–4 tbs

Rub the skin of the partridges and sprinkle inside the cavities with salt, pepper and oregano. Fill the cavities with stuffed vine leaves, wrap each bird in 1 vine leaf and then in bacon. Place in a greased roasting tin and cook, uncovered, in a preheated moderately hot oven, 200°C, 400°F, Gas Mark 6, for 5 minutes. Put the butter and half the wine into the roasting tin. Roast for a further 40 minutes, basting the birds twice during this time and replacing evaporated liquid with the remainder of the wine, until the partridges are cooked through. Arrange the partridges on a warm serving dish and keep hot.

Add a little water to the roasting tin and stir up the sediments over moderate heat. Blend in the cream and lemon rind and adjust the seasoning if necessary. Bring to the boil, stirring. Remove from the heat, stir in liqueur to taste and serve with the partridges accompanied by potato croquettes.

Above: Roast guinea fowl in sour cream sauce
Right: Braised partridges with vine leaf stuffing

Roast pheasant with sour cream
Serves 2

Ingredients	Metric-Imperial	American
1 pheasant with giblets	1 kg/2¼ lb	2¼ lb
Salt		
Streaky bacon (strips)	50 g/2 oz	4 strips
Margarine	25 g/1 oz	2 tbs
Sour cream	125 ml/4 fl oz	½ cup
Flour (all-purpose)	1 tbs	1 tbs
Few drops of lemon juice		

Rub the skin of the pheasant with salt and sprinkle some inside the cavity. Finely chop the giblets, season with salt and stuff into the cavity of the bird. Close the opening and secure with wooden cocktail sticks (toothpicks). Cover the breast of the pheasant with bacon and tie on with string.

Melt the margarine in a roasting tin and brown the bird on all sides over moderate heat. Then place, uncovered, in a preheated hot oven, 220°C, 425°F, Gas Mark 7, for 10 minutes, or until the sediment begins to brown. Add 4 tbs (5 tbs) hot water, baste the bird with it and roast for a further 15 minutes. Replace the evaporated liquid with more hot water then baste again. Roast for another 15 minutes. Stir the sour cream into the juices in the tin and cook for 10 minutes more, or until the juices run clear when you prick the flesh of the breast of the pheasant with a fine skewer. Place the bird on a warm serving dish, removing the sticks and string and the stuffing from inside the cavity. Keep the bird hot.

Loosen the sediment by stirring in a little more hot water and bring to the boil. Moisten the flour with a small amount of cold water, add to the pan and stir until boiling. Simmer for 2 minutes and add lemon juice and salt to taste. Serve with the pheasant.

Pheasant in aspic
Serves 4

Ingredients	Metric-Imperial	American
1 pheasant	1 kg/2¼ lb	2¼ lb
Salt and pepper		
Streaky bacon (strips)	40 g/1½ oz	3 strips
Butter	25 g/1 oz	2 tbs
1 onion		
1 carrot		
1 whole clove		
6 peppercorns		
Hot chicken stock (bouillon)	300 ml/½ pint	1¼ cups
Canned pineapple syrup	4 tbs	5 tbs
For the stuffing:		
Canned drained pineapple pieces	100 g/4 oz	⅔ cup
1 banana		
Lemon juice	1 tbs	1 tbs
Desiccated coconut (shredded)	2 tbs	3 tbs
Ground ginger	¼ tsp	¼ tsp
For the aspic:		
Powdered gelatine	1 tbs	1 tbs
Madeira	3 tbs	4 tbs
Salt and pepper		
Ground ginger		
Few toasted slivered almonds		

First make the stuffing. Finely chop the pineapple pieces. Peel and chop the banana. Mix the fruit with the lemon juice, coconut and ginger. Use to stuff the pheasant. Close the opening and secure with wooden cocktail sticks (toothpicks). Rub the outside of the bird with salt and pepper, cover the breast with the bacon and tie on with fine string. Melt the butter in a large flameproof pan and use to brown the pheasant on all sides. Peel and chop the onion and carrot, add to the pheasant with the clove and peppercorns and cook for 5 minutes. Add half the stock, cover the pan and place in a preheated moderately hot oven, 190°C, 375°F, Gas Mark 5, for 40 minutes. Spoon the pineapple syrup over the pheasant, cover the pan again and return to the oven for a further 10 minutes, or until the bird is cooked through. Remove from the pan and cool. Discard the cocktail sticks, bacon and trussing strings.

Pour the remaining stock into the roasting tin and stir well to loosen the sediment. Strain into a pan, skim off excess fat and allow to cool. Sprinkle the gelatine over the Madeira in a small bowl and leave to stand for 10 minutes. Make up the liquid from the roasting tin to 300 ml/½ pint (1¼ cups) with water and place in a pan. Bring to the boil, adjust the seasoning with salt, pepper and a little ginger, remove from the heat and add the gelatine mixture. Stir until it has completely dissolved.

Cool until the aspic begins to thicken then spoon carefully over the pheasant. When the first layer has set, spoon over more aspic until the bird is well covered. Pour any remaining aspic into a shallow tin and leave to set. Cut into cubes, using a crinkle cutter if possible. Serve the pheasant on a platter, garnished with aspic cubes and slivered almonds.

Left: Roast pheasant with sour cream
Right: Pheasant in aspic

Saddle of venison, with sour cream sauce

Serves 4

Ingredients	Metric-Imperial	American
1 saddle of venison with bones	1.25 kg/3¼ lb	3¼ lb
Salt		
Softened butter or margarine	50 g/2 oz	¼ cup
Streaky bacon (strips)	100 g/4 oz	8 strips
6 juniper berries		
2 onions		
Hot water	500 ml/18 fl oz	2¼ cups
Sour cream	300 ml/½ pint	1¼ cups

Below: Saddle of venison with sour cream sauce
Right: Pheasant on a bed of cabbage

For the sauce:		
Cornflour (cornstarch)	2 tbs	3 tbs
Salt		
Sugar		
Lemon juice		
Sprigs of parsley		

Remove any membrane from the venison, rub with salt then spread with butter or margarine. Lay half the bacon slices in a layer in a roasting tin, put the venison joint on top and cover with the remaining bacon. Cook, uncovered, in a preheated moderately hot oven, 200°C, 400°F, Gas Mark 6, for 10 minutes.

Crush the berries, peel and quarter the onions. Add these to the roasting tin with a little of the water. Return the pan to the oven for a further 35 minutes, basting the ingredients occasionally with the juices in the tin and adding more water as the liquid evaporates.

Spoon the cream over the saddle and cook for a further 30 minutes, or until the meat is cooked through. Transfer the venison to a warm serving dish and keep hot. If desired, remove the meat from the bones and slice before placing on the serving dish.

To make the sauce, add any remaining water to the roasting tin and stir well to loosen the sediment. Strain into a pan. Moisten the cornflour with a little cold water, add to the pan and stir until boiling. Simmer for 1 minute and season to taste with salt and sugar. Add a little lemon juice to sharpen the flavour if wished. Garnish the venison with parsley and serve with buttered noodles and Brussels sprouts. Hand the sauce separately.

Pheasant on a bed of cabbage
Serves 8

Ingredients	Metric-Imperial	American
Small potatoes	750 g/1¾ lb	1¾ lb
White cabbage	1.5 kg/3¼ lb	3¼ lb
Onions	225 g/8 oz	8 oz
2 whole cloves		
3 pheasants	1 kg/2¼ lb each	2¼ lb each
Baby carrots	225 g/8 oz	8 oz
Goose or bacon fat	100 g/4 oz	½ cup
Piece of fat bacon	225 g/8 oz	8 oz
1 bay leaf		
Chicken stock (bouillon)	125 ml/4 fl oz	½ cup
Few large sprigs of thyme		
Pork boiling ring sausage	750 g/1¾ lb	1¾ lb
Salt and pepper		
Streaky bacon (strips)	100 g/4 oz	8 strips

Scrub the potatoes, place in a pan with salted water to cover and bring to the boil. Cover and simmer for about 20 minutes, or until tender. Drain, peel and leave to cool.

Remove any rough outer leaves of the cabbage, quarter, cut out the core and then shred the leaves. Peel the onions. Press the cloves into 1 onion and chop the other. Cut one pheasant into pieces with poultry shears. Peel the carrots.

Melt the fat in a large pan and use to cook the chopped onion until transparent. Add the piece of bacon and the pheasant portions and brown on all sides. Put in the cabbage and carrots and cook, stirring frequently, for 5 minutes. Add the whole onion stuck with cloves, the bay leaf, stock and thyme. Bring to the boil, cover and simmer for 30 minutes. Put the sausage into the pan and cook for 15 minutes more.

Rub the skin and sprinkle the cavities of the remaining 2 pheasants with salt and pepper. Cover the birds with the bacon and tie on with fine string. Place in a greased roasting tin and cook, uncovered, in a hot oven, 220°C, 425°F, Gas Mark 7, for 30 minutes. Add the potatoes to the pan and turn them in the fat. Roast for a further 20 minutes, or until

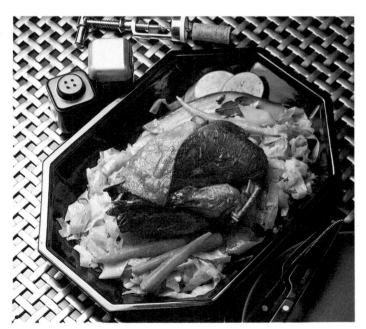

the pheasants are cooked through. Remove the trussing strings.

Slice the sausage and bacon and arrange with the cabbage mixture on a warm platter. Top with the roast pheasants. Serve the potatoes in a separate dish.

Microwave hints for preparing vegetable and fruit accompaniments for poultry and game meals

● To make a quick apple sauce, peel and core 2 large cooking apples. Slice finely into a pudding bowl, add 2 tbs (3 tbs) water and 25 g/l oz (2 tbs) butter and cook on Full Power, uncovered, for 2 minutes. Mash and stir well. Add a pinch of allspice or nutmeg, if liked.

● When preparing chips or roast potatoes, place the prepared potatoes in a bowl, cover and microwave on Full Power for 3–5 minutes, depending on the quantity, until the potatoes are thoroughly warmed through. This will reduce cooking time whether frying or roasting.

● To cook carrots, slice neatly and place in a suitable dish. Spoon over 3 tbs (4 tbs) orange juice and add a pinch of ground mace. Cover and cook on Full Power for 4 minutes then stir and test for tenderness. Cover again and cook for a further 2 minutes then test again and add salt to taste. Leave to stand for 2 minutes before serving.

● When you cook a favourite vegetable, such as Brussels sprouts, by microwave, it is easy to vary the flavour a little. Add a tsp of lemon juice, ½ tsp grated lemon rind, a pinch of allspice and generous seasoning to the water for cooking the sprouts. This produces a lemon-flavoured sauce. Vary by using orange juice instead of lemon.

● To cook green beans, trim the ends, cut long beans in half and place in a suitable container. Sprinkle with salt to taste, then add 2–3 tbs (3–4 tbs) water according to the quantity. Cover and cook on Full Power for 3 minutes. Test for tenderness, then re-cover and cook on Full Power for a further 2–3 minutes. Leave to stand, covered, for a further 2 minutes before serving, sprinkled with chopped savory.

● To cook cabbage, shred and place in a suitable bowl with 4 tbs (5 tbs) apple juice, ¼ tsp caraway seeds and a little black pepper. Mix the ingredients, cover the bowl and cook on Full Power for 3 minutes. Stir again, test for tenderness and add salt to taste. Cover and cook for a further 2–3 minutes on Full Power then leave to stand for 2 minutes before serving.

● To save time on cooking root vegetables to be used as part of a composite recipe, grate them or chop very finely. This will reduce cooking time by approximately half. Fine chopping, if appropriate, reduces time for green vegetables, but this would not apply to, say, asparagus.

● If food becomes cold after serving, because one person is late for the meal, a single portion can be covered with an inverted plate of the same size and reheated in one minute when the late-comer appears.

Ribbon noodles with seafood
Serves 5–6

Ingredients	Metric-Imperial	American
Ribbon noodles	450 g/1 lb	1 lb
Butter	40 g/1½ oz	3 tbs
For the sauce:		
1 onion		
1 clove of garlic		
Oil	1 tbs	1 tbs
Dry white wine	125 ml/4 fl oz	½ cup
1 bay leaf		
Salt and pepper		
Cooked or frozen shelled cockles or chopped clams	175 g/6 oz	1 cup
Tomatoes	450 g/1 lb	1 lb
Cooked or frozen shelled mussels	225 g/8 oz	1⅓ cups
Cooked or frozen shelled prawns (shrimp)	100 g/4 oz	⅔ cup
Drained capers	1 tbs	1 tbs
Chopped parsley	1 tbs	1 tbs

Cook the noodles in plenty of boiling salted water for about 10 minutes, until tender but still firm to the bite. Drain well, refresh briefly with cold water, drain again and return to the pan. Melt the butter and stir into the noodles. Keep hot.

To make the sauce, peel and finely chop the onion and garlic. Heat the oil in a pan and cook the onion in it until soft. Add the garlic and cook for 1 further minute. Stir in the wine and add the bay leaf with seasoning to taste. Put in the cockles or clams and simmer, stirring frequently, for about 5 minutes. Pour boiling water over the tomatoes, drain, peel, halve, scoop out the seeds and dice the flesh. Defrost the mussels and prawns if using frozen and drain off any liquid. Stir the remaining shellfish, tomato and capers into the sauce. Bring to the boil and simmer for about 3 minutes. Carefully fold together the sauce and noodles, transfer to a warm serving dish and sprinkle with parsley.

Green and white ribbon noodles with basil sauce
(Photo p. 298–299)

Serves 5–6

Ingredients	Metric-Imperial	American
Green and white ribbon noodles	450 g/1 lb	1 lb
Oil	1 tbs	1 tbs
Butter	40 g/1½ oz	3 tbs
For the sauce:		
Whipping cream	225 ml/8 fl oz	1 cup
Grated Parmesan cheese	50 g/2 oz	½ cup
Butter	25 g/1 oz	2 tbs
1 egg yolk		
Freshly ground pepper		
Finely chopped basil	2–3 tbs	3–4 tbs

Cook the noodles in plenty of boiling salted water, adding the oil, for about 10 minutes, until tender but still firm to the bite. Drain well, refresh briefly with cold water and drain again. Melt the butter and stir into the noodles. Place in a warm serving dish and keep hot.

To make the sauce, mix together the cream and cheese. Soften the butter and beat in with the egg yolk. Season to taste with pepper and mix in the basil. Pour the sauce over the noodles and serve at once.

Serving ideas: Serve with a salad of thinly sliced tomatoes dressed with a little good-quality olive oil, chopped basil and a good grinding of black pepper, or with a crisp green salad.

Ribbon noodles with spinach and ham
Serves 5–6

Ingredients	Metric-Imperial	American
Ribbon noodles	450 g/1 lb	1 lb
Oil	2 tbs	3 tbs
Butter or margarine	25 g/1 oz	2 tbs
Frozen leaf spinach	275 g/10 oz	10 oz
Salt and pepper		
Ground nutmeg		
Ham	225 g/8 oz	8 oz
1 clove of garlic		
Grated Parmesan cheese	100 g/4 oz	1 cup
6 eggs		
Whipping cream	400 ml/14 fl oz	1¾ cups

Cook the noodles in plenty of boiling salted water, adding the oil, for about 10 minutes, or until tender but still firm to the bite. Drain and return to the pan while still wet. Cover and keep hot.

Melt the butter in another pan, add the spinach and cook, stirring, until defrosted and hot. Season to taste with salt, pepper and nutmeg. Cut the ham into strips. Peel and crush the garlic. Add the ham, cheese and garlic to the eggs and cream and mix well.

Pour the egg mixture over the noodles and add the spinach. Stir over low heat for about 3 minutes, until the eggs are lightly scrambled. Adjust the seasoning if necessary and serve at once with a tomato salad.

Variations: Substitute smoked turkey breast for the ham and Cheddar or Gouda cheese for the Parmesan.

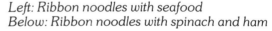

Left: Ribbon noodles with seafood
Below: Ribbon noodles with spinach and ham

Home-made noodles with pesto sauce
Serves 4

Ingredients	Metric-Imperial	American
Flour (all purpose)	about 450 g/1 lb	about 4 cups
4 egg whites		
Water	10 tbs	scant 1 cup
For the sauce:		
Pine kernels (nuts)	25 g/1 oz	¼ cup
3 cloves of garlic		
Finely chopped basil	100 g/4 oz	2 cups
Olive oil	300 ml/½ pint	1¼ cups
Grated Parmesan cheese	40 g/1½ oz	⅓ cup

Sift the flour into a bowl and make a well in the centre. Drop in the egg whites and water and mix to a dough. Knead on a lightly floured surface for 8–10 minutes, or until smooth and elastic. If the dough remains sticky, add a little more flour. Roll out the dough thinly and cut into strips about 5 cm/2 inches wide. Roll up each strip from one short side and cut this roll into very narrow strips.

Add the noodles to a large pan of boiling salted water and cook for about 5 minutes, or until tender but still firm to the bite. Drain well, refresh briefly with cold water and drain again. Return to the pan and keep hot.

To make the sauce, put the pine kernels into a frying pan and toast without adding any fat over moderate heat until golden. Leave to cool then chop. Peel and finely chop the garlic. Put the basil, garlic and pine kernels into a blender and process until smooth. With the machine on high speed, gradually add the oil in a thin stream and then the cheese. Process until the sauce is well combined. Serve the hot noodles topped with pesto sauce.

Cook's tips: If time is short, you may find it useful to keep a jar of ready-made pesto sauce in your store cupboard. This is also delicious as a topping for jacket-baked potatoes.

Other ready-made pasta sauces, available from supermarkets, include tomato, mushroom and clam, and make excellent store cupboard standbys.

In Italy, pesto sauce is made with half Parmesan and half Pecorino, another favourite Italian hard cooking cheese.

Home-made noodles with artichoke bottoms
Serves 4

Ingredients	Metric-Imperial	American
1 quantity home-made noodles (see Home-made noodles with pesto sauce)		
Canned drained artichoke bottoms	100 g/4 oz	¾ cup
Olive oil	6 tbs	½ cup
3 cloves of garlic		
3 red sweet peppers		
Chopped parsley	2 tbs	3 tbs

Cook the noodles for 5 minutes in plenty of boiling salted water, until tender but still firm to the bite. Drain well, refresh briefly with cold water and drain again. Return to the pan and keep hot.

Cut the artichoke bottoms into strips. Heat the oil in a pan, add the artichoke bottoms and fry, stirring, for 3 minutes. Peel and finely chop the garlic. Halve the peppers, remove the seeds and chop the flesh finely. Add the parsley, garlic and peppers to the pan and stir well. Cover and cook for 10 minutes, stirring occasionally. Combine the artichoke mixture with the noodles and serve piping hot.

Opposite: Home-made noodles with pesto sauce
Below: Home-made noodles with artichoke bottoms

Lasagne with young vegetables
Serves 5-6

Ingredients	Metric-Imperial	American
Boneless chicken breast	350 g/12 oz	12 oz
Lime or lemon juice	2 tbs	3 tbs
Soy sauce	1 tbs	1 tbs
Mange-tout peas (sugar)	225 g/8 oz	8 oz
Kohlrabi	225 g/8 oz	8 oz
Carrots	225 g/8 oz	8 oz
Shelled peas	225 g/8 oz	1⅓ cups
Cauliflower florets	175 g/6 oz	1 cup
Salt and freshly ground 'pepper		
Butter or margarine	25 g/1 oz	2 tbs
Flour (all-purpose)	25 g/1 oz	¼ cup
Milk	500 ml/18 fl oz	2¼ cups
Cream cheese with herbs	100 g/4 oz	½ cup
Coarsely grated Cheddar or Gouda cheese	350 g/12 oz	3½ cups
Ground nutmeg		
Snipped chives	3 tbs	4 tbs
Lasagne	225 g/8 oz	8 oz

Cut the chicken breasts into thin slices and place in a dish. Sprinkle with the citrus juice and soy sauce, cover and leave for 20 minutes.

Top and tail the mange-tout peas. Peel and thinly slice the kohlrabi and carrots. Put all the vegetables into a pan and add water just to cover plus a little salt. Bring to the boil, cover and simmer for 10 minutes. Drain well.

Melt the butter in a pan, sprinkle in the flour and stir until golden. Gradually add the milk and bring to the boil, stirring constantly. Simmer for 5 minutes. Mix in the cream cheese and a third of the grated cheese. Season to taste with salt, pepper and nutmeg. Fold in the chives.

Cook the lasagne in plenty of boiling salted water for 8 minutes. Drain well, refresh briefly with cold water and drain again. Grease an ovenproof dish with a capacity of about 2 L/3½ pints (4¼ pints). Arrange half the noodles in the dish, cover with half the chicken breast and then half the vegetables, keeping the layers as even as possible. Spoon over half the sauce. Repeat all the layers and finish by sprinkling the remaining cheese on top. Place uncovered, in a preheated hot oven, 220°C, 425°F, Gas Mark 7, for about 55 minutes. Leave for 5 minutes before cutting.

Cook's tips: This makes a perfect springtime main course, accompanied by a mixed salad.

You can also buy ready-to-use lasagne sheets, which require no pre-cooking before layering with the filling ingredients.

Use fresh vegetables in season for this dish: broad beans, celery, mushrooms and spinach would all make excellent additions.

Below: Noodle, spinach and beef bake
Opposite: Wholemeal lasagne with pine kernels

Wholemeal lasagne with pine kernels
Serves 6–8

Ingredients	Metric-Imperial	American
Wholemeal flour (wholewheat)	about 550 g/1¼ lb	about 5 cups
Salt		
6 eggs		
Olive oil	2 tbs	about 3 tbs
Tomatoes	1 kg/2¼ lb	2¼ lb
Carrots	350 g/12 oz	12 oz
Celeriac	350 g/12 oz	12 oz
Leeks	1 kg/2¼ lb	2¼ lb
Butter	100 g/4 oz	½ cup
Milk	1 L/1¾ pints	4⅓ cups
Salt		
Chopped basil	50 g/2 oz	1 cup
Whipping cream	125 ml/4 fl oz	½ cup
Grated Cheddar cheese	300 g/11 oz	2¾ cups
Pine kernels (nuts)	50 g/2 oz	½ cup
Sugar		
Cayenne pepper		

Put 450 g/1 lb (4 cups) of flour into a bowl and add the salt. Make a well in the centre and add the eggs and 2 tbs (3 tbs) oil. Mix, gradually drawing in the dry ingredients, until a ball of dough is formed. Knead on a lightly flavoured surface for 5 minutes. Form the dough into a ball again, brush it with oil and leave at room temperature for 1 hour.

Knead the dough again for 2 minutes and roll out thinly on a lightly floured surface to a rectangle measuring about 50 × 60 cm/20 × 24 inches. Cut into 16 rectangles each measuring about 15 × 12 cm/6× 5 inches.

Cook the lasagne rectangles, four at a time, in boiling salted water for 3 minutes. Remove from the pan and leave on clean tea towels to drain and cool.

Pour boiling water over the tomatoes, drain, peel and halve. Peel the carrots and celeriac and cut into thin strips about 4 cm/1½ inches long. Cook these in boiling salted water for 2 minutes. Drain, refresh with cold water and drain again. Trim and clean the leeks. Cut into 4 cm/1½ inch lengths. Cook in the same water for 1 minute. Drain, refresh and drain again, as above.

Melt the butter in a pan, sprinkle in the remaining flour and stir until golden. Gradually add the milk and bring to the boil, stirring constantly. Season well with salt and simmer for about 5 minutes. Stir in the basil and cream.

Grease a large rectangular ovenproof dish and lay 4 lasagne noodles in the base. Arrange half the leeks on top, spoon over one third of the sauce and sprinkle with a quarter of the cheese. Put 4 noodles over this, arrange the carrots and celeriac strips on top and sprinkle with half the pine kernels and another quarter of the cheese. Spoon over another third of the sauce. Lay 4 more noodles on this, put the remaining leeks on top, cover with the rest of the sauce and a third quarter of the cheese. Arrange the tomato halves, cut surfaces downwards, on the top and sprinkle these with sugar, a little cayenne, the remaining pine kernels and the last of the cheese. Place, uncovered, in a preheated moderately hot oven, 200°C, 400°F, Gas Mark 6, for about 1 hour. Leave to stand for 5 minutes before cutting.

Noodle, spinach and beef bake
Serves 4

Ingredients	Metric-Imperial	American
Spinach noodles	350 g/12 oz	12 oz
Salt and pepper		
1 clove of garlic		
1 onion		
Oil	2 tbs	3 tbs
Minced (ground) beef	450 g/1 lb	1 lb
Tomato purée (paste)	2 tsp	2 tsp
Worcestershire sauce		
Frozen chopped spinach	300 g/10 oz	10 oz
Coarsely grated Cheddar cheese	100 g/4 oz	1 cup

Cook the noodles in plenty of salted boiling water until only just tender. Drain well, refresh immediately under cold running water and drain again.

Peel and chop the garlic and onion and fry in the oil until soft and lightly coloured. Add the beef and cook, stirring, until it has lost all its pinkness. Stir in the tomato purée (paste) and season well with salt, pepper and Worcestershire sauce. Make sure the spinach is thoroughly defrosted, then drain well and season.

In a well-greased shallow ovenproof dish make a layer of half the noodles, then spoon over the beef mixture and top with the cheese. Bake, uncovered, in a preheated moderately hot oven, 200°C, 400°F, Gas Mark 6, for about 40 minutes, or until golden-brown on top.

Serving idea: Accompany with hot garlic bread.
Variations: Use half minced beef and half minced pork, and freshly grated nutmeg to season the spinach. For a vegetarian version, replace the meat with sliced mushrooms, and season these with soy sauce.
Cook's tips: Pasta bakes freeze well. It is worth making this recipe in double quantity and freezing one for later use. It will store in the freezer for up to 1 month and can be easily reheated in the microwave.

Pasta bakes are very suitable for informal buffet entertaining as they are easily eaten with a fork.

Macaroni with tangy cream cheese
Serves 2–3

Ingredients	Metric-Imperial	American
Short-cut macaroni	225 g/8 oz	2⅔ cups
Oil	1 tbs	1 tbs
Butter	2 tbs	3 tbs
Cream cheese	225 g/8 oz	1 cup
Whipping cream	125 ml/4 fl oz	½ cup
Grated Parmesan cheese	40 g/1½ oz	⅓ cup
Salt and pepper		
Sweet paprika pepper		

Cook the macaroni in plenty of boiling salted water, adding the oil, for about 10 minutes, until tender but still firm to the bite. Drain, refresh briefly with cold water and drain again.

Soften the butter and beat in the cream cheese, cream and Parmesan. Season to taste and stir into the noodles.

Transfer to a greased ovenproof dish and place, uncovered, in a preheated hot oven, 220°C, 425°F, Gas Mark 7, for about 5 minutes, or until the top is just golden brown.

Buttered macaroni
Serves 4

Ingredients	Metric-Imperial	American
Long macaroni	225 g/8 oz	8 oz
Butter	25 g/1 oz	2 tbs
Grated cheese		
Pepper or sweet paprika pepper		

Break the macaroni into finger-length pieces and cook in plenty of boiling salted water for about 10 minutes, or until tender but still firm to the bite. Drain, refresh briefly with cold water and drain again. Return to the pan. Melt the butter, pour over the noodles and toss lightly until coated. Serve sprinkled with cheese, pepper or paprika to taste.

Above: Macaroni with tangy cream cheese
Opposite: Macaroni with peas and ham

Macaroni with garlic and olive oil
Serves 5–6

Ingredients	Metric-Imperial	American
4 cloves of garlic		
Olive oil	6 tbs	½ cup
Salt		
2 canned red pimientos		
Chopped parsley	4 tbs	5 tbs
Long macaroni	450 g/1 lb	1 lb

Peel and finely chop the garlic. Heat the oil in a pan and use to fry the garlic until golden. Add a little salt. Halve the pimientos, remove any seeds and chop the flesh. Add to the pan with the parsley and cook gently for a further 2 minutes. Keep warm.

Cook the macaroni in plenty of boiling salted water for 10–12 minutes, or until tender but still firm to the bite. Drain, refresh briefly with cold water and drain again. Fold into the garlic sauce and serve immediately.

Variations: Replace the pimientos with 50 g/2 oz sliced stuffed olives or a few chopped anchovy fillets. For a more substantial dish, add some sliced salami or chorizo sausage.

Macaroni with peas and ham
Serves 3

Ingredients	Metric-Imperial	American
Long macaroni	225 g/8 oz	8 oz
Oil	1 tbs	1 tbs
Frozen peas	350 g/12 oz	2 cups
Salt and pepper		
Sugar		
Chopped parsley	2 tbs	3 tbs
Cooked ham	225 g/8 oz	8 oz
Butter	100 g/4 oz	½ cup
Grated Parmesan cheese	75 g/3 oz	¾ cup

Break the macaroni into finger-length pieces and cook in plenty of boiling salted water, adding the oil, for about 10 minutes, or until tender but still firm to the bite. Drain, refresh briefly with cold water and drain again.

Cook the peas in a little boiling salted water for 3 minutes. Drain well. Season the peas to taste with salt, pepper and sugar and mix in the parsley. Cut the ham into thin strips, mix with the peas and fold into the macaroni. Melt the butter. Serve the macaroni mixture hot, handing the melted butter and Parmesan separately.

Minced beef and pork combined (ground)	225 g/8 oz	8 oz
1 small onion		
1 clove of garlic		
1 carrot		
2 egg yolks		
Tomato purée (paste)	1 tbs	1 tbs
Dried thyme	¼ tsp	¼ tsp
Salt and pepper		
To cook and serve the ravioli:		
Oil	1 tbs	1 tbs
Butter	65 g/2½ oz	5 tbs
Grated Parmesan cheese	150 g/5 oz	1¼ cups
Chopped parsley		

To make the dough, sift the flour into a bowl and make a well in the centre. Beat together the eggs, egg whites, oil and salt and add to the flour. Mix, gradually drawing in the dry ingredients, until a ball of dough is formed. Knead on a lightly floured surface for 5 minutes.

Cover the dough with a damp cloth and leave to rest at room temperature for 10 minutes.

To make the filling, heat the oil and add the meat. Cook,

Noodles cooked in milk
Serves 4

Ingredients	Metric-Imperial	American
Milk	1 L/1¾ pints	4⅓ cups
Pinch of salt		
Butter or margarine	1 tsp	1 tsp
Medium-sized pasta shapes	250 g/9 oz	3 cups
Seedless raisins	50 g/2 oz	⅓ cup
Sugar	50 g/2 oz	¼ cup

Put the milk into a pan with the salt and butter or margarine. Bring to the boil and put in the pasta. Stir, cover and simmer for 25 minutes, or until the pasta is soft. Meanwhile, pour a little boiling water over the raisins and leave for 5 minutes. Drain and stir into the cooked noodles with the sugar.

Variations: Instead of the sugar and raisins, serve the cooked noodles sprinkled with cinnamon and sugar accompanied by cooked dried fruit salad (see picture).

Ravioli
Serves 4

Ingredients	Metric-Imperial	American
Flour (all-purpose)	about 300 g/ 11 oz	about 2¾ cups
2 eggs		
2 egg whites		
Oil	2 tbs	3 tbs
Salt	1 tsp	1 tsp
For the filling:		
Oil	1 tbs	1 tbs

stirring, until it is brown and crumbly. Peel and chop the onion and garlic. Peel and coarsely grate the carrot. Add onion, garlic and carrot to the meat and cook for a further 5 minutes. Leave to cool. Mix in egg yolks, tomato purée and thyme and season to taste.

Roll out half the dough on a floured surface to a rectangle measuring about 48 × 36 cm/19 × 14 inches. Divide the rectangle in half and set one piece aside, covered with a damp cloth. On the remaining half of dough, put small even-sized portions of the meat mixture about 6.5 cm/2½ inches apart. Using a brush and water, paint wet lines downwards and crossways between the heaps of filling. Lay the other piece of dough on top and press down all round the heaps of filling, along the dampened lines. Cut through these lines, using a fluted cutter, to form the individual ravioli. Leave on lightly floured greaseproof paper (waxed) to dry. Repeat the process using the remaining dough and filling.

Heat a large pan of boiling salted water and add the oil. Put in the ravioli and cook for 8–10 minutes, or until tender but still firm to the bite. Stir carefully now and then during cooking. Drain the ravioli well and transfer to a warm serving dish. Melt the butter and pour over the pasta. Sprinkle with Parmesan, add a little parsley if liked.

Macaroni with pepper and fig sauce
Serves 5–6

Ingredients	Metric-Imperial	American
Long thin macaroni	450 g/1 lb	1 lb
For the sauce:		
6 small sweet peppers		
1 stick of celery (stalk)		
Olive oil	4 tbs	5 tbs
Water	2 tbs	3 tbs
3 ripe figs		
Salt and pepper		

Cook the macaroni or spaghetti in plenty of boiling salted water for about 8 minutes, or until tender but still firm to the bite. Drain, refresh briefly with cold water and drain again. Return to the pan.

To make the sauce, halve, deseed and dice the peppers. Trim and chop the celery. Heat the oil in a pan, add the celery and diced pepper and cook, stirring occasionally, for 10–15 minutes, or until tender. Blend in the water. Peel and chop the figs and mix into the vegetables. Season, pour the sauce over the pasta and reheat carefully.

Cannelloni with cream cheese filling
Serves 4

Ingredients	Metric-Imperial	American
Cream cheese	350 g/12 oz	1½ cups
2 eggs		
Grated Parmesan cheese	50 g/2 oz	½ cup
Chopped parsley	2 tbs	3 tbs
Dried basil	½ tsp	½ tsp
Salt and pepper		
Cannelloni tubes	175 g/6 oz	6 oz
2 onions		
2 cloves of garlic		
Oil	3 tbs	4 tbs
Tomatoes	396 g/14 oz can	14 oz can
Dried oregano	¼ tsp	¼ tsp
Sugar		
Grated Gouda cheese	100 g/4 oz	1 cup

Mix together the cream cheese, eggs, Parmesan, parsley and basil. Season to taste with salt and pepper and place in a piping bag fitted with a plain tube (pipe). Use to fill the cannelloni tubes and arrange them side-by-side in a greased ovenproof dish.

Peel and chop the onions and garlic and fry in the oil in a pan until softened. Liquidize or sieve the tomatoes with the liquid in the can and add to the pan with the oregano. Season to taste with salt, pepper and sugar. Bring to the boil and simmer for 5 minutes.

Pour the sauce evenly over the cannelloni, sprinkle with the cheese and place in a preheated moderately hot oven, 200°C, 400°F, Gas Mark 6, for 35 minutes.

Opposite: Noodles cooked in milk
Left: Ravioli

Green tortellini with walnuts
Serves 5–6

Ingredients	Metric-Imperial	American
Shelled walnut halves	225 g/8 oz	2 cups
2–3 cloves of garlic		
Olive oil	125 ml/4 fl oz	½ cup
Whipping cream	125 ml/4 fl oz	½ cup
Salt		
Ground nutmeg		
Chopped marjoram	2 tbs	3 tbs
Green tortellini	450 g/1 lb	1 lb

Finely chop two thirds of the walnuts. Peel and chop the garlic. Heat the oil in a pan and use to fry the garlic until transparent. Add the chopped walnuts, walnut halves and cream. Season to taste with salt and nutmeg, and stir in the marjoram. Heat the sauce gently to just below boiling point. Do not allow to boil or it may curdle.

Meanwhile, cook the tortellini in plenty of boiling salted water for 20 minutes, or until tender but still firm to the bite. Drain, refresh briefly with cold water and drain again. Transfer to a warm serving dish and spoon the sauce over the top.

Tortellini with mushroom and wine sauce
Serves 2

Ingredients	Metric-Imperial	American
Beef stock (bouillon)	1 L/1¾ pints	4⅓ cups
Tortellini	100 g/4 oz	1 cup
Mushrooms	100 g/4 oz	4 oz
1 onion		
Butter	15 g/½ oz	1 tbs
Dry white wine	125 ml/4 fl oz	½ cup
Whipping cream	150 ml/¼ pint	⅔ cup
Salt and pepper		
Finely chopped parsley	1 tbs	1 tbs

Put the stock into a pan and bring to the boil. Add the tortellini, bring back to the boil and cook for about 20 minutes, or until tender but still firm to the bite. Drain, refresh briefly with cold water and drain again.

Slice the mushrooms and peel and chop the onion. Melt the butter in a pan and use to fry the onion until transparent. Put in the mushrooms and wine and cook, stirring, for 2 minutes. Stir in the cream, season to taste and bring to the boil. Put in the tortellini and simmer, stirring occasionally, for a further 3 minutes. Serve sprinkled with parsley.

Tortellini with ham and cream sauce
Serves 2

Ingredients	Metric-Imperial	American
Beef stock (bouillon)	1 L/1¾ pints	4⅓ cups
Tortellini	100 g/4 oz	1 cup
1 clove of garlic		
Whipping cream	150 ml/¼ pint	⅔ cup
Milk	3 tbs	4 tbs
Salt and pepper		
Ground nutmeg		
Meat extract		
Ham	100 g/4 oz	4 oz
Snipped chives	2 tbs	3 tbs

Put the stock into a pan and bring to the boil. Add the tortellini, bring back to the boil and cook for about 20 minutes, or until tender but still firm to the bite. Drain.

Peel the garlic, cut in half and rub the cut surfaces over the inside of a pan. Pour in the cream and milk, bring to the boil and add the tortellini. Season to taste with salt, pepper, nutmeg and a little meat extract and simmer, stirring occasionally, for 4 minutes. Meanwhile, cut the ham into strips, fold into the tortellini mixture and serve in a warm dish sprinkled with chives.

Noodles with courgette and plum sauce
Serves 5–6

Ingredients	Metric-Imperial	American
Tagliatelle noodles	450 g/1 lb	1 lb
Oil	1 tbs	1 tbs
For the sauce:		
1 large onion		
Small courgettes (zucchini)	225 g/8 oz	8 oz
1 sweet pepper		
Tomatoes	225 g/8 oz	8 oz
Plums	225 g/8 oz	8 oz
Olive oil	125 ml/4 fl oz	½ cup
Salt and pepper		
Chopped mint	1 tsp	1 tsp
Chopped basil	1 tsp	1 tsp

Cook the noodles in plenty of boiling salted water, adding the oil, for 8–10 minutes, or until tender but still firm to the bite. Drain, refresh briefly with cold water and drain again.

To make the sauce, peel the onion, top and tail the courgettes and deseed the pepper. Chop the onion, courgettes, pepper and tomatoes. Halve and stone (pit) the plums. Mix together the vegetables, fruit and olive oil and season to taste with salt and pepper. Stir in the herbs. Combine this mixture with the warm noodles and serve at once.

Opposite: Green tortellini with walnuts
Above: Tortellini with ham and cream sauce

311

Meat-stuffed cannelloni with cream sauce
Serves 3–4

Ingredients	Metric-Imperial	American
Cannelloni	225 g/8 oz	8 oz
For the filling:		
1 bread roll		
Minced beef and pork combined (ground)	225 g/8 oz	8 oz
Salt and pepper		
Dried oregano	½ tsp	½ tsp
Dried thyme	½ tsp	½ tsp
For the sauce:		
Whipping cream	150 ml/¼ pint	⅔ cup
Milk	6 tbs	½ cup
Salt and pepper		
Meat extract	½ tsp	½ tsp
Chopped basil	1 tbs	1 tbs
Grated Parmesan cheese	1 tbs	1 tbs
Butter	25 g/1 oz	2 tbs

First make the filling. Soften the bread roll in cold water then squeeze out the moisture and crumble the bread. Mix with the meat and season to taste with salt, pepper and the herbs. Fill the cannelloni with the mixture and place side-by-side in a greased shallow ovenproof dish.

To make the sauce, stir together the cream and milk and season to taste with salt and pepper, the meat extract and basil. Pour evenly over the cannelloni which must be completely covered. Sprinkle with the cheese and dot with butter. Place, uncovered, in a preheated moderately hot oven, 200°C, 400°F, Gas Mark 6, for about 30 minutes.

Baked cannelloni with beef and spinach stuffing
Serves 4

Ingredients	Metric-Imperial	American
Cannelloni	225 g/8 oz	8 oz
For the filling:		
Frozen chopped spinach	150 g/5 oz	5 oz
1 small onion		
1 clove of garlic		
Oil	1 tbs	1 tbs
Butter	15 g/½ oz	1 tbs
Minced beef (ground)	225 g/8 oz	8 oz
1 egg		
Whipping cream	1 tbs	1 tbs
Grated Parmesan cheese	2 tbs	3 tbs
Salt and pepper		
Dried oregano	½ tsp	½ tsp
For the sauce:		
1 onion		
1 clove of garlic		
Streaky bacon (strips)	50 g/2 oz	4 strips
Oil	1 tbs	1 tbs
Flour	1 tbs	1 tbs
Tomato purée (paste)	3 tbs	4 tbs
Salt and pepper		
Dried basil	½ tsp	½ tsp
Dried oregano	½ tsp	½ tsp
Beef stock (bouillon)	350 ml/12 fl oz	1½ cups
Grated Cheddar or Gouda cheese	25 g/1 oz	¼ cup
Butter	25 g/1 oz	2 tbs

First make the filling. Defrost the spinach completely. Peel and chop the onion and garlic. Heat the oil in a pan, add the onion and garlic and fry until transparent. Stir in the spinach and cook for a few minutes to evaporate the moisture. In another pan, melt the butter and use to fry the meat, stirring, until it is well browned and looks crumbly. Beat the egg with the cream and cheese, stir into the spinach mixture with the beef and season to taste with salt, pepper and the oregano. Use this stuffing to fill the cannelloni tubes.

To make the sauce, peel and finely chop the onion and garlic. Chop the bacon, put into a pan with the oil and cook until the fat runs. Add the onion and garlic and cook until transparent. Stir in the flour, then the tomato purée and season to taste with salt and pepper, the basil and oregano. Blend in the stock and stir until boiling. Simmer, stirring occasionally, for 10 minutes.

Pour a third of the sauce into a greased ovenproof dish and arrange the cannelloni in it side-by-side. Pour over the remaining sauce, sprinkle with the cheese and dot with butter. Place, uncovered, in a preheated moderate oven, 180°C, 350°F, Gas Mark 4, for 30 minutes, or until the topping is golden-brown.

Cook's tip: To fill cannelloni tubes, either use a piping bag fitted with a large plain tube (pipe), or a teaspoon, using the handle of a wooden spoon to push the filling mixture down into the tubes.

Serving ideas: Serve the cannelloni with a mixed continental salad of shredded crisp lettuce, radicchio, chicory (endive) and watercress sprigs.

Cheese-stuffed cannelloni on leaf spinach
Serves 8

Ingredients	Metric-Imperial	American
1 onion		
Oil	2 tbs	3 tbs
Frozen leaf spinach	550 g/1¼ lb	1¼ lb
Salt and pepper		
Ground nutmeg	½ tsp	½ tsp
Butter	100 g/4 oz	½ cup
Flour	100 g/4 oz	1 cup
Milk	850 ml/1½ pints	3¾ cups
Whipping cream	300 ml/½ pint	1¼ cups
Grated Emmental cheese	150 g/5 oz	1¼ cups
Cream cheese	225 g/8 oz	1 cup
Cannelloni	225 g/8 oz	8 oz
Little extra butter		

Peel and chop the onion. Heat the oil in a pan and use to fry the onion until transparent. Add the spinach and cook over low heat, stirring frequently, for 15 minutes, or until the spinach is completely defrosted. Drain off any surplus liquid and season to taste with salt, pepper and the nutmeg. Put the spinach mixture into a greased ovenproof dish.

Melt the butter in a clean pan, sprinkle in the flour and stir until golden. Whisk in 750 ml/1¼ pints (3 cups) of the milk and the cream and bring to the boil. Simmer, stirring, for 2 minutes. Season to taste with salt and pepper and stir in almost all the Emmental. Pour one third of the sauce into a bowl, cool and beat in the cream cheese. Season to taste with more salt and pepper if wished and use to fill the cannelloni.

Spoon half the remaining sauce over the spinach mixture and lay the cannelloni side-by-side on this. Stir the remaining milk into the last of the sauce and spoon evenly over the cannelloni. Sprinkle with the reserved Emmental and dot with a little butter. Bake, uncovered, in a preheated hot oven, 220°C, 425°F, Gas Mark 7, for 30 minutes. Serve with a tomato salad.

Opposite: Meat-stuffed cannelloni with cream sauce
Above: Cheese-stuffed cannelloni in leaf spinach

Tyrolean noodles with cabbage
Serves 5–6

Ingredients	Metric-Imperial	American
White cabbage	1 kg/2¼ lb	2¼ lb
2 large onions		
Pork dripping	75 g/3 oz	⅓ cup
Salt and pepper		
Ribbon noodles	275 g/10 oz	10 oz
Garlic sausage	225 g/8 oz	8 oz
Chopped parsley	1 tbs	1 tbs

Discard the rough outer leaves of the cabbage, quarter, cut out the core and shred the leaves. Wash and drain well. Peel and chop the onions.

Heat the dripping in a heavy pan and use to fry the onion until transparent. Add the cabbage, season to taste with salt and pepper and cook over low heat for 25 minutes, stirring frequently, until light brown.

Meanwhile, cook the noodles in plenty of boiling salted water for about 10 minutes, until tender but still firm to the bite. Drain, refresh briefly with cold water then drain again. Skin the sausage and cut into large dice. Combine the noodles, cabbage and sausage, adjust the seasoning if necessary and reheat, stirring frequently. Sprinkle with the parsley before serving.

Ribbon noodles with chervil sauce
Serves 4

Ingredients	Metric-Imperial	American
Green ribbon noodles	275 g/10 oz	10 oz
Butter	40 g/1½ oz	3 tbs
Tomatoes	350 g/12 oz	12 oz
Whipping cream	300 ml/½ pint	1¼ cups
Salt and pepper		
Ground nutmeg	¼ tsp	¼ tsp
Chopped chervil	1 tbs	1 tbs
Grated Parmesan cheese	25 g/1 oz	¼ cup
Few sprigs of chervil		

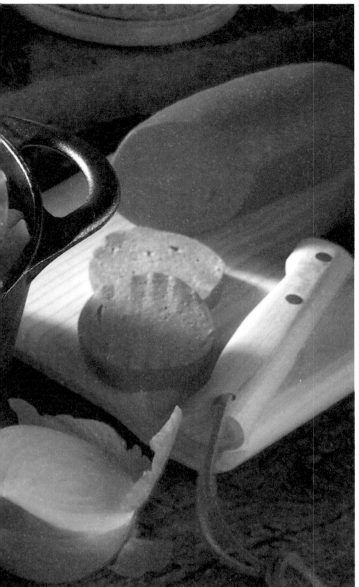

Ribbon noodles with mussels
Serves 3

Ingredients	Metric-Imperial	American
Ribbon noodles	225 g/8 oz	8 oz
Oil	1 tbs	1 tbs
Butter	65 g/2½ oz	5 tbs
Frozen shelled mussels	450 g/1 lb	1 lb
2 cloves of garlic		
Mushrooms	225 g/8 oz	8 oz
Chopped parsley	2 tbs	3 tbs
Salt and pepper		
Onion powder	½ tsp	½ tsp

Cook the noodles in plenty of boiling salted water, adding the oil, for 10 minutes, or until tender but still firm to the bite. Drain, refresh briefly with cold water and drain again. Transfer to a warm serving dish. Melt a little of the butter and pour over the noodles. Keep hot.

Defrost the mussels, keeping any liquid. Peel and finely chop the garlic. Slice the mushrooms. Melt the remaining butter in a pan, cook the garlic in it for 1 minute and add the mushrooms and parsley. Cook for a further 5 minutes, stirring frequently. Put in the mussels and reserved liquid and cook until the shellfish is hot. Season to taste with salt and pepper and the onion powder. Pour the mussel mixture over the noodles and serve immediately.

Cook's tip: Mussels in brine, available in jars from supermarkets, may be used instead of frozen mussels. Remember to rinse them well before adding to the mushroom and garlic mixture.

Cook the noodles in plenty of boiling salted water for 10 minutes, or until tender but still firm to the bite. Drain, refresh briefly with cold water and drain again. Rinse and dry the pan, melt the butter in it and return the noodles. Toss well until coated with butter.

Pour boiling water over the tomatoes, drain, peel, halve, remove the seeds and dice the flesh. Add to the noodles together with the cream (which may be lightly whipped first if desired). Stir well. Reheat gently, stirring, then season to taste with salt, pepper and the nutmeg. Just before serving fold in the chopped chervil. Serve sprinkled with Parmesan and top each portion with a sprig of chervil.

Above: Tyrolean noodles with cabbage
Right: Ribbon noodles with mussels

Spaghetti with courgette sauce
Serves 4–6

Ingredients	Metric-Imperial	American
Spaghetti	400 g/14 oz	14 oz
1 clove of garlic		
Oil	1 tbs	1 tbs
Butter	15 g/½ oz	1 tbs
For the sauce:		
1 onion		
1 clove of garlic		
Small courgettes (zucchini)	450 g/1 lb	1 lb
Oil	4 tbs	5 tbs
Chopped fresh mixed herbs	2 tbs	3 tbs
Whipping cream	125 ml/4 fl oz	½ cup
Salt and pepper		
1 'beefsteak' tomato		

First make the sauce. Peel and chop the onion and garlic. Top and tail the courgettes and cut into matchsticks. Heat the oil in a pan, add the onion, garlic and courgette and cook for about 3 minutes, stirring all the time. Mix in the herbs and the cream and season to taste with salt and pepper. Pour boiling water over the tomato, drain and peel. Cut in half, remove the seeds and dice the flesh. Stir into the courgette mixture and keep hot in the pan.

Peel and chop the remaining garlic. Cook the spaghetti in plenty of boiling salted water, adding the garlic and oil, for about 10 minutes, or until tender but still firm to the bite. Drain, refresh briefly with cold water and drain again. Rinse and dry the pan, melt the butter in it and return the spaghetti. Shake to coat well and serve topped with the courgette sauce.

Note: Other pasta shapes can be used in all these dishes, but the basic cooking time will vary according to their size. The length of cooking time is usually indicated on the pack.

Spaghetti with leeks and ham
Serves 5–6

Ingredients	Metric-Imperial	American
Leeks	750 g/1¾ lb	1¾ lb
Spaghetti	450 g/1 lb	1 lb
Oil	1 tbs	1 tbs
Butter	50 g/2 oz	¼ cup
Cooked ham	225 g/8 oz	8 oz
Salt and pepper		

Trim and thoroughly clean the leeks. Cut in half lengthways and then into slices. Wash again and drain well.

Cook the spaghetti in plenty of boiling salted water, adding the oil, for about 7 minutes. Add the leeks and cook for a further 3 minutes, or until the spaghetti is tender but still firm to the bite. Drain, refresh briefly with cold water and drain again. Rinse and dry the pan, melt the butter in it and allow to brown slightly. Cut the ham into strips and add to the pan together with the spaghetti mixture. Season to taste with salt and pepper and toss lightly. Serve with a fresh tomato sauce.

Spaghetti with walnut butter
Serves 4

Ingredients	Metric-Imperial	American
Spaghetti	275 g/10 oz	10 oz
Oil	1 tbs	1 tbs
Shelled walnut halves	75 g/3 oz	¾ cup
Butter	75 g/3 oz	⅓ cup
Salt and pepper		

Cook the spaghetti in plenty of boiling salted water, adding the oil, for 10 minutes, or until tender but still firm to the bite. Drain, refresh briefly with cold water and drain again. Rinse and dry the pan.

Chop the walnut halves coarsely. Melt the butter in the pan and fry the nuts until golden brown. Put in the spaghetti and mix well. Season to taste with salt and pepper and serve piping hot.

Left: Spaghetti with courgette sauce
Opposite: Spaghetti with leeks and ham

Spaghetti with cream sauce
Serves 2

Ingredients	Metric-Imperial	American
Spaghetti	175 g/6 oz	6 oz
Oil	1 tbs	1 tbs
Streaky bacon (strips)	100 g/4 oz	8 strips
Butter	15 g/½ oz	1 tbs
Whipping cream	150 ml/¼ pint	⅔ cup
Salt and pepper		
Ground nutmeg	½ tsp	½ tsp
Chopped basil	1 tsp	1 tsp
2 sprigs of basil		
Grated Parmesan cheese		

Cook the spaghetti in plenty of boiling salted water, adding the oil, for about 10 minutes, until tender but still firm to the bite. Drain, refresh briefly with cold water and drain again.

Chop the bacon. Rinse and dry the pan, melt the butter in it and use to fry the bacon until the fat runs. Stir in the cream, season to taste with salt and pepper and add the nutmeg. Bring to the boil, fold in the spaghetti and the chopped basil. Serve garnished with sprigs of basil and sprinkled with a little Parmesan.

Spaghetti with vegetables and cheese sauce
Serves 5–6

Ingredients	Metric-Imperial	American
Carrots	175 g/6 oz	6 oz
Courgettes (zucchini)	175 g/6 oz	6 oz
Spinach	100 g/4 oz	4 oz
Frozen peas	100 g/4 oz	⅔ cup
Spaghetti	450 g/1 lb	1 lb
Oil	1 tbs	1 tbs
Cauliflower florets	225 g/8 oz	1⅓ cups
Butter	40 g/1½ oz	3 tbs
For the sauce:		
2 onions		
Butter	40 g/1½ oz	3 tbs
Whipping cream	450 ml/¾ pint	scant 2 cups
Grated Cheddar or Gouda cheese	50 g/2 oz	½ cup
Ground nutmeg	½ tsp	½ tsp
Salt		

Peel and thinly slice the carrots. Top and tail the courgettes then slice thinly. Wash the spinach, removing any tough stalks. Defrost the peas.

Cook the spaghetti in plenty of boiling salted water, adding the oil, for 4 minutes. Put in the cauliflower florets and carrot and cook for a further 4 minutes, then add the courgettes, spinach and peas and cook for a further 2 minutes or until all the vegetables and the spaghetti are tender. Drain well and transfer to a warm serving dish. Add the butter and toss the ingredients lightly together until coated. Keep hot.

To make the sauce, peel and finely chop the onions. Melt the butter and use to fry the onion gently until transparent. Stir in the cream and cook, stirring, until slightly reduced and thickened. Stir in the cheese and when it has melted, season to taste with nutmeg and salt. Serve the sauce with the spaghetti dish.

Below: Spaghetti with cream sauce
Opposite: Spaghetti with vegetables and cheese sauce

Apple rice
Serves 4

Ingredients	Metric-Imperial	American
Cooking apples	450 g/1 lb	1 lb
Water	1 L/1¾ pints	4⅓ cups
Salt	½ tsp	½ tsp
Sugar	50 g/2 oz	¼ cup
Grated rind of ½ lemon		
Round grain rice	200 g/7 oz	scant 1 cup
Ground cinnamon mixed with sugar		

Peel, quarter, core and slice the apples. Put the water, salt, sugar and lemon rind into a pan and bring to the boil. Add the apple slices and rice and stir once. Cover and simmer for about 40 minutes, or until the rice is tender. Serve sprinkled with a mixture of cinnamon and sugar.

Variation: Cook the rice in the lemon liquid as above. Substitute tart dessert apples for the cooking apples and poach the slices lightly in water with a little lemon juice added, until tender but not falling. Drain well. Arrange layers of rice mixture and apples in a serving dish and sprinkle the top with cinnamon sugar.

Moulded rice with diced vegetables
Serves 4

Ingredients	Metric-Imperial	American
Carrots	225 g/8 oz	8 oz
Kohlrabi	175 g/6 oz	6 oz
Salted water	500 ml/18 fl oz	2¼ cups
3 whole coriander berries		
Long grain rice	250 g/9 oz	generous 1 cup
Grated Gruyere cheese	2 tbs	3 tbs
Cooked ham	350 g/12 oz	12 oz

Peel and dice the carrots and kohlrabi. Put the salted water into a pan, add the vegetables, coriander and rice and bring to the boil. Stir once, cover and simmer for about 12 minutes, or until the vegetables and rice are tender and the liquid absorbed.

Press the rice mixture into a greased bowl or ring mould then turn out on a warm serving dish. Sprinkle with the cheese. Form the ham into rolls and use to surround the rice mould.

Green rice
Serves 4

Ingredients	Metric-Imperial	American
2 green sweet peppers		
1 leek		
Oil	1 tbs	1 tbs
Long grain rice	250 g/9 oz	generous 1 cup
Milk	125 ml/4 fl oz	½ cup
Salted water	375 ml/13 fl oz	1⅔ cups
Chopped parsley	2 tbs	3 tbs

Halve the peppers, remove the seeds and cut the flesh into strips. Trim and clean the leek and cut into slices. Heat the oil in a pan and use to fry the pepper and leek for 1 minute. Add the rice, milk and salted water and bring to the boil. Stir once, cover and simmer for about 12 minutes, or until the rice is tender and the liquid absorbed.

Transfer to a strainer, refresh with cold water then drain well. Mix in the parsley and serve with brawn or cold meat.

Left: Moulded rice with diced vegetables
Opposite: Green rice

Rice with mushrooms and bacon
Serves 4

Ingredients	Metric-Imperial	American
Dried mushrooms	50 g/2 oz	2 oz
Streaky bacon (strips)	150 g/5 oz	10 strips
1 onion		
Long grain rice	250 g/9 oz	generous 1 cup
Salted water	500 ml/18 fl oz	2¼ cups
Salt and pepper		
1 lettuce		
Oil	4 tbs	5 tbs
Vinegar	2 tbs	3 tbs
Mild mustard	1 tbs	1 tbs
Sugar		
4 egg yolks		

Soak the mushrooms in hot water until plump. Cut the bacon into small strips, place in a pan and fry until golden and crisp. Remove the bacon bits from the pan. Peel and chop the onion and cook in the bacon fat until transparent. Drain and chop the mushrooms and add to the pan with the rice and water. Bring to the boil, stir once, cover and simmer for 12 minutes, or until the rice is tender and the liquid absorbed. Mix in the bacon strips.

Discard any rough outer leaves from the lettuce. Separate the remaining leaves, tearing larger ones into pieces. Place in a bowl.

Make a dressing by beating together the oil, vinegar and mustard with salt, pepper and sugar to taste. Pour over the lettuce and toss lightly. Arrange the rice mixture and lettuce salad on 4 plates. Make a hollow in the top of each mound of rice and drop in an egg yolk. Serve at once.

Liver risotto
Serves 4

Ingredients	Metric-Imperial	American
2 onions		
Margarine	50 g/2 oz	¼ cup
Long grain rice	250 g/9 oz	generous 1 cup
Chinese leaves (cabbage)	250 g/9 oz	9 oz
Hot beef stock (bouillon)	500 ml/18 fl oz	2¼ cups
Pigs' liver or calves' liver	450 g/1 lb	1 lb
Flour		
Butter	25 g/1 oz	2 tbs
Salt and pepper		

Peel and chop the onions. Melt the margarine in a pan and use to cook the onion gently until transparent. Stir in the rice and cook for 5 minutes. Discard any rough leaves from the Chinese cabbage, then shred. Wash, drain and add to the pan. Cook for 2 minutes. Pour in the hot stock, bring to the boil and stir once. Cover and simmer for 12 minutes or until the rice is tender and the liquid absorbed.

Meanwhile, cut the liver into strips and coat with flour. Melt the butter in a pan, add the liver strips and cook, stirring frequently, for 6 minutes, until brown. Season with salt and pepper. Combine the liver strips with the rice mixture.

Vegetable and herb risotto
Serves 4

Ingredients	Metric-Imperial	American
1 small onion		
Butter or margarine	25 g/1 oz	2 tbs
Long grain rice	250 g/9 oz	generous 1 cup
Hot beef stock (bouillon)	500 ml/18 fl oz	2¼ cups
Cooked or canned peas	100 g/4 oz	⅔ cup
Cooked or canned diced carrots	100 g/4 oz	⅔ cup
Chopped fresh herbs	2 tbs	3 tbs

Peel and chop the onion. Melt the butter or margarine in a pan, add the onion and fry until transparent. Stir in the rice and cook until pale golden. Pour in the stock and bring to the boil. Cover and simmer for 12 minutes, or until the rice is tender and the liquid absorbed. Fork in the peas and carrots and heat through carefully. Transfer to a warm serving dish and sprinkle with the herbs.

Microwave hint
To cook frozen fried potatoes by microwave, preheat a browning dish for 5 minutes, add 2 tbsp (3 tbsp) oil and 225 g/8 oz frozen potatoes. Cook on full power for 7 minutes, stirring gently half way through.

Opposite: Rice with mushrooms and bacon
Below: Vegetable and herb risotto

Rice with pork and celery
Serves 4

Ingredients	Metric-Imperial	American
Long grain rice	250 g/9 oz	generous 1 cup
Salted water	500 ml/18 fl oz	2¼ cups
4 sticks of celery (stalks)		
1 onion		
Oil	1 tbs	1 tbs
Minced pork (ground)	225 g/8 oz	8 oz
Salt and pepper		
Canned mushrooms	225 g/8 oz can	8 oz can
Chopped parsley	2 tbs	3 tbs

Put the rice into the salted water in a pan. Bring to the boil, stir once, cover and simmer for 12 minutes, or until the rice is tender and the liquid absorbed. Place in a warm serving dish and keep hot.

Trim the celery, remove any strings and divide thick stems in half lengthways. Cut into thin slices. Peel and roughly chop the onion. Heat the oil in a pan, add the onion and celery and cook, stirring, until the onion is transparent. Put in the meat, add a little seasoning and cook, stirring frequently, for 15 minutes. Mix in the mushrooms and liquid from the can and stir well. Cover and simmer again for a further 5 minutes. Adjust the seasoning to taste with salt and pepper. Serve with the rice, sprinkled with parsley.

Rice ring
Serves 4

Ingredients	Metric-Imperial	American
1 onion		
Butter	15 g/½ oz	1 tbs
Long grain rice	250 g/9 oz	generous 1 cup
Beef stock (bouillon)	500 ml/18 fl oz	2¼ cups
Oil	1 tbs	1 tbs
Salt		

Peel and chop the onion. Melt the butter in a pan and use to fry the onion until transparent. Add the rice, stock and oil and season to taste with salt if necessary. Bring to the boil, stir once, cover and simmer for 12 minutes, or until the rice is tender and the liquid absorbed. Press into a greased ring mould and turn out on a warm serving dish.

Spinach rice
Serves 4

Ingredients	Metric-Imperial	American
Long grain rice	250 g/9 oz	generous 1 cup
2 onions		
Butter or margarine	50 g/2 oz	¼ cup
Frozen chopped spinach	400 g/14 oz	14 oz
Salt and pepper		
Ground nutmeg		

Add the rice to a pan of salted water, bring to the boil and stir once. Cover and simmer for 12 minutes, or until the rice is tender. Drain, refresh briefly with cold water and drain again.

Peel and chop the onions. Melt the butter or margarine and use to fry the onion until soft. Add the spinach and cook, stirring frequently, for about 10 minutes, adding a little water if the mixture becomes dry. Season to taste with salt, pepper and nutmeg, add the rice and reheat carefully. Serve topped with fried eggs.

Three kings rice with hare
Serves 4

Ingredients	Metric-Imperial	American
4 small legs of hare		
1 onion		
2 bay leaves		
2 juniper berries		
Red wine	750 ml/1¼ pints	3 cups
Oil	2 tbs	3 tbs
Whipping cream	125 ml/4 fl oz	½ cup
Salt and pepper		
Sugar		
Butter	1 tbs	1 tbs
Long grain rice	250 g/9 oz	generous 1 cup
Salted water	500 ml/18 fl oz	2¼ cups
1–3 whole cloves		
½ cinnamon stick		
Chopped candied peel	75 g/3 oz	½ cup

Remove any membrane from the hare legs, wash and pat dry. Place in a dish. Peel and quarter the onion and add to the hare with the bay leaves and juniper berries. Pour over the wine, making sure that the meat is covered. Put a lid on the dish and leave in a cool place for at least 24 hours, turning the hare portions occasionally. Remove the hare and pat dry. Strain the marinade and reserve.

Heat the oil in a pan, put in the hare portions and brown on both sides. Measure 500 ml/18 fl oz (2¼ cups) of the marinade, add to the pan and bring to the boil. Cook gently for about 2 hours, putting in a little more marinade as the liquid evaporates. Remove the hare from the pan. Reduce the cooking liquid by rapid boiling until it measures about 250 ml/9 fl oz (generous 1 cup). Stir in the cream and adjust the seasoning to taste with salt, pepper and sugar. Return the hare to the sauce and keep hot.

Meanwhile, melt the butter in a separate pan, add the rice and cook until it is translucent. Pour in the salted water, add the cloves and cinnamon and bring to the boil. Cover and simmer for 5 minutes. Put in the candied peel, cover the pan again and simmer for a further 7 minutes, or until the rice is tender and the liquid absorbed. Remove the cinnamon stick before serving the rice mixture with the hare.

Opposite: Rice with pork and celery
Below: Three kings rice with hare

Baked rice layered with minced meat and sauerkraut
Serves 4

Ingredients	Metric-Imperial	American
Long grain rice	250 g/9 oz	generous 1 cup
Salted water	500 ml/18 fl oz	2¼ cups
1 clove of garlic		
1 onion		
Oil	1 tbs	1 tbs
Minced beef and pork combined (ground)	450 g/1 lb	1 lb
Salt and pepper		
Caraway seeds		
Sweet paprika pepper	5 tbs	6 tbs
Beef stock (bouillon)	350 ml/12 fl oz	1½ cups
Canned drained sauerkraut	450 g/1 lb	1 lb
Sour cream	150 ml/¼ pint	⅔ cup
Snipped chives	2 tbs	3 tbs

Put the rice into a pan, add the salted water and bring to the boil. Stir once, cover and simmer for 12 minutes, or until the rice is tender and the liquid absorbed.

Peel and chop the garlic and onion. Heat the oil in a pan, add the onion and garlic and fry until transparent. Put in the

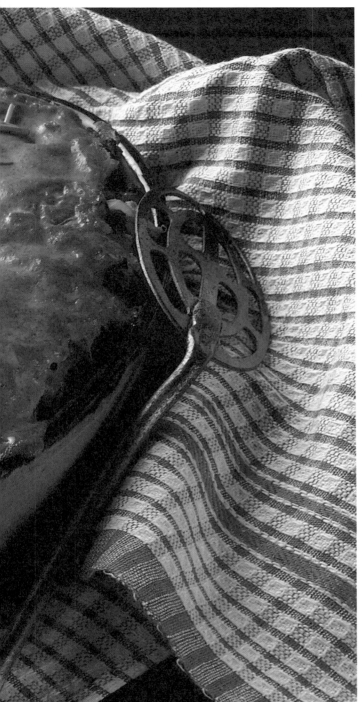

Elegant rice salad
Serves 4

Ingredients	Metric-Imperial	American
Long grain rice	40 g/1½ oz	scant ¼ cup
White wine vinegar	2 tbs	3 tbs
Dry white wine	2 tbs	3 tbs
Oil	4 tbs	5 tbs
Salt and white pepper		
Green peppercorns	1 tbs	1 tbs
Chopped dill weed	3 tbs	4 tbs
1 ripe melon such as cantaloup or ogen		
Shelled cooked prawns (shrimp)	225 g/8 oz	8 oz

Cook the rice in boiling salted water for 12 minutes, or until tender. Drain, refresh briefly with cold water and drain again. Transfer to a bowl.

Beat together the vinegar, wine and oil and season to taste with salt and pepper. Add the peppercorns and dill.

Halve the melon, cutting a vandyked edge on one half. Discard the seeds and scoop out the flesh using a ball cutter, or dice it.

Add the melon balls or dice to the rice with the prawns. Pour over the dressing and toss the ingredients together lightly. Serve piled up in one melon half.

meat and cook, stirring, until it is brown and crumbly. Season to taste with salt, pepper, a few caraway seeds and half the paprika. Pour in the stock and stir until boiling. Cover and simmer for 5 minutes.

Loosen the sauerkraut with 2 forks and arrange half of it in an even layer in the base of a greased ovenproof dish. Cover with the rice then spoon the meat mixture over this. Top with the remaining sauerkraut. Cover the dish and place in a preheated hot oven, 220°C, 425°F, Gas Mark 7, for about 30 minutes. Mix together the sour cream and remaining paprika and spoon evenly over the ingredients in the dish. Return to the oven and cook, uncovered, for a further 25 minutes. Serve garnished with chives.

Savoury potato pudding
Serves 4

Ingredients	Metric-Imperial	American
Potatoes	750 g/1¾ lb	1¾ lb
3 eggs		
Butter or margarine	75 g/3 oz	⅓ cup
Grated cheese	100 g/4 oz	1 cup
Salt	2 tsp	2 tsp
Ground nutmeg	¼ tsp	¼ tsp
To line the mould:		
Butter or margarine for greasing		
Dried breadcrumbs	2 tbs	3 tbs

Peel the potatoes and cut into pieces. Cook in lightly salted water until soft then drain and mash while still hot. Leave to cool. Separate the eggs. Reserve a little of the butter, beat the remainder until soft and gradually add to the potato with the egg yolks, cheese, salt and nutmeg. Whisk the egg whites until stiff and fold into the potato mixture.

Generously grease a large fluted heatproof mould. Put in the breadcrumbs and turn the mould until the sides and base are evenly coated. Spoon in the potato mixture but do not fill the mould more than three quarters full, to allow the pudding room to rise. Cover with foil. Stand the mould in a pan and pour in boiling water to come half-way up the sides. Cover the pan and boil gently for 1¼ hours.

Turn the pudding out on to a heated plate. Melt the reserved butter and pour over the pudding.

Potato goulash
Serves 4

Ingredients	Metric-Imperial	American
Potatoes	1 kg/2¼ lb	2¼ lb
3 onions		
Margarine	50 g/2 oz	¼ cup
Flour	40 g/1½ oz	⅓ cup
Milk	600 ml/1 pint	2½ cups
Boiling sausage	450 g/1 lb	1 lb
Chopped parsley	4 tbs	5 tbs
Apple juice	3 tbs	4 tbs
Salt and pepper		
Ground mace	½ tsp	½ tsp

Scrub the potatoes, place in a pan and add cold water just to cover. Bring to the boil, cover and simmer for 20 minutes, or until the potatoes are tender. Drain, peel while still warm and cut into thick slices.

Peel and finely chop the onions. Cook in the margarine in a large pan until transparent. Sprinkle on the flour and stir well. Blend in the milk and stir until boiling. Cook for 3 minutes. Peel and dice the sausage. Fold the sausage, potato slices, parsley and apple juice into the sauce and season to taste with salt, pepper and the mace. Serve hot.

Below: Savoury potato pudding
Opposite: Potato goulash

Potatoes in Emmental cheese

(Using a pressure cooker)
Serves 4

Ingredients	Metric-Imperial	American
Potatoes	1 kg/2¼ lb	2¼ lb
Streaky bacon (strips)	100 g/4 oz	8 strips
2 onions		
Grated Emmental cheese	100 g/4 oz	1 cup
Dried marjoram	½ tsp	½ tsp
Ground nutmeg	¼ tsp	¼ tsp
Salt and freshly ground black pepper		
Beef or chicken stock (bouillon)	300 ml/½ pint	1¼ cups
Snipped chives	2 tbs	3 tbs

Peel and dice the potatoes. Chop the bacon and place in the open pressure cooker. Heat gently until the fat runs. Peel and slice the onions and cook in the bacon fat until transparent. Add the potato, cheese, marjoram, nutmeg and salt and pepper to taste. Mix well together and pour in the stock. Close the cooker and bring to full pressure. Cook for about 12 minutes. Transfer to a warm serving dish and sprinkle with the chives.

Serving ideas: Serve the potatoes with grilled or poached fish, gammon steaks or lamb cutlets.

Potatoes cooked in stock

Serves 4

Ingredients	Metric-Imperial	American
Potatoes	1 kg/2¼ lb	2¼ lb
Beef stock (bouillon)	600 ml/1 pint	2½ cups
Salt		
Butter	15 g/½ oz	1 tbs
Chopped parsley	1 tbs	1 tbs

Peel and dice the potatoes. Bring the stock to the boil in a large pan, add the potato and cook for 10 minutes, or until tender. Season to taste with salt and stir in the butter. Sprinkle with parsley and serve with fish, ham or boiled beef.

Variation: Strips of peeled carrot may be cooked with the potatoes.

Simple mashed potatoes

Serves 4

Ingredients	Metric-Imperial	American
Potatoes	1 kg/2¼ lb	2¼ lb
Butter	75 g/3 oz	⅓ cup
Hot milk	250 ml/9 fl oz	generous 1 cup
Salt		
Ground nutmeg	½ tsp	½ tsp

Peel and dice the potatoes and place in a pan with salted water to cover. Bring to the boil, cover and simmer for about 10 minutes, or until tender.
 Drain the potatoes and mash immediately in the pan. Add the butter and hot milk and beat over gentle heat until smooth. Season to taste with salt and the nutmeg.

Variation: Decorate the mashed potato with onion rings or breadcrumbs fried in butter until golden brown.

Saucy potatoes

Serves 4

Ingredients	Metric-Imperial	American
Potatoes	1 kg/2¼ lb	2¼ lb
For the sauce:		
2 small onions		
Diced ham	50 g/2 oz	⅓ cup
Butter or margarine	40 g/1½ oz	3 tbs
Flour	40 g/1½ oz	⅓ cup
Milk	300 ml/½ pint	1¼ cups
Beef stock (bouillon)	300 ml/½ pint	1¼ cups
Salt and pepper		
Ground nutmeg		
Chopped parsley	2 tbs	3 tbs

Scrub the potatoes, place in a pan with salted water to cover and bring to the boil. Cover and simmer for about 20 minutes, or until tender. Drain and peel while still warm. Leave to cool and cut into slices.

To make the sauce, peel and chop the onions. Fry with the ham in the butter or margarine until transparent. Sprinkle in the flour and cook, stirring, until the roux is golden. Blend in the milk and stock and stir until boiling. Simmer for 5 minutes.

If preferred, strain the sauce before adding the potato slices. Reheat, season to taste with salt, pepper and nutmeg and serve sprinkled with parsley.

Herbed mashed potatoes with scrambled eggs and ham
Serves 4

Ingredients	Metric-Imperial	American
Potatoes	1 kg/2¼ lb	2¼ lb
Butter	100 g/4 oz	½ cup
Salt and freshly ground black pepper		
Snipped chives	1 tsp	1 tsp
Chopped parsley or other fresh herb	1 tsp	1 tsp
Hot milk	300 ml/½ pint	1¼ cups
Ground nutmeg	¼ tsp	¼ tsp
6 eggs		
Cold water	100 ml/4 fl oz	½ cup
Cooked ham	100 g/4 oz	4 oz

Peel the potatoes and cut into pieces. Place in a pan with just enough salted water to cover. Bring to the boil and cook, covered, for 20 minutes, or until the potatoes are tender. Drain and mash immediately.

Soften three quarters of the butter and beat into the potato with 1 tsp salt and the herbs. Pour in the hot milk, return the pan to the heat and beat until smooth and fluffy. Season to taste with pepper and nutmeg and keep hot.

Beat the eggs with the water and season to taste with salt and pepper. Cut the ham into strips. Melt the remaining butter in a shallow pan, put in the ham and egg mixture and stir over low heat until creamy. Serve at once with the mashed potato, before the eggs become dry.

Serving suggestion: Accompany with a tomato salad.

Opposite: Potatoes with Emmental cheese
Above: Herbed mashed potatoes with scrambled eggs and ham

Potato omelette
Serves 4

Ingredients	Metric-Imperial	American
Potatoes	450 g/1 lb	1 lb
2 small onions		
Streaky bacon (strips)	75 g/3 oz	6 strips
Salt and pepper		
3 eggs		
Milk	125 ml/4 fl oz	½ cup
Chopped parsley	1 tbs	1·tbs

Cook potatoes until tender, drain and peel, cool and slice.
Peel and chop onions, chop bacon. Fry bacon in omelette pan, add onion and potato. Season, fry until golden. Beat the eggs with milk and parsley. Pour over the potatoes, cook without stirring until set.

Above: Potato omelette
Opposite: Peasant's breakfast

Peasant's breakfast
Serves 4

Ingredients	Metric-Imperial	American
New potatoes	750 g/1¾ lb	1¾ lb
4 small onions		
Streaky bacon (strips)	75 g/3 oz	6 strips
Butter	25 g/1 oz	2 tbs
3 eggs		
Milk	3 tbs	4 tbs
Diced red sweet pepper	2 tbs	3 tbs
Diced cooked ham	100 g/4 oz	⅔ cup
Ground nutmeg	¼ tsp	¼ tsp
Snipped chives	3 tbs	4 tbs

Cook potatoes until tender, drain and peel, cool and slice.
Peel and chop onions and bacon. Fry in butter until onion is transparent. Add potato, cook until brown. Beat together remaining ingredients, pour over potatoes, cook without stirring until set.

	Metric-Imperial	American
Flour	2 tbs	3 tbs
3 eggs		
Salt and freshly ground black pepper		
Snipped chives	50 g/2 oz	⅔ cup
Sugar	¼ tsp	¼ tsp
Cream cheese	450 g/1 lb	2 cups
Milk	125 ml/4 fl oz	½ cup
Lemon juice	1 tbs	1 tbs
1 clove of garlic		
Cooked ham	100 g/4 oz	4 oz
Chopped parsley	1 tbs	1 tbs
White vegetable fat	150 g/5 oz	⅔ cup

Peel and finely grate the potatoes and onions. Stir in the flour, eggs and a little salt. Fold in half the chives.

Mix almost all the remaining chives with the sugar, cream cheese, milk and lemon juice. Season to taste with salt, pepper and a little lemon juice. Peel and finely chop the garlic and finely dice the ham. Stir the garlic, ham and parsley into the cream cheese mixture.

Melt a little of the fat in a frying pan, put in 2 tbs of the potato pancake mixture, press flat and fry until golden brown on both sides. Remove from the pan and make further pancakes in the same way, adding extra fat as necessary. Keep hot. To serve, place one pancake on a warm plate, spread with cheese filling, top with another pancake and sprinkle with chives.

Potatoes baked in foil
Serves 4–8

Ingredients	Metric-Imperial	American
8 medium-sized potatoes	150–175 g/ 5–6 oz each	5–6 oz each
Butter		

Scrub and dry the potatoes. Wrap individually in foil and place on a baking sheet (cookie sheet). Place in a preheated moderately hot oven, 200°C, 400°F, Gas Mark 6, for 40–60 minutes, or until the potatoes are tender when pressed.

Open the foil parcels, cut a deep cross into each potato and squeeze gently so that the top opens. Put a knob of butter on each potato.

Serving suggestion: Top with herbed cottage or cream cheese, sour cream mixed with snipped chives or grated Cheddar cheese.

Potato pancakes with cream cheese filling
Serves 4

Ingredients	Metric-Imperial	American
Potatoes	1 kg/2¼ lb	2¼ lb
2 small onions		

Potato croquettes
Serves 4

Ingredients	Metric-Imperial	American
Potatoes	750 g/1¾ lb	1¾ lb
2 egg yolks		
Cornflour (cornstarch)	2 tsp	2 tsp
Salt		
Ground nutmeg		
1 egg		
Fresh breadcrumbs	50 g/2 oz	1 cup
Oil for deep frying		

Peel the potatoes, place in a pan with salted water to cover and bring to the boil. Cover and simmer for about 20 minutes, or until the potatoes are tender. Drain well, mash and leave to cool.

Stir the egg yolks and cornflour into the potatoes and season to taste with salt and nutmeg. Beat the egg and place in a dish, have the breadcrumbs on a plate. Form the potato mixture into small rolls about 2 cm/¾ inch in diameter and 5 cm/2 inches long. Dip in the beaten egg and coat with breadcrumbs.

Heat the oil in a pan and cook the croquettes for about 2–3 minutes, until golden brown all over. Drain well on absorbent kitchen paper and serve hot.

Above: Potatoes baked in foil
Opposite: Potato pancakes with cream cheese filling

Swiss pan-fried potato cakes
Serves 4

Ingredients	Metric-Imperial	American
Potatoes	1 kg/2¼ lb	2¼ lb
Butter or margarine		
Salt		

Scrub the potatoes, place in a pan and add salted water to cover. Bring to the boil, cover and simmer for about 20 minutes, or until tender. Drain, peel and leave to cool. Grate coarsely.

Melt 40 g/1½ oz (3 tbs) butter or margarine in a pan, put in half the potatoes, sprinkle with salt and press flat. Cook until the underneath is brown. Turn, adding a little more fat to the pan. Cook again until golden brown underneath. Remove from the pan and keep hot. Make another potato cake in the same way. Divide each potato cake in half, using a metal spatula,, before serving.

Serving idea: These crispy potato cakes are delicious with fried meat and green salad, or as an accompaniment to breakfast eggs and bacon.

Grated potato pancakes
Serves 4

Ingredients	Metric-Imperial	American
Flour	450 g/1 lb	4 cups
Dried yeast	1 tbs	1 tbs
Potatoes	1 kg/2¼ lb	2¼ lb
2 eggs		
Salt	2 tsp	2 tsp
Lukewarm milk	125 ml/4 fl oz	½ cup
Seedless raisins	225 g/8 oz	1⅓ cups
Oil	200 ml/7 fl oz	scant 1 cup

Sift, flour into bowl, mix in yeast. Peel and finely grate potatoes. Combine potato with eggs, salt and milk, mix into flour and yeast. Beat in electric mixer first on medium speed then on high for 3 minutes. Stir in raisins. Cover, leave in warm place until double in size. Beat at high speed for 2 minutes.

Heat oil in pan and add mixture, a small ladleful at a time. Flatten and fry until golden on both sides.

Potato pizza
Serves 4–6

Ingredients	Metric-Imperial	American
Potatoes	1¼ kg/2¾ lb	2¾ lb
Whipping cream	300 ml/½ pint	1¼ cups
4 eggs		
Salt and pepper		
Chopped oregano	2 tsp	2 tsp
Grated Parmesan cheese	100 g/4 oz	1 cup
Butter		
Tomatoes	450 g/1 lb	1 lb
Mozzarella cheese	275 g/10 oz	10 oz
Sliced salami	100 g/4 oz	4 oz

Peel the potatoes. Combine the cream and eggs. Coarsely grate the potatoes and add to the cream mixture. Stir in salt to taste, the oregano and Parmesan. Grease an ovenproof dish, put in the potato mixture and press flat. Dot lightly with flakes of butter and place in the top of a preheated moderately hot oven, 200°C, 400°F, Gas Mark 6, for about

20 minutes. Meanwhile, slice the tomatoes and Mozzarella.

Arrange tomato slices on the pizza base, sprinkle with salt then cover with salami and finally with cheese slices. Return to the centre of the oven and bake for 20 minutes. Turn off the heat and leave the pizza in the oven for a further 5 minutes. Serve sprinkled with pepper.

Opposite: Swiss pan-fried potato cake
Above: Grated potato pancakes

339

Artichokes with vinaigrette sauce
Serves 4

Ingredients	Metric-Imperial	American
4 trimmed artichokes		
Vinegar	3 tbs	4 tbs
For the sauce:		
Oil	150 ml/¼ pint	⅔ cup
Vinegar	3 tbs	4 tbs
Prepared mustard	1 tsp	1 tsp
Chopped parsley	1 tbs	1 tbs
Snipped chives	1 tbs	1 tbs
Pinch of dried chervil		
Pinch of dried basil		
Salt and pepper		

Cover the artichokes with salted water and leave to stand for 30 minutes. Drain.

Bring a pan of salted water to the boil, put in the vinegar and artichokes and simmer, covered, for 30–40 minutes, or until a leaf will easily pull away. Leave the artichokes upside-down to drain and cool.

For the vinaigrette sauce, beat together the oil, vinegar and mustard and stir in the herbs. Season to taste with salt and pepper.

How to eat artichokes: Place each artichoke on a plate with the sauce in a small container separately. Remove each leaf, dip the lower end into the sauce and strip the fleshy part of the leaf with your teeth, discarding the remainder. When all the leaves are disposed of, remove the inedible 'choke' fibres from the artichoke bottom with a knife. Dice the artichoke bottom and eat with the remaining sauce.

Simply boiled asparagus
Serves 4

Ingredients	Metric-Imperial	American
Asparagus	1 kg/2¼ lb	2¼ lb
Salt		
Sugar		
Butter	50 g/2 oz	¼ cup
Fresh breadcrumbs	2 tbs	3 tbs

Trim the asparagus into equal lengths, cutting away any woody sections. Lay the stalks side by side in a large shallow pan. Make a small roll of crumpled foil and place underneath the asparagus tips. Pour in water to cover the stalks, leaving the tips just above the surface. Add a little salt and sugar and bring to the boil. Cover the pan and simmer for about 20 minutes, or until tender. The delicate tips of the asparagus will cook in the steam. Drain carefully, place on a warm serving dish and keep hot.

Melt the butter in a small pan and stir in the breadcrumbs. Fry until just golden brown and serve sprinkled over the asparagus.

Serving suggestion: Omit the fried crumbs, sprinkle the asparagus with chopped herbs and serve with Hollandaise sauce.

Simply cooked leeks
Serves 4

Ingredients	Metric-Imperial	American
Trimmed leeks	1 kg/2¼ lb	2¼ lb
Butter or margarine	40 g/1½ oz	3 tbs
Water	125 ml/4 fl oz	½ cup
Salt		
Ground nutmeg		
Whipping cream	2 tbs	3 tbs
Chopped parsley	1 tbs	1 tbs

Clean the leeks and cut into short even lengths. Melt the butter or margarine in a pan and turn the leek pieces in it until coated. Add the water and a little salt and nutmeg and bring to the boil. Cover and simmer for about 10 minutes, or until the leek is tender.

Stir in the cream and adjust the seasoning if necessary. Just before serving, sprinkle with parsley.

Opposite: Artichokes with vinaigrette sauce
Below: Simply cooked leeks

Broad beans with meatballs
Serves 4

Ingredients	Metric-Imperial	American
Shelled broad beans (fava or lima)	675 g/1½ lb	4 cups
Water	600 ml/1 pint	2½ cups
Salt		
For the meatballs:		
1 white bread roll		
1 onion		
Pork sausagemeat (bulk pork sausage)	225 g/8 oz	8 oz
Minced beef and pork combined (ground)	225 g/8 oz	8 oz
1 egg		
Salt and pepper		
Sweet paprika pepper		
For the sauce:		
Streaky bacon (strips)	50 g/2 oz	4 strips
1 onion		
Oil	1 tbs	1 tbs
Flour	40 g/1½ oz	⅓ cup
Tomatoes	550 g/1¼ lb	1¼ lb
Tomato purée (paste)	2 tbs	3 tbs
2 wedge portions foil-wrapped processed cheese		
Chopped parsley	2 tbs	3 tbs

Put the beans into a pan, add the water and a little salt and bring to the boil. Cover and simmer for 10–12 minutes, or until tender. Drain and reserve the cooking liquid.

To make the meatballs, soften the bread roll in cold water, squeeze out the moisture and crumble roughly. Peel and chop the onion. Mix with the sausagemeat, minced beef and pork, egg and breadcrumbs. Season with salt, pepper and paprika. Form the meat mixture into even-sized balls with floured hands.

Put the reserved liquid into a pan and bring to the boil. Add the meatballs and simmer for 7 minutes. Remove with a slotted spoon, drain and keep hot. Make up the cooking liquid to 500 ml/18 fl oz (2¼ cups) with water.

Chop the bacon and peel and chop the onion. Heat the oil in a clean pan, add the bacon and onion and cook until the onion is soft. Stir in the flour. Roughly chop three quarters of the tomatoes, add to the pan with the cooking liquid and stir until boiling. Simmer for 5 minutes. Sieve the sauce and return it to the pan. Adjust the seasoning to taste. Put in the tomato purée and cheese and reheat, stirring, until the cheese has melted.

Carefully mix the beans and meatballs into the sauce and reheat thoroughly. Peel the remaining tomatoes, quarter and scoop out the seeds. Dice the flesh and stir into the bean mixture. Transfer to a hot serving dish and sprinkle with parsley.

French beans Parma style
(Using a pressure cooker)
Serves 4

Ingredients	Metric-Imperial	American
French beans (green)	450 g/1 lb	1 lb
Mushrooms	150 g/5 oz	5 oz
Tomatoes	225 g/8 oz	8 oz
Streaky bacon (strips)	50 g/2 oz	4 strips
1 onion		
Dried savory	½ tsp	½ tsp
Pinch of dried oregano		
Beef stock (bouillon)	125 ml/4 fl oz	½ cup
Salt and pepper		
Grated Parmesan cheese	40 g/1½ oz	⅓ cup

Top and tail the beans and break into even lengths. Quarter the mushrooms. Peel and quarter the tomatoes. Chop the bacon and heat gently in the open pressure cooker until the fat runs. Peel and chop the onion and fry in the bacon fat until transparent. Add the beans, tomatoes and mushrooms, sprinkle in the herbs and pour over the stock. Season to taste with salt and pepper.

Close the cooker and bring to full pressure. Cook for about 5 minutes. Transfer to a hot serving dish and sprinkle with the cheese.

Above: French beans Parma style
Opposite: Broad beans with meatballs

Simply cooked broad beans
Serves 4

Ingredients	Metric-Imperial	American
Streaky bacon (strips)	100 g/4 oz	8 strips
3 onions		
Shelled broad beans (fava or lima)	750 g/1¾ lb	4½ cups
Dried savory	½ tsp	½ tsp
Water	125 ml/4 fl oz	½ cup
Salt		
Snipped chives	1 tbs	1 tbs

Chop the bacon, place in a pan and heat gently until the fat runs. Peel and slice the onions and divide into rings. Fry in the bacon fat until golden brown. Add the beans and savory and cook, stirring, for 2 minutes. Pour in the water, add a little salt and bring to the boil. Cover the pan, reduce the heat and simmer for about 10–12 minutes, or until the beans are tender.

Drain the beans, season with more salt if necessary and serve sprinkled with chives.

Braised tomatoes
Serves 4

Ingredients	Metric-Imperial	American
Tomatoes	450 g/1 lb	1 lb
Butter or margarine	50 g/2 oz	¼ cup
Salt and freshly ground pepper		
Chopped parsley or snipped chives	1 tbs	1 tbs

Pour boiling water over the tomatoes, drain and peel. Melt the butter or margarine in a deep frying pan with a lid. Put in the tomatoes, arranging them side by side. Season the tomatoes with salt and pepper, cover the pan and cook gently for about 10 minutes. Serve the tomatoes sprinkled with parsley or chives.

Variations: Marjoram or basil would also give a delicious flavour to these tomatoes instead of parsley or chives.
Serving ideas: Serve the tomatoes with grilled or fried steak, hamburgers or grilled fish.

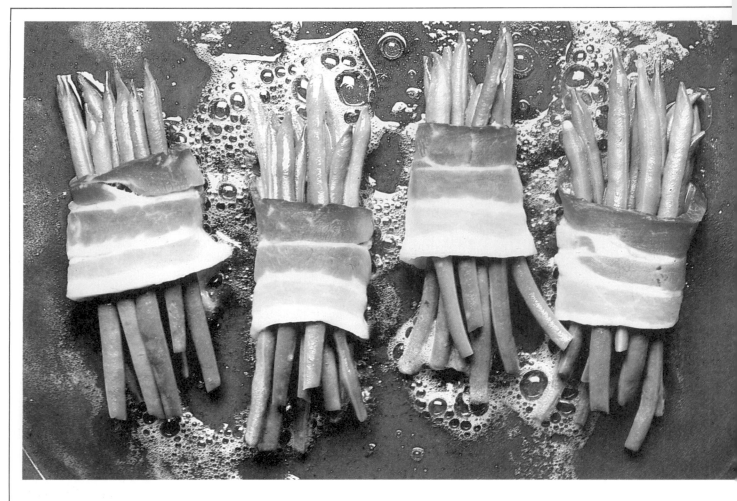

French bean bundles in bacon
Serves 4

Ingredients	Metric-Imperial	American
French beans (green)	450 g/1 lb	1 lb
Dried savory	½ tsp	½ tsp
8 rashers streaky bacon (16 strips)		
Butter	40 g/1½ oz	3 tbs

Top and tail the beans. Put them into a pan with the savory and add water almost to cover. Bring to the boil, cover and simmer for about 7 minutes, or until tender. Drain well and divide into 8 equal portions. Wrap each portion in bacon and secure with a wooden cocktail stick (toothpick).

Melt the butter in a frying pan and use to cook the bean bundles for about 3 minutes on each side, or until the bacon is cooked. Remove the sticks before serving.

Kohlrabi in cheese sauce
Serves 4

Ingredients	Metric-Imperial	American
Butter or margarine	25 g/1 oz	2 tbs
Diced kohlrabi	1 kg/2¼ lb	6 cups
Beef stock (bouillon)	300 ml/½ pint	1¼ cups
For the sauce:		
Margarine	25 g/1 oz	2 tbs
Flour	25 g/1 oz	¼ cup
2 wedge portions foil-wrapped processed cheese		
Chopped mixed herbs	1 tbs	1 tbs

Melt the butter or margarine in a pan, add the kohlrabi and cook, stirring occasionally, for 3 minutes. Add the stock, bring to the boil, cover and simmer for about 10 minutes, or until the kohlrabi is tender. Drain and reserve the cooking liquid. Keep hot.

To make the sauce, melt the margarine in a pan, sprinkle in the flour and cook, stirring, until golden brown. Make up the reserved liquid to 350 ml/12 fl oz (1½ cups) with water. Gradually add to the pan and stir until boiling. Simmer for 5 minutes. Put in the cheese and cook, stirring, until melted. Mix the kohlrabi gently into the sauce, reheat and serve sprinkled with the herbs.

Above: French bean bundles in bacon
Opposite: French beans with hollandaise sauce

French beans African style with shredded coconut
Serves 4

Ingredients	Metric-Imperial	American
French beans (green)	450 g/1 lb	1 lb
Dried tarragon	½ tsp	½ tsp
Salt		
Butter	65 g/2½ oz	5 tbs
Shredded coconut	75 g/3 oz	1 cup
Ground coriander	¼ tsp	¼ tsp
Ground turmeric	½ tsp	½ tsp
Pinch of cayenne pepper		

Top and tail the beans. Place in a pan with the tarragon and add water just to cover and a little salt. Bring to the boil, cover and simmer for about 7 minutes, or until tender. Drain well. Add 15 g/½ oz (1 tbs) of the butter and keep hot.

Melt the remaining butter in a pan and sprinkle in the coconut, coriander, turmeric and cayenne. Cook, stirring, until the coconut begins to brown. Place the beans in a warm serving dish and scatter the browned spiced coconut evenly over them.

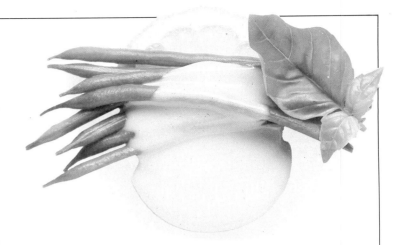

Salsify in bacon sauce
Serves 4

Ingredients	Metric-Imperial	American
Salsify (scorzonera)	1 kg/2¼ lb	2¼ lb
Water	1 L/1¾ pints	4⅓ cups
Flour	2 tbs	3 tbs
Vinegar	4 tbs	5 tbs
Water	about 350 ml/12 fl oz	1½ cups
Salt		
For the sauce:		
Streaky bacon (strips)	50 g/2 oz	4 strips
Butter	25 g/1 oz	2 tbs
Flour	25 g/1 oz	¼ cup
Milk	125 ml/4 fl oz	½ cup
1 egg yolk		
Chopped parsley		

Clean and peel the salsify. Put the water into a bowl and whisk in the flour and half the vinegar. Add the salsify and leave to stand for 10 minutes.

Put the second quantity of water into a pan with 1 tsp salt and the remaining vinegar. Drain the salsify, cut into chunks and add to the pan. Bring to the boil, cover and simmer for about 35 minutes, or until tender. Drain the salsify, reserving the cooking liquid. Keep hot.

To make the sauce, chop the bacon. Melt the butter in a pan, add the bacon and fry until golden. Sprinkle in the flour and cook, stirring, until pale brown. Make up the reserved liquid to 350 ml/12 fl oz (1½ cups) with water and add the milk. Gradually whisk this liquid into the roux and bring back to the boil. Simmer for 5 minutes. Beat the egg yolk with a little cold water, blend into the sauce and add the salsify. Reheat but do not allow to boil. If necessary adjust the seasoning with more salt.

French beans with hollandaise sauce
Serves 4

Ingredients	Metric-Imperial	American
French beans (green)	750 g/1¾ lb	1¾ lb
Dried basil	½ tsp	½ tsp
For the sauce:		
Butter	75 g/3 oz	⅓ cup
5 egg yolks		
Grated rind and juice of 1 lemon		
Water	2 tbs	3 tbs
Few drops Tabasco		
Salt and pepper		

Top and tail the beans. Place in a pan with the basil, cover with lightly salted water and bring to the boil. Cover and simmer for about 7 minutes, or until the beans are tender. Drain and keep hot.

To make the sauce, melt the butter and skim off the foam. Set aside. Place the egg yolks, lemon rind and juice, the water, Tabasco and a little salt and pepper in the top of a double boiler or a bowl over a pan of simmering water. Whisk with an electric mixer for about 5 minutes, or until foamy and slightly thickened. Remove from the heat and gradually whisk in the melted butter. Adjust the seasoning if necessary, pour the sauce over the beans and serve at once.

Microwave method
Top and tail the beans. Place in a suitable microwave dish with 125 ml/4 fl oz/½ cup water. Cover and cook on full power for 8 minutes. Allow to stand for 5 minutes.

To make the sauce; melt the butter in the microwave on full power for 2 minutes. Put the egg yolks, salt and white pepper in a pyrex bowl with 1 teaspoon of water and a few drops of lemon juice. Whisk this mixture together and gradually whisk in some of the foaming butter. Place on full power for 1 minute, remove and whisk again adding a little butter at a time. Return for 1 minute on full power and whisk again. Add a little more lemon juice and lemon rind to taste with a drop of Tabasco sauce. Whisk well and if the sauce is not yet thick enough, return to the microwave for another 30 seconds at a time until thick. Whisk constantly.

Drain the beans, sprinkle with basil and return to the microwave on full power for 3 minutes. Stir round and serve with the sauce poured over.

If the sauce has to be kept warm, stand it in a dish of hot not boiling water.

Traditional red cabbage
Serves 4

Ingredients	Metric-Imperial	American
Red cabbage	1 kg/2¼ lb	2¼ lb
1 large onion		
3 tart dessert apples		
Meat dripping	65 g/2½ oz	5 tbs
1 bay leaf		
3 whole cloves		
Salt	1 tsp	1 tsp
Sugar	1 tsp	1 tsp
Vinegar	2 tbs	3 tbs
Water	125 ml/4 fl oz	½ cup
Flour	1 tbs	1 tbs
Pepper		

Discard the rough outer leaves of the cabbage, quarter and remove the core. Finely slice the cabbage. Peel and chop the onion. Peel, quarter, core and thinly slice the apples.

Melt the dripping in a pan, and use to fry the onion until golden. Add the cabbage and apple and cook, stirring, for 2 minutes. Put in the bay leaf, cloves, salt, sugar, vinegar and water. Bring to the boil, cover and simmer for about 25 minutes.

Moisten the flour with a little cold water, stir well into the cabbage mixture and cook for a further 5 minutes. Taste and adjust the seasoning, adding extra salt, sugar and vinegar if liked, with a little pepper.

Variations: Instead of water, use red or white wine, or add 1 tbs redcurrant jelly with the sugar when cooking the cabbage.

Microwave method
Discard the rough outer leaves of the cabbage, quarter the cabbage and remove the core; slice thinly. Peel and chop the onion. Peel, quarter, core and thinly slice the apples.

Place a browning dish in the microwave for 2 minutes on full power, add the dripping and switch on for 1 minute. Stir in the onion and apples and cook for 4 minutes.

Put the cabbage in a large pyrex bowl with the bay leaf, cloves, salt, sugar, vinegar and water. Tip in the apples and onion and mix well with the cabbage, cover and cook for 10 minutes on full power. Remove and stir the ingredients well. Return to the microwave on full power for a further 10 minutes and allow to stand for 5 minutes. Taste and adjust seasoning. Do not use the flour.

French beans with mushrooms in tomato sauce
Serves 4

Ingredients	Metric-Imperial	American
French beans (green)	450 g/1 lb	1 lb
Dried thyme	½ tsp	½ tsp
Streaky bacon (strips)	75 g/3 oz	6 strips
Butter or margarine	25 g/1 oz	2 tbs
1 onion		
Mushrooms	225 g/8 oz	8 oz
Salt and pepper		
Tomatoes	350 g/12 oz	12 oz

Top and tail the beans and cut into pieces. Place in a pan with lightly salted water just to cover and add the thyme.

Bring to the boil, cover and simmer for 7 minutes, or until the beans are tender. Drain and keep hot.

Chop the bacon and heat in a large pan until the fat runs. Add the butter or margarine. Peel and finely chop the onion and cook in the fat until transparent. Slice the mushrooms, add to the pan and season to taste with salt and pepper. Cook for about 5 minutes, stirring frequently. Pour boiling water over the tomatoes, drain, peel and halve. Remove the seeds and dice the flesh. Carefully combine the beans, mushrooms and tomato in the pan and reheat thoroughly.

White cabbage with caraway seeds
Serves 4

Ingredients	Metric-Imperial	American
White cabbage	1 kg/2¼ lb	2¼ lb
1 onion		
Margarine	75 g/3 oz	⅓ cup
Caraway seeds	1 tsp	1 tsp
Water	125 ml/4 fl oz	½ cup
Salt	1 tsp	1 tsp
Cornflour (cornstarch)	1 tsp	1 tsp

Discard the tough outer leaves of the cabbage and cut it into 8 wedges. Remove the core and slice the cabbage very finely. Peel and chop the onion.

Melt the margarine in a large pan, add the onion and fry until golden. Stir in the cabbage, caraway seeds, water and salt and bring to the boil. Cover and simmer for 15 minutes. Moisten the cornflour with a little cold water, stir well into the cabbage and cook for a further 5 minutes.

Cauliflower with hollandaise sauce
Serves 4

Ingredients	Metric-Imperial	American
1 medium-sized cauliflower	about 750 g/ 1¾ lb	about 1¾ lb
Salted water	600 ml/1 pint	2½ cups
For the sauce:		
Butter or margarine	25 g/1 oz	2 tbs
Flour	25 g/1 oz	¼ cup
Cold water	2 tbs	3 tbs
1 egg yolk		
Lemon juice	2 tsp	2 tsp
Salt		

Discard any leaves from the cauliflower and remove as much of the core as possible. Wash carefully in cold water. Drain. Bring the salted water to the boil in a pan and put in the cauliflower, stem end downwards. Cover and simmer for 25 minutes, or until the cauliflower is tender. Drain, reserving the cooking liquid. Transfer the cauliflower to a warm serving dish and keep hot.

To make the sauce, melt the butter or margarine in a pan and sprinkle in the flour. Cook, stirring, until golden. Measure 300 ml/½ pint (1¼ cups) of the reserved liquid and add this gradually to the pan. Stir until boiling and simmer for 5 minutes. Meanwhile, beat together the water and egg yolk. Remove the sauce from the heat and whisk in the egg mixture. Add the lemon juice and adjust the seasoning with more salt if necessary. Pour over the cauliflower.

Variation: Instead of the sauce, make a topping by melting 50 g/2 oz (¼ cup) butter and using this to brown 2 tbs (3 tbs) breadcrumbs. Sprinkle over the cooked cauliflower.

Left: Traditional red cabbage
Above: Cauliflower with hollandaise sauce

347

Simply cooked Brussels sprouts
Serves 4

Ingredients	Metric-Imperial	American
Brussels sprouts	1 kg/2¼ lb	2¼ lb
Butter or margarine	40 g/1½ oz	3 tbs
Salt		
Ground nutmeg		

Remove the rough outer leaves from the sprouts and trim the bases. Melt the butter or margarine in a pan, add the sprouts and cook for a few minutes, stirring. Add lightly salted water just to cover and bring to the boil. Cover and simmer for 15 minutes, or until the sprouts are tender. Drain and season to taste with more salt if necessary and a little nutmeg.

Serving idea: If liked, pour more melted butter over the cooked sprouts and stir to coat.

Quickie peas in ham sauce
Serves 2

Ingredients	Metric-Imperial	American
Frozen peas	350 g/12 oz	2 cups
Water	150 ml/¼ pint	⅔ cup
Salt		
1 small onion		
Diced cooked ham	50 g/2 oz	⅓ cup
Butter or margarine	25 g/1 oz	2 tbs
Savoury white sauce mix to make	300 ml/½ pint	1¼ cups
Whipping cream	4 tbs	5 tbs
Pepper		
Ground nutmeg		

Put the peas into a pan, add the water and a little salt and bring to the boil. Cover and simmer for about 5 minutes. Drain, reserving the cooking liquid. Transfer the peas to a warm serving dish and keep hot.

Peel and chop the onion and dice the ham. Melt the butter or margarine in a pan and fry the ham and onion gently until the onion is soft. Make up the packet of sauce as directed, using the reserved liquid and the cream instead of milk. Adjust the seasoning with pepper and nutmeg if wished. Stir in the onion and ham and pour over the peas.

Simply cooked broccoli
Serves 4

Ingredients	Metric-Imperial	American
Broccoli	1 kg/2¼ lb	2¼ lb
Ground nutmeg	¼ tsp	¼ tsp
Salt		
Butter	75 g/3 oz	⅓ cup
2 hard-boiled eggs		

Trim the stalks of the broccoli. Place in a pan and add water just to cover, the nutmeg and a little salt. Bring to the boil, cover and simmer for about 10 minutes, or until the broccoli is tender. Drain carefully, transfer to a warm serving dish and keep hot.

Melt the butter and shell and chop the eggs. Pour the butter over the broccoli and serve sprinkled with the egg.

Left: Simply cooked Brussels sprouts
Opposite: Broccoli with herbed wine sauce

Broccoli with herbed wine sauce
Serves 4–6

Ingredients	Metric-Imperial	American
Broccoli	750 g/1¾ lb	1¾ lb
1 clove of garlic		
Butter	15 g/½ oz	1 tbs
Sugar	1 tsp	1 tsp
For the sauce:		
Butter	175 g/6 oz	¾ cup
4 egg yolks		
Lemon juice	2 tsp	2 tsp
Dry white wine	3 tbs	4 tbs
Few drops of		
Worcestershire sauce		
Salt and pepper		
Sugar		
Snipped chives	2–3 tbs	3–4 tbs
Chopped dill weed	2–3 tbs	3–4 tbs
Chopped thyme	1 tbs	1 tbs
Chopped basil	2–3 tbs	3–4 tbs

Trim the stalks of the broccoli. Peel and crush the garlic. Melt the butter in a pan, add the broccoli, garlic and sugar and pour over water just to cover. Bring to the boil, cover and simmer for about 10 minutes, or until the broccoli is tender. Drain carefully, transfer to a warm serving dish and keep hot. Discard the garlic.

For the sauce, melt the butter and skim off the foam. Set aside. Put the egg yolks, lemon juice, wine, Worcestershire sauce and a little salt, pepper and sugar into the top of a double boiler or a bowl over a pan of simmering water. Whisk with an electric mixer for about 5 minutes until foamy and slightly thickened. Gradually whisk the melted butter into the sauce. Fold in the herbs and adjust the seasoning to taste. Serve in a warm sauceboat with the broccoli.

Steamed savoy cabbage
Serves 4

Ingredients	Metric-Imperial	American
Savoy cabbage	1 kg/2¼ lb	2¼ lb
1 onion		
Margarine or meat		
dripping	65 g/2½ oz	5 tbs
Water	125 ml/4 fl oz	½ cup
Salt		
Cornflour (cornstarch)	2 tsp	2 tsp
Chopped parsley	1 tsp	1 tsp

Discard the rough outer leaves of the cabbage, quarter and remove the core. Finely slice the cabbage. Peel and chop the onion.

Melt the margarine or dripping in a pan and use to fry the onion until golden brown. Add the cabbage and cook for 3 minutes, stirring. Add the water and a little salt and bring to the boil. Cover and simmer for 20 minutes, or until the cabbage is soft.

Moisten the cornflour with a little cold water and stir into the cabbage. Simmer for a further 2 minutes. Taste and adjust the seasoning with more salt if necessary. Before serving, sprinkle with the parsley.

Serving ideas: Serve the cabbage with roast pork, grilled pork chops or gammon steaks, or pork sausages.
Variation: Replace the pastry with caraway seeds.
Cook's tips: In this recipe the cabbage cooks in the steam from the small amount of water added. Most vegetables benefit from steaming, as they remain crisp, colourful and full of goodness. A special expandable vegetable steamer is a useful piece of kitchen equipment.

Simply cooked garden peas
Serves 6

Ingredients	Metric-Imperial	American
Butter	40 g/1½ oz	3 tbs
Shelled peas	1 kg/2¼ lb	6 cups
Water	125 ml/4 fl oz	½ cup
Salt		
Sugar		

Melt the butter in a pan, put in the peas and cook, stirring, for 1 minute, until they are coated. Add the water and a little salt and sugar and bring to the boil. Cover and simmer for about 10 minutes, or until the peas are tender. Drain very thoroughly before serving.

Mushrooms with onion and bacon
Serves 4

Ingredients	Metric-Imperial	American
Mushrooms	1 kg/2¼ lb	2¼ lb
2 medium-sized onions		
Streaky bacon (strips)	40 g/1½ oz	3 strips
Margarine	40 g/1½ oz	3 tbs
Salt and pepper		
Chopped parsley	1 tbs	1 tbs

Slice the mushrooms, peel and chop the onions and chop the bacon. Put the bacon into a pan and heat gently. When the fat runs, add the margarine and onion and cook until the onion is golden brown. Put in the mushrooms, season with salt and pepper and cook for 10 minutes, stirring frequently. Serve sprinkled with parsley.

Purée of dried peas
Serves 4

Ingredients	Metric-Imperial	American
Dried peas	350 g/12 oz	1⅔ cups
Water	750 ml/1¼ pints	3 cups
Selection of pot vegetables		
Salt and pepper		
1 onion		
Butter or margarine, or	40 g/1½ oz	3 tbs
streaky bacon (strips)	50 g/2 oz	4 strips

Soak the peas in the water in a pan for 24 hours. Bring to the boil in the soaking liquid, cover and simmer for 1½ hours.

Clean, peel if necessary, and chop the pot vegetables. Add to the pan with a little salt and pepper and bring back to the boil. Cover and simmer for 1 further hour, or until the peas are tender.

Liquidize or sieve, return to the pan and reheat, stirring, until the purée is light and creamy. Adjust the seasoning to taste with salt and pepper and transfer to a warm serving dish. Keep hot.

Peel and slice the onion and divide into rings. Melt the butter or margarine in a pan and use to cook the onion until golden. Or finely chop the bacon and heat in a pan until the fat runs. Use this to brown the onion, and top the purée with onions and bacon bits.

Below: Simply cooked garden peas

Quick steamed mixed vegetables
Serves 4

Ingredients	Metric-Imperial	American
Baby carrots	100 g/4 oz	4 oz
Asparagus	2–3 stalks	2–3 stalks
1 kohlrabi		
1 small cauliflower		
Shelled peas	100 g/4 oz	⅔ cup
Butter or margarine	40 g/1½ oz	3 tbs
Water	125 ml/4 fl oz	½ cup
Salt		
Sugar		
Chopped parsley	1 tbs	1 tbs

Scrape the carrots and trim the asparagus, discarding any woody sections. Cut into pieces. Peel and thinly slice the kohlrabi. Divide the cauliflower into florets.

Melt the butter or margarine in a pan, add the vegetables and cook for 1 minute, stirring. Pour in the water and add a little salt and sugar. Bring to the boil, cover tightly and simmer for about 20 minutes, or until the vegetables are tender. Hardly any liquid will remain. Adjust the seasoning if necessary and serve sprinkled with parsley.

Simply cooked turnips
Serves 4

Ingredients	Metric-Imperial	American
Turnips	1 kg/2¼ lb	2¼ lb
Margarine	65 g/2½ oz	5 tbs
Sugar	1 tsp	1 tsp
Water	125 ml/4 fl oz	½ cup
Salt and pepper		
Flour	1 tsp	1 tsp
Chopped parsley	1 tsp	1 tsp

Peel the turnips and cut into thin strips about 5 cm/2 inches long. Melt the margarine in a pan, add the sugar and cook until it is golden brown. Add the turnip strips and cook, stirring, for 2–3 minutes. Mix in the water and season to taste with salt and pepper. Bring to the boil, cover and simmer for 20 minutes, or until the turnip is tender.

Moisten the flour with a little cold water, add to the pan and stir until boiling. Simmer for a further 5 minutes and serve sprinkled with parsley.

Mange-tout peas in almond butter
Serves 4

Ingredients	Metric-Imperial	American
Mange-tout peas (sugar)	550 g/1¼ lb	1¼ lb
Salt and pepper		
Butter	50 g/2 oz	¼ cup
Slivered almonds	40 g/1½ oz	⅓ cup

Top and tail the mange-tout peas and place in a pan. Add water to cover and a little salt and bring to the boil. Cover and simmer for about 5 minutes. Drain well.

Melt the butter in a pan and use to brown the almonds, stirring all the time. Add the peas and reheat, stirring. Season with more salt and pepper to taste and serve immediately.

Mange-tout peas in lemon sauce
Serves 4

Ingredients	Metric-Imperial	American
Mange-tout peas (sugar)	550 g/1¼ lb	1¼ lb
Salt and pepper		
Oil	2 tsp	2 tsp
Whipping cream	150 ml/¼ pint	⅔ cup
Natural yogurt (plain)	2 tbs	3 tbs
Finely grated rind of 1 lemon		
Sugar		
Chopped mint	2 tbs	3 tbs

Top and tail the mange-tout peas and place in a pan. Add water just to cover, a little salt and the oil. Bring to the boil, cover and simmer for 5 minutes. Drain and transfer to a warm serving dish. Keep hot.

Stir together the cream, yogurt and lemon rind. Season to taste with salt, pepper and sugar and mix in the mint. Serve with the hot peas.

Serving idea: Serve the mange-tout peas with grilled lamb cutlets or roast lamb.

Microwave method
Top and tail the mange-tout peas and put in a suitable dish with 125 ml/4 fl oz (½ cup water). Cook on full power for 5 minutes, drain and mix the oil into the mange-tout peas.

Mix together the cream, yogurt and lemon rind and season with salt and pepper and a pinch of sugar. Put in the microwave for 1½ minutes on half power. Pour over the peas and sprinkle with chopped mint.

Curried bean sprouts with mushrooms
Serves 4

Ingredients	Metric-Imperial	American
Mushrooms	225 g/8 oz	8 oz
1 onion		
Oil	1 tbs	1 tbs
Curry powder	1 tbs	1 tbs
Sweet sherry	2 tbs	3 tbs
Bean sprouts	275 g/10 oz	5 cups
Salt		

Slice the mushrooms. Peel and chop the onion. Heat the oil in a pan, add the onion and mushroom and fry, stirring gently, for a few minutes. Mix in the curry powder and sherry, and cook for a further 3 minutes. Put in the bean sprouts and continue cooking, stirring from time to time, for another 5 minutes. Season to taste with salt.

Serving idea: Serve with other dishes as part of an Indian meal.

Creamed spinach
Serves 4

Ingredients	Metric-Imperial	American
Spinach	1 kg/2¼ lb	2¼ lb
1 small onion		
Butter or margarine	40 g/1½ oz	3 tbs
Salt and pepper		
Ground nutmeg		
Cornflour (cornstarch)	1 tsp	1 tsp
Whipping cream	2 tbs	3 tbs

Wash the spinach and remove any tough stalks. Drain and place in a pan with only the water clinging to the leaves. Cover the pan and cook for about 8 minutes, shaking the pan occasionally, until the spinach is limp. Chop very finely or purée in a food processor or blender.

Peel and chop the onion. Melt the butter or margarine in a pan and cook the onion until golden. Add the spinach and season to taste with salt, pepper and nutmeg. Moisten the cornflour with a little cold water, add to the pan and cook, stirring, until thickened. Beat in the cream, adjust the seasoning if necessary and serve very hot.

Serving suggestion: Top each portion of spinach with a fried egg.

Braised cucumber in curry cream
Serves 4

Ingredients	Metric-Imperial	American
3 medium-sized cucumbers		
1 onion		
Butter or margarine		
Curry powder	½ tsp	½ tsp
Ground turmeric	½ tsp	½ tsp
Lemon juice	2 tbs	3 tbs
Sugar	1 tsp	1 tsp
Grated lemon rind	½ tsp	½ tsp
Salt and pepper		
Whipping cream	150 ml/¼ pint	⅔ cup
Little lemon juice or dry white wine		
Few sprigs of mint		

Peel the cucumbers, halve them lengthways and scoop out the seeds. Cut into 1.25 cm/½ inch wide strips. Peel and chop the onion.

Melt the butter or margarine in a pan and use to cook the onion until transparent. Sprinkle in the curry powder and turmeric and cook for 1 minute, stirring. Put in the cucumber, lemon juice, sugar, lemon rind and a little salt and pepper. Stir well, cover the pan and cook gently for 7 minutes.

Blend in the cream, add a little extra lemon juice or white wine to taste and adjust the seasoning if necessary. Reheat but do not boil. Serve garnished with mint sprigs.

Simply cooked runner beans
Serves 4

Ingredients	Metric-Imperial	American
Runner beans (English)	1 kg/2¼ lb	2¼ lb
1 medium-sized onion		
Butter or margarine	40 g/1½ oz	3 tbs
Water	125 ml/4 fl oz	½ cup
Salt and pepper		
Chopped parsley	1 tbs	1 tbs

Top and tail the beans, remove any strings and slice obliquely. Peel and chop the onion. Melt the butter or margarine in a pan, add the onion and cook until golden. Put in the beans and stir over the heat for 2 minutes. Pour in the water and season with salt and pepper. Bring to the boil, cover and simmer for 25 minutes, or until the beans are tender. Drain well, add more seasoning if wished and serve sprinkled with parsley.

Glazed carrots
Serves 4

Ingredients	Metric-Imperial	American
Baby carrots	450 g/1 lb	1 lb
Salt and pepper		
Butter	50 g/2 oz	¼ cup
Sugar	3 tbs	4 tbs
Chopped mint leaves	1 tbs	1 tbs

Scrape the carrots, place in a pan, add water just to cover and a little salt and bring to the boil. Cover and simmer for 7 minutes. Drain well.

Add the butter and sugar to the hot carrots and cook for about 10 minutes, shaking the pan frequently, until the carrots are tender and glazed. Adjust the seasoning with salt and pepper and serve sprinkled with mint.

Young carrots in egg sauce
Serves 4

Ingredients	Metric-Imperial	American
Baby carrots	1 kg/2¼ lb	2¼ lb
1 onion		
Margarine	40 g/1½ oz	3 tbs
Beef stock (bouillon)	225 ml/8 fl oz	1 cup
For the sauce:		
Butter	25 g/1 oz	2 tbs
Flour	25 g/1 oz	¼ cup
Whipping cream	2 tbs	3 tbs
Salt and pepper		
Sugar		
Lemon juice		
1 hard-boiled egg		
Chopped herbs	2 tbs	3 tbs

Scrape and dice the carrots. Peel and chop the onion. Melt the margarine in a pan, add the onion and carrot and cook, stirring, for 2 minutes. Add the stock and bring to the boil. Cover and simmer for 15 minutes, or until the carrots are tender. Drain and reserve the cooking liquid. Transfer the carrots to a warm serving dish and keep hot. Make up the cooking liquid to 350 ml/12 fl oz (1½ cups) with water.

For the sauce, melt the butter in a pan, sprinkle in the flour and cook, stirring, until golden. Gradually add the reserved liquid and stir until boiling. Simmer for 5 minutes. Remove from the heat and blend in the cream with salt, pepper, sugar and lemon juice to taste. Shell and chop the egg and add to the sauce with the herbs. Pour over the carrots and serve hot.

Microwave hint
To cook carrots by microwave, slice them neatly and place in a suitable dish. Spoon over 3 tbsp (4 tbsp) orange juice and add a pinch of ground mace. Cover and cook on full power for 4 minutes, then stir and test for tenderness. Cover again and cook for a further 2 minutes, then test again and add salt to taste. Leave to stand for 2 minutes before serving.

Opposite: Creamed spinach
Right: Glazed carrots

Savoury lentils
Serves 4

Ingredients	Metric-Imperial	American
Lentils	350 g/12 oz	1½ cups
Water	750 ml/1¼ pints	3 cups
Selection of pot vegetables		
Salt		
1 onion		
Butter	50 g/2 oz	¼ cup
Vinegar	2–3 tbs	3–4 tbs
Little sugar		

Put the lentils into a pan, pour over the water and leave to soak for 24 hours. Clean the pot vegetables, peel if necessary and chop. Add to the pan and bring to the boil. Put in a little salt, cover and simmer for 25 minutes, or until the lentils are tender.

Peel and chop the onion. Melt the butter in a clean pan and use to cook the onion gently until golden brown. Stir into the lentils and add vinegar and sugar to taste. Reheat and serve hot.

Caramelized onions with cinnamon
Serves 4

Ingredients	Metric-Imperial	American
Button onions	450 g/1 lb	1 lb
Oil	2 tbs	3 tbs
Soft brown sugar (light)	65 g/2½ oz	5 tbs
Salt		
Red wine	225 ml/8 fl oz	1 cup
Red wine vinegar	5 tbs	6 tbs
Tomato purée (paste)	2 tbs	3 tbs
Ground cinnamon		
Pinch of cayenne pepper		

Peel the onions. Heat the oil in a large pan, add the onions and cook gently, turning occasionally, for 3 minutes. Sprinkle in the sugar, add a little salt and cook, stirring now and then, until the onions are caramelized.

Combine the wine, vinegar and tomato purée and pour over the onions. Stir well and bring to the boil. Put in 2 tsp cinnamon and the cayenne, cover the pan and simmer for about 15 minutes, until the onions are tender. Remove the onions with a slotted spoon and keep hot.

Boil the liquid in the pan until well reduced and thickened. Return the onions to the sauce, turn until coated and reheat carefully. If wished, add a little more cinnamon to taste.

Serving suggestion: These caramelized onions make a good accompaniment to roast lamb or game.

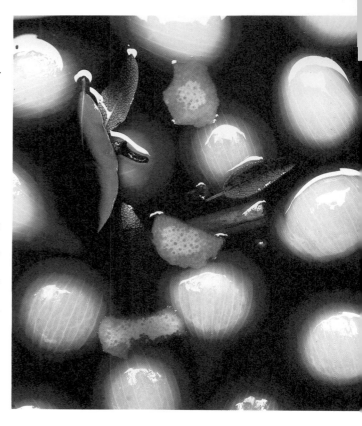

Button onions in port wine
Serves 8–10

Ingredients	Metric-Imperial	American
Button onions	1 kg/2¼ lb	2¼ lb
Red wine vinegar	225 ml/8 fl oz	1 cup
Salt	2 tsp	2 tsp
Sugar	225 g/8 oz	1 cup
8 sage leaves		
4 bay leaves		
Shredded root ginger	20 g/¾ oz	2 tbs
5 whole cloves		
10 black peppercorns		
1 stick of cinnamon		
Pared rind of 1 orange		
Port	225 ml/8 fl oz	1 cup

Peel the onions, place in a pan with water to cover and bring to the boil. Cover and simmer for 10 minutes. Remove the onions and place in cold water. Leave for 10 minutes then drain well.

Put the vinegar, salt and half the sugar into a pan and bring to the boil. Set aside. Put the remaining sugar into a clean pan and stir over moderate heat until caramelized. Carefully add the vinegar liquid and stir well until the caramel has dissolved. Put in the onions, sage and bay leaves, ginger, cloves, peppercorns, cinnamon and orange rind. Bring to the boil and simmer for 5 minutes. Remove the pan from the heat and add the port.

Pack the onions, herbs and spices into clean jars and top up with the port liquid. Cover tightly and store in a cool place for at least 2 weeks before using. Serve with meat dishes.

Onions in cream sauce
Serves 4

Ingredients	Metric-Imperial	American
Large mild onions	750 g/1¾ lb	1¾ lb
Butter or margarine	50 g/2 oz	¼ cup
Beef stock (bouillon)	125 ml/4 fl oz	½ cup
White wine	125 ml/4 fl oz	½ cup
Salt		
Sugar		
Whipping cream	2 tbs	3 tbs
Chopped parsley	1 tbs	1 tbs

Peel and slice the onions. Melt the butter or margarine in a pan and use to cook the onion gently until golden. Add the stock and wine, bring to the boil, cover and simmer for 10 minutes. Season to taste with salt and sugar and stir in the cream. Sprinkle with parsley before serving.

Simply cooked fennel
Serves 4

Ingredients	Metric-Imperial	American
Fennel (Florence)	1 kg/2¼ lb	2¼ lb
Butter	75 g/3 oz	⅓ cup
Salt		

Clean and trim the fennel. Bring a pan of lightly salted water to the boil, add the fennel, bring back to the boil and simmer, covered, for about 20 minutes, or until tender. Drain well, cut into quarters and transfer to a warm serving dish. Melt the butter, add a little salt if wished, and pour over the hot fennel.

Italian vegetable casserole
Serves 4

Ingredients	Metric-Imperial	American
1 large green sweet pepper		
3 small tomatoes		
Mushrooms	50 g/2 oz	2 oz
1 large onion		
Butter	15 g/½ oz	1 tbs
Beef stock (bouillon)	300 ml/½ pint	1¼ cups
Tomato purée (paste)	1 tbs	1 tbs
Cornflour (cornstarch)	1 tbs	1 tbs
Salt and pepper		
Garlic powder		
Whipping cream	1 tbs	1 tbs
Chopped parsley	1 tbs	1 tbs

Halve the pepper, remove the seeds and cut the flesh into large dice. Pour boiling water over the tomatoes, drain, peel, halve, remove the seeds and cut the flesh into segments. Halve the mushrooms. Peel and chop the onion.

Melt the butter in a pan, add the onion and cook until golden. Put in the pepper and mushrooms and cook, stirring frequently, for 3 minutes. Add the stock, tomato pieces and tomato purée and bring to the boil. Cook for 1 minute. Moisten the cornflour with a little cold water, add to the pan and stir until boiling. Simmer for 2 minutes and season to taste with salt, pepper and a little garlic powder. Blend in the cream and serve sprinkled with parsley.

Opposite (below): Button onions in port wine
Opposite (above): Caramelized onions with cinnamon
Below: Italian vegetable casserole

2 slices cooked ham		
5 tomatoes		
Chopped parsley	3 tbs	4 tbs
1 egg		
Cayenne pepper		
Worcestershire sauce		
Fresh breadcrumbs	2 tbs	3 tbs
Butter		
Whipping cream	125 ml/4 fl oz	½ cup
Salt and pepper		
Sweet paprika pepper		
Lemon juice		

Halve the peppers lengthways, through the stem, and remove the seeds. Sprinkle the insides with salt and pepper.

Reduce the chicken breasts to a purée in a food processor, or mince them. Dice the ham. Halve 2 of the tomatoes, scoop out the centres and reserve. Dice the flesh. Mix together the ham, diced tomato, parsley and chicken. Beat the egg lightly and add to the chicken mixture with a little cayenne and Worcestershire sauce to taste. Use to fill the pepper halves, sprinkle with breadcrumbs and dot with butter. Arrange in a greased ovenproof dish.

Pour boiling water over the remaining tomatoes, drain, peel and quarter them. Put round the peppers with the reserved tomato pulp. Season the cream with salt, pepper, paprika and lemon juice to taste and pour over the tomato pieces. Bake in a preheated moderately hot oven, 200°C, 400°F, Gas Mark 6, for 25–30 minutes, until the peppers are tender.

Stuffed baked tomatoes
Serves 4

Ingredients	Metric-Imperial	American
4 large 'beefsteak' tomatoes		
Salt and pepper		
Oil	6 tbs	½ cup
1 small onion		
1 clove of garlic		
2 hard-boiled eggs		
Soft liver pâté (liverwurst)	100 g/4 oz	4 oz
Chopped parsley	2 tbs	3 tbs
Fresh breadcrumbs	4 tbs	5 tbs

Halve the tomatoes and sprinkle the cut surfaces with salt and pepper. Heat half the oil in a pan and put in the tomatoes, cut surfaces downwards. Cook gently for 5 minutes then transfer to an ovenproof dish.

Peel and finely chop the onion and garlic. Shell and chop the eggs. Mix together the liver pâté, onion, garlic, egg and parsley. Season to taste with salt and pepper. Pile the filling on top of the tomatoes, sprinkle with a little of the remaining oil, then with the breadcrumbs and finally with the rest of the oil. Place, uncovered, in a preheated hot oven, 220°C, 425°F, Gas Mark 7, for about 15 minutes, basting once during this time with any liquid which accumulates in the dish.

Chicken-stuffed red peppers
Serves 4

Ingredients	Metric-Imperial	American
4 red sweet peppers		
Salt and pepper		
Boneless chicken breast	450 g/1 lb	1 lb

Mushroom-stuffed tomatoes
Serves 4

Ingredients	Metric-Imperial	American
8 medium-sized firm tomatoes		
Salt		
For the stuffing:		
Mushrooms	225 g/8 oz	8 oz
1 small onion		
Butter	20 g/¾ oz	scant 2 tbs
1 egg		
Fresh breadcrumbs	40 g/1½ oz	¾ cup
Chopped parsley	1 tbs	1 tbs
Salt and pepper		
Margarine	65 g/2½ oz	5 tbs
Flour	40 g/1½ oz	⅓ cup
Sugar		
Tomato purée (paste)	2 tsp	2 tsp

Cut off the tops of the tomatoes and scoop out the seeds. Press through a sieve and make the pulp up to 500 ml/18 fl oz (2¼ cups) with water. Sprinkle the insides of the tomatoes with salt.

To make the stuffing, slice the mushrooms and peel and chop the onion. Melt the butter in a pan and use to fry the onion and mushroom slices for 3 minutes, stirring occasionally. Mix in the egg and breadcrumbs, add the parsley and seasoning to taste. Fill the tomatoes with this stuffing and put on the lids.

Melt the margarine in a frying pan, arrange the tomatoes in this side by side and cook gently for 20 minutes. Transfer to a warm serving dish and keep hot.

Sprinkle the flour into the fat left in the pan and cook, stirring, until golden. Whisk in the tomato liquid and bring to the boil, stirring. Simmer for 3 minutes and season to taste with salt, pepper and sugar. Blend in the tomato purée, simmer for 1 further minute and pour the sauce into the dish round the stuffed tomatoes.

Serving ideas: Serve the mushroom-stuffed tomatoes with simply cooked white fish, or by themselves, on hot buttered toast, as a simple snack or supper dish.

Opposite: Stuffed baked tomatoes
Above: Mushroom-stuffed tomatoes

357

Salt and pepper

Ingredients	Metric-Imperial	American
Long grain rice	40 g/1½ oz	⅓ cup
Canned tuna	2 × 200 g/7 oz cans	2 × 7 oz cans
Chopped parsley	2 tbs	3 tbs
Mayonnaise	3 tbs	4 tbs
Grated rind of 1 lemon		
Chopped basil		
Few lettuce leaves		

Cut off the tops of the tomatoes and scoop out the seeds. Sprinkle the insides with salt and leave the tomatoes upside-down on a rack to drain. Cook the rice in boiling salted water for about 12 minutes, until tender. Drain and cool. Drain and flake the tuna.

Mix together the rice, tuna, parsley, mayonnaise and lemon rind. Add pepper and a little basil to taste. Use to fill the tomatoes and replace the lids. Line a serving platter with lettuce leaves and arrange the tomatoes on top.

Stuffed aubergines
Serves 4

Ingredients	Metric-Imperial	American
2–4 aubergines (eggplant)	about 750 g/ 1¾ lb	about 1¾ lb
Salt and pepper		
1 onion		
Minced lamb (ground)	225 g/8 oz	8 oz
1 egg		
1 white bread roll		
3–4 tomatoes		
Margarine	50 g/2 oz	¼ cup
Whipping cream	300 ml/½ pint	1¼ cups
Flour	2 tbs	3 tbs
Water	125 ml/4 fl oz	½ cup
Chopped parsley	1 tbs	1 tbs
Snipped chives	1 tbs	1 tbs
Grated cheese	100 g/4 oz	1 cup

Halve the aubergines lengthways, sprinkle the cut surfaces with salt and leave to stand for 30 minutes. Drain off the liquid and scoop out the flesh of the aubergines, leaving a 'shell' of about 1.25 cm/½ inch.

Finely chop the aubergine flesh. Peel and chop the onion and combine with the chopped aubergine, meat and egg. Soak the roll in water, squeeze out the moisture and crumble into the meat mixture. Add salt and pepper to taste. Use to stuff the aubergines.

Pour boiling water over the tomatoes, drain, peel and cut into wedges. Melt the margarine in a flameproof dish, add the tomato wedges and pour the cream over the top. Put in the stuffed aubergines, cover and cook gently for 40 minutes. Lift out the aubergines. Blend the flour with the water and stir into the dish with the herbs. Return the aubergines and sprinkle with cheese. Place, uncovered, in a preheated moderately hot oven, 200°C, 400°F, Gas Mark 6, for 8–10 minutes.

Meat-stuffed Spanish onions
Serves 4

Ingredients	Metric-Imperial	American
4 large mild onions	about 750 g/1¾ lb	about 1¾ lb
Salt		
Margarine	15 g/½ oz	1 tbs
Whipping cream	3 tbs	4 tbs
Lean minced beef (ground)	350 g/12 oz	12 oz
Chopped parsley	2 tbs	3 tbs

Peel the onions, place in a pan with water to cover and add a little salt. Bring to the boil, cover and simmer for about 30 minutes, or until the onions are just tender. Drain. Remove the centres, leaving a 'shell' of about 3 layers.

Melt the margarine in a flameproof pan. Chop the centres of the onions, add to the margarine and cook gently until transparent. Stir in the cream and season to taste with salt. Stand the onions in the sauce. Combine the meat and half the parsley and use to stuff the onions. Place, uncovered, in a preheated moderately hot oven, 200°C, 400°F, Gas Mark 6, for 30 minutes. Sprinkle with remaining parsley.

Tomatoes stuffed with rice and tuna
Serves 4

Ingredients	Metric-Imperial	American
8 medium-sized firm tomatoes		

Left: Meat-stuffed Spanish onions
Opposite: Stuffed aubergines

Cabbage leaf parcels with meat stuffing
Serves 4

Ingredients	Metric-Imperial	American
1 white or savoy cabbage		
For the filling:		
1 bread roll		
1 medium-sized onion		
1 egg		
Minced beef and pork combined (ground)	450 g/1 lb	1 lb
Salt and pepper		
Margarine	75 g/3 oz	⅓ cup
Hot water		
Flour	2 tbs	3 tbs

Using a pointed knife, cut out the core of the cabbage. Bring a pan of salted water to the boil, put in the cabbage and leave for a few minutes, until the outer leaves can be removed. Return the cabbage to the pan and repeat the process, until all the leaves are soft enough to come away without tearing. Trim along the central rib of each leaf to make it flat on both sides.

To make the filling, soak the bread roll in water, squeeze out the moisture and then crumble. Peel and chop the onion. Mix together the breadcrumbs, onion, egg, meat and seasoning to taste. Lay two or three cabbage leaves together on a board, put some of the filling on top and roll up into a neat parcel. Tie with fine string. Make more parcels in the same way.

Melt the margarine in a pan, add the stuffed cabbage parcels and brown them lightly on all sides. Pour in water just to come level with the top of the rolls, bring to the boil and simmer, uncovered, for about 35 minutes, adding more water to the pan as it evaporates. Lift out the cabbage parcels with a slotted spoon, drain and remove the strings. Transfer to a warm serving dish and keep hot. Blend the flour with a little cold water, add to the pan and bring to the boil, stirring constantly. Simmer for 3 minutes and adjust the seasoning to taste. Serve the sauce poured over the cabbage parcels.

Microwave method

Remove the leaves from the cabbage and discard any damaged ones. Cut the thick stalk from the larger leaves. Arrange in piles in a suitable dish with about 225 ml/8 fl oz (1 cup) of cold water. Do this in two batches. Cook the cabbage leaves for 3 minutes on full power.

To make the filling, soak the bread roll in water, squeeze out the moisture and then crumble into a bowl. Peel and chop the onion and mix with the breadcrumbs, egg, meat and seasoning.

Lay two or three cabbage leaves on a board, put some filling on top and roll into a neat parcel. Tie with fine string. Continue to make parcels until the ingredients are used.

Pour over 500 ml/1 pint (2½ cups) of tomato sauce. Cover and cook for 15 minutes at full power. Allow to stand for 5 minutes.

Remove the strings, return the cabbage parcels to the dish and cook on full power for a further 5 minutes.

You may find that it is better to cook two dishes with one layer of parcels.

Tomatoes with cheese soufflé filling
Serves 4

Ingredients	Metric-Imperial	American
8 large tomatoes		
Milk	125 ml/4 fl oz	½ cup
Blue-veined cheese	100 g/4 oz	4 oz
Cornflour (cornstarch)	2 tsp	2 tsp
2 eggs		
Salt and pepper		
Chopped tarragon	1 tbs	1 tbs

Cut off the tops of the tomatoes and scoop out the seeds. Leave upside-down on a rack to drain. Heat the milk in a pan. Mash the cheese, add to the milk and stir until blended together. Moisten the cornflour with a little cold water, add to the pan and stir until boiling. Remove from the heat and leave to cool slightly.

Separate the eggs, add the yolks to the sauce and beat well. Whip the egg whites in a clean bowl until stiff and fold into the sauce. Season with salt and pepper and fold in the tarragon. Use this mixture to fill the tomatoes then put on the lids. Arrange in a greased ovenproof dish and place, uncovered, in a preheated hot oven, 220°C, 425°F, Gas Mark 7, for about 15 minutes.

Chinese leaves with cheese
Serves 4

Ingredients	Metric-Imperial	American
1 head of Chinese leaves (cabbage)	about 1 kg/2¼ lb	about 2¼ lb
Chicken stock (bouillon)	1 L/1¾ pints	4⅓ cups
Butter	40 g/1½ oz	3 tbs
Grated cheese	50 g/2 oz	½ cup
For the sauce:		
1 small onion		
Sour cream	150 ml/¼ pint	⅔ cup
Chopped parsley	1 tbs	1 tbs
Salt and pepper		

Cut the head of Chinese leaves carefully into quarters, without allowing the quarters to fall to pieces. Put the stock into a pan and bring to the boil. Add the cabbage quarters and cook for about 10 minutes, or until tender. Drain, reserving the cooking liquid.

Grease an ovenproof dish, put in the cabbage quarters, side by side, dot with the butter and sprinkle with half the cheese.

To make the sauce, peel and chop the onion. Combine the cream, parsley, onion and seasoning to taste. Stir well together and pour over the Chinese leaves. Sprinkle with the remaining cheese and place, uncovered, in a preheated hot oven, 220°C, 425°F, Gas Mark 7, for about 15 minutes.

Opposite: Cabbage leaf parcels with meat stuffing
Below: Tomatoes with cheese soufflé filling

For the filling:

	Metric-Imperial	American
½ bread roll		
1 medium-sized onion		
1 medium-sized tomato		
Mushrooms	100 g/4 oz	4 oz
1 hard-boiled egg		
Pork boiling sausage	100 g/4 oz	4 oz
Minced beef and pork combined (ground)	100 g/4 oz	4 oz
Salt and pepper		
Ground nutmeg		
Butter or margarine	50 g/2 oz	¼ cup
Beef stock	300 ml/½ pint	1¼ cups
Cornflour (cornstarch)	4 tsp	4 tsp
Sour cream	150 ml/¼ pint	⅔ cup
Snipped chives	1 tbs	1 tbs

Peel the kohlrabi, cut off the tops and carefully scoop out the centres. Reserve 2 tbs (3 tbs) of this kohlrabi flesh to make the filling. Any remaining flesh can be used in a soup.

For the filling, soak the roll in water, squeeze out the moisture and crumble roughly. Peel and chop the onion. Pour boiling water over the tomato, drain, peel and chop. Chop the mushrooms. Shell and chop the egg. Cut the sausage into strips. Mix all these ingredients with the reserved kohlrabi and meat and season with salt, pepper and nutmeg to taste. Pack the filling into the kohlrabi 'shells', put on the lids and if necessary tie with fine string.

Melt the butter in a large shallow pan, put in the kohlrabi and allow them to brown slightly at the bottom. Pour over the stock, bring to the boil, cover and simmer for about 45 minutes. Lift out the kohlrabi, remove the strings, and transfer to a warm serving dish. Blend together the cornflour and sour cream, add to the pan and stir constantly until boiling. Pour the sauce over the kohlrabi and serve sprinkled with chives.

Baked onion rings in cream
Serves 4

Ingredients	Metric-Imperial	American
Onions	450 g/1 lb	1 lb
Butter	50 g/2 oz	¼ cup
Salt and pepper		
Few tiny sprigs of thyme		
Whipping cream	300 ml/½ pint	1¼ cups
Grated mature Gouda or Cheddar cheese	150 g/5 oz	1¼ cups
4 slices white bread		

Peel the onions, slice and divide into rings. Melt half the butter and use to cook the onions until transparent. Season with salt and pepper and place in an ovenproof dish. Sprinkle with a little thyme. Season the cream with salt to taste and pour over the onion rings. Sprinkle on the cheese.

Trim the crusts from the bread slices, cut the bread into cubes and scatter these over the cheese. Dot the remaining butter over the bread cubes and place, uncovered, in a preheated moderately hot oven, 200°C, 400°F, Gas Mark 6, for about 25 minutes, or until the bread cubes are golden.

Stuffed kohlrabi
Serves 4

Ingredients	Metric-Imperial	American
8 medium-sized kohlrabi		

Cauliflower florets in batter
Serves 4

Ingredients	Metric-Imperial	American
1 cauliflower		
1 egg		
Flour	75 g/3 oz	¾ cup
Water	100 ml/3½ fl oz	scant ½ cup
Salt		
Ground nutmeg		
Oil	5 tbs	6 tbs

Wash the cauliflower in cold water and cut into florets. Place in a pan, add lightly salted water just to cover and bring to the boil. Cover and simmer for about 10 minutes, or until the cauliflower is just tender. Drain well.

Beat together the egg, flour and water to make a rather thick batter. Season to taste with salt and nutmeg. Heat the oil in a frying pan. Dip a few cauliflower florets into the batter until coated, allow surplus batter to drain off, and add to the oil. Fry, turning frequently, until golden brown on all sides. Drain and keep hot while frying the remaining cauliflower florets in the same way.

Opposite: Baked onion rings in cream
Below: Cauliflower florets in batter

Trim the stalks of the broccoli. Place in a pan and add water just to cover and a little salt. Bring to the boil, cover and simmer for 10 minutes, or until tender. Drain carefully and transfer to a serving dish.

To make the sauce, beat together the oil, vinegar and mustard with salt, pepper and sugar to taste. Fold in the herbs and pour the sauce over the broccoli. Leave it to cool in the sauce and serve cold.

Broccoli with almond butter
Serves 4

Ingredients	Metric-Imperial	American
Broccoli	750 g/1¾ lb	1¾ lb
Salt		
Butter	75 g/3 oz	⅓ cup
Slivered almonds	50 g/2 oz	½ cup

Trim the stalks of the broccoli. Place in a pan, add water to cover and a little salt. Bring to the boil, cover and simmer for 10 minutes, or until the broccoli is tender. Drain carefully, transfer to a warm serving dish and keep hot.

Melt the butter in a pan, add the almonds and fry, stirring, until golden brown. Pour the almond butter over the broccoli and serve at once.

Broad beans in yogurt cream sauce
Serves 4

Ingredients	Metric-Imperial	American
Shelled broad beans	450 g/1 lb	2½ cups
Salt and pepper		
2–3 onions		
Butter	25 g/1 oz	2 tbs
Whipping cream	150 ml/¼ pint	⅔ cup
Chopped marjoram	1 tbs	1 tbs
Chopped savory	1 tbs	1 tbs
Natural yogurt (plain)	150 ml/¼ pint	⅔ cup

Put the beans into a pan, add water just to cover and a little salt. Bring to the boil, cover and simmer for about 10 minutes, or until tender. Drain well.

Peel and chop the onions. Melt the butter in a pan, add the onion and cook gently until transparent. Put in the beans and stir well. Cook for a few minutes. Blend in the cream and herbs and season to taste with salt and pepper. Cook for a further 2 minutes, mix in the yogurt and reheat gently before serving.

Serving suggestion: Particularly good with lamb or pork cutlets.

Broccoli with vinaigrette sauce
Serves 4

Ingredients	Metric-Imperial	American
Broccoli	750 g/1¾ lb	1¾ lb
Salt		
For the sauce:		
Oil	4 tbs	5 tbs
Vinegar	3 tbs	4 tbs
Prepared mustard	1 tsp	1 tsp
Salt and pepper		
Sugar		
Snipped chives	1 tbs	1 tbs
Chopped parsley	1 tbs	1 tbs
Chopped mint	1 tbs	1 tbs
Chopped tarragon	1 tbs	1 tbs
Chopped basil	1 tbs	1 tbs

Ham and leek rolls
Serves 4

Ingredients	Metric-Imperial	American
8 small leeks		
4 slices cooked ham		
Whipping cream	125 ml/4 fl oz	½ cup
Salt		
Ground nutmeg		
Meat extract		
Flour	1 tsp	1 tsp
Cold water	1 tbs	1 tbs

Carefully clean the leeks and trim so that they are all the same length. Place in a pan with lightly salted water to cover and cook for about 10 minutes, or until tender. Drain well. Wrap each leek in a slice of ham and arrange side by side in a greased oval ovenproof dish. Season the cream with salt, nutmeg and a little meat extract to taste and pour over the leeks. Cover the dish with a lid or foil and place in a preheated hot oven, 220°C, 425°F, Gas Mark 7, for about 15 minutes.

Remove the leeks. Moisten the flour with the water and stir well into the sauce. Return the leeks to the sauce and put the dish back into the oven, covered, for a further 10 minutes.

Serving suggestion: Serve with potatoes baked in foil (page 336).

Baked salsify rolls
Serves 4

Ingredients	Metric-Imperial	American
Salsify (scorzonera)	1 kg/2¼ lb	2¼ lb
Water	1 L/1¾ pints	4⅓ cups
Flour	2 tbs	3 tbs
Vinegar	4 tbs	5 tbs
Salted water	400 ml/14 fl oz	1¾ cups
4–8 slices Parma ham	about 400 g/14 oz	about 14 oz
For the sauce:		
Butter or margarine	40 g/1½ oz	3 tbs
Flour	40 g/1½ oz	⅓ cup
Milk or whipping cream	150 ml/¼ pint	⅔ cup
Salt and pepper		
Ground nutmeg		
Chopped dill weed	2 tbs	3 tbs
Grated mature Gouda cheese (sharp)	50 g/2 oz	½ cup

Opposite (above): Broccoli with vinaigrette sauce
Opposite (below): Broccoli with almond butter
Below: Baked salsify rolls

Clean and peel the salsify. If they are particularly thick, cut in half lengthways. Put the water into a bowl and whisk in the flour and half the vinegar. Add the salsify and leave to stand for 10 minutes.

Put the salted water into a pan and add the remaining vinegar. Drain the salsify and add to the pan. Bring to the boil, cover and simmer for about 10 minutes. Remove the salsify with a slotted spoon and drain. Keep the cooking liquid. Divide the vegetable into 4 portions and wrap each in one or two slices of ham. Arrange in a greased ovenproof dish.

To make the sauce, melt the butter or margarine in a pan, sprinkle in the flour and stir until golden brown. Measure 350 ml/12 fl oz (1½ cups) of the cooking liquid and combine with the milk or cream. Gradually blend into the roux and bring to the boil, stirring constantly. Simmer for 5 minutes. Season to taste with salt, pepper and nutmeg. Stir in the dill and pour over the salsify. Sprinkle with the cheese and place in a preheated moderately hot oven, 200°C, 400°F, Gas Mark 6, for 20–25 minutes. Serve with boiled potatoes or rice.

Variations: Chicory (endive) or celery may replace the salsify, and Cheddar cheese may be used instead of Gouda.

Below: Celery in white wine sauce
Opposite: Leeks in ham and cheese sauce

Microwave hint

To cook cabbage in the microwave cooker, shred and place in a bowl with 4 tbsp (5 tbsp) apple juice, ¼ tsp caraway seeds and a little black pepper. Mix the ingredients, cover and cook on full power for 3 minutes. Stir again, test for tenderness and add salt to taste. Cover and cook on full power for a further 2–3 minutes, then leave to stand for 2 minutes before serving.

Celery in white wine sauce
Serves 4

Ingredients	Metric-Imperial	American
Celery	1 kg/2¼ lb	2¼ lb
Water	600 ml/1 pint	2½ cups
Salt and pepper		
For the sauce:		
Butter or margarine	40 g/1½ oz	3 tbs
Flour	40 g/1½ oz	⅓ cup
1 egg yolk		
Dry white wine	3 tbs	4 tbs
Ground nutmeg		

Trim and string the celery. Cut into short lengths. Place the water in a pan and add a little salt. Bring to boil, add celery, cover and simmer for 25 minutes, or until tender. Drain, reserving liquid. Keep hot.

For the sauce, melt the butter or margarine in a pan. Sprinkle in the flour and stir until golden. Make the reserved liquid up to 600 ml/1 pint (2½ cups). Gradually whisk this into the roux and bring to the boil. Simmer for 5 minutes. Whisk the egg yolk with the wine and blend into the sauce. Remove from the heat and season to taste with salt, pepper and nutmeg. Stir the celery into the sauce and reheat without allowing it to boil.

Leeks in ham and cheese sauce
Serves 4

Ingredients	Metric-Imperial	American
8 medium-sized leeks		
Water	750 ml/1¼ pints	3 cups
Salt		
For the sauce:		
1 onion		
Butter or margarine	25 g/1 oz	2 tbs
Flour	25 g/1 oz	¼ cup
Cooked ham	225 g/8 oz	8 oz
Whipping cream	150 ml/¼ pint	⅔ cup
Grated Cheddar cheese	100 g/4 oz	1 cup
Salt and pepper		
Sugar		
Ground nutmeg		
1 egg yolk		
Lemon juice		

Trim the leeks, clean and cut into 5 cm/2 inch lengths. Put the water into a pan, add the leeks and a little salt and bring to the boil. Cover and simmer for about 15 minutes, or until the leeks are tender. Drain well, reserving the cooking liquid.

For the sauce, peel and finely chop the onion. Melt the butter or margarine in a pan and cook the onion gently until transparent. Sprinkle in the flour and cook, stirring, until the roux is golden. Whisk in 500 ml/18 fl oz/2¼ cups of the reserved liquid and bring to the boil. Simmer for 5 minutes. Dice the ham and stir into the sauce with the cream and cheese. Season to taste with salt, pepper, sugar and nutmeg. Remove from the heat and stir in the egg yolk then sharpen the flour with a little lemon juice. Add the leeks to the sauce and reheat but do not allow the sauce to boil.

Iceberg lettuce with tongue and mixed fruit
Serves 4

Ingredients	Metric-Imperial	American
1 small iceberg lettuce		
1 dessert apple		
Lemon juice	1 tbs	1 tbs
Cooked ox tongue	225 g/8 oz	8 oz
1 orange		
Black grapes	150 g/5 oz	5 oz
For the dressing:		
Whipping cream	150 ml/¼ pint	⅔ cup
Natural yogurt (plain)	150 ml/¼ pint	⅔ cup
Lemon juice	2 tbs	3 tbs
Salt and pepper		
Sugar		

Discard the rough outer leaves of the lettuce, quarter and remove the core. Separate the leaves. Peel, quarter, core and slice the apple. Sprinkle with the lemon juice to prevent discoloration. Cut the tongue into strips. Peel and segment the orange, discarding any pith. Halve the grapes and remove the pips (pits). Arrange the ingredients in layers in a salad bowl.

To make the dressing, mix together the cream, yogurt and lemon juice. Season with salt, pepper and sugar to taste. Pour over the salad and toss carefully.

Iceberg lettuce with bacon and paprika dressing
Serves 4

Ingredients	Metric-Imperial	American
1 small iceberg lettuce		
Oil	2 tbs	3 tbs
Sour cream	6 tbs	½ cup
Lemon juice	2 tbs	3 tbs
Salt and pepper		
Sugar		
Sweet paprika pepper		
Chopped parsley	2 tbs	3 tbs
1 onion		
Streaky bacon (strips)	100 g/4 oz	8 strips
Margarine	15 g/½ oz	1 tbs

Remove any rough outer leaves from the lettuce and cut it into 8 wedges. Arrange in a salad bowl.

To make the dressing, mix together the oil, cream and lemon juice and season with salt, pepper, sugar and paprika to taste. Mix in the parsley and pour over the lettuce.

Peel and chop the onion and chop the bacon. Melt the margarine in a frying pan and use to brown the onion and bacon. Sprinkle over the salad.

Left: Iceberg lettuce with tongue and mixed fruit
Below: Iceberg lettuce with bacon and paprika dressing

Iceberg lettuce and apple salad
Serves 4

Ingredients	Metric-Imperial	American
1 small iceberg lettuce		
6 sticks of celery (stalks)		
2 tart dessert apples		
Lemon juice	2 tsp	2 tsp
For the dressing:		
Whipping cream	5 tbs	6 tbs
Lemon juice	3 tbs	4 tbs
Orange juice	4 tbs	5 tbs
Ground ginger	½ tsp	½ tsp
Chopped hazelnuts (filberts)	1 tsp	1 tsp
Salt		
White pepper		
Sugar		

Discard the outer rough leaves of the lettuce and shred the remainder. Clean the celery, string if necessary and chop roughly. Peel, quarter, core and dice the apples. Sprinkle with the lemon juice to prevent discoloration. Stir the salad ingredients lightly together in a salad bowl.

To make the dressing, combine the cream, lemon juice, orange juice, ginger and nuts with salt, pepper and sugar to taste. Toss with the salad in the bowl.

Summer salad
Serves 4

Ingredients	Metric-Imperial	American
1 round lettuce (butterhead)		
1 bunch of radishes		
15 cm/6 inch length cucumber		
20 stuffed green olives		
For the dressing:		
Blue vein cheese	50 g/2 oz	2 oz
Whipping cream	2 tbs	3 tbs
Oil	3 tbs	4 tbs
Wine vinegar	2 tbs	3 tbs
Freshly ground black pepper		
Sugar		
Chopped mixed herbs such as parsley, sorrel or tarragon	1 tbs	1 tbs

Remove the rough outer leaves of the lettuce. Tear larger leaves in half and keep inner leaves whole. Wash and drain well. Trim and quarter the radishes lengthways. Halve the cucumber lengthways, scoop out the seeds and cut the flesh into slices. Finely chop 10 olives and halve the remainder. Put the lettuce, radish, cucumber and olives into a salad bowl.

To make the dressing, press the cheese through a sieve and stir in the cream, oil and vinegar. Season with pepper and sugar to taste. Fold in the chopped olives and herbs and pour over the salad.

Serving suggestion: As this type of lettuce leaf is fragile, only dress the salad immediately before serving.

Above: Summer salad
Right: Iceberg lettuce with fruit and nuts

372

Iceberg lettuce with fruit and nuts
Serves 4

Ingredients	Metric-Imperial	American
1 small iceberg lettuce		
1 grapefruit		
1 orange		
2 kiwi fruit		
For the dressing:		
Oil	4 tbs	5 tbs
Lemon juice	2 tbs	3 tbs
Wine vinegar	2 tbs	3 tbs
Caster sugar (granulated)	1 tbs	1 tbs
Chopped walnuts	50 g/2 oz	½ cup
Salt and pepper		
Few walnut halves		

Remove the rough outer leaves of the lettuce and tear inner leaves into pieces. Peel the grapefruit and orange, carefully remove the white pith and cut the flesh into thin slices. Quarter the grapefruit slices. Peel and slice the kiwi fruit. Place the lettuce and fruit in a salad bowl.

To make the dressing, mix together the oil, lemon juice, vinegar, sugar and chopped walnuts. Season to taste with salt and pepper. Pour over the salad, toss lightly and garnish with the walnut halves. Serve immediately.

Endive salad with apples
Serves 4

Ingredients	Metric-Imperial	American
1 medium head of endive		
2 tart dessert apples		
For the dressing:		
Oil	5 tbs	6 tbs
Wine vinegar	2 tbs	3 tbs
Water	4 tsp	4 tsp
Salt and pepper		
Sugar		

Trim and remove outer leaves of the endive. Halve it and chop roughly. Wash and drain well. Peel, quarter and core the apples. Cut into thin slices. Put the endive and apple together in a salad bowl.

To make the dressing, mix together the oil, vinegar and water. Season to taste with salt, pepper and sugar. Pour over the salad and serve immediately.

Lettuce with sour cream dressing

Serves 4

(Photo p. 368–369)

Ingredients	Metric-Imperial	American
2 round lettuces (butterhead)		
For the dressing:		
1 small onion		
Oil	1 tbs	1 tbs
Wine vinegar	2 tbs	3 tbs
Sour cream	4 tbs	5 tbs
Salt		
Sugar		
Chopped mixed herbs such as mint, tarragon or marjoram	2 tbs	3 tbs

Discard the rough outer leaves of the lettuces and remove the remainder of the leaves from the stalks. Tear the larger leaves in half, leaving the small inner ones whole. Wash and drain the leaves well without bruising. Place the leaves in a salad bowl.

To make the dressing, peel and finely chop the onion. Beat together the oil, vinegar and sour cream and season with salt and sugar to taste. Stir the onion and herbs into the dressing. Turn the lettuce leaves in the dressing just before serving, so that they are thoroughly coated.

Variation: Make the dressing with 3 tbs (4 tbs) oil, 2 tbs (3 tbs) lemon juice, salt to taste and the chopped herbs. Use in the same way.

Savoury banana salad

Serves 4

Ingredients	Metric-Imperial	American
4 ripe bananas		
Grapefruit juice	4 tbs	5 tbs
Cooked ox tongue	100 g/4 oz	4 oz
2 sticks of celery (stalks)		
For the dressing:		
Milk	4 tbs	5 tbs
Whipping cream	150 ml/¼ pint	⅔ cup
Sugar	1 tsp	1 tsp
Chopped rosemary	1 tsp	1 tsp
Salt		
Coarsely ground black pepper	½ tsp	½ tsp
Few drops soy sauce		
Few drops vinegar		

Peel and thinly slice the bananas into a salad bowl. Sprinkle with the grapefruit juice to prevent discoloration. Cut the tongue into strips. Trim the celery, string if necessary then slice thinly. Add the tongue and celery to the banana.

To make the dressing, stir together the milk, cream, sugar and rosemary. Season to taste with salt, pepper, soy sauce and vinegar. Pour over the salad ingredients in the bowl and toss lightly.

Below: Lettuce with sour cream dressing
Opposite: Savoury banana salad

374

Chinese leaf salad with sour cream dressing
Serves 4

Ingredients	Metric-Imperial	American
Chinese leaves (cabbage)	550 g/1¼ lb	1¼ lb
For the dressing:		
Cream cheese	25 g/1 oz	2 tbs
Whipping cream	3 tbs	4 tbs
Sour cream	3 tbs	4 tbs
Wine vinegar	2 tbs	3 tbs
Salt and pepper		
Sugar		
Chopped parsley	1 tbs	1 tbs
Snipped chives	1 tbs	1 tbs

Discard the rough outer leaves from the Chinese cabbage. Cut the head in half, then across into strips. Wash carefully, drain well and put into a salad bowl.

To make the dressing, mix together the cream cheese, whipping cream, sour cream and vinegar. Beat until smooth. Season with salt, pepper and sugar to taste. Fold in the herbs. Spoon the dressing over the salad and toss to combine.

Beat together the oil and vinegar to make a dressing. Remove the stems from the chilli peppers, halve, discard the seeds and chop the flesh roughly. Add to the dressing and allow to stand overnight. Purée the peppers and dressing in a blender.

Halve the tomatoes, remove the seeds and dice the flesh. Season with the salt. Peel and finely chop the onions. Trim the spring onions cutting back the green part to 15 cm/6 inches. Cut into rings. Combine the tomato, onion and spring onion in a salad bowl. Spoon over the dressing and mix gently. Chill for about 1 hour to allow the flavours to combine.

Colourful vegetable salad
Serves 4

Ingredients	Metric-Imperial	American
3 large corn cobs		
Shelled or frozen peas	225 g/8 oz	1⅓ cups
1 red sweet pepper		
For the dressing:		
2 medium-sized onions		
Water	225 ml/8 fl oz	1 cup
Wine vinegar	6 tbs	½ cup
Salt and freshly ground		
pepper	2 tsp	2 tsp
Sugar	3 tbs	4 tbs
Onion powder (optional)		
Chopped mixed herbs		
such as parsley, chives,		
dill weed, mint,		
watercress, chervil	3 tbs	4 tbs
Oil	2 tbs	3 tbs

Remove leaves and silk from the corn cobs. Cook in boiling salted water to cover for 10 minutes. Drain, then strip off the kernels. Leave to cool. Cook the peas in a little salted water for 10 minutes. Drain and cool. Deseed the pepper and dice the flesh. Combine the corn, peas and pepper in a salad bowl.

To make the dressing, peel and chop the onions. Mix with the water, vinegar and salt. Add pepper and sugar to taste and a little onion powder, if liked. Stir in the herbs. Fold the dressing into the salad vegetables. Finally, mix in the oil and allow to stand for 1 hour before serving.

Variation: If preferred, use 450 g/1 lb mixed frozen vegetables, defrosted at room temperature then cooked until tender, instead of the corn, peas and pepper.

Tomato salad with chilli sauce
Serves 4

Ingredients	Metric-Imperial	American
Oil	4 tbs	5 tbs
Wine vinegar	1 tbs	1 tbs
8 chilli peppers (chili)		
Tomatoes	450 g/1 lb	1 lb
Salt	1 tsp	1 tsp
2 mild onions		
1 bunch of spring onions		
(scallions)		

Above: Chinese leaf salad with sour cream dressing

377

Gourmet salad with kiwi fruit sauce
Serves 4

Ingredients	Metric-Imperial	American
1 head of fennel (Florence)	about 200 g/7 oz	about 7 oz
1 red sweet pepper		
2 courgettes (zucchini)		
3 spring onions (scallions)		
6 kiwi fruits		
Walnut or olive oil	1 tbs	1 tbs
Lemon juice	1 tbs	1 tbs
Dry sherry	2 tbs	3 tbs
Clear honey	1 tsp	1 tsp
Pinch of cayenne pepper		
1 egg yolk		
Whipping cream	4 tbs	5 tbs
Salt		

Remove the feathery green fennel leaves, chop finely and reserve. Quarter the fennel bulb and cut into thin strips. Halve the pepper, remove the seeds and cut the flesh into thin strips. Top and tail the courgettes and slice thinly. Trim and chop the spring onions. Peel 4 of the kiwi fruit and slice thinly. Arrange all these ingredients in a large salad bowl or in individual dishes.

To make the dressing, peel and roughly chop the remaining kiwi fruit. Press through a sieve and stir in the oil, lemon juice, sherry, honey and cayenne. Beat together the egg yolk and cream and fold into the sauce. Season to taste with salt. Spoon a little dressing over the salad and sprinkle with fennel leaves. Serve the remaining dressing separately.

Sweet pepper and tomato salad
Serves 4

Ingredients	Metric-Imperial	American
3 red or green sweet peppers		
1 small cucumber		
Firm tomatoes	350 g/12 oz	12 oz
For the dressing:		
Oil	4 tbs	5 tbs
Wine vinegar	4 tbs	5 tbs
Salt and pepper		
Sugar		
Chopped dill weed	1 tbs	1 tbs

Halve the peppers, remove the seeds and cut the flesh into fine strips. Peel and thinly slice the cucumber. Slice the tomatoes. Transfer these ingredients to a salad bowl.

To make the dressing, beat together the oil and vinegar with salt, pepper and sugar to taste and the dill. Pour the dressing over the salad and mix lightly. Leave to stand for at least 30 minutes before serving.

Variation: Peel and thinly slice a mild onion and add to the salad with 100 g/4 oz (1 cup) shredded white cabbage.

Opposite: Gourmet salad with kiwi fruit sauce
Below: Sweet pepper and tomato salad

Cauliflower and egg salad
Serves 4

Ingredients	Metric-Imperial	American
1 cauliflower		
For the sauce:		
2 hard-boiled eggs		
1 egg yolk		
Salt		
Oil	125 ml/4 fl oz	½ cup
Vinegar or lemon juice	2 tbs	3 tbs
Prepared mustard	1 tsp	1 tsp
Chopped mixed herbs	2 tbs	3 tbs
Salt		
Sugar		

Place the cauliflower in a pan with the stalk end downwards. Cover with lightly salted water, bring to the boil, cover and simmer for 20–25 minutes, or until tender. Drain well, divide into florets and arrange on a serving dish.

To make the sauce, shell and halve the eggs. Press the yolks through a sieve and mix with the egg yolk and a little salt. Gradually beat in half the oil, until thick. Then mix in the vinegar or lemon juice and the mustard and beat in the remaining oil. Finely chop the egg whites and fold into the sauce, with the herbs. Adjust the seasoning with salt and sugar and spoon over the cauliflower florets. Chill for 30 minutes before serving.

Cucumber salad
Serves 4

Ingredients	Metric-Imperial	American
1 large cucumber		
For the dressing:		
Oil	3 tbs	4 tbs
Vinegar	2 tbs	3 tbs
Salt and pepper		
Sugar		
1 medium-sized onion		
Chopped mixed herbs	2 tbs	3 tbs

Finely slice the cucumber. To make the dressing, beat together the oil, and vinegar with salt, pepper and sugar to taste. Peel and chop the onion and mix into the dressing with the herbs. At serving time, combine the cucumber and herb dressing and transfer to a salad bowl.

Below: Cauliflower and egg salad
Opposite: Onion and orange salad

Asparagus salad with prawns
Serves 4

Ingredients	Metric-Imperial	American
Shelled cooked prawns		
(shrimp)	225 g/8 oz	1½ cups
Cooked asparagus tips	450 g/1 lb	2¾ cups
Lettuce leaves		
For the dressing:		
Whipping cream	2 tbs	3 tbs
Medium sherry	1 tbs	1 tbs
Mayonnaise	5 tbs	6 tbs
Lemon juice		

Defrost the prawns if necessary and carefully mix with the asparagus tips.

To make the dressing, stir the cream and sherry into the mayonnaise and sharpen the flavour to taste with a little lemon juice. Arrange a bed of lettuce on a serving dish, put the asparagus and prawn salad on top and spoon the dressing over evenly.

Variations: To serve this salad as an hors d'oeuvre, peel 1 orange, divide into segments and remove the pith. Slice and mix into the salad. Spoon into orange cups before serving if liked. Alternatively, use a grapefruit, preferably a pink one, instead of the orange.

Onion and orange salad
Serves 4

Ingredients	Metric-Imperial	American
Mild onions, red-skinned		
if possible	350 g/12 oz	12 oz
3 medium-sized oranges		
For the dressing:		
Oil	3 tbs	4 tbs
Wine vinegar	1 tbs	1 tbs
Sweet sherry	2 tbs	3 tbs
Clear honey	1 tsp	1 tsp
Salt and pepper		
Chopped dill weed	1 tbs	1 tbs

Peel and slice the onions. Peel and slice the oranges, removing the pith. Place the onion and orange slices in a salad bowl.

To make the dressing, mix together the oil, vinegar, sherry and honey with salt and pepper to taste. Pour the dressing over the salad, toss lightly and sprinkle with dill. This is a refreshing salad to serve with grilled or fried meat.

Variation: Black olives would make a good addition.

Kohlrabi and radish salad
Serves 4

Ingredients	Metric-Imperial	American
4 small kohlrabi		
2 bunches of radishes		
For the dressing:		
Oil	3 tbs	4 tbs
Vinegar	4 tbs	5 tbs
Chopped mixed herbs	1 tbs	1 tbs
Salt and pepper		
Sugar		

Peel and coarsely grate the kohlrabi. Trim and thinly slice the radishes. Place the kohlrabi and radish together in a bowl.

To make the dressing, beat together the oil and vinegar and mix in the herbs. Season to taste with salt, pepper and sugar and pour over the salad ingredients. Toss lightly and leave to stand for 1 hour before serving.

Sweet pepper salad
Serves 4

Ingredients	Metric-Imperial	American
4 sweet peppers		
2 onions		
For the dressing:		
Oil	3 tbs	4 tbs
Tarragon vinegar	2 tbs	3 tbs
Salt and pepper		
Sugar		
Chopped tarragon leaves	1 tbs	1 tbs

Halve the peppers, remove the seeds and cut the flesh into strips. Peel and slice the onions. Place the ingredients in a salad bowl.

Combine dressing ingredients, pour over salad and toss lightly.

Bean salad with pine kernels
Serves 4

Ingredients	Metric-Imperial	American
Young runner beans (English)	1 kg/2¼ lb	2¼ lb
Oil	2 tbs	3 tbs
Pine kernels (nuts)	100 g/4 oz	1 cup
For the dressing:		
Oil	6 tbs	½ cup
Tarragon vinegar	3 tbs	4 tbs
Chopped oregano	2 tsp	2 tsp
Salt and pepper		
Garlic salt		

Slice beans obliquely and cook until just tender. Drain, cool and transfer to a salad bowl.

Heat the oil in a frying pan and use to cook the pine kernels until golden brown. Remove from the pan and cool.

Combine dressing ingredients, pour over beans and serve sprinkled with pine kernels.

Spinach and orange salad
Serves 4

Ingredients	Metric-Imperial	American
Young spinach leaves	225 g/8 oz	8 oz
For the dressing:		
½ orange		
Lemon juice	2 tbs	3 tbs
Oil	2 tbs	3 tbs
Salt and pepper		
Sugar		
Chopped thyme	1 tsp	1 tsp

To make the dressing carefully pare the rind from the orange half and cut into fine strips. Place in a small pan, add water just to cover and bring to the boil. Cook for 3 minutes then drain well and cool. Mix together the lemon juice and oil and season to taste with salt, pepper and sugar. Add the thyme. Peel and chop orange half, arrange in a salad bowl with spinach. Sprinkle over orange rind and dressing and serve at once.

Left: Kohlrabi and radish salad
Opposite: Spinach and orange salad

Orange and fennel salad with gin dressing

Serves 4

Ingredients	Metric-Imperial	American
Fennel (Florence)	450 g/1 lb	1 lb
3 oranges		

For the dressing:		
Oil	2 tbs	3 tbs
Vinegar	4 tbs	5 tbs
Gin	3 tbs	4 tbs
Sugar	1 tbs	1 tbs
Salt and pepper		
Garlic salt		

Remove any green feathery leaves from the fennel and reserve. Cut the fennel into thin strips and place in a bowl.

Combine dressing ingredients, pour over fennel and leave to stand for 30 minutes.

Meanwhile, peel the oranges, remove any pith and cut into slices. Arrange the orange slices and dressed fennel in a serving dish and pour over the remaining dressing. Sprinkle with fennel leaves before serving.

Confetti salad
Serves 4

Ingredients	Metric-Imperial	American
3 small onions		
Mushrooms	50 g/2 oz	2 oz
1 bunch of radishes		
1 red dessert apple		
2 hard-boiled eggs		
Canned drained		
mandarin segments	100 g/4 oz	⅔ cup
For the dressing:		
Olive oil	4 tbs	5 tbs
Lemon juice	3 tbs	4 tbs
Salt and pepper		
Sugar		
Chopped mixed herbs	3 tbs	4 tbs

Peel and slice the onions. Slice the mushrooms and trim and slice the radishes. Quarter, core and slice the apple. Shell and chop the eggs. Arrange all these ingredients and the mandarins in a salad bowl.

Combine dressing ingredients, pour over salad and toss lightly. Leave to stand for 30 minutes.

Radish salad
Serves 4

Ingredients	Metric-Imperial	American
3 bunches of radishes		
5 spring onions (scallions)		
1 dessert apple		
For the dressing:		
Oil	3 tbs	4 tbs
Tarragon vinegar	3 tbs	4 tbs
Salt and pepper		
Sugar		
Snipped chives	1 tbs	1 tbs

Trim and slice the radishes and trim and chop the onions. Peel, quarter, core and slice the apple. Place these ingredients in a salad bowl.

Combine dressing ingredients, pour over salad and toss lightly. Leave to stand for 1 hour.

Layered salad cocktail
Serves 2

Ingredients	Metric-Imperial	American
1 medium-sized onion		
1 green sweet pepper		
2–3 tomatoes		
For the dressing:		
Oil	2 tbs	3 tbs
Wine vinegar	1 tbs	1 tbs
Salt and pepper		
Sugar		

Peel and slice the onion then divide the slices into rings. Halve the pepper, remove the seeds and cut the flesh into small strips. Slice the tomatoes. Layer up the ingredients in two tall glasses.

To make the dressing, mix together the oil and vinegar with salt, pepper and sugar to taste. Pour over the cocktails before serving.

Opposite: Orange and fennel salad with gin dressing
Right: Layered salad cocktail

Celeriac salad with onion cream dressing
Serves 4

Ingredients	Metric-Imperial	American
1 head of celeriac	750 g/1¾ lb	1¾ lb
For the dressing:		
Oil	3 tbs	4 tbs
Lemon juice or vinegar	2 tbs	3 tbs
Salt		
Sugar		
1 medium-sized onion		
Whipping cream	2 tbs	3 tbs
Chopped mixed herbs	1 tbs	1 tbs

Peel and coarsely grate the celeriac. Place in a salad bowl.

To make the dressing, beat together the oil and lemon juice or vinegar with salt and sugar to taste. Peel and chop the onion, stir into the cream with the herbs. Combine with the oil mixture. Serve poured over the celeriac.

Variation: Mix the celeriac with grated apple. Instead of the sauce given above, prepare a cream dressing (see page 374) and garnish the salad with finely chopped lettuce and strips of Parma ham.

Kohlrabi salad with cream dressing
Serves 4

Ingredients	Metric-Imperial	American
Kohlrabi	750 g/1¾ lb	1¾ lb
For the dressing:		
Whipping cream	2 tbs	3 tbs
Lemon juice	2 tbs	3 tbs
Sugar		
Salt and pepper		
Chopped mixed herbs	2 tbs	3 tbs

Peel and coarsely grate the kohlrabi.

To make the dressing, stir together the cream and lemon juice and season to taste with sugar, salt and pepper. Fold in the kohlrabi, transfer to a salad bowl. Sprinkle with herbs.

Bean sprouts with chicken and avocado
Serves 4

Ingredients	Metric-Imperial	American
2 cooked chicken breast fillets	150 g/5 oz each	5 oz each
Wine vinegar	5 tbs	6 tbs
Dry sherry	2 tbs	3 tbs
French mustard	½ tsp	½ tsp
Olive oil	6 tbs	½ cup
Sugar		
Salt		
2 ripe avocado pears		
Bean sprouts	225 g/8 oz	8 oz
Coarsely ground black pepper		
Few sprigs of basil		

Skin the chicken breasts and cut into thin slices. Mix together 3 tbs (4 tbs) of the vinegar, the sherry, mustard and oil and season to taste with sugar and salt to make a smooth dressing.

Peel, halve and stone (pit) the avocados and cut into slices. Arrange the slices like fans on serving plates and sprinkle with the remaining vinegar. Arrange chicken slices and bean sprouts on the avocado. Spoon over the dressing and sprinkle the salads with pepper. Garnish with sprigs of basil and serve with French bread.

Below: Celeriac salad with onion cream dressing
Opposite: Bean sprouts with chicken and avocado

Pasta salad with ham and peas
Serves 4

Ingredients	Metric-Imperial	American
Short cut macaroni	400 g/14 oz	4²/₃ cups
Shelled peas	350 g/12 oz	2 cups
Sugar		
Cooked ham	350 g/12 oz	12 oz
4 small dill pickled cucumbers		
1 small onion		
For the dressing:		
Mayonnaise	225 ml/8 fl oz	1 cup
Natural yogurt (plain)	150 ml/¼ pint	²/₃ cup
Liquid from the jar of pickles	3–4 tbs	4–5 tbs
Chopped mixed herbs	3 tbs	4 tbs
Salt and pepper		

Cook the macaroni in plenty of boiling salted water for about 10 minutes, or until tender but still firm to the bite. Drain well, refresh with cold water and drain again. Cook the peas in boiling salted water, adding a little sugar, for about 10 minutes, or until tender. Drain well and add to the pasta. Dice the ham and pickled cucumbers and peel and finely chop the onion. Combine the ham, cucumber and onion with the pasta and peas and transfer to a serving bowl.

To make the dressing, mix together the mayonnaise, yogurt and liquid from the jar of pickles. Fold in the herbs and add salt and pepper to taste if necessary. Mix the dressing into the noodle salad and leave to stand for 30 minutes before serving.

Variations: Omit the dill pickled cucumbers and replace with 4 rings of pineapple, chopped. Replace the pickle liquid with pineapple juice from the tin. Chicken, turkey or tongue may be substituted for the ham. Other pasta shapes, such as bows or shells, may be used instead of macaroni. This salad is also good wih rice or new potatoes instead of pasta.

Pasta salad with tuna and tongue
Serves 8

Ingredients	Metric-Imperial	American
Spaghetti	450 g/1 lb	1 lb
Canned tuna	200 g/7 oz can	7 oz can
Cooked tongue	225 g/8 oz	8 oz
Drained capers	2 tbs	3 tbs
Lettuce leaves		
For the dressing:		
1 egg yolk		
Prepared mustard	1 tsp	1 tsp
Anchovy essence	1 tsp	1 tsp
Lemon juice	1 tbs	1 tbs
Salt and pepper		
Sugar	1 tsp	1 tsp
Oil	125 ml/4 fl oz	½ cup
Chopped mixed herbs	1 tbs	1 tbs
Lemon slices		
Sprigs of mint		

Break the spaghetti into small pieces and cook in plenty of boiling salted water for about 10 minutes, or until tender but still firm to the bite. Drain, refresh with cold water and drain again. Drain and flake the tuna. Cut the tongue into strips. Arrange the pasta, tuna, tongue and capers in a serving bowl lined with lettuce leaves.

To make the dressing, beat the egg yolk with the mustard, anchovy essence and lemon juice. Add a little salt and pepper and the sugar and gradually beat in the oil until the mixture is thick. Fold in the chopped herbs. Adjust the seasoning with more salt and pepper if necessary. Spoon the dressing over the salad. Remove the flesh from the lemon slices, discarding the pith. Use this to garnish the salad with sprigs of mint.

Left: Pasta salad with ham and peas
Opposite: Pasta salad with tuna and tongue

Watercress salad
Serves 4

Ingredients	Metric-Imperial	American
2 bunches of watercress		
For the dressing:		
Oil	2 tbs	3 tbs
Wine vinegar	1 tbs	1 tbs
Salt		
Sugar		
Chopped mixed herbs	2 tbs	3 tbs

Carefully wash the watercress, discarding any tough stalks. Drain well, without bruising the leaves. Place in a salad bowl.

To make the dressing, beat together the oil and vinegar with salt and sugar to taste. Stir in the herbs and pour over the watercress. Fold in gently.

Serving ideas: Serve the watercress salad with grilled steaks or chops, or as part of a combination of mixed salads for a buffet meal. It also makes a good filling for a savoury mousse set in a ring mould.

Tomato and onion salad with garlic dressing
Serves 4

Ingredients	Metric-Imperial	American
Tomatoes	450 g/1 lb	1 lb
2 large onions		
2 cloves of garlic		
1 hard-boiled egg		
Oil	3 tbs	4 tbs
Wine vinegar	2 tbs	3 tbs
French mustard	½ tsp	½ tsp
Salt and pepper		
Sugar		
Streaky bacon (strips)	75 g/3 oz	6 strips
Chopped basil	2 tbs	3 tbs

Pour boiling water over the tomatoes, drain, peel and slice. Peel and slice the onions and arrange in a salad bowl with the tomato slices. Peel and finely chop the garlic. Shell the egg, chop the white and reserve. Press the yolk through a sieve and mix well with the oil, vinegar and mustard. Add salt, pepper and sugar to taste. Stir in the garlic and pour over salad. Chop the bacon and fry until crisp. Cool, drain and sprinkle over the salad with the egg white and basil.

Salad platter with corn and tuna fish
Serves 4–6

Ingredients	Metric-Imperial	American
1 small lettuce		
1 green sweet pepper		
1 red sweet pepper		
4 large tomatoes		
1 large mild onion		
15 cm/6 inch length cucumber		
Canned sweetcorn kernels	350 g/12 oz can	12 oz can
Canned tuna fish	200 g/7 oz can plus 99 g/3½ oz can	7 oz and 3½ oz can
For the dressing:		
Whipping cream	300 ml/½ pint	1¼ cups
Tomato ketchup	3 tbs	4 tbs
Milk	3 tbs	4 tbs
Salt and pepper		
Sugar		
Chopped parsley	1 tbs	1 tbs
Chopped dill weed	1 tbs	1 tbs
Snipped chives	1 tbs	1 tbs

Remove the outer leaves from the lettuce. Tear the larger leaves in half and leave small ones whole. Wash and drain well. Deseed the peppers and cut the flesh into strips. Slice the tomatoes. Peel and slice the onion. Thinly slice the cucumber. Drain the corn and tuna and flake the fish roughly. Arrange all the ingredients on a large platter.

To make the dressing, stir together the cream, ketchup and milk and season to taste with salt, pepper and sugar. Spoon the dressing over the salad and sprinkle with herbs.

Tomato and tuna salad
Serves 4

Ingredients	Metric-Imperial	American
Tomatoes	450 g/1 lb	1 lb
2 large onions, red-skinned if possible		
Canned tuna fish in oil	200 g/7 oz can	7 oz can
For the dressing:		
Oil	3 tbs	4 tbs
Red wine vinegar	2 tbs	3 tbs
Salt and pepper		
Sugar		
Chopped parsley	2 tbs	3 tbs

Slice the tomatoes. Peel and slice the onions and divide the slices into rings. Flake the tuna and place, with the oil from the can, in a salad bowl with the tomato slices and onion rings.

To make the dressing, beat together the oil and vinegar and season to taste with salt, pepper and sugar. Pour over the salad, mix thoroughly and leave to stand for 30 minutes to allow the flavours to combine. Sprinkle with the parsley before serving.

Carrot salad with walnuts
Serves 4

Ingredients	Metric-Imperial	American
Carrots	750 g/1¾ lb	1¾ lb
Coarsely chopped walnuts	75 g/3 oz	¾ cup
Few lettuce leaves		
For the dressing:		
Lemon juice	5 tbs	6 tbs
Walnut or olive oil	4 tbs	5 tbs
Caster sugar (granulated)	3 tbs	4 tbs
Salt and pepper		
Few lemon slices		

Peel and finely grate the carrots. Place in a bowl with the nuts.

To make the dressing, beat together the lemon juice, oil and sugar and season to taste with salt and pepper. Stir into the carrot and nut mixture. Chill for 15 minutes.

Arrange lettuce leaves on 4 small plates, divide the salad among them and garnish with lemon slices.

Left: Tomato and onion salad with garlic dressing
Below: Broccoli cocktails

Broccoli cocktails
Serves 4

Ingredients	Metric-Imperial	American
Broccoli	225 g/8 oz	8 oz
3 tomatoes		
Camembert cheese	150 g/5 oz	5 oz
Few lettuce leaves		
For the dressing:		
Whipping cream	150 ml/¼ pint	⅔ cup
Pernod	4 tsp	4 tsp
Salt and pepper		
Chopped pistachio nuts	1 tbs	1 tbs

Divide the broccoli into florets and cook in boiling salted water for about 10 minutes, or until tender. Drain well and allow to cool. Divide the broccoli into bite-sized pieces and reserve a few for decoration. Pour boiling water over tomatoes, drain, peel and chop. Dice cheese. Line four cocktail glasses with lettuce, divide salad among them.

Stir together cream and Pernod and season to taste. Pour over cocktails, decorate with reserved broccoli florets and sprinkle with nuts.

Spanish salad platter
Serves 4

Ingredients	Metric-Imperial	American
1 lettuce		
15 cm/6 inch length cucumber		
1 medium-sized mild onion		
3 'beefsteak' tomatoes		
Canned anchovy fillets	50 g/2 oz can	2 oz can
5 hard-boiled quails' eggs		
20 stuffed green olives		
For the dressing:		
Olive oil	6 tbs	½ cup
Tarragon vinegar	4 tbs	5 tbs
Salt and pepper		
Sugar		
Chopped parsley	1 tbs	1 tbs

Remove the outer leaves from the lettuce. Tear larger leaves in half and keep small ones whole. Wash and drain well. Thinly slice the cucumber. Peel and slice the onion and divide the slices into rings. Cut each tomato into 8 wedges. Drain the anchovies and soak the fillets in water for 10 minutes if too salty. Drain well again. Shell the quails' eggs. Halve the eggs and olives. Combine all these ingredients in a salad bowl.

To make the dressing, beat together the oil and vinegar and season to taste with salt, pepper and sugar. Fold into the salad and chill for 1 hour. Serve sprinkled with the parsley.

Variation: Replace the anchovies with sardines.

Chicken salad
Serves 4

Ingredients	Metric-Imperial	American
Cooked chicken breast fillets	350 g/12 oz	12 oz
Canned mandarin orange segments	300 g/11 oz can	11 oz can
Canned sliced mushrooms	225 g/8 oz can	8 oz can
Canned asparagus tips	175 g/6 oz can	6 oz can
For the dressing:		
1 egg yolk		
Wine vinegar	1 tbs	1 tbs
French mustard	1 tsp	1 tsp
Salt and pepper		
Sugar		
Oil	125 ml/4 fl oz	½ cup

Cut the chicken breasts into strips, discarding the skin if preferred. Drain the mandarins, mushrooms and asparagus and place in a bowl with the chicken.

To make the dressing, beat together the egg yolk, vinegar, mustard and a little salt, pepper and sugar, using an electric mixer if possible. When the consistency is that of thin cream, gradually beat in the oil. Adjust the seasoning if necessary. Carefully fold the dressing into the chicken mixture and chill for 30 minutes. Serve with a leafy green salad.

Cook's tip: This salad is quick to assemble from store cupboard items, but you may of course use fresh, lightly cooked mushrooms and asparagus.

Fennel salad
Serves 4

Ingredients	Metric-Imperial	American
2 heads of fennel (Florence)		
3 tomatoes		
For the dressing:		
1 clove of garlic		
1 onion		
Juice of 1 lemon		
Oil	3 tbs	4 tbs
Salt and pepper		
Sugar		
Snipped mustard and cress	1 tbs	1 tbs
Chopped walnuts	1 tbs	1 tbs

Trim the fennel, reserving any green feathery leaves. Cut the fennel into thin strips. Pour boiling water over the tomatoes, drain, peel and quarter. Place in a salad bowl with the fennel.

To make the dressing, peel and crush the garlic and peel and chop the onion. Beat together the lemon juice and oil and season to taste with salt, pepper and sugar. Fold into the salad. Sprinkle with cress, nuts and fennel leaves.

Opposite: Spanish salad platter
Above: Fennel salad

Tomato and radish salad
Serves 4

Ingredients	Metric-Imperial	American
2 punnets of mustard and cress		
1 bunch of radishes		
4 tomatoes		
Salt and pepper		
For the dressing:		
Oil	3 tbs	4 tbs
White wine vinegar	3 tbs	4 tbs
French mustard	1 tsp	1 tsp
Sugar		

Wash the cress, drain well and remove the leaves from the stalks. Use these to line a flat dish or plate. Trim and slice the radishes. Slice the tomatoes and arrange in a ring round the edge of the dish. Sprinkle with salt and pepper. Put the radish slices in the centre of the dish.

To make the dressing, beat together the oil, vinegar and mustard with sugar to taste. Spoon over the salad.

Herbed cream cheese on cress
Serves 4

Ingredients	Metric-Imperial	American
Butter	75 g/3 oz	⅓ cup
Cream cheese	225 g/8 oz	1 cup
Whipping cream	1 tbs	1 tbs
Grated lemon rind	1 tsp	1 tsp
1 clove of garlic		
Chopped thyme	1 tsp	1 tsp
Chopped parsley	1 tbs	1 tbs
Chopped dill weed	1 tbs	1 tbs
Snipped chives	1 tbs	1 tbs
Chopped borage leaves (optional)	1 tbs	1 tbs
Chopped lemon balm	1 tbs	1 tbs
Chopped basil	1 tbs	1 tbs
1 punnet of mustard and cress		

Soften the butter and beat together with the cream cheese until smooth. Stir in the cream and lemon rind. Peel and chop the garlic, stir into the cream cheese mixture with all the chopped herbs. Place in a small bowl and chill for 4–5 hours.

Wash the watercress, drain well and take the leaves from the stalks. Use these to line a plate and turn the cheese mixture out on top.

Note: If any of the herbs are unobtainable, increase the quantity of others, to make up the same amount.

Opposite: Herbed cream cheese on cress and tomato and radish salad

Chicken, grape and cheese salad
Serves 4

Ingredients	Metric-Imperial	American
Green and black grapes	350 g/12 oz	12 oz
Cooked chicken breast fillets	225 g/8 oz	8 oz
Hard cheese such as Gouda or Cheddar	225 g/8 oz	8 oz
Drained canned sliced mushrooms	175 g/6 oz	1 cup
For the dressing:		
1 egg yolk		
French mustard	2 tsp	2 tsp
Wine vinegar	2 tbs	3 tbs
Salt and pepper		
Sugar		
Oil	125 ml/4 fl oz	½ cup
Natural yogurt (plain)	3 tbs	4 tbs

Halve the grapes and remove the pips (pits). Reserve some of the grapes for decoration. Cut the chicken breasts into strips and cut the cheese into slices and then into small squares. Reserve some of the grapes for the garnish and put the remainder into a salad bowl with the chicken, cheese and mushrooms.

To make the dressing, beat the egg yolk, mustard and vinegar together with salt, pepper and sugar to taste. Gradually beat in the oil and when thick, add the yogurt. Spoon the dressing over the salad and mix carefully. Garnish with the reserved grapes.

Variation: Use Danish Blue or Stilton cheese instead of Gouda or Cheddar.

Mixed salad with cream dressing
Serves 4

Ingredients	Metric-Imperial	American
1 small or ½ large lettuce		
2 medium-sized tomatoes		
½ red sweet pepper		
½ green sweet pepper		
½ large mild onion		
1 bunch of radishes		
12.5 cm/5 inch length cucumber		
For the dressing:		
Whipping cream	150 ml/¼ pint	⅔ cup
Sour cream	150 ml/¼ pint	⅔ cup
Milk	5 tbs	6 tbs
Tomato ketchup	2 tbs	3 tbs
Salt		
Sweet paprika pepper		
Sugar		
Chopped mixed herbs such as cress, parsley, chives	3 tbs	4 tbs

Discard the rough outer leaves of the lettuce, tear large leaves into pieces and keep tender small leaves whole. Wash and drain well. Slice the tomatoes. Deseed the peppers and cut the flesh into strips. Peel the onion and slice thinly. Trim and slice the radishes and slice the cucumber. Put the salad ingredients into a bowl.

To make the dressing, beat together the creams, milk and tomato ketchup and season to taste with salt, paprika and sugar. Fold in the herbs. Spoon the dressing over the salad or hand separately as preferred.

Ham and egg salad
Serves 4

Ingredients	Metric-Imperial	American
2 hard-boiled eggs		
Cooked ham	75 g/3 oz	3 oz
½ red sweet pepper		
For the dressing:		
Whipping cream	150 ml/¼ pint	⅔ cup
Lemon juice	1 tsp	1 tsp

Carrot, celery and apple salad with yogurt dressing
Serves 4

Ingredients	Metric-Imperial	American
4 sticks of celery (stalks)		
Carrots	225 g/8 oz	8 oz
2 dessert apples		
Lemon juice	1 tsp	1 tsp
For the dressing:		
Natural yogurt (plain)	150 ml/¼ pint	⅔ cup
Whipping cream	3 tbs	4 tbs
Lemon juice	2 tbs	3 tbs
Clear honey	1 tsp	1 tsp
French mustard	½ tsp	½ tsp
Salt and pepper		
Cooked ham or boneless chicken breast	100 g/4 oz	4 oz
Slivered almonds	1 tbs	1 tbs
A little mustard and cress (optional)		

Trim the celery, remove any strings then slice thinly. Peel and coarsely grate the carrots. Peel, quarter and core the apples then slice thinly. Sprinkle with lemon juice. Divide the celery, carrot and apple among 4 salad plates.

To make the dressing, beat together the yogurt, cream, lemon juice, honey and mustard and season to taste with salt and pepper. Chop the ham and stir into the dressing with the almonds. Spoon over the salad portions. If liked, chop the mustard and cress and sprinkle over the salads.

Worcestershire sauce	1 tsp	1 tsp
Salt and pepper		
Sugar		
Snipped chives	1 tbs	1 tbs

Shell and slice the eggs and cut the ham into strips. Deseed the pepper and cut the flesh into strips. Place in a bowl, pour over boiling water to cover then drain well. Place in a salad bowl with the egg and ham.

To make the dressing, mix the cream with the lemon juice and Worcestershire sauce. Season to taste with salt, pepper and sugar. Pour over the salad ingredients, toss lightly and sprinkle with the chives.

Above: Mixed salad with cream dressing
Right: Carrot, celery and apple salad with yogurt dressing

397

Salt herrings in cream sauce
Serves 4

Ingredients	Metric-Imperial	American
4 salt herrings		
4 onions		
2 pickled cucumbers (dill pickles)		
Whipping cream	350 ml/12 fl oz	1½ cups
Vinegar	6 tbs	½ cup
Mustard seeds	½ tsp	½ tsp
Peppercorns	½ tsp	½ tsp
1 bay leaf		
Sprigs of parsley		

Clean the herrings and soak them in cold water to cover for 24 hours, changing the water twice during this time.

Rinse the fish in cold water, discard the gills and heads and remove the inner black skin. Rinse again then remove the backbone with as many of the other bones as possible. Divide each into 2 fillets then each fillet into 3 pieces.

To make the sauce, peel and slice the onions and slice the pickled cucumbers. Put the cream in a bowl and stir in the vinegar, mustard seeds, peppercorns, bay leaf, onion and pickled cucumber. Put in the herring, cover and marinate 24 hours. Serve masked with the sauce and garnish with parsley.

Rollmops
Makes 12

Ingredients	Metric-Imperial	American
6 salt herrings		
2 gherkins (small dill pickles)		
2 onions		
French mustard	1 tbs	1 tbs
Drained capers	1 tbs	1 tbs
6 peppercorns		
2 bay leaves		
Water	125 ml/4 fl oz	½ cup
Vinegar	125 ml/4 fl oz	½ cup

Soak the herrings in cold water to cover for 24 hours, changing the water twice during this time.

Rinse the fish in clean cold water, discard the gills and heads and remove the inner black skin. Rinse again then cut along the backbone of each fish and remove it with as many of the other bones as possible. Divide each herring into 2 fillets. Chop the gherkins and peel and chop the onions.

Spread each herring fillet with mustard then top with a little gherkin and onion and a few capers. Roll up and secure with wooden cocktail sticks (toothpicks).

Place the rollmops in an earthenware dish with the peppercorns and bay leaves. Combine the water and vinegar, pour over the fish rolls then cover and leave to stand in a cool place for 4–6 days before serving.

Microwave method

If salt herrings are not available rollmops can be made with fresh herrings in the microwave.

Rinse the fish under cold water, discard the gills and head. Slit down the stomach, remove the insides and wash thoroughly again. Open up the fish and place on a flat board with the backbone facing upwards. Press down on the backbone hard, turn the fish over and release the bone with a sharp knife. Divide the fish into 2 fillets and remove any bones which are still on the fish.

Chop the gherkins and peel and chop the onions. Spread each herring fillet with mustard and then top with a little gherkin, onion and a few capers. Roll up and secure with wooden cocktail sticks (toothpicks).

Place the rollmops in a suitable dish with the peppercorns and bay leaves. Mix the water and vinegar and pour over the fish. Cook, covered, on full power for 10 minutes. Allow to stand for 5 minutes. Cook for a further 10 minutes. Cool and baste the herring with the liquid. Cover and leave in the refrigerator for 24 hours before using.

Left: Salt herrings in cream sauce
Below: Gourmet smoked salmon

Gourmet smoked salmon
Serves 4

Ingredients	Metric-Imperial	American
4 eggs		
Milk	2 tbs	3 tbs
Snipped chives	2 tbs	3 tbs
Salt and pepper		
Butter or margarine	15 g/½ oz	1 tbs
8 slices of smoked salmon		
Lettuce leaves		
Cooked or canned asparagus tips		
Stuffed green olives		
Sprigs of watercress		

Beat together the eggs, milk and chives and season to taste with salt and pepper. Melt the butter or margarine in a frying pan, pour in the egg mixture and stir until set. Leave to cool.

Divide the scrambled egg among the smoked salmon slices and roll them up. Arrange lettuce leaves on a platter, top with the salmon rolls and garnish with asparagus tips, sliced olives and sprigs of watercress. Serve with buttered toast.

Salmon with tartare sauce
Serves 4

Ingredients	Metric-Imperial	American
Lemon juice	2 tbs	3 tbs
4 salmon steaks	225 g/8 oz each	8 oz each
Salt and pepper		
For the sauce:		
Mayonnaise	4 tbs	5 tbs
Sour cream	4 tbs	5 tbs
2 hard-boiled eggs		
Snipped chives	1 tbs	1 tbs
Chopped parsley	1 tbs	1 tbs
Chopped dill weed	1 tsp	1 tsp
Salt and pepper		
Few lettuce leaves		
Oil	1 tsp	1 tsp

Sprinkle the lemon juice over the salmon steaks and leave them to stand for 20 minutes.

Season the fish with salt and pepper. Generously butter 4 pieces of foil, each large enough to enclose a salmon steak loosely. Place a steak on each piece of foil then fold up the sides and crimp the edges together to make airtight parcels. Arrange the parcels on a baking sheet (cookie sheet) and cook in a preheated hot oven, 220°C, 425°F, Gas Mark 7, for 25 minutes. Leave the fish to cool, still in the foil.

To make the sauce, mix together the mayonnaise and cream. Shell and finely chop the eggs and stir into the mayonnaise mixture with the chives, parsley and dill. Add salt and pepper if necessary.

Line a serving dish with lettuce leaves. Unwrap the salmon steaks, place on the lettuce and brush the fish lightly with oil. Serve with buttered toast, handing the sauce separately. Garnish the salmon steaks with parsley sprigs.

Stuffed matjes herring fillets
Serves 4

Ingredients	Metric-Imperial	American
1 tart dessert apple		
White wine	125 ml/4 fl oz	½ cup
4 matjes herring fillets		
Cranberry sauce	4 tbs	5 tbs
Whipping cream	150 ml/¼ pint	⅔ cup
Chopped dill weed	1 tbs	1 tbs

Peel and core the apple then cut it into 4 slices. Heat the wine in a small pan and use to cook the apple slices until just tender. Do not allow them to break up. Leave to cool in the wine liquid.

Drain the apple slices and arrange on a platter. Roll up the herring fillets and place one, upright, on each apple slice. Spoon cranberry sauce into the top of each herring roll. Add about 2 tbs (3 tbs) of the wine liquid to the cream, spoon over the fish rolls and sprinkle with the dill. Serve at once with brown bread and butter.

Microwave hint
Yogurt makes the basis of a good sauce for white fish. Purée cooked courgette (zucchini) or spinach in a blender with yogurt, lemon juice, salt and pepper. Transfer to a suitable dish and cook on medium power for 3 minutes. Pour over the cooked fish and serve.

Below: Salmon with tartare sauce
Right: Stuffed matjes herring fillets

Prawns with Pernod cream
Serves 4

Ingredients	Metric-Imperial	American
Water	750 ml/1¼ pints	3 cups
Salt	1 tsp	1 tsp
Pepper	½ tsp	½ tsp
Aniseeds	2 tsp	2 tsp
12 uncooked Mediterranean or Dublin Bay prawns (jumbo shrimp)		
Lettuce leaves		
Chopped pistachio nuts		
For the cream:		
Whipping cream	150 ml/¼ pint	⅔ cup
Pernod	4 tsp	4 tsp
Pinch of ground ginger		
Salt		

Place the water in a pan with the salt, pepper, aniseeds and prawns. Bring to the boil, cover and simmer for 10 minutes. Drain the prawns and shell them while still warm. Leave to cool. Arrange the prawns on lettuce leaves in a serving dish and sprinkle with the nuts.

To make the Pernod cream, mix together the cream, Pernod and ginger and season to taste with salt. Serve with the prawns accompanied by buttered toast.

Below: Prawns with Pernod sauce
Above right: Carp with sauce vinaigrette
Right: Avocado coupes

Carp with sauce vinaigrette
Serves 4

Ingredients	Metric-Imperial	American
1 cleaned carp, weight	1¾ kg/3¾ lb	3¾ lb
Salt and pepper		
Tomato wedges		
Lemon slices		
For the sauce:		
Oil	175 ml/6 fl oz	¾ cup
Vinegar	3 tbs	4 tbs
2 hard-boiled eggs		
Chopped parsley	2 tbs	3 tbs
Snipped chives	1 tsp	1 tsp
Pinch of dried basil		
Pinch of dried chervil		
Salt and pepper		

Wash the fish thoroughly and dry on absorbent kitchen paper. Rub the skin and inside the cavity with salt and pepper. Have ready a sheet if heavy duty foil, or use a double thickness of kitchen foil, which should be large enough to enclose the fish easily. Grease the foil, place the carp on it and seal the foil edges to make an airtight parcel which encloses the fish loosely. Place on a baking sheet and cook in a preheated hot oven, 220°C, 425°F, Gas Mark 7, for 50 minutes. Transfer the cooked fish to a serving dish and cool. Garnish with tomato wedges and lemon slices.

Skin the smoked trout and the eel and discard any bones. Remove the heads of the bucklings. Cut all the smoked fish into bite-sized pieces.

Line a platter with lettuce leaves and arrange the herring rolls and fish pieces attractively on it, putting the shellfish in the centre. Garnish the dish with sprigs of dill.

Avocado coupes
Serves 4

Ingredients	Metric-Imperial	American
4 matjes herring fillets		
8 stuffed green olives		
1 carton of mustard and cress		
1 small onion		
Whipping cream	2 tbs	3 tbs
2 ripe avocados		

Soak the matjes fillets in water for 2 hours then drain and dry on absorbent kitchen paper. Cut into strips. Slice the olives and cut the leaves from the cress. Peel and chop the onion. Mix together the herring strips, olive slices, onion, cream and almost all the cress.

Halve and stone (pit) the avocados. Divide the herring mixture among the avocado halves and sprinkle with the remaining cress. Serve at once before the avocado flesh becomes discoloured.

Microwave hint
To make a thickened sauce to serve with fish, blend 1–2 tsp cornflour (cornstarch) with a little water, add to the juices left in the dish when you remove the cooked fish, whisking well. Cook at Full Power, uncovered, for 2 minutes. Whisk again, ensuring that the sauce has boiled. If not, return to the cooker for a further 1 minute. Spoon over the fish and serve.

To make the sauce, whisk together the oil and vinegar. Shell and finely chop the eggs. Add to the oil mixture with the parsley, chives, basil and chervil. Season to taste with salt and pepper. Serve the sauce with the fish accompanied by new potatoes.

Mixed smoked fish platter
Serves 8–10

Ingredients	Metric-Imperial	American
3 matjes herring fillets		
Creamed horseradish from a jar	3 tbs	4 tbs
4 smoked trout fillets		
Smoked eel	225 g/8 oz	8 oz
Smoked bucklings	450 g/1 lb	1 lb
Smoked mackerel fillets	450 g/1 lb	1 lb
Smoked salmon slices	225 g/8 oz	8 oz
Lettuce leaves		
Shelled cooked prawns (shrimp)	225 g/8 oz	8 oz
Sprigs of dill weed		

Soak the matjes fillets in cold water for 2 hours. Drain and dry on absorbent kitchen paper. Spread each fillet with horseradish, roll up and secure with a wooden cocktail stick (toothpick).

Fillets of hare in puff pastry
Serves 6–8

Ingredients	Metric-Imperial	American
1 saddle of hare, weight	675 g/1½ lb	1½ lb
Dried thyme	½ tsp	½ tsp
Dried rosemary	½ tsp	½ tsp
Lemon juice	1 tbs	1 tbs
Oil	2 tbs	3 tbs
Salt and pepper		
Butter	40 g/1½ oz	3 tbs
10 stoned prunes (pitted)		
10 button mushrooms		
Sausagemeat (bulk **sausage)**	225 g/8 oz	8 oz
Brandy	1 tbs	1 tbs
Chopped pistachio nuts	1 tbs	1 tbs
Frozen puff pastry	450 g/1 lb	1 lb
1 egg yolk		
Milk	1 tsp	1 tsp

Carefully separate the fillets and the remaining hare flesh from the bones of the saddle. Remove any membrane from the meat, wash and dry on absorbent kitchen paper. Place in a bowl and sprinkle with the thyme, rosemary, lemon juice and oil. Cover and chill for 24 hours, turning the meat pieces twice during this time.

Remove the hare meat from the marinade, drain and season with salt and pepper. Melt the butter in a frying pan, add the hare pieces and fry until brown on all sides. Leave to cool. Chop the prunes and 4 of the mushrooms and mix both these into the sausagemeat with the brandy and pistachio nuts.

Defrost the pastry at room temperature then roll out and trim to a rectangle measuring about 60 cm/24 inches by 35 cm/14 inches. Take half the sausagemeat mixture and form into a rectangle measuring about 20 cm/8 inches by 7.5 cm/3 inches. Put this in the centre of the pastry. Top with the larger pieces of hare and then with the smaller pieces and the remaining mushrooms, putting these in a line down the centre between the pieces of hare, like a 'backbone'. Form the remaining sausagemeat mixture into a rectangle as above and place on the hare meat. Fold up the pastry, dampen the edges and seal firmly together.

Place the pastry parcel on a dampened baking sheet (cookie sheet) with the seam downwards. Cut fancy shapes from the pastry trimmings. Beat the egg yolk with the milk, brush the pastry parcel all over with this egg wash then position the pastry shapes and brush these also with egg wash. Cut 2 or 3 small steam vents if wished. Bake, uncovered, in a preheated moderately hot oven, 200°C, 400°F, Gas Mark 6, for 35 minutes, or until golden brown. Leave to cool. Cut into fairly thick slices and arrange on a serving platter. If liked, garnish with pistachio nuts.

Cream cheese with cucumber and black olives

Serves 2

Ingredients	Metric-Imperial	American
Curd cheese (sieved cottage)	100 g/4 oz	½ cup
Whipping cream	150 ml/¼ pint	⅔ cup
2 cloves garlic		
15 cm/6 inch length of cucumber		
Salt and pepper		
Few lettuce leaves		
Few black olives		
Olive oil	¼ tsp	¼ tsp

Beat the cheese until soft and gradually beat in the cream. Peel and chop the garlic. Peel and very finely dice the cucumber. Stir the garlic and cucumber into the cheese mixture and season to taste with salt and pepper.

Arrange lettuce leaves on 2 serving plates and top with the cheese mixture. Sprinkle with the olive oil and garnish with black olives.

Left: Fillets of hare in puff pastry
Below: Cream cheese with cucumber and black olives

Lamb shoulder with dried fruit stuffing

Serves 8

Ingredients	Metric-Imperial	American
Water	300 ml/½ pint	1¼ cups
Madeira	125 ml/4 fl oz	½ cup
1 stick of cinnamon		
3 whole cloves		
Dried fruit salad	450 g/1 lb	1 lb
1 boned shoulder of lamb, weight	1.75–2 kg/ 4–4½ lb	4–4½ lb
Salt and pepper		
Sweet paprika pepper		

Put the water into a pan and add the Madeira, cinnamon stick, cloves and fruit salad. Bring to the boil, cover and simmer for 10 minutes. Leave to cool and drain off any excess liquid.

Trim off excess fat from the lamb. Rub the meat, including inside the cavity, with salt, pepper and paprika. Place on a large sheet of foil and fill with most of the fruit. Close the opening and tie the meat into a neat shape with fine string. Fold up the foil, seal to make an airtight parcel. Place on a baking sheet (cookie sheet). Cook in a preheated moderately hot oven, 200°C, 400°F, Gas Mark 6, for 1½ hours. Remove from the oven and leave to cool, still in the foil.

Unwrap the stuffed shoulder, slice and arrange on a platter. Garnish with the remaining fruit before serving.

Meat balls with Roquefort stuffing
Serves 4

Ingredients	Metric-Imperial	American
1 bread roll		
Minced beef (ground)	450 g/1 lb	1 lb
1 onion		
1 clove of garlic		
Oil	1 tbs	1 tbs
2 eggs		
Chopped parsley	2 tbs	3 tbs
Tomato ketchup	2 tbs	3 tbs
Salt and pepper		
Roquefort cheese	100 g/4 oz	4 oz
Fresh breadcrumbs	50 g/2 oz	1 cup
Fat or oil for frying		

Soak the roll in cold water then squeeze out the moisture. Crumble into a bowl and add the beef. Peel and finely chop the onion and garlic. Heat the oil in a frying pan and use to cook the onion and garlic until transparent. Add to the meat mixture with the eggs, parsley and ketchup. Mix very well together and season to taste with salt and pepper.

Cut the cheese into 22–24 small pieces. Divide the meat mixture into the same number of portions and form each into a ball, enclosing a piece of cheese. Coat the meat balls in breadcrumbs.

Heat oil or fat in a deep pan until it will brown a cube of day-old bread in 1 minute. Cook the meatballs in batches for about 5 minutes, until golden brown. Drain well on absorbent kitchen paper and serve hot or cold.

from which the backbone was removed, with a sharp knife. Rub the meat all over with salt and pepper.

Peel and finely chop the onions and garlic and mix with the mustards and herbs. Fill the opening in the joint with stuffing and spread the remainder over the top. Tie into a neat shape with fine string and place on a large sheet of foil. Fold up the sides of the foil and seal to make an airtight parcel.

Place on a baking sheet (cookie sheet) and cook in a preheated moderately hot oven, 200°C, 400°F, Gas Mark 6, for 1¾ hours. Allow to stand for 15 minutes then open back the foil and leave the meat to cool completely. Take off the trussing strings, slice the pork carefully and arrange on a platter for serving. Garnish with chervil leaves and tomato 'waterlilies' if wished.

Veal miniature escalopes
Serves 8

Ingredients	Metric-Imperial	American
8 small veal escalopes	75 g/3 oz each	3 oz each
Olive oil	3 tbs	4 tbs
Salt and freshly ground black pepper		
8 slices Parma ham		
16 sage leaves		
Dry white wine	125 ml/4 fl oz	½ cup

Beat out the escalopes as thinly as possible. Heat the oil in a frying pan, and use to cook the escalopes in batches, for about 2 minutes on each side or until done to taste. Sprinkle with salt and pepper. Add the ham and sage leaves to the fat remaining in the pan and fry the ham slices for 1 minute on each side.

Lay a sage leaf on each escalope, top with a slice of ham then fold the escalope crossways and secure with a wooden cocktail stick (toothpick). Top each stuffed escalope with another sage leaf and arrange on a platter.

Pour the wine into the juices remaining in the pan and heat, stirring up the sediment. Spoon over the escalopes and serve hot or cold with French bread and a tomato salad.

Pork with herbed crust
Serves 8

Ingredients	Metric-Imperial	American
Boned saddle of pork	1½ kg/3¼ lb	3¼ lb
Salt and freshly ground black pepper		
For the crust:		
2 onions		
1 clove of garlic		
English (hot) mustard	2 tbs	3 tbs
Herbed French mustard	2 tbs	3 tbs
Chopped mixed herbs	50 g/2 oz	1 cup

Remove the skin and excess fat from the pork. Make a cut down the centre of the joint a little deeper than the cavity

Above: Pork with herbed crust; Meat balls with Roquefort stuffing; Veal miniature escalopes

Saddle of venison en croûte
Serves 4

Ingredients	Metric-Imperial	American
Boned saddle of venison	750 g/1¾ lb	1¾ lb
Butter	15 g/½ oz	1 tbs
Pepper and salt		
3 onions		
Streaky bacon (strips)	100 g/4 oz	8 strips
Mushrooms	100 g/4 oz	4 oz
Chopped basil	1 tbs	1 tbs
Chopped sage	½ tsp	½ tsp
Chopped marjoram	½ tsp	½ tsp
Frozen puff pastry	350 g/12 oz	12 oz
1 egg yolk		
Milk	2 tsp	2 tsp

Remove any membrane from the meat. Melt the butter in a pan and use to brown the meat on all sides. Remove it from the pan, sprinkle with pepper and leave to cool. Peel and chop the onions and chop the bacon and mushrooms. Add the onion, bacon and mushrooms to the fat remaining in the pan and cook, stirring frequently, until the onion is transparent. Leave to cool. Mix in the herbs and season to taste with salt and pepper.

Defrost the pastry at room temperature and roll out to a rectangle three times as long and as wide as the joint of venison. Spread about a quarter of the filling in the centre of the pastry and place the venison on this.

Cover the meat with the remaining filling. Fold up the

pastry round the joint, moisten the edges and seal well together. Transfer the pastry-wrapped venison to a dampened baking sheet (cookie sheet) with the seal underneath.

Beat the egg yolk with the milk and brush over the pastry parcel. Cut fancy shapes from the trimmings to decorate the parcel, put in position and brush these with egg wash. Bake, uncovered, in a preheated hot oven, 220°C, 425°F, Gas Mark 7, for 30 minutes. Lay a sheet of foil over the pastry parcel, reduce the oven heat to moderately hot, 200°C, 400°F, Gas Mark 6, and cook on for a further 15 minutes. Leave to cool.

Cut the venison en croûte into fairly thick slices and arrange on a serving dish. If wished, garnish the dish with canned pear halves filled with cranberry sauce.

Above: Saddle of venison en croûte and garnished venison medallions
Opposite: Prawn and avocado cocktails

Garnished venison medallions
Serves 8

Ingredients	Metric-Imperial	American
8 venison medallions	75 g/3 oz each	3 oz each
Salt		
Lemon juice		
Dried rosemary		
4–8 rashers of streaky bacon (strips)		
Butter	40 g/1½ oz	3 tbs
Brandy	2 tbs	3 tbs
Chicken liver pâté	150 g/5 oz	5 oz
Whipping cream		
For the garnish:		
Kiwi fruit slices		
Sliced cooked mushrooms		
Green grapes		
Mandarin orange segments		
Pistachio nuts		
Sprigs of parsley		

Sprinkle the venison medallions with salt, lemon juice and rosemary. Wrap a whole or half rasher of bacon, according to size, around each medallion and either tie with fine string or secure with wooden cocktail sticks (toothpicks).

Melt the butter in a frying pan and use to cook the bacon-wrapped medallions for 3 minutes on each side, or until done to taste. Transfer to a plate, sprinkle with half the brandy and leave to cool. Arrange the bacon-wrapped medallions on a serving plate and carefully remove the string or sticks.

Beat the pâté with the cream and remaining brandy until smooth. Place in a piping bag fitted with a star tube (pipe). Top each medallion with creamed pâté and garnish with mushroom slices, fruit pieces, nuts and parsley sprigs before serving.

Prawn and avocado cocktails
Serves 4

Ingredients	Metric-Imperial	American
2 ripe avocados		
Lemon juice	1 tbs	1 tbs
For the filling:		
Butter	15 g/½ oz	1 tbs
Whipping cream	2 tbs	3 tbs
Milk	1 tbs	1 tbs
Chopped dill weed	1 tsp	1 tsp
Salt and pepper		
Sugar		
Worcestershire sauce		
Few drops of lemon juice		
3 medium-sized tomatoes		
Shelled cooked prawns (shrimp)	100 g/4 oz	4 oz
Onion salt		
Few lettuce leaves		
Lemon slices		
Sprigs of dill		

Halve the avocados and remove the stones (pits). Scoop out the flesh leaving a 'shell' of about 6 mm/¼ inch thickness. Dice the removed flesh. Sprinkle the diced avocado and avocado 'shells' with lemon juice.

To make the filling, melt the butter and stir in the cream, milk and dill. Season to taste with salt, pepper, sugar, Worcestershire sauce and lemon juice.

Halve the tomatoes, scoop out the seeds and dice the flesh. Stir the tomato, shellfish and diced avocado into the cream mixture. Leave to stand for 10 minutes.

Sprinkle the insides of the avocado 'shells' with onion salt and fill with the shellfish mixture. Arrange the lettuce leaves on a serving dish, top with the avocado cocktails and garnish with lemon slices and sprigs of dill.

Artichoke bottoms piped with pâté
Serves 4–5

Ingredients	Metric-Imperial	American
Chicken liver pâté	150 g/5 oz	5 oz
Whipping cream	2 tbs	3 tbs
Brandy	1 tbs	1 tbs
8–10 drained canned artichoke bottoms		
Kiwi fruit slices		
Chopped tarragon		

Beat the pâté with the cream and brandy until smooth. Place in a piping bag fitted with a star tube (pipe).

Arrange the artichoke bottoms on a serving dish and pipe pâté mixture on top of each. Quarter kiwi fruit slices and use to garnish the artichokes then sprinkle with tarragon.

Cream cheese stuffed eggs
Serves 4

Ingredients	Metric-Imperial	American
4 hard-boiled eggs		
Cream cheese	100 g/4 oz	½ cup
Whipping cream	1 tbs	1 tbs
Salt and pepper		
Sweet paprika pepper		
A few shelled cooked		

prawns (shrimp)
Lemon slices
Sprigs of dill weed

Shell the eggs, cut in half lengthways and scoop out the yolks. Press these through a sieve and beat into the cheese and cream until smooth. Season to taste with salt, pepper and paprika. Place in a piping bag fitted with a star tube (pipe).

Arrange the egg white 'cups' on a serving dish, pipe in the cheese mixture and garnish with prawns, quartered lemon slices and sprigs of dill.

Veal garnished with aspic and maraschino cherries
Serves 4

Ingredients	Metric-Imperial	American
4 veal medallions		
Salt and pepper		
Butter	15 g/½ oz	1 tbs
Brandy	1 tbs	1 tbs
Calves' liver pâté	75 g/3 oz	3 oz
Whipping cream	1 tbs	1 tbs
Chopped aspic jelly		
Maraschino cherries		
Canned drained mandarin oranges		
Thyme leaves		

Press or beat the medallions slightly and form each into a neat shape. Season, then fry in butter for about 3 minutes on each side. Sprinkle with brandy, leave to cool.

Beat the pâté with the cream until smooth then place in a piping bag fitted with a star tube (pipe). Top each medallion with pâté mixture and garnish the dish with chopped aspic, quartered cherries, mandarin segments and thyme.

Fricassée of veal in a rice ring
Serves 4

Ingredients	Metric-Imperial	American
Boneless veal	675 g/1½ lb	1½ lb
Chicken stock (bouillon)	750 ml/1¼ pints	3 cups
1 medium-sized onion		
3 whole cloves		
Butter or margarine	40 g/1½ oz	3 tbs
Flour	40 g/1½ oz	⅓ cup
1 egg yolk		
Milk	2 tbs	3 tbs
Salt and pepper		
Sugar		
Lemon juice		
1 rice ring (see page 324)		

Dice the veal and place in a pan with the stock. Bring to the boil and skim. Meanwhile, peel the onion and stick with the cloves. Add it to the pan, bring back to the boil, cover and simmer for 45 minutes, or until tender. Drain off stock, reserving 500 ml/18 fl oz (2¼ cups). Discard onion and cloves.

Melt the butter or margarine in a separate pan and add the flour. Stir until the roux is golden then gradually add the reserved stock and bring to the boil, stirring constantly. Simmer for 5 minutes. Add the meat and heat through. Remove the pan from the heat. Beat the egg yolk with the milk and stir briskly into the veal mixture. Reheat if necessary but do not allow the fricassée to boil. Season with salt, pepper and sugar to taste and sharpen the flavour with a little lemon juice. Spoon into the rice ring.

Opposite: Veal garnished with aspic and maraschino cherries; Cream cheese stuffed eggs; Artichoke bottoms piped with pâté

Garnished beef fillet slices
Serves 16

Ingredients	Metric-Imperial	American
2 fillets of beef cut from the centre	1 kg/2¼ lb each	2¼ lb each
Oil	4 tbs	5 tbs
Salt and pepper		
For the garnishes:		
Suggestion 1.		
12 canned drained apricot halves		
12 maraschino cherries (cocktail)		
Sprigs of mint		
Suggestion 2.		
Cooked green peas	225 g/8 oz	1⅓ cups
Powdered gelatine	1 tsp	1 tsp
Water	2 tbs	3 tbs
Whipping cream	150 ml/¼ pint	⅔ cup
Salt and pepper		
Ground nutmeg		
Mushroom ketchup		
2 medium-sized tomatoes		
Sprigs of parsley		
Suggestion 3.		
1–2 ripe mangoes		
6 walnut halves		
Suggestion 4.		
Goose or chicken liver pâté	75 g/3 oz	3 oz
12 canned drained mandarin orange segments		
Chopped pistachio nuts		
Suggestion 5.		
Butter	100 g/4 oz	½ cup
Chicken livers	225 g/8 oz	8 oz
Salt and pepper		
Chopped mixed herbs		
Madeira or sherry	1 tbs	1 tbs
1 hard-boiled egg		
3 stuffed green olives		
Suggestion 6.		
Canned drained mandarin orange segments	100 g/4 oz	⅔ cup
Chopped pistachio nuts		
For the aspic:		
Water	4 tbs	5 tbs

Powdered gelatine	1 tbs	1 tbs
Clear canned beef consommé	425 ml/15 fl oz can	15 fl oz can
Sherry	2 tbs	3 tbs

Remove the membrane from the fillets. Heat the oil in a large frying pan and use to brown each fillet on all sides. Season with salt and pepper and transfer to a roasting tin. Pour the contents of the frying pan over the fillets and cook, uncovered, in a preheated hot oven, 220°C, 425°F, Gas Mark 7, for about 30 minutes, turning the fillets and basting several times during cooking. Remove from oven, cool, then cut each into 17–18 slices. Garnish as follows:

Suggestion 1.
Take 6 slices of fillet. Fill each apricot half with a cherry and place 2 halves on each fillet slice. Garnish with mint.

Suggestion 2.
Take 6 slices of fillet. Purée the peas and then press the purée through a sieve. Sprinkle the gelatine over the water in a small bowl and leave to stand for 10 minutes. Place over hot water and stir until the gelatine has completely dissolved. Beat into the pea purée. Lightly whisk the cream, fold into the pea mixture and season to taste with salt, pepper, nutmeg and a little mushroom ketchup. Pipe on to fillet slices, garnish with chopped tomato and parsley.

Suggestion 3.
Take 6 slices of fillet. Peel the mangoes and remove the stone (pit). Cut the flesh into 12 long slices. Arrange 2 slices in the shape of a cross on each slice of meat. Garnish with the walnut halves.

Suggestion 4.
Take 6 slices of fillet. Chill the pâté then cut into 6 slices. Lay each on a slice of meat and top with 2 mandarin segments. Garnish with pistachio nuts.

Suggestion 5.
Take 8 slices of fillet. Heat 15 g/½ oz (1 tbs) of the butter in a frying pan and use to cook the livers for about 3 minutes, turning them frequently. Season with salt and pepper and sprinkle on the herbs. Purée and cool. Cream the remaining butter until soft and beat in the liver purée. Adjust the seasoning again and add the Madeira or sherry. Place in a piping bag fitted with a star tube (pipe). Make a large rosette of liver mixture in the centre of each slice of meat. Shell and slice the egg and slice the olives. Top each rosette with a slice of egg and a slice of olive.

Suggestion 6.
Take 3 slices of fillet. Divide the mandarin segments among the fillet slices and sprinkle with pistachio nuts.

To make the aspic, place the water in a bowl and sprinkle on the gelatine. Leave to stand for 10 minutes. Heat the consommé in a pan, add the softened gelatine and stir until it has completely dissolved. Add sherry, cool and when syrupy, pour into a plate and chill until set. Cut into dice with a sharp knife. If wished, brush the syrupy aspic over the decorated fillet slices before allowing it to set.

Carefully arrange all the garnished fillet slices on a serving platter and decorate the dish with aspic dice.

Camembert canapés
Serves 4

Ingredients	Metric-Imperial	American
1 egg		
Camembert cheese	225 g/8 oz	8 oz
Flour	1 tbs	1 tbs
Slivered almonds	75 g/3 oz	¾ cup
Butter		
8 slices of French bread		
Canned drained pineapple pieces		
Canned drained mandarin orange segments		

Beat the egg and place in a shallow dish. Slice the cheese. Dust each slice first with flour, then dip in the egg and finally coat all over in almond flakes.

Melt 40 g/1½ oz (3 tbs) butter in a frying pan and use to fry the coated cheese slices until the almonds are golden brown. Remove from the pan, drain on absorbent kitchen paper and cool. Butter the bread, cover with the almond cheese slices and garnish with pieces of pineapple and orange. Arrange on a platter for serving.

Opposite: Garnished beef slices
Below: Camembert canapés

Cold duck with fresh figs
Serves 4

Ingredients	Metric-Imperial	American
1 duck	1½ kg/3 lb 5 oz	3 lb 5 oz
Salt and pepper		
Hot water	300 ml/½ pint	1¼ cups
Cold water	1 tbs	1 tbs
Powdered gelatine	1 tsp	1 tsp
Port	1 tbs	1 tbs
Sprigs of mint		
4–6 fresh figs		

Rub the skin of the duck with salt and sprinkle a little inside the cavity. Place the duck, breast upwards, in a roasting tin and cook, uncovered, in a preheated moderately hot oven, 200°C, 400°F, Gas Mark 6, for 30 minutes, pricking the bird below the wings and legs twice during this time to encourage the fat to run.

Pour off the accumulated fat from the tin then add half the hot water and return the bird to the oven for a further 1 hour, basting from time to time and adding the remaining water to the tin as the liquid evaporates. Brush the duck skin with salted cold water, raise the temperature of the oven to hot, 220°C, 425°F, Gas Mark 7, and cook the duck for a further 10 minutes, to crisp the skin. Transfer the bird to a plate and leave to cool. Scrape up the sediment in the tin,

strain the juices into a pan and spoon off surplus fat.

Put the cold water in a small bowl and sprinkle on the gelatine. Leave to stand for 10 minutes. Add to the juices in the pan and stir until the gelatine has completely dissolved, if necessary placing the pan over gentle heat. Stir in the port, add salt and pepper to taste and pour the mixture into a plate. Chill until set.

Loosen the duck breast meat from the carcase, slice and then carefully arrange back on the carcase. Place the duck on a serving dish and garnish with mint sprigs. Cut a deep cross in the top of each fig and peel back the four 'petals'. Dice the aspic and use to garnish the duck with the figs.

Pheasant terrine with truffles
Serves 6–8

Ingredients	Metric-Imperial	American
1 pheasant, weight	1¼ kg/2¾ lb	2¾ lb
Brandy	3 tbs	4 tbs
1 small onion		
1 clove of garlic		
Streaky bacon (strips)	450 g/1 lb	1 lb
Boneless lean pork	450 g/1 lb	1 lb
Port	3 tbs	4 tbs
1 egg		

	Metric-Imperial	American
Whipping cream	150 ml/¼ pint	⅔ cup
Chopped mixed herbs	1 tsp	1 tsp
Salt and pepper		
Truffles	25 g/1 oz	1 oz
For the aspic:		
Powdered gelatine	2 tsp	2 tsp
Water	1 tbs	1 tbs
Canned consommé	125 ml/4 fl oz	½ cup
Port	4 tsp	4 tsp
Chopped pistachio nuts	1 tbs	1 tbs

Have the poulterer bone the pheasant. Place the breast fillets in a dish, pour the brandy over them, cover and leave to stand for 1–2 hours.

Peel and chop the onion and garlic and mince with half the bacon, the pork and remaining pheasant flesh. Mix in the port, egg, cream and herbs and season with salt and pepper to taste. Very finely chop two thirds of the truffles and fold into the meat mixture.

Choose a terrine with a lid and a capacity of about 1¾ L/3 pints (3¾ pints) and line with most of the remaining bacon slices. Put in half the meat mixture, lay the pheasant fillets on top and cover with the rest of the meat mixture. Level the top then fold over the ends of the bacon strips lining the terrine and put the rest of the bacon on top. Cover with the lid and place the terrine in a roasting tin. Pour in water to come half-way up the side of the terrine. Cook in a preheated moderately hot oven, 200°C, 400°F, Gas Mark 6, for 1¾ hours, adding more water to the tin as necessary during cooking. Remove the terrine from the oven, take off the lid and pour off excess fat. Cover with foil and weight the top of the terrine. Leave to cool and then chill for at least 24 hours.

To make the aspic, sprinkle the gelatine over the water in a small bowl. Leave to stand for 10 minutes. Pour the consommé into a pan with the port. Bring to the boil, remove from the heat and stir in the softened gelatine until it has completely dissolved. Thinly slice the remaining truffles and use, with the pistachio nuts, to garnish the terrine. Pour the aspic over the top and leave to set before serving.

Variation: As an alternative to truffles, use dried Chinese mushrooms, soaked and pre-cooked.

Herbed cold roast beef
Serves 8–10

Ingredients	Metric-Imperial	American
Top rump of beef	2 kg/4½ lb	4½ lb
2 cloves of garlic		
Salt and pepper		
French mustard	2 tbs	3 tbs
Dried herbs of Provence	2 tsp	2 tsp

Make small cuts all over the fat surface of the meat. Peel and crush the garlic and rub into the meat. Sprinkle it with salt and pepper. Spread the meat with mustard and then sprinkle with the herbs. Place in a greased roasting tin and cook, uncovered, in a preheated hot oven, 220°C, 425°F, Gas Mark 7, for 40 minutes, or until done to taste.

Leave the meat to cool and then cut into slices and arrange on a platter for serving.

Avocados with Roquefort cream
Serves 4

Ingredients	Metric-Imperial	American
2 ripe avocados		
Whipping cream	150 ml/¼ pint	⅔ cup
1 small onion		
Salt and pepper		
Roquefort cheese	75 g/3 oz	3 oz
Few lettuce leaves		
Black olives		

Halve and stone (pit) the avocados then scoop out the flesh leaving a 'shell' of about 6 mm/¼ inch thickness. Mash the avocado flesh until smooth then beat in most of the cream. Peel and grate the onion and fold into the avocado mixture. Season to taste with salt and pepper.

Mash the cheese with the remaining cream and when smooth, fold into the avocado mixture. Place in a piping bag fitted with a large star tube (pipe). Fill the avocado shells with the Roquefort cream and serve on a plate, garnished with lettuce leaves and olives.

Opposite: Cold duck with fresh figs
Below: Avocados with Roquefort cheese

Rémoulade sauce
Serves 4–6

Ingredients	Metric-Imperial	American
2 hard-boiled eggs		
1 egg yolk		
Sugar	1 tsp	1 tsp
Salt		
Oil	125 ml/4 fl oz	½ cup
Vinegar or lemon juice	2 tbs	3 tbs
French mustard	1 tsp	1 tsp
Drained capers	1 tbs	1 tbs
2 canned anchovy fillets		
2 gherkins (small dill pickles)		
Green peppercorns	2 tsp	2 tsp
Chopped mixed herbs	2 tbs	3 tbs

Shell the hard-boiled eggs, halve, remove the yolks and press these through a sieve into a bowl. Mix in the egg yolk, sugar and salt to taste. Gradually beat in half the oil and when the mixture thickens, beat in the vinegar or lemon juice, the mustard and remaining oil.

Chop the capers, anchovy fillets and gherkins and crush the green peppercorns with a knife tip. Add all these to the sauce with the herbs. Chop the hard-boiled egg white and fold in. Adjust the seasoning with more salt if necessary.

Below: Rémoulade sauce
Opposite: Cold smoked fish platter

Beef n' bean soup
Serves 8–10

Ingredients	Metric-Imperial	American
Skirt of beef (flank)	225 g/8 oz	8 oz
Boneless lean pork	225 g/8 oz	8 oz
Pork dripping	50 g/2 oz	¼ cup
Onions	225 g/8 oz	8 oz
Salt and pepper		
Sugar		
Hot paprika pepper		
Tabasco pepper sauce		
Chilli sauce		
Cayenne pepper		
Madeira	2 tbs	3 tbs
Beef stock (bouillon)	1 L/1¾ pints	4⅓ cups
1 leek		
1 red hot pepper		
2 carrots		
Piece of celeriac	100 g/4 oz	4 oz
Canned red kidney beans	425 g/15 oz can	15 oz can
Canned cannellini beans	425 g/15 oz can	15 oz can

Dice the beef and pork. Melt the dripping in a pan and use to brown the meat on all sides. Peel and halve the onions and add to the pan. Fry for a few minutes. Season to taste with salt, pepper, sugar, a little hot paprika, Tabasco, chilli sauce and cayenne. Stir in the Madeira and stock and bring to the boil. Cover and simmer for 15 minutes.

Meanwhile, trim, clean and slice the leek, quarter the pepper and remove the seeds, and peel the carrots and celeriac and cut into strips. Add the vegetables to the soup, bring back to the boil. Cover and simmer for 45 minutes. Add the red and white beans to the pan with the liquid from the cans, stir well and simmer, covered, for a further 5 minutes. Adjust the seasoning if necessary.

Cold smoked fish platter
Serves 6

Ingredients	Metric-Imperial	American
Selection of smoked fish such as smoked bucklings, smoked fillets of trout, smoked mackerel fillets, smoked salmon slices, total weight	1 kg/2¼ lb	2¼ lb
Hard-boiled egg halves		
Canned anchovy fillets		
Gherkins (small dill pickles)		
Radish slices		
Tomato baskets or 'roses'		
Lemon slices		
Sprigs of parsley		
Sprigs of watercress		

Arrange the chosen selection of fish attractively on a platter. Garnish with eggs, anchovy fillets, gherkins, radish slices, tomato baskets or 'roses' and lemon slices. Finish with sprigs of herbs before serving.

Serving ideas: Accompany the smoked fish with a horse-radish cream. To make this, combine 2 tbs/3 tbs creamed horseradish from a jar with 150 ml/¼ pint/⅔ cup sour cream. Stir in the finely grated rind of ½ lemon and a pinch of sugar. Transfer to a small dish and chill before serving. Accompany with wholemeal or pumpernickel bread.

Mushroom salad
Serves 4–6

Ingredients	Metric-Imperial	American
Mushrooms	450 g/1 lb	1 lb
Salt and pepper		
Sliced roast beef	225 g/8 oz	8 oz
2 hard-boiled eggs		
For the dressing:		
Oil	4 tbs	5 tbs
Herbed vinegar	2 tbs	3 tbs
Whipping cream	4 tbs	5 tbs
Tomato ketchup	2 tbs	3 tbs
Brandy	1 tsp	1 tsp
Salt and pepper		
Sweet paprika pepper		
Sugar		
Chopped parsley	2 tbs	3 tbs

Quarter the mushrooms and place in a pan with just enough water to cover. Bring to the boil, cover and simmer for 10 minutes. Drain and leave to cool. Season with salt and pepper. Cut the beef into strips and shell and coarsely chop the eggs. Combine the mushrooms, beef and egg.

To make the dressing, beat together the oil, vinegar, cream, ketchup and brandy and season to taste with salt, pepper, sweet paprika and sugar. Stir in the parsley. Fold into the mushroom mixture and chill for 20 minutes. If wished, garnish the salad with hard-boiled egg slices and sprigs of parsley before serving.

Serving idea: Accompany with garlic bread.

Chocolate pudding
Serves 4

Ingredients	Metric-Imperial	American
Butter or margarine	50 g/2 oz	¼ cup
Caster sugar (granulated)	150 g/5 oz	⅔ cup
Vanilla essence (extract)	1 tsp	1 tsp
3 eggs		
Rum essence (extract)		
Pinch of salt		
Instant coffee powder	1 tsp	1 tsp
Cornflour (cornstarch)	40 g/1½ oz	⅓ cup
Cocoa powder	3 tbs	4 tbs
Baking powder	1 tsp	1 tsp
Milk	4 tbs	5 tbs
Fresh breadcrumbs	100 g/4 oz	2 cups
Ground almonds	25 g/1 oz	¼ cup

Cream the butter or margarine with the sugar and vanilla essence until light and fluffy. Gradually beat in the eggs, rum essence, salt and coffee. Sift together the cornflour, cocoa and baking powder. Fold into the mixture alternately with the milk, most of the breadcrumbs and the almonds.

Grease a pudding bowl and sprinkle with the remaining breadcrumbs. Turn in the pudding mixture. Cover with foil and crimp the edges well under the rim of the bowl. Stand this in a pan and pour in boiling water to come halfway up the sides of the bowl.

Cover the pan and keep the water boiling gently for 1½ hours, adding more boiling water if necessary during cooking. Turn out on a warm dish and serve with an almond-flavoured sauce.

Nut pudding with apricot sauce
Serves 4

Ingredients	Metric-Imperial	American
Hazelnut kernels (filberts)	100 g/4 oz	1 cup
Sweet baby rusks	100 g/4 oz	4 oz
5 eggs		
Butter	100 g/4 oz	½ cup
Caster sugar (granulated)	100 g/4 oz	½ cup
Grated rind of 1 lemon		
Pinch of salt		
Whipping cream	150 ml/¼ pint	⅔ cup
For the sauce:		
Canned apricots	425 g/15 oz can	15 oz can
Apricot liqueur	2 tbs	3 tbs

Spread the hazelnuts on a baking sheet (cookie sheet) and place, uncovered, in a preheated moderately hot oven, 200°C, 400°F, Gas Mark 6, for 10 minutes. Cool then rub off the skins. Grind the rusks and hazelnuts as finely as possible. Separate 3 of the eggs.

Cream the butter until soft then gradually beat in half of the sugar, the remaining 2 eggs, the 3 egg yolks, lemon rind and salt. Stir in the cream and almost all the rusk mixture. Whisk the egg whites in a clean bowl until stiff then gradually add the remaining sugar, a tablespoon at a time, whisking vigorously after each addition. Fold into the nut mixture.

Grease a fluted ring mould and sprinkle with the reserved rusk mixture. Spoon in the pudding. Stand the mould in a roasting tin and pour in boiling water to come halfway up the side of the mould. Cook, uncovered, in the moderately hot oven for about 1 hour, or until firm to the touch. Invert the mould over a warm serving dish and cover with a damp cloth for 5 minutes. This should release the pudding. Remove the mould.

To make the sauce, drain the apricots then purée and mix in the liqueur and enough of the fruit syrup to give a pouring consistency. Spoon over the hot pudding or hand separately. Serve at once.

Morello cherry and curd cheese bake
Serves 4

Ingredients	Metric-Imperial	American
3 eggs		
Caster sugar (granulated)	100 g/4 oz	½ cup
Curd cheese (sieved cottage)	450 g/1 lb	1 lb
Semolina	75 g/3 oz	½ cup
Lemon juice	2 tbs	3 tbs
Canned stoned morello cherries (pitted)	425 g/15 oz can	15 oz can

Separate the eggs. Whisk together the egg yolks and sugar until light and creamy. In a separate bowl mix together the cheese, semolina and lemon juice. Stir into the egg mousse.

Whisk the egg whites in a clean bowl until stiff and fold in. Drain the cherries, reserving the syrup, stir in lightly, then transfer to a greased shallow ovenproof dish. Bake, uncovered, in a preheated moderately hot oven, 200°C, 400°F, Gas Mark 6, for 25 minutes, or until golden brown on top. Serve with the cherry syrup and whipped cream.

Stuffed baked apple pudding
Serves 6

Ingredients	Metric-Imperial	American
6 small dessert apples		
White wine	2 tbs	3 tbs
Caster sugar (granulated)	4 tbs	5 tbs
Redcurrant jelly		
1 egg		
Cornflour (cornstarch)	1 tbs	1 tbs
Milk	300 ml/½ pint	1¼ cups
½ vanilla pod		

Peel and core the apples and place in a greased ovenproof dish. Brush with the wine and sprinkle with 1 tbs of the sugar. Cover and place in a preheated moderately hot oven, 200°C, 400°F, Gas Mark 6, for 35 minutes. Fill the centres of the apples with redcurrant jelly. Raise the oven heat to hot, 220°C, 425°F, Gas Mark 7.

Separate the egg and mix together the yolk, cornflour, 1 tbs of the remaining sugar and 2 tbs (3 tbs) of the milk. Put the rest of the milk into a pan with the vanilla pod and bring to the boil. Pour into the cornflour mixture and stir briskly. Return to the pan and stir constantly until boiling. Remove from the heat, take out the vanilla pod and pour the mixture over the apples in the dish.

Whisk the egg white in a clean bowl until stiff then whisk in the rest of the sugar. Spoon over the vanilla cream and place, uncovered, in the hot oven for 5 minutes, until the top is just turning golden brown.

Microwave method
Peel and core the apples and place in deep microwave dish. Brush with the wine and sprinkle with 1 tbs of the sugar. Cover with a lid or clingwrap and cook on full power for 10 minutes.

Take the apples out of the oven and fill the centres with redcurrant jelly. Return on full power for a further 5 minutes.

Separate the egg and mix the yolk with the cornflour, 1 tablespoon of the remaining sugar and 2 tbs (3 tbs) of the milk. Put the rest of the milk with the vanilla pod in a bowl and heat on full power for 5 minutes. Pour some of the milk into the egg mixture and then return all the mixture to the bowl. Mix well. Return to the microwave on full power for 3 minutes, stir and cook for a further 2 minutes. Remove the vanilla pod if the sauce is thick enough and pour the mixture over the apples in the dish. Return to the microwave for 3 minutes on full power.

Whisk the egg white in a clean bowl until stiff then whisk in the remaining sugar. Spoon over the vanilla cream and place under a hot grill until the top turns golden brown.

Peaches in white wine with soufflé topping
Serves 4

Ingredients	Metric-Imperial	American
4 peaches		
White wine	125 ml/4 fl oz	½ cup
Clear honey	2 tbs	3 tbs
Lemon juice	1 tsp	1 tsp
½ cinnamon stick		
3 eggs		

Pour boiling water over the peaches, drain and peel. Halve and remove the stones (pits).

Place the wine in a pan with the honey, lemon juice and cinnamon stick. Bring to the boil, put in the peach halves and simmer for 4 minutes. Drain the fruit and arrange in a greased ovenproof dish. Boil the syrup to reduce slightly then discard the cinnamon stick.

Separate the eggs and whisk the yolks into the peach syrup. Whisk the whites in a clean bowl until stiff and fold into the mixture. Spoon over the peaches to make an even layer. Place, uncovered, in a preheated moderately hot oven, 200°C, 400°F, Gas Mark 6, for 15 minutes.

Left: Nut pudding with apricot sauce
Below: Peaches in white wine with soufflé topping

Cinnamon pudding
Serves 4

Ingredients	Metric-Imperial	American
Milk	450 ml/¾ pint	scant 2 cups
Pinch of salt		
Semolina	125 g/4½ oz	¾ cup
Butter	100 g/4 oz	½ cup
Caster sugar (granulated)	100 g/4 oz	½ cup
Vanilla essence (extract)	2 tsp	2 tsp
3 eggs		
1 packet vanilla blancmange powder (pudding)	33 g/1¼ oz	1 ¼ oz
Ground cinnamon	1 tsp	1 tsp
Seedless raisins	50 g/2 oz	⅓ cup
Ground almonds	25 g/1 oz	¼ cup
Fresh breadcrumbs	2 tbs	3 tbs

Reserve 5 tbs (6 tbs) of the milk, put the remainder into a pan and bring to the boil. Remove from the heat, sprinkle in the salt and semolina and stir well. Leave to stand for about 15 minutes, stirring frequently.

Meanwhile, cream the butter in a bowl and gradually add the sugar, vanilla essence and eggs, beating vigorously all the time. Beat this mixture into the semolina while it is still warm. Mix together the reserved milk, blancmange powder and cinnamon and stir into the semolina mixture together with the raisins and almonds.

Grease a metal ring mould with a capacity of about 1½ L/2½ pints (3⅓ pints) and sprinkle with the breadcrumbs. Pour in the pudding mixture to fill the mould two-thirds full. Cover with foil, crimping this well under the rim of the mould. Place in a pan and pour in boiling water to

Breadcrumb pudding
Serves 4

Ingredients	Metric-Imperial	American
Day-old bread rolls	225 g/8 oz	8 oz
Hot milk	350 ml/12 fl oz	1½ cups
2 eggs		
Butter or margarine	100 g/4 oz	½ cup
Caster sugar (granulated)	100 g/4 oz	½ cup
Ground almonds	50 g/2 oz	½ cup
Seedless raisins	50 g/2 oz	⅓ cup
Pinch of salt		
Grated rind 1 lemon		
Fresh breadcrumbs	2 tbs	3 tbs

Cut the rolls into small pieces and place in a bowl. Pour over the hot milk and leave to stand until cool, stirring occasionally.

Separate the eggs. Place the butter or margarine in a bowl and beat until soft. Gradually beat in the sugar, egg yolks, bread and milk, almonds, raisins, salt and lemon rind. Whisk the egg whites in a separate bowl until stiff and fold into the raisin mixture.

Grease a pudding bowl or dish and sprinkle with the breadcrumbs. Pour in the raisin mixture and cover with foil, crimping this well under the rim of the bowl. Place in a pan and pour in boiling water until it reaches about 2.5 cm/ 1 inch below the rim of the bowl.

Cover the pan and keep the water boiling gently for about 1 hour and 10 minutes. Turn the pudding out on a dish and serve hot or cold with a sherry or wine sauce.

Tip: The rolls may be partly replaced by cake crumbs in which case the sugar should be reduced slightly.

come halfway up the sides of the mould. Cover the pan and keep the water boiling gently for 1½ hours, adding more boiling water to the pan during cooking if necessary. Turn the pudding out on a warm plate and serve with stewed plums.

Cinnamon pudding
Right: Breadcrumb pudding

Moulded rice pudding with cherry sauce
Serves 4

Ingredients	Metric-Imperial	American
Milk	500 ml/18 fl oz	2¼ cups
Pinch of salt		
½ stick of cinnamon		
Round grain rice	150 g/5 oz	¾ cup
Vanilla essence (extract)	2 tsp	2 tsp
3 eggs		
Caster sugar (granulated)	75 g/3 oz	⅓ cup
Grated rind of ½ lemon		
Lemon juice	2 tbs	3 tbs
Chopped or ground almonds	75 g/3 oz	¾ cup
Fresh breadcrumbs	2 tbs	3 tbs
For the sauce:		
Canned stoned cherries (pitted)	425 g/15 oz can	15 oz can
Cornflour (cornstarch)	2 tbs	3 tbs

Put the milk into a pan with the salt and cinnamon stick. Bring to the boil, sprinkle in the rice, bring back to the boil and stir once. Cover and simmer for about 20 minutes, or until the rice is tender. Remove from the heat, take out the cinnamon stick, stir in the vanilla essence and leave to cool.

Separate the eggs and place the yolks in a bowl with the sugar, lemon rind and juice. Whisk until thickened and creamy. Fold in the rice mixture and almonds. Whisk the egg whites until stiff and fold into the rice mixture.

Grease a pudding bowl and sprinkle with the breadcrumbs. Fill with the rice mixture and cover with foil, crimping this well under the rim of the bowl. Place in a pan and add boiling water to come about half-way up the sides of the bowl. Put on the lid and keep the water boiling gently for about 1 hour, adding more boiling water to the pan during cooking if necessary. Turn out on a warm dish.

To make the sauce, drain the syrup from the cherries into a pan. Moisten the cornflour with a little of the syrup, add to the pan and stir until boiling and thickened. Roughly chop the cherries, add to the sauce and heat through. Serve with the rice pudding.

Biscuit crumb pudding
Serves 4

Ingredients	Metric-Imperial	American
Milk	300 ml/11 fl oz	1⅓ cups
Biscuit crumbs (broken cracker)	150 g/5 oz	1⅔ cups
Butter or margarine	50 g/2 oz	3 tbs
Caster sugar (granulated)	2 tbs	3 tbs
2 eggs		
Vanilla essence (extract)	2 tsp	2 tsp
Few drops of almond essence (extract)		
Few drops of lemon essence (extract)		
Pinch of salt		
1 packet vanilla blancmange powder (pudding)	33 g/1¼ oz	1¼ oz
Baking powder	2 tsp	2 tsp
Candied lemon peel	40 g/1½ oz	1½ oz
Sultanas (seedless white raisins)	40 g/1½ oz	¼ cup
Finely chopped walnuts	25 g/1 oz	¼ cup
Fresh breadcrumbs	2 tbs	3 tbs

Reserve 3 tbs (4 tbs) of the milk and heat the remainder.

Place the biscuit crumbs in a bowl, pour over the hot milk and leave to stand until cool. The crumbs will be soft.

Place the butter or margarine in a bowl and add the sugar. Beat well until light and fluffy then gradually beat in the eggs, essences and salt. Stir in the soaked crumbs. Combine the blancmange powder and baking powder and stir into the crumbs mixture with the reserved milk. Chop the peel and add to crumb mixture with sultanas and walnuts.

Grease a pudding bowl and sprinkle with the breadcrumbs. Turn in the pudding mixture. Cover with foil, crimping it well under the rim of the bowl. Place in a pan and pour in boiling water to come halfway up the sides of the bowl. Put on the lid and keep the water boiling gently for about 1 hour, adding more boiling water to the pan during cooking if necessary.

Left: Moulded rice pudding with cherry sauce
Right: Ground rice pudding

Ground rice pudding
Serves 6–8

Ingredients	Metric-Imperial	American
Milk	750 ml/1¼ pints	3 cups
Butter	150 g/5 oz	⅔ cup
Caster sugar (granulated)	25 g/1 oz	2 tbs
Ground rice	250 g/9 oz	1½ cups
6 eggs		
Slivered almonds	150 g/5 oz	1¼ cups
Chocolate dots (chips)	100 g/4 oz	⅔ cup
Fresh breadcrumbs	2 tbs	3 tbs

Place the milk in a pan with the butter and sugar and bring to the boil. Sprinkle in the rice and stir well then remove from the heat. Separate the eggs and beat the yolks into the rice mixture. Whisk the egg whites in a clean bowl until stiff and fold in carefully with the almonds and chocolate dots.

Grease a ring mould and sprinkle with the breadcrumbs. Turn in the pudding mixture and cover with foil, crimping this well under the rim of the mould. Place in a pan and pour in boiling water to come half-way up the side of the mould. Put on the lid and keep the water boiling gently for 2 hours, adding more boiling water if necessary. Remove and cool. Turn out on a dish and serve with canned cherries.

Lemon pudding
Serves 2–3

(Photo p. 420–421)

Ingredients	Metric-Imperial	American
Lemon juice	5 tbs	6 tbs
Grated rind of 1 lemon		
1 egg		
Cornflour (cornstarch)	50 g/2 oz	scant ½ cup
Water	4 tbs	5 tbs
Caster sugar (granulated)	100 g/4 oz	½ cup
1 banana		

Reserve 1 tsp of the lemon juice and make the remainder up to 250 ml/9 fl oz (generous 1 cup) with warm water. Stir in the lemon rind and place in a pan. Separate the egg. Blend the cornflour with the water, sugar and egg yolk. Heat the lemon liquid, add the cornflour mixture and stir vigorously until boiling and thickened. Remove from the heat. Peel and slice the banana. Whisk the egg white in a clean bowl until stiff and fold into the lemon pudding with most of the banana slices. Spoon into individual dishes and leave to cool. Sprinkle the remaining banana slices with the reserved lemon juice. Decorate the puddings with the banana slices and add a sprinkling of pistachio nuts if wished. Serve with wafers.

Fruit pudding
(Using a pressure cooker)
Serves 8

Ingredients	Metric-Imperial	American
Dried pear halves	225 g/8 oz	8 oz
Dried peach halves	225 g/8 oz	8 oz
Dried stone prunes (pitted)	175 g/6 oz	6 oz
Water	400 ml/14 fl oz	1¾ cups
Flour (all-purpose)	200 g/7 oz	1¾ cups
Baking powder	4 tsp	4 tsp
Caster sugar (granulated)	25 g/1 oz	2 tbs
Vanilla essence (extract)	2 tsp	2 tsp
Ground mixed spices	¼ tsp	¼ tsp
Cherry liqueur	1 tbs	1 tbs
Coarsely chopped hazelnuts (filberts)	65 g/2½ oz	⅔ cup
Chopped candied lemon peel	65 g/2½ oz	scant ½ cup
Seedless raisins	100 g/4 oz	⅔ cup
Fresh breadcrumbs	1 tbs	1 tbs

Place the dried fruit in a pan and pour the water over. Leave to soak overnight. Bring the fruit to the boil in the soaking liquid and cook for 2 minutes. Drain, reserving the liquid. Cool the fruit then chop coarsely.

Sift the flour with the baking powder into a bowl and make a well in the centre. Put in the sugar, vanilla essence, spices, cherry liqueur and 150 ml/¼ pint (⅔ cup) of the reserved liquid, making this up with water if necessary. Mix until the dough is smooth. Stir in the chopped fruit, nuts, peel and raisins.

Grease a pudding bowl with a capacity of about 1½ L/ 2½ pints (3⅓ pints) and sprinkle with the breadcrumbs. Turn in the pudding mixture and cover with lid or foil, crimping this well under the rim of the bowl. Place in the open cooker and pour in water to come one third of the way up the sides of the bowl. Close the cooker, bring to low pressure and cook for 1 hour and 5 minutes. Reduce the pressure at room temperature before opening. Turn the pudding out on a warm dish and serve with a vanilla or wine sauce.

Microwave hint
To avoid overnight soaking for dried pear halves, peach halves and prunes, place in a bowl, cover with boiling water and microwave on Full Power for 1 minute. Leave to stand for 5 minutes, then drain before using.

Microwave hint
Do not use crystal glass in the microwave cooker as it contains a small proportion of lead and may crack during heating.

Peach crown
Serves 4–6

Ingredients	Metric-Imperial	American
4 firm peaches		
Caster sugar (granulated)	175 g/6 oz	¾ cup
Vanilla essence (extract)	2 tsp	2 tsp
Warm water	350 ml/12 fl oz	1½ cups
Sweet white wine or cider	400 ml/14 fl oz	1¾ cups
3 eggs		
Cornflour (cornstarch)	65 g/2½ oz	½ cup
Cold water	6 tbs	7 tbs

Pour boiling water over the peaches, drain and peel. Cut in half, remove the stones (pits) and place the fruit in a pan with the sugar, vanilla essence and warm water. Bring to the boil then simmer until the peaches are tender. Lift out the peaches and drain well.

Measure the peach syrup and make up to 250 ml/9 fl oz (generous 1 cup) with more water if necessary. Add the wine or cider and bring to boiling point. Separate the eggs and whisk the egg whites in a clean bowl until stiff. Mix the yolks with the cornflour and cold water. Add to the pan and stir vigorously until boiling and thickened. Remove from the heat and fold in the whipped egg whites.

Lightly oil a ring mould and arrange the peach halves in it with the rounded side downwards. Pour over the egg mixture and leave to cool and then chill. Carefully loosen the edge of the crown and turn out on a serving dish. Decorate with whipped cream if wished.

Variation: Instead of the peaches substitute plums, pears or apricots.

Left: Fruit pudding
Above: Peach crown

Praline ring
Serves 4–6

Ingredients	Metric-Imperial	American
For the praline:		
Butter	2 tbs	3 tbs
Sugar	65 g/2½ oz	5 tbs
Chopped almonds	100 g/4 oz	1 cup
For the pudding:		
2 packets vanilla blanc-mange powder, each	33 g/1¼ oz	1¼ oz
Caster sugar (granulated)	75 g/3 oz	⅓ cup
Cold milk	125 ml/4 fl oz	½ cup
Hot milk	1 L/1¾ pints	4⅓ cups
For the sauce:		
Canned apricots	225 g/8 oz can	8 oz can
½ orange		
Orange liqueur	2 tbs	3 tbs

To make the praline put the butter and sugar into a pan and heat, stirring, until the sugar has melted and turned golden brown. Stir in the almonds and continue cooking and stirring until the caramel and nuts are browned. Pour on to an oiled baking sheet (cookie sheet) and leave to cool. Reduce to a coarse powder in a grinder or food processor.

Mix together the blancmange powder, caster sugar and cold milk. Blend in the hot milk then pour into a pan and stir until boiling. Simmer as directed on the pack. Rinse a ring mould with cold water and pour in the blancmange. Leave to cool and then chill.

Meanwhile, make the sauce. Drain the apricot syrup into a pan. Thinly pare the rind of the orange and cut this into very fine shreds. Add to the pan and bring to the boil. Simmer for 5 minutes. Stir in the liqueur and leave to cool.

Turn out on a dish and sprinkle with the praline. Fill the centre with apricots and serve with the sauce.

Individual caramel custards
Serves 4

Ingredients	Metric-Imperial	American
Butter	1 tsp	1 tsp
Caster sugar (granulated)	175 g/6 oz	¾ cup
Milk	500 ml/18 fl oz	2¼ cups
4 eggs		
Vanilla essence (extract)	1 tsp	1 tsp
Pinch of salt		

Melt the butter in a pan, sprinkle in half the sugar and stir over the heat until the sugar caramelizes. Spoon into 4 individual ovenproof dishes.

Place the milk in a pan and bring to boiling point. Meanwhile, whisk the eggs with the vanilla essence, remaining sugar and the salt. Pour on the boiling milk, whisking vigorously. Divide among the caramel-lined dishes then stand these in a roasting tin. Pour in hot water to come half-way up the sides of the dishes and cook, uncovered, in a preheated moderate oven, 180°C, 350°F, Gas Mark 4, for 25 minutes, or until lightly set. Leave to cool. Turn out.

Apricot cream
Serves 4

Ingredients	Metric-Imperial	American
Apricots	550 g/1¼ lb	1¼ lb
Sweet white wine	225 ml/8 fl oz	1 cup
Sugar	50 g/2 oz	¼ cup
Short cinnamon stick		
Pared rind of ½ a lemon		
1 packet vanilla blancmange powder (pudding)	33 g/1¼ oz	1¼ oz
Milk	125 ml/4 fl oz	½ cup

Quarter and stone (pit) the apricots. Place in a pan with the wine, sugar, cinnamon stick and lemon rind. Bring to the boil, stir once then cover and simmer for 10 minutes. Remove the cinnamon stick and lemon rind. Purée the fruit mixture and return to the rinsed pan. Place over low heat.

Combine the blancmange powder and the milk until smooth. Add to the apricot purée and stir until thickened.

Transfer to a fluted mould previously rinsed wih cold water. Leave to cool, then chill well. Turn out.

Left: Praline ring
Below: Apricot cream

keep the water boiling gently for 1 hour, adding more boiling water during cooking if necessary. Turn the pudding out on to a warm dish and serve with a wine sauce.

Yogurt jelly
Serves 4

Ingredients	Metric-Imperial	American
Cold water	5 tbs	6 tbs
Powdered gelatine	1 tbs	1 tbs
Milk	125 ml/4 fl oz	½ cup
Natural yogurt (plain)	300 ml/½ pint	1¼ cups
Caster sugar (granulated)	75 g/3 oz	⅓ cup
Vanilla essence (extract)	1 tsp	1 tsp
Grated rind and juice of ½ lemon		
Chocolate vermicelli (sprinkles)		

Put the water into a small bowl and sprinkle on the gelatine. Leave to stand for 10 minutes, place over simmering water and stir until the gelatine has completely dissolved.

Beat together the milk, yogurt, sugar, vanilla essence, lemon rind and juice. Stir about 3 tbs (4 tbs) of the milk mixture into the dissolved gelatine, then whisk this into the remaining milk mixture. Transfer to a dish and leave to set. Sprink with chocolate vermicelli.

Almond or hazelnut pudding
Serves 4

Ingredients	Metric-Imperial	American
Butter	100 g/4 oz	½ cup
Caster sugar (granulated)	100 g/4 oz	½ cup
Vanilla essence (extract)	1 tsp	1 tsp
3 eggs		
Pinch of salt		
Few drops of almond essence (extract)		
Ground almonds or hazelnuts	50 g/2 oz	½ cup
Flour	150 g/5 oz	1¼ cups
Cornflour (cornstarch)	50 g/2 oz	½ cup
Baking powder	2 tsp	2 tsp
Milk	3 tbs	4 tbs
Fresh breadcrumbs	1 tbs	1 tbs

Cream the butter with the sugar in a bowl until light and fluffy. Gradually add the vanilla essence, eggs, salt, almond essence and nuts, beating constantly. Sift the flour with the cornflour and baking powder. Fold into the creamed mixture with the milk.

Grease a ring pudding mould and sprinkle with the breadcrumbs. Transfer the pudding mixture to the mould and level the top. Cover with foil and crimp well under the rim of the bowl. Place in a pan and pour in boiling water to come halfway up the sides of the mould. Cover the pan and

Black Forest cherry cream
Serves 4

Ingredients	Metric-Imperial	American
Morello cherries	450 g/1 lb	1 lb
Caster sugar (granulated)	150 g/5 oz	⅔ cup
Vanilla essence (extract)	4 tsp	4 tsp
Kirsch	6 tbs	½ cup
3 eggs		
Milk	350 ml/12 fl oz	1½ cups
Cornflour (cornstarch)	3 tbs	4 tbs
Pinch of salt		
Whipping cream	300 ml/½ pint	1¼ cups
1 large chocolate flake		

Remove the stalks and stones (pits) from the cherries. Place in a bowl, sprinkle over two thirds of the sugar, 1 tsp of the vanilla and half the Kirsch. Stir lightly and leave to stand for 2 hours.

Separate the eggs. Put the milk in a pan with the cornflour, egg yolks, remaining sugar and salt. Stir constantly until boiling then leave to cool, stirring occasionally. When cold stir in the rest of the Kirsch and vanilla. Whisk the egg whites in a clean bowl until stiff and whip the cream separately. Fold the egg whites and half the cream into the mixture.

Layer up cherries and syrup and the vanilla cream in a glass serving dish, ending with a circle of cherries. Place the remaining whipped cream in a piping bag fitted with a star tube (pipe) and use to decorate the dessert. Crumble the chocolate flake and sprinkle over the top.

Semolina pudding

Serves 4

Ingredients	Metric-Imperial	American
Vanilla custard powder (pudding)	2 tbs	3 tbs
Semolina	25 g/1 oz	scant ¼ cup
Caster sugar (granulated)	50 g/2 oz	¼ cup
2 eggs		
Milk	600 ml/1 pint	2 cups

Mix together the custard powder, semolina and sugar. Separate the eggs and add the yolks and 75 ml/3 fl oz (⅓ cup) of the milk to the semolina mixture.

Place the remaining milk in a pan and bring to the boil. Add the semolina mixture and bring back to the boil, stirring constantly. Remove from the heat. Whisk the egg whites in a clean bowl until stiff then fold into the hot pudding mixture. Transfer to a fluted mould previously rinsed with cold water. Leave to cool, and then chill well. Turn out the pudding on a serving dish and, if wished, decorate with rosettes of cream. Serve with cooked fruit or a fruit syrup.

Semolina and vanilla pudding

Serves 4

Ingredients	Metric-Imperial	American
Milk	400 ml/14 fl oz	1¾ cups
Pinch of salt		
Semolina	100 g/4 oz	⅔ cup
Butter	75 g/3 oz	⅓ cup
Caster sugar (granulated)	65 g/2½ oz	5 tbs
3 eggs		
Vanilla essence (extract)	1 tsp	1 tsp
Few drops of lemon essence		
Vanilla custard powder (pudding)	2 tbs	3 tbs
Baking powder	1 tsp	1 tsp
Seedless raisins	2 tbs	3 tbs
Fresh breadcrumbs	1 tbs	1 tbs

Reserve 3 tbs (4 tbs) of the milk and place the remainder in a pan with the salt. Bring to the boil and remove from the heat. Sprinkle in the semolina and stir well. Set aside.

Cream the butter with the sugar in a bowl until light and fluffy then gradually beat in the eggs, vanilla and lemon essences. Stir in the semolina mixture.

Blend the custard powder with the reserved milk and baking powder. Add to semolina mixture with raisins.

Grease a pudding bowl and sprinkle with the breadcrumbs. Pour in the mixture then cover with foil, crimping it well under the rim of the bowl. Place in a pan of boiling water to come halfway up the side of the bowl. Put on the lid and keep the water boiling gently for 1¼ hours, adding more boiling water if necessary. Turn out and serve hot.

Left: Almond or hazelnut pudding
Below: Semolina pudding

Lime jelly
Serves 6

Ingredients	Metric-Imperial	American
3 limes		
Caster sugar (granulated)	700 g/7 oz	scant 1 cup
White rum	4 tbs	5 tbs
Powdered gelatine	1 tsp	1 tsp
1 packet lime jelly (jello)		
Strawberries	450 g/1 lb	1 lb

Grate the rind from one of the limes then squeeze the juice. Mix the rind and juice with almost all of the sugar and the rum. Add water to make this mixture up to 500 ml/18 fl oz (2¼ cups). Place 2 tbs (3 tbs) water in a small bowl, sprinkle on the gelatine and leave to stand for 10 minutes. Put 300 ml/½ pint (1¼ cups) of water in a pan and bring to boiling point. Break up the jelly and add to the pan placing the pan over gentle heat. Stir until the jelly is dissolved. Add to the rum liquid with the gelatine and stir well. Pour a thin layer into the base of a ring mould and allow to set.

Thinly slice 1 more lime and cut the slices in half. Arrange these half slices on the jelly in the mould. Pour a little more jelly on top and leave to set again. Pour in the rest of the jelly and chill until firmly set.

Dip the mould quickly in hot water and turn the jelly out on a serving dish. Hull and halve the strawberries, place in the centre of the lime ring and sprinkle with the remaining sugar. Thinly slice the last lime, halve the slices and use to garnish the ring. Serve with cream.

Buttermilk jelly with cream
Serves 4–6

Ingredients	Metric-Imperial	American
Water	125 ml/4 fl oz	½ cup
Powdered gelatine	1 tbs	1 tbs
Buttermilk	450 ml/¾ pint	2 scant cups
Caster sugar (granulated)	75 g/3 oz	⅓ cup
Vanilla essence (extract)	2 tsp	2 tsp
Grated rind of 1 lemon		
Lemon juice	3 tbs	4 tbs
Whipping cream	125 ml/4 fl oz	½ cup
Grated chocolate		

Put the water into a small bowl and sprinkle on the gelatine. Leave to stand for 10 minutes then put the bowl over a pan of hot water and stir until the gelatine has completely dissolved.

Mix together the buttermilk, sugar, vanilla essence, lemon rind and juice and mix in the dissolved gelatine. Whip the cream until thick and fold most of it into the buttermilk mixture. Pour into a glass serving dish or into individual dishes and leave to set.

Decorate with the reserved cream and grated chocolate. Serve with small biscuits (cookies).

Chocolate jelly
Serves 4

Ingredients	Metric-Imperial	American
Water	3 tbs	4 tbs
Powdered gelatine	1 tbs	1 tbs
Milk	450 ml/¾ pint	scant 2 cups
Plain chocolate (semi-sweet)	100 g/4 oz	4 oz
Sugar	2 tbs	3 tbs

Put the water into a small bowl and sprinkle on the gelatine. Leave to stand for 10 minutes.

Pour the milk into a pan, bring to the boil and remove from the heat. Break the chocolate into pieces, add to the milk with the sugar and soaked gelatine and stir well until the gelatine has completely dissolved and the chocolate has melted. Transfer to a serving dish and leave to cool. Chill well before serving.

Variation: As the jelly begins to thicken, whip 125 ml/4 fl oz double cream (½ cup heavy cream) until thick and fold in evenly.

Microwave hint
Soften gelatine that has set before you are ready to use it in the microwave. Heat on Medium Power for 30 seconds, then stir carefully.

Grape and mint jelly
Serves 4

Ingredients	Metric-Imperial	American
1 packet lime jelly (jello)		
Water	150 ml/¼ pint	⅔ cup
Apple juice	300 ml/½ pint	1¼ cups
Crème de menthe	2 tbs	3 tbs
Green grapes	225 g/8 oz	8 oz
For the sauce:		
Sour cream	150 ml/¼ pint	⅔ cup
Clear honey	1 tbs	1 tbs

Place the jelly in a pan with the water and apple juice. Heat gently, stirring, until the jelly has dissolved. Remove from the heat and stir in the liqueur. Leave to cool until warm.

Halve the grapes and remove the seeds (pits). Divide among 4 stemmed glasses. Pour the warm jelly mixture over the grapes and chill until set.

To make the sauce, warm the honey until it is runny then stir into the cream. Place in a small jug and serve with the jellies.

Microwave hint
When a small amount of hot water is required, for example, to make up a stuffing mix or to melt gelatine, put the measured water in a cup, place in the cooker and heat on full power for 45 seconds. Use as required.

Left: Lime jelly
Above: Grape and mint jelly

Strawberry jelly
Serves 4–6

Ingredients	Metric-Imperial	American
Water	125 ml/4 fl oz	½ cup
Powdered gelatine	1 tbs	1 tbs
Strawberries	450 g/1 lb	1 lb
Caster sugar (granulated)	100 g/4 oz	½ cup
White wine	125 ml/4 fl oz	½ cup
Lemon juice	2 tbs	3 tbs
Whipped cream		

Put the water into a small bowl and sprinkle on the gelatine. Leave to stand for 10 minutes then place the bowl over a pan of hot water and stir until the gelatine has completely dissolved.

Hull the strawberries and cut in half. Sprinkle with the sugar and leave to stand until the juice begins to run. Take two thirds of the sugared berries and mash with a fork. Stir in the dissolved gelatine, wine and lemon juice. Transfer to a glass serving dish or into individual dishes and chill until set. Serve decorated with whipped cream and the reserved strawberries.

Apricot dessert with cinnamon cream
Serves 4–6

Ingredients	Metric-Imperial	American
Ripe apricots	1 kg/2¼ lb	2¼ lb
White wine or apple juice	125 ml/4 fl oz	½ cup
Caster sugar (granulated)	100 g/4 oz	½ cup
Cold water	3 tbs	4 tbs
Powdered gelatine	1 tbs	1 tbs
Lemon juice	1 tbs	1 tbs
Apricot liqueur	1 tbs	1 tbs
Whipping cream	150 ml/¼ pint	⅔ cup
Icing sugar (confectioners')	1 tsp	1 tsp
Ground cinnamon		

Pour boiling water over the apricots, drain and peel. Cut the fruit in half and remove the stones (pits). Purée three quarters of the apricots with the wine or apple juice and the caster sugar and cut the remainder into strips.

Put the water into a bowl and sprinkle on the gelatine. Leave to stand for 10 minutes then place over hot water and stir until the gelatine has completely dissolved. Stir into the fruit purée with the fruit strips, lemon juice and apricot liqueur. Divide among serving plates and chill well.

Whip the cream with the icing sugar and place in a piping bag fitted with a star tube (pipe). Decorate the desserts with rosettes of cream and sprinkle these with cinnamon.

Kiwi fruit jelly with gourmet sauce
Serves 6–8

Ingredients	Metric-Imperial	American
6 kiwi fruit		
Cornflour (cornstarch)	40 g/1½ oz	⅓ cup
White wine	225 ml/8 fl oz	1 cup
Apple juice	300 ml/½ pint	1¼ cups
Sugar	75 g/3 oz	⅓ cup
1 strip pared orange rind		
Vanilla essence (extract)	½ tsp	½ tsp
Orange liqueur	2 tbs	3 tbs
For the sauce:		
Whipping cream	150 ml/¼ pint	⅔ cup
Advocaat	4 tbs	5 tbs
Vanilla essence (extract)	½ tsp	½ tsp
Caster sugar (granulated)	1 tsp	1 tsp

Peel the kiwi fruit and cut 4 good slices from one fruit. Reserve these for the garnish. Carefully purée two thirds of the remainder without breaking the small black seeds. Roughly chop the rest.

Moisten the cornflour with a little of the wine. Place the rest of the wine in a pan with the apple juice, sugar and orange rind and bring to the boil. Add the cornflour mixture and stir until boiling and thickened.

Stir in the vanilla essence and liqueur and remove from the heat. Discard the orange rind. Fold in the chopped kiwi fruit and the purée. Pour into a glass serving dish or into individual dishes and chill.

To make the sauce, stir together the cream, egg liqueur, vanilla essence and sugar. Pour over the fruit jelly and decorate with the reserved kiwi fruit slices.

Microwave hint
Sugar dissolves more quickly if it is warmed before adding to liquid. Place the sugar in a shallow dish and cook on full power for about 3 minutes, stirring halfway through. Don't overheat as the sugar may discolour or burn if it gets too hot.

Left: Apricot dessert with cinnamon cream
Right: Sherried fruit jelly

Sherried fruit jelly
Serves 4–6

Ingredients	Metric-Imperial	American
Dried apricots	225 g/8 oz	8 oz
Green grapes	225 g/8 oz	8 oz
Sweet sherry	225 ml/8 fl oz	1 cup
White grape juice	500 ml/18 fl oz	2¼ cups
Caster sugar (granulated)		
Water	6 tbs	½ cup
Powdered gelatine	4 tsp	4 tsp
Vanilla essence (extract)	2 tsp	2 tsp
Whipping cream	300 ml/½ pint	1¼ cups

Cut the apricots into quarters. Halve the grapes and remove the pips (pits). Place the fruit in a pan and pour over the sherry and grape juice. Leave to stand for 12 hours. Bring the fruit mixture to the boil with sugar to taste. Simmer for 2 minutes. Place the water in a small bowl and sprinkle on the gelatine. Leave to stand for 10 minutes.

Stir in the soaked gelatine until it has completely dissolved. Mix in the vanilla essence.

Rinse a ring mould with cold water and turn in the fruit mixture. Leave to cool and then chill until firm. Turn out on a serving dish. Whip the cream with 1 tbs sugar and a few drops of vanilla essence (extract) if wished. Place in a piping bag fitted with a star tube (pipe) and surround the jelly with rosettes of cream.

Brussels orange cream
Serves 6–8

Ingredients	Metric-Imperial	American
Water	3 tbs	4 tbs
Powdered gelatine	1 tbs	1 tbs
4 egg yolks		
Caster sugar (granulated)	100 g/4 oz	½ cup
Grated rind of 1 orange		
Orange juice	300 ml/½ pint	1¼ cups
Orange liqueur	3 tbs	4 tbs
Whipping cream	350 ml/12 fl oz	1½ cups
Orange slices		
Pistachio nuts		

Put the water into a bowl and sprinkle on the gelatine. Leave to stand for 10 minutes.

Place the egg yolks, most of the sugar, the orange rind and juice in the top of a double boiler or in a bowl over a pan of simmering water and whisk until thickened. Remove from the heat, whisk until cool and stir in the orange liqueur. Whip two thirds of the cream in a bowl until thick and fold into the orange mixture.

Lightly oil a mould and pour in the orange cream. Chill until set. Stiffly whip the remaining cream with the rest of the sugar. Turn the mould out on a serving plate, decorate with the halved orange slices, sweetened cream and pistachio nuts.

Wine cream with pistachio nuts
Serves 6

Ingredients	Metric-Imperial	American
Water	3 tbs	4 tbs
Powdered gelatine	1 tbs	1 tbs
4 egg yolks		
Caster sugar (granulated)	100 g/4 oz	½ cup
Vanilla essence (extract)	4 tsp	4 tsp
White wine	300 ml/½ pint	1¼ cups
Grated rind of 1 lemon		
Ground pistachio nuts	50 g/2 oz	½ cup
Whipping cream	350 ml/12 fl oz	1½ cups

Chopped pistachio nuts	25 g/1 oz	¼ cup
1 small bunch of grapes		

Place the water in a small bowl and sprinkle on the gelatine. Leave to stand for 10 minutes then place the bowl over a pan of hot water and stir until the gelatine has completely dissolved.

Pour the egg yolks in a bowl with the sugar and vanilla essence and whisk well until creamy. Gradually whisk in the wine, lemon rind and ground pistachio nuts. Stir in the dissolved gelatine, whip the cream until stiff and fold in gently. Pour into a serving dish and chill until set.

Sprinkle the chopped pistachio nuts on the wine cream in the shape of a vine leaf and decorate with the grapes.

Strawberry and Marsala mousse
Serves 4–6

Ingredients	Metric-Imperial	American
Strawberries	750 g/1¾ lb	1¾ lb
Marsala	2–4 tbs	3–5 tbs
Caster sugar (granulated)	150 g/5 oz	⅔ cup
Grated lemon rind	2 tsp	2 tsp
Water	3 tbs	4 tbs
Powdered gelatine	scant 1 tbs	1 tbs
4 egg yolks		
Vanilla essence (extract)	2 tsp	2 tsp
Whipping cream	300 ml/½ pint	1¼ cups

Hull the strawberries. Purée one third of the fruit and combine with 2 tbs (3 tbs) Marsala, one third of the sugar and half the lemon rind. Make up to 350 ml/12 fl oz (1½ cups) with more Marsala if necessary.

Put the water in a small bowl and sprinkle on the gelatine. Leave to stand for 10 minutes. Place over hot water and stir until the gelatine has completely dissolved.

Place the egg yolks in a bowl with the remaining sugar and vanilla essence. Whisk until thickened. Whisk in the strawberry purée mixture and dissolved gelatine. Chill until the mixture just begins to set. Stiffly whip half the cream and fold in evenly. Chill until set.

Slice the remaining strawberries, divide among serving dishes and sprinkle with the rest of the lemon rind. Top with scoops of mousse. Lightly whip the remaining cream and serve with the desserts. Each portion can be decorated with a whole strawberry if wished.

Chocolate mousse
Serves 4–6

Ingredients	Metric-Imperial	American
Orange	1	1
Plain chocolate (semisweet)	100 g/4 oz	4 squares
Butter	2 tbs	2 tbs
Eggs	4	4
Pinch of salt		

Finely grate the orange rind, being careful not to remove any of the white pith. Break the chocolate into pieces and melt in the top of a double boiler over simmering water.

Immediately pour the melted chocolate into a heavy-based pan and add the butter and orange rind. Stir until the butter melts.

Separate the eggs. Add the yolks to the chocolate, stirring vigorously with a wooden spoon to prevent the mixture from boiling. Remove from the heat. Cool.

Add a pinch of salt to the egg whites and whisk until stiff. Fold in one or two tablespoons of the egg whites to lighten, then fold in the remainder. Pour into a serving bowl and chill for 3 hours before serving. Serve with cream if desired.

Vanilla milk fondue
Serves 4–6

Ingredients	Metric-Imperial	American
6 egg yolks		
Caster sugar		
(granulated)	100 g/4 oz	½ cup
Milk	500 ml/18 fl oz	2¼ cups
½ vanilla pod		
Fruit liqueur	2–3 tbs	3–4 tbs
Selection of fresh fruit		
such as strawberries,		
grapes, kiwi fruit,		
bananas, oranges,		
pears, peaches,		
apricots, raspberries,		
apples	1 kg/2¼ lb	2¼ lb

Place the egg yolks and sugar in a bowl and whisk until beginning to thicken. Put the milk into a pan with the vanilla pod. Bring to the boil and simmer for 3 minutes. Remove from the heat, discard the vanilla pod and whisk in the egg yolk mixture. Reheat, stirring constantly, but do not allow to boil. Remove from the heat and add liqueur to taste.

Prepare the chosen fruit, peeling where necessary and removing any stones (pits) or cores. Cut into bite-sized pieces. Transfer the vanilla fondue to a fondue dish and serve hot or cold with the fruit pieces. Provide fondue forks for dipping. Serve with boudoir biscuits (ladyfingers).

Wine cream with meringue topping
Serves 4–6

Ingredients	Metric-Imperial	American
6 eggs		
Dry white wine	300 ml/½ pint	1¼ cups
Cornflour		
(cornstarch)	4 tsp	4 tsp
Caster sugar		
(granulated)	150 g/5 oz	½ cup
Lemon juice	2 tbs	3 tbs
Vanilla essence		
(extract)	2 tsp	2 tsp
Slivered almonds	4 tbs	5 tbs

Separate the eggs and place the yolks in the top of a double boiler or in a bowl over a pan of simmering water with the wine, cornflour, most of the sugar and the lemon juice. Whisk, if possible with an electric mixer, until thickened. Remove from the heat and whisk until cold. Transfer to an ovenproof dish.

Whisk the egg whites in a clean bowl until stiff then gradually whisk in the remaining sugar and the vanilla essence. Place in a piping bag fitted with a star tube (pipe) and make a trellis of meringue on top of the cream. Sprinkle with the almonds.

Cook, uncovered, in a hot oven, 220°C, 425°F, Gas Mark 7, for 5–10 minutes, or until the meringue is turning golden brown. Serve at once.

Mango cream
Serves 4–6

Ingredients	Metric-Imperial	American
Water	5 tbs	6 tbs
Powdered gelatine	1 tbs	1 tbs
1 large or 2 smaller ripe		
mangoes, weight	400 g/14 oz	14 oz
Champagne or sparkling		
white wine	300 ml/½ pint	1¼ cups
Lemon juice	2 tsp	2 tsp
Caster sugar		
(granulated)	75 g/3 oz	⅓ cup
Whipping cream	225 ml/8 fl oz	1 cup

Place the water in a small bowl and sprinkle on the gelatine. Leave to stand for 10 minutes. Place over hot water and stir until the gelatine has completely dissolved.

Meanwhile, peel the mango and purée the flesh, discarding the stone (pit). Combine with the wine, lemon juice and sugar. Stir well so that the sugar dissolves. Stir 3 tbs (4 tbs) of the mango mixture into the dissolved gelatine then add this to the remaining mixture and stir well. Chill until beginning to thicken. Whip the cream and fold in evenly. Place in a glass serving dish or in individual dishes and chill until set.

Walnut and orange cream
Serves 4

Ingredients	Metric-Imperial	American
Cold water	4 tbs	5 tbs
Powdered gelatine	1 tbs	1 tbs
2 eggs		
Warm water	2 tbs	3 tbs
Caster sugar (granulated)	75 g/3 oz	1/3 cup
Orange juice	225 ml/8 fl oz	1 cup
Milk	150 ml/1/4 pint	2/3 cup
Orange liqueur	3 tbs	4 tbs
Whipping cream	300 ml/1/2 pint	1 1/4 cups
Chopped walnuts	75 g/3 oz	3/4 cup

Place the cold water in a small bowl and sprinkle on the gelatine. Leave to stand for 10 minutes. Place over hot water, stirring until the gelatine has completely dissolved.

Separate the eggs and place the yolks in a bowl with the warm water and sugar. Whisk vigorously until light and creamy. Gradually whisk in the orange juice, milk and two thirds of the liqueur, then the dissolved gelatine. Chill until the mixture begins to thicken.

Whisk the egg whites in a clean bowl until stiff and whip the cream separately. Fold the egg white, most of the cream and almost all the nuts into the liqueur mixture. Transfer to a serving dish or individual glasses and chill until set.

Whip the remaining liqueur into the rest of the cream. Decorate with rosettes of liqueur cream with pieces of nut.

Fig and lemon cream
Serves 4

Ingredients	Metric-Imperial	American
Canned figs	425 g/15 oz can	15 oz can
1 packet lemon whipped dessert mix		
Milk	150 ml/1/4 pint	2/3 cup
Single cream (light)	150 ml/1/4 pint	2/3 cup

Drain the figs well, reserve 4 for the decoration and divide the rest among 4 dessert dishes.

Make up the dessert mix as directed with the milk and cream combined. Spoon over the figs in the dishes and leave to set for 5 minutes. Cut the reserved figs into quarters without actually separating them at the base. Open out and lay a 'star' of fig on top of each dessert.

Left: Vanilla milk fondue
Below: Walnut and orange cream

Bavarois with orange liqueur
Serves 6

Ingredients	Metric-Imperial	American
Water	3 tbs	4 tbs
Powdered gelatine	1 tbs	1 tbs
8 egg yolks		
Caster sugar (granulated)	75 g/3 oz	⅓ cup
Vanilla essence (extract)	2 tsp	2 tsp
Orange liqueur	125 ml/4 fl oz	½ cup
Lemon juice	2 tbs	3 tbs
Whipping cream	450 ml/¾ pint	scant 2 cups
3 oranges		
Strawberries	450 g/1 lb	1 lb
Chopped pistachio nuts	25 g/1 oz	¼ cup

Place the water in a small bowl and sprinkle on the gelatine. Leave to stand for 10 minutes.

Place the egg yolks in the top of a double boiler or in a bowl over a pan of simmering water. Add two thirds of the sugar, the vanilla essence, orange liqueur and lemon juice. Whisk constantly, if possible with an electric mixer, until beginning to thicken. Add the softened gelatine and whisk until it has completely dissolved. Stand the container in a bowl of cold water, stirring frequently, until cool. Whip the cream and fold in evenly. Leave to set.

Peel the oranges, remove pith and divide into segments. Hull and halve strawberries. Sprinkle with remaining sugar.

At serving time, arrange the fruit on serving plates and sprinkle with pistachio nuts. Arrange bavarois on top.

Diplomat cream
Serves 6

Ingredients	Metric-Imperial	American
Vanilla custard powder (pudding)	2 tbs	3 tbs
Caster sugar (granulated)	75 g/3 oz	⅓ cup
Pinch of salt		
Milk	600 ml/1 pint	2½ cups
Chopped candied lemon, citron or orange peel	40 g/1½ oz	¼ cup
Seedless raisins	75 g/3 oz	½ cup
Sultanas (white raisins)	50 g/2 oz	⅓ cup
Water	4 tbs	5 tbs
Whipping cream	300 ml/½ pint	1¼ cups

Vanilla essence (extract)	2 tsp	2 tsp
Icing sugar (confectioners')	2 tsp	2 tsp
12 Boudoir biscuits (ladyfingers)		
Rum	3 tbs	4 tbs
Grated chocolate	50 g/2 oz	½ cup

Mix together the custard powder, two thirds of the sugar, the salt and 6 tbs (½ cup) of the milk. Heat the remaining milk to boiling point, pour into the bowl and mix well.

Return to the pan and stir constantly until boiling. Simmer for 3 minutes, stirring. Remove from the heat and leave to cool, stirring frequently to prevent a skin forming.

Place the peel, raisins, sultanas and water in a pan and bring to the boil. Simmer until the fruit mixture has absorbed all the water. Cool.

Meanwhile, whip the cream with the vanilla essence and icing sugar. Fold into the cold custard. Place the biscuits with the sugared surface downwards and sprinkle with the rum.

Place one third of the custard cream in the base of a glass dish and top with 3 boudoir biscuits, one third of the fruit mixture and of the chocolate. Add a second layer of the custard cream then three more biscuits. Reserve a small quantity of the fruit mixture and sprinkle over the rest and the remaining chocolate. Lay the 3 biscuits on top, spoon on the rest of the custard and sprinkle with reserved fruit.

Left: Bavarois with orange liqueur
Above: Diplomat cream

443

Paradise grapefruit cups
Serves 4

Ingredients	Metric-Imperial	American
2 grapefruit		
1 packet lemon whipped dessert mix	100 g/4 oz	4 oz
Milk	150 ml/¼ pint	⅔ cup
Single cream (light)	125 ml/4 fl oz	½ cup
4 lemon slices		

Cut the grapefruits in half with a sharp pointed knife giving a vandyked edge. Scoop out the flesh, and remove all the pith. Cut the flesh into small pieces, then drain well.

Make up the dessert mix as directed using the milk and cream combined. Leave to thicken slightly then fold in the grapefruit flesh. Pile into the grapefruit 'shells', and serve each portion decorated with a lemon slice.

Pear charlotte
Serves 4

Ingredients	Metric-Imperial	American
Water	3 tbs	4 tbs
Powdered gelatine	1 tbs	1 tbs
1 packet chocolate flavour blancmange powder (pudding)	33 g/1¼ oz	1¼ oz
Caster sugar (granulated)	75 g/3 oz	⅓ cup
Milk	500 ml/18 fl oz	2¼ cups
16 boudoir biscuits (ladyfingers)		
Canned pear halves	225 g/8 oz can	8 oz can
Whipping cream	300 ml/½ pint	1¼ cups
Grated milk chocolate (sweet)	25 g/1 oz	¼ cup

Put the water in a small bowl and sprinkle on the gelatine. Leave to stand for 10 minutes.

Mix together the blancmange powder, sugar and 6 tbs (½ cup) of the milk in a bowl. Heat the remaining milk in a pan to boiling point. Pour into the bowl and mix well. Return to the pan and stir constantly until boiling. Remove from the heat and stir in the softened gelatine until it has completely dissolved. Leave to cool, stirring frequently.

Grease a ring mould with a diameter of about 24 cm/9½ inches and line with a strip of greaseproof (waxed) paper. Cut the boudoir biscuits in half. Line the mould with the biscuits, sugared surface towards the tin. Drain the pear halves and cut into large pieces.

Whip the cream until stiff. When the blancmange starts to thicken, fold the cream in evenly. Pour into the biscuit-lined mould. Press the pear pieces into the soft filling so that they are not visible. Chill until firm. Unmould onto a plate and remove the paper strip. Sprinkle with chocolate.

Gingered bananas with Cointreau cream
Serves 4–6

Ingredients	Metric-Imperial	American
3 bananas		
3 pieces of preserved ginger		
Orange juice	4 tbs	5 tbs
Cointreau	2 tbs	3 tbs
For the cream:		
Water	2 tbs	3 tbs
Powdered gelatine	2 tsp	2 tsp
Milk	125 ml/4 fl oz	½ cup
½ vanilla pod		
2 egg yolks		
Caster sugar (granulated)	1 tbs	1 tbs
Whipping cream	300 ml/½ pint	1¼ cups
Cointreau	3 tbs	4 tbs
Little crumbled chocolate flake or grated chocolate		

Peel the bananas, cut 2 in half lengthways and then slice each banana. Coarsely chop the ginger. Place bananas and ginger in a bowl with the orange juice and Cointreau and stir lightly. Leave to stand while making the cream.

Put the water in a small bowl and sprinkle on the gelatine. Leave to stand for 10 minutes. Place the milk in a pan with the vanilla pod and bring to the boil. Simmer for 5 minutes and remove the vanilla pod. Leave the milk to cool slightly then place in the top of a double boiler or in a bowl over a pan of simmering water and add the egg yolks and sugar. Whisk over the hot water, if possible using an electric mixer, until thickened. Whisk in the softened gelatine until it has completely dissolved. Remove from the heat and place the container in a bowl of cold water, stirring occasionally, until cool. As soon as the mixture begins to thicken, whip the cream and fold in with the liqueur.

Divide the banana mixture among serving dishes and top with the Cointreau cream. Sprinkle with chocolate and serve at once.

Variation: Replace the Cointreau with orange juice to make an extra special dessert for children or people who prefer an alcohol free dessert.

Microwave hint
Frozen orange juice or other fruit juices may be thawed in their container. Remove the metal lid and place the open container in the microwave cooker. Heat on full power for 30 seconds. Check and repeat the process if necessary.

Left: Paradise grapefruit cups
Below: Gingered bananas with Cointreau cream

Apricot compôte with baroque cream
Serves 6

Ingredients	Metric-Imperial	American
Ripe apricots	1 kg/2¼ lb	2¼ lb
Caster sugar (granulated)	150 g/5 oz	⅔ cup
Grated rind of 1 lemon		
Lemon juice	3 tbs	4 tbs
Apricot liqueur	6 tbs	½ cup
Water	3 tbs	4 tbs
Powdered gelatine	1 tbs	1 tbs
6 egg yolks		
Vanilla essence	½ tsp	½ tsp
Whipping cream	450 ml/¾ pint	scant 2 cups

Quarter the apricots and remove the stones (pits). Place in a pan with two thirds of the sugar, the lemon rind and juice and cook gently, covered, for 15 minutes. Do not stir or the fruit will break up. Sprinkle with the liqueur, leave to stand for 5 minutes then drain the fruit and reserve the liquid. Divide most of the cooked apricots among 6 glass dishes and chill. Reserve a few pieces of the fruit for decoration.

Place the water in a small bowl and sprinkle on the gelatine. Leave to stand for 10 minutes.

Put the egg yolks in a bowl with the remaining sugar, the vanilla essence and 3 tbs (4 tbs) of the reserved liquid. Whisk vigorously until creamy.

Heat the remaining reserved liquid in a pan, add the softened gelatine and stir until it has completely dissolved. Gradually add to the egg yolk mixture, whisking constantly. Leave to stand and when the mousse begins to thicken, whip the cream and fold in evenly. Spoon over the apricots in the dishes and chill. Decorate with reserved apricots.

Royal yogurt cream
Serves 4

Ingredients	Metric-Imperial	American
Water	3 tbs	4 tbs
Powdered gelatine	1 tbs	1 tbs
Natural yogurt (plain)	150 ml/¼ pint	⅔ cup
Milk	125 ml/4 fl oz	½ cup
Vanilla essence (extract)	2 tsp	2 tsp
Lemon juice	2 tbs	3 tbs
Caster sugar (granulated)	75 g/3 oz	⅓ cup
Whipping cream	125 ml/4 fl oz	½ cup
Chocolate vermicelli (sprinkles)		

Place the water in a small bowl and sprinkle on the gelatine. Leave to stand. After 10 minutes, place over hot water and stir until the gelatine has completely dissolved.

Mix together the yogurt, milk, vanilla essence, lemon juice and sugar until the sugar has dissolved. Stir 3 tbs (4 tbs) into the dissolved gelatine then add this to the yogurt mixture and stir well. When it begins to thicken, whip the cream and fold in evenly. Transfer to a glass serving dish or into individual glasses and chill until set. Serve sprinkled with vermicelli.

Cherry cream mould
Serves 12

Ingredients	Metric-Imperial	American
Canned stoned morello cherries (pitted)	3 × 425 g/15 oz cans	3 × 15 oz cans
Cherry or pear liqueur	6 tbs	½ cup
Icing sugar (confectioners')	50 g/2 oz	scant ½ cup
Water	5 tbs	6 tbs
Powdered gelatine	4½ tsp	4½ tsp
Whipping cream	1 L/1¾ pints	4⅓ cups
Vanilla essence (extract)	4 tsp	4 tsp

Drain the cherries. Pour the liqueur over them, then sift half the sugar on top, stir and leave to stand for at least 1 hour.

Put the water in a small bowl and sprinkle on the gelatine. Leave to stand for 10 minutes then place over hot water and stir until the gelatine has completely dissolved.

Sift the remaining sugar into a bowl, add the cream and vanilla essence and whip until just stiff. Add 2 tbs (3 tbs) into the dissolved gelatine then add this to the whipped cream and fold in thoroughly, mix in the cherries and soaking liquid. Transfer to a large mould, cover and chill overnight.

At serving time, dip the mould in warm water and turn the cherry cream out on a dish. If liked, decorate with a few fresh cherries. The cherry syrup can be thickened with arrowroot and served as a sauce with the mould.

Left: Apricot compôte with baroque cream
Below: Cherry cream mould

Port macaroons with raspberry cream and strawberries
Serves 4–6

Ingredients	Metric-Imperial	American
Strawberries	450 g/1 lb	1 lb
Grated rind and juice of 1 lime		
Caster sugar (granulated)	200 g/7 oz	scant 1 cup
Water	2 tbs	3 tbs
Powdered gelatine	1½ tsp	1½ tsp
Raspberries	225 g/8 oz	8 oz
3 egg yolks		
Orange liqueur	225 ml/8 fl oz	1 cup
Whipping cream	300 ml/½ pint	1¼ cups
Ratafia biscuits (miniature almond macaroons)	200 g/7 oz	7 oz
Port	4 tbs	5 tbs

Hull and then halve or quarter the strawberries. Place in a bowl, sprinkle with the lime juice and one third of the sugar and leave to stand for 2 hours.

Put the water in a small bowl, sprinkle on the gelatine and leave to stand for 10 minutes. Place over hot water and stir until the gelatine has completely dissolved.

Place the raspberries in a pan with 2 tbs (3 tbs) water and half the remaining sugar. Bring to the boil, stir and then press through a sieve.

Whisk the egg yolks with the last of the sugar until thickened. Fold in the raspberry purée then add the orange liqueur and dissolved gelatine. When the mixture begins to thicken, whip the cream and fold in half of it. Chill. Sprinkle the ratafias with the port and leave to stand for 1 hour.

Divide three quarters of the ratafias among 4 serving dishes, top with strawberries and syrup and then with raspberry cream. Decorate with the remaining ratafias, the lime rind and the rest of the whipped cream.

Bilberry bavarois
Serves 6

Ingredients	Metric-Imperial	American
Cold water	150 ml/¼ pint	⅔ cup
Powdered gelatine	2 tbs	7 tsp
Bilberries from a jar	2 × 425 g/ 15 oz jars	2 × 15 oz jars
Icing sugar (confectioners')	200 g/7 oz	1¾ cups
Lemon juice	1 tbs	1 tbs
6 egg yolks		
Warm water	2 tbs	3 tbs
Whipping cream	450 ml/¾ pint	scant 2 cups

Put the cold water into a small bowl and sprinkle on the gelatine. Leave to stand for 10 minutes. Place over hot water and stir until the gelatine has completely dissolved.

Drain the bilberries well, reserving a few for decoration. Combine the rest with half the sugar and the lemon juice and purée in a blender or food processor. Stir in the dissolved gelatine.

Place the egg yolks, warm water and remaining sugar in a bowl and whisk vigorously until thickened. Fold in the bilberry purée. When it begins to thicken, whip the cream and fold in most of it. Transfer to a mould previously rinsed with cold water and chill until firm.

Turn the bavarois out on a plate and serve decorated with the remaining cream and reserved bilberries.

Apples in ginger cream
Serves 4–6

Ingredients	Metric-Imperial	American
2 large cooking apples		
Dry white wine	125 ml/4 fl oz	½ cup
Cold water	3 tbs	4 tbs
Powdered gelatine	scant 1 tbs	1 tbs
2 egg yolks		
Caster sugar (granulated)	100 g/4 oz	½ cup
Grated rind of 1 lemon		
Chopped preserved ginger	75 g/3 oz	½ cup
Whipping cream	300 ml/½ pint	1¼ cups
2 pieces of preserved ginger		
4–6 thin slices of dessert apple		

Peel the cooking apples, quarter and remove the cores. Slice and place in a pan with the wine. Cover and cook gently until the apple is soft. Beat until smooth.

Put the water in a small bowl and sprinkle on the gelatine.

Stir in the apricot purée, lemon juice, apricot liqueur and dissolved gelatine. When the mixture starts to thicken, whip the cream and fold in with two thirds of the apricot strips. Leave to set.

Press the raspberries through a sieve and stir in the remaining sugar and the raspberry liqueur. Serve portions of the apricot cream topped with raspberry sauce and decorate with the rest of the apricot strips.

Variation: If raspberries are unavailable, substitute strawberries and replace the liqueur with orange juice.

Leave to stand for 10 minutes. Place over hot water and stir until the gelatine has dissolved. Stir into the apple purée.

Whisk the egg yolks, sugar and lemon rind together in a bowl until light and creamy. Fold into the apple mixture.

Chill until beginning to thicken then whip the cream and fold in with the chopped ginger. Divide among sundae dishes. Slice the pieces of ginger and use to top the desserts. Decorate each portion with a slice of apple and serve.

Apricot cream with raspberry sauce
Serves 4

Ingredients	Metric-Imperial	American
Very ripe apricots	750 g/1¾ lb	1¾ lb
Cold water	3 tbs	4 tbs
Powdered gelatine	1 tbs	1 tbs
6 egg yolks		
Caster sugar (granulated)	150 g/5 oz	⅔ cup
Warm water	2 tbs	3 tbs
Vanilla essence (extract)	½ tsp	½ tsp
Lemon juice	1 tbs	1 tbs
Apricot liqueur	2 tbs	3 tbs
Whipping cream	300 ml/½ pint	1¼ cups
Raspberries	225 g/8 oz	8 oz
Raspberry liqueur	1 tbs	1 tbs

Pour boiling water over the apricots, drain, peel, halve and remove the stones (pits). Purée two thirds and cut the remainder into strips.

Put the cold water in a small bowl and sprinkle on the gelatine. Leave to stand for 10 minutes. Place over hot water and stir until the gelatine has completely dissolved.

Whisk the egg yolks with most of the sugar, the warm water and vanilla essence in a bowl until light and creamy.

Quick peach delight
Serves 4

Ingredients	Metric-Imperial	American
Canned peach slices	225 g/8 oz can	8 oz can
2 packets vanilla whipped dessert mix	100 g/4 oz each	4 oz each
Cold milk	500 ml/18 fl oz	2¼ cups
Whipping cream	300 ml/½ pint	1¼ cups
Plain chocolate (semi-sweet)	100 g/4 oz	4 oz

Drain the peach slices well. Make up the dessert mixes with the milk as directed and pour into 4 glass serving dishes. Leave to set. Whip half the cream and place in a piping bag fitted with a star tube (pipe).

Arrange the peach slices in a fan on each dessert. Decorate with large rosettes of cream.

To make the sauce, break up the chocolate and melt in a bowl over a pan of hot water. Remove from the heat and stir in the remaining unwhipped cream. Spoon the warm chocolate sauce over the desserts. If preferred to use the sauce cold, stir in 2 tbs (3 tbs) milk before it cools.

Red wine cream with macaroons and grapes
Serves 4

Ingredients	Metric-Imperial	American
Cold water	3 tbs	4 tbs
Powdered gelatine	1 tbs	1 tbs
4 egg yolks		
Icing sugar (confectioners')	150 g/5 oz	1¼ cups
Sweet red wine	125 ml/4 fl oz	½ cup
Whipping cream	350 ml/12 fl oz	1½ cups
Black grapes	225 g/8 oz	8 oz
Ratafia biscuits (small almond macaroons)	100 g/4 oz	4 oz
Brandy or rum	1–2 tbs	2–3 tbs

Put the water in a small bowl and sprinkle on the gelatine. Leave to stand for 10 minutes. Place over hot water and stir until the gelatine has completely dissolved.

Place the egg yolks in a bowl and sift over the sugar. Whisk vigorously until light and creamy. Whisk in the wine and dissolved gelatine. Chill until the mixture begins to thicken, then whip the cream and fold in.

Halve the grapes and remove the seeds (pits).

Put a layer of wine cream into 4 dessert glasses and add some of the grapes and ratafias. Sprinkle with a little brandy or rum and repeat the layers until the ingredients are used up. Serve with extra whipped cream.

Chocolate foam pudding
Serves 4

Ingredients	Metric-Imperial	American
Cold water	1 tbs	1 tbs
Powdered gelatine	1 tbs	1 tbs
Whipping cream	225 ml/8 fl oz	1 cup
Plain chocolate (semi-sweet)	150 g/5 oz	5 oz
Hot water	3 tbs	4 tbs
2 egg whites		
Chocolate dots (chips)		

Put the cold water in a bowl and sprinkle on the gelatine. Leave to stand for 10 minutes. Add 2 tbs (3 tbs) of the cream, place the bowl over hot water and stir until the gelatine has completely dissolved.

Break up the chocolate and place in a bowl with the hot water. Stand the bowl over hot water and stir until the chocolate melts. Leave to cool, stirring occasionally.

Whip the remaining cream until thick then whisk in the dissolved gelatine and continue whisking until stiff. Stir in the chocolate mixture. Whisk the egg whites in a clean bowl until stiff and fold in carefully. Transfer the chocolate foam to a glass serving dish or individual dishes and when set decorate with chocolate dots.

Left: Quick peach delight
Above: Red wine cream with macaroons and grapes

Hints for preparing desserts in a microwave

● To soften hard ice-cream ready for serving, microwave on Medium Power for 15 seconds. Test the consistency with a fork and repeat the process if necessary. Do not extend the heating time without testing as the ice-cream could melt and lose its fluffy texture.

● To soften sugar that has gone hard in the carton or packet, place in the cooker together with a jug containing 150 ml/¼ pint (⅔ cup) hot water. Cook on Full Power for 2–3 minutes, according to the size of the pack of sugar. Break the lumps up with a fork. Repeat the process if necessary.

● When using heatproof glass or ceramic containers in the microwave cooker, make sure they have no metal trim or screws in lids. Remember to remove any detachable handles too.

Cinnamon cream with fig compôte
Serves 8–10

Ingredients	Metric-Imperial	American
8–12 ripe figs		
Port	125 ml/4 fl oz	½ cup
Lemon juice	3 tbs	4 tbs
Caster sugar (granulated)	100 g/4 oz	½ cup
Cornflour (cornstarch)	1 tsp	1 tsp
Whipping cream	450 ml/¾ pint	scant 2 cups
2 cinnamon sticks		
1 vanilla pod		
Cold water	5 tbs	6 tbs
Powdered gelatine	4½ tsp	4½ tsp
6 eggs		
Brandy	2 tbs	3 tbs
Ground cinnamon		
Chocolate flakes		

Remove the stems from the figs and cut the fruit into quarters. Place the port in a pan with the lemon juice, 1 tbs of the sugar and the cornflour. Stir until boiling then add the fig quarters and cook gently for 5 minutes. Leave to cool.

Put the cream into another pan with the cinnamon sticks and vanilla pod. Bring to the boil and simmer for 10 minutes. Strain the cream, rinsing the vanilla pod and reserving this for future use.

Meanwhile, put the water in a small bowl and sprinkle on the gelatine. Leave to stand for 10 minutes then place over hot water and stir until the gelatine has completely dissolved. Stir into the spiced cream.

Separate the eggs and whisk the yolks with remaining sugar, brandy and 1 tsp ground cinnamon until thickened. Whisk in the spiced cream then stand the bowl in cold water and stir until the mixture is cold. Whisk the egg whites in a clean bowl until stiff. When the cream begins to thicken, fold in one third of the egg white and then the remaining two thirds. Chill. Serve portions of the cinnamon cream and fig compôte on plates, add short lengths of chocolate flake and sprinkle with extra cinnamon to taste.

Coffee chocolate mousse
Serves 4

Ingredients	Metric-Imperial	American
Plain chocolate (semi-sweet)	150 g/5 oz	5 oz
4 eggs		
Caster sugar (granulated)	50 g/2 oz	¼ cup
Coffee liqueur	2 tbs	3 tbs
Instant coffee powder or granules	1 tsp	1 tsp
Whipping cream	150 ml/¼ pint	⅔ cup

Break up the chocolate, place in a bowl over hot water and stir until melted.

Separate 3 of the eggs. Put the yolks in the top of a double boiler or into a bowl over a pan of simmering water with the remaining egg, the sugar, coffee liqueur and instant coffee. Whisk, if possible using an electric mixer, until thickened. Remove from the heat and whisk for a further 5 minutes.

Whisk the egg whites in a clean bowl until stiff and whip the cream separately. Fold these into the chocolate mixture. Transfer to individual glasses and chill.

Coffee cheese creams with liqueur
Serves 4

Ingredients	Metric-Imperial	American
Cream cheese	275 g/10 oz	1¼ cups
4 egg yolks		
Instant coffee powder or granules	1 tbs	1 tbs
Brandy	4 tsp	4 tsp
Icing sugar (confectioners')	4 tbs	5 tbs
Coffee liqueur	125 ml/5 tbs	⅓ cup
Chocolate curls		

Place the cheese in a bowl and beat until soft. Gradually beat in the egg yolks, one at a time. Dissolve the coffee in the brandy and beat into the cheese mixture. Sift the icing sugar over the top and continue beating until the cheese cream is glossy.

Place in a piping bag fitted with a star tube (pipe). Pipe the cheese cream in long spirals into 4 stemmed glasses then chill. At serving time, spoon coffee liqueur over the creams and sprinkle with chocolate curls.

Tip: To make chocolate curls, melt plain (semi-sweet) chocolate and spread on a laminated board to cool. Do not chill. Hold a large straight-bladed sharp knife with one hand on the handle and one securing the tip, and shave curls from the chocolate by scraping the knife across the surface at an angle.

Golden cream with double fruit purée
Serves 8

Ingredients	Metric-Imperial	American
8 egg yolks		
Caster sugar (granulated)	75 g/3 oz	⅓ cup
Grated rind of 1 lime		
Lime juice	1 tbs	1 tbs
Dry vermouth	2 tbs	3 tbs
Vanilla essence (extract)	2 tsp	2 tsp
Pinch of salt		
Cold water	3 tbs	4 tbs
Powdered gelatine	4 tsp	4 tsp
Whipping cream	350 ml/12 fl oz	1½ cups
2 egg whites		
Icing sugar (confectioners')	3 tbs	4 tbs
3 kiwi fruit		
Raspberries	225 g/8 oz	8 oz

Whisk the egg yolks with the caster sugar, lime rind and juice, vermouth, vanilla essence and salt using an electric mixer if possible, until thick. Put the water in a small bowl and sprinkle on the gelatine. Leave to stand for 10 minutes then place the bowl over a pan of hot water and stir until the gelatine has completely dissolved. Whisk into the egg yolk mixture. Whip the cream until thick. Whisk the egg whites in a clean bowl until stiff. Fold the cream and egg whites into the egg yolk mixture.

Lightly oil 8 individual dishes or moulds and divide the cream mixture among them. Cover and chill until set. Turn the creams out on serving plates.

To make the purée, sift the icing sugar, peel and chop the kiwi fruit and purée with one third of the icing sugar. Purée the raspberries with the remaining icing sugar then sieve the purée. Spoon a little of each purée over the creams and serve at once.

Microwave hint
Citrus fruits will yield more juice if put whole in the microwave cooker. Heat on full power for 1–3 minutes (depending on the quantity) before squeezing the juice.

Left: Cinnamon cream with fig compôte
Below: Golden cream with double fruit purée

Winter fruit salad
Serves 4

Ingredients	Metric-Imperial	American
4 large oranges		
2 pomegranates		
Fresh dates	100 g/4 oz	4 oz
Pine kernels (nuts)	50 g/2 oz	½ cup
Lemon juice	3 tbs	4 tbs
Orange liqueur	125 ml/4 fl oz	½ cup
Amaretto	4 tsp	4 tsp
Icing sugar (confectioners')	1 tsp	1 tsp
Grated rind of 1 orange		

Peel the oranges and divide into segments, removing all pith. Halve the pomegranates, scoop out the flesh and seeds with a spoon. Cut the dates into strips, discarding the stones (pits). Toss the pine kernels in a dry frying pan over moderate heat until golden brown. Leave to cool. Combine the fruit and pine kernels in a glass serving dish.

Combine the lemon juice, orange liqueur, Amaretto, icing sugar and orange rind and pour over the fruit mixture. Cover and chill well before serving.

Gooseberry compôte
Serves 4

Ingredients	Metric-Imperial	American
Green gooseberries	450 g/1 lb	1 lb
Water	125 ml/4 fl oz	½ cup
Sugar		
Almond essence (extract)	½ tsp	½ tsp

Top and tail the gooseberries. Place the water in a pan with 100 g/4 oz (½ cup) sugar and heat, stirring until the sugar has dissolved. Put in the fruit, bring to the boil then cover and simmer until the berries are tender but not breaking up. Do not stir during cooking.

If more sugar is needed, drain the hot syrup into a bowl, stir in extra sugar to taste and when it has dissolved, pour the syrup back over the fruit. Add the almond essence. Chill.

Greengage compôte
Serves 4

Ingredients	Metric-Imperial	American
Greengages (greengage plums	450 g/1 lb	1 lb
Water	125 ml/4 fl oz	½ cup
Sugar		
Grated nutmeg		

Wash the greengages if necessary and remove the stems. Place the water in a pan with 75 g/3 oz (⅓ cup) sugar and bring to the boil. Add the greengages, cover and simmer until the fruit is tender. If more sugar is needed, drain the syrup into a bowl, stir in extra sugar to taste and pour the syrup back over the fruit. Add grated nutmeg to taste, and if liked a little plum liqueur. Cool, and chill before serving.

Apple compôte
Serves 4

Ingredients	Metric-Imperial	American
Dessert apples	450 g/1 lb	1 lb
Water	225 ml/8 fl oz	1 cup
Sugar		
Lemon juice		

Peel and quarter the apples, remove the cores and cut into thick slices. Place in a pan with the water and 50g/2 oz (¼ cup) sugar and heat, stirring, until the sugar has dissolved. Bring to the boil, cover and simmer until the apples are tender. Leave to cool, then add the lemon juice.

Plum compôte
Serves 4

Ingredients	Metric-Imperial	American
Plums	450 g/1 lb	1 lb
Water	125 ml/4 fl oz	½ cup
Sugar		
1 cinnamon stick		
3 whole cloves		

Halve and stone (pit) the plums and place in a pan with the water, 50 g/2 oz (¼ cup) sugar and spices. Boil, cover and simmer until tender.

Above clockwise from left: Greengage compôte; Gooseberry compôte; Apple compôte; Plum compôte

Microwave hint

To bottle plums or greengages by microwave, wash and remove the stones (pits) from 1 kg/2¼ lb plums. Place 450 g/1 lb caster sugar (granulated sugar) in a 1.8 kg/4 lb bottling jar with 300 ml/½ pint (1¼ cups) water. Microwave on full 1234 for 4 minutes and stir to dissolve the sugar. Add the plums, cover with pierced cling film and cook on full power for 5 minutes, then on medium power for 5 minutes. Put on the sealing ring and lid, then leave to cool. Check the seal when the jar is cold.

Pour the remaining wine over the portions of fruit then spoon over the sabayon. Decorate with the reserved redcurrants and serve at once.

Rhubarb meringue
Serves 6

Ingredients	Metric-Imperial	American
Rhubarb	1 kg/2¼ lb	2¼ lb
Caster sugar (granulated)	275 g/10 oz	1¼ cups
Grated rind of 1 lemon		
Margarine	40 g/1½ oz	3 tbs
Sweet biscuit crumbs (cookie)	200 g/7 oz	2⅓ cups
Vanilla essence	4 tsp	4 tsp
2 egg whites		

Clean the rhubarb and cut into 2.5 cm/1 inch lengths. Put into a pan and sprinkle over half the sugar. Heat gently until the juice begins to run, shaking the pan occasionally, then stir in the lemon rind, cover and cook gently for about 10 minutes, or until the rhubarb is soft.

Meanwhile, melt the margarine in a frying pan and add the biscuit crumbs and just over half the remaining sugar. Stir until golden brown then remove from the heat, sprinkle over the vanilla essence and stir in.

Grease an ovenproof dish and layer up the rhubarb and biscuit crumb mixtures, ending with a layer of crumbs. Whisk the egg whites in a clean bowl until stiff, gradually add the rest of the sugar, a tablespoon at a time, whisking well after each addition until the meringue is firm and glossy. Spread over the ingredients in the dish. Place, uncovered, in a preheated hot oven, 230°C, 450°F, Gas Mark 8, for about 5 minutes, or until the meringue is golden brown.

Berry salad with sabayon
Serves 4

Ingredients	Metric-Imperial	American
Raspberries	225 g/8 oz	8 oz
Redcurrants	225 g/8 oz	8 oz
Caster sugar (granulated)	3 tbs	4 tbs
2 egg yolks		
1 egg		
Lemon juice	1 tbs	1 tbs
Medium dry sparkling white wine	250 ml/9 fl oz	generous 1 cup

Reserve 4 small clusters of redcurrants for the decoration and remove the remainder from the stems. Top and tail if preferred. Divide the raspberries and redcurrants among 4 stemmed glass dishes. Sprinkle with one third of the sugar and chill.

Place the egg yolks in the top of a double boiler or in a bowl over a pan of simmering water with the egg, remaining sugar, lemon juice and half the wine. Whisk with an electric mixer until creamy.

Orange slices with almonds
Serves 4

Ingredients	Metric-Imperial	American
3 oranges		
Butter	25 g/1 oz	2 tbs
Sugar	2 tbs	3 tbs
Slivered almonds	40 g/1½ oz	⅓ cup
Grand Marnier	4 tbs	5 tbs
Lemon juice	1 tbs	1 tbs

Thinly pare the rind of 1 orange and cut the rind into very fine shreds. Squeeze the orange juice and reserve. Peel and slice the remaining oranges, discarding any pith.

Melt the butter in a frying pan, sprinkle in the sugar and almonds and stir until the nuts are golden brown. Add the orange rind and orange slices to the pan and cook the slices for about 3 minutes, turning them once.

Pour in the liqueur and when it is warm, ignite. As soon as the flames die down, stir in the reserved orange juice and the lemon juice and serve at once accompanied by whipped cream or vanilla ice cream.

Whole figs with vodka
Serves 4–6

Ingredients	Metric-Imperial	American
Canned figs	2 × 425 g/ 15 oz cans	2 × 15 oz cans
Vodka	150 ml/¼ pint	⅔ cup
Green peppercorns	5 tsp	5 tsp
Whipping cream	150 ml/¼ pint	⅔ cup

Drain the figs, reserving the syrup. Combine this with the vodka. Put the figs into a bowl, add most of the peppercorns and pour over the vodka syrup. Cover and chill for at least 8 hours.

Divide the fruit mixture among small serving dishes. Whip the cream, use to top the desserts and sprinkle with the remaining peppercorns before serving.

Fruit with nut ice cream
Serves 4

Ingredients	Metric-Imperial	American
2 oranges		
2 grapefruit		
Green grapes	75 g/3 oz	3 oz
Black grapes	75 g/3 oz	3 oz
Amaretto	2 tbs	3 tbs
Lemon juice	1 tbs	1 tbs
Caster sugar (granulated)	2 tbs	3 tbs
Nut ice cream	500 ml/18 fl oz	generous 1 pint
Slivered almonds	75 g/3 oz	¾ cup

Peel the oranges and grapefruit, remove all the white pith, and divide into segments. Halve the grapes, remove the seeds (pits), and combine all the fruit in a bowl. Sprinkle

with the amaretto, lemon juice and sugar. Allow to stand for at least 30 minutes to allow the flavours to combine.

Divide the fruit mixture among 4 dessert dishes. Scoop out balls of ice cream, and arrange one on top of each portion. Serve sprinkled with the almonds.

Left: Berry salad with sabayon
Below: Whole figs with vodka

Strawberry yogurt dessert
Serves 4

Ingredients	Metric-Imperial	American
Strawberries	450 g/1 lb	1 lb
Caster sugar (granulated)		
Natural yogurt	300 ml/½ pint	1¼ cups
Lemon juice	1 tbs	1 tbs
Toasted slivered almonds or chocolate curls		

Hull and halve the strawberries, place in a bowl and sprinkle with sugar to taste. Cover and chill for 2 hours.

Mix together the yogurt, 1 tbs sugar and the lemon juice. Pour over the strawberry mixture and serve decorated with almonds or chocolate curls.

If a sweeter dessert is preferred, increase the sugar.

Above: Strawberry yogurt dessert
Right: Stuffed peaches

To prepare the topping, add the sugar to the cream with the vanilla essence and whip until stiff. Fold in the nuts. Serve the fruit mixture topped with pistachio cream.

Stuffed peaches
Serves 4

Ingredients	Metric-Imperial	American
2 peaches or 4 drained canned peach halves		
Peach brandy	150 ml/¼ pint	⅔ cup
Whipping cream	300 ml/½ pint	1¼ cups
Cornflour	2 tsp	2 tsp
Caster sugar (granulated)	1 tbs	1 tbs
1 egg yolk		
Water	3 tbs	4 tbs
Vanilla essence		
Strawberries	225 g/8 oz	8 oz
Grated rind of 1 lemon		

Pour boiling water over fresh peaches, drain and peel. Halve and stone (pit) the peaches and place in a bowl. Sprinkle with the peach brandy, cover and chill.

Mix together 3 tbs (4 tbs) of the cream, the cornflour and sugar. Place the remaining cream in a pan and bring to the boil. Add the cornflour mixture and stir until boiling. Remove from the heat. Beat the egg yolk with the water and vanilla and whisk into the sauce. Divide among 4 serving dishes. Hull and purée the strawberries and stir in the lemon rind.

Place a peach half, rounded side downwards, in each dish of vanilla cream. Stir any liquid from the bowl into the strawberry purée. Spoon this into the hollows in the peach halves before serving.

Tipsy apricots with pistachio cream
Serves 4–6

Ingredients	Metric-Imperial	American
Ripe apricots	1 kg/2¼ lb	2¼ lb
Caster sugar (granulated)		
Grated rind of 1 lemon		
Short cinnamon stick		
Apricot liqueur	125 ml/4 fl oz	½ cup
For the cream:		
Caster sugar	2 tsp	2 tsp
Whipping cream	300 ml/½ pint	1¼ cups
Few drops of vanilla essence (extract)		
Chopped pistachio nuts	25 g/1 oz	¼ cup

Halve and stone (pit) the apricots, place in a pan and sprinkle with 3 tbs (4 tbs) sugar. Cover and leave to stand for 1 hour. Add the lemon rind and cinnamon stick, bring just to the boil then cover and simmer until the apricots are tender. Discard the cinnamon stick. Add more sugar to the fruit if wished, stir this in gently then add the liqueur and leave to cool.

Stuffed pineapple halves with meringue topping
Serves 4

Ingredients	Metric-Imperial	American
2 small ripe pineapples		
Cream cheese	275 g/10 oz	1¼ cups
Caster sugar (granulated)	1 tbs	1 tbs
Rum		
4 egg whites		
Icing sugar		
(confectioners')	2 tbs	3 tbs

Halve the pineapples lengthways, remove the flesh from the skin and chop, discarding any woody core. Beat the cheese until soft and stir in the chopped pineapple, the caster sugar and rum. Pile the mixture back into the pineapple 'shells'

Whisk the egg whites in a clean bowl until stiff. Sift over the icing sugar and whisk until the meringue is firm. Place in a piping bag fitted with a star tube (pipe). Cover the cheese filling with meringue. Stand the stuffed pineapple halves on a baking sheet (cookie sheet) and bake, uncovered, in a preheated moderately hot oven, 200°C, 400°F, Gas Mark 6, for 5 minutes or until the ridges of the meringue turn golden brown. Serve immediately, decorated with maraschino cherries if wished.

Bananas with almond snow
Serves 4

Ingredients	Metric-Imperial	American
4 bananas		
Lemon juice	1 tbs	1 tbs
1 egg white		
Caster sugar (granulated)	50 g/2 oz	¼ cup
Ground almonds	50 g/2 oz	½ cup

Carefully slit the skin of the bananas lengthways on opposite sides, without cutting the fruit. Remove one half of the banana skin. Prick the exposed banana flesh lightly with a cocktail stick (toothpick) and sprinkle with the lemon juice.

Whisk the egg white in a clean bowl until stiff then gradually add the sugar, a tablespoon at a time, whisking vigorously after each addition until the meringue is firm and glossy. Fold in the almonds. Transfer to a piping bag fitted with a star tube (pipe).

Pipe the almond snow to cover the exposed banana flesh. Arrange the bananas on the grid of a grill pan (broiler) and cook under high heat for about 5 minutes, until golden.

Below: Stuffed pineapple halves with meringue topping
Right: Sweet cheese dip for seasonal fruit

Sweet cheese dip for seasonal fruit
Serves 4

Ingredients	Metric-Imperial	American
Cream cheese	225 g/8 oz	1 cup
Orange juice	6 tbs	½ cup
Vanilla essence (extract)	1 tsp	1 tsp
Icing sugar (confectioners')	1 tbs	1 tbs
Fruits in season such as strawberries, cherries, peaches, apricots, grapes, pears, apples, mangoes, melons		
Lemon juice		

Beat the cheese until soft then add the orange juice and vanilla essence. Sift the icing sugar over the top and beat until the mixture is smooth. Place in a serving dish and chill.

Prepare the chosen fruit and divide into bite-sized pieces. Sprinkle pears or apples with lemon juice to prevent discoloration. Thread a selection of fruit pieces on to wooden cocktail sticks (toothpicks) and serve with the cheese dip.

Orange segments with avocado purée
Serves 4

Ingredients	Metric-Imperial	American
5 oranges		
2 ripe avocados		
Caster sugar (granulated)	2 tbs	3 tbs
Few drops of vanilla essence (extract)		
Orange liqueur	1 tbs	1 tbs

Peel 4 of the oranges and divide into segments, removing all the pith. Reserve any juice. Squeeze the juice from the last orange. Arrange the segments on 4 plates. Chill.

Halve and stone (pit) the avocados and scoop out the flesh. Purée with the orange juice, sugar, vanilla essence and liqueur. Place in a piping bag fitted with a star tube (pipe). Top each plate of orange segments with a long spiral of avocado purée and decorate with maraschino (cocktail) cherries if wished.

Caramelized fresh pineapple
Serves 4

Ingredients	Metric-Imperial	American
1 large fresh pineapple		
Water	125 ml/4 fl oz	½ cup
Sugar	200 g/7oz	scant 1 cup
1 vanilla pod		

Halve the pineapple lengthways and cut out the hard woody

Pineapple with raspberry cream
Serves 8

Ingredients	Metric-Imperial	American
Raspberries	225 g/8 oz	8 oz
Whipping cream	300 ml/½ pint	1¼ cups
Icing sugar (confectioners')	3 tbs	4 tbs
1 large fresh pineapple		

If wished, reserve a few raspberries for the decoration. Purée and then sieve the remainder of the raspberries. Whip the cream until stiff and fold in the raspberry purée. Sift the icing sugar over the top and fold in thoroughly. Divide the raspberry cream among 8 small stemmed glasses.

Divide the pineapple lengthways into 8 wedges and cut out the hard woody core. Cut the flesh of each piece of pineapple from the skin in one piece then slice the flesh and arrange on the pineapple skin, off-setting the slices against each other. Decorate with the reserved fruit and serve with the raspberry creams.

Left: Orange segments with avocado purée
Below: Pineapple with raspberry cream

centre. Using a sharp pointed knife, remove the pineapple flesh from the skin and cut into bite-sized pieces. Reserve the pineapple 'shells'.

Put the water, sugar and vanilla pod into a pan and heat, stirring, until the sugar has dissolved. Simmer for 3 minutes then add the pineapple pieces, bring back to the boil and simmer for a further 3 minutes. Remove the pineapple with a slotted spoon and place on a wire rack over a baking sheet (cookie sheet) and leave to drain really well. Collect the syrup which has dripped from the pineapple and return to the pan. Bring to the boil and cook gently until the syrup begins to turn golden. Remove the vanilla pod.

Place the pineapple shells on a serving dish. Dip each piece of pineapple into the caramel until coated, allow excess caramel to drip off then place the coated fruit in the shells. Serve with whipped cream flavoured with a little rum.

Iced pistachio creams with strawberry purée
Serves 4

Ingredients	Metric-Imperial	American
2 peaches		
Whipping cream	300 ml/½ pint	1¼ cups
Chopped pistachio nuts	50 g/2 oz	½ cup
Apricot or strawberry liqueur	150 ml/¼ pint	⅔ cup
Strawberries	225 g/8 oz	8 oz

Pour boiling water over the peaches, drain, peel then halve and remove the stones (pits).

Whip the cream until stiff and fold in the pistachio nuts and 3 tbs (4 tbs) of the fruit liqueur. Put a layer of pistachio cream into 4 small rounded cups or bowls. Put a peach half on each layer of cream, with the hollow side upwards. Put 1 tsp of fruit liqueur into each peach half. Top with the rest of the pistachio cream. Place the moulds in a freezer for about 1 hour.

Meanwhile, make the fruit purée. Hull the strawberries then mash with a fork and press through a sieve. Sti in the remaining fruit liqueur and chill.

At serving time, loosen the half-frozen pistachio creams from the moulds with a knifeblade and turn out on plates. Top with the strawberry purée and serve at once.

Cinnamon parfait
Serves 4–6

Ingredients	Metric-Imperial	American
Milk	300 ml/½ pint	1¼ cups
2 cinnamon sticks		
Sugar	150 g/5 oz	⅔ cup
Water	125 ml/4 fl oz	½ cup
3 egg yolks		
Pinch of salt		
Ground cinnamon	1 tsp	1 tsp
Whipping cream	450 ml/¾ pint	scant 2 cups

2 large milk chocolate flakes
Little extra ground cinnamon

Place the milk in a pan and bring to the boil. Add the cinnamon sticks and leave to stand for 30 minutes. Strain and reserve the cinnamon milk.

Place the sugar and water in a pan and heat gently, stirring, until the sugar has dissolved. Boil until syrupy. Place the egg yolks in a bowl and add the hot sugar syrup in a thin stream, whisking vigorously all the time, until thick. Whisk in the cinnamon milk, salt and ground cinnamon. Whip the cream until thick and fold into the cinnamon mixture. Transfer to a bowl or mould and freeze overnight.

At serving time, dip the mould into hot water then turn out on a plate. Decorate with crumbled chocolate flake and a sprinkling of ground cinnamon.

South Seas coconut coupe
Serves 4

Ingredients	Metric-Imperial	American
Butter	25 g/1 oz	2 tbs
Caster sugar (granulated)	2 tbs	3 tbs
Shredded coconut	2 tbs	3 tbs
Whipping cream	3 tbs	4 tbs
Raspberries	350 g/12 oz	12 oz
Vanilla ice cream	500 ml/18 fl oz	generous 1 pint

Melt the butter in a pan and add the sugar and coconut. Heat, stirring, but do not allow the mixture to brown. Stir in the cream, remove from the heat and set aside. Defrost the raspberries if using frozen.

Scoop the ice cream into 4 serving dishes and top with the raspberries and then with the buttered coconut. Serve with rolled ice cream wafers.

Kiwi fruit dessert
Serves 4

Ingredients	Metric-Imperial	American
Butter	40 g/1½ oz	3 tbs
Slivered almonds	2 tbs	3 tbs
Sugar	4 tbs	5 tbs
Calvados or brandy	2 tbs	3 tbs
Orange juice	2 tbs	3 tbs
Ground cinnamon		
6 kiwi fruit		
Walnut ice cream	500 ml/18 fl oz	generous 1 pint

Melt the butter in a pan and use to fry the almonds until golden. Sprinkle in the sugar and stir until it turns golden brown. Mix in the Calvados or brandy and the orange juice. Add cinnamon to taste.

Peel the kiwi fruit and cut into thick slices. Cut the ice cream into large cubes and divide among 4 plates. Top the cubes with kiwi fruit slices and then with the caramelized almonds. Decorate with any remaining kiwi fruit slices and caramelized almonds, and if liked serve with orange segments.

Simple vanilla ice cream
Serves 4

Ingredients	Metric-Imperial	American
2 egg yolks		
Caster sugar (granulated)	75 g/3 oz	⅓ cup
Vanilla essence	1 tsp	1 tsp
Whipping cream	300 ml/½ pint	1¼ cups

Place the egg yolks in a bowl with the sugar and vanilla and whisk until thickened and creamy. Whisk the cream in a separate bowl until stiff and fold into the egg mousse. Transfer to a shallow container and freeze until firm.

Scoop the ice cream into dishes and if liked serve with sugared berries and ice cream wafers.

Microwave hint
Make fresh egg pouring custard in a dish or glass measuring jug standing in a bath of hot water which comes half way up the sides. Always stir frequently. The custard is ready when it coats the back of a spoon.

Left: Iced pistachio creams with strawberry purée
Above: Kiwi fruit dessert

Strawberry tartlets
Serves 6–8

Ingredients	Metric-Imperial	American
Strawberries	450 g/1 lb	1 lb
Caster sugar (granulated)	2 tbs	3 tbs
6–8 large ready-made pastry tartlet cases		
Strawberry ice cream	500 ml/18 fl oz	generous 1 pint
Whipping cream	150 ml/¼ pint	⅔ cup
Grenadine syrup (pomegranate)		

Hull the strawberries and divide in halves or quarters according to size. Sprinkle with the sugar and leave to stand for about 10 minutes, until the juice begins to run.

Divide the strawberries among the pastry tartlet cases and top with scoops of ice cream. Whip the cream and use to decorate the filled tartlets. Spoon a little grenadine syrup over the top of the ice cream and serve at once.

Microwave hint
To make a coloured glaze to enhance the appearance of a fruit-filled flan, add 2 drops of food colouring to the glaze while it is still warm – orange for peaches and apricots, red for strawberries, green for gooseberries and so on.

Festive surprises
Serves 4

Ingredients	Metric-Imperial	American
Strawberries	225 g/8 oz	8 oz
Icing sugar (confectioners')	2 tbs	3 tbs
Fruit in season such as cherries, mandarin oranges, bananas, melons, strawberries		
Neapolitan ice cream (layered pistachio/strawberry/vanilla)	500 ml/18 fl oz	generous 1 pint

Hull the strawberries, mash with a fork and then sieve. Sift the icing sugar over the top and mix well.

Prepare the fruit and divide into bite-sized pieces. Thread a selection of fruit pieces on wooden cocktail sticks (toothpicks).

Cut the ice cream into four slices and place in dessert dishes. Spoon over the strawberry sauce and serve immediately with the fruit 'spears'.

Variation: Use raspberries or loganberries in place of the strawberries for the sauce.

Iced soufflé
Serves 4

Ingredients	Metric-Imperial	American
4 eggs		
Caster sugar (granulated)	50 g/2 oz	¼ cup
Vanilla essence (extract)	2 tsp	2 tsp
Grated rind and juice of 1 orange		
Orange liqueur	4 tbs	5 tbs
Whipping cream	300 ml/½ pint	1¼ cups
Little cocoa powder for sprinkling		

Separate 3 of the eggs and place the yolks in a double boiler or in a bowl over a pan of simmering water. Add the remaining whole egg, the sugar, vanilla essence, orange rind and juice and the liqueur. Whisk over the hot water, if possible using an electric mixer, until thickened and creamy. Remove from the heat and continue whisking until cool.

Whisk the egg whites in a clean bowl until stiff. Whip the cream until thick. Fold the egg whites and cream into the egg mousse then transfer to a soufflé dish slightly too small to accommodate the entire mixture. When the dish is four fifths full, make a folded strip of greaseproof paper (waxed) and insert this between the mixture and the dish so that it extends at least 2.5 cm/1 inch above the rim.

Pour in the remaining soufflé mixture. Freeze for about 3 hours, or until firm. Remove the paper collar and sift over a little cocoa powder.

Raspberry foam with vanilla ice cream
Serves 4

Ingredients	Metric-Imperial	American
Raspberries	225 g/8 oz	8 oz
Port	3 tbs	4 tbs
Caster sugar (granulated)	4 tbs	5 tbs
Vanilla essence (extract)		
2 eggs		
Raspberry liqueur or kirsch	1 tbs	1 tbs
Vanilla ice cream	500 ml/18 fl oz	generous 1 pint

Put the raspberries into a pan with the port and three quarters of the sugar. Heat gently, stirring, until the mixture boils then simmer for 4 minutes. Press through a sieve into the top of a double boiler or into a bowl over a pan of simmering water. Add a little vanilla essence to taste then put in the remaining sugar, the eggs and liqueur. Whisk over the hot water, if possible using an electric mixer, until thick and foamy. Remove from the heat and cool slightly.

Cut the ice cream into chunks and divide among 4 serving dishes. Spoon the warm foamy sauce over the top and serve.

Left: Strawberry tartlets
Above: Iced soufflé

467

Pineapple parfait
Serves 4

Ingredients	Metric-Imperial	American
1 large fresh pineapple		
2 egg yolks		
Caster sugar (granulated)	50 g/2 oz	¼ cup
Vanilla essence (extract)	½ tsp	½ tsp
Whipping cream	225 ml/8 fl oz	1 cup
Icing sugar (confectioners')	75 g/3 oz	¾ cup
Few drops of lemon juice		

Remove the top of the pineapple, including the leafy crown. Carefully cut out the pineapple flesh, discarding the woody core, and cut the flesh into pieces. Purée the pineapple pieces and set aside.

Place the egg yolks in a bowl with the sugar and vanilla essence and whisk, using an electric mixer if possible, until smooth and creamy. The sugar grains should have dissolved. Fold in the pineapple purée.

Whip the cream until thick. Sift the icing sugar over the top and stir in lightly. Fold in the fruit purée mixture and sharpen the flavour with a few drops of lemon juice if desired. Fill the pineapple with the parfait and put excess mixture into a dish. Wrap the fruit in foil and cover the dish. Freeze both until firm.

Just before serving, remove the foil, turn the pineapple on its side and cut downwards into four slices, using a very sharp knife. Place the slices on serving dishes. If liked, scoop small balls from the dish of parfait and arrange on the pineapple slices. Alternatively, sprinkle with toasted shredded coconut.

Aphrodite's ice cream
Serves 2

Ingredients	Metric-Imperial	American
1 ripe mango		
Orange liqueur	2 tbs	3 tbs
Pistachio ice cream	250 ml/9 fl oz	generous 1 cup
Whipping cream	125 ml/4 fl oz	½ cup
Few pistachio nuts		

Halve the mango and remove the stone (pit). Carefully loosen the flesh and cut into pieces. Sprinkle with the liqueur.

Cut the ice cream into cubes and divide between the mango 'shells'. Place on serving plates. Whip the cream, spoon over the filled mango shells and sprinkle with pistachio nuts. Serve immediately.

Tipsy strawberry ice cream
Serves 6–8

Ingredients	Metric-Imperial	American
Strawberries	750 g/1¾ lb	1¾ lb
Caster sugar (granulated)	100 g/4 oz	½ cup
Amaretto	3 tbs	4 tbs
Advocaat	3 tbs	4 tbs
Whipping cream	300 ml/½ pint	1¼ cups

Hull and halve the strawberries and reserve a few for decoration. Purée the remainder and stir in the sugar, amaretto liqueur and advocaat. Whip the cream until stiff, reserve a little for decoration and fold the rest into the strawberry mixture. Transfer to a suitable container, cover and freeze until firm.

To serve, scoop out balls of the ice cream into dishes and decorate each portion with some of the reserved strawberries and piped rosettes of whipped cream.

Ice cream Suzette
Serves 4

Ingredients	Metric-Imperial	American
2 oranges		
10 cubes of sugar		
Orange juice		
Butter	15 g/½ oz	1 tbs
Lemon juice	2 tbs	3 tbs
Orange liqueur	3 tbs	5 tbs
Vanilla ice cream	500 ml/18 fl oz	generous 1 pint

Rub the oranges all over with the sugar cubes to remove the zesty layer of rind. Squeeze the juice from both oranges and make up to 150 ml/¼ pint (⅔ cup) with more juice.

Melt the butter in a small frying pan, add the sugar cubes and heat, stirring, until the sugar dissolves and turns golden. Put in the orange and lemon juices and bring to the boil, stirring. Boil until reduced by about one quarter. Remove from the heat and stir in the liqueur.

Cut the ice cream into dice, divide among 4 heatproof glasses and pour the hot sauce over the top. Serve at once.

Left: Pineapple parfait
Right: Tipsy strawberry ice cream

Pistachio parfait
Serves 4

Ingredients	Metric-Imperial	American
Pistachio nuts	75 g/3 oz	¾ cup
Milk	300 ml/½ pint	1¼ cups
Grated orange rind	1 tbs	1 tbs
Grated rind of 1 lime		
Sugar	150 g/5 oz	⅔ cup
Water	125 ml/4 fl oz	½ cup
3 egg yolks		
Whipping cream	350 ml/12 fl oz	1½ cups
Strawberries	350 g/12 oz	12 oz
Orange juice	2 tbs	3 tbs

To make the parfait, thinly slice a few of the shelled pistachio nuts and grind the remainder. Heat the milk with a little of the orange rind and the lime rind. Add the ground pistachio nuts and remove from the heat.

In another pan, bring the sugar and water slowly to the boil, stirring until the sugar has dissolved, then boil to reduce by one third. Whisk the egg yolks in a bowl until creamy, and slowly add the hot sugar syrup, whisking constantly until the mixture begins to thicken. Then gradually add the hot milk mixture, stirring all the time. Lower the pan into a bowl of cold water and stir briskly until the mixture is cool.

Stiffly whip two thirds of the cream and fold into the pistachio mixture.

Transfer the parfait to a bowl, cover and freeze for 1 hour. Remove and beat well with a whisk then freeze again for at least 3 hours.

Hull and halve the strawberries, sprinkle with the orange juice, and divide between 4 dessert glasses. Defrost the parfait, until soft enough to scoop portions over the strawberries. To make the orange topping, stiffly whip the remaining cream, stir in the rest of the orange rind and spoon over the parfait. Decorate with the pistachio slices and more coarsely grated orange rind if desired.

Paw-paw and ginger salad with walnut ice cream
Serves 4

Ingredients	Metric-Imperial	American
2 paw-paws		
2 dessert apples		
Lemon juice	1 tbs	1 tbs
Ruby port	3 tbs	4 tbs
2 pieces preserved ginger		
Raspberries	100 g/4 oz	4 oz
Walnut ice cream	500 ml/18 fl oz	generous 1 pint
Chopped walnuts	40 g/1½ oz	⅓ cup

Quarter the paw-paws, discard the seeds (pits), remove the flesh from the skin and cut into small pieces. Peel and quarter the apples. Core, and cut into pieces. Mix the prepared fruit and sprinkle with the lemon juice and port. Thinly slice the ginger and add to the fruit mixture with the raspberries. Allow to stand for 20 minutes for the flavours to combine. Divide between 4 dessert glasses.

Scoop out balls of ice cream, and arrange one on top of each portion of fruit. Decorate with chopped walnuts.

Nectarine Melba
Serves 4

Ingredients	Metric-Imperial	American
4 ripe nectarines		
Raspberries	225 g/8 oz	8 oz
Vanilla essence (extract)	2 tsp	2 tsp
Caster sugar (granulated)		
Whipping cream	300 ml/½ pint	1¼ cups
Vanilla ice cream	500 ml/18 fl oz	generous 1 pint
Chopped pistachio nuts	40 g/1½ oz	⅓ cup

Dip the nectarines first into boiling water, then into cold water and remove the skins. Halve, and discard the stones (pits). Press the raspberries through a sieve, and stir in the vanilla essence and sugar to taste. Stiffly whip the cream with 1 tbs sugar and place in a piping bag fitted with a large star tube (pipe).

Divide the ice cream between 4 dessert dishes. Place 2 nectarine halves, cut sides downwards, on each portion and spoon over the raspberry purée. Decorate with rosettes of whipped cream and sprinkle with pistachio nuts.

Microwave hint
For a meringue mixture suitable for microwave cooking, add 1 tsp cornflour (cornstarch) and a pinch of cream of tartar to every 3 egg whites. Spread over the pie to be covered, taking it right up to the edge. Cook on medium power for 3 minutes to set. Place under a preheated grill (broiler) for a further 2 minutes to brown the surface if required.

Left: Pistachio parfait
Right: Paw-paw salad with ginger and walnut ice cream

471

Peach sorbet
Serves 6

Ingredients	Metric-Imperial	American
Peaches	1 kg/2¼ lb	2¼ lb
Peach brandy		
Caster sugar (granulated)	250 g/9 oz	generous 1 cup
Egg whites	2	2

Pour boiling water over the fresh peaches, drain and peel. Halve and stone (pit) the peaches, then purée in a blender or food processor. Put the purée in a measuring jug and top up with the peach brandy to make 600 ml (1 pint/2½ cups).

Add the sugar to the purée and mix well until the sugar is completely dissolved. Pour into a freezer tray and freeze until mushy.

Remove the mixture from the freezer, turn into a bowl and beat to break down any ice crystals. Whisk the egg whites until stiff, then fold into the mixture. Return to the freezer and freeze until solid. Soften for about 10 minutes in the refrigerator before scooping into tall glasses to serve.

Variation: Well drained canned peach halves can be used if fresh are out of season.

Champagne sorbet
Serves 6

Ingredients	Metric-Imperial	American
Caster sugar (granulated)	225 g/8 oz	generous 1 cup
Water	600 ml/1 pint	2½ cups
Champagne	150 ml/¼ pint	⅔ cup
Lemon juice	1 tbs	1 tbs
Egg whites	2	2

Put the sugar and water in a pan and heat gently, stirring until the sugar completely dissolves. Bring to the boil and simmer for 10 minutes without stirring. Do not let the mixture colour. Remove from the heat and cool.

Add the Champagne and lemon juice to the syrup, then pour into a freezer tray and freeze until mushy.

Remove the mixture from the freezer, turn into a bowl and beat to break down any ice crystals. Whisk the egg whites until stiff, then fold into the mixture. Return to the freezer and freeze until solid. Soften for about 10 minutes in the freezer before scooping into tall glasses to serve.

Below clockwise from left: Redcurrant sorbet; Peach sorbet; Mint sorbet; Forest fruit; Champagne sorbet

Neapolitan surprise
Serves 4

Ingredients	Metric-Imperial	American
Milk	500 ml/18 fl oz	2¼ cups
Caster sugar (granulated)	4 tbs	5 tbs
Grated rind of ½ lemon		
Pinch of salt		
Round grain rice	100 g/4 oz	⅔ cup
2 eggs		
Neapolitan ice cream	500 ml/18 fl oz	generous 1 pint
Lemon juice	1 tsp	1 tsp

Place the milk in a pan with half the sugar, the lemon rind and salt. Bring to the boil, add the rice then bring back to boiling point, stirring. Cover for 20 minutes stirring occasionally. Allow to cool slightly. Separate the eggs, and beat the yolks into the rice while it is still warm. Divide among 4 heatproof dishes and chill. Cut the ice cream into slices and arrange on the rice mixture.

Whip the egg whites until very stiff, then whisk in the rest of the sugar and the lemon juice. Place in a piping bag fitted with a star tube (pipe) and pipe swirls of meringue over the top of each dish, covering the ice cream completely. Place under a hot grill (broiler) for a few minutes until the ridges of the meringue turn golden. Serve immediately.

Redcurrant sorbet
Serves 8

Ingredients	Metric-Imperial	American
Redcurrants	900 g/2 lb	2 lb
Water		
Caster sugar (granulated)	250 g/9 oz	generous 1 cup
Egg whites	2	2

Reserve a handful of redcurrants for decoration and purée the remainder in a blender or food processor. Put the purée in a measuring jug and top up with water to make 600 ml (1 pint/2½ cups).

Add the sugar to the purée and mix well until the sugar is completely dissolved. Pour into a freezer tray and freeze until mushy.

Remove the mixture from the freezer, turn into a bowl and beat to break down any ice crystals. Whisk the egg whites until stiff, then fold into the mixture. Return to the freezer and freeze until solid. Soften for about 10 minutes in the refrigerator before scooping into tall glasses. Serve decorated with the reserved redcurrants.

Variation: Replace the redcurrants with blackcurrants and use blackcurrant liqueur instead of water to top up the purée.

Apricots with chocolate ice cream
Serves 4

Ingredients	Metric-Imperial	American
8 – 12 ripe apricots		
Butter	15 g/½ oz	1 tbs
Slivered almonds	50 g/2 oz	½ cup
Sugar	5 tbs	6 tbs
Chocolate ripple ice cream	500 ml/18 fl oz	generous 1 pint
Coffee liqueur	4 tbs	5 tbs

Pour boiling water over the apricots, drain and peel. Halve and discard the stones (pits). Cut the fruit into pieces.

Melt the butter in a pan and use to fry the almonds, stirring, until golden. Sprinkle in the sugar and heat until it has melted. Stir in the apricot pieces, cover and cook for about 5 minutes. Leave to cool.

Divide the apricot mixture among 4 dessert plates. Scoop balls from the ice cream and place on each portion. Spoon over the liqueur before serving.

Peach purée with muesli and ice cream
Serves 2

Ingredients	Metric-Imperial	American
Canned peach slices	225 g/8 oz can	8 oz can
Chocolate ripple ice cream	250 ml/9 fl oz	generous 1 cup
Muesli with fruit and nuts	50 g/2 oz	½ cup
Chopped walnuts or hazelnuts (filberts)	25 g/1 oz	¼ cup

Drain the peaches and purée with just enough of the syrup from the can to give a pouring consistency. Cut the ice cream into 4 wedges and divide between 2 dessert plates. Surround with the purée and sprinkle with the muesli and nuts.

Vanilla parfait with foamy port sauce
Serves 4–6

Ingredients	Metric-Imperial	American
2 eggs		
Whipping cream	125 ml/4 fl oz	½ cup
Pinch of salt		
6 egg yolks		
Icing sugar (confectioners')	65 g/2½ oz	scant ⅔ cup
Vanilla essence (extract)	½ tsp	½ tsp
Strawberries	450 g/1 lb	1 lb
Caster sugar (granulated)	2 tbs	3 tbs
Orange liqueur	3 tbs	4 tbs
Port	125 ml/4 fl oz	½ cup

Separate the 2 eggs. Put the cream into a pan, add the salt and bring to the boil. Remove from the heat. Place 4 egg yolks in a bowl and sift over half of the icing sugar. Whisk until creamy then gradually add the hot cream and the vanilla essence, whisking all the time. Leave to cool.

Whisk the egg whites in a clean bowl until stiff. Sift the remaining icing sugar and gradually add to the egg whites, a tablespoon at a time, whisking vigorously after each addition until the meringue is firm and glossy. Fold into the egg yolk mixture. Transfer to a savarin mould and freeze for 1 hour, stirring twice during this time. Then freeze for about 4 hours, or until firm. Chill a serving plate.

Hull the strawberries, place in a bowl, sprinkle with the caster sugar and liqueur. Leave to stand for 2 hours, stirring gently now and then.

Put the port in the top of a double boiler or in a bowl over a pan of simmering water. Add the remaining 4 egg yolks

and whisk over the hot water until the sauce is creamy.

Turn the parfait out on the cold plate, fill the centre with the strawberries and syrup and pour the port sauce over.

Paw-paw sorbet
Serves 2

Ingredients	Metric-Imperial	American
1 paw-paw		
Grapefruit juice	125 ml/4 fl oz	½ cup
Icing sugar (confectioners')	40 g/1½ oz	⅓ cup
Sparkling rosé wine		

Halve the paw-paw and discard the seeds (pits). Scoop out the flesh and purée it with the grapefruit juice and icing sugar. Transfer to a shallow container and freeze for 2–3 hours, stirring occasionally. The sorbet should not be frozen solid.

Divide the sorbet between 2 tall glasses and top up with sparkling rosé wine.

Orange cream cheese with fruit ice
Serves 2

Ingredients	Metric-Imperial	American
Cream cheese	100 g/4 oz	½ cup
Lemon juice	1 tsp	1 tsp
Orange juice	1 tbs	1 tbs
Caster sugar (granulated)	1 tbs	1 tbs
Fruit ice cream	250 ml/9 fl oz	generous 1 cup
Corn flakes	4 tbs	4 tbs

Cream the cheese with the lemon and orange juices then beat in the sugar. Divide between 2 dessert dishes and cover with slices of ice cream. Serve sprinkled with the corn flakes.

Peach Melba
Serves 4

Ingredients	Metric-Imperial	American
Raspberries	350 g/12 oz	12 oz
4 canned peach halves		
Vanilla ice cream	500 ml/18 fl oz	generous 1 pint
Whipped cream		

Purée the raspberries then sieve the purée if a smooth sauce is preferred. Thinly slice each peach half. Cut the ice cream into cubes and divide among 4 dessert dishes. Place a 'fan' of peach slices on each portion and top with raspberry purée. Decorate with whipped cream before serving.

Left: Vanilla parfait with foamy port sauce

INDEX